RESEARCH HANDBOOK ON CRITICAL LEGAL THEORY

RESEARCH HANDBOOKS IN LEGAL THEORY

Research Handbooks in Legal Theory are designed to provide original and sophisticated discussions from an international and expert range of contributors. The volumes in this important series cover key topics within the field as well as major schools of thought, and also explore the application of legal theory to different areas of law. Comprising specially commissioned chapters from leading academics each *Research Handbook* brings together cutting-edge ideas and thought-provoking contributions and is written with a wide readership in mind. Equally useful as reference tools or high-level introductions to specific topics, issues, methods and debates, these *Research Handbooks* will be an essential resource for academic researchers and postgraduate students.

Titles in this series include:

Research Handbook on Feminist Jurisprudence
Edited by Robin West and Cynthia Grant Bowman

Research Handbook on Critical Legal Theory
Edited by Emilios Christodoulidis, Ruth Dukes and Marco Goldoni

Research Handbook on Critical Legal Theory

Edited by

Emilios Christodoulidis

Ruth Dukes

Marco Goldoni

School of Law, University of Glasgow, Glasgow, UK

RESEARCH HANDBOOKS IN LEGAL THEORY

Cheltenham, UK • Northampton, MA, USA

© The Editors and Contributors Severally 2019

All rights reserved. No part of this publication may be reproduced, stored in a retrieval system or transmitted in any form or by any means, electronic, mechanical or photocopying, recording, or otherwise without the prior permission of the publisher.

Published by
Edward Elgar Publishing Limited
The Lypiatts
15 Lansdown Road
Cheltenham
Glos GL50 2JA
UK

Edward Elgar Publishing, Inc.
William Pratt House
9 Dewey Court
Northampton
Massachusetts 01060
USA

A catalogue record for this book
is available from the British Library

Library of Congress Control Number: 2019945345

This book is available electronically in the Elgaronline
Law subject collection
DOI 10.4337/9781786438898

ISBN 978 1 78643 888 1 (cased)
ISBN 978 1 78643 889 8 (eBook)

Typeset by Columns Design XML Ltd, Reading
Printed and bound in Great Britain by TJ International Ltd, Padstow, Cornwall

To Megan Dyer, 1994–2019

Contents

List of contributors ix
Preface xi

PART I

1 Critical theory and the law: reflections on origins, trajectories and conjunctures 2
  Emilios Christodoulidis
2 Critical legal realism in a nutshell 27
  Dennis M. Davis and Karl Klare

PART II

3 Critical legal feminisms 45
  Rosemary Hunter
4 Critical race theory 63
  Mathias Möschel
5 Queer in the law: critique and postcritique 79
  Mariano Croce
6 Marxism and the political economy of law 95
  Emilios Christodoulidis and Marco Goldoni
7 Critical theory of the state 114
  Bob Jessop
8 Law and the public/private distinction 135
  Scott Veitch
9 Rhetoric, semiotics, synaesthetics 151
  Peter Goodrich
10 Law and deconstruction 166
   Johan van der Walt
11 The ethical turn in critical legal thought 181
   Louis E. Wolcher
12 Law is a stage: from aesthetics to affective aestheses 201
   Andreas Philippopoulos-Mihalopoulos
13 The responsibilities of the critic: law, politics and the Critical Legal Conference 223
   Costas Douzinas
14 Law in the mirror of critique: a report to an academy 238
   Kyle McGee

PART III

15	Property law *Paddy Ireland*	260
16	Ideology and argument construction in contract law *Richard Michael Fischl*	283
17	Critical copyright law and the politics of "IP" *Carys J. Craig*	301
18	A different kind of 'end of history' for corporate law *Lilian Moncrieff*	324
19	Critical labour law: then and now *Ruth Dukes*	345
20	Social rights *Fernando Atria and Constanza Salgado*	363
21	Between persecution and reconciliation: criminal justice, legal form and human emancipation *Craig Reeves, Alan Norrie and Henrique Carvalho*	379
22	Facticity as validity: the misplaced revolutionary praxis of European law *Michelle Everson and Christian Joerges*	407
23	Critical law and development *Fiona Macmillan*	428
24	International economic law's wreckage: depoliticization, inequality, precarity *Nicolás M. Perrone and David Schneiderman*	446
25	Can transnational law be critical? Reflections on a contested idea, field and method *Peer Zumbansen*	473
26	Critical legal theory and international law *Bill Bowring*	495
27	Nihilists, pragmatists and peasants: a dispatch on contradiction in international human rights law *Margot E. Salomon*	509

Index   525

Contributors

Fernando Atria – Professor, School of Law, Universidad de Chile

Bill Bowring – Professor of International Law and Human Rights, Birkbeck College, University of London

Henrique Carvalho – Associate Professor, School of Law, University of Warwick

Emilios Christodoulidis – Chair of Jurisprudence, University of Glasgow

Carys J. Craig – Associate Professor of Law, Osgoode Hall Law School, York University

Mariano Croce – Associate Professor of Political Philosophy, Sapienza Università di Roma

Dennis M. Davis – Judge of the High Court of South Africa and Honorary Professor of Law, University of Cape Town

Costas Douzinas – Professor of Law, Birkbeck College, University of London

Ruth Dukes – Professor of Labour Law, University of Glasgow

Michelle Everson – Professor of Law, Birkbeck College, University of London

Richard Michael Fischl – Professor of Law, University of Connecticut

Marco Goldoni – Senior Lecturer in Legal Theory, University of Glasgow

Peter Goodrich – Professor of Law and Director of the Program in Law and Humanities, Cardozo School of Law, New York

Rosemary Hunter – Professor of Law and Socio-Legal Studies, University of Kent

Paddy Ireland – Professor of Law, University of Bristol Law School

Bob Jessop – Distinguished Professor of Sociology, University of Lancaster

Christian Joerges – Professor Emeritus of Law and Society, Hertie School of Governance

Karl Klare – George J. & Kathleen Waters Matthews Distinguished University Professor, Northeastern University School of Law

Fiona Macmillan – Professor of Law, Birkbeck College, University of London; Visiting Professor of Law, University of Roma Tre

Kyle McGee – Lawyer, Delaware, USA

Lilian Moncrieff – Lecturer in Law, University of Glasgow

Mathias Möschel – Associate Professor of Comparative Constitutional and Human Rights Law, Central European University

Alan Norrie – Professor, School of Law, University of Warwick

Nicolás M. Perrone – Assistant Professor, Durham Law School

Andreas Philippopoulos-Mihalopoulos – Professor of Law and Theory, University of Westminster, London

Craig Reeves – Lecturer in Law, Birkbeck College, University of London

Constanza Salgado – Lecturer, Universidad Ibáñez, Chile

Margot E. Salomon – Associate Professor, Law Department, London School of Economics and Political Science; Director, Laboratory for Advanced Research on the Global Economy, LSE Human Rights.

David Schneiderman – Professor, Faculty of Law, University of Toronto

Johan van der Walt – Professor of Philosophy of Law, University of Luxembourg

Scott Veitch – Paul KC Chung Professor in Jurisprudence, University of Hong Kong

Louis E. Wolcher – Professor of Law Emeritus, University of Washington

Peer Zumbansen – Professor of Law at Kings College London and Director of the Transnational Law Institute

Preface

Critical theory, characteristically linked with the *politics* of theoretical engagement, covers the manifold connections between theory and praxis. As the editors of this Handbook, we saw our task as that of capturing faithfully the broad range of those connections as far as legal thought is concerned. We were keen to retain an emphasis both on the politics of theory, and on the notion of theoretical engagement as reflexive about its own main assumptions and aware of its embeddedness in history and culture. We were also keen to maintain the emphasis on *legal* thought. The discourse of law presents the critic with a significant challenge. Interpretative leeway – so crucial to a politics of theory that is driven by the exigency to envisage what presents itself as natural *otherwise*, to instil contingency where there is givenness, to counter the appearance of necessity – has to work against the logic of the institution. The institution of law, with its deep structures, the functional requirements that tie it to stability, entrenchment and the reproduction of expectations along given pathways, does not lend itself readily to the critical imagination. This is what makes critical legal thought so distinctive and so exacting.

It was our ambition to confront the logic of the institutional with its specific challenges right across the broad field of legal thought that suggested to us the particular structure of this Handbook. A first part of the volume looks at the question of definition and tracks the origins and development of critical legal theory along its European and North American trajectories: its roots in Western Marxism in the former case, and in realism and the revolt against formalism in the latter case. The second part of the volume looks at thematic connections between the development of legal theory and other currents of critical thought: feminism, Marxism, critical race theory, varieties of postmodernism, and so on, as well as the various 'turns' (ethical, aesthetic, political) of critical legal theory. The third part looks at particular fields of law, addressing the question how the field has been shaped by critical legal theory and – additionally or alternatively – what critical approaches reveal about the field, with a decided focus on opportunities for social transformation. Mostly by design, but partly for reasons outwith our control, the selection of fields discussed in Part III has no claim to comprehensiveness, but instead offers several important and interesting examples of the significance of critical legal approaches to legal scholarship, legal discourse and legal reasoning.

When we first accepted the publisher's invitation to edit this collection, we were excited at the opportunity but did not anticipate quite how rewarding it would prove to be to work together with our friends and colleagues in completion of the task. We owe each of the contributors a very big thank you. Additionally, we acknowledge the invaluable editorial assistance provided by Donald Buglass. Without his patience, hard work and dedication, the project would surely have faltered far in advance of the finishing line.

EC, RD, MG
Glasgow, November 2018

PART I

1. Critical theory and the law: reflections on origins, trajectories and conjunctures

Emilios Christodoulidis

1. A BRIEF ARCHAEOLOGY

The tradition of critical theory has its roots in Hegelian Marxism. While its organising insight can be clearly traced back to Marx, its systematic development, if 'systematic' does not overstate the development of this dispersed and diasporic tradition, does not begin until the end of the First World War. We will look sequentially first at the origins – Marx's profound debt to Hegel and to Feuerbach as expressed in the *1844 Manuscripts* and the *Theses on Feuerbach* respectively – then at a brief history of some of the postwar trajectories of its diaspora. Second, we will identify key moments of the critical–theoretical enterprise, the basic premises of critical theory construction, by providing an inventory of terms and a (necessarily brief) explanation of them: the constitutive relationship of theory to practice or *praxis*; the *dialectic* and in particular the moment of *negation*; the idea of theory's task of *mediation* as it is situated and embedded in history and the materiality of social reproduction; the *genealogical* viewpoint; and finally the specific reflexivity that develops and is expressed in and as *immanent critique*. Third, we will visit these concepts and the ways they interrelate by way of a close reading of Max Horkheimer's essay on 'traditional and critical theory', a text that, despite certain limitations, allows the *differentia specifica* of critical theory to emerge. Finally we apply these insights to law, to look at whether and how legal method might carry the organising premises of critical thinking into the organisation of law's semiotic field, into legal discourse and legal practice. The analysis here is somewhat skeletal; it falls to the rest of the volume to develop the themes of critical theory along a rich variety of legal trajectories.

Already one is likely to encounter the objection that the critical project was inaugurated by Kant rather than Hegel, because it was Kant who famously answered his own question 'what is Enlightenment' with the injunction 'dare to inquire' ('*sapere aude*'), which releases 'man from his self-inflicted immaturity' by placing knowledge on a critical footing. Hegel objects that Kant's conception of critique is self-defeating. For him, Kant's categorical severance of *what is* (*Sein*) from *what ought to be* (*Sollen*) undercuts the critical project by withdrawing from it the comprehension it requires to figure *as* critique. Hegel introduces the dialectic to remedy the devastating disjunction that we might call, with Johan van der Walt,[1] Kant's incurable hermeneutic deficit, and what from the point of view of critique is an incorrigible incomprehension. We will say

---

[1] See Christodoulidis and van der Walt, 'Critical Legal Studies: Europe', in Dubber & Tomlins (eds) *Oxford Handbook of Historical Legal Research*, Oxford University Press, 2018.

more on this later, in looking at how critical theory promises to recollect the fragments of the 'real' in terms of the 'rational'. In the meantime Hegel invites us to note a second crucial shortcoming of Kant's critical project. What can duty (*Pflicht/Sollen*) *mean* for us, he asks, in the realm of *pure reason*, if it is not conceptualised as a *response* to the *historical circumstances* in which we are called to act? The dialectical method is introduced by Hegel to remedy both shortcomings: both to sustain a relationship between what is and what ought to be, and at the same time to locate it within the historical situation, that is, in relation to finite circumstances. Only when embedded in this way does the critical project acquire its necessary purchase in the world. The Marxian notion of immanent critique, as situated in the concrete material practices that reproduce society, pivots on this key insight that emerged from Hegel's critique of Kant.

We will pick up the strand of 'immanence' again, of course, as that which drives critical theory methodologically. But first, to radicalise, with Marx, that first prong of critique regarding the bridging of the domains of 'is' and 'ought', we turn to his engagement no longer with Hegel but with Feuerbach, with whom Marx was in the process of settling his accounts in 1845 when he produced that explosive text that came to be known as the *Theses on Feuberbach*. It emerges most clearly in the famous '11th thesis', in which Marx argues that '[t]he philosophers have only interpreted the world, in various ways; the point is to change it'. Marx of course does not mean that philosophers should cease to try to understand the world; he means that comprehension engages them in a task whose requirements are significantly steeper than ordinarily assumed. The 11th thesis tells them that their attempt to understand cannot be and should not be divorced and distinguished from an *activity* that has a certain *telos*, which alone for Marx yields *objective* truth. As he puts it in the second thesis: 'The question whether objective truth can be attributed to human thinking is not a question of theory but is a practical question.' Herbert Marcuse, who was influential in introducing the work of the Frankfurt School to the US academy, puts it nicely nearly a century later: 'What exists is not immediately and already rational but *must be brought to reason.*'[2]

We will have a lot more to say about praxis and its relationship to theory in the next section, but we can already discern in the invitation to *bring to reason* something of an 'active element in cognition', as Max Horkheimer put it. Hegel insists on a distinction between the terms Understanding (*Verstand*) and Reason (*Vernunft*) that may help to elucidate the modality of the *critical* intervention. The activity of 'bringing to Reason' involves an ambitiously synthetic activity that contrasts with the more superficial, commonsensical perception of the *givenness* of phenomena as discrete and separate entities. *Reason* asks the question of what is the mode of their *individuation*, what *evaluative* criteria are deployed to individuate facts and events that appear as given at the level of simple *Understanding*: evaluative because they carry a judgement over salience regarding the criteria of selection. And then, to return to Marcuse, now with even clearer echoes of Hegel: 'As the given world [is] bound up with rational thought and, indeed, ontologically dependent on it, all that contradicts reason or is not rational

---

[2] Marcuse, Herbert, 'Philosophy and critical theory', *Negations* 6.1 (1989): 147–54, emphasis added.

is posited as something that has to be overcome. *Reason [is thereby] established as a critical tribunal.*'³

It would not be an exaggeration to say that these two poles – of *reason* and *praxis* – are what the dialectic spans, poised to 'probe the forcefield' between consciousness and being, subject and object, in Adorno's formulation.⁴ Adorno along with Horkheimer was at the forefront of the recovery of this Hegelian Marxism as the Frankfurt Institute for Social Research (the 'Frankfurt School'), established in 1923, took a radical turn towards Marxism in the 1930s (only to turn away from it after the Second World War). The rediscovery of the early Marx of the 'Paris Manuscripts' of 1844, a text that was first published more than half a century after it was written, was crucial to the rise of critical theory after the First World War, with its key emphasis on praxis, precipitated by George Sorel's theorisation of workers' spontaneous political action and Rosa Luxemburg's theorising of the *auto-gestion* of revolutionary workers' councils.⁵ In terms of the *philosophical* turn to Marx, the great Hegelian Marxist Georg Lukács was hugely influential in the 1920s with the publication of the *History of Class Consciousness*, as was Karl Korsch with *Marxism and Philosophy*. These works raised a distinct, and distinctly heterodox, voice against the orthodoxy of the socialist thought of the Third International, critical because of the constitutive connection to praxis (more on this soon) and echoing the early Marx, who had argued, against the givens and assumptions that founded bourgeois society, that in fact the *only* given was humankind's ability to forever create itself anew.

In this introduction to the rise of critical theory in Europe, both the history of that rise and the theoretical trajectories and work of its protagonists, fascinating as they are, will be kept to a minimum, in order to reserve some space for conceptual analysis. A few words are nevertheless necessary to identify a tradition that stems from the work of Marx in the 1840s and spans a number of generations after him. The annals of critical theory in its European trajectory would include the influential work of Lukács and that of the Italian 'school' (De la Volpe, Colletti), of which Antonio Gramsci was the towering figure. The emphasis in the tradition drawing from Gramsci was predominantly on the *political* moment of the production of political unity as the latter proceeds through processes of 'condensation' and 'distension'⁶ of social forces and the mobilisation of *collective subjects* which provide the 'efficient cause' of the development of the material constitution – a theme radicalised later in the work of the leftists of the *Operaismo* and *Autonomia* movements that emerged out of the Italian trade unions. Perhaps one could extend the reach, though their inclusion is highly controversial given their clear anti-Hegelianism, to a current of critical thought at the École Normale Superieure in Paris, around the leading figure of Louis Althusser – a current that would include Nicos Poulantzas, Étienne Balibar and Alain Badiou, and the recently much

---

³ ibid 937, emphasis added.
⁴ Quoted in Jay, Martin, *The Dialectical Imagination*, University of California Press, 1973, at p54.
⁵ Sorel, Georges, *Reflections on Violence*, Cambridge University Press, 1999/1908.
⁶ See among others Laclau, Ernesto and Chantal Mouffe, *Hegemony and Socialist Strategy*, Verso, 1985.

celebrated work of Jacques Rancière.[7] The work of Foucault at the ENS developed largely in dialogue with that tradition. But most crucially the key protagonists and representatives of critical theory are the theorists of the Frankfurt School, which emerged during the Weimar Republic when the Institute for Social Research was set up in Frankfurt, and brought within its ambit important thinkers such as Herbert Marcuse, Erich Fromm, Karl Lowenthal and Walter Benjamin, under the directorship of Horkheimer and Adorno. After the war, some of the protagonists returned from exile to the Institute, and their thinking took a 'negative' turn away from the notion that the dialectic might deliver emancipation. After Auschwitz, Adorno would largely surrender political critique to the 'aesthetic turn', while for Horkheimer the prospect of emancipatory action became increasingly remote in the face of the instrumental logic of bourgeois society.

Today critical theory spans a heterogeneous field. On the one hand we have the second and third generations of the Frankfurt School, orbiting the key figure of Jürgen Habermas. Alongside him worked his contemporaries Alfred Schmidt and Albrecht Wellmer, and among the exponents of the third generation were Axel Honneth, Peter Burger, Oskar Negt, Claus Offe and Hauke Brunkhorst. Habermas' highly influential 'communicative turn' was aimed at redirecting critical theory towards a theory of Reason achieved now as *mutual understanding*, pursued in a political dialogue that, given its conditions, presupposes and aspirationally achieves the equal competence of all who enter it. But democracy in the form of communicative reason arguably gives up on the tradition's Marxist legacy, divesting it of much of its radicalism, to reconcile it, eventually, to law in the form of the 'co-originality' and mutual implication of democracy and rights, public and private autonomy. Pitted against this development we find the critical projects of deconstruction (Derrida infinitely closer to Adorno and of course Benjamin than to Habermas) and other currents of poststructuralist and postmodern thought. Many of these currents are discussed in contributions to this collection.

Perhaps the changes and mutations of critical thought tracked in the above are not only to be expected but are actually *faithful* to a thinking that locates itself in history, in a way that makes its insights forever partial, provisional and incomplete. For the purposes of gathering the assumptions that are shared by the many currents of critical theory, and that therefore underpin and inform its very identity, its self-proclaimed historicism is one such shared assumption. The term *immanence* captures this with its understanding of reason as located in history and its refusal to cast reflexivity as something that might lift itself above the situation that informs its iteration. 'Conjuncture' is the term that, in the radical tradition, typically captures both situatedness and opportunity. If immanence is the first pole, the second is the *emancipatory* element of theory: theory is the activity of 'bringing to reason' by confronting the contradictions and tautologies with the explanatory frames within which they are encountered and which supposedly provide the coordinates of meaningful engagement and action. While how 'immanent critique' navigates this tension is a key theme that we will visit later

---

[7] For competing accounts of the significance of this tradition see Badiou, Alain, 'The adventure of French philosophy', *NLR* 35 [2005] 67–77, and Lecourt, Dominique, *The Mediocracy: French Philosophy since the Mid-1970s*, Verso, 2002.

on, for present purposes we note that in the move that invokes, confronts and potentially transcends the context of its iteration, critique places itself on a certain boundary. In its insistence that the givenness of phenomena, the ways in which the fragmented world installs itself as the necessary context of action, *may* be navigated, critical theory renegotiates the boundary between contingency and necessity. In the third section of this chapter we will see that Horkheimer identifies 'necessity [as] a critical concept'[8] that 'contains a protest against the order of things'.[9] By this he means that its reach is not given, but that it harbours political contestation ('protest') by those whose horizon of action it reduces. The term 'liminal' connects the critical insight with thinking the border, in an understanding of 'liminality' as that which concerns the distribution of necessity and contingency across it.

Despite the continuities we are in the process of tracking, there is one staggering difference between the earlier generations of Marxist thinkers on the one hand, and the exponents of Western Marxism after the First World War on the other. It has to do with the question of revolutionary *agency*, or how to conceptualise the *subject* of praxis. Between the 1840s and the 1920s, the working class was the projected bearer of the revolutionary project. At the time of the resurgence of critical theory after the war, the subject was already becoming a question to itself. As the issue of how to conceptualise revolutionary agency under conditions of the rise of mass culture, the multiple fragmentations of the working classes across the globe, anti- and postcolonial struggle, and so on became increasingly problematic, critical theory took two different directions, both Hegelian, but of a radically different tenor. In the first, more mainstream expression, the question of agency is recast as a *struggle for recognition*, with a view to exploring the structures of reciprocity and agonistic engagement that embed actors in social contexts and habitats.[10] In the second, more radical *marxisant* expression, with an emphasis not on agonism but on antagonism, the critical gaze largely turned away from theorising the 'subject' and towards theorising the 'event' of revolutionary action. Alain Badiou is a recent example of this tendency,[11] while for Jacques Rancière, who is much closer to the Hegelian roots (and Lukács' idea of an emergent subjectivity), it is in the *event* of staging resistance that revolutionary *agency* is *enacted*.[12] It may be worth noting here that Rancière's intriguing turn owes much to his resistance to the lesson of his teacher Althusser,[13] and he dedicated much of his earlier ethnographic work to recovering the workers' own revolutionary voice in order to let them, so to say, speak for themselves. Against Althusser's dogged structuralism, where the 'subject' is never more than the surface phenomenon produced by the structure (the 'absent

---

[8] Horkheimer, Max, 'Traditional and critical theory', in *Critical Theory: Selected Essays*, Continuum, 1932/1976, p. 230.

[9] ibid 229.

[10] Honneth, Axel, *The Struggle for Recognition: The Moral Grammar of Social Conflicts*, MIT Press, 1996.

[11] Badiou, Alain, *Being and Event*, A&C Black, 2007.

[12] Rancière, Jacques, *Disagreement: Politics and Philosophy*, University of Minnesota Press, 1999.

[13] Rancière, Jacques, *Althusser's Lesson*, Continuum, 2011. For his return to the Marxism that Althusser rejected, see Rancière, 'Le concept de critique et la critique de l'économie politique des "manuscrits de 1844" au "Capital"', in *Lire le Capital*, PUF, 1998.

cause'), and where the subject position that the proletariat is 'called' to inhabit is an ontological support or 'placeholder' in a field that 'always-already' represents the economy of capital,[14] Rancière's is an attempt to carve out another stage for revolutionary agency. The struggle for recognition here, unlike in Honneth and the later Frankfurt School(s), involves 'a class giv[ing] itself a name, in order to exhibit its situation and respond to the discourse of which it is the object'.[15] The reflexive name-giving, however improbable, is set against the recursive folding back into the processes of misrecognition that underlie identity formation under capitalism. The significance of these acts of forging speaking positions against available distributions must be borne in mind today: they are key to how the critical project understands the processes of subject formation, and the distribution of attention and disregard that they entail.

2. AN INVENTORY OF TERMS

This section looks at terms that are pivotal to the conceptual range and novelty of critical theory. It attempts to provide an understanding of them, and track key interdependencies between them.

2.1 Praxis

Critical theory borrows the term for 'action' from Aristotle, who distinguishes praxis from the contemplative *theoria*. But it realigns it: praxis is no longer contrasted with theory, as in Aristotle, but dialectically tied to it in a relation of mutual constitution. In this relation neither concept precedes the other: 'the old question – which has priority? – is meaningless as it is posed', insisted Marcuse. We saw in discussing the 11th thesis that, against the reduction of reason to surface understandings that 'interpret the world', Marx argued that reason was properly deployed in thematising the 'existent' with the view to forging social change.[16] The thematisation calls forth the facts and events as relevant to the telos of restoring rationality to a 'sunken' world, if we can extend Schelling's beautiful formulation to capture something of the ruinous effects of capitalism.[17] Against the irrationalities with which class society is fraught, irrationalities that emerge as contradictions, tautologies and impasses, against the irrationality of

---

[14] See Althusser, L., *Lenin and Philosophy*, New York, 1971.

[15] Faure, A. and J. Rancière, *La parole ouvrière*, Paris, 2007, p. 9.

[16] The connection is clearly a great deal more subtle than what Ernst Bloch, the highly original Marxist theorist, found 'misconstrued' in America under the banner of pragmatism, 'which derives from an area altogether remote from Marxism, spiritually inferior, and indeed alien to it', despite the fact that it is being 'constantly latched on to, as though it were identical to American cultural barbarism. The basis of American pragmatism is the view that truth is essentially nothing more that the social utility of ideas.' Bloch, Ernst, *On Karl Marx*, Verso, 2018/1968, p. 90.

[17] 'Does not everything announce a sunken life? ... The whole earth is an enormous ruin, whose animals dwell in it as ghosts, and men as spirits, and where many hidden forces and

a system that promises justice as it relentlessly delivers injustice, the aim of the philosopher of the 11th thesis is to restore a properly human rationality. On the one hand, theory equips practice with its coordinates; on the other, practice situates and resituates theory within new coordinates that will inform its possibilities anew. A dialectic develops between theory and practice in a dynamic process that is caught up in history and in the making of history.

The theory/practice distinction installs a border between the two terms, across which the dialectic operates. The boundary is, so to say, that which gives *traction*. Theory measures itself against its ability to rationalise practice, and practice emerges as meaningful with the help of theory. The dialectic keeps them combined and in tension. Any asymmetry that installs itself between theory and practice can work both ways. A deficit on the pole of practice leaves theory as mere contemplation of, and apology for, the status quo; a deficit on the side of theory leaves practice underdetermined. The latter is a more difficult deficit to appreciate, so an example might be helpful – an example, that is, of theory failing to give adequate expression to praxis as self-determined activity. In *The Making of the English Working Class*, Edward Thompson described the communities of handloom weavers in Lancashire and Yorkshire at the end of the eighteenth and the beginning of the nineteenth centuries that sustained independent forms of production and exchange 'without the distortions of masters and middlemen'[18] but were unable to protect and maintain those forms in the face of the advancing capitalist economy. Alasdair MacIntyre makes the important point that what these communities lacked was a 'theory that would have successfully articulated their practice' of solidarity in the organisation of production and that would have equipped them epistemologically to resist the supposed inevitability of the defeat of their very own principles of association emerging out of jointly held conceptions of the common good. They lacked the theory that would help them to articulate, as he puts it, 'virtues adequate to the moral needs of resistance'.[19] The demands placed on theory are steep here, and for MacIntyre it is not Marxism that will meet them. Because if Marx offers a theory of resistance for the weavers – he was indeed impressed by the militancy of the uprising of another community of weavers, in Silesia in 1844 – *it engages them as proletarians*, a constituency incongruous to them in their professional association, not attuned to the life form that made their engagement and resistance meaningful, and, crucially, one that already assumes the defeat of their form of past life. I am reminded of a similar deficit that Tom Nairn attaches to the 'revolutionary explosion' of May 1968. If 1968 failed, he says, it 'failed because it was too novel, and inevitably dwarfed most of the circumstances around it. It was heavy with a significance too great for our times to bear, a premonitory significance which the events of May could only sketch in

---

treasures are held fast as if by unseen powers or magic spells.' Schelling, *Werke*, 1927, quoted in Anderson, *Considerations of Western Marxism*, p. 81.

[18] Thompson, Edward Palmer, *The Making of the English Working Class*, Open Road Media, 1963/2016, at p. 295.

[19] In the 1994 text 'Theses on Feuerbach: a road not taken', included in K. Knight, *The MacIntyre Reader*, 1998, at 232. This point is also developed in MacIntyre, A., 'Epistemological crises, dramatic narrative and the philosophy of science' *The Monist* 60 (1977): 453.

outline.'[20] How eloquent the incomprehension that attaches to that surge of collective action: of an event that broke with the theoretical models available to interpret it. Practice here was *in advance*, to paraphrase Rimbaud on the Paris Commune. And the responsibility that befalls theory, once conscious that it lags behind, is to lend praxis expression in terms that are *adequate to it*, and in time that is still opportune!

If the unity of theory and praxis is what is distinctive of Marxist *method*, it is also what threads together the variants of critical theory, and collects the tradition around a common premise. So far I have attempted to show how the connection can be conceived at the level of conceptual analysis and the rationalising, emancipatory *gesture* (that is, action) of the theoretical undertaking. But there is a second level at which the connection between theory and praxis is forged, and this level explicitly links theory to *collective* action. It can be read in Marx's own rejection of pure theoretical work as a means of social change,[21] his conception of a humanism that comprehends itself in action. And it is renewed and enhanced in the insistence that the unity of theory and practice finds its culmination and completion in the mass revolutionary movement. If today this connection, with few exceptions, appears increasingly remote (see section 1), one must remember that for the generation of thinkers that immediately followed Marx and Engels the connection with practice was part of the lived reality of theoretical engagement; clearly in the case of Lenin and Luxemburg, of course, but also for the subsequent generation, among whom Lukács wrote the constitution of the Hungarian communist party and Gramsci organised the workers' insurgencies of 1919 and 1920, when he led the Turin factory councils, and then founded and led the Italian Communist party in the mid-1920s.[22] The examples are numerous. It was only after the Second World War and perhaps, ironically, with the Frankfurt School of Critical Research itself that had proclaimed with Adorno that 'theory is a form of practice and practice itself is an eminently theoretical concept'[23] that the connection with praxis was renounced, while the communist parties of Europe's South sustained an often difficult relationship with 'their' theorists (as for example in the tense relationship of Althusser to the PCF). And yet the connection with practice remains the task against which critical theory measures itself, not in the relatively easy lexical identification ('theory *is* practice') but in the difficult articulation that demands a certain synchronicity between the two, that demands, in other words, that theory does not outpace the real historical rhythm of popular mobilisation or substitute for the masses' own modalities of engagement and self-understanding, while remaining alive and relevant to those processes.

---

[20] Quattrocchi, Angelo, and Tom Nairn, *The Beginning of the End: France, May 1968*, Verso, 1998.

[21] 'Just as philosophy discovers its material weapons in the proletariat, so the proletariat discovers its intellectual weapons in philosophy' (a contribution to the critique of Hegel's Philosophy of Right).

[22] For Perry Anderson, 'it is a token of his greatness' that Gramsci 'alone embodied in his person a revolutionary unity of theory and practice, of the type that had defined the classical heritage'. In Anderson, *Considerations of Western Marxism*, Verso, 1976, p. 45.

[23] Adorno, T, *Negative Dialectics*, Routledge, 1966/1990, p. 144.

2.2 The Dialectic and the Role of Negation

While the dialectic is absolutely central to critical theory, even at the outset a question presents itself over its designation as *method* or *system*.[24] 'System' ties it too closely to Hegelian philosophy, where it receives its most profound statement but at the same time becomes *locked* into a logic of history; 'method' on the other hand invokes means–ends thinking that not only belittles its constitutive (rather than instrumental) significance to critical theory but also begs the question of what *ends* critical theory deploys the dialectic as the *means of*. However we describe it, nevertheless it is the dialectic that lends critical theory its very dynamic, and places it within the movement of history that it is tasked to at once understand and intervene in.

Against both the metaphysics of systematic philosophy, of which Hegel's was the last major iteration, and empiricism's invitation to the 'commonsensical', critical theory invites the observer to hold up to reason the givens of experience, the understanding of factual situations, replete as they come with antinomy and contradiction. No fact situation is to be deemed final or complete in itself, but always should be seen as an instantiating aspect of the total situation as it is caught up in historical change. 'Men make their own history', Marx famously remarked in the *18th Brumaire*, 'but not under conditions of their own choosing'. Theory delineates that which opens up meaningfully as the field for praxis, the constraints it must navigate and the vistas it may yet uncover. For the interplay to be maintained, the gravity of the factual situation, the *'mere immediacy* of the empirical world' (Lukács), needs to be suspended for alternatives to be glimpsed and, once comprehended, acted upon. This glimpse – the *'Augenblick'* – takes, in Lukács, an altogether different significance,[25] but we cannot presently follow him along that path.

We will remain instead with the significance of *the negative* in the unfolding of the dialectic. The dialectic, as is well known, moves from an initial positive (thesis) through its rejection (antithesis) to a transcendent synthesis or 'sublation' (*Aufhebung* in Hegel) that maintains both moments, and *preserves* the transcended in the act of overcoming it. These, for Hegel, are the markers of the unfolding of reason in history, and the concept of negation, while crucial to that unfolding, is nonetheless transitory, subject in turn to its own negation as history moves forward towards its *telos*. Against Hegel's projection of this smooth passage through the negative, Marx fastened onto the contradictions that persisted in the *reality* of capitalism, identifying negation as constitutive to the formation of subjectivity (degradation reaches its acme with the dehumanisation and objectification of the proletariat: the negative form of absolute deprivation of the 'Nothing that would become Everything'),[26] and suggesting leverage in the *unresolved* contradiction that – as negation – sets reality against itself.

---

[24] On this see Jameson, Fredric, *Valences of the Dialectic*, London, Verso, 2009.

[25] Lukács, Georg, *History and Class Consciousness: Studies in Marxist Dialectics* (R. Livingstone, trans), London: Merlin, 1971/1923.

[26] See Marx, *A Contribution to the Critique of Hegel's Philosophy of Right*. On the constitutive role of negation see also the chapter on critical legal theory and Marxism in this volume.

Taking up Marx's insight, the theorists of the Frankfurt School also fastened onto the moment of negation, and insisted on viewing critical theory as the site of the *negative* thrust of Reason. In their earlier work, indeed, the *critical impulse* sustained itself in its opposition to the order of society as it appears, insistent on the nonidentity of the actual and the rational, and installing itself, as *intervention*, in that faultline between the two. 'A given social order based upon a system of abstract labour and the integration of needs through the exchange of commodities is *incapable of asserting and establishing a rational community*', argued Marcuse. The contradiction cannot be 'sublated' by means of pursuing the systemic logic of bourgeois society; it requires a utopian moment (utopian because unavailable in the given situation) and therefore a commitment to negativity. Horkheimer will also warn in 1942: 'Dialectics is not identical with development … [Social revolution] is not the acceleration of progress but rather the jumping out of progress [der Sprung aus dem Fortschritt heraus].'[27] And later: 'The new society arises from praxis. It goes back to 1871, 1905, and other events. The revolution has a tradition on whose continuation theory is dependent.'[28]

But where Marxism never abandons the idea that the extreme degradation and alienation visited on the proletariat will become the point of dialectical reversal, the critical theorists of Frankfurt – writing in the shadow of the rise of Nazism – came largely to abandon the idea that an emancipatory dialectic might be forged out of the situation they faced, and became increasingly insistent on the moment of negation without sublation. In other words, where the conditions offered no possibility of being put to question against any credible alternative or potentiality, the dialectic was blocked.[29] Horkheimer wrote in *The Eclipse of Reason* that 'inasmuch as subject and object, word and thing cannot be integrated under present conditions, we are driven by the principle of negation to attempt to salvage relative truths from the wreckage of false ultimates'.[30]

2.3 Mediation and Ideology

We will remain with the meaning and use of negation but generalise it beyond the extraordinary circumstances of the rise of fascism, and across the very ordinary operation of capitalist social reproduction. In a letter to Carl Lowenthal in 1934, Adorno wrote of 'the agonising development of the capitalist total situation whose

---

[27] Quoted in Jay, *The Dialectical Imagination*, p. 157.
[28] Horkheimer, Max, *Autoritärer Staat: Aufsätze 1939–1941*, de Munter, 1967, at p. 138.
[29] 'Their legacy would be to place the very notions of historical subjectivity and the idea of an emancipatory dialectic between subject and object in question. Their coauthored essay on *The Dialectic of Enlightenment* (1944) already commenced with an equation of subject-formation and reification. The subject itself is as such a product of reification and dominance and can therefore not be invoked for purposes of contemplating a revolutionary de-reification of social relations, they argued. *Negative Dialectics* (1966) is one of the crucial statements of critical theory's despairing withdrawal from the philosophy of the subject.' Christodoulidis & Van der Walt, 'Critical legal theory: European perspectives', in *The Oxford Handbook of Legal Research* (forthcoming).
[30] Horkheimer, Max, *The Eclipse of Reason*, Continuum Books, 1974/1947, at p. 183.

horrors exist so essentially in the precision of the mechanism of *mediation*'.[31] We are already familiar with the term 'mediation' and what it expresses for us. Here are some examples: the operation of the capitalist economy and the material reproduction of society are constitutively *mediated* by legal, political, moral and economic concepts that simultaneously organise the network of commodity exchange and *give it expression* as the coordination of acts of freedom and autonomous agency; the operation of the labour market that secures the extraction of surplus value *is expressed* as freely contracted labour, and so on. There are key features of material organisation of society that are thereby distorted, misrepresented, eclipsed or elided in the process of giving them expression. Critical theory here measures itself against the *operation of ideology*.

If ideology in common parlance usually means a body of ideas and beliefs, in the understanding of critical theory it is related to a *function*. This function is to sustain relations of domination through a move at the level of representation.[32] Marx invites us to think about how real relations are represented and lived, and locates ideology as that system of representation that mediates man's relationship to the material conditions of his life. Ideology here names a certain misrepresentation, a certain misreading of the conditions that allows the continuation of a system of domination that presents itself as free. As John Thompson has put it:

> the concept of ideology calls our attention to the ways in which meaning is mobilized in the service of dominant individuals and groups, that is, the ways in which the meaning constructed and conveyed by symbolic forms serves to establish and sustain structured social relations from which some individuals and groups benefit more than others.[33]

There is a connection here between material production and the control of intellectual production, but that is not all. Ideology covers the multitude of ways in which capitalism diffuses resistance and critique through subtle moves and strategies at the level of representation. To reproduce itself over time, capitalism must ensure that relations of production are reproduced, and that class struggle is prevented from irrupting in a way that might challenge the capitalist distribution of advantage.

Our earlier *insistence on negation*, and the stance of 'being-against' that it informs, can be comprehended as levelled against the ways in which systems of meaning and dominant representations are mobilised ideologically to install false givens and assumptions at the point of recovery of the meaning of the possibilities of association. Critical theory faces a difficult task against the pervasiveness of ideology, especially when the dominant interests it serves combine in *hegemonic* constellations.[34] Organised and transmitted through the network of predominantly cultural institutions, the system

---

[31] In Jay, *The Dialectical Imagination* at p. 66, my emphasis.

[32] Here is Marx in *The German Ideology*: 'The class which has the means of material production at its disposal, has the control at the same time over the means of intellectual production, so that thereby, generally speaking, the ideas of those who lack the means of intellectual production are subject to it.' (1846/1932, p. 176).

[33] Thompson, John B., *Studies in the Theory of Ideology*, University of California Press, 1984, at p. 73.

[34] For the meaning of hegemony see Gramsci, Antonio, *Prison Notebooks*, Columbia University Press, 1992/1931.

of power becomes hegemonic to the extent that it can minimise the level of repression it requires in order to secure its continuation, because the organisation of the totality of dialectical mediations in such constellations extracts allegiance and secures consent. How, asks Marcuse in *One-Dimensional Man*,[35] might the negative thrust of reason be asserted in a society that thus controls the consciousness of its members? Ultimately its achievement will be to allow language to voice the protest of the oppressed, and prevent it from mutating into a stream of affirmations or at best concessions before 'false ultimates'. Our discussion has revolved around the question of how a *critical* reflexivity might be forged out of these inert or suppressed material, the resources of the society in which we find ourselves, the ideas, stock of meanings, interpretation of history and imaginaries that contain them: a critical reflexivity that may be able to resist the reproduction of the systemic givens.

Critique strives to put itself at some distance from the conceptual forms that determine identity and action, if what is given over to 'understanding' (*Verstand*) by the dominant imaginary is to be prevented from establishing itself as unquestioned and unquestionable context for thought and action. In a crucial sense this involves the introduction of contingency where there is necessity. Certainly, as we discussed already, the reflexive move is emphatically *not* a stepping *outside* of the context that might afford an objective (as opposed to class-inflected) view, but always carries the partiality of contextually situated and historically conditioned perspectives. But where founding assumptions carry self-evidence into the imaginary constitution of society by mobilising specific systems of signification and material support, critical theory demands the recognition of the contingency of those foundations. This is both key to critical thinking and one of its steepest requirements – one that Althusser, for one, thought impossible in relation to the fundamentals of capitalist relations.[36] Marx's analysis of the fetish phenomenon was for him a case in point: if the commodity form installs itself from the outset as the very way in which we conceptualise social relations, action and agency, then they cannot be stepped behind to recover them in a nonalienated form.

The distinction in fact of what is necessary and what contingent lies at the heart of the task that critical theory sees itself as addressing, sometimes described as 'anti-necessitarian' thinking.[37] The idea is to resist the temptation to describe the realm of freedom from the vantage point of (supposed) necessity; to resist the argument, typically, that *given* human nature, *such* are the options available for the exercise of freedom. Famously, for example, Thomas Hobbes extracted the reason for the constitution of civil society from the givenness of human nature. The granting of absolute sovereignty to the Leviathan connects to what motivates human behaviour –

---

[35] Marcuse, Herbert, *One-Dimensional Man: The Ideology of Advanced Industrial Society*, Sphere Books, 1964.

[36] For Althusser's rejection of the Hegelian tradition and the direct reconnection with the scientific theory of historical materialism, see *Reading Capital*. For Althusser, Hegelian 'historicism was a ideology in which society becomes a circular expressive totality, history a homogeneous flow of linear time, philosophy a self-consciousness the historical process, capitalism a universe essentially defined by alienation, communism a state of true humanism beyond alienation.' See Anderson, *Considerations on Western Marxism*, p. 70.

[37] See e.g. Unger, Roberto Mangabeira, *False Necessity: Anti-Necessitarian Social Theory in the Service of Radical Democracy*, Cambridge University Press, 1987.

fear, *given the nature of man* that makes '[him] wolf to man' and the 'natural state' as that of 'constant fear, and danger of violent death; and the life of man solitary, poor, nasty, brutish and short'. An argument that begins with the supposed 'givenness' of the nature of 'man' and what moves him allows the constitution of civil society to be understood as coincident with its subjugation to the sovereign. In other words, at the point of the recovery of the meaning of civil society, a point that cannot be stepped back from, is installed the necessity of its subjugation. The assumptions over necessity, whatever their content, across the theories of social contract premise the 'political' on necessary assumptions about human nature. To this Marx responds with an argument that attributes near infinite plasticity to the possibilities of human association.

But to return to the key term under scrutiny, the focus and stake of 'mediation' are the processes of meaning construction. If, as we read it above, the 11th thesis aimed to elevate Understanding to Reason, it was because understanding of the world, the observation of reality, is never immediate to itself; it is instead mediated through categories, structures and conceptual schemes. These mediations are of course abstractions; they select and classify the 'raw' material of observation, individuate events, establish causal connection, generalise specific features of the situation while suppressing others, and in that mediation they configure the real. The creation of meaning occurs in terms of specific imaginaries, with their vocabularies and rules of signification. It also occurs in the context of specific sets of social relations, institutional arrangements and processes of social reproduction. In both senses meaning construction is always *in media res*: situated in history, partial and perpetually incomplete. It may appear surprising that critical theory directs us to the mediating function that involves abstraction, since Marx famously denounced precisely capitalism's transformation of concrete labour into 'abstract labour', the concreteness of social life into the abstract lawlike forms of exchange-dependent civil society. But what Marx was denouncing in these abstractions was not abstraction itself, which is a constitutive moment of thought, but the specificity of bourgeois abstractions that involve specific substitutions: of use value for exchange value, of living labour for dead labour, of social being for individualism, and so on. Critical theory calls for attention to the fact and the nature of mediation; understands it as historical and therefore as revisable; and in that sense is both attuned to the ways in which social change might be pursued and more importantly attuned to the distinction between what is contingent, and could therefore be thought of, thematised and undertaken otherwise, and what is not.

But if negation invites us to resist ideology and hold the *present* up to reason, because it divests realities of the self-evidence with which they present themselves to our understanding, it fulfils a similar function when it comes to the *past*. Here the emphasis of the critical project is on how reason fixes its gaze on, and uncovers, the past. For this we turn to another important concept of the lexicon of critical theory, that of *genealogy*.

2.4 Genealogy

'A true dialectics was the attempt to see the new in the old instead of simply the old in the new', wrote Adorno in the *Metacritique*.[38] This is clearly not a statement to the effect that 'history matters', as easy references to the notion of genealogy so often assume. It is instead a dialectical intervention in the temporal dimension of the present/past: it alerts us to the fact that every new constellation that we inhabit as political actors repositions us before the challenge – and renewed capacity – to read the past as it becomes available to our understanding at each turn. This repositioning introduces a new level of contingency across the temporal dimension of meaning construction. It works against the assumption that the contingency of the future is set before and against the determinism of the present and the past. Instead the 'active' role of the contestation of the past in the present sets the latter, too, on a contested basis; a certain fluidity is introduced across both borders (past/present/future) and along the entire axis of the temporal. And if genealogy is often associated with 'subjugated knowledges', as the literature on and around Foucault frequently reminds us, it is the *disruptive* thrust of genealogy that allows their recovery *against* the way in which dominant historical trajectories establish lineages and causal continuities that 'subjugate' them.

'What I would call genealogy', Foucault famously wrote in 1977, '[is] a form of history which can account for the constitution of knowledges, discourses, domains of objects, etc, without having to make reference to a subject which is either transcendental in relation to a field of events or runs in empty sameness throughout the course of history'.[39] For Foucault (who takes his inspiration from Nietzsche), 'there is nothing primary to interpret': everything is already interpretation. If genealogy is a history of the series of interpretations, it is also a history of how things have come to be seen as objective. The genealogist, Foucault puts it memorably, is tasked with 'recognis[ing] the events of history, its jolts, its surprises, its unsteady victories and unpalatable defeats'; tasked with understanding the 'hazardous play of dominations'[40] against what comes to install itself as the apparent objectivity of the present. That is why Foucault's emphasis is on the events of history, and that is why his genealogy is *disruption*: a contingency read back into histories to destabilise them at the junctures where they assert objectivity and constitute themselves as a knowledge. Let us be clear about this point of method: the *genealogical* coupure allows us to cut into historical trajectories to look at how, at crucial junctures, certain options were discarded and certain options were installed as conditions of the range of further developments. With attention focused on how discourses harness the power of truth, genealogy points to the contingent constitution of those objectivities. Accordingly, a profound possibility and urgency attaches to the genealogical method: *urgency* because histories – in their paradigmatic form – are caught up in trajectories that *offer nothing as alternative*; and profound *possibility* because genealogical method holds the historical framework itself

---

[38] Quoted in Jay, *The Dialectical Imagination*, at p. 69.
[39] Foucault, Michel, *Language, Counter-Memory, Practice: Selected Essays and Interviews*, Cornell University Press, 1977, p. 144.
[40] ibid, p. 148.

to question in a way that both exposes the points of foreclosure on which current certitudes depend, and directs historical insight back to the discarded histories of those certitudes.

Foucault's genealogy is tied to what he calls the archaeological method. What the archaeology 'excavates' along the temporal path-dependency of meaning are the junctures where determinants set the present on its path. It asks: what were the possibilities and contingencies that might have been thereby passed over, elided or obscured? And while Foucault was most interested in uncovering the histories of discursive formations as a series of interpretations on which 'violent or surreptitious' direction was 'imposed',[41] he points critical theory in the directions of what it means to reappropriate the past, 'bend it to [a different] will' and restore it to alternative interpretations that might challenge current certitudes; to return the past, as it were, to its potentiality.[42] A critical intervention of this kind addresses the question of the conditions of possibility of the formation of knowledges; it addresses, in other words, the gathering work that explanatory frameworks and contexts perform, with their specific forces of rationalisation at play. Rationalisation would include here the range of classifications, causalities, imputations, the array of techniques of selection, through which the past is rendered operative for the present. And in a move that today we associate with the notion of deconstruction, it attempts to trace their genesis and operation; if the past is going to be released from such determination, to question their functionality; and, if negation is still what drives critical intervention, to thereby render them inoperative. Only in this way will the *fore*closing of options be resisted, and an enhanced reflexivity restored to the present in a way that equips it to revisit the distinction between necessity and contingency outwith the seemingly intractable path-dependencies that hold the present captive to the past.

3. IMMANENT CRITIQUE: THEORY AS 'GENUINE FORCE'

In Max Horkheimer's essay of 1932,[43] *traditional* and *critical theory* are contrasted in a series of stark binaries. The inaugurating move of *traditional theory* involves the separation of questions of fact from questions of value, research from evaluation, description from prescription. In 'traditional theory', conceptual systems (methodologies) that organise our knowledge of the world receive correction according to their own criteria of salience and weight, in accordance, that is, to their capacity to sustain their own internal coherence. The observer perceives herself as passive in the act of reception, as if, says Horkheimer, s/he brings nothing to the process. At the same time the perceived fact stands independently of *the act* that recognises it as fact. For

---

[41] To quote the passage in full: 'If interpretation is the violent or surreptitious appropriation of a system of rules, which in itself has no essential meaning, in order to impose a direction, to bend it to a new will, to force its participation in a different game ... then the development of humanity is a series of interpretations' (Foucault, 'Nietzsche, Genealogy, History').

[42] Returning the past to its potentiality is the aspiration that sustains Agamben's method in *Signatura rerum. Sur la méthode*, Vrin, 2008.

[43] Horkheimer, 'Traditional and critical theory'.

Horkheimer, this dual misapprehension misses the crucial insight that 'facts which are presented to our senses' are '*socially pre-formed* in two ways: through the historical character of the object perceived and through the historical character of the perceiving organ'.[44] The perceived fact is, in effect, codetermined by ideas and concepts. The act of perception is clearly connected, says Horkheimer, with material processes of production that effect 'the mediation of the factual through the activity of society as a whole'.[45] But it is 'easy at this point to confuse two questions: the mediation of the factual through the activity of society as a whole, and the question of the influence of the measuring instrument'.[46] Both are relevant but in distinct ways. 'As man reflectively records reality, he separates and rejoins pieces of it, and concentrates on some particulars while failing to notice others.' It is these processes of selection, of disassembling and reassembling the 'pieces', with the full complement of anticipatory assumptions, projected path-dependencies, and 'hidden conflicting forces', that Horkheimer suggests that 'traditional theory' misses or elides in the perception and representation of the world of ordered concepts that forms its object. Take bourgeois society, he suggests, 'in which the life of the society proceeds from the economy only at the cost of excessive friction, in a stunted form and almost, as it were, accidentally'.[47] The problem is, he says with extraordinary foresight, that 'contemporary political economics are unable to derive practical profit from the fragmentary questions they discuss'.[48]

Against the fragmentation that pervades traditional theory, a fragmentation that is constitutive of the fundamental divisions (fact/value, subject/object) through which it operates and therefore unaddressable by it, Horkheimer will invite the *critical* recuperation of reason. The critical engagement 'leads to a re-assignment of degrees of relative importance to individual elements of the theory, forces further concretisations and determines which [scientific insights] are significant for critical theory at any given time'.[49] 'The world that is given to the individual is the product of the activity of society as a whole.'[50] A crucial insight about the unity of theory emerges in this suggestion of the recuperation of reason. In the face of everything that has been said about fragmentation above, the unity of theory is only achievable vis-à-vis the unity of the situation that confronts it. This dialectical tie is crucial for the role of theory that confronts, under capitalist conditions, a reality riddled by contradiction, in other words a reality that *cannot* be theorised as a unity. And the importance of this insight is this: the fact that theory in its current conjuncture cannot achieve the sufficient level of internal coherence vis-à-vis contradiction does not make *it* deficient; instead the recuperation of reason forces the theoretical undertaking not in the direction of *internal* critique and the readjustment of its own methodological assumptions, but in the

---

[44] ibid 200.
[45] ibid 201.
[46] ibid 200–1.
[47] ibid 203.
[48] ibid 228.
[49] ibid 234.
[50] ibid 200.

direction of making rational the disunity that confronts it, equipped now with the reality-transforming force of *immanent* critique.

What would the self-awareness of thought[51] – what we have called its *reflexivity* – achieve confronted with its object under conditions of fragmentation, substitution, and so on – conditions, that is, of *disunity*? How might this stunted reflexivity – available to 'understanding' – be recuperated as self-awareness in the reflexivity of reason? Since 'theory [as] a unified whole has its proper meaning only in relation to the contemporary situation',[52] the task against which the critical attitude measures itself is to achieve 'its proper meaning' by addressing in a *coherent* way what in effect confronts it as a *dispersal* of social totality. Inevitably theory will be drawn into an 'evolution' as a result. It might be useful to note that this was never an issue for Kant's critical enterprise. For Kant, the primary transcendental move of critical thought, which is the transcendental condition of knowledge, presupposes the existence of its object and reflects on the *a priori* that conditions the possibility of our knowledge of it. To Kant the question of the 'evolution' of theory *in tandem* with the reality it comprehends is in any case lost, since the things-in-themselves are unavailable to perception and to any sense of equivalence to the concepts that mediate them. To Hegel the transcendental moment, the overcoming of Reason's limitation, is a matter of history or of the 'cunning of reason'. It is only with the Left-Hegelians, and Marx in particular, that 'reason comes to stand over against itself [that is, over against its instantiations] in *purely critical fashion*'.[53] The Hegelian moment allows us to recover the critical vein in Marxism from the standpoint of its own philosophical foundation.

But we do not need to dwell further on the philosophical foundations for present purposes. Instead, let us return to the task that philosophical critique sets itself in view of the thesis, Marx's 11th thesis, that lies at its root. All theory, critical or traditional, derives its statements about real relationships from basic universal concepts. But unlike traditional theory, in critical theory these universal concepts do not install themselves on one side of the distinction between diagnosis and cure, description and prescription, but on the boundary itself. Because if in traditional theory the object is not affected by the theory that describes it, critical theory casts its descriptions (its universal concepts) as relevant to its own emancipatory function vis-à-vis necessity. That is why Horkheimer says that 'a consciously critical attitude is part of the development of society'; because the diagnosis of the pathology is not independent of its overcoming. The judgement passed on the 'necessity' inherent in the previous course of events engages also a struggle to change it from 'a blind to a meaningful necessity'. Hence for Horkheimer, as we saw, 'necessity is a critical concept';[54] and that is why 'it contains a protest against the order of things'.[55] Where in traditional theory 'necessity means the independence of the event from the observer',[56] critical theory as the 'tribunal of

---

[51] ibid 209.
[52] ibid 238.
[53] ibid 204.
[54] ibid 230.
[55] ibid 229.
[56] ibid 230.

reason' theorises a world in which the necessity of an object becomes the necessity of a 'rationally mastered event'.

And that is also why 'the tension between the concept and being', theory and the social world, 'is inevitable and ceaseless'. Critical theory installs itself in the instituting gap between the two and what drives it is not some *speculative* commitment to coherence, but to a deficit that is *experienced* by social actors, as alienation. 'The critical theorist finds himself *confronted* with the real experience of disharmony or alienation.' The transmission of theory is aroused by prevailing injustice, says Horkheimer, 'today, when the whole weight of the existing state of affairs is pushing mankind towards the surrender of all culture and relapse into darkest barbarism'.[57] Much of Horkheimer's critical enterprise is directed to tracking the 'productive' tension between processes he deems 'objective' and the 'subjective' experience they generate in those who find themselves subject to them. The embeddedness in experience is crucial for immanent critique in this respect: it means that the representation of discrepancy and contradiction is not merely an *expression* of historical reality but a force of *change* within it. 'Immanence' always-already implicates the historically poised, necessarily unfinished nature of human engagement, which suggests that the engagement is not something subjects can stand back from, but one that comes upon them with the 'force of present distress' which they need to 'make rational'.[58] The emphasis in all this is on the experiential dimension, the lived experience of suffering. 'I do not know', Horkheimer wrote, 'how far metaphysicians are correct ... But I do know that they are usually impressed only to the smallest degree by what men suffer.'[59] The incomprehensibility of suffering as such calls forth a response by the subject.

The response may take – and indeed, at least at first, it often does – the form of pure negation: an injunction that *this is unjust*. In an important essay, Paul Ricoeur identified that very injunction as one that crucially *precedes* the theories of justice that one might engage to justify it and lend it weight. 'The cry *"it is unfair"*,' he writes, 'often indeed expresses a clearer intuition regarding the true nature of society and the place that violence still holds within it, than any discourse over what justice rationally or reasonably requires'.[60] This temporal 'anomaly' connotes something important about the crucial function of negation as we developed it above. Let us return to it, now with the help of a real example.

In autumn 2005, the deaths of two young people in the Parisian suburb of Clichy-sous-Bois sparked rioting on an unprecedented scale. In a period of a few weeks the riots had spread to banlieues across France. In and around these suburban ghettos insurgent crowds burned cars, damaged buildings and clashed with police. The scale of the violence was such that it resulted in the French government's decision to implement emergency laws dating from the Algerian war of independence. The reactions from

---

[57] ibid 241.
[58] ibid, see 215.
[59] In Jay, *The Dialectical Imagination*, at p. 46.
[60] This is what Paul Ricoeur says in a tantalisingly short extract from his *L'acte de Juger*: 'Nous n'accédons au sens de la justice que par le détour de la protestation contre l'injustice. Le cri: "C'est injuste!" exprime bien souvent une intuition plus clairvoyante concernant la nature véritable de la société, et la place qu'y tient encore la violence, que tout discours rationnel our raisonable sur la justice.' In Ricoeur, *Le Juste*, Paris, Esprit, 1995, p. 190.

both government and public intellectuals were characteristically damning. For the prominent Gaullist intellectual Alain Finkielkraut, the riots sprang from a religiously motivated hate for the Republic; Nicolas Sarkozy, at the time Interior Minister, adopted 'warlike semantics', promising France that he would get rid of the 'thugs', the 'rabble' ('les débarrasser des voyous … de la racaille') and using the metaphor of a 'Kärcher' (a high powered cleaning hose) when speaking of his intentions to clean the suburbs of the 'scum' inhabiting these areas.[61]

If on the one side the *malaise des banlieues* was offered only misrecognition ('religious hatred', 'thuggery'), if it was altogether denied the dignity of the signifier 'resistance' to the violence of systemic marginalisation that generated it, on the other side the normative dynamics of the uprisings were neither harnessed nor structured into meaningful political claim or strategy by the insurgents. Nor was there anything like collective agency.[62] As far as the *banlieusards* were concerned, their action was played out on the field of negation: their objection to the advancing diminishment of life chances took the form of an objection – '*not this*' – whose 'expression' was violence. A political claim for recognition had not yet been fashioned or articulated. We might venture the suggestion that the 'not yet' at stake here is the stake of critical theory. Since we have explored at some length above the meaning of *negation* and the forging of its own particular understanding of *reflexivity* at the juncture of theory and praxis, let us attempt to see how this might elucidate for us the *meaning* of the uprisings. What negation marks is a break with the *understandings* that have been offered to rationalise the situation. To borrow a formulation from the increasingly influential work of Jacques Rancière, it is a break with the available 'distribution of the sensible', the way in which political discourse attributes meaning to actions and events. But negation does not yet equip the insurgency with a 'scheme of interpretation' or of 'intelligibility'; it does not equip it with an alternative signification. At the level of negation it is merely a marker of a normative gap between the normative language available and a social experience of the diminishment of life chances. At one level, then, the insurgents' action is an injunction against the ways in which the available categories of political rationality (democracy, rights, equality) fail to collect rationally, and to give expression to, *their* experience *as* French citizens. This falling short of the categories available to signify the dispossession experienced registers only as a suffering that cannot find articulation. And the mobilisation, thematised from the point of view of political order (the 'order of the police', Rancière calls it) as a meaningless lashing out, has no language to dignify it as anything but that. This inadequacy walls in the suffering as necessary, written into the lives of the inhabitants of the ghettos, and immanent with the full weight of the impasse.

It is on this terrain that critical theory's promise of recuperation is inscribed. But inscription presupposes a register, and it finds it only in the categories (citizenship,

---

[61] See *Libération*, 31 October 2005.
[62] In his work on the sociology of the uprisings, Michel Kokoreff states that the riots 'ont marqué une entrée en politique des jeunes non seulement animés par le désir de détruire mais par une volonté de confrontation'. See Kokoreff, Michel, 'Sociologie de l'émeute. Les dimensions de l'action en question', *Déviance et Société* 30 (2006): 521–33, at 528 and Kokoreff, Michel, *Sociologie des émeutes*, Paris, Payot, 2008.

rights, and so on) that the action attempts to place in doubt. This is the moment of immanent critique. It is immanent in the sense described above, as carried in the experience of the dispossessed, and thus engaging them normatively. And it is immanent, too, to the language available to describe that experience, the language of rights, democracy and equality. Its challenge is to articulate and exploit *contradiction*: that which erupted as negation seeks a register in a language that might rationalise it as the political order's simultaneous *promise* and *denial* of speaking position (citizenship) and claim (rights, equality, justice). Resistance seeks articulation in terms of the very categories that the action places in doubt. If the inscription succeeds, then it gains purchase in a system that promises but is *incapable* of delivering speaking position or justice to the insurgents, because its promise is undercut at the level of its material foundation of exploitative relations of capitalist production. 'Incapable' is an important word here; unlike 'likely', it carries a structural limitation. Equality is structurally undercut in a system that organises production along class lines: it is at once offered and denied; recognition is a lie where constituencies of the citizenry become superfluous as producers of value; less abstractly, a capitalist labour market cannot deliver on the promise of 'full employment' because a market – in order that it be able to optimise supply and demand – requires a structural element of unemployment to maintain itself *as* a market. In all these cases the promise hits upon a constitutive limitation, and in this respect, critique distinguishes itself from criticism as simply directed to rectify inconsistencies.[63] In contrast, the object of critique is to expose contradiction and offers neither rectification nor reconciliation. It is instead poised against the 'wrong' where the wrong attaches to the very 'recognition order' that organises the semiotic field, and also the meaning of resistance to it. At this point the circle closes and theory fastens on to transformative praxis – because the solution *has to be* transcendent to the system that harboured it.

Is it incidental, then, that it is at this juncture that bourgeois theory most vocally rails against the connection of political action to suffering? The theoretical objection is raised with predictable anxiety whenever the solution is carried in the mode of engagement of those who have suffered the injustice on their skin, so to speak – from the 'sans-cullottes' who forced their wretchedness on the streets of Paris during the French Revolution, to the insurgents of the banlieues. Hannah Arendt warns repeatedly in *On Revolution*, with palpable alarm, that if you build a political theory on suffering, you end up with Robespierre and the Terror. It is a measure of her influence in the Anglo-American academy that this argument has been taken up as a credo by political theorists of the antidialectical bend; and yet all theoretical endeavour *can* and *will be* judged on its politics, even where its demand is presented, as so very eloquently in Arendt, at the metalevel of theory construction.

At this point we might conclude this short excursus with another reference to Marx on Feuerbach, this time the fourth thesis, where he writes about the 'cleavages and self-contradictions' that circulate at the level of secular society, a society 'both [to be] understood in its contradiction and revolutionized in practice'. Critical theory attempts

---

[63] Rancière's distinction between politics/police is a powerful expression of the impasse that invites 'dissensus' as the form of its transcendence, while J-F Lyotard's *Le Différend* remains the most devastating account of the impossibility of such a move.

to navigate this terrain of the nexus with praxis as appropriate to the conjunctures in which it finds itself. At no point has the reflexivity of theoretical reason lifted itself above history and the specific coordinates that determine the horizon of meaning. The first, semiotic, route took us through the processes of meaning construction, and the 'mediation' of factual situations through concepts that read them no longer as *series* of phenomena but as *combinations*, mediated and related within larger semantic fields and subfields. Critical thought found its opportunity in the irreducible contradictions that it attempted to 'bring to reason': contradictions between the promise of equality and the reproduction of an ever widening inequality; between the promise of inclusion and the reality of marginalisation; between the promise of dignity and the infliction of exploitation; between the promise to protect the right to work and the generalisation of job insecurity and underemployment, and so on. By tracking, fastening onto and 'exploiting' the contradictions that the imaginary constitution of society incurs, the critical method is able to engage actors normatively in forms of contestation of the reality of their situation. Negation, we saw, was a first step to resisting the necessity of the situation, and critique one to imagining the situation otherwise. And against the false givens of traditional theory, critical theory harboured 'the idea of a theory that becomes a 'genuine force,' revolutionising agency (or 'the self-awareness of the subjects')[64] in the social dimension, and in the substantive dimension establishing that the theoretical elaboration of a state of affairs is indeed a step towards changing it.

4. CRITICAL THEORY AND THE LAW

This final section consists in a brief, suggestive rather than systematic, attempt to carry over some of the key insights of critical theory into legal thought. The history of critical legal theory as it emerged in Europe in the way described above ties it constitutively, on the one hand, to the state, as the form of the political organisation of society, and on the other to the political economy, as the site of its material reproduction. In reference to the state, critical theory thematises the institution of law as that which organises and mediates the relation of the state to civil society. The other constitutive reference, to the political economy, typically grounds this tradition of thinking about the law in the materiality of the practices of social production and reproduction. It is in these connections, of the institution of law to the domains of the state and of the political economy, that critical legal theory locates the function of law, with the emancipatory potential it affords on the one hand, and the obstacles to emancipation which it imposes on the other.

Neither of these two constitutive references – to the state and to material production – can be taken today to have the meaning they had for previous generations of critical theorists. The demand that theory confront its current historical conjuncture remains one of Marx's most valuable legacies, and such an effort today would demand that we turn – as far as the political economy is concerned – to the modalities and expressions

---

[64] 'La praxis qui révolutionne la realité' wrote the young Lukács in his *Dialectique et Spontaneité*, only recently unearthed (in 2001) in the ancient archives of the Lenin Institute in Moscow.

of capitalist renewal, its new forms of flexible accumulation, the staggering growth of financialisation, the fragmentation of labour and the new forms of its exploitation, and so on, and – as far as the state is concerned – to the new functions of the state in the era of global flows, the new linkages of states and capitals, the articulations and disarticulations of state steering functions, and so on. As far as critical *legal* thinking is concerned, it involves a massive reorientation to the new modalities of organisation (and dispersal) of economic and political power.

How the organising categories of critical theory described above cross the institutional threshold into legal thinking is a question addressed across the range of the contributions to this book. Let me revisit briefly the key terms of our inventory (of section 2) in order to point out some possible connections, as well as the profound difficulty and effort it takes for critical theory to pierce the institutional veil. In each case the conceptual reach of the law and its connection to practice appears to be disciplined by law's function. And against this disciplining effect, the critical undertaking confronts particular difficulties that relate to the *institutional* nature of law.

First, critical theory's connection to praxis must negotiate what we might identify as the constitutive limitations of the institutional. Institutions reduce the contingency of human interaction; they entrench models of social relationships, and, in doing so, hedge in imaginative political uses and opportunities. To *understand* the law, it appears to be emphatically the case, is *not to change* it. Second, critical theory's *dialectical imagination* comes up again and again against the dominant (and severely antidialectical) paradigms, on the one hand, of its autonomous or 'pure' self-reproduction (Kelsen, Luhmann), and on the other, of its heteronomous dependence on politics and the exception (Schmitt, Agamben). Third, the very particular *mediation* of legal meaning is achieved through the ways in which it puts concepts in connection and in sequence and oversees application through the regulation of procedure. At once both enabling and limiting, these substantive and procedural rules deliver what Niklas Luhmann calls the '*reduction-achievement*', which is law whose malleability is controlled through secondary rules that contain it and orient it to its proper function to channel and stabilise expectations. To secure this function the legal system needs to maintain a relative balance of stability and innovation, or, more precisely, to reproduce structures of normative expectations through controlled innovation. Innovations can only be grafted onto what already exists, and what already exists sets the thresholds of what might count as relevant information, what – and under what circumstances – may count as a 'surprise' in the system that might lead it to vary expectations. The legal observer will appreciate that the balanced renewal of law, of what is new and what business as usual, can only lean so far in the direction of variety without jeopardising the function of the law that must at some level meet the exigencies of the rule of law, and yield to protected expectations. Fourth, if genealogy calls us to unpick the law at the joints at which it establishes and renews its repertoire of reasons, it must first confront law's powers of 'homology'[65] and the unique methods it has to marshal the past in support of current arrangements, radically limiting our ability to reimagine or disentrench it except

---

[65] I have discussed the mechanisms of 'homology' and 'deliberate deadlock' in a previous paper: Christodoulidis, E., 'Strategies of rupture', *Law & Critique* 1 (2009).

in piecemeal ways.[66] Because of course the law overwhelmingly reactivates known ground. The pattern of what can be varied, what contested comes heavily predetermined, not because the borders of law are heavily policed (though they are that too) but because structures of expectations release opportunities of variation selectively on the back of what is entrenched as invariant. Hovering above the reproduction of legal expectations along given pathways is the requirement of coherence, cutting away at genealogy at its core. Granted, there is nothing deterministic about the givenness of context (contexts *are* reconfigured as selections are made), but it is also counterproductive to exaggerate the leverage that critique is afforded under the conditions of normative closure and legal self-reference.

And yet, improbable as its conditions appear, critical theory has a vital role to play in legal thought, enhanced by the urgent need for its intervention in law's field of the reproduction of ideology and advantage. It is because law is steeped in tautology, paradox and contradiction that critical legal thinking can graft itself on the fault lines of law's articulations.[67] Tautology is renewed in the grand positivisms of the day that define *the law as what the law says it is*, a circularity that becomes productive for the unity of the legal system at the point where rules lock into the system of law through (secondary or constitutional) rules that recognise them as rules. Critical theory might address these 'joints' at which the constitutional discourse walls itself in, in a gesture of immunisation. Paradox emerges as law's other-reference to the interests, persons and domains that it is called to regulate, mediated exclusively through its own self-reference. Contradictions emerge at the point at which the law, as tied to the processes of the material reproduction of society, couches in the universality of its categories the partiality of its distributions. Critical insight can address such operations, both where paradox institutes a gap and where contradiction conceals the elision it performs.

Let me end with three examples, three exemplary contradictions, with a view to identifying what the application of immanent critique might deliver in each case. The emphasis, remember, is on the experiential dimension. This is to say that legal actors confront the deficits in theory construction as experiential deficits, and therefore their engagement in the legal situation is not something that they can stand back from but is one that, remember, comes upon them with the 'force of present distress' which they need to 'make rational'. It is the lived dimension that is the potential site of disruption of the economy of representation that would otherwise organise meaning, seal it over and, in this state of self-immunisation, place it out of reach.

A first contradiction famously arises between constituent and constituted power. Here, pitched at the most abstract level of the constitutional register, a certain irresolution installs itself: constitution-*making* comes within a pregiven context of

---

[66] Christopher Tomlins writes of 'a disenchanting mode of historical analysis, that strips [law] of its metaphysical dignity, unity, and coherence by exposing law as the outcome of mundane and profane processes and interests'. Tomlins, C., 'After critical legal history: scope, scale, structure', *Annual Review of Law and Social Science* 8 (2012): 31, 37.

[67] I refer here to the way that Hans Lindahl develops the idea that 'questionability' grafts itself onto the faultlines of law to carve a space also for radical innovation. See Lindahl, Hans, *Fault Lines of Globalization: Legal Order and the Politics of A-Legality*, Oxford University Press, 2013.

'recognition' that alone establishes its objective meaning as 'constitution'. Constitutional discourse thus forever folds back the constituent into the representational space of the constituted, which means that 'constituent power' comes harnessed to the constitutional order at the point of the very recovery of its meaning as constituent. A form of deadlock that is 'constitutive' of legal agency and legal opportunity underlines the constitution of democratic capitalism and leaves constitutively immune the regime of property and rights that it sanctions. To the extent that the articulation of the two moments is understood as giving expression to *democratic* constitutionalism, and it is this that provides the key ground of legitimacy to the constitutional order, immanent critique in this context would fasten onto the democratic dimension and insist on the transformative dimension of the democratic impulse as both promised and arrested in bourgeois constitutionalism.[68]

A second set of contradictions appears between categories of rights – civil, political and social. It is largely conceded in the literature that social rights are incongruous to capitalism and its particular structures of opportunity and reward, which accounts for the fact of their marginalisation, even eradication under austerity regimes, or their 'elevation' to aspirational status. Where the market does *all* the work of allocating value to resources among possible uses, the distribution of resources with the explicit aim to meet needs is, from the point of view of market thinking, *irrational*. What does it mean to insist on the incongruity, and to act on this assumed 'irrationality'? I have suggested that if social rights are beset by the contradiction between capitalism and democracy, we should explore the significance of their constitutional iteration, as enunciated – that is, with constitutional force – and as unyielding to their subjugation to the logic of civil and property rights.[69] With the urgent appeal not to displace the antinomic significance of social constitutionalism, we might think of the use of immanent critique here as the insistent strategic use of social rights aiming to import a real contradiction from which the system cannot retract.[70]

A third example might focus on the use of immanent critique in terms of criminal procedure. The most spectacular instance relates to Jacques Vergès' 'strategy of rupture' in the context of the criminal trial.[71] Vergès' defence of Nazi criminal Klaus Barbie before the French courts in 1987 consisted in the maximal use of the

---

[68] See Lindahl, Hans, 'Possibility, actuality, rupture: constituent power and the ontology of change', *Constellations* 22:2 (2015): 163–74. Also Christodoulidis, E., 'Constitutional irresolution: law and the framing of civil society', *European Law Journal* 9:4 (2003), special issue: 401–32, and Christodoulidis, E., 'Against substitution: the constitutional thinking of dissensus', in Martin Loughlin and Neil Walker (eds) *The Paradox of Constitutionalism: Constituent Power and Constitutional Form*, Oxford University Press, 2007, pp. 189–208.

[69] Christodoulidis, E., 'Social rights constitutionalism: an antagonistic endorsement', *Journal of Law and Society* 44.1 (2017): 123–49.

[70] A Foucauldian reading of incongruity along these lines is suggested by Ben Golder: '[Foucault's] invocations of rights are strategic in this *incongruous* sense as they are situated within the spaces of political formation but are intended to resist and go beyond that formation, to transcend it.' In B. Golder, 'Foucault's critical (yet ambivalent) affirmation: three figures of rights', *Social & Legal Studies* 20:3 (2011): 283–312, at 295.

[71] Vergès, Jacques and Amar Bentoumi, *De la stratégie judiciaire*, Les éditions de minuit, 1968.

'*tu quoque*', in a way that would directly confront the French with their hypocritical denunciation of a crime that Vergès claimed underpinned their own colonial legacy – and particularly the national policy during the Algerian War. The strategy of rupture aimed to undercut and reconfigure the historical and didactic nature of the trial, increase its responsive range, renegotiate past alliances and reopen wounds.

To conclude, let me recapitulate what I take to be features of critique that, in the Marxist tradition at least, identify it as *immanent* critique. Normative expectations are part of institutional frameworks that inform actors' perception of social reality. Immanent critique aims to generate *within* these institutional frameworks contradictions that are *inevitable* (they can neither be displaced nor ignored), *compelling* (they necessitate action) and *transformative*, in that (unlike internal critique) the overcoming of the contradiction does not restore, but transcends, the 'disturbed' framework within which it arose. Against 'hegemonic' reasoning, which allows legal reason to organise and reproduce meaning within given structures and thereby to secure those structures' continuation, critical theory pushes it to go beyond those patterns of reproduction and forces transgression, in a move that – to return to Marx, with whom we began – might 'enable the world to clarify its consciousness in waking it from its dream about itself'.[72]

---

[72] Letter to Arnold Ruge, September 1843.

2. Critical legal realism in a nutshell
Dennis M. Davis and Karl Klare

For about 20 years beginning in the mid-1970s, diverse progressive approaches in the United States found a gathering point for dialogue and political energy in the Critical Legal Studies movement (CLS or "the crits"). CLS was influenced by and influenced other schools of the period, such as critical race theory, critical feminist legal thought, queer legal theory, and Third World approaches to international law. CLS generated a profusion of new scholarship focused initially on class and labor,[1] race and slavery,[2] sex and gender,[3] legal history,[4] practice,[5] and pedagogy,[6] and eventually covering a wide range of legal subjects and fields. Crits participated with others in many forms of legal and political activism; they also launched numerous initiatives to transform legal education. CLS no longer exists as an organized movement, but strands of CLS thinking continue to influence legal scholarship in the US and elsewhere.

We use "critical legal realism" (CLR) to refer to a major branch of CLS that pursued two "theory" projects in tandem. One was to promote the reception in US legal thought of modernist and postmodernist social and cultural theory.[7] The other was to recover and extend techniques of legal criticism developed by the Legal Realists and their predecessors,[8] going back to sociological jurisprudence and the revolt against formalism at the turn of the twentieth century in the US and Europe.[9] Legal Realism faded into retirement as an intellectual movement after World War II. The Realists' progressive political orientation and antiformalist pyrotechnics were forgotten, and their texts were no longer studied. A bland version of Realism drained of critical purchase came to be mainstreamed and embedded into the collective unconscious of American lawyers. Most US law students now absorb a clichéd rendering by osmosis. Liberal,

---

[1] See, e.g., Hyde; Klare 1978; Stone.

[2] See, e.g., Freeman; Klare 1982b; Tushnet. For an account of the relationship of CLS and Critical Race Theory, see Crenshaw et al.

[3] See, e.g., Mary Joe Frug 1985; Olsen 1983; Schneider; Schneider et al; Taub & Schneider.

[4] See, e.g., Gordon; Horwitz 1977.

[5] See, e.g., Bellow; Gabel & Harris; Simon.

[6] See, e.g., Feinman & Feldman; Kennedy 1983; Klare 1979b, 1982a.

[7] Works by Karl Marx, Max Weber, Georg Lukács, Antonio Gramsci, the Frankfurt School, Herbert Marcuse, Karl Polanyi, Jean-Paul Sartre, Ferdinand de Saussure, Claude Lévi-Strauss, Jean Piaget, and Michel Foucault were particularly influential.

[8] Leading thinkers associated with Legal Realism included Felix Cohen, Morris Cohen, William O. Douglas, Jerome Frank, Felix Frankfurter, Robert Hale, Walton Hamilton, and Karl Llewellyn. Douglas and Frankfurter ascended to the Supreme Court during Roosevelt's New Deal. Excellent accounts of Legal Realism appear in Kennedy 1993 and Singer 1988. For a collection of original sources, see Fisher et al.

[9] Central figures in the US were Oliver Wendell Holmes, Louis Brandeis, Roscoe Pound, Wesley Hohfeld, and Benjamin Cardozo.

centrist, and conservative jurists alike opportunistically deploy Realist-style analytics today, usually without knowing the provenance.

CLR resurrected the critical approaches described above and sought to apply them systematically in a wide range of substantive contexts, in policy as well as doctrinal argument, and in private (Kennedy 1976, 1991; G. Frug 1989) as well as public law (Klare 1978; Freeman 1978; G. Frug 1980). CLR was preoccupied with legal arguments of a certain type, namely, arguments that mistakenly or falsely proclaim the legal necessity of an outcome. "Mistaken" in this context means that the claim of the necessity of the outcome is invalid within its own frame of reference because a different, even conflicting outcome can also be justified within the stated premises and analytical framework. (We use "formalist error" to refer to this kind of mistaken claim of legal necessity.) CLR showed that jurists and scholars frequently made false claims for the legal necessity of baneful outcomes, thereby rationalizing domination, inequality, and injustice. Lawyers' work in this mode played and continues to play an important role in constructing and legitimating unjust social arrangements. To sustain this claim, CLR demonstrated that legal discourses and legal reasoning are more open-textured than is suggested by ritual insistence on the "necessity" of legal outcomes. In showing this, CLR also revealed emancipatory possibilities in lawyers' work (Klare 1979a, 1998).

This chapter outlines CLR's main claims and approaches, beginning with critical analytics and the salience of legal culture, proceeding to ideas about the legal construction of the social order, and concluding with transformative possibilities in legal work.

1. LEGAL OUTCOMES ARE UNDERDETERMINED BY LEGAL REASONING

So-called legal reasoning consists of the practiced use by legal actors (judges, attorneys, and others) of a stylized repertoire of rhetorical strategies and argumentative techniques to produce the appearance of the legal necessity of an outcome. Legal reasoning is not an algorithm; it is a set of discursive practices—practices that evoke, enact, and create meanings within a semiplastic, culturally specific medium or legal culture.

"Legal culture" and "legal consciousness" refer to the characteristic thought processes, habits of mind, and argumentative repertoires shared by a group of lawyers at a given time and place (see Kennedy 1980). A legal culture takes shape from its participants' shared experiences of training and socialization, the basic concepts that organize their legal thinking and work, what they regard as appropriate methods of solving legal problems and generating legal knowledge, whether and how they draw conceptual links between different fields of law, what counts for them as a persuasive legal argument, what types of argument they deem *ultra vires* the professional discourse of lawyers (although the argument type might be valid in another discipline such as political philosophy), what their view is of the appropriate role and demeanor of judges and other key legal actors, what enduring political and ethical commitments influence their professional discourse, and what understandings of and assumptions about human possibility and social organization they share. The discursive configuration of a legal culture gives content to, but also constrains, the legal imagination of its participants, the types of questions they are capable of asking, and, therefore, the range of answers that they can provide. Legal culture is semiautonomous from philosophical outlook and political ideology (understood in conventional "left"/"right" terms). Judges who disagree sharply about the political issues of the day may share a common legal culture. Legal cultures are not necessarily homogeneous; they may unify or fragment over time.

Legal actors deploying the conventional routines of argument within a particular legal culture often find that the legal authorities and texts with which they work are not infinitely plastic. Legal materials can exhibit qualities of rigidity and firmness. Sometimes a norm or rule simply will not yield to a skilled lawyer's best efforts to interpret it in a certain way. Legal reasoning is not a mere façade masking decisions self-consciously made on other grounds. Sometimes discursive conventions observably constrain decision making and influence outcomes, particularly in democratic societies in which fidelity to law is a powerful norm. Legal traditions are internalized in training. Legal education socializes students into culturally specific ways of thinking. It frequently happens that many or most participants in a legal culture will agree that only one interpretation of given materials (or a narrow range of interpretations) or only one solution to a problem (or a narrow range) is plausible. Legal outcomes are often highly predictable; many cases play out as "routine." If this were not so, law practice as we know it would be impossible.

On the other hand, lawyers also regularly find that the analytical repertoire, argumentative conventions, and legal materials do not constrain quite as tightly as students and beginners imagine. The core CLR claim is that it is often possible to destabilize the settled beliefs of a legal community, in which case the experience of "bindingness" or constraint imposed by the legal materials may weaken or dissolve. Lawyers might make an effort to destabilize settled understandings because something important is at stake or perhaps because they have been exposed to a different legal culture. When lawyers step back and interrogate a widely shared understanding, they are often able to justify a radically different or even contrary understanding of what the legal materials imply using perfectly respectable and accepted tools of legal reasoning presently residing in the legal culture. Destabilization initiatives are not always successful. Whether and when a powerful sense of constraint will unfreeze cannot be predicted, but neither is the experience uncommon.

We emphasize the modest nature of the indeterminacy thesis because this is often misunderstood. It is not a global claim about intrinsic properties of language, reason, texts, or interpretation. CLR did not claim that it is impossible to construct a relatively determinate system of legal reasoning, or that the tools of legal reasoning can never yield results that lawyers will agree are legally correct, or that any authority or text can or may appropriately be given any meaning a legal interpreter wishes to impose on it. Critics sometimes argue that the theory of legal indeterminacy leads inexorably to nihilism and the view that "anything goes" or that any legal result is as valid as any other. This criticism is demonstrably false. That judges should be self-conscious and transparent about the values they bring to their work does not imply that they are free to decide simply by consulting their philosophical assumptions or by enacting their personal ("arbitrary") preferences. More philosophically, CLR does not disdain reason; rather, it challenges the misuse of reason and the exaggeration of its powers. Without positing a transcendental ego, reason can criticize values, interrogate social practices, deepen self-consciousness, and inform judgment. Critical theory embraces dialogue based on good-faith reason giving and attempts to persuade by appeal to social experience, empathy, and solidarity. It distinguishes between good/persuasive legal arguments and bad/unconvincing legal arguments.[10]

2. A LEGAL ACTOR'S SENSE OF BEING 'BOUND' IS BETTER UNDERSTOOD AS AN *EXPERIENCE* OF THE LEGAL MATERIALS AND TOOLS OF REASONING THAN AS AN *ENTAILMENT* OF THEM

What we call legal constraint is best understood as a kind of experience that lawyers have of legal materials. Legal necessity is an "effect" that "is the product of work in the legal medium" (Kennedy 2014: 126). As noted, legal actors often possess a high degree of confidence and little if any doubt that the materials and reasoning conventions require a particular outcome without any interpretive input on their part. What lawyers cannot do with the tools presently available to us is to *prove* that the materials entail the posited result. The possibility of destabilization of settled understandings cannot be ruled out. At the same time, lawyers cannot prove that legal work within the discursive frame can always destabilize settled understandings.

Lawyers' ordinary conversation suggests that they imagine legal concepts to possess inherent or self-defining content that we can apprehend. The conviction that a given legal concept must be understood in a certain way may be so powerful—so much a matter of "common sense" within a legal culture—that lawyers will attribute the meaning to the norm rather than to their experience, understanding, or interpretation of the norm.[11] "Mechanical" rule application is common in most if not all legal cultures. Lawyers may authentically and in good faith reject any suggestion that their conclusions reflect interpretive work by them. But legal texts and concepts do not have voice, and they cannot speak to us. They cannot define, apply, or revise themselves without some sort of activity of the human mind (whether or not this is apparent to our consciousness). Activity of mind occurs and cannot but occur within a culturally constructed medium; accordingly, the "known" is never entirely separable from the perspective of the "knower." Whether a given set of legal materials entails a proposed legal outcome is something we cannot know (or deny) with certainty.

---

[10] See Klare 2015; see generally Singer 1984.
[11] On the phenomenon of "reification," see Berger & Pullberg and Berger & Luckmann.

3. EMPTY PROPOSITIONS, TAUTOLOGIES, GAPS, CONFLICTS, AND AMBIGUITIES PERMEATE LEGAL RULES AND DISCOURSES

Professionally respectable work within the discursive medium of a legal culture shows that legal rules and maxims are often unrevealing because they are empty or tautological (Felix Cohen 1935),[12] and that legal argument is often pliant because permeated with gaps, conflicts, and ambiguities. A "gap" arises when it appears that no extant norm was intended to apply to the circumstances at hand. A "conflict" is a situation in which two or more norms or lines of authority plausibly apply to a legal problem, and the respective norms or authorities would, if applied, produce different outcomes. "Ambiguity" is present when it appears that the canonical authorities applicable to a legal situation have more than one possible meaning, and the plausible meanings of the authority or norm point in different directions with respect to the outcome.

Critical analytics of both the earlier generations and of contemporary CLR revealed the pervasiveness of empty general propositions, tautologies, gaps, conflicts, and ambiguities in field after field of law. The Realists and their predecessors demonstrated that the accepted canons of legal decision making (deduction, induction, adhering to precedent, weighing the equities, resort to underlying purposes, and so on) cannot entirely close the gaps, resolve the conflicts, or make the ambiguities go away. This is why the existing rules, authorities and decision procedures do not, by themselves, yield determinate outcomes and why a member of the legal community can often make competent, plausible arguments that the rules and authorities point in multiple, even conflicting directions.

4. LAWYERS PARTIALLY CONSTRUCT THE LAW TO WHICH THEY SAY THEY ARE BOUND AND OWE FIDELITY

Because empty propositions, tautologies, gaps, conflicts, and ambiguities are pervasive, legal argument regularly passes through and is inflected at "bend points" intermediate between the norms or rules and the outcomes. At a bend point, the line of argument veers in one rather than another direction compatible with the norm in question, with path-dependent and outcome-determinative consequences. Often the inflection amounts to leaning one way or the other in terms of conflicting perspectives already solidly embedded in the legal materials (for example, individualism versus altruism, security of expectation versus freedom of action). These bend points are ports of entry for philosophical convictions, cultural sensibilities, unconscious assumptions, or what for a given judge is simply "common sense." World views play, and cannot but play, a routine role in legal decision making. This is not necessarily illicit, nor does it mean that judges exceed their rightful authority or arbitrarily inject personal convictions into

---

[12] See Holmes: 3 ("empty general propositions ... teach[ ] nothing but a benevolent yearning" (referring to the familiar maxim *sic utere*)).

the process. Complicated questions, unnecessary to address here, arise as to whether and when the values, assumptions, and sensibilities that influence judges at the bend points in argument are properly described as "legal" or "extralegal," or sometimes one, sometimes the other. But even taking the most expansive view of what counts as "legal," the culturally bounded perceptions, sensibilities, and experiences judges bring into adjudication at the bend points eventually overflow the repertoire of legal reasoning.

"Abuse of deduction," the formalist's vice, lies in the faith (or expressed faith) that deduction, induction, analysis of legal purposes, or some other neutral decision procedure reveals a determinate solution to a legal problem that is insulated from the socially constructed sensibilities and/or contestable, intermediate choices that inflect legal argument, when in fact it is the case that professionally respectable work can justify an equally plausible, alternative outcome. In this situation, decision makers who sincerely believe that the authorities require them to rule a certain way are mistaken. Their error may be innocent or motivated. Depending on their level of self-consciousness and sophistication and upon what they disclose to the public in their written opinions, their error may be in bad faith.

Lawyers and judges partially construct the law to which they say they are bound and owe fidelity. They shape the legal materials not only through choices made at bend points in individual cases but more generally in choices they make about how to allocate and deploy their interpretive energies—a scarce resource (Kennedy 1997). That judges place their own imprint on the law in their encounters with the legal materials over time poses difficult questions about the legitimacy of adjudication in representative democracies.

5. THE ACCEPTED INTERPRETIVE MAXIMS OF A LEGAL CULTURE FREQUENTLY POINT TOWARD CONFLICTING OUTCOMES IN A GIVEN CASE

Consider Karl Llewellyn's discussion of precedent and *stare decisis* (1930: 56–69). According to conventional wisdom, the common law practice of adhering to precedent carries forward the accumulated wisdom of the past, promotes legal stability and predictability, fosters equal treatment of like cases, and restricts judges to their proper role subordinate to the legislature. Precedent-following achieves these desiderata by constraining and steering decision makers' choices. Llewellyn demonstrated, however, that the practice of adhering to precedent is not the constraining decision procedure it is often made out to be. Rather, it is a repertoire of rhetorical maneuvers that allow decision makers to claim *either* that they are bound by prior authorities *or* that they are free to depart from them. Even in its most traditional understanding, the principle of *stare decisis* sometimes constrains judges and sometimes gives them freedom of motion.

For one thing, there is the problem of the pervasiveness of conflicts, previously discussed: "[I]n any case doubtful enough to make litigation respectable the available authoritative premises—i.e., the premises legitimate and impeccable under the traditional legal techniques—are at least two, and ... the two are mutually contradictory as applied to the case in hand" (Llewellyn 1931: 1239). A more fundamental source of tension between constraint and freedom within *stare decisis* is that the method contains within itself potentially conflicting mandates with respect to prior authorities. The decision maker is bound to adhere to a past authority but only when past authority is "on point"; distinguishable past authority does not bind and may be disregarded. The injunction to "follow applicable precedent" tells us how to proceed once we know that a given precedent is or is not "on point." It does not and cannot tell us *whether* a given precedent is "on point." From one view, an authority appears applicable and may therefore be taken as binding. But from another, the precedent is distinguishable, in which case the advocate or decision maker may escape its binding ties without abandoning *stare decisis*. The discursive repertoire of precedent-following provides practitioners with a scalpel to cut free from unfavorable precedent. At the same time, a familiar understanding in common law systems is that the "holding" of a prior case encompasses the reasons relied upon or necessary to reach the result. In this aspect of precedential reasoning practitioners have a platform upon which to expand the scope and binding power of favorable precedents. *Stare decisis* bears less resemblance to an algorithmic decision procedure and more to a toolbox containing two equally legitimate and dogmatically correct operating procedures—namely, distinguishing and extending precedent. In any given case, these steering mechanisms point in opposite directions. *Stare decisis* does not and cannot tell us which of these devices to employ on a given occasion.[13]

Stare decisis is—but is no more than—an invitation to deploy a catalogue of argumentative clichés. Whether or not the legal actor appreciates this, applying the common law method to a new case involves conscious or unconscious choices ("interpretation" or "the exercise of judgment") concerning the facts in the earlier case, the facts here, the meaning of the prior case, the meaning of the new situation, the evolution of social context, and the purposes to be served by and the likely effects of legal rules. The *stare decisis* toolkit contains numerous maxims (such as "the precise facts of the case control its meaning"), each of which is canceled out by an equally valid countermaxim (such as "extract and apply the *ratio decidendi*"). The method of reasoning from precedents does not contain its own criteria for determining which maxim to follow. The conventions of legal reasoning by precedent-following certainly influence lawyers' work methods and patterns of thought, often quite powerfully, but frequently the capacity of the conventions and maxims to steer decision makers to a determinate conclusion runs out. Resolution of the case then becomes, consciously or otherwise, a matter of choice and judgment upon which contestable ethical and political considerations inevitably bear.

---

[13] Common law systems also accept that precedent may be "overruled" under some circumstances, but the discursive conventions contain only spongy criteria as to when overruling is appropriate (e.g. "times have changed"). In *Payne v. Tennessee*, 501 U.S. 808 (1991), the US Supreme Court described *stare decisis* as a "principle of policy," not an "inexorable command." The Court said that *stare decisis* has greatest weight "in cases involving contract and property rights, where reliance interests are involved" but is less compelling in cases involving procedural and evidentiary rules. On that understanding, the Court felt comfortable overruling constitutionally grounded precedents of criminal procedure that barred capital sentencing based on certain evidence and, having done so, it ordered a man's execution.

Llewellyn found the same maxim/countermaxim pattern in the canons of statutory interpretation and other contexts. CLR work later generalized Llewellyn's observations by showing that across a wide range of legal fields and contexts, for every maxim or argument type in the discursive repertoire, one can usually find an equally respectable, although equally formulaic, countermaxim or argument type that cuts in the opposite direction with respect to the outcome of a given case.

6. AS LEGAL ACTORS UNDERSTAND THEM, MANY BASIC NORMS AND PRINCIPLES REFLECT OR EMBRACE COUNTERVAILING VALUES WITH POTENTIALLY CONFLICTING IMPLICATIONS FOR OUTCOMES IN CASES TO WHICH THEY APPLY

The pattern of conflicting considerations and maxims surfaces in purposive or "policy" reasoning as well as in doctrine (Kennedy 1976). It is a common experience for legal actors to agree that a particular norm or principle governs a case but to find that the norm or principle embodies conflicting values and purposes with contradictory implications. Determining what the norm or principle implies for the case then involves (consciously or unconsciously) leaning in the direction of one or the other of the embedded values or policies.

For example, lawyers understand "private property" to embody the idea that owners may utilize their property in a self-interested manner. Seen in this light, ownership implies privileges and entitlements. But lawyers also typically understand "private property" to embody the idea that owners are entitled to be protected from the uses that other owners make of *their* property. Seen this way, ownership implies duties to use one's property so as to protect neighbors or even strangers. Which implication of property should predominate in any instance—the self-interested or the altruistic—is ultimately a matter of judgment, indeed, a judgment of public policy. "[P]roperty [is] a symbol for the conclusion that certain patterns of behavior are to be enforced between people for the benefit of society as a whole."[14] That the concept of private property may have conflicting implications for the resolution of a particular controversy does not mean that it is impossible to reach a conclusion or that anyone's judgment is as good as anyone else's. It does mean that the concept of private property by itself cannot tell us whether, in a particular case, I may use my land without regard to the interests of others, or whether I must use my land so as to respect the interests of others. Drawing "deductions" or "entailments" from the concept of property always involves an element of circular reasoning. "It is incorrect to say that the judiciary protect[s] property; rather they call[ ] that property to which they accord[ ] protection" (Hamilton & Till: 536).

Similarly, "freedom of contract" promotes the values of personal liberty and autonomy, but it also requires constraints on liberty in order to protect legitimate expectations (interests typically invoked by the phrase "commercial certainty and predictability"). In every contract judgment, the court in effect strikes a balance

---

[14] Student Note: 489–90. See also Felix Cohen 1954.

between the promisor's freedom of action and the promisee's expectations and reliance. Contractual freedom affords individuals a zone of liberty in which to self-order their own affairs, but to defend "freedom of contract" in strictly libertarian terms without attending to the coercive side is unpersuasive. The promisee in every contract case proclaims fidelity to private ordering while seeking to mobilize the power of the state to coerce the promisor to do something the latter would prefer not to do. We may tell losing defendants that their own liberty and autonomy are vindicated by the court's judgment enforcing the contract, but what they experience is that the sheriff seizes their property if they do not pay up. Whether the government should deploy its power in this way is always ultimately a question of public policy (Morris Cohen 1933: 586).

A standard argument for enforcing voluntary agreements is that doing so maximizes aggregate welfare. But contract litigation arises because a previous agreement is no longer utility maximizing for one of the parties or because a party can no longer afford to perform. Whether blanket enforcement of all agreements that happen to be entered enhances aggregate welfare is a hopelessly complicated empirical question (Singer 1988a: 484–5). In any event, no contract regime enforces all agreements, and no contract regime compels breaching defendants to repair the full extent of the consequences of their breach. Contract law contains many excuses for nonperformance, limitations on damages for breach, and doctrines permitting recovery by breaching plaintiffs, undoubtedly reflecting an intuition that contract enforcement can sometimes produce suboptimal outcomes. How and to what extent a given contract regime vindicates the expectation interest boils down to "no more than a series of economic policy choices by the state."[15] Whether, when, and to what extent the state should impose its coercive power on a contract defendant in order to vindicate the plaintiff's expectations and/or reliance always ultimately involves judgments that cannot be deduced from the idea of contractual freedom because that idea encompasses conflicting notions of desirable policy.[16]

7. LEGAL NORMS AND OUTCOMES ARE UNDERDETERMINED BY SOCIAL STRUCTURE AND POLITICAL IDEOLOGY

CLR's crossfertilization of American critical legal traditions and modernist social theory led to the insight that particular "types" of society—whether capitalist, socialist, or other—do not possess an inbuilt structure that tightly determines the legal regime in place (Unger 1983: 567–70 & 660–5). The law/society relationship is much more indeterminate, somewhat in the same way that the legal authority/legal outcome relationship is indeterminate (Kennedy 1979: 362 note 56, Gordon 1984: 75–81). A social or economic institution—say, a market for the purchase and sale of labor power in a capitalist society—can be legally structured in a wide variety of ways based on different, foundational rule sets (Steinfeld 1991). These rule sets may have quite different distributive consequences, for example, as between workers and employers. In a general way, one might attribute the content and distributive effects of a particular

---

[15] Mensch: 760 (footnote omitted) (discussing classic text of Fuller & Perdue).
[16] For these paragraphs, see generally Kennedy 1985: 958–67.

rule set—for example, the law of contractual offer and acceptance in late nineteenth century England—to the type of society in which it appears (industrial capitalism, in this example). But the attribution would tell us very little about the shape and content of the rules or possible alternative configurations. Moreover, the claim would be circular. One cannot provide a coherent description of late nineteenth century English industrial capitalism—the social type to which the content of the rules is supposedly attributed—without discussing the legal rules that partially construct and constitute that social order.

As with the indeterminacy of legal reasoning, the claim about indeterminacy in the law/society relationship is modest. It is not an argument that a given social type is compatible with any legal arrangement imaginable or that the characteristics of and challenges facing a society in a given historical period have no bearing on the shape of legal rules. A particular, historically grounded rule set may follow recognizable patterns or observe a kind of culturally specific logic. The modest claims are, first, that we cannot identify core social structures (such as "the relations of production") that tightly determine legal institutions, and second, that legal rules, practices, and cultures are central to identifying what we mean by a given social order and its characteristic arrangements (such as "the relations of production").

Along similar lines, the precise legal implications of a general political viewpoint or ideology—say, "conservatism" or "leftism" or Marxism or neoliberalism—are relatively indeterminate. Progressive lawyers who see themselves as sharing overarching political values frequently find themselves in sharp disagreement about the appropriate institutional or legal resolution of a problem. As we pursue these disagreements, the "legal" sometimes inflects the "political." As Duncan Kennedy argued, rule choices emerge from "interaction between the legal materials, understood as a constraining medium, and the ideological projects of judges [or advocates]." The resulting legal decisions "should be understood neither as simply the implications of authority nor as the implications of the ideological projects, but as a compromise" (Kennedy 1997: 19).

8. LEGAL RULES AND PRACTICES OFTEN PLAY A SIGNIFICANT ROLE IN CONSTRUCTING SOCIAL LIFE; ADJUDICATORS BEAR SOME RESPONSIBILITY FOR THE EFFECTS OF THEIR DECISIONS

Social systems are organized or "constructed" by humanly crafted and culturally transmitted norms, discourses, and practices which, in modern societies, are frequently embodied in legal rules. These norms, practices, and rules can have significant effects on human conduct, experience, and belief. Law is endogenous to human behavior and interaction. The relationships and identities that fill daily life—family; employment; gender and sexual relationships and identities; race hierarchies; buying, selling, and owning, and so on—are *always already legally constituted*. All institutions and power dynamics in contemporary societies are at least partially constituted by rules of law. There is no natural, "prelegal" or "law-free" domain of social interaction in modern societies. People act, transact, believe, desire, and aspire as they do in part because of the powers, authorities, immunities, expectations, and entitlements established in law.[17] Adjudicators bear some responsibility for the social impact of their decisions, whether or not they are aware of or acknowledge the cumulative effects their choices produce on the texture of social life and the distribution of power and wellbeing.

For example, markets are structured by legal ground rules that define capacity to contract, allocate property entitlements, distinguish voluntary exchange from coerced transfer, divide the outputs of joint productive activity, and so on. There is no such thing as "the" market; there are only "markets," discrete institutional arrangements, each structured by a particular set of background rules. Likewise, there cannot be a "free market," if what is meant by that is a market unregulated by law. Legal decision makers do not face a choice between "staying out of" or "intervening in" markets. Law is always "in" from the start; markets are always already structures and practices shaped by law. The important questions are what approaches the law should take in constructing markets and with what effects.

Similarly, families and family life are structured by largely taken for granted background norms, which in modern societies are embodied in legal rules. The family is regulated by numerous legal rules that determine what constitutes a family, who may marry, how decisions are taken within families, which family members have capacity to contract or own property, in what ways parents may control children, and so on. No family is "private" or "independent of" or "autonomous from" the state, if what is meant by these phrases is a social unit the composition and inner workings of which are untouched by law (Olsen 1983, 1985).

The socially constitutive power of law is at work not only when legal rules establish an entitlement or obligation but also when the law refrains from doing so or is simply silent, thereby privileging legal subjects to act in certain ways that affect the lives of others. Much vintage Realist writing was directed at problematizing the classical act/no act distinction (see Hale 1943, 1946). People interpret their experience and conduct themselves "in the shadow" of background rules of law. Where the rules impose no limits or obligations on some aspect of social or economic interaction, the resulting distributive effects may properly be attributed to the community or the state in the sense that it is always possible that someone will call attention to and challenge the gap or omission and make a proposal for legal change.

9. RULES OF LAW DISPOSE DISTRIBUTIVE STAKES

The legal ground rules of social and economic interaction often significantly affect distributive outcomes in transactions and relationships (such as employer/employee, owner/neighbor, landlord/tenant, seller/consumer, husband/wife) that implicate the pursuit of wellbeing (sustenance, income, knowledge, fulfillment, and so on). Defining entitlements, privileges, liabilities, and immunities in one way rather than another may

---

[17] "I am not persuaded that there is, in the modern State, any right which exists which is not ultimately sourced in some law, even if it be no more than an unarticulated premise of the common law[.]" *Du Plessis v. De Klerk*, 1996 (5) BCLR (CC), at par [79] (Mahomed DP concurring).

produce quite different consequences for the distribution of power and welfare and, therefore, for people's lived experience and quality of daily life. For example, the particular rule set in place may favor employers vis-à-vis employees, sellers vis-à-vis buyers, landlords vis-à-vis tenants and husbands vis-à-vis wives. With differently formulated background legal rules, we might observe over the long run different power relationships and a different distribution of wellbeing.

Private law rules empower some actors while disempowering and subordinating others. For example, private law establishes ground rules that govern how one acquires assets and how one may use one's assets and legal endowments in interaction with others. P, a landowner, negatively affects the interests of Q, a malnourished, homeless person, by denying Q's request for rent-free access to P's property and/or edible yield. Though grievous harm or even death may result, P is nevertheless privileged to refuse Q's request pursuant to the public policy decisions embodied in the common law of property, namely, that normally owners may exclude strangers and that, if push comes to shove, the local authorities will use force to uphold owners' privilege to exclude (Morris Cohen 1927; Hale 1923, 1943).[18]

Realist writing revealed that so-called freedom of contract consists of negotiation conducted and agreements made within a legally structured framework of mutual pressure and coercion. Offerees consent to a bargain in order to avoid negative consequences that offerors may inflict upon them by withholding what the offeror owns and the offeree desires or needs, which might include the necessities of life (Morris Cohen 1927). However, an offeror may also desire or need what an offeree has. A "price" is a metric of the relative strength of the coercive powers which law puts at the parties' disposal, respectively. Sellers' revenue is the sum of the prices that others are willing to pay in order to induce sellers to refrain from utilizing their legally granted power to withhold access to what they own and others need or desire. The social distribution of income reflects the relative balance of the legal powers of coercion granted by law to the various members of the community.[19]

For example, legal rules privilege employers to deny workers access to opportunities to earn income unless the workers agree to accept the employers' wage offers. A system of private property and "free" contract therefore endows employers with significant power to coerce prospective employees. Of course, where industrial action is immune from liability and/or affirmatively protected, law grants the workers a reciprocal coercive power to withhold what the employer requires (profit-generating labor power) unless the employer agrees to the workers' wage demands. The wage level is neither unilaterally imposed by the employer, nor does the employee "freely" consent to it. Employer offers and worker responses are channeled by law-structured economic

---

[18] But see *State v. Shack*, 58 N.J. 297, 277 A.2d 369 (1971) (farm owner may not exclude attorney and poverty worker seeking entry to assist resident farm laborers; property rights must serve "human values" and cannot be applied so as to deprive vulnerable persons of what is essential to their health, welfare, and dignity).

[19] See Hale 1923: 478 ("[t]he distribution of income ... depends on the relative power of coercion which the different members of the community can exert against one another. Income is the price paid for not using one's coercive weapons").

pressures. The wage bargain reached in a given case reflects the relative balance of the employers' and the workers' legally authorized powers to coerce each other.

Courts say that they only enforce agreements entered into "freely" and that they decline to enforce "coerced" arrangements. The Realists argued that all bargains combine aspects of choice and aspects of coercion. "[C]oercion, including legal coercion, lies at the heart of *every* bargain."[20] Contract doctrines such as fraud, duress, undue influence, and unconscionability supposedly show us a bright line between "freely chosen," enforcementworthy bargains and "coerced" bargains that do not merit enforcement. In fact, these doctrines mark the blurred, porous, and ever shifting boundaries between coercive behaviors which the community is prepared to accept as normal and those which it is not. When a court announces that it will withhold enforcement because a particular bargain resulted from "coercion" rather than voluntary agreement, the court is using the ostensibly fact-based concept of coercion as an emblem for a moral conclusion or intuition, namely that it would be unfair to enforce the bargain. "Doctrines of duress are intended to raise precisely the question whether it is 'rightful' to use particular types of pressure for the purpose of extracting an excessive or disproportionate return."[21] To paraphrase Hamilton and Till, it is incorrect to say that the courts enforce voluntary bargains but deny enforcement of coerced bargains; rather, they call "voluntary" or "consensual" the bargains they will enforce, and call "coerced" those which they are not prepared to enforce.

10. RULES OF LAW DISPOSE CULTURAL AND IDEOLOGICAL STAKES

Legal practices and discourses create and privilege meanings that contribute to the store of culturally available symbols and artefacts that comprise the medium in which people interpret their experiences. To the extent that they are salient and diffused in society, legal discourses and practices orient consciousness and construct identities. For example, legal practices that treat women in certain ways and legal discourses that explain and justify such treatment induce people to believe that such treatment is appropriate to the identity of "being a woman" (see Mary Joe Frug 1985, 1992).[22]

Here again, the law produces effects by its gaps and silences as well as by its more overt content. A assaults his wife, B. No liability ensues because the jurisdiction observes a strong doctrine of interspousal tort immunity. Predictably, B files no action against A. The police make no intervention. No court is ever called upon to adjudicate A's conduct or enforce a sanction against him. As traditionally understood, no governmental action has occurred. Conventionally, A's conduct is considered without reference to the immunity rule. But if social and historical context are brought into the picture, one can draw a connection between A's conduct and longstanding rules that

---

[20] Mensch: 764 (italics in original) (relying on classic Legal Realist texts).
[21] Dawson: 288. See generally Hale 1943.
[22] The strand of argument concerning the "legal constitution of the subject" played little role in the work of the Legal Realists or their predecessors. It reflects the influence of modernist social theory on CLR.

subordinate women, and the effects of such rules on popular and police attitudes toward domestic violence. That for centuries the legal system placed little or no inhibition on spousal abuse likely contributed something to male socialization and the incidence of abuse. If the jurisdiction has a constitution committed to gender equality, the presence of the tort immunity ("state nonaction") should in principle be subjected to constitutional scrutiny for compatibility with the equality guarantee.[23]

Sometimes in history, legal discourses have widespread cultural and psychological impact at grassroots level. Legal discourses—even traditionalist legal discourses—can be repositories of oppositional values and emancipatory aspirations that can be tapped in times of social conflict. The more familiar cultural effect of law is to legitimate the status quo, that is, to induce people to believe that existing social arrangements are fair or, at any rate, the best we can do. Elite legal discourses tend to naturalize the background rules that sustain unjust social arrangements. These discourses often function as legitimating ideology. A common ideological effect of legal discourses is to induce people to consent to their own domination.

11. INTERROGATION OF BACKGROUND LEGAL RULES MAY REVEAL TRANSFORMATIVE POSSIBILITIES

Many legal rules that play a role in structuring social and economic life reside very far in the background of legal and popular consciousness—so far back that such rules are virtually invisible and often not even recognized as legal rules at all. Even lawyers tend to forget that each and every legal rule is a humanly crafted artefact. An example is the default rule of property law by virtue of which the employer owns the commodities produced through the joint activity of management and labor (Fischl 1987: 527–8). There is nothing natural or eternal about this principle of social organization; it was centuries in the making. A similarly invisible rule is the default principle of family law that parents have custody of their children and determine the children's place of residence. It takes mental effort to recall that this is, in fact, a legal rule. This rule makes obvious sense under most circumstances, but it may produce negative consequences in some situations. Some children suffer preventable abuse because this elementary rule of family law discourages relatives, friends, and neighbors from acting appropriately to rescue children from domestic violence.

Critical legal approaches open imaginative and political space for projects to interrogate and reenvision our legal contexts with a motive to transform them. Background rules of law matter. We can bring them out of the background and into the foreground to spotlight their distributional consequences. Casting a critical light on background rules may unfreeze and destabilize their coded ideological content. In the context of conducive political mobilization and resistance, the rules can be revised to aim at more egalitarian, democratic, caring, and ecologically sound outcomes and the establishment and continuous revision of a legal, social, and economic infrastructure

---

[23] "[E]very social practice … in some way relies upon and is sanctioned by a legal rule that can—in suitable circumstances—be subjected to constitutional review." Van der Walt: 665.

designed to enable all people to enjoy ample and meaningful prospects for self-realization. CLR invites us to regard criticizing and contesting background rules, and working to alter them, as practices essential to fashioning a more just and egalitarian world.

BIBLIOGRAPHY

Bellow, Gary (1977) "Turning Solutions into Problems: The Legal Aid Experience," *NLADA Briefcase*, 34:106–22.
Berger, Peter L. & Luckmann, Thomas (1966) *The Social Construction of Reality: A Treatise in the Sociology of Knowledge*, Garden City, NY: Doubleday & Co.
Berger, Peter & Pullberg, Stanley (1966) "Reification and the Sociological Critique of Consciousness," *New Left Review*, I/35:56–71.
Cohen, Felix (1935) "Transcendental Nonsense & the Functional Approach," *Columbia Law Review*, 35:809–49.
Cohen, Felix (1954) "Dialogue on Private Property," *Rutgers Law Review*, 9:357–87.
Cohen, Morris (1927) "Property & Sovereignty," *Cornell Law Quarterly*, 13:8–30.
Cohen, Morris (1933) "The Basis of Contract," *Harvard Law Review*, 46:553–92.
Crenshaw, Kimberlé, Gotanda, Neil, Peller, Gary & Thomas, Kendall, eds, "Introduction," *Critical Race Theory: The Key Writings that Formed the Movement*, New York: The New Press, 1995, pp. xiii–xxxii.
Dawson, John P. (1947) "Economic Duress—An Essay in Perspective," *Michigan Law Review*, 45:253–90.
Feinman, Jay & Feldman, Marc (1985) "Pedagogy and Politics," *Georgetown Law Journal*, 73:875–930.
Fischl, Richard Michael (1987) "Some Realism about Critical Legal Studies," *University of Miami Law Review*, 41:505–32.
Fisher, William, Horwitz, Morton, & Reed, Thomas A. (eds) (1993) *American Legal Realism*, New York & Oxford, UK: Oxford University Press.
Freeman, Alan (1978) "Legitimizing Race Discrimination through Antidiscrimination Law: A Critical Review of Supreme Court Doctrine," *Minnesota Law Review*, 62:1049–1119.
Frug, Gerald (1980) "The City as a Legal Concept," *Harvard Law Review*, 93:1057–1154.
Frug, Gerald (1989) "A Critical Theory of Law," *Legal Education Review*, 1:43–57.
Frug, Mary Joe (1985) "Re-Reading Contracts: A Feminist Analysis of a Contracts Casebook," *American University Law Review*, 34:1065–1140.
Frug, Mary Joe (1992) *Postmodern Legal Feminism*, New York & London: Routledge.
Fuller, Lon L. & Perdue, W.R. (1936) "The Reliance Interest in Contract Damages: 1," *Yale Law Journal*, 46:52–96.
Gabel, Peter & Harris, Paul (1982–3) "Building Power and Breaking Images: Critical Legal Theory and the Practice of Law," *New York University Review of Law & Social Change*, 11:369–411.
Gordon, Robert W. (1984) "Critical Legal Histories," *Stanford Law Review*, 36:57–125.
Hale, Robert (1923) "Coercion & Distribution in a Supposedly Non-Coercive State," *Political Science Quarterly*, 38:470–94.
Hale, Robert (1943) "Bargaining, Duress, & Economic Liberty," *Columbia Law Review*, 43:603–28.
Hale, Robert (1946) "Prima Facie Torts, Combination & Non-Feasance," *Columbia Law Review*, 46:196–218.
Hamilton, Walton & Till, Irene (1933) "Property," *Encyclopedia of Social Science*, 12:528–38.
Hohfeld, Wesley N. (1913) "Some Fundamental Legal Conceptions as Applied in Judicial Reasoning," *Yale Law Journal*, 23: 16–59.
Holmes, Jr., Oliver Wendell (1894) "Privilege, Malice, and Intent," *Harvard Law Review*, 8:1–14.
Horwitz, Morton J. (1977) *The Transformation of American Law, 1780–1860*, Cambridge, MA & London: Harvard University Press.
Horwitz, Morton J. (1992) *The Transformation of American Law 1870–1960: The Crisis of Legal Orthodoxy*, Oxford, UK & New York: Oxford University Press.
Hyde, Alan (1982), "Beyond Collective Bargaining: The Politicization of Labor Relations under Government Contract," *Wisconsin Law Review*, 1982:1–41.
Kennedy, Duncan (1976) "Form and Substance in Private Law Adjudication," *Harvard Law Review* 89:1685–1778.

Kennedy, Duncan (1979) "The Structure of Blackstone's *Commentaries*," 28 *Buffalo Law Review*, 28:205–382.
Kennedy, Duncan (1980) "Towards an Historical Understanding of Legal Consciousness: The Case of Classical Legal Thought," *Research in Law and Society* 3:3–24, reprinted in *The Rise & Fall of Classical Legal Thought*, Washington, DC: Beard Books, 2006.
Kennedy, Duncan (1983) *Legal Education and the Reproduction of Hierarchy: A Polemic against the System*, Cambridge, MA: Afar, republished New York & London: New York University Press, 2004.
Kennedy, Duncan (1985) "The Role of Law in Economic Thought: Essays on the Fetishism of Commodities," *American University Law Review*, 34:939–1001.
Kennedy, Duncan (1986) "Freedom & Constraint in Adjudication: A Critical Phenomenology," *Journal of Legal Education*, 36:518–62.
Kennedy, Duncan (1991) "A Semiotics of Legal Argument," *Syracuse Law Review*, 42:75–116.
Kennedy, Duncan (1993) "The Stakes of Law, or Hale & Foucault!" in *Sexy Dressing Etc.*, Cambridge, MA & London: Harvard University Press.
Kennedy, Duncan (1997) *A Critique of Adjudication*{fin de siècle}, Cambridge, MA & London: Harvard University Press.
Kennedy, Duncan (2001) "Legal Formalism," in Neil J. Smelser & Paul Baltes, eds-in-chief, *Encyclopedia of the Social and Behavioral Sciences*, Amsterdam: Elsevier, 13:8634–7.
Kennedy, Duncan (2014) "The Hermeneutic of Suspicion in Contemporary American Legal Thought," *Law Critique*, 25:91–139.
Klare, Karl (1978) "Judicial Deradicalization of the Wagner Act and the Origins of Modern Legal Consciousness, 1937–1941," *Minnesota Law Review*, 62:265–339.
Klare, Karl (1979a) "Law-Making As Praxis," *Telos*, 40:123–35.
Klare, Karl (1979b) "Contracts Jurisprudence and the First-Year Casebook," *New York University Law Review*, 54:876–99.
Klare, Karl (1982a) "The Law-School Curriculum in the 1980s: What's Left?" *Journal of Legal Education*, 32:336–92.
Klare, Karl (1982b) "The Quest for Industrial Democracy and the Struggle against Racism: Perspectives from Labor Law and Civil Rights Law," *Oregon Law Review*, 61:157–200.
Klare, Karl (1998) "Legal Culture and Transformative Constitutionalism," *South African Journal on Human Rights*, 14:146–88.
Klare, Karl (2015) "Critical Perspectives on Social and Economic Rights, Democracy, and Separation of Powers," in Helena Alviar García, Karl Klare, & Lucy A. Williams, eds, *Social and Economic Rights in Theory and Practice: Critical Inquiries*, London & New York: Routledge, pp. 3–22.
Llewellyn, Karl N. (1930) *The Bramble Bush: On Our Law & Its Study*, Dobbs Ferry, NY: Oceana Publications, Inc.
Llewellyn, Karl N. (1931) "Some Realism about Realism—Responding to Dean Pound," *Harvard Law Review*, 44:1222–64.
Llewellyn, Karl N. (1989) *The Case Law System in America* (Michael Ansaldi trans.) (originally published 1933), Chicago & London: University of Chicago Press.
Llewellyn, Karl N. (1960) "Remarks on the Theory of Appellate Decision & the Rules or Canons About How Statutes Are to Be Construed," *Vanderbilt Law Review*, 3 (1949–50):395–406, reprinted in *The Common Law Tradition*, Boston & Toronto: Little, Brown & Co., 1960.
Mensch, Betty (1981) "Freedom of Contract as Ideology," *Stanford Law Review*, 33:753–72.
Olsen, Frances E. (1983) "The Family and the Market: A Study of Ideology and Legal Reform," *Harvard Law Review*, 96:1497–1578.
Olsen, Frances E. (1985) "The Myth of State Intervention in the Family," *University of Michigan Journal of Law Reform*, 18:835–64.
Schneider, Elizabeth M. (1986) "Describing and Changing: Women's Self-Defense Work and the Problem of Expert Testimony on Battering," *Women's Rights Law Reporter*, 9:195–222.
Schneider, Elizabeth M., Jordan, Susan B., & Arguedas, Cristina C. (1978) "Representation of Women Who Defend Themselves in Response to Physical or Sexual Assault," *Women's Rights Law Reporter*, 4:149–63.
Simon, William (1984) "Visions of Practice in Legal Thought," *Stanford Law Review*, 36:469–507.
Singer, Joseph W. (1984) "The Player and the Cards: Nihilism and Legal Theory," *Yale Law Journal* 94:1–70.
Singer, Joseph W. (1988a) "Legal Realism Now," *California Law Review*, 76:465–544.
Singer, Joseph W. (1988b) "The Reliance Interest in Property," *Stanford Law Review*, 40:611–751.

Steinfeld, Robert J. (1991) *The Invention of Free Labor: The Employment Relation in English and American Law and Culture, 1350–1870*, Chapel Hill, NC & London: University of North Carolina Press.

Stone, Katherine Van Wezel (1981) "The Post-War Paradigm in American Labor Law," *Yale Law Journal*, 90:1509–80.

Student Note (1970) "Unemployment as a Taking without Just Compensation," *Southern California Law Review*, 43:488–515.

Taub, Nadine & Schneider, Elizabeth N. (1982) "Perspectives on Women's Subordination and the Role of Law," in David Kairys (ed.), *The Politics of Law: A Progressive Critique*, New York: Pantheon Books, pp. 117–39.

Tushnet, Mark V. (1981) *The American Law of Slavery 1810–1860: Considerations of Humanity and Interest*, Princeton, NJ: Princeton University Press.

Unger, Roberto (1983) "The Critical Legal Studies Movement," *Harvard Law Review*, 96:561–675.

Van der Walt, André (2005) "Transformative Constitutionalism and the Development of South African Property Law—Part 1," *Tydskrif vir die Suid-Afrikaanse Reg*, 4:655–89.

PART II

3. Critical legal feminisms
Rosemary Hunter

1. INTRODUCTION

A glance at this volume's table of contents illustrates the need for feminist critique of critical legal theory. Less than one quarter of the authors are women. Moreover, women are particularly underrepresented in Parts I and II, which deal with theoretical approaches as opposed to areas of law. At least feminism rates a mention, which is an achievement of the past 30 years. But the experience of being the token feminist remains an all too familiar one. In the undergraduate Jurisprudence and Legal Theory module on which I recently taught, my three hours of lectures on feminist legal theory represented a tiny incursion in an otherwise unrelieved diet of (mostly dead, white) male theorists and jurisprudes. But the continuing marginalization of women and of feminism is as much a feature of left/critical legal scholarship as it is of mainstream/liberal legal scholarship.

Feminist critical legal theory, however, goes well beyond concerns about women's inequality and underrepresentation in legal scholarship. This chapter outlines the typical preoccupations of critical legal feminisms, and the methods and tools upon which they draw. There is considerable diversity within the field, encompassing scholars who would identify variously as postmodern or poststructuralist, psychoanalytic, critical race, postcolonial/decolonial and/or queer feminists, sometimes in combination with materialist and/or sociolegal orientations. However, the key commonality among critical legal feminisms is that they engage in critique in three directions simultaneously: critique of law, critique of other ('malestream') critical theories (critical legal theory, critical race theory, left political theory generally) and critique of other ('mainstream') feminisms (white/middle class/liberal and structuralist feminisms). To a greater or lesser extent, critical legal feminisms have also moved beyond critique to develop transformative projects, alternative visions or more tentative reconstructive agendas in law.

At the outset, then, it is necessary to distinguish between critical legal feminisms and the general 'feminist critical project in law'. The hallmark of all critical approaches is their attention to the operations of power and power relations, and this is certainly true of feminist legal theory in general, which is described by Maria Drakopoulou as 'predicated upon a belief that an intimate and singular relationship exists between the workings of law and women such that law has particular and negative effects on women's social being'.[1] In other words, feminist legal scholars are generally critical of

---

[1] Maria Drakopoulou, 'Clio's Forgotten Consciousness: History and the Question of Feminist Critique in Law' (2013) 38 A Fem LJ 3, 9.

the ways in which law contributes to, reinforces and is complicit in women's social oppression. They have advanced various theories as to how and why law has this effect, and correspondingly have advanced various proposals as to how law may be reformed to empower women, promote women's equality and end their subordination. As discussed below, one of the markers of critical legal feminisms is that they are, at the very least, sceptical of the prospects for, in Audre Lorde's famous phrase, 'using the master's tools to dismantle the master's house'. Critical legal feminisms thus include critiques of law reform, and in particular of feminist law reform projects.

The second key distinction between critical legal feminisms and other strands of feminist legal scholarship is their rejection of theoretical grounding in a unitary subject. As Deborah Rhode put it in an early essay, critical legal feminists 'have sought to fuse a political agenda that is dependent on both group identity and legalist strategies with a methodology that is in some measure skeptical of both'.[2] Since she wrote in 1990, that scepticism in both respects has profoundly deepened, but has also been productive of new methodologies which at that time could scarcely have been envisaged.

2. CRITICAL LEGAL *FEMINISM*

The origin stories of critical legal feminist movements in different locations, such as the 'fem-crits' and critical race feminists in the USA and the British critical legal feminists, are remarkably congruent in time – the mid to late 1980s – and in content – the experience of marginalization, tokenism and/or dismissal by the critical legal 'malestream'. As Carrie Menkel-Meadow tells the US fem-crit story, women got sick of being ghettoized at critical legal studies (CLS) conferences into sessions on 'feminist theory and the law' which men didn't attend.[3] Rhode begins her essay mentioned above as follows:

> The piece grows out of an invitation to offer a feminist perspective for an anthology on critical legal studies. Such invitations are problematic in several respects. Almost any systematic statement about these two bodies of thought risks homogenizing an extraordinarily broad range of views. Moreover, providing some single piece on the 'woman question' perpetuates a tradition of tokenism that has long characterized left political movements.[4]

Anne Bottomley gives a strikingly similar account in the British context:

---

[2] Deborah L. Rhode, 'Feminist Critical Theories' (1990) 42 Stan L Rev 617, 619.

[3] Carrie Menkel-Meadow, 'Feminist Legal Theory, Critical Legal Studies, and Legal Education or, "The Fem-Crits go to Law School"' (1988) 38 J Leg Ed 61, 63. See also Phyllis Goldfarb, 'From the Worlds of "Others": Minority and Feminist Responses to Critical Legal Studies' (1992) 26 New Eng L Rev 683; Robin West, 'Jurisprudence and Gender' (1988) 55 U Chi L Rev 1; Nikol G. Alexander-Floyd, 'Critical Race Black Feminism: A "Jurisprudence of Resistance" and the Transformation of the Academy' (2010) 35 *Signs* 810 (noting that Black feminist legal theorists have also criticized the racial limitations of CLS).

[4] Rhode (n 2) 617 (footnote omitted).

When a small group of us were asked, some years ago, to contribute a chapter on feminism to a collection on critical legal studies, we chose to present a paper which centred on a series of challenges to both established and critical law work. The editor immediately came back to us and said that what was actually required was that we describe and introduce to the readers the feminist agenda. We refused to do this and wrote a second version of the paper arguing that feminism was not to be thought of as only having a validity if we could produce a neat coherent account of it within standard scholastic terms and that what we wanted to do was to lay down a challenge to the ways in which 'they' were willing to apprehend feminism.[5]

Likewise, Kimberlé Crenshaw's groundbreaking article 'Demarginalizing the Intersection of Race and Sex: A Black Feminist Critique of Antidiscrimination Doctrine, Feminist Theory and Antiracist Politics',[6] while criticizing feminist theory for its whiteness (of which more below), also criticized the failure of antiracist policy discourses to 'embrace the experiences and concerns of Black women'.[7] In a US Law School seminar on critical race theory in the mid-1990s, I recall being frustrated by the absence of attention to gender issues, and outraged by the crude sexism of some of the materials presented as exemplary representations of racial minority experience in America. As with the fem-crits, Crenshaw's challenge was not simply a call for the inclusion of Black women within already established analytical structures. Rather, critical legal feminists have insisted upon the need for a fundamental shift in critical analytical frameworks.

Thirty years on, while fundamental shifts have arguably occurred within feminist theory, the fundamental shift in the gendering of critical legal theory is still awaited. As suggested in the introduction to this chapter, the concerns articulated by Crenshaw and the fem-crits remain salient. A contemporary example is provided by claims, in the wake of Brexit and the election of Donald Trump, that identity politics are to blame for the failure of the left to mobilize a successful challenge to neoliberalism. As Sarah Keenan points out, such claims fail to recognize 'the racialized and gendered structure of labour' and, in positing the lives and interests of white men as the neutral ground on which common interests can and should be built, constitute a form of white male identity politics. In Keenan's critical race feminist analysis, Brexit and Trump are explained as moves to restore white men to their historically 'rightful' position of ownership and membership of national space. Challenges and mobilizations therefore need to proceed from that understanding rather than reproducing the same consignment of gender and race to the margins of consideration.[8]

---

[5] Anne Bottomley, 'Shock to Thought: An Encounter (of a Third Kind) with Legal Feminism' (2004) 12 Fem LS 29, referring to Anne Bottomley, Susie Gibson and Belinda Meteyard, 'Dworkin; Which Dworkin? Taking Feminism Seriously' (1987) 14 JLS 47.

[6] Kimberlé W. Crenshaw, 'Demarginalizing the Intersection of Race and Sex: A Black Feminist Critique of Antidiscrimination Doctrine, Feminist Theory and Antiracist Politics' [1989] U Chi Legal F 139.

[7] Ibid 140.

[8] Sarah Keenan, 'Identity Politics and Property in the Trump/Brexit Era' (2017) 7(2) *feminists@law*; citing in particular Katherine Franke, 'Making White Supremacy Respectable. Again' (*Los Angeles Review of Books Blog*, 21 November 2016) http://blog.lareviewofbooks.org/essays/making-white-supremacy-respectable/ accessed 4 April 2018.

3. *CRITICAL* LEGAL FEMINISM

As outlined in the introduction, the two respects in which critical legal feminisms depart from more orthodox legal feminisms is in their commitment to antiessentialism and their problematization of feminist law reform efforts. Antiessentialism entails the acknowledgement that there is no singular Woman or 'women's experience' to provide a grounding for feminist theorizing or political action. This position has its origins in two separate strands of feminist analysis, although they have by now become significantly intertwined. First, critical race and lesbian feminist theorists pointed out that mainstream feminist theory tended to assume the experiences and represent the interests of white, heterosexual women, and failed to take into account the specificities of Black and lesbian women's lives. Second, poststructuralist feminists argued that all subjects are unstable and contingent, and are constructed in discourse rather than possessing fixed identities.[9] While liberal, radical and some materialist legal feminists found these arguments destabilizing and dangerous, posing a threat to the very possibility of feminist legal politics, critical legal feminisms have embraced them and worked through their implications.

One implication, as noted by Anne Bottomley, is that feminist legal scholars are usefully reminded not to present feminist legal theory as a coherent project recognizable as part of a shared, mainstream scholarly enterprise. While the legal academy values coherence and unity, critical legal feminisms insist on the diversity of the feminist project. Bottomley argues that it is preferable to see feminism as 'a force, a movement of potentials rather than an identity', or as 'an imperative, and a field of activity within which we pursue our many divergent interests and needs, held together, loosely, by our common recognition of ourselves as challengers of the status quo, and a commitment to try and hear clearly the many voices within the field and enter into many conversations with them/us'.[10]

A second implication is that feminist legal scholars need to attend to the discursive effects of legal feminism, to examine the feminist scholar (not just the woman-as-victim) as an object of study, and the construction of knowledge in which she participates.[11] This point has been made in particular in relation to the fetishization of Third World women in Western feminist scholarship, where they are treated as 'an object of study or a subject to be rescued and rehabilitated by the feminist mission'.[12] Brenda Cossman, for example, writes of the need to exercise care in deploying Western feminist concepts in non-Western contexts, to interrogate their explanatory value and force in historically and materially specific locations. This process provides an

---

[9] For considerable elaboration of this discussion, see Rosemary Hunter, 'Deconstructing the Subjects of Feminism: The Essentialism Debate in Feminist Theory and Practice' (1996) 6 A Fem LJ 135.

[10] Bottomley (n 5) 59–60. See also Berta Esperanza Herdandez-Truyol, 'The LatIndia and Mestizajes: Of Cultures, Conquests and LatCritical Feminism' (1999) 3 *Journal of Gender, Race and Justice* 63.

[11] Bottomley, ibid 56. For sustained illustrations see Ratna Kapur, *Erotic Justice: Law and the New Politics of Postcolonialism* (Glass House Press 2005); Juliet Rogers, *Law's Cut on the Body of Human Rights: Female Circumcision, Torture and Sacred Flesh* (Routledge 2013).

[12] Kapur, ibid 4.

opportunity not just to ask what is culturally specific in the non-Western context, but also to ask what is culturally specific about the Western concept, and to find an inbetween space of cultural hybridity from which to theorize further. According to Cossman, Western feminists must recognize not only the partiality of their own perspectives but the effects of imposing those partial perspectives on the world. Conversely, bringing difference to the centre means giving it the power to shape the theoretical and interpretive terrain, a strategy she refers to as 'scattering' feminist legal studies.[13]

A third implication is that feminist efforts to reform the law are problematized, since there is no singular woman or women's experience whom feminists can claim to represent or on whose behalf they can argue. One of the principal projects of mainstream legal feminism, from the first wave feminists of the late nineteenth and early twentieth centuries to the liberal and radical feminists of the 1970s onwards, has been the effort to reform the law so as to eliminate overt discrimination against women (first wave) and to ameliorate women's social conditions and bring an end to social inequality (second wave). It is this project which is profoundly destabilized by antiessentialism's fragmentation of the feminist subject. Drakopoulou locates the origins of the feminist politics of legal reform in the nineteenth century *episteme*, which for the first time made possible the creation of knowledge by and about women, and hence enabled feminists to generalize from their own experience to women's shared condition.[14] This knowledge, in turn, resulted in the formulation of legal reform proposals, initially to bring divergent legal representations of women into line with feminist representations, and later to address divergent representations of women in other social discourses. 'Law's promise to materialize women's dreams of a better life' became its 'siren call', which persisted even after the feminist claim to knowledge about women in general came into question in the late twentieth century.[15]

Additional objections to feminist law reform projects have been compellingly articulated by Carol Smart, most notably in her book *Feminism and the Power of Law*.[16] Smart maintains that law should certainly be understood as a site of feminist struggle, but not as a tool of feminist struggle. Her focus is on the discursive power of law and, specifically, on law as a discourse which claims to speak the Truth about women,[17] and which systematically disqualifies other knowledges, including those of feminism and of women themselves. Far from living up to its claims to right wrongs and to empower the disadvantaged, law is harmful to women. Thus, feminist calls for legal intervention and legal change could make matters worse. Not only is it likely that law reform will be ineffective in solving the social problem, but constant appeals to law

---

[13] Brenda Cossman, 'Turning the Gaze Back on Itself: Comparative Law, Feminist Legal Studies and the Postcolonial Project' [1997] Utah L Rev 525, 533, 536–7, 539. See also Anne Orford, 'Feminism, Imperialism and the Mission of International Law' (2002) 71 Nord J Intl L 275.
[14] Maria Drakopoulou, 'Feminism and the Siren Call of Law' (2007) 18 Law & Crit 331.
[15] Ibid 359–60.
[16] Carol Smart, *Feminism and the Power of Law* (Routledge 1989). See also Carol Smart, *Law, Crime and Sexuality: Essays in Feminism* (Sage 1995).
[17] See also Carol Smart, 'The Woman of Legal Discourse' (1992) 1 Soc & Leg Stud 29; Kapur (n 11).

simply enhance the power of law and hence the power and authority of its damaging Truth claims. Feminist law reform projects accord too much power and significance to law, confirm its place in the hierarchy of knowledge and accept all of its claims about being a force for good, providing justice for women, being able to represent the truth about women and being the primary way in which women's claims can be legitimized. Smart argues that rather than constantly turning to law, feminists should 'resist the move towards more law and the creeping hegemony of the legal order'.[18] Law's assertions of universal Truths about women need to be contested by means of local and particular knowledges generated by women in specific contexts. Resistant discourses and alternative visions and accounts need to be articulated in legal forums, and there is also a need to pay attention to other discursive sites responsible for reproducing women's oppression.

A further critique of feminist law reform has revolved around the dangers of feminist concerns being coopted by wider conservative, neoliberal, governance and/or security agendas. However, there is a need to distinguish in this respect between critical legal feminisms, which acknowledge the critique as a form of reflexivity about their own practice, and critics of feminism who tend to locate the faults in an 'other' feminism from which they distance themselves, often by means of pejorative labels (such as 'carceral feminism' or 'governance feminism') and often with the implication that all feminism is tarred with the same complicit brush.[19] Examples of the former include Jane Scoular's work on the legal regulation of prostitution,[20] and Dianne Otto's analysis of feminist strategies in international law. Otto argues that while employing the language of crisis can be useful to feminist efforts to have a problem taken more seriously, this needs to be weighed against the risk of the cooptation of feminist ideas to serve crisis governance. The language of crisis 'securitises the issue, prioritising militarism over progressive social change and law over politics, and making it possible for law to extend its empire deeper into the everyday lives of women and men, reducing the space for "life itself"'.[21] Moreover, feminists must engage politically as well as legally, paying attention to structural inequalities, doing the political groundwork to enable women to mobilize new legal provisions, 'actively contesting the constraints of crisis thinking and remaining aware of the unpredictability of law and the contingency of its certainties'.[22]

---

[18] Smart (1989) (n 16) 5.

[19] See, for example, Janet Halley, *Split Decisions: How and Why to Take a Break from Feminism* (Princeton University Press 2006); Elizabeth Bernstein, 'Militarized Humanitarianism Meets Carceral Feminism: The Politics of Sex, Rights, and Freedom in Contemporary Antitrafficking Campaigns' (2010) 36 *Signs* 45. See also Ratna Kapur, 'Pink Chaddis and SlutWalk Couture: The Postcolonial Politics of Feminism Lite' (2012) 20 Fem LS 1.

[20] Jane Scoular, 'What's Law Got to Do With It? How and Why Law Matters in the Regulation of Sex Work' (2010) 37 JLS 12; Jane Scoular, *The Subject of Prostitution: Sex Work, Law and Social Theory* (Routledge 2015).

[21] Dianne Otto, 'Remapping Crisis Through a Feminist Lens' in Sari Kouvo and Zoe Pearson (eds), *Feminist Perspectives on Contemporary International Law* (Hart Publishing 2011) 92.

[22] Ibid 78.

4. CRITICAL *LEGAL* FEMINISM

Critical legal feminist engagements with law (as opposed to law reform) have been, as the above discussion would suggest, extremely diverse. At the risk of simplifying, systematizing and omitting, this section focuses on three characteristic forms of engagement and the methods of critique and resistance employed in each case. These are: the immanent critique of liberal legalism; the critique of law's marginalizing and exclusionary tendencies; and the critique of law's discursive power, its role in governmentality and its production of gendered, raced, classed, colonial, sexual and embodied subjects.

4.1 The Immanent Critique

Feminist legal scholars have long sought to puncture law's inflated view of itself (and liberal legal scholarship's inflated view of law) by arguing that law is not what it seems or claims to be. Law's claims to universality, rationality and objectivity have been thoroughly debunked, and its claim to be a neutral arbiter standing outside society and politics has been demolished.[23] These arguments are, of course, staples of critical legal theory generally. What makes them feminist is that the debunking, demolition and exposure have been achieved – and have proved particularly easy to achieve – by the juxtaposition of law with women's lives. This juxtaposition quickly reveals law's masculinity and partiality, women's exclusion from legal subjectivity and the role of law as a player in the politics of gender.

Critical legal feminisms have made several specific contributions to this debate. First, they have complexified the juxtaposition between law and women's lives in line with their insistence on the diverse, intersectional and unstable nature of women's experience. Thus, they have shown how the particular forms and manifestations of legal partiality, historicity and gender politics inevitably vary given the heterogeneity of women's lives, and hence are experienced differently by women at different times and in different locations. Second, they have highlighted incoherence, inconsistencies, discontinuities and contradictions in law.[24] While law might represent itself as monolithic and seamless, this image also falls apart under close critical scrutiny. From the perspective of legal subjects, law is not a system or a singular thing but is fragmented and diverse. It follows that these features may be open to exploitation and provide opportunities for resistance.[25] However, law's discontinuities include gendered, raced and classed gaps between its stated commitments (such as rights guarantees and prohibitions of harm) and its actual delivery (where enforcement may be categorically withheld, limited, nonexistent or prohibitively expensive). Smart's contestation of the claim that law is a force for good was noted above. According to Smart, from a

---

[23] See, for example, Margaret Davies, 'Feminism and the Idea of Law' (2011) 1(1) *feminists@law*.
[24] Smart (1989) (n 16).
[25] Davies (n 23).

feminist perspective, law is neither a force for good, nor a force (effective in bringing about the objective of equality for women) at all.[26]

Third, critical legal feminists have argued that while the various claims made by liberal law are unsustainable, those claims are made with the purpose of establishing and reinforcing law's own power and authority. Within Western metaphysics the qualities of universality, objectivity, coherence and rationality are highly valued. By associating itself with these terms, law asserts its own high value and the superiority of its knowledge as compared to other knowledges – and in particular to the knowledge produced by women, which is consistently associated with the devalued term in each binary: particular, subjective, incoherent and irrational. This focus on the self-interest inherent in law's self-representations – on its performativity and material existence[27] – marks a shift from earlier feminist theorizing which tended to see law as purely instrumental, that is, as operating in the interests either of men (generally the white middle and upper class men who act within law and who constitute its privileged subjects) or of patriarchy as a system. Within the critical feminist account, law's claims to power and authority and to the superiority of its knowledge are certainly associated with masculinity (as well as with whiteness, imperialism and heterosexuality) but the masculine power of law is understood as hegemonic rather than as either a historical artefact or a totalizing force.

4.2 The Critique of Exclusion

While the immanent critique focuses on the processes of exclusion from the perspective of law, the critique of exclusion is a sociolegal rather than a jurisprudential argument, focusing on the experience of exclusion, oppression and subjugation from the perspective of the excluded. Critical race feminism has played a particularly prominent role in this critique, with its concern to give 'voice to those who have been excluded from the discourse of dominant legal theory' and to challenge 'the laws and the legal institutions that have played a central role in the creation and the reification of social hierarchies'.[28] This is also a critique of law's abstraction, its refusal to notice the bodies and lives on which it operates, its race and gender blindness which make it blind to the social dynamics and harms of gender and race.[29]

One of the methods of critical race feminism which has been important in this critique has been the use of genres of writing outside the realms of traditional legal scholarship, such as irony, storytelling and narratives of personal experience, to draw attention to subjectivity and disrupt the legal (and scholarly) 'view from nowhere'.[30]

---

[26] Smart (1989) (n 16).
[27] Davies (n 23).
[28] Angela Onwuachi-Willig, 'Foreword: This Bridge Called Our Backs: An Introduction to "The Future of Critical Race Feminism"' (2006) 39 UC Davis L Rev 733, 736.
[29] Margaret E. Montoya, '*Mascaras, Trenzas y Greñas*: Un/Masking the Self While Un/Braiding Latina Stories and Legal Discourse' (1994) 17 Harv Women's LJ 185. See also Sherene Razack, Malinda Smith and Sunera Thobani (eds), *States of Race: Critical Race Feminism for the 21st Century* (Between the Lines 2010).
[30] For example, Alexander-Floyd (n 3) 811–12; Montoya, ibid; Patricia Williams, *The Alchemy of Race and Rights* (Harvard University Press 1991).

(See also Möschel, 'Critical Race Theory', this volume.) Another has been a conscious embrace of the complexity, multiplicity and multidimensionality of marginalized experience, together with a search for interconnections and strategic coalitions and a commitment to practising hybridity or *mestizaje*,[31] as described by Cossman above. Notably, this is not a search for or assertion of an 'authentic' Other identity; racial, religious or cultural essentialism are as much to be eschewed as gender essentialism.[32]

Critical race and postcolonial feminists have also advocated 'looking to the bottom'[33] or 'moving theory to the intersection':[34] a commitment to building theory from the lives and experiences of excluded rather than dominant groups, and to living with and valuing difference 'beyond accommodation'.[35] As Karin van Marle has observed, this entails a demand not simply to add more voices on the margins, but to destabilize current systems and the culture and privilege attached to them and to redefine what the centre is. She adds that it is very unlikely that law will be able or willing to do this.[36] Nevertheless, critical legal feminists have attempted to engage in an epistemology of resistance to counter the epistemic violence and injustice of legal exclusion, involving the production not just of different but of resistant knowledges. This might include insisting upon relationality and the recognition of power relations within groups and communities against law's decontextualized, atomistic individualism,[37] or exploring 'the theoretical and disruptive possibilities that the subaltern subject brings to law'.[38]

An example of moving theory to the intersection is the reconceptualization of equality in terms of 'complex equality', as explained by Karin van Marle. The concept of formal equality is central to the rule of law and to liberal legal claims of objectivity, impartiality and consistency. Yet this concept (treating like cases alike) has been shown by feminists to be simply a means of reinforcing sedimented privilege and power, since the question of 'likeness' comes to be judged by reference to the status quo of social difference and inequality. 'Complex equality', by contrast, is a critical, nonessentialist concept which demands that a multiplicity of values and rights come into play in the interpretation of equality in any given context, depending on whether the type of discrimination at issue is moral, political and/or material. The analysis would also pay attention to complex life experiences, intersectionality and the part played by other structures and institutions. Van Marle further suggests combining it with the idea of

---

[31] Hernandez-Truyol (n 10) 65.
[32] See, for example, Kapur (n 11) esp ch 3; Moira Dustin and Anne Phillips, 'Whose Agenda Is It? Abuses of Women and Abuses of "Culture" in Britain' (2008) 8 *Ethnicities* 405; Pragna Patel, 'Faith in the State? Asian Women's Struggles for Human Rights in the UK' (2008) 16 Fem LS 9.
[33] Mari J. Matsuda, 'Looking to the Bottom: Critical Legal Studies and Reparations' (1987) 22 Harv Civ Rts-Civ Lib L Rev 323.
[34] Crenshaw (n 6).
[35] Karin van Marle, 'Holding Out for Other Ways of Knowing and Being' (2017) 7(2) *feminists@law*. The phrase 'beyond accommodation' is from Drucilla Cornell, *Beyond Accommodation: Ethical Feminism, Deconstruction and the Law* (Routledge 1991).
[36] Van Marle, ibid 5.
[37] Samia Bano, 'Diversity, Knowledge and Power' (2017) 7(2) *feminists@law*. See also Nicola Lacey, *Unspeakable Subjects: Feminist Essays in Legal and Social Theory* (Hart Publishing 1998).
[38] Kapur (n 11) 3.

'ethical equality', which entails a recognition of the impossibility of law and equality to serve justice fully, and hence creates an incentive actively to pursue better ways of serving justice and recognition of the need for continuing responsibility and judgement.[39] These concepts take a position of openness rather than closure or fixed solutions, and further expose the partial perspectives embedded in liberal law.

4.3 The Critique of Law's Discursive Power

The 'postmodern turn' in critical legal feminisms has involved relocating the starting point of analysis from 'women's experience' to the discursive processes by which gender and women's experience are constructed. In this analysis, law is viewed as a discourse which, like other normalizing discourses, is involved in the construction of gender and hence in producing male and female subjectivities. Smart describes law in this context as a 'technology of gender', and traces the legal construction of categories such as the single mother.[40] Similarly Mary Joe Frug notes the way in which law produces women's bodies as 'naturally' of a particular type: terrorized – 'a body that has learned to scurry, to cringe and to submit'; maternalized – 'a body that is "for" maternity'; and sexualized – 'a body that is "for" sex with men, a body that is "desirable" and also rapable, that wants sex and wants raping'.[41]

One of the implications of this approach is the need to examine 'what law is doing' in any given instance.[42] This can be seen, for example, in Doris Buss's examination of the 'analytical, epistemological and ontological work' done by the notion of 'rape as a weapon of war'. Within this trope, she asks, what stories of rape and other forms of violence are made visible and which are not? What can be known about sexualized violence and what cannot? Answering these questions, she finds, illuminates postconflict justice mechanisms as spaces within which gender norms and identities are defined and reiterated, often in conservative ways, with victims and aggressors constructed in essentialized terms which fail to capture the nuances of ethnicity, identification, gender, contexts, actions and negotiations.[43]

A further implication is that law cannot be understood in isolation from other social discourses which participate in the governance of subjects. As Jane Scoular puts it, law is part of wider processes which constitute certain subjects as objects of knowledge and targets for governance, and which then authorizes and informs systems of governance that act on these subjects.[44] Sometimes law actively works in conjunction with other disciplinary configurations such as medicine and the 'psy' professions,[45] and sometimes it simply authorizes and enforces ideas derived from elsewhere. In this context,

---

[39] Karin van Marle, 'Haunting (In)Equalities' in Rosemary Hunter (ed), *Rethinking Equality Projects in Law: Feminist Challenges* (Hart Publishing 2008).
[40] Smart (n 17). See also Scoular (2010) (n 20) 26–8.
[41] Mary Joe Frug, *Postmodern Legal Feminism* (Routledge 1992) 129–30.
[42] Scoular (2010) (n 20) 28.
[43] Doris Buss, 'Rethinking "Rape as a Weapon of War"' (2009) 17 Fem LS 145.
[44] Scoular (2015) (n 20) 19.
[45] See, for example, Smart (1989) (n 16) 14–20, ch 3; Rosemary Hunter, 'Judicial Diversity and the "New Judge"' in Hilary Sommerlad, Sonia Harris-Short, Steven Vaughan and Richard Young (eds), *The Futures of Legal Education and the Legal Profession* (Hart Publishing 2015).

focusing attention on the legal manifestations of a problem may miss the broader issue. For example, Mary Joe Frug argues in relation to Catharine MacKinnon and Andrea Dworkin's antipornography campaign that the attempt to use law to end pornography was misplaced. 'If women's oppression occurs through sex, then in order to end women's oppression in its many manifestations, the way people think and talk and act about sex must be changed.' On the contrary, she observes, 'the ordinance advocates relentlessly utilized and exploited traditional ideas and language regarding sex in all aspects of the campaign'. Pornography and people's attitudes to it were reduced to simple dichotomies, whereas pornography which represents women's sexuality differently might in fact have greater value in shifting the discourse.[46] As Nicola Lacey notes, critical legal feminists need to develop and act upon 'a theoretical understanding of how law relates to other powerful institutions and discourses'[47] in each of their areas of critique.

As discussed earlier, the acknowledgement of law's discursive power means that critical feminist engagements with law need to contest and challenge its power to define and limit women.[48] On this view, law is a site of political and discursive struggle over sex differences and competing visions of women's place in the world.[49] The tools of struggle include critical discourse analysis and deconstruction, in particular the deconstruction of binary thinking with its embedded gender hierarchies.[50] (See further Van de Walt, 'Deconstruction', this volume.) Particular binaries which have been the target of critical feminist deconstruction, as well as those noted earlier in relation to the immanent critique of law, include the public/private distinction,[51] and the victimization/agency dichotomy.[52] Consistent with their understandings of the complexity, contingency and situated nature of subjectivity and the diversity of lived experience, critical legal feminists have been concerned to destabilize fixed positions and attend to context, particularities and ambivalence, including the articulation of agency under conditions of oppression,[53] the relational and contingent nature of autonomy and the possibility of other subject positions altogether. Ratna Kapur, for example, has sought to move beyond the victim/agent dichotomy by making discursive space and visibility for erotic subjects.[54]

---

[46] Frug (n 41) 152. See also Smart (1989) (n 16). And on pornography which represents women's sexuality differently, see, for example, Sara Janssen, 'Sensate Vision: From Maximum Visibility to Haptic Erotics' (2015) 5(2) *feminists@law*.

[47] Lacey (n 37) 180.

[48] Smart (1989) (n 16).

[49] Frug (n 41) 126; Kapur (n 11) 5; Cossman (n 13) 531.

[50] Drakopoulou (n 1) 11–12; Menkel-Meadow (n 3) 71; Maggie Troup, 'Rupturing the Veil: Feminism, Deconstruction and the Law' (1993) 1 A Fem LJ 63.

[51] See, for example, Frances E. Olsen, 'The Myth of State Intervention in the Family' (1985) 18 U Mich J L Reform 835; Frances E. Olsen, 'Constitutional Law: Feminist Critiques of the Public/Private Distinction' (1993) 10 Const Commentary 319; Kapur (n 11) ch 2.

[52] See, for example, Kapur, ibid ch 4; Anastasia Vakulenko, *Islamic Veiling in Legal Discourse* (Routledge 2012).

[53] For example, Bano (n 37) 7; Scoular (2015) (n 20); Van Marle (n 39) 129.

[54] Kapur (n 11) ch 4.

The obvious question that arises in this context concerns the implications of deconstruction for feminism. How can feminists assert the superiority of feminist as opposed to legal knowledge, and isn't that knowledge equally subject to deconstruction? Margaret Davies and Nan Seuffert argue that while knowledge cannot be validated or legitimized on the basis of reason or power, it may still be valued on political and ethical grounds. Knowledge that challenges existing inequalities or oppressions should be valued over knowledge which perpetuates them or assumes they do not exist, although such value must always be understood as situated and contingent rather than universal.[55]

5. BEYOND CRITIQUE

To the extent that critical legal feminisms hold onto a sense of political and ethical injustice, then, there is a constant imperative to move beyond critique, but to what? The desire for justice has been met on the one hand by the formulation of utopian projects, such as Drucilla Cornell's envisioning of the recovery of a specifically feminine imaginary through deconstruction, and the transformation of the legal sphere to guarantee to women the freedom to determine themselves as sexed beings.[56] While utopian projects are themselves inevitably the subjects of critique,[57] Van Marle has argued for the importance of being an idealist, of holding out hope for the possibilities of a plural jurisprudence, which would heed 'other ways of being' and diverse and multiple knowledges and truths, without expectations that this will ever be fully realized. As suggested earlier, the vision of an unrealizable ideal may nevertheless act as a spur to greater efforts to do better and to guard against complacency and self-satisfaction.[58]

At the same time, other critical legal feminists have been willing to engage, albeit tentatively and self-reflexively, in normative projects. Rejecting any strategy or approach, including legal reformism, out of hand would appear to contradict the postmodern rejection of grand theory and its strictures about the contingency of knowledge. Rather, feminists should think about the potential usefulness of any strategy in the particular context or circumstances.[59] As Nicola Lacey notes, decentring law makes sense only if intervention in other discourses would be likely to be more politically productive or if the creation of alternative feminist practices offers in the long run the possibility of political progress as opposed to further marginalization.[60] Thus, legal reform initiatives should not be categorically struck from the list of potential feminist strategies, but should not be used in isolation and should be treated

---

[55] Margaret Davies and Nan Seuffert, 'Knowledge, Identity and the Politics of Law' (2000) 11 Hastings Women's LJ 259, 273–4.

[56] Drucilla Cornell (n 35); *The Philosophy of the Limit* (Routledge 1992); *Transformations: Recollective Imagination and Sexual Difference* (Routledge 1993); *The Imaginary Domain* (Routledge 1995).

[57] See, in particular, Lacey (n 37) ch 7.

[58] Van Marle (n 35).

[59] Lacey (n 37) 176.

[60] Ibid 185–6.

with caution, including thinking carefully about potential side effects and acknowledging that the ultimate outcomes may be indeterminable in advance.[61] In this context, Dianne Otto invokes Foucault's warning that 'nothing is an evil in itself but everything is dangerous'.[62]

Contrasting conclusions about the value of legal reform may be seen, for example, in critical feminist work by Yvette Russell and Adrian Howe on criminal law. Russell's psychoanalysis of rape law suggests law's continuing complicity in its own failure to provide justice to raped women, 'because it is structurally invested, for its own survival and coherence, in the exclusion and erasure of woman's voice, which represents the possibility of a plural form of being and thinking and is thus a fundamental challenge to the legitimacy of law'.[63] No amount of further tinkering with the law of rape, nor efforts to implement it more effectively, will have any impact on the fundamental structure of law's sexual indifference (its recognition only of a masculine legal subject). In this context, rather than investing all our efforts in making the law work better, feminists need to diversify our approach to find other ways to acknowledge and address the harms of rape for women.

Howe, on the other hand, engages in a self-reflexive interrogation of her desire to abolish the defence of provocation, animated by 'feminist and queer anger about the law of provocation's victim-blaming narratives', while at the same time being critically aware of 'the deeply problematic history of the power to punish'. In particular, in the Australian context in which she is working, this includes

> the disproportionate number of Aboriginal women killed in domestic homicides as well as the over-representation of Aboriginal people in Australian prisons. How then, at the political level, can she advocate a law reform that would result in increased murder convictions, and presumably longer prison sentences, for men, including Aboriginal men, who kill their wives? … What is the best theoretically-informed political strategy … while remaining cognisant that poststructuralism problematises both law and law reform?[64]

Having noted that malestream commentators have frequently dismissed her abolitionist stance as polemical, and observed how the denial of the right to be angry is used as a mechanism of subordination, she finds an 'ethical basis for poststructuralist feminist anger about the provocation defence'.[65] Drawing on Adriana Cavarero, she argues that

> the standard provocation tale is a man's tale of his aggravation by a 'what', traditionally a nagging, unfaithful or departing wife, more recently a man making an unwanted sexual advance to another man. This 'what' can never be a 'who', a subject, a 'you'. On the other hand, without the victim, the killer cannot become the provocation defence's narratable

---

[61] Ralph Sandland, 'Between "Truth" and "Difference": Poststructuralism, Law and the Power of Feminism' (1995) 3 Fem LS 3.

[62] Dianne Otto, 'Introduction: Embracing Queer Curiosity' in Dianne Otto (ed), *Queering International Law: Possibilities, Alliances, Complicities, Risks* (Routledge 2018).

[63] Yvette Russell, 'Woman's Voice/Law's *Logos*: The Rape Trial and the Limits of Liberal Reform' (2017) 42 A Fem LJ 273.

[64] Adrian Howe, 'Provoking Polemic: Provoked Killings and the Ethical Paradoxes of the Postmodern Feminist Condition' (2002) 10 Fem LS 39, 40–1.

[65] Ibid 60.

subject. The provocation narrative thus reveals the fundamental dependency of the killer's story of intolerable provocation on the other, the silenced victim. In a provocation case, only the killer's story is narrated, allowing him, the *sexed* who, to become a 'narratable self' while the victim – whether female or feminised – is reduced to an annihilated 'what'. As such the provocation narrative is a narrative, utterly ethically bankrupt.[66]

On the basis of this analysis, Howe concludes that law reform to abolish the defence of provocation is the only way to shift the discourse of the criminal trial and avoid the erasure of the victim through the defence narratives it invites.

The question of whether to take a normative approach is accompanied by questions about the content of normative strategies and again there is no straightforward answer. If one maintains a commitment to the value of multiple knowledges and perspectives, any approach will necessarily be diverse and complex. As Davies and Seuffert observe:

> We are faced with the strategic choice between complying in the legal preference for a single approach or policy, or attempting to reflect situations in all of their difficulty, complexity, and non-rationality (which may appear to be less effective in the short term). As feminist legal thinkers are only too well aware, there is no easy solution to this dilemma, leaving us to work simultaneously on many fronts ... [T]he project of resistance to [law's] totalizing tendencies is an ongoing and essential one.[67]

Similarly, Van Marle notes that

> The response to any call for transformation, any critique on present systems and arrangements is a demand for a fully worked out plan. We find ourselves in a time where it feels more than ever that there is no space for talking about things, for dialogue, deliberation and most importantly, reflection.[68]

Resources for critical feminist reconstruction may be drawn from a variety of sources, including sociolegal studies of alternative practices, understandings of legality and social imaginaries, as well as 'those doctrinal principles and discursive images which are less dominant yet which fracture and complicate the seamless web imagined by orthodox legal scholarship'.[69] Jane Scoular advocates pragmatic and strategic engagement with legal norms, using the concepts and structures that the system provides, although with the same health warnings applied to engagement with law reform: without universalizing, with awareness of the likelihood of unforeseen consequences, and acknowledging that outcomes cannot accurately be predicted.[70] In relation to prostitution, she points to three feminist legal interventions which have enhanced the legal subjectivity and hence also, at least potentially, the material wellbeing of sex workers. One has been the establishment of sex workers as legally rapable subjects, that is, as having the capacity *not* to consent, and hence falling within the protection (fragile though it may be) of the law of rape. A second has been the establishment of the 'right

---

[66] Ibid 61.
[67] Davies and Seuffert (n 55) 289.
[68] Van Marle (n 35) 10–11.
[69] Lacey (n 37) 11, 159–63; Bano (n 37) 11.
[70] Scoular (2015) (n 20) 23–4, 122–3.

to have rights', the constitution of sex workers as citizens entitled to invoke the protections of public law in ways that are relevant to their lives. A third has been the rethinking of workers' rights to encompass the specific experiences and needs of sex workers. This has not simply involved taking a position in the old binary debate as to whether prostitution should be conceived of as legitimate labour or illegitimate patriarchal exploitation, but rather has involved thinking about workers' rights from the perspective of sex workers (shifting the centre) as a demand to reformulate the scope of workers' rights more broadly, which in turn may operate to the benefit of many other precarious and marginalized workers.[71] In line with the discussion above, Scoular reiterates the modesty of her objectives:

> A final point to make by way of clarification is that these examples do not constitute a programme for law reform. They are simply examples of ways in which law has been utilised constructively to advance the interests of sex workers and to reconfigure the subject of prostitution. They demonstrate that law can be utilised in ways that create space for struggle and may produce better outcomes for some.[72]

More ambitiously than Scoular, Prabha Kotiswaran offers a sustained attempt to produce a coherent albeit localized reconstructive project, again in the context of sex work. Kotiswaran carefully considers which feminist and other theoretical resources appear most useful in the particular local contexts of sex work in various Indian cities, from the perspective of sex workers themselves (based on her sociological and ethnographic research), and situating law within a broader analysis of political economy. Her inquiry includes a hypothetical economic analysis to test and assess the potential distributional consequences of alternative law reform and regulatory proposals. Finding none of the existing options satisfactory, she develops a 'postcolonial materialist feminist theory of sex work', and formulates different proposals based on this theory to achieve normative redistributive goals. Notably, she suggests that regulatory models may need to be tailored to specific sex markets rather than there being a single national law. And she also identifies the important role played by unions and membership organisations in promoting and defending sex workers' rights and wellbeing, regardless of the actual terms of the law.[73]

Feminist judgment projects are another reconstructive approach which has taken off in the past decade.[74] These projects involve the rewriting of existing judicial

---

[71] Ibid ch 5.
[72] Ibid 148.
[73] Prabha Kotiswaran, *Dangerous Sex, Invisible Labour: Sex Work and the Law in India* (Princeton University Press 2011).
[74] Women's Court of Canada, 'Rewriting Equality' (2006) 18(1) Can J Women & L; Rosemary Hunter, Clare McGlynn and Erika Rackley (eds), *Feminist Judgments: From Theory to Practice* (Hart Publishing 2010); Heather Douglas, Francesca Bartlett, Trish Luker and Rosemary Hunter (eds), *Australian Feminist Judgments: Righting and Rewriting Law* (Hart Publishing 2014); Kathryn M. Stanchi, Linda L. Berger and Bridget J. Crawford (eds), *Feminist Judgments: Rewritten Opinions of the United States Supreme Court* (Cambridge University Press 2016); Máiréad Enright, Julie McCandless and Aoife O'Donoghue (eds), *Northern/Irish Feminist Judgments: Judges' Troubles and the Gendered Politics of Identity* (Hart Publishing 2017); Elisabeth McDonald, Rhonda Powell, Māmari Stephens and Rosemary Hunter (eds), *Feminist*

decisions from a feminist perspective, imagining the judgment that would have been written by a feminist judge sitting on the bench alongside the original judges and making her judgment at the same time. This construct, with its attempt to produce alternative, equally plausible judgments, involves finding the gaps, discontinuities and indeterminacies within law and exploiting their deconstructive potential for feminist purposes.

While individual judgments take different feminist approaches – not all of them critical as defined in this chapter – the general project of rewriting judgments might be seen as a critical one. While the feminist judgment projects do not decentre law, they certainly decentre the iconic figure of the judge, and by embodying law differently they draw attention to the embodied subjectivity of all judges.[75] Second, and centrally, they engage in discursive struggle over legal constructions of gender, contesting the disempowering constructions of Woman and women in the original cases and writing alternative accounts of women's lives, subjectivities and possibilities into legal texts. This is particularly evident in the Northern/Irish feminist judgments project, which demonstrates in its selection of judgments how judges in the Republic of Ireland and Northern Ireland have contributed to the gendered politics of national identity. The alternative feminist judgments tackle head-on the narrow subject positions created for women and 'others' in this process, counterposing a much wider and more open array of subjectivities and potentialities. The feminist judgments collectively exemplify the ways in which it might be possible for law to recognize and respond to, rather than marginalizing and excluding, diversity and the particularities of lived experience at the intersections of gender, race, religion, colonialism, culture, age, (dis)ability, sexuality, pregnancy, motherhood, socioeconomic status and immigration status (as well as the justice claims of nonhuman entities). The focus on judgments rather than legislation also means that false universalism may more readily be avoided, with judgments generally being careful to address the case before the court and to avoid potentially dangerous generalizations which may inadequately represent the concerns of and do violence to those who are differently situated. Placing the relevant women or 'others' at the centre of judgments often involves telling the story and constructing the facts differently and reasoning from context rather than in the abstract. In many cases, shifting those previously excluded to the centre also compels a shift in legal doctrine.

The critical credentials of the feminist judgment projects have been called into question on the basis that they are 'too narrow in addressing the problem of justice' and too focused on 'the instrumentality of "impact"'. This critique proceeds from a position firmly within the utopian camp which prefers to emphasize the incalculability of judgment and the infinite unknowability of justice. Justice, on this view, is beyond this

---

Judgments of Aotearoa New Zealand: Te Rino – A Two-Stranded Rope (Hart Publishing 2017); Loveday Hodson and Troy Lavers (eds), *Feminist Judgments in International Law* (Hart Publishing 2019); Sharon Cowan, Chloë Kennedy and Vanessa E Munro (eds), *Scottish Feminist Judgments: (Re)Creating Law From the Outside In* (Hart Publishing 2019).

[75] Margaret Davies, *Law Unlimited: Materialism, Pluralism and Legal Theory* (Routledge 2017). See also Margaret Davies, 'The Law Becomes Us: Rediscovering Judgment' (2012) 20 Fem LS 167.

world and beyond our power to comprehend – an 'encounter with [the] experience of the sublime even though it "evades our grasp"'.[76] (See further Wolcher, 'The Ethical Turn in Critical Legal Thought', this volume.) As the discussion above might indicate, many critical legal feminists would not accept this grand, abstract theory of justice, or accept it as the only possible meaning of justice. Moreover, the argument ignores the way in which prefigurative practices, as enactments of an imagined future in the present, may unsettle the taken for granted nature of both present and future.[77] As such, they may operate as a kind of halfway house, or a hybrid, between critique and utopianism.

6. CONCLUSION

Critical legal feminisms are a collection of diverse approaches to legal critique, which tend to share a concern also to critique other critical legal theories (for their marginalization of gender) and other feminisms (for their assumption of an essentialized and exclusive feminist subject). In line with their commitments to contingency, multiplicity and localized knowledges, they do not constitute a project or a programme, are not collectively coherent and are not necessarily concerned to maintain theoretical purity. All engage with law's discursive constructions of gender and marginalized subjectivities and most are also, at least to some degree, concerned with how diverse material lives are and can be lived in the domain of law. Some focus on critique while others may posit alternative utopian visions and/or reconstructive projects and agendas in law, though remaining mindful of the uncertainties and potential pitfalls of doing so. Reconstructive projects and agendas in critical legal theory remain more elusive.

BIBLIOGRAPHY

Anne Bottomley, Susie Gibson, Belinda Meteyard, 'Dworkin; Which Dworkin? Taking Feminism Seriously' (1987) 14(1) *Journal of Law and Society* 47–60.
Drucilla Cornell, *Beyond Accommodation: Ethical Feminism, Deconstruction and the Law* (Routledge 1991).
Kimberlé W. Crenshaw, 'Demarginalizing the Intersection of Race and Sex: A Black Feminist Critique of Antidiscrimination Doctrine, Feminist Theory and Antiracist Politics' [1989] *University of Chicago Legal Forum* 139.
Mary Joe Frug, *Postmodern Legal Feminism* (Routledge 1992).
Rosemary Hunter, 'Deconstructing the Subjects of Feminism: The Essentialism Debate in Feminist Theory and Practice' (1996) 6 *Australian Feminist Law Journal* 135.
Ratna Kapur, *Erotic Justice: Law and the New Politics of Postcolonialism* (Glass House Press 2005).
Nicola Lacey, *Unspeakable Subjects: Feminist Essays in Legal and Social Theory* (Hart Publishing 1998).

---

[76] Stewart Motha, 'Mistaken Judgments' in Austin Sarat, Lawrence Douglas and Martha Umphrey (eds), *Law's Mistakes* (University of Massachusetts Press 2016).
[77] See Davies (2017) (n 75) 16–17; Davina Cooper, 'Transforming Markets and States through Everyday Utopias of Play' [2017] *Politica & Società* 187; Davina Cooper, 'Prefiguring the State' (2017) 42 *Antipode* 335.

Deborah L. Rhode, 'Feminist Critical Theories' (1990) 42 *Stanford Law Review* 617.
Carol Smart, *Feminism and the Power of Law* (Routledge 1989).
Adrien Katherine Wing (ed.), *Critical Race Feminism: A Reader* (NYU Press, 2nd ed 2003).

4. Critical race theory
*Mathias Möschel**

Dating from the late 1980s, critical race theory is one of the youngest movements or theories in the panorama of critical scholarship. In section 1, this contribution will briefly look at its origins in the United States; in section 2 it will describe its main tenets, elements, and theoretical tools; and in section 3 it will conclude with a discussion of the latest developments in this area.

1. ORIGINS

Critical race theory (hereinafter CRT) has been classified among postmodern legal movements, alongside critical legal studies (hereinafter CLS), feminist legal theory (hereinafter FLT), law and economics, and law and literature.[1] Two points are important to note from this classification: first, CRT originated in the United States; second, within that context, it developed in American law schools in the late 1980s.[2] The reason for classifying these various strands of jurisprudence as postmodern is that, unlike prior "modern" approaches, the postmodern ones do not try to analyze law from one universally true vantage point but rather dissect it from different angles. For example, FLT considers law in terms of what it does to women; law and economics looks at the economic implications of law; and critical race theory looks at law to or from the bottom,[3] that is, through the lens of racial minorities in the United States.

However, CRT's postmodernity is determined not only by whose nonuniversal vantage point is taken to look at law but also by the variety of intellectual sources that its authors have used. European philosophers such as Antonio Gramsci and Michel Foucault; postcolonial thinkers such as Frantz Fanon and Aimé Césaire; American

---

* Parts of this contribution are based, to a greater or lesser degree, on Chapter 2 of this author's *Law, Lawyers and Race: Critical Race Theory from the United States to Europe* (Routledge, 2014).

[1] On this classification see Gary Minda, *Postmodern Legal Movements* (NYU Press 1995).

[2] These are the main factors distinguishing it from other related theoretical work on race and ethnicity that has been written outside of the United States and outside of the legal context, but that has a similar name. See Philomena Essed and David Theo Goldberg (eds), *Race Critical Theories* (John Wiley & Sons 2001).

[3] Expressions taken from two founding pieces of CRT: Mari J. Matsuda, 'Looking to the Bottom: Critical Legal Studies and Reparations' (1987) 22 *Harvard Civil Rights – Civil Liberties Law Review* 323 and Derrick A. Bell Jr., *Faces at the Bottom of the Well: The Permanence of Racism* (Basic Books 1992).

radical thinkers and personalities such as Sojourner Truth, W.E.B. Du Bois, Frederick Douglass, and Martin Luther King, Jr; as well as feminist (legal) theory and the Black Power and Chicano Movements of the 1960s and 1970s, have provided inspiration for a broad body of literature.[4]

Various factors and events have been identified as providing the necessary backdrop allowing for CRT to emerge and leading to its birth in the late 1980s. Some have credited student movements at University of California, Berkeley,[5] or at Harvard Law School,[6] as providing the necessary terrain for the emergence and the establishment of CRT in top law schools. Others have instead focused on the faculty side of the matter by considering the broader academic context of the 1970s in which white Marxist and socialist professors were denied tenure and therefore had the time to spread their "radical" ideas during their un(der)employment, thus contributing to the rise of both CLS and CRT.[7]

There is little doubt about the turning point and the actual "official" birth moment of CRT in the framework of CLS. In 1986, radical CLS feminists organized a conference critiquing the patriarchy inside the CLS movement and asked CLS academics of color to organize a similar event around the topic of race in CLS. Radical feminism and CLS thus provided the intellectual and political openings within which CRT was able to develop and thrive, albeit not without difficulties. In 1987, during the tenth National Critical Legal Studies Conference, entitled "Sounds of Silence: Racism and the Law," some of the future CRT scholars raised a minority critique of CLS scholarship regarding the silence on race.[8] These critiques were not welcomed by all CLS scholars; some found it difficult to analyze their scholarship and position through the lens of White domination and racialism. And in fact, arguably the incapacity of CLS to adequately address or internalize these critiques led to its end.[9]

---

[4] See in this sense Richard Delgado and Jean Stefancic, *Critical Race Theory: An Introduction* (3rd edn, NYU Press 2017) 5. For more complete bibliographical references to (early) CRT literature (as well as Latino/a critical scholarship) see: Richard Delgado and Jean Stefancic, 'Critical Race Theory, An Annotated Bibliography' (1993) 79 *Virginia Law Review* 461; Richard Delgado and Jean Stefancic, 'Critical Race Theory, An Annotated Bibliography 1993, A Year of Transition' (1995) 66 *University of Colorado Law Review* 159; and Jean Stefancic, 'Latino and Latina Critical Theory: An Annotated Bibliography' (1997) 85 *California Law Review* 1509.

[5] Sumi Cho and Robert Westley, 'Critical Race Coalitions: Key Movements that Performed the Theory' (2000) 33 *U.C. Davis Law Review* 1377.

[6] Kimberlé W. Crenshaw, 'The First Decade: Critical Reflections, or "A Foot in the Closing Door"' (2002) 49 *UCLA Law Review* 1343, 1344–54.

[7] Richard Delgado, 'Liberal McCarthyism and the Origins of Critical Race Theory' (2009) 94 *Iowa Law Review* 1505.

[8] See more in detail on this story Kimberlé W. Crenshaw et al (eds), *Critical Race Theory: The Key Writings that Formed the Movement* (The New Press 1995) xiv–xvii.

[9] Paul Brest, 'Plus Ça Change' (1993) 91 *Michigan Law Review* 1945.

Instead, CRT began to thrive. In 1989, the first independent CRT workshop took place in Madison, Wisconsin, and the name "critical race theory" was invented.[10] From then on, for some time annual workshops were organized,[11] and a number of separate symposia or conferences were held at different times, leading to additional publications and exchanges.[12] Even when the annual CRT workshops stopped taking place regularly, CRT's legacy continued, partly thanks to LatCrit, which began to organize annual conferences.[13]

2. MAIN TENETS

The different workshops, conferences, and other meetings between scholars, have helped to develop a vast and diverse body of literature. It is hard to boil down this doctrinally and methodologically eclectic legal scholarship to one canonical unity. Indeed, this open-ended approach partly reflects the necessity of favoring identity over substantive criteria so as to create a safe space and a platform from which to engage in racial struggle.[14] Hence, it can be said that the main aim of CRT is not to develop a coherent, methodologically flawless theoretical framework, but in some ways it is rather an academic political enterprise. However, even political action needs some main ideas around which to develop its program, and CRT scholars have over the years defined such ideas, tenets, and goals.

These were in part identified and later refined during the Second Workshop, where discussion was organized around a seven-point description of CRT's proposed tenets, according to which CRT:

> holds that racism is endemic to, rather than a deviation from, American norms;
>
> bears skepticism towards the dominant claims of meritocracy, neutrality, objectivity and color-blindness;
>
> challenges ahistoricism, and insists on a contextual and historical analysis of the law;
>
> challenges the presumptive legitimacy of social institutions;
>
> insists on recognition of both the experiential knowledge and critical consciousness of people of color in understanding law and society;

---

[10] Crenshaw, 'The First Decade' (n 6) 1354–60 and Charles R. Lawrence III, 'Foreword: Who Are We? And Why Are We Here? Doing Critical Race Theory in Hard Times', in Francisco Valdes, Jerome McCristal Culp and Angela Harris (eds), *Crossroads, Directions, and a New Critical Race Theory* (Temple University Press 2002) xii.
[11] On these early workshops see Stephanie Phillips, 'The Convergence of the Critical Race Theory Workshop with LatCrit Theory: A History' (1999) 53 *University of Miami Law Review* 1247.
[12] See e.g.: (2002) 71 *UMKC Law Review* 227–527; (2004) 61 *Washington and Lee Law Review* 1485–1799; and (2005) 11 *Michigan Journal of Race and Law* 1–273.
[13] For a list of those conferences see www.latcrit.org/content/conferences/.
[14] Crenshaw, 'The First Decade' (n 6) 1362–3.

is interdisciplinary and eclectic (drawing upon, inter alia, liberalism, post-structuralism, feminism, Marxism, critical legal theory, post-modernism, pragmatism), with the claim that the intersection of race and the law overruns disciplinary boundaries; and

works toward the liberation of people of color as it embraces the larger project of liberating oppressed people.[15]

Put differently, CRT tries to challenge popular, mainstream beliefs about racial injustice, namely that (a) "blindness to race will eliminate racism," that (b) "racism is a matter of individuals, not systems," and that (c) "one can fight racism without paying attention to sexism, homophobia, economic exploitation, and other forms of oppression and injustice."[16] Some of the main intellectual tools and terms that have been developed by critical race scholars and that will be described in further detail below are, for example, "interest convergence,"[17] "unconscious racism,"[18] and "intersectionality";[19] to some extent, "colorblindness" and its critique have also played a central role in CRT's conceptual toolkit.[20]

Methodologically, legal narrative allowed to bring personal experience into academic writing and legal analysis. The main idea is that (academic) legal writing and jargon silence minorities' visions and experience and that through legal narrative and storytelling those voices can finally be heard and provide a sort of counterhegemonic account of law and its effects. For this reason, one will find that many CRT writings start with a (personal) story or are wholly written as a story.[21] Moreover, CRT scholars have always insisted that, despite their scholarly origins, work in the area is and should always be grounded in praxis and should ultimately benefit racial minorities.[22] Even 30 years after its official origins, these goals and tenets stand at the core of the CRT project and most CRT scholars would still subscribe to them.

---

[15] See Phillips, 'The Convergence of the Critical Race Theory Workshop with LatCrit Theory' (n 11) 1250.

[16] Francisco Valdes, Jerome McCristal Culp and Angela Harris, 'Battles Waged, Won, and Lost: Critical Race Theory at the Turn of the Millennium', in Valdes, McCristal Culp and Harris (eds), *Crossroads* (n 10) 1.

[17] Derrick A. Bell Jr., 'Brown v. Board of Education and the Interest Convergence Dilemma' (1980) 93 *Harvard Law Review* 518.

[18] Charles R. Lawrence III, 'The Id, the Ego, and Equal Protection: Reckoning with Unconscious Racism' (1987) 39 *Stanford Law Review* 317.

[19] Kimberlé W. Crenshaw, 'Demarginalizing the Intersection of Race and Sex' (1989) *University of Chicago Legal Forum* 139 and Kimberlé W. Crenshaw, 'Mapping the Margins: Intersectionality, Identity Politics, and Violence against Women of Color (1991) 43 *Stanford Law Review* 1241.

[20] See e.g. Neil Gotanda, 'A Critique of "Our Constitution is Colorblind"' (1991) 44 *Stanford Law Review* 1.

[21] See e.g. Patricia Williams, *The Alchemy of Rights* (Harvard University Press 1991) and Derrick A. Bell Jr., *Faces at the Bottom of the Well: The Permanence of Racism* (Basic Books 1992).

[22] See e.g. Eric K. Yamamoto, 'Critical Race Praxis: Race Theory and Political Lawyering Practice in Post-Civil Rights America' (1997) 95 *Michigan Law Review* 821 and Adrienne Katherine Wing, 'Civil Rights in the Post 911 World: Critical Race Praxis, Coalition Building, and the War on Terrorism' (2003) 63 *Louisiana Law Review* (2003) 717.

Having outlined some of the main tenets, terms and methods that have become associated with CRT over the years, it is necessary to go into more detail on certain aspects that have come to shape CRT. In fact, despite the seeming methodological eclecticism, two critiques have come to stand out as informing or serving as a baseline for CRT scholarship. The first is a critique of civil rights and antidiscrimination law and the second is a critique of CLS. On the one hand, (future) CRT scholars were dissatisfied and frustrated with the limitations of the liberal civil rights movement.[23] In their opinion, the traditional approaches—from marching, to developing new litigation strategies, to filing amicus briefs—had not achieved racial reform,[24] especially because American courts had started dismantling some of the civil rights movement's achievements. On the other hand, they were also dissatisfied with the predominantly white leftist CLS movement's "trashing" of rights and with its failure to address the race factor in its analyses.[25] Put differently, CRT brought "a left intervention into race discourse and a race intervention into left discourse."[26] In a third point, I will briefly outline some other important aspects of CRT that have come to shape its scholarship.

2.1 Critiques of Civil Rights/Antidiscrimination Law

Among the writings that functioned as pathbreaker and catalyst for this line of CRT scholarship even before its birth, one can find the late Derrick A. Bell Jr's two essays dealing with *Brown v. Board of Education*,[27] the two landmark US Supreme Court judgments that had abolished legal segregation in American public schools.[28] In the first, Bell critiqued elite liberal public interest lawyers for focusing excessively on integration and desegregation without taking into account their clients' aims, namely to obtain quality education for their children.[29] In his second essay he argued that the outcome in *Brown* can be explained not so much by the fact that America became enlightened and profoundly wanted to overcome its own institutional racism, but rather that, for a limited time period, the interests of Whites converged with those of Blacks.[30] Hence, the outcome in *Brown* can only be understood when looking at what interests Whites had in this decision. Bell offers three arguments to explain why white interests

---

[23] Crenshaw et al (eds), *Critical Race Theory* (n 8) xiv–xvii.
[24] See Richard Delgado and Jean Stefancic, 'Introduction', in Richard Delgado and Jean Stefancic (eds) *Critical Race Theory: The Cutting Edge* (Temple University Press 2000) xvi.
[25] Crenshaw et al (eds), *Critical Race Theory* (n 8) xxii–xxiii.
[26] ibid xix.
[27] Derrick A. Bell Jr. is considered the founding father of CRT. See Charles R. Lawrence III, 'Doing the "James Brown" at Harvard: Derrick Bell as Liberationist Teacher' (1991) 8 *Harvard Blackletter Journal* 263.
[28] *Brown v Board of Education (Brown I)*, 347 U.S. 483 (1954) and *Brown v Board of Education (Brown II)*, 349 U.S. 294 (1955).
[29] Derrick A. Bell Jr., 'Serving Two Masters: Integration Ideals and Client Interests in School Desegregation Litigation' (1976) 85 *Yale Law Journal* 470.
[30] Bell Jr., 'Brown v. Board of Education' (n 17) 518.

68 *Research handbook on critical legal theory*

may have converged with those of Blacks at the time: first, by showing its commitment to equality, America made a strategic political move in the Cold War struggle with communist countries over influence in the developing world;[31] second, a growing fear of disillusionment and anger on the part of Black people, and in particular Black soldiers who had fought in the name of freedom and equality during World War II and then still faced discrimination in their own country, may have been an unspoken motivation behind the *Brown* decisions; and third, Whites realized that the rural south had to become industrialized, and segregation represented an obstacle in this process.[32]

Another founding article belonging to this strand was authored by Alan Freeman,[33] an exponent of CLS who argued that antidiscrimination law as interpreted by the US Supreme Court adopted the perpetrator's rather than the victim's perspective and thus failed to address the structural aspects of race discrimination by focusing on the actions of individuals. A third early piece that needs to be mentioned here was written by Charles R. Lawrence III,[34] and specifically critiqued the requirement of discriminatory intent as it was introduced by the US Supreme Court in *Washington v. Davis*,[35] thus heavily limiting the applicability of disparate impact. Moreover, Lawrence here coined the term "unconscious racism" by arguing that conscious intent cannot adequately explain racial discrimination because in American society racial bias is endemic in its social practices, and in the interaction of culture, psychology, and context.

These (early) critiques of civil rights decisions set out by CRT theorists were subsequently confirmed by the developments in the US Supreme Court's case law on race, and in particular its dismantlement of affirmative action policies and laws supposed to protect racial minorities which started with *Bakke*,[36] continuing in various forms in *Croson*,[37] *Adarand*,[38] the twin cases *Grutter* and *Gratz*,[39] *Parents Involved*,[40] *Ricci v.*

---

[31] This aspect has been confirmed by Mary L. Dudziak, 'Desegregation as a Cold War Imperative' (1988) 41 *Stanford Law Review* 61 and Mary L. Dudziak, *Cold War Civil Rights: Race and the Image of American Democracy* (Princeton University Press 2001).
[32] ibid 524–5.
[33] Alan David Freeman, 'Legitimizing Racial Discrimination through Anti-Discrimination Law: A Critical Review of Supreme Court Doctrine' (1978) 62 *Minnesota Law Review* 1049.
[34] Lawrence III, 'The Id, the Ego, and Equal Protection' (n 18) 317.
[35] *Washington v Davis*, 426 U.S. 229 (1976).
[36] *Regents of the University of California v Bakke*, 438 U.S. 265 (1978) (declaring race-based affirmative action programmes unconstitutional by holding that affirmative action in higher education can only be justified for diversity purposes but not to remedy past discrimination, and that quotas are not sufficiently narrowly tailored to achieve that goal).
[37] *City of Richmond v J.A. Croson Co.*, 488 U.S. 469 (1989) (applying strict scrutiny to the city of Richmond's minority set-aside programme, which gave preference to minority business enterprises in the awarding of municipal contracts).
[38] *Adarand Constructors, Inc. v Peña*, 515 U.S. 200 (1995) (extending strict scrutiny also to racial classifications used by the federal government).
[39] *Grutter v Bollinger*, 539 U.S. 306 (2003) (upholding an affirmative action programme at a law school thus confirming the *Bakke* holding on using diversity); *Gratz v Bollinger*, 539 U.S. 244 (2003) (striking down an affirmative action programme because it came too close to functioning like a race-based quota, i.e. not being too narrowly tailored).
[40] *Parents Involved in Community Schools v Seattle School District No. 1*, 551 U.S. 701 (2007) (striking down a plan assigning students to public schools solely for the purpose of

DeStefano,[41] *Shelby County v. Holder*,[42] and the two *Fisher* judgments.[43] CRT scholars have critiqued some of these judgments inter alia from the point of view of colorblindness and/or that of postracialism, which will be discussed below.[44]

The case law described here has left in place fairly little of what was designed during the 1960s in order to combat race discrimination. Diversity justifications in higher education are still valid, albeit for a limited time if one is to believe and follow Justice O'Connor, who in her majority opinion stated that in 25 years such measures should no longer be necessary/constitutional.[45] Some provisions of the Civil Rights Act, such as the disparate impact ones, also still allow for race-based remedial action, despite Justice Scalia's concurring opinion in *Ricci* in which he explicitly framed a potential contrast between remedies to address potential disparate impact with the Equal Protection Clause and the principle of colorblindness inscribed into it by the Supreme Court itself.[46] The Voting Rights Act itself also still remains in place, albeit almost as an empty shell. The Supreme Court has gradually ripped the teeth out of the civil rights legislation, leaving it with little bite. It has done so by holding that any racial classification per se is discriminatory regardless of its purpose, and by establishing a symmetrical correspondence between the normative use of race to exclude people from society and the use of race as an instrument to combat racial discrimination. In its most extreme version, it does not make any distinction between race used in a benign way and race used in a discriminatory and stigmatizing way. In other words, colorblindness in American law will view "treat[ing] a Dixiecrat Senator's decision to vote against Thurgood Marshall's confirmation in order to keep African Americans off the Supreme Court as on a par with President Johnson's evaluation of his nominee's race as a positive factor."[47] As a consequence of the US Supreme Court's ideology, except in very few situations, race is today normatively off-limits and suspect, regardless of its use.

---

achieving racial integration and balance because not amounting to a compelling state interest and not being narrowly tailored).

[41] *Ricci v DeStefano*, 557 U.S. 557 (2009) (interpreting the Civil Rights Act and requiring a higher standard for employers to take what the Supreme Court frames as race-based remedial actions so as to avoid disparate impact claims).

[42] *Shelby County v Holder*, 570 U.S. __ (2013) (declaring unconstitutional Section 4(b) of the Voting Rights Act which contained the coverage formula to identify the voting districts that would be under federal supervision due to past racial discrimination).

[43] *Fisher v University of Texas (Fisher I)*, 570 U.S. 133 (2013) (establishing that lower courts had failed to apply strict scrutiny standards to a Texas state law reserving study spots in Texas public universities to all those who graduated among the best 10 per cent of each public school regardless of their scores and grades which *de facto* functioned like an affirmative action programme) and *Fisher v University of Texas (Fisher II)*, 579 U.S. __ (2016) (finding that the lower courts had correctly applied the strict scrutiny standards outlined in *Fisher I* and upholding diversity in higher education as a compelling state interest).

[44] See e.g. Girardeau A. Spann, 'The Dark Side of Grutter' (2004) 21 *Constitutional Commentary* 221; Cheryl I. Harris and Kimberly West-Faulcon, 'Reading *Ricci*: Whitening Discrimination, Racing Test Fairness' (2010) 58 *UCLA Law Review* 73.

[45] *Grutter* (n 39) 343.

[46] *Ricci* (n 41), Scalia J concurring.

[47] *Adarand* (n 38), Stevens J dissenting.

However, in the area of critique of civil rights and antidiscrimination law, it is not only the Supreme Court's restrictive and increasingly colorblind interpretation of civil rights legislation and the constitutional Equal Protection Clause that CRT scholars have observed and critiqued. In other areas affecting racial minorities, a similar trend has been scrutinized. This is the case for the area of hate speech or racial insults as interpreted in connection with the freedom of speech in American constitutional law. Again, from a minority point of view, in the early 1950s the US Supreme Court upheld, albeit by a narrow five to four majority, a conviction for hate speech of a white supremacist who had distributed leaflets accusing blacks of rape, robbery, and other violent crimes, among other things.[48] However, since then the US Supreme Court has interpreted freedom of speech as authorizing hate speech unless it poses a clear and present danger of violence.[49] CRT scholars have critiqued this trend because this broad interpretation of free speech has a particularly pernicious effect on racial minorities and tends to favor the position of the white, male majority, and because words can indeed wound and cause direct psychological harms in the form of mental and emotional distress as well as pecuniary loss and physical damages.[50]

Undoubtedly, in their critique of civil rights and antidiscrimination law and its colorblind turn, CRT scholars have certain things in common with liberal scholars. Nevertheless, there is a difference in their explicit and unapologetic adoption of a racial minority's point of view by critiquing case law as continuing to perpetrate, in different ways, White supremacy. More traditional liberal scholars are much less comfortable in articulating such positions.

2.2 Critique of CLS

The novelty of CRT does not only reside in its critiques of liberal civil rights and freedom of speech jurisprudence. Indeed, to some extent colorblindness and civil rights critiques had already been advanced by other academics, who were not necessarily affiliated with CRT. CLS played a particularly important role here. Indeed, one of the early "founding" pieces by Alan Freeman discussed above is, strictly speaking, from someone traditionally belonging to the realm of CLS rather than to CRT.

As a first critique, CRT scholars disagree in particular with the rights-critical approach, sometimes referred to as the "rights-trashing" approach, of CLS. As was shown earlier, this is a result of the indeterminacy approach to law that is taken by CLS. On the one hand, CRT scholars share the Crits' skepticism toward the liberal vision of the rule of law and the view that rights discourses are indeterminate, that legal ideals can be manipulated, and that both tend to legitimate (racial) hierarchy and the status quo based on inequalities of wealth and power by means of seemingly neutral

---

[48] *Beauharnais v Illinois*, 343 U.S. 250 (1952).
[49] See e.g. *Brandenburg v Ohio*, 395 U.S. 444 (1969), *National Socialist Party of America v Village of Skokie*, 432 U.S. 43 (1977) and *R.A.V. v City of St. Paul*, 505 U.S. 377 (1992).
[50] See for all: Richard Delgado, 'Words that Wound: A Tort Action for Racial Insults, Epithets and Name Calling' (1982) 17 *Harvard Civil Rights Civil Liberties Law Review* 133 and Mari J. Matsuda et al (eds), *Words that Wound: Critical Race Theory, Assaultive Speech and the First Amendment* (Westview Press 1993).

structured legal argumentation. On the other hand, CRT disagrees with the critiques on rights put forward by some CLS scholars. One part of those critiques states that rights are unstable because they are highly dependent on their social setting; that they do not produce determinate outcomes; that they transform real experiences into empty abstractions; and that the use of rights discourse prevents real social transformation.[51] Such transformation cannot occur because law is the expression of the ruling class's domination. Rights and rights discourse are one way in which this hegemony is being legitimized, thus inducing people to ultimately accept the domination. Due to the underlying ideology, rights cannot function as a means toward radical social transformation.

According to CRT scholars, this rights-critical position disregards the value which a rights discourse may still hold for people of color. In fact, rights are the most powerful instrument in the hands of the underprivileged and oppressed in seeking to protect themselves. Discarding rights as a hegemonic tool deprives minorities not only of an instrument against oppression but also of "a symbol too deeply enmeshed in the psyche of the oppressed to lose without trauma and much resistance."[52] Thus, CRT scholars highlight how rights are not only an external instrument, but deeply engrained and even constitutive of identities and the human psyche. Viewing rights as simply an external matter provides a limited view of the individual as a closed, monological subject, isolated from outside social and institutional influences, or in a position where such influences only provide inputs driving autonomous decisions. In this sense liberal theory and CLS share a similar position, and CRT scholars contested the Crits as mostly white, male university professors who teach at major law schools and who did not see or understand the internal aspect and symbolic relevance of rights to racial minorities and how the individual self is shaped by the relations with others and the recognition granted in the form of rights by the community.[53] Moreover, discarding rights deprives racial minorities of their only tool to respond to white domination and oppression, even though CRT scholars are quite aware that—to use Audre Lorde's essay title—"The Master's Tools Will Never Dismantle the Master's House."[54] Hence, substituting rights with some other alternative solution will only leave racial minorities worse off. By trashing rights, one ultimately risks disempowering the racially oppressed without addressing or even touching White supremacy.

This first critique leads to, and in some ways already contains, CRT's second major objection to CLS. In fact, according to the former, CLS literature fails to adequately address the role of racism as hegemony, as a tool to establish racial domination and White supremacy in American history, and the fact that this type of racial hegemony was established by means of coercion and not by consent. While the Crits' analysis is helpful in understanding the limited transformative potential which law, and in particular antidiscrimination law, can have in a hegemonic context, it bypasses the issue of racial hegemony. This specific type of domination and hegemony is different

---

[51] Mark Tushnet, 'An Essay on Rights' (1984) 62 *Texas Law Review* 1363.
[52] Williams, *The Alchemy of Rights* (n 21) 165.
[53] See Costas Douzinas and Adam Geary, *Critical Jurisprudence* (Hart 2005) 179–202.
[54] Audre Lorde, 'The Master's Tools Will Never Dismantle the Master's House', in *Sister Outsider* [1984] (Ten Speed Press 2007) 110–13.

from the one assumed by CLS. While the latter posits an ideologically induced consent to establish hegemony, racial hegemony has never been about consenting to and accepting domination. It has been mostly about coercion. Moreover, CLS rarely, if ever, analyzed racism as a form of hegemony and therefore exaggerated the role of liberal ideology as hegemonic force while not considering racism's role in white domination. Given that CLS and CRT speak of two different types of hegemony, the Crits' analysis might not fit, leading to the conclusion that there might even be some aspects in liberalism and in rights that appeal to racial minorities because they have a liberationist and transformative potential.[55] This in turn leads back to CRT scholars' rights critique aimed at CLS.

However, CRT scholars did not only highlight awareness of racial domination's role or its absence in CLS literature and conscience. It also addressed a certain intellectual and racially determined divide within CLS. The traditional Crit is a white male professor more concerned with deconstructive critique of law and the theoretical aspects of the intellectual endeavor. On the contrary, academics of color associated with CLS cannot remain indifferent, cannot forget or omit their respective communities of belonging, and cannot be oblivious to the practical, everyday implications of the work done. This ultimately leads to a divide, a cleavage along the color line, where the theoretical side of CLS is white and the practical one is predominantly colored. To make matters worse, there was a sense that the line of this divide coincided with the theoretical, white side silencing and using the practical, colored side by forcing minority scholars to speak in a certain language which did not reflect their experiences, by excluding them from relevant dialogues, and on top of that by appropriating some of the cultural references in their writings.[56]

Hence, CRT's objections to CLS introduced a reconstructive minority perspective which does take rights and race into account instead of discarding them or not factoring them into the analysis. The Crits' negative, *de*-constructive, theoretical project is not sufficient for CRT scholars but has to be followed, accompanied, and integrated by a positive, *re*-constructive, practical program. Some of the pieces cited earlier under the heading of critique of antidiscrimination law and of alternative constitutional analyses detail what this program looks like and demonstrate how CRT scholars have helped to shape this school of thought and distinguish it from its predecessor.

2.3 Other Important CRT Tenets

Beyond the two fundamental aspects described here, there are two other important points in CRT scholarship that are worth highlighting. The first concerns CRT's rejection of essentialism and a strong strand of Critical race feminism from its beginnings. Indeed, Critical race feminists posited that racial subordination cannot be

---

[55] Kimberlé W. Crenshaw, 'Race, Reform, and Retrenchment: Transformation and Legitimation in Anti-Discrimination Law' (1988) 101 *Harvard Law Review* 1331, 1356–69.
[56] Harlon L. Dalton, 'The Clouded Prism' (1987) 22 *Harvard Civil Rights Civil Liberties Law Review* (1987) 435, 435–45.

fully understood if it does not take other types of subordination into account and if it does not move away from essentialist positions that have the effect of marginalizing rather than helping to build coalitions.[57] As an example, antiracist and feminist discourses focus too much on either one or the other subordinating elements and do not analyze how they interact or intersect with each other. Hence, nowadays Critical race theorists speak about "intersectionality," following two pathbreaking articles by Kimberlé W. Crenshaw.[58] In these pieces she highlights how feminist and antiracist movements have marginalized the experience of women of color because they both operate as if women's experiences and the experiences of people of color were mutually exclusive, without ever intersecting. This attitude has led to two problematic aspects. The first resides in the legal arena of antidiscrimination legislation, where courts fail to recognize the rights and interests of black women due to the structure of antidiscrimination law, which forces them to frame their claims either as race or as sex discrimination but not both at the same time. Similar difficulties then emerge also at the political level, where black women's claims and voices are marginalized in the context of feminist campaigns dominated by white women and in antiracist campaigns dominated by black men.[59]

The second important strand of CRT scholarship concerns the analysis of whiteness and what is today probably more broadly referred to as "Whiteness studies."[60] Instead of focusing on how law and society had ultimately constructed and subordinated Blacks and other races in the US context, here the focus of attention is shifted or, more accurately, projected onto the majority, to see whiteness itself as the result of (an ongoing) legal and historical construction which continuously evolved and ultimately kept benefiting from the subordination of other groups and races. CRT's contribution in this area is to analyze and unveil the specific ways in which law contributed to the construction of whiteness and of who was deemed to be white, and in which structural ways whiteness has been not only socially but also legally protected and enforced. Two publications can be seen as constituting pathbreakers in this area. The first, by Cheryl Harris, argues that whiteness functions like some sort of property right, which the legal system created and protects to this day.[61] The second, by Ian Haney López,[62] analyzes

---

[57] See Angela P. Harris, 'Race and Essentialism in Feminist Legal Theory' (1992) 42 *Stanford Law Review* 581.

[58] Crenshaw, 'Demarginalizing' (n 19) 139–167 and Crenshaw, 'Mapping the Margins' (n 19) 1241–99.

[59] Indeed, she calls this aspect 'political intersectionality'. Crenshaw, 'Mapping the Margins', ibid. 1251 et seq.

[60] See e.g. Richard Delgado and Jean Stefancic (eds), *Critical White Studies: Looking Behind the Mirror* (Temple University Press 1997).

[61] Cheryl I. Harris, 'Whiteness as Property' (1993) 106 *Harvard Law Review* 1707.

[62] Ian F. Haney López, *White by Law* (revised 10th anniversary edn, NYU Press 2006).

the case law of the US Supreme Court, which, in a number of cases,[63] had to determine whether individuals asking for US citizenship were deemed to be white, because until 1952 that was a criterion to become a naturalized American.

This section has briefly described some of CRT's main tenets and analyses as they developed in its early days. Nevertheless, CRT has been in an expansive mode, and some of the most important developments of this expansion will be described in the next section of this contribution.

3. DEVELOPMENTS

Since its inception, CRT has been expanding and developing along various different axes. First of all, there has been an expansion in terms of analyzed groups. Indeed, there were some early critiques that Critical race theorists had focused too heavily on what was called the "Black/White Binary,"[64] namely the experience of Black Americans and their experience of White supremacy. This arguably marginalized or ignored the specific experiences of racism by law faced for example by Native Americans, Asian Americans, or Chicanos/Latinos, and also by LGBTQI racial minorities. As a result, today distinct bodies of literature have emerged, whose writers have at times identified as LatCrit,[65] NativeCrit or TribalCrit,[66] AsianCrit,[67] and/or QueerCrit,[68] and who have nevertheless retained the overarching themes of CRT, with which they retain good relations.[69]

Second, there has been a geographical spread of CRT's analyses. Whereas initially one could speak of a certain parochialism and focus on the American reality, today CRT has crossed various borders. Indeed, there are various publications applying CRT's tools and analyses to other regional, national, or local contexts,

---

[63] *Ozawa v United States*, 260 U.S. 178 (1922) (denying American naturalization to a Japanese applicant) and *United States v Thind*, 261 U.S. 204 (1922) (denying American naturalization to an Indian applicant).

[64] Juan F. Perea, 'The Black/White Binary Paradigm of Race: The "Normal Science" of American Racial Thought' (1997) 85 *California Law Review* 1213.

[65] For a good overview of this vast body of literature see: Francisco Valdés, 'Afterword. Coming Up: New Foundations in LatCrit Theory, Community and Praxis' (2012) 48 *California Western Law Review* 505.

[66] See e.g. Robert A. Williams, Jr., *Like a Loaded Weapon: The Rehnquist Court, Indian Rights, and the Legal History of Racism in America* (University of Minnesota Press 2005).

[67] See e.g.: Robert S. Chang, *Disoriented: Asian Americans, Law, and the Nation State* (NYU Press 1999).

[68] See e.g.: Dean Spade, *Normal Life: Administrative Violence, Critical Trans Politics and the Limits of Law* (2nd edn, Duke University Press 2015).

[69] In this sense, Delgado and Stefancic, *Critical Race Theory: An Introduction* (n 4) 4.

such as Brazil and Latin America,[70] Canada,[71] Japan,[72] South Africa,[73] the United Kingdom,[74] France,[75] Germany,[76] Hungary,[77] Italy,[78] Serbia,[79] Sweden,[80] and more generally continental Europe.[81]

Third, there has been an expansion in terms of material scope, in the sense that, from the legal arena, CRT has managed to spread and merge into other scientific domains of the social sciences and humanities. This is only partly surprising. On the one hand, CRT analyzed how white domination plays out in and through law in the United States. This was an angle that scholars working on related issues in other scientific disciplines, such as ethnic and racial studies, Whiteness studies, cultural studies, and/or more broadly sociology, history, philosophy, and/or political sciences could relate to and had actually already been using. On the other hand, it certainly helped that CRT had drawn inspiration from nonlegal material and movements which facilitated crossfertilization and spread into other scientific domains. One domain where this spread has been particularly visible and explicit is education,[82] but the same overlaps

---

[70] See e.g. Tanya Katerí Hernández, *Racial Subordination in Latin America: The Role of the State, Customary Law and the New Civil Rights Response* (Cambridge University Press 2013).

[71] Carol A. Aylward, *Canadian Critical Race Theory: Racism and the Law* (Fernwood Publishing 1999).

[72] Debito Arudou, 'Japan's Under-Researched Visible Minorities: Applying Critical Race Theory to Racialization Dynamics in a Non-White Society' (2015) 14 *Washington University Global Studies Law Review* 695.

[73] Joel M. Modiri, 'Towards a (Post)Apartheid Critical Race Jurisprudence: Divining Our Racial Themes' (2012) 27 *South African Public Law* 231.

[74] Namita Chakrabarty, Lorna Preston and John Preston (eds), *Critical Race Theory in England* (Routledge 2014).

[75] Hourya Bentouhami and Mathias Möschel (eds), *Critical Race Theory: une introduction aux grands textes fondateurs* (Dalloz 2017).

[76] See e.g. Cengiz Barskanmaz, 'Rassismus, Postkolonialismus und Recht – Zu einer deutschen *Critical Race Theory*?' (2008) 41 *Kritische Justiz* 296.

[77] Domokos Lázár, 'Critical Race Theory – A magyar kritikai rasszelméleti mozgalom elméleti megalapozása', (2016) *Themis* 92–115.

[78] See e.g. Kendall Thomas and Gianfrancesco Zanetti (eds), *Legge, razza e diritti. La Critical Race Theory negli Stati Uniti* (Diabasis 2005).

[79] Maja Davidovic, 'Rectification of Racial Discrimination during WWII: The Case of Restitution Laws in Serbia', (2017) 4 *Contemporary Southeastern Europe* 105.

[80] Laura Carlson, 'Racism under the Law: Rethinking the Swedish Approach through a Critical Race Theory Lens' (2013) 2 *Ragion pratica* 491.

[81] Mathias Möschel, *Law, Lawyers and Race: Critical Race Theory from the United States to Europe* (Routledge 2014).

[82] See e.g. Laurence Parker, Donna Deyhle and Sofia Villenas (eds), *Race Is … Race Isn't: Critical Race Theory and Qualitative Studies in Education* (Westview Press 1999); Adrienne D. Dixson and Celia K. Rousseau, *Critical Race Theory in Education* (Routledge 2006) and Ed Taylor, David Gillborn and Gloria Ladson-Billings (eds), *Foundations of Critical Race Theory in Education* (Routledge 2009).

and crossfertilization can be found, for instance, in psychology,[83] (mental) health,[84] economics,[85] literature,[86] music,[87] and sports.[88]

The risks inherent in all this expansion and success could have been that CRT's analyses get flattened and lose their cutting edge. But the expansion has also been accompanied by a deepening of certain substantial analyses. Beyond the already mentioned nuances on the analysis of racial domination by LatCrit, Asian Crit, and/or Native Crit, there are two areas in which CRT has been particularly active recently.

The first one is linked to the election of the United States' first Black President, Barack Obama, in 2008, and the related debate on whether or not America had now become postracial. Whereas Critical race theorists certainly welcomed the election, they had certain misgivings about what this postracial rhetoric could do at the intellectual, political, and jurisprudential levels. One of their main concerns is that the postracial turn would allow a new alignment of the conservative colorblind discourse with (white) liberal progressive positions that had always been ambivalent about raceconscious measures. In other words, the latter, who had so far rejected colorblind ideology, might ultimately be persuaded to rally behind the new "cool" position of postracialism which promotes the same idea that race is over in the United States, albeit in different clothes.[89] One of the first comprehensive analyses of postracialism and its constitutive elements at the discursive intellectual and political level comes from Sumi Cho.[90] Other Critical race theorists have analyzed postracialism's (negative) impact

---

[83] Gary Blasi, 'Advocacy against the Stereotype: Lessons from Cognitive Social Psychology' (2002) 49 *UCLA Law Review* 1241 and Gregory S. Parks, Shayne Jones and W. Jonathan Cardi (eds), *Critical Race Realism* (The New Press 2008).

[84] Tony N. Brown, 'Race, Racism, and Mental Health: Elaboration of Critical Race Theory's Contribution to the Sociology of Mental Health' (2008) 11 *Contemporary Justice Review* 53 and Chandra L. Ford and Collins O. Airhihenbuwa, 'Critical Race Theory, Race Equity, and Public Health: Toward Antiracism Praxis' (2010, supp. 1) 100 *American Journal of Public Health* 30.

[85] Devon Carbado and Mitu Gulati, 'The Law and Economics of Critical Race Theory' (2003) 112 *Yale Law Journal* 1757.

[86] Toni Morrison, 'Playing in the Dark: Whiteness and the Literary Imagination', in Delgado and Stefancic (eds) *Critical White Studies* (n 60) 79–84.

[87] John O. Calmore, 'Critical Race Theory, Archie Shepp, and Fire Music: Securing an Authentic Intellectual Life in a Multicultural World' (1992) 65 *Southern California Law Review* 2129 and Jonathan A. Beyer, 'Second Line: Reconstructing the Jazz Metaphor in Critical Race Theory' (2000) 88 *Georgetown Law Journal* 537.

[88] Kevin Hylton, *'Race' and Sport. Critical Race Theory* (Routledge 2009), and by the same author 'How A Turn to Critical Race Theory Can Contribute to Our Understanding of "Race", Racism and Anti-Racism in Sports' (2010) 45 *International Review for the Sociology of Sport* 335.

[89] See for a more detailed analysis of this point Kimberlé W. Crenshaw, 'Twenty Years of Critical Race Theory: Looking Back to Move Forward' (2011) 43 *Connecticut Law Review* 1253, 1310–36.

[90] Sumi Cho, 'Post-Racialism' (2009) 94 *Iowa Law Review* 1589.

on employment antidiscrimination litigation post-Obama's election,[91] and how postracialism affects racial performance in the workplace,[92] as well as in prisons.[93] The theorists have suggested, inter alia, that the argument that the United States has become a postracial society itself constitutes a form of systemic discrimination.[94]

The second area in which CRT has become active is connected with another societal development that has made the headlines over the past years: policing and racial profiling in conjunction with the Black Lives Matter movement. Issues of racial justice in criminal law had been far from absent in earlier CRT analyses,[95] but they came to assume a particular urgency, renewed vigor, and focus, also due to the fact that CRT was never "only" a theory but always considered itself linked to praxis, to a community, and to social/racial movements. In this sense, CRT scholars have analyzed the most recent developments in the domain with particular attention, linking it to the broader themes that had already been developed some 30 years earlier.[96]

One last word should be given to the recent election of President Trump. In certain ways, it confirmed some of CRT's main tenets: race and racism are a permanent feature of American society and law. The election of President Obama did not and could not change that fact.

BIBLIOGRAPHY

Bell, Derrick A., Jr. *Faces at the Bottom of the Well: The Permanence of Racism* (Basic Books 1992).
Bell, Derrick A., Jr., *Race, Racism, and American Law*, 6th ed. (Aspen Publishers 2008).
Crenshaw, Kimberlé W., *et al* (eds) *Critical Race Theory: The Key Writings that Formed the Movement* (The New Press 1995).
Delgado, Richard and Stefancic, Jean (eds) *Critical White Studies: Looking Behind the Mirror* (Temple University Press 1997).
Delgado, Richard and Stefancic, Jean, *Critical Race Theory: An Introduction*, 3rd ed. (NYU Press, 2017).
Haney López, Ian, *White by Law*, revised 10th anniversary ed. (NYU Press 2006).
Matsuda, Mari J., *et al* (eds) *Words That Wound: Critical Race Theory, Assaultive Speech and the First Amendment* (Westview Press 1993).
Möschel, Mathias, *Law, Lawyers and Race: Critical Race Theory from the United States to Europe* (Routledge 2014).

---

[91] Angela Onwuachi-Willig and Mario L. Barnes, 'The Obama Effect: Understanding Emerging Meanings of "Obama" in Anti-Discrimination Law' (2012) 87 *Indiana Law Journal* (2012) 325.

[92] Devon Carbado and Mitu Gulati, *Rethinking Race in Post-Racial America* (Oxford University Press 2013).

[93] Ian F. Haney Lopez, 'Post-Racial Racism: Racial Stratification and Mass Incarceration in the Age of Obama', (2010) 98 *California Law Review* 1023.

[94] Girardeau Spann, 'Disparate Impact' (2010) 98 *Georgetown Law Journal* 1133.

[95] See e.g. Richard Delgado, 'Rodrigo's Eighth Chronicle: Black Crime, White Fears – On the Social Construction of Threat' (1994) 80 *Virginia Law Review* 503 and Devon Carbado and Cheryl I. Harris, 'Undocumented Criminal Procedure' (2011) 58 *UCLA Law Review* 1543.

[96] See e.g. Charles R. Lawrence III, 'The Fire This Time: Black Lives Matter, Abolitionist Pedagogy and the Law' (2015) 65 *Journal of Legal Education* 381 and Angela Onwuachi-Willig, 'Policing the Boundaries of Whiteness: The Tragedy of Being out of Place from Emmett Till to Trayvon Martin' (2017) 102 *Iowa Law Review* 1113.

78 Research handbook on critical legal theory

Taylor, Ed, Gillborn, David and Ladson-Billings, Gloria (eds) *Foundations of Critical Race Theory in Education* (Routledge 2009).
Valdes, Francisco, McCristal, Culp Jerome and Harris, Angela (eds) *Crossroads, Directions, and a New Critical Race Theory* (Temple University Press 2002).
Williams, Patricia, *The Alchemy of Rights* (Harvard University Press 1991).
Williams, Robert A. Jr, *Like a Loaded Weapon: The Rehnquist Court, Indian Rights, and the Legal History of Racism in America* (University of Minnesota Press 2005).
Wing, Adrien Katherine (ed.) *Global Critical Race Feminism* (NYU Press 2000).

5. Queer in the law: critique and postcritique
Mariano Croce

1. INTRODUCTION

Since their inception, queer theories have had a remarkable influence on how we think of law's effects on social reality. In particular, in the past three decades the debates and polemics that have arisen in this burgeoning subject area have shed a critical light on how the law grants social speakability and political agency to forms of sexuality and types of relationships that become 'respectable', insofar as they gain access to legal recognition and state protection. As this access comes at a price, queer theorists acknowledge the importance of legal recognition, but are alert to its costs. This is why they have variously explored the tacit dynamics of negotiation and adjustment that this recognition requires. This chapter homes in on such a notable contribution to the analysis of these tacit dynamics. It commences by illustrating the meaning of the queer as a signifier and why it has become such an important field of study. Although reductive, for the sake of clarity I will look at three lines of the queer lineage (to wit, Freudo-Marxism, radical constructivism and antisocial theories) and will briefly foreground how they think of law and its relation to sexuality. I will then focus almost exclusively on the second line insofar as it captures the ambivalence of legal recognition. To cut deeper into this ambivalence, I will touch upon the same sex marriage debate and will dwell on the heated contrapositions that still surround it. This discussion will tease out the fine line between resignification and assimilation; that is, how claims to legal recognition affect the law in a transformative manner and to what extent these very claims are reabsorbed into a constrictive lexicon that effaces the challenging character of same sex sexuality. The chapter will conclude by gesturing to a more recent version of the queer (postcritical queer theory), one that draws significantly from the second line but innovates it in some significant respects.

2. SIGNIFYING THE QUEER AND THE QUEER AS A SIGNIFIER

Saying 'queer' is saying something with respect to which nothing can be put in its place. Queer is a *displacement*, and because of that, it is inextricably linked to the critique of the social. This is the 'contestatory' meaning that the term 'queer' was assigned within academia the first time it was launched in 1990, when Teresa de Lauretis (1991) organized the conference 'Queer Theory: Lesbian and Gay Sexualities' at the University of Santa Cruz (California). The juxtaposition of 'queer' and 'lesbian and gay' was a deliberate provocation, as it marked a 'critical distance' from flourishing lesbian and gay studies (de Lauretis, 1991, p.iv). De Lauretis intended to question the idea that male and female homosexuality belong to the same form of sexuality and that they should be contrasted with the other, prevalent form, namely, heterosexuality. By doing so, she wanted not to introduce a common viewpoint to describe multiple forms of sexuality, but to acknowledge an irreducible multiplicity in such a way that sexuality could never be confined to this or that taxonomy.

In the same year, two seminal books in queer theory were published: Eve Kosofsky Sedgwick's *Epistemology of the Closet* and Judith Butler's *Gender Trouble: Feminism and the Subversion of Identity*. Though these latter books do not employ the term 'queer', they are generally recognized as cornerstones of queer theory. Needless to say, these theorists owe a debt to Michel Foucault's (1990) groundbreaking studies on sexuality as the genealogical map of a signifier that gives rise to processes of subjectivation. Foucault's investigation was devoted to a history that is not made up of universals or natural kinds, as he conceived of history as a series of discourses on sexuality, criminality, madness and other objects (see Chignola 2018). Discourses are productive of practices that give an objective form to their products and naturalize them into (seemingly) transhistorical entities. In this Foucauldian sense, the queer arose as a mobilization of the conventional signifiers that traditionally defined sexuality and shored up the binary divisions male/female and straight/gay. This is why 'queer' is a fluctuating signifier averse to sedimentations of meaning and the stabilization of references. As Sedgwick (1994: 7–8) comments:

> That's one of the things that 'queer' can refer to: the open mesh of possibilities, gaps, overlaps, dissonances and resonances, lapses and excesses of meaning when the constituent elements of anyone's gender, of anyone's sexuality aren't made (or can't be made) to signify monolithically. The experimental linguistic, epistemological, representational, political adventures attaching to the very many of us who may at times be moved to describe ourselves as (among many other possibilities) pushy femmes, radical faeries, fantasists, drags, clones, leatherfolk, ladies in tuxedoes, feminist women or feminist men, masturbators, bulldaggers, divas, Snap! queens, butch bottoms, storytellers, transsexuals, aunties, wannabes, lesbian-identified men or lesbians who sleep with men, or … people able to relish, learn from, or identify with such. Again, 'queer' can mean something different: a lot of the way I have used it so far in this dossier is to denote, almost simply, same-sex sexual object choice, lesbian or gay, whether or not it is organized around multiple criss-crossings of definitional lines.

Thus, meaning is the main field where the queer operates for the erosion of typological distinctions that have long served as surreptitious forms of classification setting the threshold of the normal. However, it rapidly spread to infiltrate a variety of scholarly fields where the same distinctions had heavily influenced the production of knowledge. Philosophy,[1] sociology,[2] anthropology,[3] literary criticism,[4] legal studies,[5] political

---

[1] See e.g. Jagose (1997); Hall and Jagose (2012); Bernini (2017).
[2] See e.g. Seidman (1994).
[3] See e.g. Boellstorff (2007).
[4] See e.g. Spargo (2016).
[5] See e.g. Leckey and Brooks (2010).

science,[6] international law,[7] international relations,[8] business studies,[9] urban studies,[10] citizenship studies,[11] migration studies,[12] and other disciplines have abundantly drawn from queer critiques of prevailing sexual norms as a sharp methodology creating awareness of invisible classificatory distinctions that make certain phenomena visible and others invisible. This chapter will look at the intersection of the queer and the law through the lens of this *visibility mechanism* whereby the law makes some sexual phenomena visible, thus speakable, and confines others to silence.

3. THE QUEER LINEAGE: A TRIPARTITION

For a start, I think it will be of help to introduce a distinction that is likely to add some clarity to the genealogy of the queer. Lorenzo Bernini (2017a) distinguishes three major 'lines' of the queer lineage: Freudo-Marxism, radical constructivism and antisocial theories. Freudo-Marxism by and large emerges as the convergence of Wilhelm Reich's (1945) and Herbert Marcuse's (1966) political theorizing, or better, the encounter between Marxism and psychoanalysis. By virtue of this theoretical alliance, it advocates freedom of the natural supply of erotic desires repressed by capitalism. Freudo-Marxism importantly influenced liberation movements in the 1960s and the 1970s. For example, Italian theorist and activist Mario Mieli (1980), in one of the most interesting instances of this approach, drew on Marcuse's theorizing to make the case that all human beings are originally 'transsexual' – although he distinguished between *original* and *manifest* transsexuality, where the former expresses humans' basic plurality of erotic tendencies. For him, human beings faithful to their nature indistinctly feel sexual desires towards people of the male and female sex. In Mieli's view, the liberationist project should strive to erase the repression mechanisms that constrain sexual identities and hence to free human beings' original 'schizophrenic' desire. In one way or another, Freudo-Marxism longs for the effacement of all binary distinctions, with a view to returning to humanity's mythical original bisexuality. In this sense, although this approach is of great interest because of the way in which it captures the tie between various forms of domination (particularly the capitalist, the patriarchal and the heterosexist ones), it is at odds with an idea of the queer as deliberate indeterminacy and fluctuation.

The second line, radical constructivism – which I will consider in some detail later on – got under way from the opposite assumption, that sexuality is all about indeterminacy and fluctuation. While the queer cannot obviously be confined to this line, it has long epitomized it, for the founding authors whom I mentioned at the outset belong to this scholarly strand. The chief difference between Freudo-Marxism and

---

[6] See e.g. Smith and Lee (2014).
[7] See e.g. Otto (2018).
[8] See e.g. Weber (2016).
[9] See e.g. Rumens (2015).
[10] See e.g. Bell and Binnie (2004).
[11] See e.g. Bell and Binnie (2000); Stychin (2003).
[12] See e.g. Chávez (2013).

radical constructivism lies in the fact that for Freudo-Marxists there is a truth to sexuality, an original reality of it, that can be uncovered and liberated. This is a naturalist tenet with which constructivism dispensed. In this sense, Bernini (2017b) sensibly defines this form of constructivism as 'radical' because it embraces Foucault's approach to sexuality in order to prove that gender is not the cultural interpretation of sex, and that sex does not reflect humans' biology. Not only gender but also sex is the outcome of a sexual dispositif that is productive of a grid of intelligibility which tends to be naturalized and to be mistaken for an alleged truth of nature. At the same time, unlike Freudo-Marxist approaches, these theories do not perceive themselves as a path to the liberation of humanity and human sexuality in particular. Rather, as I noted above, radical constructivism introduces elements for a critique of conventional meanings as well as the invisible forms of exclusion and classification they are built upon. Despite this, they are by no means apolitical. Theorists of this line advocate and carve out spaces for resistance and counterpractices that can never be entirely erased and are located in the interstices of the less visible. The circulation of these energies allows the construction of new, more liveable sexual subjectivities and new, more open communities of recognition. As we will see below, this conceptualization has important bearings on how the law is conceptualized and the way in which it operates on the social.

Scholars belonging to the third line – antisocial theories – move away from both other lines. On the one hand, they reject the Freudo-Marxist idealization of a path to a liberated and common sexuality, and its corollary that gay sexuality will one day cease to be a minority practice. On the other, they denounce the naïve optimism of radical constructivists and their belief in an always possible resistance to the power that makes gay sexuality aberrant. Yet, while nowadays the hope for sexual redemption is on the wane, it is especially the prevalence of post-Foucauldian queer theory that antisocial authors lament. Leo Bersani (2010: 39) comments that 'the way in which the Foucauldian suspicion of sexual essences has been picked up by queer theorists has made me almost nostalgic for those very essences'. Bersani thinks that the idea that sexuality is the product of a disciplinary project tempers sexuality's inherent disturbance. No progressive tinge marks one's being homosexual: '[G]ay men are no less socially ambitious, and, more often than we like to think, no less reactionary and racist than heterosexuals. To want sex with another man is not exactly a credential for political radicalism.' In short, antisocial theories deny there being a path to sexual liberation or practices of resistance to domination in one's sexual practices, especially same sex ones. Sexual drives disturbingly dominate the subject, as the nonerotic percolates into the erotic and the death drive saturates sexuality. This is why sexual minorities will always be deemed to be deviant, while no politically correct conception of sexuality is ever consistent. Lee Edelman (2004: 31) goes so far as to pit the whole ideology of reproduction against the queer: '[T]he Child as futurity's emblem must die … the queer comes to figure the bar to every realization of futurity, the resistance, internal to the social, to every social structure or form' (Edelman 2004: 4).

Because of the specific political potential of radical constructivism and the way in which its advocates engage with conceptualizing the law, I will mainly concentrate on this line of the queer lineage; the contrast with the other lines will be useful for a better understanding of its limits.

4. HOW NORMS WORK

Needless to say, if the queer is regarded as the route to liberation from a bourgeois, capitalist society (as Freudo-Marxists believe), or alternatively if it is regarded as a disturbing sexual practice that will never find acceptance within mainstream society (as antisocial theorists submit), the role of the law within the queer turns out to be less than liminal. In the former case, the law is by and large a superstructure contributing to the crystallization and promotion of a repressed binary, heterosexist sexuality. In the latter case, it is the queer that has to steer clear of social legitimation and legal recognition, as same sex attracted people are called upon to embrace the aberration of their own sexual drives. In either case, the law is something of no avail to queer people. It has to be either eradicated or repudiated. This is not the case with radical constructivists, who generally believe that no disciplinary device can ever completely obliterate all residues of resistance and liveability. Like every technique of government, the law is crossed by an ambivalence that makes it a disciplinary instrument as well as a potential source of contestation and subversion. Exploring this ambivalence will offer a glimpse into the productive tension that (from a constructivist vantage point) the queer creates in the legal domain.

If the subject is a product of disciplinary powers unleashed through a variety of dispositifs, then also the legal device is a vehicle for productive forces. This is clearly key to the understanding of how law operates. The law is by no means mere normative regulation of preexisting practices, but is a subject formation device. Says Butler (2004: 41):

> It is important to remember at least two caveats on subjection and regulation derived from Foucaultian scholarship: (1) regulatory power not only acts upon a preexisting subject but also shapes and forms that subject; moreover, every juridical form of power has its productive effect; and (2) to become subject to a regulation is also to become subjectivated by it, that is, to be brought into being as a subject precisely through being regulated. This second point follows from the first in that the regulatory discourses which form the subject of gender are precisely those that require and induce the subject in question.

At the same time, Butler amends this Foucauldian insight, as the regulation of gender is not a mere instance of regulatory power – for law always seizes on preexisting social norms that filter the legibility of sexual practices. This is why she distinguishes *rules* from *norms* and emphasizes the fact that the latter are embedded in the practices they govern. With an inadvertent nod to legal thinkers such as Karl Llewellyn and Carl Schmitt,[13] Butler (2004: 41) takes norms to be generalizations of the conducts with which they are intertwined, as 'normalizing principle[s] in social practice' that most often 'remain implicit, difficult to read, discernible most clearly and dramatically in the effects that they produce'. In other words, norms provide a *grid of intelligibility* that makes certain practices (appear as) normal. This means that a norm can be analytically separated from the practices in which it is embedded, while it is exactly this potential separation that perpetuates the norm as a replicable standard which people's conducts

---

[13] Affinities with Butler's conceptions are discernible in Llewellyn's (1940) theory of law-jobs and Schmitt's notion of normality as the concrete basis of legal norms.

ought to comply with. Gender, according to Butler, operates as a norm that dictates a way of parsing experience – one that screens off the relation of generalization between norm and practice.

If this is the case, the legal system enjoys a limited creative power. If law wants to be effective, it has to feed off the deep-seated relation between a practice and its internal normalizing principle. A truly effective legal system is primarily interested in reinforcing normality and its cognitive effect on people's perception and appreciation of the social world. Not only does this explain why, in the famous debate on pornography and hate speech, Butler insisted that legal rules prohibiting particular offensive conducts are destined to be ineffective or even to reinforce the unstated cognitive underpinnings that nurture a particular criminalized practice; it also makes sense of the difficult relation between one's seeking legal protection and one's abiding by the normative standards on which legal protection relies. While discussing people diagnosed with gender identity dysphoria who seek legal recognition of their status, Butler (2004: 82) writes:

> [O]ne should approach the diagnosis strategically. One could then reject the truth claims that the diagnosis makes, that is, reject the description it offers of transsexuality but nevertheless make use of the diagnosis as a pure instrument, a vehicle for achieving one's goals. One would, then, ironically or facetiously or half-heartedly submit to the diagnosis, even as one inwardly maintains that there is nothing 'pathological' about the desire to transition or the resolve to realize that desire. But here we have to ask whether submitting to the diagnosis does not involve, more or less consciously, a certain subjection to the diagnosis such that one does end up internalizing some aspect of the diagnosis, conceiving of oneself as mentally ill or 'failing' in normality, or both, even as one seeks to take a purely instrumental attitude toward these terms.

As much as the specific topic of this juncture is the recognition of gender identity dysphoria, the ambivalence it teases out captures the ambivalence of the queer's relation to the legal. In a way that recalls Wendy Brown's (2000) refined analysis of the ineliminable ambivalence of women's rights, legal recognition is something which the queer population 'cannot not want'. On this account, the main problem is how legal measures are formulated in such a way as to enable dismantling subordination and subjection, and when, on the contrary, the law reabsorbs and weakens defiant political claims. For the paradoxical nature characterizing the legal device is that it entails 'some specification of our suffering, injury, or inequality lock us into the identity defined by our subordination, while rights that eschew this specificity not only sustain the invisibility of our subordination, but potentially even enhance it' (Brown 2000: 232).

5. MARRIAGE: OPPORTUNITY OR TRAP?

The marriage debate offers a telling example of the ambivalence I illustrated above. It marked a turning point in the queer community, within and outside of academia, which also marked a shift in the struggle for sexual equality (see e.g. Cooper 2004 ch. 5; Hull 2006; Polikoff 2008; Barker 2013). In a way, the 'stampede toward marriage' (Franke 2004: 1418) signalled the erosion of liberationist political platforms and the emergence of a liberal orientation of the gay community. As far as law is concerned, it can be described as a movement *from the outside to the inside*. The collapse of a joint project of liberation revolving around the common idea of a liberated society, in conjunction with a set of far reaching socioeconomic and political changes, weakened efforts towards a comprehensive revolution involving all sites of oppression and inequality. At the same time, the battle for liberation fragmented into a series of inward-looking battles to better the conditions of specific social groups. This produced a radical change in the role that the gay and lesbian community attributed to legal reform. Liberation movements, such as the Gay Liberation Front ((1973)1978) in their celebrated *Manifesto*, presented the law as something that 'makes sure that cottagers and cruisers will be zealously hunted, while queer-bashers may be apprehended, half-heartedly after the event' – a repressive machinery that hunts queer people down and makes their lives unliveable. However, as William Eskridge (2013) pithily comments, less radical gays, lesbians and bisexuals steadily moved 'from "outlaws" to "in-laws"'. Between the 1990s and the beginning of the twenty-first century, advocacy groups and civil society organizations came to the conclusion that equality litigation was more effective than political subversion and that they required grassroots mobilization and political alliances. This led to a consequence-laden transition that, in queer terms, could be represented as a movement from a condition of legal unspeakability to one of legal speakability.

This change in queer people's attitude to the law caused a break with those who were more sceptical of the law's porosity to genuine reforms. The same goes for the academic field, where scholars have been involved in heated debates on the viability of same sex marriage as a battering ram to open the path to previously excluded sexualities and forms of relationships. While Freudo-Marxists, in line with the Marxian tradition, generally believe that legal norms are *ideological* in the sense that they only benefit the dominant class, whereas dominated people are by and large unaware of this, antisocial theorists on the whole hold the opinion that liberal law and its horizon of inclusiveness nurtures a culture of heterosexist and realized reproduction that makes no room for queerness. While this blunt rejection of law as a form of redress is obviously not espoused by constructivists, their approach to this contested political instrument is ambivalent.

As Didi Herman (1990) persuasively illustrates in her analysis of the frictions generated within the lesbian community about the (alleged) advantages of marriage, two positions come to a head. One is the idea that existing institutional structures, enshrined in law, can be subverted as the legal system is forced to change and to recognize the lives and rights of discriminate groups. This subversion is not confined to the legal realm, as it is likely to alter the social perception of what a group is as well as the value of their existence. Thus having the law change through the recognition of same sex marriage means making the life of lesbians and gays symbolically relevant to the community at large. In this sense, affecting the complex symbolic universe that lies behind legal regulation is believed to affect people's perception of what counts as worthwhile. The alternative view is much more dubious of legal change through marriage. Same sex marriage is claimed to reassert a conventional ideal of relationships and state-sponsored unions, one that liberation movements wanted to do away with as it was a major source of oppression of women and homosexual people. As I will clarify below, radical and leftwing critics of gay marriage affirm that current legal developments relative to marriage and unions are affected by biases that theorists define as 'heteronormative' (Warner 1993), whereby the form and structure of nonheterosexual relationships are modelled on existing heterosexual ones, and 'homonormative' (Duggan 2003), whereby queer individuals struggle to gain access to those state institutions that erstwhile liberationist movements viewed as the root cause of their oppression.

6. LEGAL GLORIFICATION VERSUS QUEER RESIGNIFICATION

The same sex marriage debate gestures to a fruitful problematization of the nature of social change through law. It significantly echoes a more fundamental sociotheoretical question that still needs to be settled. It is the question of whether practices, as basic constituents of everyday life, acquire their specific meaning only within the broader sociocultural context, or whether it is the meaning of the sociocultural context that depends on the combination of its various practices (see Croce 2015). In the former case, the transformation of the various components of a particular social context calls for a much more orchestrated struggle to tear down the basic structures of this context. In the latter case, changing one component is believed to have the capacity to create instability, and thus to ignite partial changes which, though small, can combine with just as small changes in other components. This sociotheoretical question is at the root of the ambivalent attitude of the second queer line to the law.

A good entry point to this issue is Butler's interesting critique of Pierre Bourdieu's view of social change. It all began with Butler's (1997) rejection of Bourdieu's (1991) study of how linguistic interactions work. Bourdieu regarded the linguistic field as something that needs previous authorization for one to perform a successful speech act. An order or a request proves successful not on account of the linguistic structure of the particular speech act, but because it grafts onto social classifications that preestablish who can issue an order or make a request. Put otherwise, the success of performative utterances rests on prior classifications and distribution of power that determine the relative positions of the speaker and the listener. One's order is obeyed or one can make someone minister because the one who issues the order and confers the charge is previously authorized. This is what Bourdieu calls the 'magic' of performative speech acts – 'magic' because what really makes language work is concealed behind a linguistic structure that appear to be autonomous from concrete social relations. This magic dissolves, says Bourdieu, as soon as one draws attention to the social field that structures people's positions to each other and distributes power in such a way that this distribution gets reflected in the success of speakers' linguistic performances.

The idea of one's linguistic performances as conditional on a previous authorization bespeaks a conception of the social world that allows little change in its components unless the whole context is subverted. In Bourdieu's portrayal, the distinct constituents of the social are granted no genuine autonomy, nor do their movements ever prompt change on their own. The meaning and position of the constituents of the social both have a structural dependence on the context in which they occur. Importantly, the same applies to the law, and particularly to the special branch governing the family:

The juridical institution promotes an ontological glorification. It does this by transmuting regularity (that which is done regularly) into rule (that which must be done), factual normalcy into legal normalcy, simple familial *fides* (trust), which derives from a whole effort to sustain recognition and feeling, into family law, sustained by a whole arsenal of institutions and constraints. In this way the juridical institution contributes *universally* to the imposition of a representation of normalcy according to which *different* practices tend to appear *deviant*, anomalous, indeed abnormal, and pathological (particularly when medical institutions intervene to sustain the legal ones). (Bourdieu 1987: 846)

All that enjoys a status of normality has undergone a process of ontological glorification that granted it its proper place. The 'proper' of sexual practices hinges on the structure that this process has set up and continues to foster. The consequence of this view is particularly relevant to the law's effects of transformation on social reality – for the law's glorified structure allows using its means and tools only insofar as people who have recourse to it accept its categories *before* they gain access to them. As Bourdieu (2001: 120) asks: 'How can people revolt against a socially imposed categorization except by organizing themselves as a category constructed according to that categorization, and so implementing the classifications and restrictions that it seeks to resist?' In other words, the language of the dominated is (most of the time inadvertently) conditional on the hegemonic language of the dominants. As a result, for the former's claims to be heard and accepted, they always have to use the latter.

Michael Warner's (1999) pioneering critique draws on a similar, sceptical understanding of the possibilities of change through law. He isolates two orders of defects of same sex marriage recognition. On the one hand, marriage tends to reduce same sex rights to a matter of individual preferences and downplays the public character of the important transition occurring in the queer field. Along with other critics of the 'domesticating' effects of seeking access to marriage, he laments a noticeable change in queer people's attitude. While previous liberation struggles engaged with a multiplicity of oppressions not exclusively related to sexuality and thus could team up with the struggles of other excluded or marginalized populations, today's longing for marriage makes the queer population self-interested and obsessed with the legitimacy of their unions.[14] Yet, on top of these effects on those who want to marry, marriage also affects those who cannot, or do not want to, get married. As Mark Graham (2004: 24) maintains, the institution of marriage constructs

---

[14] Cheshire Calhoun (2000: 29) makes an interesting case regarding the conflict that subsists between lesbians' interest in getting married and women's interest in the end of patriarchal male–female relationships. She speculates that 'it is a mistake for feminists to assume that work to end gender subordination will have as much payoff for lesbians as it would for heterosexual women. Only a political strategy that keeps clearly in mind the distinction between gender oppression and lesbian and gay subordination – as well as the potential for conflict between feminist and lesbian political strategies – could have such a payoff'. This provoking argument is all the more interesting insofar as many genealogies of the queer glue feminism and lesbianism together.

the unmarried as lacking this virtue ... It controls sexuality by prescribing marriage as its proper place. Further, it confers social, economic, and cultural capital on the wedded couple. As a result, marriage, in its present form, is not good for queers, it is not good for unmarried heterosexuals, and it is often not good for heterosexual women.

On the other hand, other queer theorists are more cautious about any such 'either/or' positions. For example, Herman (1990: 809) contends that 'it may be helpful to distinguish between various kinds of rights ... their initiating processes, and the way a social movement takes up a particular rights struggle as a political mobilizer'. More attention should be paid to 'particular circumstances where rights claims are necessary, strategic, and even empowering, and acknowledge that the acquisition of formal rights may be a pre-condition for more substantive or fundamental change'. Carlos Ball (2005: 372) stresses even more adamantly the virtues of seeking a type of legal recognition which is not only and immediately beneficial to same sex people: '[T]he struggle for same-sex marriage has led to the recognition of many different types of relationships ... that have begun to weaken somewhat the hegemonic domination enjoyed by the institution of marriage over intimate relationships.' In this light, the broader scope of same sex equality stands a good chance of success if and only if same sex couples are steadfastly treated 'as deserving of marriage, in its privileged state, especially as feminists who want to end the gendered limitations imposed by traditional marriage' (Cox 2004: 279). In brief, deconstructing the privilege attached to marriage entails recognizing its status as a privilege and extending it to all those who have to be recognized as deserving it. This is why sociological analysis of challenges to heteronormativity should be less reductive and should be sensitive to more nuanced forms of transformative resistance (Bartholomay 2018).

While insisting on this innate ambivalence of law's effects that make marriage a successful political weapon, Kathleen Hull (2006: 198) builds exactly on Bourdieu's conception of law as that which confers official visibility and thus makes social entities speakable. Same sex marriage holds 'the potential to shake up existing power relations by shifting the schemas and resources of the institution of marriage to a new set of previously marginalized relationships', for these practices enact 'a form of legality outside the official law, an effort to invest same-sex commitments with law-like powers and qualities'. In other words, same sex marriage ignites a broader interaction between official and unofficial law that infiltrates the former from within and challenges the preeminence accorded to a particular configuration of the social world. Rejecting the law as a whole, as some radical queer critics recommend, only because of its reifying nature ends up reinforcing this nature and putting those who take this stance out of the frame of political visibility that the law grants. On the contrary, a strategic attitude to law's allocation of speakability opens up fissures for a variety of populations that are out of the law's reach.

Be this as it may, queer theorists generally exhibit some discomfort with what is normal in the here and now. The normal – that is, widespread institutions and values as well as the classifications and hierarchies that underpin them – is to be dissected and debunked, presented as a historical configuration that produced oppression in those who were denied social speakability and political visibility. The issue at stake, therefore, is how to revise the normal and make it more porous to the range of marginalized forms of sexuality and relationships. While it goes without saying that this short sketch of the debate can hardly answer the question of whether legal recognition can be advantageous or harmful, in these pages my concern has been with the second queer line's ambivalent attitude to the law and social change generally. This is why I would like to conclude this chapter with a quick excursion into a queer understanding of social change that is more positive and affirmative as to the transformative potential of ambivalence.

7. POSTCRITICAL QUEER POTENTIAL

A variation of the queer that does not completely jettison the legacy of radical constructivism but locates it in a more hopeful conception of social transformation is what might be dubbed 'postcritical' queer theory. One of its keystones is Sedgwick's take on 'paranoid readings', as she argues that most queer literary criticism, including her own, pivoted on a 'paranoid–schizoid' position. In her postcritical frame, Rita Felski (2015: 35–6) salutes Sedgwick's moving away from paranoia as a break with a tendency that has long marked the relationship between queer theory and social critique. This longstanding relationship fostered the idea that while

> all-powerful forces are working behind the scenes, the critic conjures up ever more paralyzing scenarios of coercion and control. Like the clinically paranoid individual, she feeds off the charge of her own negativity, taking comfort in her clear-eyed refusal of hope and her stoic awareness of connections and consequences invisible to others.

Sedgwick censures the link between the so-called hermeneutics of suspicion (whose celebrated initiators are Marx, Nietzsche and Freud) and the queer penchant for paranoia. The paroxysm of suspicion surfaces in the social critic's conviction that there are occult and opaque mechanisms governing what people do and think without their being aware of them. The social critic therefore feels tasked with uncovering these mechanisms and with making people aware of their tacit effects.

The connection between suspicion and paranoia manifests itself under the guise of a compulsion to recover the concealed meaning of things with an eye to unveiling that which is hidden – the true meaning of those mechanisms that have people do things they would not otherwise do. This injunction to excavate and unearth, criticize and censure, morphs into prototypical modes of the critique of the social such as historicization, defamiliarization, denaturalization – all of them being means to the end of revealing the facticity and constructedness of social objects. All that surrounds social subjects and shapes their social context is the outcome of a construction that hardly leaves visible traces and hence commands a suspicious attitude in order for it to become less and less familiar to us. While familiarity implies taking things for granted and leaving their constructed nature unquestioned, unfamiliarity allows taking some distance from social objects to bring to light their historical, fictitious character as well as to deconstruct the (seeming) relation they have to the (alleged) nature of things.

Nonetheless, however reflective and revealing this critical attitude may be, it easily turns into a form of paranoia that is all the more contagious and takes on a 'self-evident imperative force: the notation that even paranoid people have enemies is wielded as if its absolutely necessary corollary were the injunction "so you can never be paranoid enough"' (Sedgwick 2003: 127). According to 'paranoid' queer critics, the idea that things have a nature of their own and that this nature mandates specific conducts can be discredited only through the constant scrutiny of the suspicious attitude. Still, in this way, constructedness is opposed too hastily to nature and creates a polarization that disqualifies all identities. As Felski (2015: 80) points out, the antinaturalistic attitude of suspicion demotes interiority 'to a deceptive façade', so much so that it erects 'a forbiddingly high wall between ordinary language and the ethos of critique'. If what people believe their sexual identity to be represents a mere effect of construction, then the only thing they can do is mistrust their perception and follow the clue of the critic who tells them what they really are. Critique and paranoia, glued together, yield general scepticism about all that is taken for granted, but it 'is one thing to point out that certain ideas are bad and also taken for granted. It is another to conclude that they are bad because they are taken for granted – in other words, that anything taken for granted is an agent of domination' (Felski 2015: 80).

To leave behind the paranoid attitude, Sedgwick (2003: 149) advances the notion of *reparative readings* – ones that are additive and accretive as they 'assemble and confer plenitude on an object that will then have resources to offer to an inchoate self'. Reparative readings are oriented to pleasure and open to surprise, whether negative or positive. They reject the destructive aversion to all that surrounds us with an aspect of naturalness and dismisses the distrustful orientation to construction. Much in the same vein, by taking stock of Bruno Latour's (2005) 'science of the particular', Felski's postcritique invites dismissal of the permanent temptation of sociological reduction.[15] Phenomena should never be reduced to epiphenomena, but should be invested with an affect that opens up to encounters loaded with transformative potential.[16] It is in a similar sense that Davina Cooper (2013: 42–3) conjures a broader notion of queer, one that releases it as a potential:

> While some understand the term as a synonym for *gay* and others treat the term as one of sexual deviance, queer also functions as a refusal of identification, deliberately gesturing toward that which cannot be named or rendered intelligible or normal. But even this gesture depends for its success on familiarity and notice. Queer may not seek to represent a cohort of people in the sense of rendering them transparent and knowable, but it still seeks recognition – whether of its own conceptual parameters (what counts as queer) or in the challenge it presents to other forms of thought and practice.

---

[15] Latour's (2005: 137) methodological memo reads: '(I)t is the attempt at imitating a false view of the natural sciences that bogs down the social ones: it is always felt that description is too particular, too idiosyncratic, too localized. But, contrary to the scholastic proverb, there is science only of the particular. If connections are established between sites, it should be done through more descriptions, not by suddenly taking a free ride through all-terrain entities like Society, Capitalism, Empire, Norms, Individualism, Fields, and so on. A good text should trigger in a good reader this reaction: "Please, more details, I want more details." God is in the details, and so is everything else – including the Devil. It's the very character of the social to be specific. The name of the game is not reduction, but irreduction. As Gabriel Tarde never tired of saying: "To exist is to differ".'

[16] On the origins of the so-called affective turn in queer studies, see Sedgwick (2003); Cvetkovich (2003); Ahmed (2004).

This juncture insists on the *proximity* between the queer and the ordinary in a way that is both critical and affective. In order to exercise a vital, potentially transformative critique, one's posture cannot be based on distance, unfamiliarity and refusal. Fertile exchanges between the ordinary and the queer are likely to occur only in the frame of a 'critical proximity' (Cooper 2013: 9) whereby those who give life to experimental modes of living continue to be party to the social world in which they spend significant portions of their lives. The queer, then, is uncoupled from an oppositional resistance to domination and becomes a more practical attitude to everyday life, one by which people perform quotidian practices in an ambitiously counterhegemonic manner. The queer is an orientation to one's daily doings that also traverses sexuality but energetically disseminates imaginative resources. This type of queer requires neither complete refusal of mainstream social life nor assimilation into the sphere of respectable sexuality. Rather, the queer comprises a set of practical sites where all people, whether gay or straight, are invited to do what they do regularly in a more imaginative way – a way that prompts people to *desire better* and to *desire more*. This is why scholars who regard the queer as fragments of concrete, viable utopias devote their attention to actual spaces where 'queer' lines are produced, 'lines that emerge when particular sites are considered in relation to unexpected concepts' (Cooper 2013: 13): experimental sexual places, democratic schooling systems, alternative trade schemes, public performances, anarchic food producers and so on.

The queer as critical proximity and active engagement in practical contexts overcomes the limits of radical constructivism as well as those of the other lines of the queer lineage, especially when it comes to the issue of legal visibility. Ambivalence about law is no longer a strategic attitude to something that is potentially dangerous and thus is to be navigated with suspicion. Certainly, minor-stream practices always face public invisibility, neglect or even hostility, and yet this is no longer pure stigma – for it opens a fissure between the queer and the ordinary that mobilizes the production of transformative conceptual resources. As this attitude is not oppositional, the status of *minority* practice may prove an advantage, because the queer remains an interstice that can be traversed transitorily by all those who are curious to engage in a particular type of practice (whether sexual, educational, political or of another nature). This version of the queer never claims to change one's life as a whole, let alone to upturn society as a whole. In this regard, it does not share the Freudo-Marxian impulse to smash society and build a new one. Nor does it indulge in the pleasure of being the object of hatred and repulsion, as antisocial theorists recommend. The resignification of this more hopeful queer is an amendment to radical constructivism insofar as it locates it in the material practices where new meanings are produced. Resignification does not arise out of a resistance to law, but from people's concrete experience of doing things in a different way. If this is the case, it is particularly interesting to appreciate the 'nuances, subtleties, quirks, variations, and tonal differences' (Felski 2015: 79) that characterize people's recourse to law. There are ways that inevitably reinforce the hegemonic lexicon of standard heterosexist binaries and ways that force the law to take different directions.

Therefore, a postcritical queer approach invites us to *look at the particular* to appreciate how individuals handle their critical proximity with the ordinary and by doing so ignite a dialectic between adaptation and creativity: how they couch their claims, the ends they pursue, how they navigate the legal lexicon, how they bend norms in order to describe themselves with a language that is audible to a broader range of people. This postcritical queer attitude at the same time demands and favours a methodological change in the law. Legal recognition should cease to operate as a mechanism that confers legibility on social subjects through a series of predefined, fixed labels – for these labels are often foisted upon people seeking recognition, to the extent that those people alter the perception of their own relationships and the practice of their sexuality in order to fit those categories (see e.g. Lessard 2004; Diduck 2007; Swennen and Croce 2015). Instead, legal recognition should work as an *ethnographer* alert to how 'actors incessantly engage in the most abstruse metaphysical constructions by redefining all the elements of the world' (Latour 2005: 51). This attunement to how people construct and arrange their relationships would be able to turn legal recognition into a connector and stabilizer, a technical tool that helps people define their relationship with reference to a set of specialized categories (see Swennen and Croce 2017). Law is well equipped to trace and account for how people get in touch with one another and create their own normative networks, and how they verbalize these networks in ways that can be stabilized with recourse to a legal proxy. There would still be much ambivalence, as legal recognition always inevitably changes the settings it enters, but it would permit people to adapt to law's categories in a creative manner – one that would infiltrate society at large through law to extend indefinitely the gamut of normalities.

BIBLIOGRAPHY

Ahmed, Sara (2004) *The Cultural Politics of Emotions*, Routledge.
Ball, Carlos A. (2005) 'This Is Not Your Father's Autonomy: Lesbian and Gay Rights from a Feminist and Relational Perspective', *Harvard Journal of Law and Gender* 28: 345.
Barker, Meg and Langdridge, Darren (eds) (2010) *Understanding Non-Monogamies*, Routledge.
Barker, Nicola (2013) *Not the Marrying Kind: A Feminist Critique of Same-Sex Marriage*, Palgrave.
Bartholomay, Daniel J. (2018) 'What, Exactly, Are We Measuring? Examining Heteronormativity in Relation to Same-Gender Marriage', *Social Compass* (Early View), DOI: 10.1111/soc4.12563.
Bell, David and Binnie, Jon (2000) *The Sexual Citizen: Queer Politics and Beyond*, Polity.
Bell, David and Binnie, Jon (2004) 'Authenticating Queer Space: Citizenship, Urbanism and Governance', *Urban Studies* 41(9): 1807.
Bernini, Lorenzo (2017a) *Queer Apocalypses: Elements of Antisocial Theory*, Palgrave.
Bernini, Lorenzo (2017b) *Le teorie queer. Un'introduzione*, Mimesis.
Bersani, Leo (2010) 'Is the Rectum a Grave?' in *Is the Rectum a Grave? And Other Essays*, University of Chicago Press.
Boellstorff, Tom (2007) 'Queer Studies in the House of Anthropology', *Annual Review of Anthropology* 36: 18.
Bourdieu, Pierre (1987) 'The Force of Law: Toward a Sociology of the Juridical Field', *Hastings Law Journal* 38: 814.
Bourdieu, Pierre (1991) *Language and Symbolic Power*, Harvard University Press.
Bourdieu, Pierre (2001) *Masculine Domination*, Stanford University Press.
Brown, Wendy (2000) 'Suffering Rights as Paradoxes', *Constellations* 7(2): 230.
Butler, Judith (1997) *Excitable Speech: A Politics of the Performative*, Routledge.
Butler, Judith (2004) *Undoing Gender*, Routledge.
Calhoun, Cheshire (2000) *Feminism, the Family, and the Politics of the Closet: Lesbian and Gay Displacement*, Oxford University Press.

Chávez, Karma R. (2013) *Queer Migration Politics: Activist Rhetoric and Coalitional Possibilities*, University of Illinois Press.
Chignola, Sandro (2018) *Foucault's Politics of Philosophy: Power, Law, and Subjectivity*, Routledge.
Cooper, Davina (2004) *Challenging Diversity: Rethinking Equality and the Value of Difference*, Cambridge University Press.
Cooper, Davina (2013) *Everyday Utopias: The Conceptual Life of Promising Spaces*, Duke University Press.
Cox, Barbara (2004) 'Marriage Equality Is Both Feminist and Progressive', *Richmond Journal of Law and the Public Interest* 17(4): 707.
Croce, Mariano (2015) 'Homonormative Dynamics and the Subversion of Culture', *European Journal of Social Theory* 18(1): 3.
Croce, Mariano (2018) *The Politics of Juridification*, Routledge.
Cvetkovich, Ann (2003) *An Archive of Feelings: Trauma, Sexuality and Lesbian Public Cultures*, Duke University Press.
de Lauretis, Teresa (1991) 'Queer Theory: Lesbian and Gay Sexualities. An Introduction', *Differences: A Journal of Feminist Cultural Studies* 3(2): iii.
Diduck, Alison (2007) '"If Only We Can Find the Appropriate Terms to Use the Issue Will Be Solved": Law, Identity and Parenthood', *Child and Family Law Quarterly* 19(4): 458.
Duggan, Lisa (2003) *The Twilight of Equality? Neoliberalism, Cultural Politics, and the Attack on Democracy*, Beacon.
Edelman, Lee (2004) *Queer Theory and the Death Drive*, Duke University Press.
Eskridge, William N. (2013) 'Backlash Politics: How Constitutional Litigation Has Advanced Marriage Equality in the United States', *Boston University Law Review* 93: 275.
Foucault, Michel (1990) *The History of Sexuality, Vol. 1*, Vintage Books.
Franke, Katherine M. (2004) 'The Domesticated Liberty of Lawrence v. Texas', *Columbia Law Review* 104: 1399.
Gay Liberation Front ((1973) 1978) 'Manifesto'. Available at http://www.fordham.edu/halsall/pwh/glf-london.asp
Graham, Mark (2004) 'Gay Marriage: Whither Sex? Some Thoughts from Europe', *Sexuality Research and Social Policy*, 1(3): 24.
Hall, Donald E. and Jagose, Annamarie (2012) *The Routledge Queer Studies Reader*, Routledge.
Herman, Didi (1990) '"Are We Family?": Lesbian Rights and Women's Liberation', *Osgoode Hall Law Journal* 28(4): 789.
Hull, Kathleen E. (2006) *Same-Sex Marriage: The Cultural Politics of Love and Law*, Cambridge University Press.
Jagose, Annamarie (1997) *Queer Theory: An Introduction*, New York University Press.
Latour, Bruno (2005) *Reassembling the Social: An Introduction to Actor-Network Theory*, Oxford University Press.
Leckey, Robert and Brooks, Kim (2010) *Queer Theory: Law, Culture, Empire*, Routledge.
Lessard, Hester (2004) 'Mothers, Fathers and Naming: Reflections on the Law Equality Framework and Trociuk v British Columbia (Attorney General)', *Canadian Journal of Women and the Law* 16: 165.
Llewellyn, Karl N. (1940) 'The Normative, the Legal, and the Law-Jobs: The Problem of Juristic Method', *Yale Law Journal* 49: 1355.
Marcuse, Herbert (1966) *Eros and Civilization: A Philosophical Inquiry into Freud*, Beacon Press.
Mieli, Mario (1980) *Homosexuality and Liberation: Elements of a Gay Critique*, Gay Men's Press.
Otto, Dianne (2018) *Queering International Law: Possibilities, Alliances, Complicities, Risks*, Routledge.
Polikoff, Nancy (2008) *Beyond (Straight and Gay) Marriage: Valuing All Families under the Law*, Beacon Press.
Reich, Wilhelm (1945) *The Sexual Revolution: Toward a Self-Regulating Character Structure*, Farrar, Straus and Giroux.
Rumens, Nick (2016) 'Towards Queering the Business School: A Research Agenda for Advancing Lesbian, Gay, Bisexual and Trans Perspectives and Issues', *Gender, Work & Organization* 23(1): 36.
Schmitt, Carl (2004) *On the Three Types of Juristic Thought*, Praeger.
Sedgwick, Eve Kosofsky (1994) *Tendencies*, Routledge.
Sedgwick, Eve Kosofsky (2003) *Touching Feeling: Affect, Pedagogy, Performativity*, Duke University Press.
Seidman, Steven (1994) 'Queer-Ing Sociology, Sociologizing Queer Theory: An Introduction', *Sociology* 2(2): 166.

Smith, Nicola J. and Lee, Donna (2014) 'What's Queer About Political Science?' *The British Journal of Politics and International Relations* 17(1): 49.

Spargo, Tamsin (2016) 'Queer Literary Criticism', in *The Wiley Blackwell Encyclopedia of Gender and Sexuality Studies*, Blackwell, pp. 1–5.

Stychin, Carl F. (2003) *Governing Sexuality: The Changing Politics of Citizenship and Law Reform*, Hart Publishing.

Swennen, Frederik and Croce, Mariano (2015) 'The Symbolic Power of Legal Kinship Terminology: An Analysis of "Co-motherhood" and "Duo-motherhood" in Belgium and the Netherlands', *Social & Legal Studies* 25: 181.

Swennen, Frederik and Croce, Mariano, 'Family (Law) Assemblages: New Modes of Being (Legal)', *Journal of Law and Society* 44(4): 532.

Warner, Michael (ed.) (2003), *Fear of a Queer Planet: Queer Politics and Social Theory*, University of Minnesota Press.

Weber, Cynthia (2016), *Queer International Relations: Sovereignty, Sexuality and the Will to Knowledge*, Oxford University Press.

6. Marxism and the political economy of law
Emilios Christodoulidis and Marco Goldoni

1. MARX ON LAW: A REDUCTIVE CONCEPTION?

The chapter navigates the complex and diffuse field of the Marxist theory of law in order to argue that we can retrieve from it a *critical* understanding of law. The main problem that such an endeavour faces is posed by the widely held view that Marxism entertains a reductionist view of law, one that only ever conceptualises law as a *surface* phenomenon, reflecting, or at best sanctioning, the *deeper dynamic* of the capitalist organisation of production. If that assumption holds then the mobilisation of law in the direction of a critique of capitalism is already undercut from the outset.

The chapter looks at the prevalent reductionist view in the first section, by exploring two of its more sophisticated articulations. Next it turns to legal theory, and more specifically to two of the twentieth century's most influential theorists, Carl Schmitt and Hans Kelsen, to see whether they have resisted the reductionist understanding; it concludes that they have not. The third section attempts a reconstruction of the legal theory of Marx with a view to retrieving a critical–political moment irreducible to the economic structure – the reconstruction is picked up again in the final section with an eye to the post-Gramscian thinking about constituent power as the question of the space left to political action (and class struggle) in capitalist legal orders. The intervening section, section 4, looks at how the question of the legal institution in its relationship to capitalism was addressed in the context of regimes that purported to have overcome capitalism, and more specifically the early Soviet debates over the continuing relevance of law to the 'socialist' organisation of society. A reductionist understanding of law as the handmaid of capitalist reproduction would see it 'withering away', and yet law endured, and not merely as 'administration'. In the process we observe that Marxist legal theory has often produced, as in the case of Pashukanis, sophisticated analyses of the constitutive role played by law in the organisation of society.

But let us take the argument gradually. The most frequent criticism that Marxist legal theory has had to face has been directed to its reductionist view of the role of law in the formation and consolidation of the social order. Schematically put, the core of the critique states that according to the predominant Marxist legal–theoretical position, the law operates as a tool functional to the strengthening of capital's interests and, of course, their legitimacy. Such criticism is not devoid of textual evidence. The argument that law is an institution that belongs to the superstructure, ultimately determined by the material forces that operate in the economic base, was first developed by Marx in *The German Ideology*. On this understanding, the economy is the *base* of every society, determining its shape and the nature of its institutions. Law, as located among the institutions of the superstructure, is very much *in keeping with* the base that conditions of the mode of production. Its operation thus broadly reflects the necessities of the mode of production and its function is to sustain and regulate *capitalist* economic and social relations. But already this is improbably reductive to be attributed to Marxism. If the economic base determines *in the last instance* the kind of institutions we have in the superstructure, the role of the superstructure is not confined to simply reflecting the economic relations of society. For Louis Althusser,

> Marx has at least given us the 'two ends of the chain', and has told us to find out what goes on between them: on the one hand, *determination in the last instance* by the (economic) mode of production; on the other, the *relative autonomy* of the superstructures and their specific effectivity. (Althusser 2005, 111)

The first of these formulations – 'in the last instance' – was in fact offered by Engels by way of a clarification and against a pure reductionist reading that would see a one-to-one correspondence between economic forms and legal forms. Production, clarifies Engels, is the determinant factor, but only 'in the last instance': 'More than this neither Marx nor I have ever asserted.' Anyone who 'twists this' so that it says that the economic factor is the only determinant factor 'transforms that proposition into a meaningless, abstract, empty phrase'.[1] Regarding the second formulation – the 'relative autonomy of law' – the qualification involves the movement, function, and therefore also efficacy of law as conceived of independently of the base: 'relative' because determined in the last instance, but 'autonomous' nonetheless in that law manages its own reproduction.[2]

---

[1] And further: 'The economic situation is the basis, but the various elements of the superstructure the political forms of the class struggle and its results: to wit constitutions established by the victorious class after a successful battle, etc., juridical forms, and then even the reflexes of all these actual struggles in the brains of the participants, political, juristic, philosophical theories, religious views and their further development into systems of dogmas – also exercise their influence upon the course of the historical struggles. and in many cases preponderate in determining their form …' (Engels, in his letter to Bloch, 1890, English translation available here: https://www.marxists.org/archive/marx/works/1890/letters/90_09_21.htm).

[2] How are these new terms arranged? On the one hand, the structure (the economic base: the forces of production and the relations of production); on the other, the superstructure (the State and all the legal, political and ideological forms). We have seen that one could nevertheless attempt to maintain a Hegelian relation (the relation Hegel imposed between civil society and the State) between these two groups of categories: the relation between an essence and its phenomena, sublimated in the concept of the 'truth of …'. For Hegel, the State is the 'truth of' civil society, which, thanks to the action of the Ruse of Reason, is merely its own phenomenon consummated in it. For a Marx thus relegated to the rank of a Hobbes or a Locke, civil society would be nothing but the 'truth of' its phenomenon, the State, nothing but a Ruse which Economic Reason would then put at the service of a class: the ruling class. Unfortunately for this neat schema, this is not Marx. For him, this tacit identity (phenomenon-essence-truth-of …) of the economic and the political disappears in favour of a new conception of the relation between determinant instances in the structure–superstructure complex which constitutes the essence of any social formation. And famously: 'the economic dialectic is never active in the pure state; in History, these instances, the superstructures, etc. – are never seen to step respectfully aside when their work is done or, when the Time comes, as his pure phenomena, to

But concerns remain over whether this is enough to dispel the determinism and the one-directionality of the economy–law relation. Take the *Preface to the Critique of Political Economy*, where, in one of the most discussed passages of his work, Marx notes in characteristically deterministic fashion that 'the mode of production of material life conditions the general process of social, political and intellectual life. It is not the consciousness of men that determines their existence, but their social existence that determines their consciousness' (Marx 2005, 426). The organisation of the modes and relations of production dictates historical development, and the law as a product of such development, the latter too often presented as a 'reflex' of the underlying dynamics of the process of production: 'At a certain stage of development, the material productive forces of society come into conflict with the existing relations of production or – this merely expresses the same thing in legal terms – with the property relations within the framework of which they have operated hitherto' (Ibid). This last quote has often been highlighted as proof of Marx's advocacy of a reductive view of the legal order, where property relations are mere instantiations of an already constituted set of modes and relations of production. According to this interpretation, other legal institutions (such as the family) are also seen as reflexes of underlying structures of production (such as modes and relations). The *German Ideology* is usually read as a paradigmatic text of this reductive view: in it, Marx attacks directly a certain way of understanding the law as the product of an act of pure will, an idea which he denounces as 'the legal illusion', and which makes him suspicious of purely positivist descriptions of law. Marx rejects altogether the conception of law which makes it the outcome of a purely autonomous political decision. And yet the *German Ideology* contains a clear and important distinction between two conceptions of the law, first as Will and then as Power. Marx's efforts are often directed to dismissing the will-based conception of law by linking the law back to the concrete relations of power from which it emanates, and in the context of which even those who find themselves in an advantageous position cannot simply deploy the law to impose their arbitrary will freely. The will of those empowered by the structure of social relations cannot but be conditioned by the 'real relations' which are the source of their power:

> The individuals who rule in these conditions – leaving aside the fact that their power must assume the form of the state – have to give their will, which is determined by these definite conditions, a universal expression as the will of the state, as law, an expression whose content is always determined by the relations of this class, as the civil and criminal law demonstrates in the clearest possible way: just as the weight of their bodies does not depend on their idealistic will or on their arbitrary decision, so also the fact that they enforce their own will in the form of law, and at the same time to make it independent of the personal arbitrariness of each individual among them, does not depend on their idealistic will'. (Marx 1976, 327)

This is an instantiation of Marx's concern *qua* materialist author to go beyond the phenomenal world in order to retrieve the logic of the principles that animate that world. In the third volume of *Capital*, this methodology is summarised in a context in

---

scatter before His Majesty the Economy as he strides along the royal road of the Dialectic. From the first moment to the last, the lonely hour of the "last instance" never comes.'

which the discussion revolves around the main pillars of modern political economy: 'But all science would be superfluous if the outward appearance and the essence of things directly coincided' (Marx 1991b, 897). This statement sums up in an elegant way both how Marx addresses the relation between the material and the phenomenal (matter and appearance) and how he tries to overcome Hegel's idealist take on historical development. Though still a matter of intense debate among Marxists, this point might mark an essential difference between the two thinkers. While in Hegel History is animated by the Idea which takes *form* in its unfolding in such a way that it is difficult to imagine a disjunction between the two without sacrificing the rationality of reality, in Marx the relation comes across as more ambiguous.[3] As we shall argue, within the perimeter of Marx's works there is room to recover a *richer* – though never *systematic* – conception of law without having to abandon the critique of political economy. But before we explore this, a few words on how the reception of this reductive interpretation of the place and function of the law consolidated a particular understanding of Marxist legal theory, with the help of two, key, examples.[4]

Ferdinand Lassalle, in a much-celebrated essay on the essence of constitutions (Lassalle 2002), provides an exemplary case of the deterministic analysis of the law. For Lassalle the constitutional is a layer that supervenes on a deeper dynamic. He famously remarked that the formal constitutional order is only a cover ('a mask') of the real constitution, the former (sometimes pejoratively referred to by him as a 'piece of paper') fully conditioned by the latter. Extrapolating from this, the law quickly becomes the site of registration of the underlying relations of power. To the question 'what is the nature of the constitution?', Lassalle replies with the following definition: 'a constitution is the fundamental law proclaimed in a country which disciplines the organization of public rights in that nation' (Ibid). This is because, fundamentally, Lassalle thinks that 'constitutional questions are not primordially legal questions, but a matter of relations of force' (Ibid). By stating that the constitution is the fundamental law of the country, Lassalle assumed that it has higher force than ordinary law and that it provides for its own grounding, so that 'it must be none other than what it is. Its basis will not permit it to be otherwise' (Ibid). The nature of lawmaking is here purified from any contingency – *in other words, from its political origins* – and associated with the idea of necessity. The grounding of the constitution has to be found 'always and exclusively in the real effective relations among social forces in a given society' (Ibid). Yet, this definition of the constitutional order is problematic, because it assumes that the real constitution becomes law only when codified in written form and with the introduction of explicit sanctions: 'These actual relations of force are put down on paper, are given written form, and after they have been thus put down, they are no longer simply actual relations of force but have now become *laws*, judicial institutions, and whoever opposes them is punished' (Ibid). But this leaves open the question of the

---

[3] While this discussion is beyond the scope of this chapter, let us note nonetheless that the idea of appearance does not exhaust social reality but this recognition does not entail the complete dismissal of the form of law. Otherwise, instead of the law reduced to will, we would have the law reduced to the undergirding economic relations.

[4] In the field of *political theory* this view was expressed in a clear way in the work of Karl Kautsky at the end of the nineteenth century. The seminal reference is Engels and Kautsky 1977.

legal force of the real constitutional order, which in his work is never fully answered. In Lassalle's account, the formal constitution represents the juridification of the 'real' relations of power, or, in the most trivial sense, it is just the registration or codification of the real constitution. Lassalle is adamant in stating that the formal constitution is stable and lasting 'only when it corresponds ... to the real constitution, that is, to the real relations among social forces' (Ibid). Otherwise, it is just a sham constitution. Be that as it may, according to Lassalle the relation between material and formal is that of overdetermination of the former over the latter. In other words, Lassalle maintains that the social organisation of production is already shaped and achieved prepolitically and, perhaps, prelegally. At best, one could say that the formal legal order operates as part of the justificatory ideological apparatus. The key message of this Marxist approach to law is that the constitution of society is represented as independent from the formal constitutional order, and that the latter simply codifies ex post an underlying relation of forces. Relations of production are placed at the centre of the analysis, but they are represented as static and set up from the perspective of capital's primacy. The limit of such a rigid materialist take is that it underestimates the political potential of both legal and subjectivity formation. How those relations came to take up those particular *modes* and *forms* is never made into a question of political and legal analysis.

The second example derives from the work of the historian Charles Beard (1913) on the economic origins of the American constitution. Breaking away from the interpretation of the American constitution as the first experiment in modern political science, Beard focuses on the economic interests which were at the forefront of the Founding Fathers' concerns in order to identify the grounds of that constitutional order. In a clear methodological statement, he is careful not to reduce the analysis to the personal motivations of the involved actors:

> The purpose of such an inquiry is not, of course, to show that the Constitution was made for the personal benefit of the members of the Convention. Far from it. Neither is it of any moment to discover how many hundred thousand dollars accrued to them as a result of the foundation of the new government. The only point here considered is: Did they represent distinct groups whose economic interests they understood and felt in concrete, definite form through their own personal experience with identical property rights, or were they working merely under the guidance of abstract principles of political science? (Ibid, ii)

And while Beard's particular emphasis is on the materialist dimension of the constitution, the materialism that informs the historical work is largely reductive. A Marxian critique of the political economy does indeed shadow Beard's masterpiece, but it never hones it adequately to the importance of valorisation processes (that is, how value is generated) and a labour-centred understanding of class struggles. As in the case of Lassalle, little attention is given to the role of political agency of the involved classes and the role of the law in constituting the field of struggle. This lack becomes evident in the underestimation of the role of slavery in the process of valorisation and the parallel overestimation of what he defines as 'personalty' (that is, mobile capital represented by investments in securities, commerce, manufacturing) in contrast to the other major interest of the time, 'realty' (that is, capital invested in agricultural production). In brief, Beard introduces a simplified and deterministic narrative of the rise and development of the American legal order where legal constructs that are

100 *Research handbook on critical legal theory*

essential for the shaping of the American political economy are (either ignored or) taken as a direct reflection of already established economic relations.

Against such deterministic understandings of the law, our aim is to show that Marxian (a term preferred to 'Marxist' as connoting a materialist but not reductionist methodology) legal theory can still provide precious epistemic insights for a more accurate understanding of the legal order. In brief, we will retrieve those conceptions that avoid falling into the trap of reductive determination of the relation between the base and the superstructure. Some Marxist legal scholars might have adopted some version of that form of reductionism, but Marxism is a rich constellation that offers more nuanced conceptions which are still – if not increasingly – relevant. In particular, we intend to highlight how Marx's methodology – the critique of the political economy – can be extended usefully to the study of law while, at the same time, maintaining a complex idea of the legal order as internal to society, that is, against the dominant liberal understanding of law as an external tool applied over society, and a building block of social relations. Instead of an ossified conception of the relation between base and superstructural law, such a mapping offers the potential of critique as leverage for change. In brief, the critique of law and political economy is, first of all, a science of the contradictions and tensions affecting the legal regime of concretely organised modes and relations of productions, but also a study of the ambivalent role of law within that system. This presents two major concerns: the *first* relates to the study of the production and reproduction of society under the conditions of modern political economy and the essential role of the law in the organisation and development of those two poles of production (in brief, the materiality of the legal order); the *second* relates to the study of the transformative potential of the law as force and instrument of social change, with a special emphasis on the conception of constituent power, or, more accurately, on the material conditions for the emergence of constituent power (Christodoulidis 2007). For these purposes, we assume that, once a reductionist account of the law has been sidestepped, the critique of the political economy is still a core component of critical legal theory.

2. CLASSIC CHALLENGES TO MARXIST LEGAL THEORY: KELSEN AND SCHMITT

Among the reasons for the rather marginal impact of Marxism on the legal theory of the twentieth century are two important criticisms that were levelled against it by two of the most influential legal thinkers of the century, Kelsen and Schmitt.[5]

In a collection of essays on the communist theory of law, Hans Kelsen famously attacked Marx for a series of contradictions and antinomies that affect his conception of law (Kelsen 1955). Among many arguments, Kelsen puts forward two connected, major criticisms that would not only deprive Marx's methodology of any validity, but also deny any critical relevance to a Marxist approach to the study of law. First, Kelsen thinks that it is not possible to state *at the same time* that the law as 'superstructural' is

---

[5] While Marxism has been extremely important in moral and political philosophy, it has not enjoyed the same relevance in legal philosophy.

fully determined by the economic base to the point that it is simply a mirror or a reflex of what happens at the material level of production, and also that it is ideological (Kelsen here understands ideology in the pejorative sense of the term, that is, as a product of false consciousness). For Kelsen, Marx cannot state that the law is ideological (false) if it is at the same time the mirror of the material reality.[6] Second, and related, is the argument that it is unsustainable to view law as a reflex of the underlying material reality, because it does not take into account the *normativity* of the law, which in effect reduces legal theory to legal sociology.[7] Here, Kelsen harbours a basic methodological disagreement with Marx: to comprehend legal norms as a mirror effect of a concrete reality is to miss the point of the normativity of law because

> first, the legal norm must be established and only then may there be a real behaviour corresponding to this norm, that is, a real behaviour similar to that prescribed or permitted by the legal norm. Hence, it is the real behaviour which, analogous to the mirror, reflects the legal norm or the behaviour which, prescribed or permitted by the legal norm, is the content of this norm'. (Ibid, 15)

The disagreement here runs deep, and while Kelsen's 'reversal' forces Marx's conception of law into an impasse, the type of pure normativism that is advocated by Kelsen is the type of abstraction that the young Marx found fatally flawed in Hegel's conception of the state. But the disagreement does not stop there. In Marx's legal theory Kelsen discerns at work another essential tenet of the former's more general philosophy, of which Kelsen is highly critical: it is the distinction between the *essence* of social reality and the *appearance* of its visible forms: 'Reality has, so to speak, two layers: an external, visible, but illusive and hence ideological reality; and an internal, invisible ... but true, "real" reality' (Ibid, 17–18).

There can be little doubt that Kelsen's critique of Marx should be taken seriously. Marx's thinking about law is not systematic, and Kelsen is careful to point to contradictions that his own strong defence of the institution of law avoids. Nonetheless, there is arguably enough material in Marx's works to shield off the objections. While Kelsen's criticisms of Marx all turn on the Marxist reduction of law to a superstructural phenomenon, there is, as we shall see, a different understanding of the function of law in Marxism that treats it as determining (rather than determined) and constitutive (rather than other-reflective). But even if confined to the superstructure, Kelsen's idea of ideology as false representation misses the functional element of the concept (of ideology) in Marx, which, ironically not unlike the *Pure Theory*, never collapses the law into pure technique.

Another important criticism levelled against Marx in legal theory comes from the late work of Carl Schmitt. While as a political thinker Schmitt goes some way to endorsing the key idea of class struggle as a political concept,[8] he maintains a profound

---

[6] See the analyses by Guastini 1982 and Manero 1986.

[7] This is why, according to Kelsen, a Marxist legal theory is doomed to fail: 'it substitutes a normative interpretation of law with a structural analysis of the conditions which make possible for a normative system to emerge and be effective': Kelsen 1955, 202.

[8] Schmitt 2007, 38. Much has been written in the past three decades on the ambiguous relation between a Marxist conception of politics and Schmitt. See, for example, Mouffe 1999.

scepticism of Marx as a theorist of law. In a couple of short articles republished in the English translation as an appendix to the *Nomos of the Earth* (Schmitt 2006, 324–5), Schmitt criticised Marx's view of the formation of the legal order as excessively reductive in light of the emphasis and primacy attributed by him to modes and relations of production. The charge is clear: the critique of the political economy obfuscates the origin and the modality of development of the legal order (*nomos*), and in this way the political dimension of the legal order is reduced to the reflection of an economic structure. According to Schmitt, the main mistake that Marx makes is to put the organisation of production at the inception of the process. As is well known, according to Schmitt the right sequence of the creation and development of legal orders is different: appropriation – distribution – production. The point for him is that the legal order's birth originates in an initial act of theft (an original appropriation), an origin that reveals the ineradicable *political* nature of each and every legal order. The beginning is, according to Schmitt, a genuine political moment, where a decision to appropriate (usually, but not necessarily, land) sets up the main principles of the incipient legal order and its main lines of conflict. Following this reconstruction, Marx confused the relation of cause and effect between appropriation and production because of his own reductive blend of economism and sociologism. For this reason, Schmitt thinks that Marxists' and liberals' conceptions of law are affected by the same problem. They both believe that the organisation of the legal order is a reflection of processes of production and distribution. In their view, the legal order does not enjoy any autonomy and, most importantly, it does not really have a political content in the Schmittian sense.

As an accusation of reductionism against Marx, it is doubtful that Schmitt's critique holds up to closer scrutiny. First, as Schmitt himself recognises, Marx is fully aware of the crucial importance of the original appropriation at the beginning of the capitalist phase of accumulation. The last chapters of the first volume of *Capital* are devoted to describing the intimate link between appropriation and accumulation, with its devastating effects on human beings and nature. The original appropriation sets up capitalist legal orders by granting a first channel of accumulation of wealth. While Marx does not build a systematic conception of the role of law in the phase of the original appropriation, it seems quite evident that his reconstruction implies at least two important points. First, the coercion entailed by the act of dispossessing the inhabitants of the land or appropriating commons is a feature of state law; chapter 28 of volume 1 of *Capital*, for example, details the creation of the wage labourer in England through legislation. Second, appropriation is not the effect and production the cause; when Marx affirms that the original accumulation is the outcome of the capitalist mode of production, he does not mean that one is the effect and the other the cause. In fact, in another chapter of the same part (chapter 26), he states that the original accumulation 'is not the result of the capitalist mode of production but its point of departure' (Marx 1991a, 876). Remarkably for the author of *Political Theology*, Schmitt misses Marx's use of a theological metaphor to explain the role of the original appropriation as the constitutive element of capitalist production: 'this primitive accumulation plays approximately the same role in political economy as original sin does in theology' (Ibid).

But the insight regarding law's function is not limited to the original appropriation; for Marx each and every mode and set of relations of production is the outcome of a legally organised way of appropriating. In fact, across his work, references to the constitutive role of property as a *legal* relation play a remarkable role. More precisely, appropriation is not conceived as a derivative moment which consolidates a concrete mode of production and a set of distributive principles. To the contrary, Marx often alludes to the fact that the mode of appropriation and the mode of production are deeply intertwined from the outset. The mode of production of capitalism cannot be disconnected meaningfully from the mode of appropriation of the surplus value generated by labour. But in order to appropriate surplus value, it is necessary to have a legal system which turns labour into an exchangeable commodity (turns it into labour force), and a legal formalisation of property (in particular, the legal *form* of capitalist private property) which makes room for the acquisition of dead labour under the form of accumulation of wealth.[9] Marx's discovery, at this stage, can be seen in the definition of the relation between capital and labour in terms of property relations in a process dictated by the imperative of valorisation. Law is not only an expression of the underlying material production of value. It is a historical *prius* for the existence of these processes of production. Of course, law is neither the *only* constitutive factor nor a *sufficient* one; and yet it remains *necessary* for the establishment of capitalist social relations.

3. MARX AND THE POLITICAL ECONOMY OF LAW: A RECONSTRUCTION

The best place, perhaps, to begin a reconstruction of Marx's critical theory of law is an often neglected text: *The Critique of Hegel's Doctrine of the State* (Marx 2005, 57–198). This is Marx's unfinished first manuscript, which appeared only later (in 1927) in the Soviet Union. Besides offering us Marx's most extensive account of his complex but decisive relation with Hegel,[10] it also contains his most elaborated statement on the law, the role of property, the form of government and the state. The key idea that Marx extrapolates from Hegel is to be found in the productive effects of *negation*. The dialectic unfolding of history is indeed moved by the power of negation (see also Chapter 1, supra). But a key difference already emerges at this stage, one which turns Hegel's insight on the formation of consciousness on its head: negation is the constitutive act for the formation of subjectivity.[11] Famously, Marx will translate this intuition into the idea that history is made by and through class struggle, moved by

---

[9] This is the difference between the legal form of individual private property (whose content is linked to individual labour) and capitalist private property, 'which rests on the exploitation of alien, but formally free labour': Marx 1991a, 928.

[10] Marx's intellectual debt to Hegel is undeniable, but it does not prevent him from harshly criticising the German philosopher in this unfinished work.

[11] This might explain why many Marxist scholars would later find Foucault's work on resistance and subjectivity so intriguing: see, among many, Chignola 2018.

a class that draws constitutively on the *negation* of its identity, role and speaking position in the extant order.

For the legal theorist, the main challenge is to understand the place of the law within the historical developments brought about by class struggle. The critique of Hegel's dialectic, applied to the philosophy of law, reveals two key aspects of Marx's thought that are central to the materialist aspect of his methodology. First is the rejection of Hegel's version of the dialectic method as prone to mystification, at two levels. The first mystification (referred to by Marx as 'mystique of reason') is the equivalence established by Hegel between being and thought, the real and the rational. This equivalence entails a double inversion. At one level, being is reduced to thought and hence the concrete is denied autonomous reality. At another level, reason becomes an absolute and self-sufficient reality. In order to assume autonomous existence, the idea has to be embodied, it has to be carried into concrete existence. Such a move corresponds to the inversion of the order and meaning between subject and predicate. The universal is turned into a category of its own and guarantor of its own existence, while the subject becomes a mere manifestation of the idea. Commenting on §279 of the *Philosophy of Right*, Marx notes: 'Hegel makes the predicates, the objects, autonomous, but he does this by separating them from their real autonomy, *viz*, their subject. The real subject subsequently appears as a result whereas the correct approach would be to start with the real subject and then consider its objectification' (Ibid 78). Hegel's 'mystical' approach to the real fundamentally denies its material existence. The second major mystification concerns Hegel's idealised concept of the state. While, according to Hegel, the state is an achieved synthesis of ethics (*Sittlichkeit*) and morality beyond civil society, that is, a rational expression of the Spirit, Marx (whose conception of the state remained notoriously underdeveloped) takes it to be a complex field whose formation and growth are intimately linked to the development of capitalism.[12] Although later described as the political agent of the bourgeoisie, and despite the lack of a fully-fledged theory, Marx's concept of the state hints at its constitutive role in both allowing capitalism to flourish and serving as an internal limit to certain forms of accumulation.

In light of the previous remarks, it is not surprising that, unlike Hegel, Marx does not see the law as necessarily rational. However, this judgment does not imply that the legal order ought to be classified as a superstructural feature of the political economy nor as a tool which can be used in infinite ways according to the needs of capital. If the legal order resists such reductions, it is because its form does not lend itself easily to manipulation. Instead, there are important passages in Marx's oeuvre which allow us to imagine a more active, and at times even constitutive, role for the law. These passages, although not systematic, suggest that capitalist development is not dictated by a mechanical dialectic, or that law is properly understood to fall on the side of *structure* rather than *agency*. In other words, the political economy of capitalist societies evolves because its central engine is class struggle. This is the true political core of capitalist

---

[12] The definition of the state is famously left unaddressed by Marx. There are tensions among parts of his work, but this lack of clarity has not impeded Marxist scholarship to develop a rich and diversified constellation of analysis over the state. For a reconstruction of Marxist theories of the state see the chapter by Bob Jessop in this handbook.

developments. To acknowledge its centrality is to acknowledge that all actors involved in the struggle can play an active or reactive role. It is not necessarily capital that is 'in charge' of the development of the social order. Labour too can impose constraints on capital and forces, by, for example, forcing innovation as a way to defuse or alleviate class struggle.[13]

Another vivid example of the capacity for agency of labour can be found in *Capital*, in the chapter on the legislation on the working day. The reconstruction of the struggle around labour time, both for young persons and children, is obviously a crucial theme for the exploitation (and the relation between productivity and surplus value) of labour force. Marx connects legislation (a modern form of law) with class struggle in the most direct way: 'The establishment of a normal working day is therefore the product of a protracted and more or less concealed civil war between the capitalist class and the working class.' Hence, a precious lesson can be learned: legislation is not inherently the reflection of the interests of the owners of means of production as, unlike a 'pompous catalogue of the inalienable rights of man', it establishes the moment the time of the worker is its own and not for sale any longer (Marx 1991a, 412 & 416). This chapter of *Capital* illustrates two important points. First, it clearly indicates that class struggle can be driven by labour's initiative and can shape legislation (but also lawmaking in general) in a way that is not completely overdetermined by capital's interests. Second, it shows that law (in this case, in the form of legislation) is not exclusively an instrument in the hands of owners of means of production for the moulding of labour relations in favour of their own interests. Law is embedded in class struggle and whether it can be bent or used in different ways remains a question of internal constraints (meaning: internal to the form of the law) and external social context (meaning: economic incentives and culture).

These points raise broader issues, of course, some of which we will pick up again in the final section. In the meantime, however, we will take a short detour through 'proletarian law'. What this detour achieves is to reflect further on the relationship of law to the economy under conditions where the law's dependence on the underlying capitalist economic structure is, at least theoretically, no longer at issue. Would law 'wither away' as a result (along with the state structure) once the transitional period to socialism had been effected? The question obviously raises complex issues about the autonomy of the institution of law even beyond the historical situation in question, and also allows us to explore, in the case of the most famous jurist, Evgeny Pashukanis, one of the most sophisticated analyses of the constitutive role played by law in the organisation of society.

4. 'PROLETARIAN LAW'

It is interesting to see how the embeddedness of law in the social organisation, as well as its structuring function, were tested in the concept of proletarian law. *Tested* because if law was inevitably tied to the logic of bourgeois rule, then should it not 'disappear'

---

[13] The classic insight is offered by Tronti 2010.

alongside the 'withering away' of the bourgeois state, once socialism had done away with the requirement to sustain relations of private property?

Key among the Soviet legal scholars of the early decades of 'actually existing socialism' (both died during the 1930s) were Piotr Stuchka and Evgeny Pashukanis. Both were careful readers of Marx, both took from him the idea that with the advent of communism the state would 'wither away' and both were keen to explore what it means to organise human society without legal forms. Both struggled to justify the continued persistence of 'proletarian law' at a time when Stalin had already announced that socialism had been achieved in the Soviet Union. Marx had of course predicted in the late writings (the 'Critique of the Gotha programme') that bourgeois law would continue into the first phase of communism, and there was a widespread consensus that law and the exercise of state power would be necessary during the *transitional* period of the 'dictatorship of the proletariat'. But with the transition effected, there could be no grounds for maintaining the structure of bourgeois law, and the notion of proletarian law could be maintained at best only to describe the forms of administrative/technical regulation, not to undergird and sustain the regime of private property. But in the hands of Stalin 'socialist legality' acquired staying power that both Stuchka and Pashukanis found impossible to reconcile with Marxist thinking about the law – a failure that Pashukanis paid for with his life during the purges of 1936 (Stuchka had died a few years earlier of natural causes.)[14]

Pashukanis' staggering contribution to Marxist legal theory is contained in his 1924 masterpiece *The General Theory of Law and Marxism*. Its central insight was to transfer into legal theory Marx's analysis of the fetish-form of labour. Marx famously identified the mystifying element of the fetishisation of labour in the form that labour took under capitalist conditions: that of the commodity. In other words, capital calls forth (wage) labour as always-already invested in the form of the commodity. The mystification consists in this: that as always-already there is no stepping behind the appearance of labour as commodity to retrieve it in its unalienated form. Pashukanis transfers the logic of this process to the form of law. Consequently, the logic of production and exchange that constitutes the political economy based on the exploitation of wage labour acquires the mystifying form of private law as the latter sanctions the relationship between holders of property in capital and labour respectively. Fetishism names the phenomenal forms in which the social processes are experienced by the agents. Those forms of bourgeois law cannot be stepped behind to recover the

---

[14] Among the many interpreters of Marx's reflection on law, Stuchka's main contribution assumed as starting point the recognition of the protean nature of law. Accordingly, he relies on three different levels of analysis: the first one is defined as 'the concrete juridical form', the second as the 'abstract form' of the law (which is legislation), and the third is the 'intuitive form' as ideological form. In particular, Stuchka sees in Marx's unsystematic notes on law the underdeveloped conception of a juridical order with clear social origins because law is a system of social relations: 'law is not only a set of norms ... but a system, an order of social relations' (in Stuchka 1988, 134ff). In his *State and Law in the Socialist Construction* (ibid, 188ff) he distinguishes between Marxist conception of law as a legal order distinct from law as modern legislation. This insight is based on the idea that law is proper to any class-based society and not only to modern capitalism.

relationships of production in terms that are not already constitutively complicit with capitalist representations.

Take the key concept of the subject of rights. For Pashukanis 'every sort of juridical relationship is a relationship between subjects', the subject constituting the 'atom of juridical theory'. The intersubjectivity that law constitutes is one that conceives social relations as relations between possessors of commodities, and the subject positions instituted by law are the nodal points in the network of exchange for the circulation of commodities. A right is the form in which possession is recognised, the nexus between subjects and their rights is proprietal, and law provides for an intersubjectivity of formally equal subjects who meet to mediate their conflicts and strike their deals around the pursuit of rights. It is the exchange of equivalents by free subjects that is expressed in juridical relations. The juridical element enters at the point of the identification and opposition of interests. Here is Pashukanis:

> A basic prerequisite for legal regulation is the conflict of private interests. This is both the logical premise of the legal form and the actual origin of the development of the legal superstructure. Human conduct can be regulated by the most complex regulations, but the juridical factor in this regulation arises at the point when differentiation and opposition of conflicts begins. (Ibid, 81)

Pashukanis' main emphasis is on private law and he sees criminal and public law as derivative extensions – derivative in the sense that in both cases the law serves to buttress and reproduce class exploitation under the guise of neutrality, a neutrality that, in situations when class conflict becomes acute, gives way to overt class oppression. While there is secondary literature on his analyses in these legal fields, it is fair to say that Pashukanis' main contribution to legal theory centres on private law.

If we return briefly to the earlier problématique of the relation between base and superstructure, and the place of law, we note that Pashukanis clearly circumvents the reduction of the (superstructural) legal phenomenon to any underlying real relation. For him the categories of bourgeois law are constitutive rather than epiphenomena of economic relations because they provide the formal representation of subjects as possessors of either labour or capital. Subjects are constituted in the form of law. Furthermore, for relations of production to be carried out and reproduced as the production of commodities, these relations have to be fashioned, and *are* fashioned in the form of law. The material premises of legal relations cannot be distinguished or separated from their expression through that form (of law), and as a result the logic of supervenience does not obtain.

Since for Pashukanis law is an inherently bourgeois phenomenon that organises social relations among property holders, it would 'wither away' under socialism. Under socialist conditions, where the social bond would assume a different logic and form, and while social organisation would still require regulation, law in the form of rights and legal entitlements would disappear, and only technical forms of regulation would remain. The running of the trains would still need to be regulated, even if under socialism the law would not need to settle disputes between companies, shareholders, consumers and investors, or maintain any relationship of equivalency between labour expenditure and compensation therefore, because, for Pashukanis, 'an end will have been put to the form of the equivalent relationship'. 'The withering away of the categories of bourgeois law will mean the withering away of law altogether, that is to say the disappearance of the juridical factor from social relations' (Pashukanis 1978, 61). As Chris Arthur puts it in his excellent introduction to the *General Theory*:

> Pashukanis' bold perspective on the revolutionary development of post-capitalist society forces criticism to go beyond sniping at abuses or denouncing the current *content* of legal norms. The revolutionary overthrow of capitalist forms of social organisation cannot be grasped in terms of a quantitative extension of existing rights; it forces us to project a qualitative supersession of the form of law itself. (Ibid, 9–10)

It is something of a historical irony that Pashukanis was 'disappeared' by the Stalinist regime for pushing Marx's radical insight about commodity fetishism to its legal application and expression as legal fetishism. By the mid-1930s Stalin had consolidated his grip on power and deployed the state apparatus to sustain it; the adoption of the New Economic Programme (NEP) had required a clear suspension of the critique of private property, with the Party's Tenth Congress proclaiming that 'enterprise and local initiative must be given manifold support and developed at all cost'.[15] In the meantime the defeat of the Left Opposition (headed by Trotsky) in the late 1920s had meant that the strong Marxist line of critique of the early period had given rise to a market-friendlier approach coupled with the brutality of state terror. The following statement of Stalin's henchman Prosecutor-General Vyshinsky countered the 'withering away thesis' with the statement: 'History demonstrates that under socialism law is raised to the highest level of development.' For Vyshinsky, 'the state [is] an instrumentality in the hands of the dominant class [that] creates its law, safeguarding and protecting specifically the interests of that class'. And thus 'our laws are the expression of the will of our people as it directs and creates history under the leadership of the working class'.[16] These strong statements in support of 'proletarian law' assume that the institution of law is neutral and can be filled with any given class content according to the will of the dominant class. What was missed is Pashukanis' insight that it is the very form of law as tied to the institution of subjectivity and private right that overdetermines content and ties the institution inexorably to the structure and logic of commodification.

5. BETWEEN STRUCTURE AND AGENCY: THE QUESTION OF CONSTITUENT POWER

That the juridical concept of the subject was key to Pashukanis' general theory and focus of his critique was not incidental; the question of subjectivity, the question whether the collective subject would be in a position to carry the emancipatory project or whether it was inexorably caught in the logic of bourgeois rule, has always been central to Marxist thought, and, once again, it hinges on an antireductionist view of the political economy of law. With the Hegelian strand of Marxism the subject would come

---

[15] Quoted in Head 2007, 102.
[16] Quoted in Berman 1963, 55.

into its own as agent of emancipation, in the dialectical unfolding of History. But such faith in the redemptive role of history was tested on a number of fronts. The 'negative dialectic' associated with the Frankfurt School, while steeped in Hegelian thought, afforded the subject no 'transcendence' from its capture in the capitalist imaginary, especially under conditions of fascism and (later in the work of Horkheimer in particular) 'really existing socialism'; in both cases negation remained the constitutive moment (see section 3 of this chapter). And the promise that the subject of history would transcend the condition of that entrapment in the very undertaking of collective, revolutionary praxis (a theory most intriguingly put forward by Lukács) was rebutted in the emphatically anti-Hegelian currents of Marxism associated with the rise of structuralist thought. For structuralists, the unfolding of subjectivity in history would only ever repeat the logic of the reproduction of the structure of capitalism, and it was naïve to assume that the subject would be in a position to resist the reification that ran alongside it with the development of capitalism. Among the most important instances of this line of thought are the theories that emanated from the École Normale Supérieure in Paris around the key figure of Louis Althusser, perhaps the most typical exponent of the anti-Hegelian, structuralist current of Marxism, with its emphasis on the structural determination of subject positions and possibilities of action *without* dialectical overcoming. Reading *Capital* closely, Althusser takes from Marx the notion that the fetish phenomenon – the commodity form – on which capitalist exchange is based arises as cooriginal with what may be envisaged as the possibilities of human association under capitalist conditions.[17] It cannot be stepped back from, or put to question dialectically. In one of his most quoted essays, on the function of 'ideological state apparatuses', Althusser distinguishes between forms of capitalist state repression (police, prison service, military) and ideological forms that operate behind the backs of agents, as it were, in calling them forth ('*interpellating*' them is his term) under specific descriptions to occupy subject positions that reproduce the relations of production according to the logic and the exigencies of capitalism. The subject of these relations is not in a position to step behind the ideological forms and put them to question because they inform constitutively what it means to be a 'free' subject and what it means to exercise those freedoms. The constitutional imaginary of bourgeois democracy cannot be put to question by actors who rely on its *semiosis* of freedom, subjecthood and self-determination to make sense of their social experience. To contest bourgeois democracy was to transcend those terms, and with them the juridical condition of the construction of sense, a condition that a successful revolution alone could deliver.

A similar impasse relating to the subject position is theorised in the tradition of revolutionary syndicalism in Italy and the post-Gramscian currents of the autonomist syndicalist movements. The central question for them became how to claim a speaking position for the subject that breaks with the system of capitalist social reproduction. For Antonio Negri, the most famous theorist among the radicals of the workers' movements, the (collective) revolutionary subject, as wielder of constituent power, must remain underdetermined and resist subsumption under the dominant symbolic order. To

---

[17] Note the important overlap with Pashukanis at this point, though Althusser makes no explicit reference to the Bolshevik theorist. For one of the most interesting works combining both Pashukanis and Althusser, see Edelman 1979.

pick up the thread of this incongruent representation, we will need to go back to a certain Italian current of Marxism out of which Negri's work grew: the 'operaismo' movement of the 1960s that formed the springboard for the later 'autonomist' current of Italian Marxism in the 1970s, in which Negri was a leading figure. What is distinctive about the autonomist movement is the centrality within it of a project of working class *self-valorisation*, and with this self-valorisation, crucially, a resistance to accept the hegemonic representational orders of capitalism, a refusal to define the movement through its (capitalism's) vocabularies. What this entailed was the rather paradoxical refusal to identify the revolutionary-subject-to-be – the working class – through work, since the system of work, they argued, provides a context within which the self-identification of the proletariat as potential revolutionary subject is always-already undercut. That is because, to put it in the terms Marx used in the Manifesto, 'a class of labourers, live only so long as they find work, and find work only so long as their labour increases capital' (1996, 7). At the conceptual level, the possibility for *self*-identification of the working class is cancelled in this undertaking. Thus, practically, political action for the Autonomia was undertaken in terms of refusal to work, wildcat strikes, spontaneous slowdowns, acts of sabotage, bad-faith reformism (the political programme of demanding more from management than management could possibly deliver, and so on). And Negri called upon this 'project of destruction' to undo the symbolic grip that capitalism exerted on the proletariat with its control – at the very point of the recovery of meaning – of the vocabularies and representational orders within which self-valorisation might have taken place. The injunction of Operaismo and then Autonomia to undertake political praxis 'dal punto di vista operaio' becomes tragically both urgent and impossible because that point of view forever slips back to existing schemata, and makes alternatives visible only in terms of dislocations it marks rather than any consistent programme of 'self-valorisation'. 'We find ourselves', protests Negri, 'with a revolutionary tradition that has pulled the flags of the bourgeoisie out of the mud' (Negri 1991, 37). Like the Marx of the *18th Brumaire*, his call is to 'let the dead bury the dead'. And yet, despite its tragic contradiction, for Negri it is of paramount importance to remain with the project of self-valorisation.

The most interesting work as far as legal theory is concerned is undertaken in the field of constitutional and labour law (Negri 1994; 2005). If 'to speak of constituent power is to speak of democracy', as Negri puts it in the opening sentence of his early work on the concept (*Il potere costituente*, translated as *Insurgencies*), the fact that it appears as constitutional, that is, comes always-already implicated with constitutional form, means that democracy is already straitjacketed to the conditions and limitations of capitalist legality. To be valid, popular will must be imputed to the constitution that establishes the conditions under which the popular will can be expressed *as* sovereign. Law and democracy are reconciled only via the suppression of a paradox that impacts on constitution making as never, inevitably, fully democratic, if democracy *ex hypothesi* must remain sovereign to contest and determine the conditions of its exercise. The tradition of thinking about revolution – a tradition that also informs Negri's work – in the variety of its instantiations typically returned to the promise of *constituent power* to face up to precisely that reflexive question. 'What is constituent power from the perspective of juridical theory?' asks Negri, whose priority of course lies with constituent power as an expression of the potentiality *to break with* the logic of capitalist reproduction. Here is Negri (1999, 2):

> [The constituent] is the source of production of constitutional norms – that is, the power to make a constitution ... in other words the power to establish a new juridical arrangement ... This is an extremely paradoxical definition: ... Never as clearly as in the case of constituent power has juridical theory been caught in the game of affirming and denying, absolutising and limiting that is characteristic of its logic (as Marx continually affirms.)

Negri tracks a sequence of reductions, inflicted by juridical reason in the context of its 'taming' and instrumentalising the constituent, and in the process inflicting 'every type of distortion': 'Constituent power must itself be reduced to the norm of the production of law; it must be incorporated into the established power. Its expansiveness is only shown as an interpretative norm, as a form of control of the State's constitutionality, as an activity of constitutional revision.'

In this the juridical 'covers over and alters the nature of constituent power ... This is how the juridical theory of constituent power solves the allegedly vicious circle of the reality of constituent power. But isn't closing political power within representation nothing but the negation of the reality of constituent power?' (Negri 1999, 3–4).

The 'interpreters of law' are at pains to maintain the 'vitality' of the system, while navigating that vitality away from any kind of dangerous democratic excess. Among the jurists, for Negri it is only Schmitt who posed the question of constituent power 'with extraordinary intensity' (Ibid, 24). In fact, the 'constituent' is preserved in Schmitt in the logic of the decision, that is never purely of the order of the 'constituted'. But in tying it to the logic of the exception, Schmitt 'capitulates to the force of an attraction that is by now devoid of principles' (Ibid, 21). In this way, the question of constituent power is rightly disentangled from the grip of the exception and replaced in the material context of radical social change.

6. CONCLUSION

The fall of the Berlin Wall, the loud proclamations of the 'end of History', and the rise of globalisation and its supranational and international legal forms initially at least appeared to have pushed Marxist thinking aside for good. Critical legal scholars often preferred alternative views on the law, borrowing from different traditions and schools.[18] While often recognised as the main source of inspiration for critical thought, critical legal scholars have often dismissed (at times with good reason) central tenets of Marx's work (for example, dialectic materialism) and borrowed their conceptual apparatuses from other disciplines. In the process they also neglected one of Marx's key contributions: the materialist understanding of the social order. It is our contention

---

[18] See, for an overview, the chapters on deconstruction, aesthetics and postcritique in this Handbook.

that legal analysis can still benefit – in the current condition of financial sovereignty, more than ever – from the renewal of this materialist conception of the law and of its forms.

Let us highlight three methodological tenets of a materialist conception of law. First, the materialist study of law must maintain the political economy clearly within its sights, in terms of the analysis of production, reproduction and creation of value. Let us be clear: production and reproduction have to be tied to a broad, not a rigid, definition of labour. That is to say that a materialist analysis of the law should go well beyond the boundaries of a political economy based on waged labour. A second clarification follows: the legal analysis will have to take into account the political economy of the *concrete* legal order, as only in this way is it possible to retrieve how the production of economic value determines what counts as labour. That is to say, the forms of the legal order and its institutions will have to be studied against the background of the logic of valorisation concretely (and differentially) at play each time. It has been a key argument throughout this chapter that the formation of the legal order has to be understood as itself a field of struggle, and not as the *outcome* of the operation of the political economy.

The second tenet of the materialist study of law stems directly from the first and concerns the relation between the legal order and society. The materialist study of law cannot begin with the assertion of a difference between the economic base and the superstructure, because it studies the law and its forms as *internal* to the production and reproduction of the social order.[19] Accordingly, law is immanent to the social order, not an epiphenomenon of the economic order, and class struggle both shapes and is shaped by legal instruments. The emphasis on the ordering properties of law and its internal connection with class struggle implies a relative autonomy of the legal field,[20] and the recognition of the contingency of certain legal decisions (that is, legal arrangements could have been otherwise) which leaves open the potential for a genuine political imagination.[21]

The third point, which is a consequence of the above recognition of the solidity and at the same time contingency of the legal order, concerns the value of legal critique. Here, the task of a material study of law is, first of all, to study the legal and political institutions of a concrete regime of valorisation and, second, to imagine and theorise alternative institutions. For this reason, the theory of constituent power remains an essential component of the materialist study of law. An accurate reconstruction of the main tenets of the legal order and its procedures is a precondition for conceiving alternative avenues for political and legal action.

---

[19] This type of analysis is very close to two influential sociolegal approaches to legal studies. The first one is inspired by Gramsci (see Gill 2008) and the second by legal institutionalism (see Romano 2017).

[20] See Poulantzas 2015. Poulantzas maintains the necessary political unity of every capitalist social order and he assumes that the state is its guarantor. However, the state is the condensation of certain social forces around a number of objectives, assuming that these forces are capable of political organisation and action.

[21] An example of work in this vein is Rancière 2012.

BIBLIOGRAPHY

Althusser, Louis (2005) *For Marx*, London: Verso.
Beard, Charles (1913) *An Economic Interpretation of the Constitution of the United States*, New York: Macmillan, 1913.
Berman, Harold (1963) *Justice in the USSR*, Cambridge MA: Harvard University Press.
Chignola, Sandro (2018) *Foucault's Politics of Philosophy*, Abingdon: Routledge.
Christodoulidis, Emilios (2007) 'Against Substitution: The Constitutional Thinking of Dissensus', in Loughlin, Martin & Walker, Neil (eds), *The Paradox of Constitutionalism*, Oxford: Oxford University Press, 189–208.
Edelman, Bernard (1979) *Ownership of the Image*, Abingdon: Routledge.
Engels, Friedrich & Kautsky, Karl (1977) 'Juridical Socialism' (or. 1887), 7 *Politics & Society* 199–220.
Gill, Stephen (2008) *Power and Resistance in the New World Order*, Basingstoke: Palgrave.
Guastini, Riccardo (1982) 'La ambigua utopia: Marx criticato da Kelsen', 9 *Sociologia del diritto* 5–22.
Head, Michael (2007) *Pashukanis: A Critical Reappraisal*, Abingdon: Routledge.
Kelsen, Hans (1955) *The Communist Theory of Law*, New York: Praeger.
Lassalle, Ferdinand (2002) 'On the Essence of Constitutions' (or. ed. 1862), available at www.marxists.org/history/etol/newspape/fi/vol03/no01/lassalle.htm
Manero, Juan (1986) 'Sobre la crítica de Kelsen al Marxismo', 3 *Doxa* 191–231.
Marx, Karl (1976) *The German Ideology*, New York: Progress Publishers.
Marx, Karl (1991a) *Capital. Vol I*, London: Penguin.
Marx, Karl (1991b) *Capital. Vol III*, London: Penguin.
Marx, Karl (2005) *Early Writings*, London: Penguin.
Mouffe, Chantal (ed.) (1999) *The Challenge of Carl Schmitt*, London: Verso.
Negri, Antonio (1991) *The Savage Anomaly: The Power of Spinoza's Metaphysics and Politics*, Minneapolis: University of Minnesota Press.
Negri, Antonio & Hardt, Michael (1994) *Labour of Dionysus*, Minneapolis: University of Minnesota Press.
Negri, Antonio (1999) *Insurgencies: Constituent Power and the Modern State*, Minneapolis: University of Minnesota Press.
Negri, Antonio (2005) *Books for Burning*, London: Verso.
Pashukanis, Evgeni (1978) *The General Theory of Law and Marxism*, London: Pluto Press.
Poulantzas, Nicos (2015) *State, Power, Socialism*, London: Verso.
Rancière, Jacques (2012) *Proletarian Nights*, London: Verso.
Romano, Santi (2017) *The Legal Order*, Abingdon: Routledge.
Schmitt, Carl (2006) *The Nomos of the Earth*, New York: Telos Press.
Schmitt, Carl (2007) *The Concept of the Political*, Chicago: University of Chicago Press.
Stuchka, Peteris (1988) *Selected Writings on Soviet Law and Marxism*, Armonk, NY: Sharpe.
Tronti, Mario (2010) *Operai e capitale*, Roma: Derive & Approdi.

7. Critical theory of the state
Bob Jessop

Any discussion of the form, functions and effectivity of law from a state-theoretical perspective should adopt a similar approach to both. This discussion implies at least some differentiation between law and the state – a distinction that is not always made or that, if made, can still lead to onesided analyses or conflation. Thus, while some analyses of the state in constitutional terms reduce its form and competences to those inscribed in law, others reduce law to a simple tool of state power, with illegal actions always a political option. I therefore begin with an account of the state as a social relation and then consider its implications for law. Key issues include the historical specificity of the state and law in capitalist societies, the institutional boundaries of the state (including the division between the public and private spheres) and the capitalist market economy, the relation between the form and functions of the state and law in normal conditions and crisis periods and the implications of globalization for the character of law and the nature of state power. Many other topics could also be considered.

For a long time, the dominant tradition in critical state theory was Marxism-Leninism. This treats the state as an essentially repressive instrument whose control enables the economically dominant class to exercise its dictatorship over subordinate classes. It was also argued that the nature of the capitalist state corresponded to its changing economic base. Thus, while liberal competitive capitalism was associated with a bourgeois democratic order, the growth of imperialism and the subsequent onset of the so-called general crisis of capitalism have provoked political reaction and prompted authoritarian and fascistic tendencies in the state. This approach usually sees law as an automatic reflection or explicit complement of the economic base in the sphere of private law, and it treats public law as a coercive instrument of political class domination manipulated by the dominant class or class fraction. In most cases juridical ideology is also presented as a leading (if not the leading) form of mystification and legitimation of economic and political power relations. And, just as Marxism-Leninism argues that different stages in capitalist development are reflected in changes in the nature and functions of the state, it also claims that law and the rule of law are undermined by the spread of imperialism and the 'general crisis of capitalism' (for an extended review, see Jessop 1982).

What is involved in a critical theory of the state? A useful starting point (but only a starting point, not an end point) is the Continental European tradition of general state theory (*allgemeine Staatstheorie*). This identifies three elements of the state: (1) a clearly demarcated core territory; (2) a politically organized coercive, administrative and symbolic apparatus with both general and specific powers; and (3) a permanent or stable population on which the state's political authority and decisions are regarded – at least by that apparatus, if not those subject to it – as legally binding. All three elements have obvious constitutional and legal aspects, including issues of external and internal sovereignty, the mutual recognition of statehood and the legitimacy of governments, the juridicopolitical architecture of the state apparatus and its competencies, the demarcation of the private and public spheres and definition of the rights and obligations of the state's subjects or citizens. Other topics include the legal aspects of failed, collapsed, shadow or rogue states. Some commentators add a fourth element: the state idea, which defines the nature and purposes of the state and provides a reference point for concerted state action. On this basis, I have suggested the following four-element definition of the state:

> The core of the state apparatus comprises a relatively unified ensemble of socially embedded, socially regularized, and strategically selective institutions and organizations (*Staatsapparat*) whose socially accepted function is to define and enforce collectively binding decisions on the members of a society (*Staatsvolk*) in a given territorial area (*Staatsgebiet*) in the name of the common interest or general will of an imagined political community identified with that territory (*Staatsidee*). (Jessop 2015: 49)

This definition includes formal and substantive features and also indicates the historical and social contingencies of the state and state power. This opens several paths to critical state theory, inviting questions on such topics as the sources of the state's ability to act *as if* it were a unified subject, the social biases inscribed in the form and competences of the state apparatus, the sources of juridical and political legitimacy, the origins and effects of legitimacy crises, the demarcation of frontiers and the juridico-political and sociospatial organization of the territory controlled by a state, struggles to define the nature and purpose of the state, and so on. Such questions are often posed in critical state theory from a class or capital-theoretical perspective but can also be raised from other critical standpoints. Here I will focus on these perspectives but locate them within the framework of analysis of the form and function of the law and the state. I begin with Karl Marx.

1. KARL MARX ON LAW AND THE STATE

Marx did not develop a coherent theory of these topics. He adopted different approaches for different purposes, leaving a fragmented, incomplete, ambiguous and inconsistent theoretical legacy. This has not stopped efforts to reconstruct *the* Marxian theory of the state based on some of the broad assertions about the class nature of the state and state power in Marx's presentation of the materialist approach to history. But these assertions were revealed as too sweeping whenever Marx undertook specific theoretical and historical analyses of state forms, political regimes, policies and interventions, and/or explored how the exercise of state power reflected the changing balance of class and nonclass forces in different periods and conjunctures.

Marx's early work described how specific laws or state actions served as instruments of class rule. For example, his articles for the *Rheinische Zeitung* in 1842–3 presented a radical moral as well as social critique of the use of legal and administrative power to advance specific propertied interests or to defend the state itself.[1] In other contexts, however, he analysed how state managers could exploit stalemated class conflicts or political crises to gain autonomy and employ state power to reimpose 'law and order', engineer social change, or pursue their own narrow and often parasitic interests. Marx's examples of this phenomenon included Caesarism, absolutism and Bismarckism. But this view was presented most famously in his studies of France in the 1850s and 1860s under Louis Bonaparte (for a general overview of his views on state autonomy, see Draper 1977: 311–590). These contrasting views have prompted much debate but actually distract attention from Marx's key contributions in this area.

A more significant and enduring account was first presented in the *Critique of Hegel's Philosophy of Law* (Marx 1975a) and the *Introduction to the Critique of Hegel's Philosophy of Right* (Marx 1975b). These texts were based on intensive reading on the history of states and societal development in Europe and the USA, the English and French revolutions, and political and constitutional theory (see Marx 1981). In critiquing Hegel, Marx presented the state as an alienated form of political organization based on the separation of rulers and ruled. This separation takes different forms in different class-based modes of production. Regarding the emerging bourgeois social formation, Marx argued against Hegel that it rested on the institutional separation of (a) the 'public sphere', with the state at its centre, in which politics is oriented to the collective interest; and (b) 'civil society', which is dominated by private property and individual self-interest. Thus, to Hegel's claim that the modern state could and would represent the common, organic interests of all members of society, Marx replied that it could represent only an 'illusory' community of interest that obscured the continuing antagonisms, crass materialism and egoistic conflicts of a society based on private property and waged labour. Hegel seemed unaware that the fundamental contradictions in civil society would undermine attempts to secure political unification and social cohesion. True emancipation and a true community of interests required the abolition of private property. Marx refined these views over 40 years and presented them in increasingly materialist rather than philosophical terms. His clearest statement of this assessment occurs in his analysis of the 1871 Paris Commune as a radically new form of political organization that sought to abolish the separation of rulers and ruled (see Marx 1989). The separation of rulers and ruled and its instantiation in particular economic, legal and political forms is the key to reading Marx's work on law, the state and state power.

In *Capital*, Volume III, Marx encapsulated this concern as follows:

> The specific economic form, in which unpaid surplus-labour is pumped out of direct producers, determines the relationship of rulers and ruled, as it grows directly out of production itself and, in turn, reacts upon it as a determining element. Upon this, however, is founded the entire formation of the economic community which grows up out of the production relations themselves, thereby simultaneously its specific political form. It is always the direct relationship of the owners of the conditions of production to the direct producers ... which reveals the innermost secret, the hidden basis of the entire social

---

[1] For example, K. Marx, 'Debates on the law on the thefts of wood', MECW, vol. 1, pp. 224–63; 'Justification of the correspondent from the Mosel', MECW, vol. 1, pp. 332–58.

structure and with it the political form of the relation of sovereignty and dependence, in short, the corresponding specific form of the state. (1978a: 777–8)

This 'form analysis' approach implies that the social relations of production *shape* the social relations of domination and servitude. Thus, a political order based on the rule of law, equality before the law and a unified sovereign state naturally 'fits' or 'corresponds with' an economic order based on private property, the wage relation and profit-oriented, market-mediated exchange. Only in the capitalist mode of production are classes defined through relations of production that are disembedded from broader institutional forms (such as the family or kinship, political bonds or religion). This 'frees' workers to sell their labour power on the labour market, but also turns them into 'wage slaves'. There is a dual relation at work here. In the *labour market*, we find 'a very Eden of the innate rights of man. There alone rule Freedom, Equality, Property and Bentham' (1976a: 186). In the *labour process*, however, we find economic exploitation and the despotism of capital. A similar duality occurs in the constitutional state based on the rule of law. Marx indicated this in his 1844 'Draft Plan for a Work on the Modern State', writing that '[a]ll elements exist in duplicate form, as civic elements and [those of] the state' (1976b: 666). Thus, on the one hand, a constitutional state guarantees the innate rights of men, whatever their class position, based on ending feudal and guild privileges; on the other hand, it defends the interests of capital in general when these are threatened even as it claims to maintain order in the national interest. In this sense, class conflicts may be transposed from the economic into the political sphere but, reflecting the institutional separation of the two spheres, they normally take different forms in each.

These remarks indicate that form analysis is not 'merely formal' or superficial: 'social forms' have significant material effects. While political society may be 'the official expression' of civil society (1982: 96), it is nonetheless a mediated, refracted expression. The fundamental – and fundamentally contradictory – separation-in-unity of the economic and political moments of class domination means that the legal and political spheres do not directly reflect the antagonisms in civil society. Specific state policies cannot be read off directly from current economic conditions. Thus, while noting the role of economic circumstances, conflicts, contradictions and crises, Marx also considered how policies, politics and political regimes were shaped by the motley diversity of state forms, political regimes, political discourses and the changing balance of political forces (for example his analyses of class struggles in France and the Eighteenth Brumaire of Louis Bonaparte: Marx 1978b, 1979).

Marx also explored how form problematizes function. For example, in *The Class Struggles in France, 1848–1850*, he highlighted a fundamental contradiction at the heart of a democratic constitution. Whereas it gives *political power* through universal suffrage to the proletariat, peasantry and petty bourgeoisie, whose *social slavery* the constitution is to perpetuate, it sustains the *social power* of the bourgeoisie by guaranteeing private property rights even as they lose direct control over the state. 'From the ones [the subordinate classes] it demands that they should not go forward from political to social emancipation; from the others that they should not go back from social to political restoration' (1978b: 79). This raises the key question of how the antagonisms and conflicts between capital, landlords and workers (and other classes, such as peasants) can be held within the political unity formed by the state.

A possible solution consistent with Marx's historical analyses but not spelt out explicitly is that this is possible on two conditions. First, economic class struggles must be confined within the logic of the market (that is, for workers, over wages, hours, working conditions, prices) and moderated or suspended if this threatens capital accumulation. Second, political class struggles must be confined within the logic of a constitutional struggle for electoral majorities to influence policies legitimated by the (illusory) general or national interest of the state's citizens. Interesting examples of these principles at work are Marx's analyses of the repeal of the Corn Laws (1976a: 15, 286ff, 667–9) and the introduction of factory legislation to control hours, working conditions and the use of child and female labour (1976a: 283–307, 483–505). However, when workers use their economic power to challenge political authority (for example, through a general strike) and/or workers use political power to challenge market relations (for example, by expropriating property rights without compensation), bourgeois domination is fundamentally threatened. This may trigger an open war of class struggle through which the dominant classes seek to suspend the democratic constitution or concentrate power in an executive that escapes democratic control. Marx discussed this in various cases but especially in relation to France.

Marx's form analytical approach has been very influential in Marxist legal and state theory. In particular, the principal concern of the so-called capital logic school is to derive the *form* of the capitalist state from the nature of capital and/or to establish those *functional prerequisites* of accumulation whose satisfaction must be mediated through state activity. However, there is little agreement about the best starting points for such a derivation or the most significant aspects of the form and functions of the capitalist state. But there is general agreement among the better examples of this school that one should not move directly from high levels of abstraction to the analysis of specific political conjunctures: it is essential to examine the complex system of mediations that intervenes between the most abstract determinations and the immediacy of the concrete situation. This qualification is important and also applies to 'form analyses' of the legal system, and is recognized in the best examples of Marxist legal theory that start from the question of form.

2. EVGENY PASHUKANIS ON CAPITALIST LAW AND THE STATE

Marx's substantive analyses and method of presentation inspired Pashukanis (1891–1937) to ask:

> why does the dominance of a class take the form of official state domination? Or, which is the same thing, why is not the mechanism of state constraint created as the private mechanism of the dominant class? Why is it dissociated from the dominant class – taking the form of an impersonal mechanism of public authority isolated from society? (1978: 139)

His explanation for this constitutive absence of class as an explicit organizing principle of the capitalist type of state is that the bourgeoisie does not hold – or need to hold – a legal monopoly of power (1978: 185). He developed his analysis in two steps. First, he derived the specific historical form of bourgeois law from the essential qualities of commodity circulation under capitalism. He recalled Marx's observation that commodities cannot go to market and perform exchanges by themselves (1976a: 94–5). This requires subjects who enter into voluntary contractual relations in their capacities as owners of those commodities. Marx himself concluded that the economic relation between commodities must be complemented with a juridical relation between wilful subjects (Marx 1976a: 178–9). Pashukanis built on this argument to trace the coevolution of the legal subject as the bearer of rights and the commodity as a bearer of exchange value. He concluded that the logic of juridical concepts corresponds to the logic of the social relations of commodity-producing society. Only with the full development of commodity production did every person become 'man' (sic) in the abstract, all labour become socially useful labour in the abstract, every subject become an abstract legal subject, and the legal norm assume the pure form of abstract universal law. This occurs because the constant circulation of commodities facilitates a clear differentiation between the legal bearer of ownership rights and the objects in which alienable rights are held. Thus, while the precapitalist legal subject was a concrete individual with specific customary privileges, the legal subject of bourgeois society is the universal abstract bearer of all manner of claims. The kernel of the legal subject is the commodity owner, but the formal attributes of freedom and equality rooted in the economic sphere are readily generalized in other areas of civil society and the state (Pashukanis 1978: 109–33 and *passim*).

If the first step was to derive the specific form of bourgeois law, the second was to derive the specific form of the bourgeois state as an impersonal apparatus of public power that was distinct from the private sphere of civil society. Pashukanis posited that a constitutional state based on the rule of law (*Rechtsstaat*) is required by the nature of market relations among free, equal individuals. These must be mediated, supervised and guaranteed by an abstract collective subject with the authority to enforce rights in the interests of all parties to legal transactions. However, although the *Rechtsstaat* introduces clarity and stability into the bourgeois legal system, both are still rooted in capitalist relations of production (1978: 63–4, 80, 94, 104, 188).

Pashukanis's approach can also be applied to the modern tax state (*Steuerstaat*). A tax state gets revenue from its general power to levy taxes on the activities and subjects of an essentially private economic order, and this depends on its monopoly of coercion and its ability to set the currency in which taxes are paid. State revenues derive from taxes or loans guaranteed by the power to levy taxes. This distinguishes the capitalist type of state from states that use their own productive property to generate resources for use or sale (whether through strategic resources, such as oil or gas, through state-owned productive property, or sovereign wealth funds) and from private economic agents, individual or corporate, who must earn money through their own economic activities or valorize their own property before they can obtain goods and services from the market. Only with the rise of the constitutional state based on the rule of law which accompanied capitalist development in the West were taxes transformed: first, from payments linked to precisely circumscribed tasks undertaken by the state into general contributions to state revenue spendable on any legitimate task; second, from extraordinary, irregular and overwhelmingly short-term imposts into regular and permanently levied taxes; and third, from payments that the monarch had to secure through negotiation to payments that effectively became compulsory (cf Krätke 1984). Interestingly, this third feature is now in decline because transnational firms and banks as well as many wealthy households can now choose how to present their accounts for tax purposes and may 'offshore' wealth and income beyond the formal reach of local, national or even supranational states.

Pashukanis has been criticized for deriving the form of bourgeois law from commodity circulation rather than from capitalist production. But other critical theorists have shown how the bourgeois legal order is overdetermined through the commodification of labour power and the resulting need to define the legal and political framework for orderly class relations (e.g., Tuschling 1976 on law and production relations; Fine 1984 on democracy and the rule of law; Kay and Mott 1982 on the labour contract; Buckel 2007 on legal subjectification). Another problem is that Pashukanis starts his derivation from commodity relations, which provides a plausible explanation for the form of private law and the impersonal authority of the capitalist state over the market economy. But this starting point cannot explain the nature of public law. Thus, he has been criticized for imposing a spurious unity on the legal order by generalizing illegitimately from the economic region to all legal relations. However, his key claim was that the legal form is suitable whenever there is a conflict of private interests (1978: 81–2). He does not generalize beyond this argument. Moreover, while Pashukanis does posit a certain unity among legal relations as a precondition of the general theory of law, he emphasizes that the unity of private and public laws is historically constituted, largely formal, inherently contradictory and particularly unstable (1978: 47, 60, 96, 101–6, 137, 167, 176–7). Indeed, this fragile unity depends on the elaboration of a general juridicopolitical ideology shared by the administrative and judicial apparatuses (1978: 40–1, 42–3, 68, 76–7, 93–4, 139–40, 146, 148–9, 167). Finally, Pashukanis has been charged with ignoring the major part played by repression in the legal order and the bourgeois state. However, not only did he fully subscribe (rightly or wrongly) to the Marxist-Leninist view of the state as a machine for class repression (see, for example, Lenin 1964) and emphasize the role of *raison d'état* and naked expediency in certain fields of operation (especially in periods of open class war); he also highlighted the self-contradictory appearance of law as subjective freedom coupled with external regulation and, indeed, tended to give greater weight to the role of organized violence than to individual will in the sphere of public law (particularly in the field of criminal law) (1978: 62–3, 89, 97, 137–8, 162, 167, 173).

The work of Pashukanis and his epigones represents a significant advance on the crude economism and/or simple-minded voluntarism of a Marxism-Leninism that ignores form in favour of content and then reduces the latter to an effect of the material base and/or class will. But it is one thing to show the formal correspondence between the basic forms of law, the legal order and the *Rechtsstaat* and their various functions at the level of the pure mode of production, and another to explain the historical constitution and periodization of legal forms, how their specific content and efficacy is shaped and how they are overdetermined through other social forms and/or forces.

3. ANTONIO GRAMSCI ON HEGEMONY

In contrast to Pashukanis, Gramsci (1891–1937) was more interested in the substantive modalities of state power than the state's formal juridicopolitical features. He suggested that the modern state in its integral sense (*lo stato integrale*) includes 'elements which need to be referred back to the notion of civil society (in the sense that one might say that the State = 'political society + civil society', in other words, hegemony armoured with coercion)' (1971: 263). He therefore studied the state as a complex social relation that articulates state *and nonstate* institutions and practices around particular economic, political and societal imaginaries, projects and strategies. 'Civil society', a domain of ostensibly 'private' institutions, organizations and movements, was an integral part of the state and, *a fortiori*, of politics and policy.

In this context, Gramsci identified two main modes of class domination: force and hegemony. Force involves the use of a coercive apparatus to bring the mass of people into conformity and compliance with the demands of a specific mode of production. It can be employed by private groups (for example, fascist squads) as well as state organs, and its mobilization and impact depend on economic and ideological factors as well as police and military considerations. Hegemony involves the creation and reproduction of the 'active consent' of dominated groups by the ruling class through their exercise of political, intellectual and moral leadership. The ruling class must take systematic account of popular interests and demands; shift position and make compromises on secondary issues to maintain support in an inherently unstable and fragile system of political relations (without, however, sacrificing essential interests); and organize this support to attain 'national' goals that also serve the fundamental long-term interests of the dominant class. Just as the moment of force is institutionalized in an array of coercive apparatuses, hegemony is crystallized and mediated through a series of ideological apparatuses dispersed throughout the social formation. Thus, although the government engages in hegemonic practices, they mostly occur outside it. Indeed, Gramsci suggests that they occur mostly in civil society or the sphere of so-called private bodies, such as the Church, trade unions, schools, the mass media or parties, and that they are actualized by intellectuals, whose role is to elaborate ideologies, educate the people, organize and unify social forces and secure the hegemony of the dominant group. Note that Gramsci discussed intermediate forms between direct force and hegemony. These include absorption of the leaders of subaltern organizations and movements, piecemeal reforms to preempt revolution and fraud-corruption (see Gramsci 1971: 80–2, 95, 105–20, 230–2).

Gramsci's work has inspired a wide range of theoretical reflections and empirical research on struggles over hegemony and juridicopolitical responses to crises of hegemony. Thus, while his approach says less about the form of law in bourgeois societies, it offers many insights into how law works and its role in securing class domination. An influential British example is the series of analyses by Stuart Hall and collaborators on the place of law, the police, judicial apparatuses, and so on, in the articulation of bourgeois hegemony. They argued that this position changes across different stages in capital accumulation and different forms of state, illustrating their claim from legal despotism in the emergent agrarian capitalist state of eighteenth-century England and the rule of law in the liberal state of nineteenth century industrial capital (Hall et al. 1978: 186–94, 206–8; cf. Hay et al. 1975; Thompson, 1975). They also investigated the changing role of 'policing' (in its widest sense) in the postwar British state as it engaged in a general 'law and order' campaign in the 1970s to reinforce the element of coercion in bourgeois rule to compensate for the decline in spontaneous consent (Hall et al. 1978: 272–97; for a critique, see Jessop et al., 1988). Gramsci's work has also been influential in the field of subaltern studies, which used Gramscian concepts and methods to study the legal and administrative forms of colonial rule in the Indian subcontinent and elsewhere (for a good summary, see Prakash 1994).

A further development is the respecification of Gramsci's approach in more contemporary theoretical terms. Thus, Jessop has suggested that the state in its integral sense comprises 'government + governance in the shadow of hierarchy'. The last term in this definition denotes the indirect influence that states may exercise over other actors or forces in political and civil society through the real or imagined threat of executive or legislative action where these forces challenge their political authority. This respecification suggests that state power (a) involves state capacities unique to the state (such as its constitutionalized monopoly of organized coercion, tax powers, legal sovereignty, and positive law), its role in mobilizing and allocating money and credit, and its strategic use of intelligence, statistics and other kinds of knowledge to guide politics and policies; (b) depends on the state's capacity to mobilize active consent or passive compliance from forces situated and/or operating beyond its legally defined juridicopolitical boundaries, using modes of governance or governmentalization that penetrate the wider society; and (c) includes contested practices of metagovernance or *collibration* to strategically rebalance modes of government and governance to improve the effectiveness of indirect as well as direct state intervention and/or alter the balance of forces within and beyond the state (Jessop 2015; Meuleman 2008). Metagovernance is not a purely technical or technocratic process but, as with other aspects of state power, involves efforts to secure and/or rework a wider 'unstable equilibrium of compromise' organized around specific objects, techniques and subjects of government/ governance. Those engaged in metagovernance may redraw the inherited public–private divide, alter the forms of interpenetration between the political system and other functional systems, and modify the relations between these systems and civil society in the light of their (perceived) impact on state capacities.

Rephrased in these terms, Gramsci's notion of the integral state retains its relevance to class analysis but can be extended to other aspects of the state and state power, enabling links to more mainstream forms of political and administrative analysis. The concept of 'government + governance in the shadow of hierarchy' can, for example, inform thinking about the polity, politics and policy and assist in the disambiguation of notions such as politicization. First, the nature of the *polity* is shaped by the 'lines of difference' drawn between the state and its 'constitutive outside', whether this comprises an unmarked residuum external to the political sphere (such as state vs society, public vs private) or one or more marked spheres with their own institutional order, operational logics, subjects and practices (e.g., the religious, economic, legal, educational or scientific fields). This is more productive analytically than the notion of 'political society + civil society'. Moreover, politicization extends the frontiers of the polity (penetrating or colonizing the nonpolitical sphere[s] and subordinating it/them to political factors, interests, values and forces). Analogously, *depoliticization* rolls these frontiers back, and *repoliticization* reintegrates depoliticized spheres into the political (Jessop 2014). Their overall significance for politicization broadly considered nonetheless depends on how they are connected to changes in politics and policy.

4. NICOS POULANTZAS ON THE STATE AS A SOCIAL RELATION

Poulantzas (1936–79) studied law but later wrote on many aspects of capitalism. Law nonetheless kept a central place in his theoretical and political analyses. Building on Marx and Gramsci, he posited that 'the state is a social relation'. Less elliptically, this implies that state power is the form-determined (institutionally mediated) condensation of a shifting balance of forces oriented to the exercise of capacities and powers associated with particular political forms and institutions as these are embedded in the wider social formation (Poulantzas 1978). This argument was already present in his earlier analyses, albeit not yet phrased in explicitly strategic-relational terms, and I present the earlier work and then comment on later developments.

4.1 On Private Individuation and Public Unity

In his early legal analyses, Poulantzas criticized previous Marxist work for failing to specify a distinctive theoretical object of legal inquiry. Marxists had too often reduced law to a reflex of the economic base or treated it in a hyperpoliticized way as an embodiment of the will of the dominant class. Poulantzas responded that law must be studied in terms of its specific place and function within capitalist reproduction (1964, 1965a, 1966a, 1967). Thus, economically, he noted how law sanctions social relations of production and exploitation by representing them as legal rights attached to private property, organizes the sphere of circulation through contractual and commercial law and regulates the state's intervention in the economic field (1974: 322–4; cf 1973: 53, 163, 214, 228; 1975: 39, 191). It also interpellates economic agents as individual juridical subjects rather than as members of antagonistic classes. This 'isolation effect' encourages competition among individuals, trades or sectors for economic advantage by distracting attention from overarching class relations (1973: 130–1, 213–14, 275–6, 310; 1978: 63-70, 86–8). Conversely, the isolation effect produced by law and juridico-political ideology also provides the basis for a 'unifying effect' in the 'public' sphere (1973: 132). The sovereignty of a liberal democratic *Rechtsstaat* with its distinctive hierarchical bureaucratic framework requires political forces to compete for power in the name of the people-nation. In this sense, the juridicopolitical superstructure unifies those whom it has first disunified. Poulantzas argued that the capitalist state represents itself as the strictly political, public unity of the people-nation considered as the abstract sum of formally free and equal legal subjects. It is concerned with managing and reducing class antagonisms, and securing social cohesion (1973: 125, 133–4, 188–9, 215–16, 276–81, 288–91, 348–50; 1978: 49, 58, 63–5, 86–8). This analysis recalls Pashukanis's account of the impersonal nature of authority in the capitalist state, but Poulantzas provides more detail on the institutional architecture of the formal, general, universal and codified rational-legal norms (1973: 216, 226–7, 332, 347–50; 1975: 186; 1978: 59, 65, 76–7, 80–2, 88–91). He also notes that the rule of law and parliamentary sovereignty underpin the rational-legal legitimation of political class domination in bourgeois societies.

Moreover, as noted above, Poulantzas also draws on Gramsci's analyses of hegemony. He explores this in two respects: the unification of dominant class fractions into a coherent, enduring power bloc and the struggle to win active consent from the 'popular masses' by presenting its own interests as those of the entire people-nation. This involves the continual negotiation of interests within the power bloc as well as concessions to the economic-corporate demands of the dominated classes (1973: 137, 190–1). In addition, echoing Marx's comments on the fundamental contradiction in the democratic constitution, Poulantzas argued that the capitalist state must prevent the dominated classes from overcoming their economic isolation and social fracturing and engaging in political mobilization to overthrow the capitalist order (1973: 136–7, 140–1, 188–9, 284–89; 1975: 97–8, 157–8; 1978: 127, 140–1). His analysis of the formation of the power bloc and its hegemony is also a response to Marx's problem of how the dominant classes can abstain from demanding 'political restoration' (that is, attacking the political rights of subaltern classes) while retaining its social power.

Poulantzas argued that juridicopolitical ideology dominates the wider ideological field during the stage of liberal capitalism. It provides the ideological matrix of individuation necessary to capital accumulation as well as the matrix of people-nation that orients political and ideological struggles (1973: 206–10; 1974: 76–8; 1975: 286–99; 1978: 28). Moreover, even during ideological crises, juridicopolitical ideology often influences the forms in which the dominated classes live their revolt against exploitation and oppression (1973: 195, 213, 221–3, 310–12, 356–7; 1978: 86–9, 236). In monopoly capitalism, with its primacy of the political order rather than of free markets, the dominant ideological framework becomes economic growth. Securing this becomes crucial to the legitimacy of state power as well as the capitalist order. When these are threatened by economic and political crises, there is a further shift towards authoritarian populism and statism (see below).

4.2 Normal States and Exceptional Regimes

The significance of law and juridicopolitical ideology for state forms and political class struggles emerges clearly in Poulantzas's contrast between 'normal' states and 'exceptional' regimes. Drawing on Gramsci, Poulantzas argued that the former correspond to conjunctures in which bourgeois hegemony is stable and secure; the latter correspond to a crisis of hegemony (1973: 293; 1974: 11, 57–9, 72, 298, 313; 1976: 92–3). Representative democratic institutions facilitate the organic regulation and reorganization of 'unstable equilibria of compromise' in the power bloc as well as between this bloc and the popular masses. This inhibits major ruptures or breaks in the overall reproduction of bourgeois society. In contrast, the 'exceptional' regime develops in order to reorganize the power bloc and its relations with the people in response to a political and ideological crisis that cannot be resolved through normal democratic means. They suspend elections (with the possible exception of plebiscites or referendums), ban or control competing political parties, undermine autonomous mass organizations, dissolve or supervise private ideological apparatuses and employ coercion to restore the rule of capital (1973: 226; 1974: 152, 314–18, 330; 1976: 9, 92, 129). They also tighten executive control over the legislature and judiciary and centralize power at the expense of regional and local territorial authorities (1973: 333–49; 1974: 315–16, 327–30; 1975: 274–6; 1976: 50, 100–1; 1978: 58–60). In these circumstances the transfer of political power is less regulated by the constitution and legal constraints and depends on which part of the executive is dominant, such as the military, the bureaucracy, a fascist party, the political (or religious) police, and so on (1973: 226–7, 311; 1974: 320–4; 1978: 87–92).

However, all of these moves tend to 'congeal' the balance of forces prevailing at the time at which the exceptional regime was established and make it inflexible in the face of new disturbances and contradictions (1976: 30, 38, 48–50, 90–3, 106, 124). Poulantzas suggests that exceptional regimes will vary in their flexibility/rigidity depending on the extent to which: (a) a political apparatus is present to concentrate and channel mass support; (b) transmission belts and parallel power networks facilitate rapid changes in the distribution of power and thereby enable shifts in the balance of forces among competing interests or groups; and (c) the power bloc can secure support for its actions through a national-popular ideology that permeates key sections of the dominated as well as dominant class(es) (1974: 105–6, 128–9, 251–6, 329–30, 331; 1976: 83–5, 124). He cites fascism as approximating these conditions and military dictatorships as the form of regime most distant from them. Where these conditions are absent, the internal contradictions of the state apparatus are intensified, and it becomes harder to deal with economic and political crises (1976: 49–50, 55–7, 76–84, 94, 120–1, 124–6).

4.3 Authoritarian Statism

Poulantzas's analyses of 'exceptional' regimes influenced his later discussion of the changes in the 'normal' state. The new form of capitalist state is 'authoritarian statism' and its basic developmental tendency is 'intensified state control over every sphere of socio-economic life combined with radical decline of the institutions of political democracy and with draconian and multiform curtailment of so-called "formal" liberties' (1978: 203–4). Specifically, Poulantzas argued that the principal elements of 'authoritarian statism' comprise: first, a transfer of power from the legislature to the executive and the concentration of power within the latter; second, an accelerated fusion between the three branches of the state – legislature, executive and judiciary – accompanied by a decline in the rule of law (1973: 303–7, 310–15; 1975: 173; 1978: 222–5, 227–8); third, the concentration of power in prime ministerial or presidential offices, including their staffs (1973: 311–14; 1978: 221–28, 233, 238); fourth, the functional decline of political parties as the privileged interlocutors of the administration and the leading forces in organizing hegemony; fifth, the rise of a dominant 'state' party that acts as a political commissar at the heart of the administration and ensures its subordination to the summits of the executive and transmits the authoritarian state ideology to the popular masses, thereby reinforcing the plebiscitary legitimation of the new state form (1978: 233–7); sixth, the growth of a reserve repressive parastate apparatus whose role is preemptive policing of popular struggles and other threats to bourgeois hegemony (1978: 210, 212); and seventh, the growth of parallel networks that crosscut the formal organization of the state and exercise a decisive share in its activities (1978: 217–31). Poulantzas also argued that certain 'exceptional' features develop alongside the normal elements of this regime in response to the permanent instability of bourgeois hegemony and the general intensification of the inherent tendencies towards political and state crisis.

4.4 Law and the State

Poulantzas recognized that, despite the close relation between juridical structures (law) and political structures (the state), they are distinct, relatively autonomous levels, whose concrete combination depends on the mode of production and the social formation under consideration (1973: 42n). He focused on changes in their articulation linked to different phases of capitalism and/or periods of hegemonic stability or crisis. For example, he identifies a decline in the rule of law that accompanies the rise of monopoly capitalism. This has three aspects. First, in managing economic crises, law can no longer be confined to general, formal and universal norms enacted by parliament as the embodiment of the general will of the people-nation. Instead, legal norms are specified by the administration for particular conjunctures, situations and interests, and even their initial formulation has passed almost entirely from parliament to the administration (1978: 218–19). Second, a trend towards particularistic regulation reflects the imperatives of detailed economic intervention and the permanent instability of monopoly hegemony within the power bloc and over the people. Third, there is a rise in the preemptive policing of the potentially disloyal and deviant, which substitutes for the judicial punishment of clearly defined offences against the law (1978: 219–20). This said, the decline in the rule of law is not from a prior condition of perfect legality. Poulantzas argues that many state activities are not covered by juridical regulation and that the state also transgresses its own legality and allows for a certain rate of violation in other cases. Indeed, the monopoly of violence enjoyed by the state means that it can modify the law or suspend its operation when necessary to secure class domination. This is especially clear in exceptional regimes. In short, Poulantzas concludes that the state is a functional unity of legality and illegality and should not be reduced to a purely juridical structure (1978: 83–8).

4.5 Critique and Assessment of Poulantzas

Inspired by Marx and his own legal training, Poulantzas recognizes the institutional separation of the profit-oriented, market-mediated capitalist economy, the legal system with its private and public moments, and the state. In particular, he had the legal concepts necessary to explore the historical specificity of bourgeois law and its distinctive role in reproducing capitalist social relations. He could therefore investigate the juridical and political fields of capitalist societies in their own terms based on the twin 'isolation' and 'unifying' effects of juridicopolitical ideology and institutional separation on the nature and dynamic of economic and political class struggle. While drawing on Marx's form analytical account of law in the economic and political fields, Poulantzas also integrated Gramsci's analyses of hegemony and class agency into his analysis. This combination of form analysis and class analysis left uncertainties about the famous (or notorious) role of economic determination as compared to the role of legal and political struggles in these two distinctive fields with their own logics, stakes and imaginaries. This is a major problem for Marxist analysis more generally and is often fudged by invoking the merely placeholding concept of the 'relative autonomy' of law and the state. This is the name of the problem, not the answer. Poulantzas developed an answer in the 1970s based on his account of the state as a social relation. Instead of using the more structural concept of relative autonomy, which reifies the institutional separation of the economic and political, he emphasized that, in strategic-relational terms, their articulation depends on the balance of forces mobilized by different strategies to coordinate them in a practically adequate or organic manner rather than one that is arbitrary, rationalistic and willed (cf Gramsci 1971; Jessop 1983; Jessop 2015). In other words, form analysis sets out the terrain on which these struggles occur; an analysis of the changing balance of political forces and the projects behind which they are mobilized explains the contingently necessary mechanisms in and through which these forces make their own history, but not in circumstances of their own choosing.

This is related to other difficulties. On the one hand, despite Poulantzas' growing recognition of the prodigious incoherence of state policies and the socialist potential of 'formal' liberties, he neglects the political indeterminacy of the institutional structure of the state in favour of stressing that, in essence, it is a bourgeois form. This leaves little room for the influence of political struggle on class domination. On the other hand, despite his insistence, with Pashukanis, on the constitutive absence of class from the bourgeois state and his argument that its relation to civil society is refracted through the individuation and differential fragmentation of social agents, he overlooks the implications of the 'isolation effect' for the nature of the struggle for hegemony in favour of a class reductionist account of political forces and ideologies. Rather than exploring the contingent relation between political forces and/or ideologies and the requirements of capital accumulation in particular conjunctures, Poulantzas often ascribes a necessary class belonging to political parties and other apparatuses and/or to specific ideologies, and also neglects the role of nonclass (for example, gender, ethnic, youth) movements in the struggle for intellectual, moral and political leadership. Yet, if one accepts his claims concerning the role of individuation and social fracturing in the constitution of civil society and the bourgeois state, then the influence of nonclass forces must assume a central place in political analysis along with an account of the specific effects of the institutional arrangements of the state. In this sense the theoretical promise of his work is betrayed in the attempt to explain everything in terms of a few principles at a high level of abstraction, rather than admit that the Marxist tenet of the overdetermined nature of specific conjunctures implies a certain degree of underdetermination at less concrete and complex levels.

Other problems occur in his highly original account of 'normal' states and 'exceptional' regimes. However, the arguments for the alleged benefits of 'normal' forms are largely asserted and depend for proof on the contraindications of 'exceptional' regimes. This is partly rooted in an underdeveloped notion of hegemony. These problems are accentuated in Poulantzas' discussion of 'authoritarian statism'. Not only does he present it as a hybrid of normal and exceptional elements (presumably articulated under the dominance of the normal elements), he also insists that authoritarian statism leads to a decline in representative democracy (the theoretically typical or normal form of bourgeois state) without specifying how it substitutes new forms of democratic participation and thereby remains 'normal'. All the evidence he adduces points to the decline of democracy and not its internal transformation. It is also unclear whether authoritarian statism is really a *new* state form (involving a break or rupture with the interventionist state) or if it simply represents an intensification of features of the interventionist state in the face of more frequent and/or durable economic and political crises (for further criticisms, see Jessop 1985).

This said, Poulantzas certainly developed one of the richest theoretical studies of the law, state and juridicopolitical ideology available in contemporary Marxism. He established, more successfully than other Marxist theorists, the close articulation between these three fields and their implications for the linkage between the economic and juridicopolitical regions. Moreover, rather than restricting himself to a narrow analysis of the law and/or legal ideology in terms of fetishism, he demonstrated how they provide the matrix for the institutional framework of the capitalist state as a *Rechtsstaat* and for the characteristic form of bourgeois politics as a struggle for hegemony. In this sense, while he recognizes that law is a relatively autonomous sphere of bourgeois social formations with its own distinctive impact, he also provides the means to locate its place within the overall system of bourgeois domination. This represents a significant advance on the 'capital logic' school and, as indicated in his account of 'normal' and 'exceptional' states, has great theoretical potential.

5. FOUCAULT AS A GENEALOGIST OF STATECRAFT

Foucault is renowned for his criticisms of state theory and advocacy of a bottom-up approach to social power as well as for his hostility to orthodox Marxism and communism. But this did not exclude interest in state power, as is evidenced in his lectures on governmentality and biopolitics in *Society Must Be Defended* (2003), *Security, Territory, Population* (2008) and *The Birth of Biopolitics* (2009).

Notably, Foucault developed the problematic of government to explore the historical constitution and periodization of the state and the important strategic and tactical dimensions of power relations and their associated discourses. For, in rejecting various essentialist, transhistorical, universal, and deductive analyses of the state and state power, Foucault created a space for exploring its 'polymorphous crystallization' in and through interrelated changes in technologies of power, objects of governance, governmental projects and modes of political calculation. Indeed, he argued that 'the state is nothing more than the mobile effect of a regime of multiple governmentalities' (2008: 79). He proposed:

> it is likely that if the state is what it is today, it is precisely thanks to this governmentality that is at the same time both external and internal to the state, since it is the tactics of government that allow the continual definition of what should or should not fall within the state's domain, what is public and what private, what is and what is not within the state's competence, and so on. So, if you like, the survival and limits of the state should be understood on the basis of the general tactics of governmentality. (2008: 109)

This poses important issues of statecraft understood not just as the exercise of sovereign power (its conventional referent) but as the complex art of 'governance of governance' within and beyond the (changing) formal boundaries of the state. Foucauldian scholars study problem definition, power asymmetries, domination and the political effects of specific modes of calculation, institutional assemblages and social practices. A key aspect of governmentality is how it (re-)defines some issues as private, technical or managerial, removing them from overtly political decision making and contentious politics.

He analysed it as an emergent and changeable effect of incessant transactions, multiple governmentalities, perpetual *statizations* (2008: 79):

> An analysis in terms of power must not assume that state sovereignty, the form of the law, or the over-all unity of a domination, is given at the outset; rather, these are only the terminal forms power takes ... power must be understood in the first instance as the multiplicity of force relations immanent in the sphere in which they operate and that constitute their own organization; as the process which, through ceaseless struggles and confrontations, transforms, strengthens, or reverses them; as the support which these force relations find in one another, thus forming a chain or a system, or, on the contrary, the disjunctions and contradictions that isolate them from each other; and, lastly, as the strategies in which they take effect, whose general design or institutional crystallization is embodied in the state apparatus, in the formulation of the law, in various social hegemonies. (2008: 92–3)

In this context, the art of government, or governmentality, is said to involve 'the ensemble constituted by the institutions, procedures, analyses, and reflections, the calculations and tactics that permit the exercise of this quite specific, albeit very complex form of power, which has, as its principal target, population; as its main form of knowledge, political economy; and, as its essential technical means, apparatuses of security' (2008: 111). Foucault regards the state as a relational ensemble and treats governmentality as a set of practices and strategies, governmental projects and modes of calculation that operate on something called the state. This something is the terrain of a nonessentialized set of political relations, however, rather than a universal, fixed, unchanging phenomenon. In this sense, while the state is pregiven as an object of governance, it also gets reconstructed as government practises change (2008: 5–6).

His Collège de France lectures from 1975 to 1979 identified three forms of government: sovereignty, disciplinarity and governmentality. The first is associated with the medieval state based on customary law, written law and litigation and concerned with control over land and wealth; the second with the rise of the administrative state of the fifteenth and sixteenth centuries based on the disciplinary regulation of individual bodies in different institutional contexts; and the third with the increasingly governmentalized state, which dates from the late sixteenth century and came to fruition in the nineteenth century, when state concern was focused on controlling the mass of the population on its territory rather than controlling territoriality as such (2008: 221; cf, with the same sequence but other dates, 2003: 37–9, 249–50). Expanding this account, Foucault traced governmental concerns back to sixteenth century interest in the administration of territorial monarchies; to sixteenth and seventeenth century development of new analyses and forms of 'statistical' knowledge, that is, knowledge of the state, in all its elements, dimensions and factors of power; and, finally, to the rise of mercantilism, cameralism and *Polizeiwissenschaft* (2008: 212). Accordingly, the governmental state arose from the governmentalization of the state rather than the statization of society and was based on continual (re-)definition of state competences and the division between public and private (2008: 220–1).

He noted that the modern state's disciplinary techniques originated in dispersed local sites well away from the centres of state power in the *Ancien Régime* and well away from emerging sites of capitalist production and had their own distinctive disciplinary logics. Thus, disciplinary normalization focused on the conduct of persons who were not directly involved in capitalist production (for example, those in asylums, prisons, schools, barracks).

Nonetheless, second, Foucault recognized that some technologies and practices were selected and integrated into other sites of power. Thus, while *Discipline and Punish* (1977) mostly emphasized the *dispersion* of power mechanisms, the first volume of the *History of Sexuality* (1979) began to explore how different mechanisms were combined to produce social order through a strategic codification that made them more coherent and complementary. In this text and a roughly contemporary lecture series, *Society Must Be Defended*, Foucault links this explicitly to bourgeois recognition of their economic profitability and political utility (1979: 114, 125, 141; 2003: 30–3).

Third, he explored how existing power relations were not only codified but also consolidated and institutionalized. Foucault notes how the immanent multiplicity of relations and techniques of power are 'colonised, used, inflected, transformed, displaced, extended, and so on by increasingly general mechanisms and forms of overall domination ... and, above all, how they are invested or annexed by global phenomena and how more general powers or economic benefits can slip into the play of these technologies of power' (2003: 30–1).

The articulation of the economic and political should not be explained in terms of functional subordination or formal isomorphism (2003: 14). Instead it should be studied in terms of functional overdetermination and a perpetual process of strategic elaboration or completion. The former occurs when 'each effect – positive or negative, intentional or unintentional – enters into resonance or contradiction with the others and thereby calls for a readjustment or a re-working of the heterogeneous elements that surface at various points' (1980: 195). In describing the strategic elaboration or completion of a general line, Foucault invoked concepts such as 'social hegemonies', 'hegemonic effects', 'hegemony of the bourgeoisie', 'meta-power', 'class domination', 'polymorphous techniques of subjugation', 'sur-pouvoir' (or a 'surplus power', analogous to surplus value), 'global strategy', and so forth. He also gave a privileged role to the state as the point of strategic codification of the multitude of power relations and the apparatus in which the general line is crystallized (e.g., 2003: 27, 31–5; cf 1980: 122, 156, 189, 199–200; 1982: 224). For example, the rise of the population–territory–wealth nexus in political economy and of the police created the space for the revalorization and rearticulation of disciplines that had emerged in the seventeenth and eighteenth centuries, such as schools, manufactories, armies, and so on (2008: 217–19).

6. CONCLUSIONS

Much of the literature (and much political discourse) presupposes a separation between the economy and politics, the market and the state.[2] From a critical political economy viewpoint, this is misleading – not because there is no separation but because this separation must be related to the overall structure and dynamic of capitalist social formations. The separation depends on the variable lines of demarcation between the economy, law and politics and their structural and strategic significance. Structurally, this separation is the condition for trade in free markets and the rational organization of production and finance as well as the existence of a constitutional state based on the rule of law. Strategically, differential accumulation depends on the use of economic *and extra-economic* resources to create the conditions of profitable accumulation and/or to socialize losses. As noted above, this depends on the capacity of specific social forces in a context of variable institutional separation of these spheres to secure the continued reciprocal interdependence of 'market' and 'state' as complementary moments in the reproduction of the capital relation. A key factor here is the relation between different forms of private and public law as a significant matrix within which these governance practices occur. In this sense, law and the state are never absent from the process of capital accumulation, whether in stability or crisis: even *laissez-faire* is a form of state intervention because it implicitly supports the outcome of market forces (cf. Gramsci 1971). Law and the state both provide general external conditions of production, distribution, circulation and consumption. The state also allocates money, credit and resources to different economic activities, and helps to frame and steer production, distribution and trade; it is also involved in organizing and reorganizing class alliances among dominant class fractions and disorganizing subordinate classes and forces, whether through divide and rule tactics or through articulating a national-popular interest that transcends particular class interests (Gramsci 1971; Poulantzas 1978).

There are important legal aspects to the state as defined in *allgemeine Staatstheorie* and as considered in its inclusive sense (*lo stato integrale*), that is, political society + civil society. But this does not mean that it can be analysed purely from a constitutional or legal perspective. Thus, Joachim Hirsch, one of the leading German Marxist state theorists, affirms that the bourgeois state codifies the norms of commodity exchange and monetary relations, and ensures their clarity, stability and calculability. Yet he adds that the state constantly breaches the rule of law through its resort to executive measures to secure specific material conditions required for capital accumulation. It is also prepared to use force outside the framework of law to secure bourgeois rule whenever the proletariat threatens the foundations of the capitalist order. Freedom, equality and the rule of law are only one side of bourgeois rule: its other side is *raison d'état*, class bias and open violence. Both facets are essential to the reproduction of bourgeois society (Hirsch 1978: 64–5).

What can critical state theory bring to the analysis of law, the state and juridicopolitical ideology? An appropriate starting point here is the form of law considered in abstraction from its specific content. As a *sui generis* theoretical object this involves the

---

[2] The following arguments draw heavily on my earlier work on state theory (e.g., Jessop 1982, 1985, 2000, 2015).

constitution of a subject endowed with rights and/or obligations that are justiciable before a rational-legal apparatus empowered to use coercion in the implementation of its judgments. In turn this permits analysis in terms of the interpellation of juridical subjects, the nature of rational-legal discourse, the conditions of existence of the legal form and the effectiveness of intervention through the law. On this basis one can also develop the concept of a legal order as a determinate form of societalization involving the generalization of the legal form to all social relations. Neither the study of the basic form of law nor that of the legal order should involve reducing them to epiphenomena of the economic region: at most, one could investigate their economic conditions of existence and their reciprocal influence on the economic region. That the commodification of labour power may well be necessary for the development of an autonomous legal order no more implies that law is reducible to the economic region than the fact that certain legal forms are necessary if commodities are to circulate means that the economy is reducible to the legal field. In this sense, introducing economic determinations into analyses of law requires us to consider their complex articulation and to avoid any unilateral reduction of one to the other. We should also note that analyses at this level of abstraction (whether confined to the legal region or extended to its articulation with other regions) will inevitably be relatively indeterminate in their implications for specific conjunctures. This relative indeterminacy, or underdetermination, can be progressively eliminated through more detailed specification of the explanandum and its conditions of existence and effectiveness.

This means a progressive shift from the primacy of form to an emphasis on the content of law and legal order. This approach need not involve the 'essentialization' of law that assumes a determinate, albeit abstract, essence of law and suggests that deviations therefrom at more concrete, complex levels are inessential. On the contrary, it implies that the appearance of a 'pure' legal discourse or 'legal' order is as much the product of the interaction of diverse causal mechanisms as the existence of hybrid forms of discourse and/or societal organization. It is only in these terms that we can begin to understand the decline of law or the growth of 'authoritarian statism', as well as the conditions that favoured the classic *Rechtsstaat*. In short, it is only in these terms that we can investigate the functional unity of legality and illegality in the bourgeois state and begin to explain their relative significance in securing bourgeois domination in different situations. The studies reviewed above provide us with important guidelines in this endeavour, but it should be obvious that there is still much work to be done at all levels of legal analysis.

BIBLIOGRAPHY

Buckel, S. (2007) *Subjektivierung und Kohäsion. Zur Rekonstruktion einer materialistischen Theorie des Rechts*, Weilerswist: Verbruck Wissenschaft.
Draper, H. (1977) *Karl Marx's Theory of Revolution: State and Bureaucracy, vol. 1*, New York: Monthly Review Press, 1977.
Fine, Robert (1984) *Democracy and the Rule of Law*, London: Pluto.
Foucault, M. (1977) *Discipline and Punish*, London: Allen Lane.
Foucault, M. (1979) *History of Sexuality, vol. 1: An Introduction*, London: Allen Lane.
Foucault, M. (1980) *Power/Knowledge: Selected Writings and Other Interviews 1972–77*, Brighton: Wheatsheaf.

Foucault, M. (1982) 'How is power exercised?', in H.L. Dreyfus and P. Rabinow (eds), *Michel Foucault: Beyond Structuralism and Hermeneutics*, Brighton: Harvester, 216–26.
Foucault, M. (2003) *Society Must Be Defended: Lectures at the Collège de France, 1975–6*, Basingstoke: Macmillan.
Foucault, M. (2008) *Security, Territory, Population: Lectures at the Collège de France, 1977–8*, Basingstoke: Macmillan.
Foucault, M. (2009) *The Birth of Biopolitics: Lectures at the Collège de France, 1978–9*, Basingstoke: Macmillan.
Gramsci, A. (1971) *Selections from the Prison Notebooks*, London: Lawrence and Wishart.
Hall, S., Critcher, R., Clarke, J. and Roberts, B. (1978) *Policing the Crisis*, London: Macmillan.
Hirsch, J. (1978) 'The state apparatus and social reproduction', in J. Holloway and S. Picciotto (eds), *State and Capital*, London: Arnold, 57–107.
Jessop, B. (1982) *The Capitalist State: Marxist Theories and Methods*. Oxford: Martin Robertson.
Jessop, B. (1983) 'Accumulation strategies, state forms, and hegemonic projects', *Kapitalistate*, 10, 89–111.
Jessop, B. (1985) *Nicos Poulantzas: Marxist Theories and Methods*, London: Macmillan.
Jessop, B. (2000) 'On recent Marxist theories of law, the state, and juridico-political ideology', *International Journal of the Sociology of Law*, 8(4), 339–68.
Jessop, B. (2010) 'Another Foucault effect? Foucault on governmentality and statecraft', in U. Bröckling, S. Krasmann and T. Lemke (eds), *Governmentality: Current Issues and Future Challenges*, New York: Routledge, 56–73.
Jessop, B. (2014) 'Repoliticizing depoliticization: theoretical preliminaries on some responses to the American and Eurozone debt crises', *Policy & Politics*, 42(2), 207–23.
Jessop, B. (2015) *The State: Past, Present, Future*. Cambridge: Polity.
Jessop, B., Bonnett, K., Bromley, S. and Ling, T. (1988) *Thatcherism: A Tale of Two Nations*, Cambridge: Polity.
Kay, G. and Mott, J. (1982) *Political Order and the Law of Labour*, London: Macmillan.
Krätke, M. (1984) *Kritik der Staatsfinanzen: Zur politischen Ökonomie des Steuerstaats*, Hamburg: VSA.
Lenin, V.I. (1964) 'The state and revolution', in *Lenin: Collected Works, vol. 25*, Moscow: Progress Publishers, 381–492.
Marx, K. (1975a) 'Contribution to the Critique of Hegel's *Philosophy of Law*', MECW, vol. 3, 3–129.
Marx, K. (1975b) 'Contribution to the Critique of Hegel's *Philosophy of Law*, Introduction', MECW, vol. 3, 175–87.
Marx, K. (1976a) *Capital, Volume I*, MECW, vol. 35.
Marx, K. (1976b) 'Draft plan for a work on the modern state', MECW, vol. 4, 666.
Marx, K. (1978a) *Capital, Volume III*, MECW, vol. 37.
Marx, K. (1978b), 'The class struggles in France, 1848–1850', MECW, vol. 10, 45–146.
Marx, K. (1979) 'The Eighteenth Brumaire of Louis Bonaparte', MECW, vol. 11, 99–197.
Marx, K. (1981) 'Kreuznacher Hefte 1-5', MEGA, vol. IV/2, 9–278.
Marx, K. (1982), 'Letter to Pavel Vasilyevich Annenkov in Paris', 28 December 1846, MECW, 38, 95–106.
Marx, K. (1986) 'The rule of the Pretorians', MECW, vol. 15, 464–7.
Marx, K. (1989) 'Second draft of the Civil War in France', MECW, vol. 22, 519–51.
Marx, K. and F. Engels (1975) 'The German ideology', MECW, vol. 5, 21–93.
Pashukanis, E.V. (1978) *A General Theory of Law and Marxism*, London: Ink Links.
Poulantzas, N. (1964) 'L'examen marxiste de l'état et du droit actuels: la question de l'alternative', *Les Temps Modernes*, 219/220, 274–302.
Poulantzas, N. (1965a) '*La Critique de la Raison Dialectique* de Sartre et le droit', *Archives de Philosophie du Droit*, 10, 83–106.
Poulantzas, N. (1965b) 'Préliminaires à l'étude de l'hégémonie dans l'état', *Les Temps Modernes*, 234, 862–96, and 235, 1048–69.
Poulantzas, N. (1967) 'A propos de la théorie marxiste du droit', *Archives de Philosophie du Droit*, 12, 145–62.
Poulantzas, N. (1973) *Political Power and Social Classes*, London: NLB (1968).
Poulantzas, N. (1974) *Fascism and Dictatorship*, London: NLB (1970).
Poulantzas, N. (1975) *Classes in Contemporary Capitalism*, London: NLB (1974).
Poulantzas, N. (1976) *Crisis of the Dictatorships*, 2nd edn, London: NLB.
Poulantzas, N. (1978) *State, Power, Socialism*, London: Verso.
Prakash, G. (1994) 'Subaltern studies as postcolonial', *American Historical Review*, 99(5), 1475–90.
Thomas, P. (1994) *Alien Politics: Marxist State Theory Retrieved*, London: Routledge.

Tuschling, B. (1976) *Rechtsform und Produktionsverhältnisse*, Frankfurt/Main: EVA.
Thompson, E.P. (1975) *Whigs and Hunters*, London: Merlin.

8. Law and the public/private distinction
Scott Veitch

If, according to Karl Klare, *'There is no "public/private" distinction'* (Klare, 1982, 1361, emphasis in original), why would he write a long article dedicated to understanding its role in labour law? Indeed, if legal realists and then critical legal scholars have variously debunked the distinction as unwarranted, incoherent and implausible, why would anyone *now* write an article about it? Klare's answer to this kind of question is instructive: 'What does exist is a series of ways of thinking about public and private that are constantly undergoing revision, reformulation, and refinement … The public/private distinction poses as an analytical tool in labor law, but it functions more as a form of political rhetoric used to justify particular results' (ibid). This is the insight critical scholars follow, not just in labour law, but across all areas of enquiry into legal doctrines and institutions which sustain illegitimate inequalities: that there is a politics to the rhetorical deployment of the distinction through which determinate power relations produce, reproduce and rationalise harmful results. The distinction may be descriptively untenable, in other words, but it does conceptual work and has real effects. *This* is why it matters, and this is why critical legal scholars have been, and remain, interested in it.

This chapter consists of three parts. The first two analyse the claim that it is the public quality of state law that is essential to the existence of what is deemed private, whether in 'private law' or with respect to 'private interests' or the meaning of 'private life'. Two contrasting thematisations of this problematic are examined. The first, drawing on Marx, is a critique which argues that the public realm and the differentiation between public and private which it invokes operate ideologically to legitimate exploitation. The second treats the juridical deployment of the public/private distinction as necessary in the defence of human dignity against the operation of economic or scientific calculation. The final section considers the ways in which critical legal scholarship is engaged with the question of the public, and the public in law, insofar as its critique of contemporary power relations demands that the question of political community must be addressed directly.

1. THE MATTER OF THE PUBLIC

We may helpfully contrast two readings of the relation between public and private with respect to the realm of law. One claims that there is a necessary public quality to law in the western state tradition that simultaneously transcends and guarantees all other juridical forms and relations, including those of private law and the interests it protects. This *sui generis* quality persists through variations in historical, material and social contexts and supplies a function – to secure reason, personhood and dignity – not reducible to any other social institution or rationality. We will come to this in the following section. The other claims that the public quality of the state and its law is merely epiphenomenal; the real root and meaning of this public quality are to be found in the material relations of production whose dominant interests the state is there to represent and serve.

We will consider both of these in more detail in a moment. But before we do so we must consider a fundamental challenge to this whole problematic – for the first challenge to the public/private distinction is also potentially the most devastating: that there is no distinction because there is *no public* power or realm that is different from any private realm or any other kind of power. The 'publicness' of the 'public' as something autonomous will play an essential role in thinking about the public/private distinction particularly with respect to the commonly taken for granted realms of public authority, public law and the public nature of political institutions such as the state. But the challenge to any and all such claims consists in the simple, bubble-bursting observation of the child in the story who – for all the talk, belief, drama and activity to the contrary – saw that 'the Emperor has no clothes'. The child sees through the charade of pomposity and deference of public officialdom as just that: a charade. Thinking and acting otherwise depends on a confidence trick, an effort of make-believe, stemming either from fear or a fabricated desire to see other than what your eyes are telling you. Writ large, seeing though the charade of the public realm as something qualitatively different means seeing that all its 'officials' – the Emperor, the king or queen, the judge or lord or lady – are just ordinary people, like you and me and everyone else, and that their public airs and graces are no more and no less than a self-serving fiction. A woman with a crown on her head or a man with a wig on his are simply women and men dressed up, and it doesn't matter whether they are sitting on a throne or up on a dais, or attending a fancy dress party. The 'public' persona of office is every bit as fanciful as Santa Claus – in fact, *all* he has are his fancy clothes. And as Robert Burns said of all such 'tinsel show': 'The man o' independent mind, He looks an' laughs at a' that' (Burns, 1795).

But to maintain such a radical scepticism arguably fails to account for how the force of these inventions, or 'institutional facts', makes a difference in the world of a very specific kind. Given its often underexamined status in thinking about the public/private distinction, it is thus worth enquiring further into how the 'public' comes about, how it is sustained and what its effects are. We might begin with David Hume's observations:

> Nothing appears more surprising to those who consider human affairs with a philosophical eye, than the easiness with which the many are governed by the few; and the implicit submission, with which men resign their own sentiments and passions to those of their rulers. When we enquire by what means this wonder is effected, we shall find, that, as Force is always on the side of the governed, the governors have nothing to support them but opinion. It is, therefore, on opinion only that government is founded; and this maxim extends to the most despotic and most military governments, as well as to the most free and most popular. (Hume, 1987, 32)

States, their institutions and officials, may exist only by force of opinion, but they exist nevertheless. 'What is problematic', writes Pierre Bourdieu, reflecting on this passage from Hume, 'is the fact that the established order *is not* problematic' (Bourdieu, 1998,

56, emphasis in original). To address the public quality of law and the state thus requires focusing on their actual operations rather than on their own legitimation narratives. What is required, in other words, is a broader account of how the 'wonder' and 'opinion' Hume identified are generated and maintained. But the difficulty in doing so is that, as Bourdieu notes, so deeply ingrained as natural, given and commonsensical are notions of the state's public authority that it is almost impossible to think apart from them. Indeed, its presence begins already in childhood (before, so to speak, the honest little anarchist of Andersen's tale can do too much damage to the Imperial State), with the state's role in public education being central to it: 'School is the state school where young people are turned into state persons … Walking to school, I was walking into the state … regulated and registered and trained and finished and perverted and dejected, like everyone else' (Bourdieu, 35, quoting Thomas Bernhard). It might once have been possible to challenge this, to walk out of the state into a nonstate space, just as it was once the case that one could go to the market and thereafter leave it. But so successful is its power, its omnipresence, that leaving seems impossible: one is never not in some state-organised law space or time, never not subject to some state-sponsored jurisdiction, just as one can never now truly leave the marketplace because we carry our access to it, and its access to us, constantly around with us in our pockets or bags in the form of smartphones, laptops and bank cards.

The formation of 'opinion' in the matter of the public, so insistently and for such duration, is a key part of what makes it so difficult to think outwith the state. In sociological terms the process embodies (literally, says Bourdieu) two aspects of symbolic violence: the state '*incarnates* itself simultaneously in objectivity, in the form of specific organisational structures and mechanisms, and in subjectivity, in the form of mental structures and categories of perception and thought' (Bourdieu, 40, emphasis added). The category of the public that attaches to the modern state is set in mind through an effort so great that its effects have come to appear effortless. Ideas, technologies, symbols, modes of mental and physical disposition, combine to ensure that the public is installed as public in a way that is both natural and naturally transcendent. The effects of this cannot be overstated. As John Trudell, speaking about the experience of indigenous people in the United States, notes:

> They have interfered in our lives since the moment we were born. Look at America. You have to pay to be born, and you have to pay to be buried. That tells you a lot about our freedom. And if they've gotten it into our consciousness to accept *that*, then we've got a lot of work to do. We really do. (Trudell, 1980, original emphasis; see also Williams 1990)

Securing national, territorial jurisdiction as state or 'common' law is effected through a multiplicity of legal and nonlegal techniques. These embrace symbolic forms of 'cultural and linguistic unification' which deploy the idea of the universal to uneven ends. Just as the state is, with respect to competing legal jurisdictions, a jealous state, so natural or professional languages secure one 'dialect' as universal, valorising one set of standards of linguistic competence to designate the others as inferior. 'The prisons', writes Tom Leonard, are 'full of many voices/but never the dialect of the judges' (Leonard, 1995, 17). And, he adds, 'In dismissing the language [of the many], one dismisses the existence of its users – or rather, one chooses to believe that they have dismissed themselves' (ibid 41). That latter observation affirms the degree to which the double structuring noted by Bourdieu succeeds in securing, in Hume's terms, the 'implicit submission' of the governed. It is the generalised result of a combination of universalism and an objective discriminatory particularism:

> given that the universalization of requirements thus officially instituted does not come with a universalization of access to the means needed to fulfill them, this fosters both the monopolization of the universal by the few and the dispossession of all others, who are, in a way, thereby mutilated in their humanity. (Bourdieu, 1998, 46–7)

The state as public actor thus differentiates itself from private actors with respect to the meaning and consequences of its actions in ways that are simultaneously universal and discriminatory, life affirming and life destroying. Nowhere is this more decisive than on the vast scale of human suffering directly and continuously inflicted by states, including democratic ones, on populations of innocents. The personal becomes political here insofar as personal harms are whitewashed in the name of the state. So while domestically a private citizen killing another citizen may be charged with murder and, if found guilty, sentenced to imprisonment, by contrast, the state literally gets away with murder by calling it another name. The killing of innocent women, men and children in the name of the state (by the USA alone, for example: 100,000 instantly in Hiroshima and Nagasaki, up to two million in Vietnam, and in the present century already tens of thousands in Afghanistan and Iraq) comes with no legal consequence for those who plan, organise and execute such mass deaths. As these and many other examples testify, publicly sanctified killing of the guiltless succeeds for those who commit it. The 'public' quality of the state in causing such extensive damage with impunity is 'normalised' as the necessary adjunct to the qualitatively distinct nature of the state: its particularised universalism. This is so even as it fails entirely to account for the fact that the suffering of innocent victims acknowledges no difference whatever between public and private rationalisations. Instead, with each and every death the meaning *for the killers* is redeemed as necessary or, at a push, regrettable, through the transformative touch of the public. From the latter perspective people's personal, private lives are always potentially political: killing with impunity by the million is a central facet of the redemptive powers of modern public authority (see Veitch 2007).

That one might detect in this miraculous capacity of the public realm a religious aspect should be no surprise, for the inheritance is clear. As Schmitt noted:

> All significant concepts of the modern theory of the state are secularized theological concepts not only because of their historical development – in which they were transferred from theology to the theory of the state, whereby, for example, the omnipotent god became the omnipotent lawgiver – but also because of their systematic structure, the recognition of which is necessary for a sociological consideration of these concepts. The exception in jurisprudence is analogous to the miracle in theology. (Schmitt, 1985, 36)

Such transference transmits to the state projections of (religious) fantasy and incorporates them in functionally useful ways. Even a nominally secular state can, for its greater glorification or insurance, retain religious dogma to augment, mythologise and inure its power, as when subjects learn to sing that God will save their Queen, or that the God 'in whom we trust' will provide additional security to the nation and its dollar. Illusory as such fantasies may be, they are nonetheless, in Habermas's terms, 'objective illusions' in that they have real effects on those who believe them (as well as those who would not) (Habermas, 1987, 329).

In this sense, the theological dimension of the state's function does an immense amount of work in establishing the coordinates and meanings of the public/private distinction and the 'political rhetoric' that attends its deployment. Marx wrote incisively about this in his early essay critiquing Bauer on the 'Jewish Question', arguing that the limits of Bauer's notion of freedom lay in failing to see the distinctive functioning of the political state and its own religiosity:

> when man liberates himself politically, he liberates himself by means of a detour, through the medium of something else, however necessary that medium may be. It follows finally, that man, even when he proclaims himself an atheist through the intermediary of the state – ie, when he proclaims the state to be atheist – still retains his religious prejudice, just because he recognizes himself only by a detour through an intermediary. Religion is precisely the recognition of man by detour, through an intermediary. The state is the intermediary between man and his freedom. As Christ is the intermediary onto whom man unburdens of his divinity, all his religious bonds, so the state is the mediator onto which man transfers all his Godlessness and all his human liberty ... The relation of the political state to civil society is just as spiritual as the relations of heaven to earth. (Marx, 1843, 44–5)

Freedom by detour is that which allows the state to function as a transcendent mediator, sanctifying *as equal* citizens who are in reality unequal. But this was no mere charade; it required a sophisticated and successful operation that depended on simultaneously politicising and depoliticising what counted both as public *and* private. And it was their posited opposition that explained not only the continued influence of dominant material interests but, just as importantly, the nature of the public *as* public. The significance of this is brought out in the following passage which discusses the removal of property qualifications on voting, and the issue of whether this introduces a new kind of equality that does away with the influence that inequalities in property once maintained. Marx argues to the contrary:

> [T]he political annulment of private property has not only not abolished private property, it actually presupposes it. The state does away with difference in birth, class, education, and profession, when it declares birth, class, education, and profession, to be unpolitical differences, when it summons every member of the people to an equal participation in popular sovereignty without taking the differences into consideration, when it treats all elements of the people's real life from the point of view of the state. Nevertheless, the state still allows private property, education, and profession, to have an effect in their own manner – that is, as private property, as education, as profession, and make their particular natures felt. Far from abolishing these factual differences, its existence rests on them as a presupposition, it only feels itself to be a political state and asserts its universality by opposition to these elements. (ibid, 45)

In other words (those of Burns), 'the rank is but the guinea's stamp', but this stamp is a symbolic seal of distinction that lifts wealth and private property above their ordinary influence. It does so by protecting that ordinary influence through ensuring their inviolability as the *opposite* of influence in the public sphere. Where universal equality is recognised in and by the state, commodified power appears as mere corruption. So money can have no influence in the state; it is excluded by definition. And this is how it has its influence.

Yet the 'guinea's stamp' is not only symbolic. The stamp is coercive too, backed by the power of the state which has in modernity acquired, in Weber's terms, 'a monopoly on the legitimate use of physical force' (Weber, 1948/1919, 78). But this monopoly may not be all it seems. In particular, while private property relies on the coercive power of the state, it also relies on its distribution (that is, coercion's distribution) to owners. This is a form of argument that was taken up by legal realists, particularly in the work of Robert Hale and Morris Cohen. When the state 'protects a property right', argues Hale, '[p]assively it is abstaining from interference with the owner when he deals with the thing owned; actively it is forcing the non-owner to desist from handling it, unless the owner consents' (Hale, 1923, 471). This insight is taken up most starkly when Hale considers the coercive role of the law of property in material and labour practices, detailing how the combination of ownership and coercion is central to securing the subjugation of labour power. People must eat to live, writes Hale, but those who legally own foodstuffs or their means of production are entitled to keep them unless they are offered payment:

> There is no law to compel them to part with their food for nothing. Unless, then, the non-owner can produce his own food, the law compels him to starve if he has no wages, and compels him to go without wages unless he obeys the behests of some employer. It is the law that coerces him into wage-work under penalty of starvation.

Property law protects the private interests of owners not simply in the sense of securing noninterference with their property – it is doing this that, in turn, allows market forces to operate as precisely that: *forces*, generated within the legally organised market affecting social relations in compulsive ways. The private law of property thus coerces people into the market or workplace, or else they starve from lack of access to necessities of food or the means to produce it. This is the *'law-made* dilemma', says Hale, 'of starvation or obedience' (473, emphasis added). Given the public role of the state in licensing such coercion, there is *no difference* with respect to the operation of force between a supposedly 'free' market and a welfarist one. To believe otherwise is to accept the lie of the 'laissez faire' economy. It is to believe that freedom of property in ownership and exchange decreases coercion and compulsion. But the reality of the free market based in private property is otherwise, as Hale shows and as most workers know only too well. That this is another, if different, form of political sovereignty over people's private lives should be recognised too. With a remarkable prescience for our own times, Cohen concludes: 'we must not overlook the fact that dominion over things is also *imperium* over our fellow beings ... There can be no doubt that our property laws do confer sovereign power on our captains of industry and even more so on our captains of finance' (Cohen, 1927, 13).

The coercively organised distribution of coercion from state to private actors (be they individuals or corporations) has likewise been an important theme of critique for feminist scholars and activists who have opened to contestation the supposedly fixed categories of public and private that have, as categories, been 'fixed' only in the sense that loaded dice are fixed. This work has resulted in at least some measure of success in changing attitudes as well as laws. Seeking to undo the harms perpetrated by the functionally similar licensing of state coercion to 'private' actors, feminists have shown how gender constructions and relations are deeply implicated in the structuring of social, political and economic inequality. Following on from Marx's observations, critical feminist analyses attributed to liberal political theory in particular a number of distinctions and effects, key among which was that between public and private. This was one of a number of dualities or dichotomies through which liberal theory was deemed to perceive the world and through which power was arranged and deployed to serve the interests of patriarchy. These dualities treated the public sphere as the arena of reason, abstraction, objectivity and neutrality, organised and enforced by legal regulation according to respect for individual rights under the doctrine of the rule of law. By contrast, the private sphere was variously deemed to be that of the family, of the domestic or of civil society, within which affect, emotion, particularity and subjectivity operated without the intervention of state law (e.g. Olsen 1983).

One of the challenges faced by feminist legal scholarship in addressing the distinction between public and private has been well noted by Nicola Lacey. She points out that if the distinction turns out to be incoherent and 'hopelessly indeterminate', then the 'theoretical critique of the public/private distinction undermines our critique of its power ... It is extremely difficult, in other words, to engage in critique of the public/private dichotomy or its effects without speaking as if it had an analytic and empirical validity which the critique denies' (Lacey, 1998, 84–5). So at a descriptive or sociological level there is, she argues, in reality no neat separation of social institutions that maps on to the public/private distinction. With respect, for example, to the idea that the family is the quintessential locus of the private sphere, 'a moment's thought reveals that many aspects of family life are hedged around with legal regulation – marriage, divorce, child custody, social welfare' and so on (ibid, 74). Similarly, and while clearly sympathetic to feminist critiques, Lacey describes the mapping of women's lives to the private sphere as equally problematic: 'the suggestion that women have lived their lives exclusively or even mainly in the private sphere of the family is unsustainable. Working class women in particular have worked outside the home to a far greater degree than the public/private critique has tended to acknowledge' (76).

The strength of the feminist critique therefore lies not in attaining better or more accurate descriptions of the differences between public and private; rather, it is to trace the deployment of the distinction as (in Klare's terms) 'political rhetoric' operating to the detriment of women. This is best seen in the way that it works in a *normative* and *ideological* manner, and here the feminist critique is for Lacey incisive:

> It exposes the way in which the ideology of the public/private dichotomy allows government to clean its hands of any *responsibility* for the state of the 'private' world and *depoliticises* the disadvantages which inevitably spill over the alleged divide by affecting the position of the 'privately' disadvantaged in the 'public' world. (77, emphasis in original)

This describes well the technique that lies at the heart of the power of deployment of the public/private distinction. In line with the observations of Hale and Cohen, the general point, Lacey notes, is that 'abstention amounts to a form of regulation ... decisions *not* to regulate made by state or other institutions with the power to do so are every bit as much *political* decisions as are decisions to regulate' (75, emphasis in original). Sovereign power is thus organised *and* dispersed here in ways that are not in any sense natural or commonsensical, but ideologically driven. If there is no value-independent way of describing what is private and what public, then the enforced demarcation between the two is a matter of political will. As a matter of critique, what is required is to unveil the workings of this technique with a view to challenging their 'normalising' operations, coercive underpinnings and detrimental effects. And this requires opening to genuine political contestation the meaning and significance of what counts as valuable in people's lives. For, as Lacey and other feminist writers have argued, it is not the case that there is no worth in, for example, attributing value to privacy as something to be protected. Whether with respect to bodily integrity or to family life, arguing for the distinctive quality and value of privacy may be an important means of protecting people from state or corporate surveillance and control. What matters, however, is that decisions about these values should be challengeable politically and not left in place as natural or necessary – for these latter claims will themselves be the deposit of prior political decisions or structures, and it is precisely through their coercive depoliticisation that much of their harm continues and is rationalised. This is why strategies of politicisation remain central to feminist critique.

We have considered some of the potentially multiple and varied sources that sustain the 'public', and identified some of the effects that this category can have. As shown by examples as different as mass killing in the name of the state and the ongoing rationalisations of material and gendered inequality, the private realm – of grief, injustice and personal suffering – has never been distinct but has always either been constituted by or drawn unstoppably into the political through the operation of sovereign political right and its selective distribution. In all these instances the 'public' organises, delivers and justifies a coercive sponsoring of determinate social relations in the interests of the few to the detriment of the many.

And yet there is a competing understanding to be offered about the relation between public and private and what is done in the name of the public and its state form. It is time to turn, then, to the ways in which proponents have reasoned their accounts of public authority more positively – for these too have a significant bearing on what may be understood as 'private' and on the changing relationship between the two.

2. THE JURIDICAL AS INCALCULABLE AND ITS DECLINE

The relation between public and private finds another dimension to its lineage in the west through the conceptual work and influence of Roman law. This gets exemplary articulation in Justinian's *Digest* as formulated by Ulpian: 'There are two branches of legal study: public and private law. Public law is that which respects the establishment of the Roman commonwealth, private that which respects individuals' interests, some matters being of public and others of private interest' (*Digest*, I.1.2). As glossed by Alain Supiot, these 'interests' do not work on the same plane; they are qualitatively different. The 'body of law' – the *corpus iuris* – has, he argues, two 'positions' whose 'mutual adjustment' is crucial to the specificity of law and its anthropological function in the west (Supiot, 2013, 130). This *mutuality* of public and private is of a very particular sort: 'private interests in the horizontal plane [are] *dependent* on the stability (*status*) of the public institution in the vertical one …' Rather like the vertically inclined poles holding up a tent that make the shape of the structure and the space within it possible, so private (horizontal) interests depend for their *juridical* form on the (vertical) 'stability of the public institution'. Law's 'publicness', Supiot maintains, thus has a *sacred* element ('*jus in sacris*') that distinguishes the *res publica* from all those other private interests and things which the law can protect. The 'public' cannot be thought of as the collection or aggregate of private interests or individuals. There must be a definite if mutually related hierarchy: the 'subordination of private to public is what makes the structure of law intelligible and dependable' (ibid).

On this account, law's 'dogmatic' or 'anthropological' function acts as a precondition which cannot be removed without the collapse of the juridical as such. Historically this function has been given concrete content in all manner of legitimatory terms, from natural law to the divine right of kings and the general will. But whatever terms it uses, the function is always the same: to provide an institution for the 'incalculable' protection of personality, dignity and reason. It is incalculable in the sense that it is not reducible through commensuration to empirical forces or the criteria of other social systems. Human dignity, for example, cannot be measured against price or efficiency, and the institution of law is there to make sure this does not occur. Supiot draws on Kant to express this: 'In the kingdom of ends everything has either a price or a dignity. What has a price can be replaced by something else as its equivalent; what on the other hand is above all price and therefore admits of no equivalent has a dignity' (Kant 1993/1785, 40). If the public (vertical) dimension of law collapses then the forms of reason, personhood and dignity made possible by law immediately become hostage to the play of nonjuridical forces whose criteria of validation may invoke anything from economic or scientific calculation to racial profiling. As the history of totalitarian regimes shows, the human damage such reductions can cause is horrific. Whether in the fascist treatment of Jews or the self-styled communist abolition of legal ordering entirely, the replacement of legal categories of dignity or personhood with the administration of 'things' produces devastating human effects. That the history of western modernity too was complicit in the reduction of human dignity to price, most obviously in the form of slavery and the forced removal of millions of Africans to the Americas, is testament to the fact that western law was for centuries no less susceptible to the collapse of its anthropological function.

Today, the effects of reducing juridical categories to economic commensuration and criteria arguably constitutes one of the most potentially significant challenges to this function. As Lon Fuller once observed: 'Before the principle of marginal utility nothing is sacred; all existing arrangements are subject to being reordered in the interest of increased economic return' (Fuller, 1969, 28). To avoid sacrificing the protection of dignity on the altar of price and profit it is, for Supiot, only through maintaining the hierarchical structure of mutuality of public and private law that a double structure of reciprocity – between government and citizen and between citizen and citizen – can be instituted that resists efforts at commensurating and calculating with dignity or personality. It is precisely because 'calculation is not thinking', writes Supiot, that 'all human beings must be referred to an authority that vouches for their identity and symbolizes that they are not to be treated like a thing' (Supiot, 2007, xi, 13). It is then the irreducibly public *capacity* of law, and the dignity appropriate to *homo juridicus*, that is what makes the *rule of law*, in EP Thompson's famous phrase, 'an unqualified human good'. For, as Thompson concludes, 'to deny or belittle this good is, in this dangerous century when the resources and pretensions of power continue to enlarge, a desperate error of intellectual abstraction' (Thompson, 1975, 266).

That such goods are achievable primarily through legal means is a matter to which we will return in the final section. Before doing so we might supplement the challenges to *homo juridicus* that Supiot has indicated by noting how a number of sociological features in modern social relations make an understanding of what is public and what private more complex. To choose only one example, Ulrich Beck noted several years ago:

> The private sphere is not what it appears to be: a sphere separated from the environment. It is the outside turned inside and made private, of conditions and decisions made elsewhere, in the television networks, the educational system, in firms, in the labour market, or in the transportation system, with general disregard of their private, biographical consequences. (Beck 1986, 133)

The effects of this 'outside turned inside' have only been exacerbated by the development, since Beck wrote these words, of internet and smart technologies whose effect is to further challenge any actual or possible separation between public and private. Nonetheless, the force and function of what Beck identifies remains constant. As he observed: 'it is precisely individualized private existence which becomes more and more obviously and emphatically dependent upon situations and conditions that completely escape its reach' (Beck, 1986, 131). Contemporary discourses of responsibilisation, resilience and mindfulness are symptoms of precisely such a phenomenon. These discourses have not only proliferated and become dominant within workplace practices and expectations, but have also (as Bourdieu might have predicted) become increasingly instituted and ingrained as mentalities in places of formative education. From school through to college or university, 'learning to labour' now means being trained to be responsible and mindful for oneself, to become resilient within the system that will inevitably determine individuals' life chances. When we add increasing personal debt to all this, it is clear that private mentalities and personal opportunities are being shaped not to the contours of genuine individual choice, but to those of an omnivorous market. That these attitudes should be seen as a pragmatic and sensible preparation for youngsters – of taking responsibility for effects over which they have no control – confirms the entirely paradoxical situation of 'implicit submission' (Hume again) that is to be doggedly inculcated as a realism that precludes imagining alternatives. Be resilient, it seems to say, but not *too* resilient.

While this is true at the level of ensuring deferential individual mentalities – what Lordon (2014) has extensively examined as the formation of 'willing slaves of capital' – it may also be observed at the level of institutional structures. We can refer here to Supiot's account of the 'refeudalization' he describes in the transformation of the 'public–private relation' today. Essentially, he argues, contrary to the public state acting as an independent guarantor, a structurally distinct institution whose function is, as we have seen, to ensure the autonomy of the *res publica* and respect for dignity, today we are witnessing a collapse of that structure through the inversion of the hierarchy between public and private. In this new arrangement, 'government and law would give way to governance and contract' in the specific sense that 'the state should be transformed into a means of maximizing one's individual utilities' (Supiot, 2013, 132–3). Whether or not Supiot's grander claims about the history of the autonomy of the public realm are thought plausible, this need not detract from the insights he offers into the changing form and content of institutions going on today. With respect to form, the inversion sees the instantiation of calculation and measurement geared to efficiency as the key indicator of value. To be accountable, we might put it, no longer requires giving an account – it requires *counting*: counting things, attitudes, performances, and so on. Hence we witness the massive proliferation in quantification techniques whose symptoms are the formulation of league tables in everything from preschools to hospitals to rule of law indices. It does not matter that these tables and results offer (and can have) no insight into the integrity, specificity or complexity of these social practices. What matters are the headline results, the determination of winners and losers. As was said of the 'body count' as a measure of American progress in the war in Vietnam in the 1960s, 'If you can't count what's important, you make what you can count important'. Hand in hand with the 'privatisation' of public or common goods (education, health, welfare) asserted through political projects of proclaimed inevitability, these changes in form are symptoms of exchange value's dominance, and ones which in turn affect the content of the practices and institutions themselves, from educational to governmental and legal practice.

With respect to changes in legal content, for example, Supiot cites legal forum shopping – 'the international market of legal rules' – as an example of how the inverted hierarchy of public and private changes the way in which law's purpose is understood. In allowing 'private persons to choose the public framework most likely to maximise their individual utilities … ultimately, the only law which holds is that of the pursuit of individual interest' (Supiot, 2013, 136; see also Veitch 2018). This results in negotiation and dealmaking becoming the dominant form of legal practice, rather than any notion of legality as (in Fuller's terms) the subjection of human conduct to the governance of rules. The effects of this shift are, as is perhaps only to be expected, unevenly distributed since they introduce a new (old) form of governance, the network, that signals the reconfiguration of private interest at the expense of the public. Across workplaces, national and transnational economies and government bureaucracies, the rise of chains of loyalties – to bosses, administrators and, most importantly, to creditors – signifies the reintroduction of status, and bonds of allegiance become the *modus vivendi* of the contemporary network. Taken together, this results in a new form of dependency, in the conditional burdening of the dependent's benefits with obligations to the superior, that are reminiscent, argues Supiot, of the feudal bond. In other words, the modern network society 'does not mark the culmination of individual freedom, but rather the reemergence of feudalism … it subjects people to fulfilling objectives rather than observing rules' (Supiot, 2013, 140). Doubly bound to personal ties and 'governance by numbers' (Supiot, 2018), under conditions of economic precarity the personal makes its reappearance as dependency, not autonomy; the administration of people and things, not of law.

If this is so, then the question arises as to what a (legal) politics of the public might still have to offer by way of critical analysis. It is to this question that we now turn.

3. RENEWAL

Critical legal scholars have an interest in the public realm. Not remaining beholden to the coercive power and discriminatory operation of dominant private interests, of 'privatisation' programmes and of the refeudalisation of social relations requires engaging at some point with the potential and the idea of the public. This may take the form of political strategies of the kind we have seen associated with feminist jurisprudence. Alternatively, or additionally, it may take the form of policy proposals for public ownership, public control or public accountability in the name of the people. Whatever form it takes, however, it demands utilising public, political contestability as the test for assigning public and private value generally. On this reading, any and all uses of coercion, and not only those associated with the state and the market, must be tested politically and publicly with respect to the designation of values worth protecting, whether as private or collective. In order to assess the significance of this dimension we turn to the work of Jurgen Habermas, which, arguably at least with respect to the analysis of the critical public sphere, has remained true to the earlier impetus of the Frankfurt School. If the public sphere invites a hermeneutical understanding and not merely a categorical one, we can nonetheless observe a second order dimension about form and potentiality in the public sphere that consists, as we will now see, in the fact that it is more than the mere *content* expressed in actors' self-understanding that is significant in this area of enquiry and activity.

In its Arendtian understanding, the public sphere is traced back to its Attic roots, and stands constructed as the brightly lit stage on which citizens engage one another directly and as equals in public deliberation. Here 'public-spiritedness' demands participation in the goods of the *common* realm, whose practice is its own end and not those of any particular or private self-interests. In clear contrast to this understanding, the contemporary 'public sphere' is often seen to be replete with powerful interests and forms – none more so than those associated with the distortions of the 'popular' media – in which interest groups seek out recognition, advantage and profit. So our question here is whether that is all that can now be said of the public sphere: does it remain always and only a projection of interests, susceptible to capture and hijack by the most powerful lobbies, or do there exist further capabilities that are not exhausted by those projections and susceptibilities? To explore the latter possibility, there are three potentialities in the public sphere that may be briefly considered. These are drawn from part of the work of Habermas (1996), though they by no means capture all or even most of what he has to say on the topic. The potentialities may be described as those associated with latency, dependency and the mode of actualisation in the public sphere.

According to Habermas,

> Public opinion can be manipulated but neither publicly bought nor publicly blackmailed. This is due to the fact that a public sphere cannot be 'manufactured' as one pleases. Before it can be captured by actors with strategic intent, the public sphere together with its public must have developed as a structure that stands on its own and reproduces itself *out of itself*. (1996: 364, original emphasis)

The temporal dimension here signals a priority – '*Before* it can be captured' – that has an important qualitative aspect: the public and the public sphere do not emerge as an agglomeration of private realms or a tally of private interests. Rather, for Habermas, the mode of formation (and reproduction) of the public sphere 'remains latent in the constituted public sphere – and takes effect again only in moments when the public sphere is mobilized' (ibid). In other words, even if the public sphere is open to domination by particular interests, it nonetheless remains a site where the appearance of an as yet unconstituted public can always occur. This latent potency, of a self-renewable 'public', is not the creation of the competition and compromise of particular interests but carries its own specific potential that may be tapped to counter and transform existing power relations.

This is further evidenced by the potential associated with a specific *dependency*, which also appears as core to the existence of the public sphere. For Habermas, 'the endogenous mobilization of public sphere activates an otherwise latent dependency built into the internal structure of every public sphere, a dependency also present in the normative self-understanding of the mass media: the players in the arena owe their influence to the approval of those in the gallery' (382). (The Arendtian overtones of stage, actors and audience resonate clearly in Habermas's depiction of the public sphere in this formulation.) Hence even where there may be, for example, an overbearing sense of the money-driven saturation of media content or political lobbying, there is never any guarantee that approval will not be withheld, that the audience will not turn its back and walk out or turn off. If not exactly a mutuality, then this latent dependency – in part induced by the need for power itself to *appear*, in whatever guise – and the potential it carries are similarly not reducible to private influence and competition. Such dependency, in other words, means the public sphere always has the capacity to make demands for critical transformation at the level of commonality and community, qualities and forms that cannot be manufactured or bought in their entirety.

The third potentiality rests in the mode of actualisation of deliberation in the public sphere. Engagement in the public sphere has a second order significance, which exists beyond the mere articulation of positions in debate. As Habermas notes:

> Whatever the manifest content of their public utterances, the performative meaning of such public discourse at the same time actualizes the function of an undistorted political public sphere as such … Actors who know they are involved in the *common* enterprise of reconstituting and maintaining structures of the public sphere as they contest opinions and strive for influence differ from actors who merely use forums that already exist. (369–70, emphasis in original)

With respect to political debate, for example, the 'dual orientation' of actors' public engagement may be geared to 'directly influenc[ing] the political system', but – and this is the decisive point – 'at the same time [actors] are also reflexively concerned with revitalizing and enlarging civil society and the public sphere as well as with confirming their own identities and capacities to act' (369–70). It is precisely this dual orientation that embodies the distinctively 'public' quality of the public sphere and its political potential. With respect to the mode of actualisation of deliberation, the public sphere instantiates a reflexivity that the competition of strategically geared self-interest does not and cannot. On this account, public sphere activities, their modes of articulation and debate, *do* have a distinctive quality: their second order significance cannot be quantified, nor counted and commodified. And this is precisely why they have been characterised as the 'carriers of the potentials of cultural modernity' (370).

These three potentialities significantly challenge the view that the public sphere is reducible to the play of private interests. For if the latter *were* true, then it also follows that no common or communal critical project could be invoked or would find resonance. There would be nothing beyond the calculations of self-interest, nothing beyond the aspirations offered by the charmless solipsism of liberal economic analysis, nothing to be thought (of) 'in common'. But it is precisely these mindsets and practices that the potentialities of the public sphere can work to disturb.

Under current conditions, however, these claims are not free from further challenge. There are two major sources of vulnerability that may be noted. The first is described by Habermas himself, and comes from a perhaps surprising source. That is, while the quality of the public sphere has its own claimed distinctiveness, it is not only threatened by intrusions of private interest and power, but is susceptible to a weakening caused by the effects of *public* institutions on what appear as nonpublic forms. In certain circumstances, Habermas argues,

> a panoptic state not only directly controls the bureaucratically desiccated public sphere, it also undermines the private basis of this public sphere. Administrative intrusions and constant supervision corrode the communicative structure of everyday contacts in families and schools, neighbourhoods and local municipalities ... Communicative rationality is thus destroyed *simultaneously* in both public and private contexts of communication. (369, emphasis in original)

The public sphere, in other words, is vulnerable not only to attacks directed at it, but also to a diminution in the capabilities of actors and activities across all forms of social relations. A major source of these threats is readily identifiable with (and this is the irony) nominally public, state or administrative, intrusions. But *pace* Habermas they are not limited to such origins. Those aspects of power that would operate through positive or productive modes, rather than in a deductive manner (of the state bureaucratic kind), may exacerbate this vulnerability. Hence disciplinary or biopolitical forms (of the kind analysed by Foucault), as well as those network forms noted in the previous section, may also succeed in 'corrod[ing] the communicative structure of everyday contacts'. In line with Supiot's earlier observations on contemporary neofeudalism, the 'private basis of the public sphere' may be vulnerable not only to state administrative intrusions but also to a range of practices and techniques that cut across public/private dimensions and leave both more susceptible than an optimistic constitutional democratic account would present.

The second vulnerability is different, and in a sense more radical. Here the danger arises not so much from some putative collapse of the public and private – from whichever place it originated – but from the role that law plays as the dominant contemporary form of thinking the relation between the two. It will be recalled that on Marx's account, the universal equality that was postulated – and in reality experienced – at the level of the state itself depended on the material reality of inequality and exploitation rooted in alienated labour and capitalist production. The state was, as we noted, a detour to emancipation, but emancipation got stuck there since the state and its underlying 'nonpolitical' ground determined and limited what could count as emancipation.

This insight points us towards the more profound vulnerability of the 'public' as a locus for common political action today. The concern here is not that it is captured by private interests, nor that it is a particular interest that is falsely universalised. Rather, it is that where 'the public' registers or acts predominantly in a legally defined way, then it too is forced to work through an institutionalised detour that naturalises a certain juridical *modus operandi*. As Legrand puts the point succinctly in the context of European legal integration, 'for every problem, there appears to be a solution and the solution is almost always law' (Legrand 2006: 14). The postindustrial west has been proclaimed as the 'age of rights', which exhibits what Loughlin describes as the dual movement of the politicisation of law and the legalisation of politics (Loughlin 2000, ch 13). Under this description, 'the public' can be seen to be increasingly organised *as* juridical. This condition has therefore a historical specificity of great import: as Habermas observes, 'Today legal norms are what is left from a crumbled cement of society ... Law stands as a substitute for the failures of other integrative mechanisms – markets and administrations, or values, norms, and face-to-face communications' (Habermas, 1999, 937). Where this is so, the public sphere of rights and dignities which is achieved brings with it a new kind of ambivalence. For it is at one and the same time an extraordinarily highly regulated politics in this sense: the tracks along which freedom can be enacted are already laid.

The danger to 'the public' as carrier of the latent potential for communal political practice lies not in its particular content – striated as that may be by powerful interests – but in its form. The juridical security established in the democratic constitutionalism of a market society understands law and legal categories as the best, perhaps the only, institutional form for deliberating and pursuing common goods. But the dominance of *homo juridicus* may come with a price. An 'unruly public' is no longer to be considered a political force or public movement that might 'carry the potential of modernity', but is rather something to be feared, like a Hobbesian state of nature. Where the public sphere may only be the legally underwritten and operationalised public sphere, the vulnerability of its more profound potential lies precisely in the reduction of political imagination to legal imagination.

To reassert the 'public' therefore means to be open not only to the dialectic of politicisation and depoliticisation, but to the politicisation of law in ways that may strain the legal settlement and categories that have themselves become normalised as forces for good. The *potential* of the public sphere – latency, dependency and the mode of actualisation – invokes the possibilities of an 'unconstituted public' as an expression of or figure for the carrier of movements that progress through unprepared ways and unexpected dissonances. Where these movements are, conversely, limited to legal categories, no matter how inventive, then 'the public' loses its unruly energy and potential and with it the potential to repoliticise what is deemed valuable as public *and* private. It is precisely this potential that is at stake in thinking about the public and the public in law today. And if this sense of the public is not only imaginative but imaginary, does that matter? Of course it does. This is part of its vulnerability. But then again, that alone is its power.

BIBLIOGRAPHY

Beck, U., 1986, *Risk Society*, London, Sage.
Bourdieu, P., 1998, *Practical Reason: On the Theory of Action*, Stanford, Stanford University Press.
Burns, R., 1795, 'A Man's a Man for a' That' available at www.robertburns.org/works/496.shtml (last accessed 31/10/18).
Cohen, M.R., 1927, 'Property and Sovereignty' 13 *Cornell Law Review*, 8–30.
Habermas, J., 1987, *The Theory of Communicative Action*, Volume 2, Cambridge, Polity.
Habermas, J., 1996, *Between Facts and Norms* (trans. W. Rehg) Cambridge, MA: MIT Press.
Habermas, J., 1999, 'Between Facts and Norms: An Author's Reflections', 76 *Denver University Law Review* 937.
Hale, R., 1923, 'Coercion and Distribution in a Supposedly Non-Coercive State', 38 *Political Science Quarterly*, 470–8.
Hume, D., 1987, 'Of the First Principles of Government' [1741], in *Essays Moral, Political, and Literary*, Indianapolis, Liberty*Classics*.
Hunt, A., 1986, 'The Theory of Critical Legal Studies', 6:1 *Oxford Journal of Legal Studies*, 1–45.
Kant, I., 1993/1785, *Groundwork for the Metaphysics of Morals*, Indiana, Hackett.
Klare, K., 1982, 'Public/Private Distinction in Labor Law' 130 *University of Pennsylvania Law Review*, 1358.
Lacey, N., 1998, *Unspeakable Subjects*, Oxford, Hart.
Legrand, P., 2006, 'Antivonbar' 1:1 *Journal of Comparative Law*, 14.
Leonard, T., 1995, *Reports from the Present: Selected Work 1982–1994*, London, Jonathan Cape.
Lordon, F., 2014, *Willing Slaves of Capital: Spinoza & Marx on Desire*, London, Verso.
Loughlin, M., 2000, *Sword and Scales*, Oxford: Hart.
Marx, K., 1843, 'On the Jewish Question', in D. McLellan, *Karl Marx: Selected Writings*, 1977, Oxford, Oxford University Press.
Olsen, F.E., 1983, 'The Family and the Market: A Study of Ideology and Legal Reform', 96 *Harvard Law Review*, 1497–1578.
Schmitt, C., 1985, *Political Theology*, Cambridge, MA, MIT Press.
Trudell, J., 1980, 'We Are Power', www.historyisaweapon.com/defcon1/trudellwearepower.html
Supiot, A., 2007, *Homo Juridicus*, London, Verso.
Supiot, A., 2013, 'The Public-Private Relation in the Context of Today's Refeudalization', 11 *I-CON*, 129–45.
Supiot, A., 2018, *Governance by Numbers*, London, Bloomsbury.
Thompson, E.P., 1975, *Whigs and Hunters*, New York, Pantheon.
Veitch, S., 2007, *Law and Irresponsibility: On the Legitimation of Human Suffering*, Abingdon, Routledge.
Veitch, S., 2018, 'Duty Free' in D. Matthews and S. Veitch, eds, *Law, Obligation, Community*, Abingdon, Routledge.
Weber, M., 1948/1919, 'Politics as a Vocation', in Gerth and Mills, eds, *From Max Weber: Essays in Sociology*, London, Routledge.
Williams, R.A., 1990, *The American Indian in Western Legal Thought: Discourses of Conquest*, Oxford, Oxford University Press.

9. Rhetoric, semiotics, synaesthetics
Peter Goodrich

> It is obviously in the realm of the cinema that *détournement* can attain its greatest effectiveness and, for those concerned with this aspect, its highest beauty.[1]

The principal impetus of contemporary critical legal theory is towards an exit from law. Melancholegalism, the saturnine sense of the failings of critique and the powerlessness of theory drive more inventive and younger scholars, wary of the title of jurist, into genres, styles, identities and offices far removed from classical legalism. In one sense, the critical exodus is motivated by a desire for the other – the illusion that literature, film, comics, creative writing, or philosophy, psychoanalysis, ethics, aesthetics, science or semiotics, will somehow fill the hole that exists at the heart of law. Such an oedipal drive is unlikely to succeed.[2] Nothing will fill the gap, but there is another facet to the exit orientation, this war in the virtual libraries, that does portend significance and change. Recognition of the limits of critique, the inutility of the hermeneutics of suspicion, has fostered a creativity of affect and expression. Such exuberance of discursive expression potentially promises, to borrow the language of the Melbourne school, a breakup of jurisdictions and multiplication of offices.

The second and plural feature of contemporary critical legal theory is that of an expanded rhetoric and accompanying reinvention and revivification of the figure of the jurist as an affective, embodied and precarious inhabitant of mobile and minor jurisprudential offices. The horizons may seem limited and the political possibilities constrained – and there is nothing new about that – but getting mobile, walking, taking law on the bus, bicycling through lawscapes, egressing into street art, parodic protests, novella and further performances, all indicate a rhetoric of the body in motion, as practice, habitus and inhabitation. The phenomenological attempt to occupy redefined offices thus suggests a material change, a shift of focus that is simultaneously inward – incarnadine, affective, synaesthetic – and exterior, because it is concerned with expression of this change, with the body as exteriority, as the motive of the outside, as engagement in a world without an outside. The cohering feature of the move to occupy office in a critically reflexive fashion is thus one of attention to the doings, the rhetorical actions, *elocutio* or delivery of law, in the broken up, global domains of new social media, radical relays, changed positions and altered sites of the jurist's new web archive, presence and engagements.

---

[1] Guy Debord, 'A User's Guide to Détournement', in *Complete Cinematic Works* (AK Press: 2003) 209.

[2] On which, see Maria Aristodemou, *Law, Psychoanalysis, Society: Taking the Unconscious Seriously* (Routledge: 2014) ch. 2 on law and lack, and especially pp. 15–16 on epistemophilia and the hopeless quest for truth through 'other' disciplines.

The stream of new media, the enhanced scope of potential modes of appearance in the social, the elision of news and entertainment, places ever greater emphasis upon the image as the immediacy and immediate impact of even an office as minor as that of the critical jurist, the scholar who seeks to think and teach law in a humanistic fashion. The breakup of the legal archive, the dissipation of the text of law into the crucible of online presences and web optimized viewings, the ethereal quality of the norm in a floating world, what Bottici terms imaginal politics, all suggest that an expanded rhetoric of law is now necessary, a semiotics of juristic transmission, an oratory of the image.[3] As the boundaries of legal texts become blurred, and as new media increasingly intrude and extricate law from its historically confined sites of expression and performance, it is the theatricality of juridism, the play of the norm, the atmosphere of lawyering, that is increasingly the appropriate object of our affections. It is this trajectory of an expanded rhetoric and the increasingly semionautical excursions of juristic office holders that this chapter will address. Everyone likes a map, and so, starting with the passage from rhetoric to semiotics, analysis will then move to the theatrocracy of contemporary governance, on to imaginal law, and will then conclude with a prospectus of the impact of new media upon critical legal theory and its transmission of legality.

1. RHETORIC TO SEMIOTICS

Rhetoric does not die. It contracts and expands, morphs and shifts, adopts the cover of different schema and tropes, but above all subsists because rhetoric is the law. It is this point that Barthes makes most effectively in his account of the 'ancient rhetoric' as a necessarily continuing form: 'what does it mean that all our literature, formed by Rhetoric and sublimated by humanism, has emerged from a politico-juridical practice (unless we persist in the error that limits rhetoric to the "Figures")?'[4] For Barthes, the critical project was here that of reviving a forgotten rhetoric, passing on its classical Latin forms, as a mode of challenging a criticism that had grown oblivious to the play of the law in the linguistic form of modern humanistic disciplines and institutions. The argument was that rhetoric, which classically was a combination of technique, teaching, science, ethic, social practice and ludic practice, had fallen into desuetude and had died. The cause was what Genette, in an article published in the same journal issue as Barthes' essay, termed rhetoric restrained.[5] Rhetoric had been contracted into an academic pedagogy, a didactic discipline that addressed only the figures of speech and even then was restricted by what Genette terms a 'tropological reduction'. Ethics,

---

[3] Chiara Bottici, *Imaginal Politics: Images beyond Imagination and the Imaginary* (Columbia University Press: 2013). See further on image and imaginal, Emanuele Coccia, *Sensible Life: A Micro-Ontology of the Image* (Fordham University Press: 2016).

[4] Barthes, 'The Old Rhetoric – An *Aide Mémoire*', in *The Semiotic Challenge* (Farrar, Strauss, Giroux: 1988) 92. Originally published as 'L'Ancienne rhétorique. Aide Mémoire' (1970) 16 *Communications* 172.

[5] Gérard Genette, 'Rhetoric Restrained' [1970] in *Figures of Literary Discourse* (Columbia University Press: 1982). For a comprehensive defence of rhetoric against such restrictions, see Brian Vickers, *In Defence of Rhetoric* (Oxford University Press: 1988).

social practice, the ludic and political dimensions of discourse, the theatrical quality of institutional enactments were all expelled in the name of reason, science and law conceived as carried by lucid, neutral and transparent linguistic means. We were rhetors without knowing it, orators who could not admit it. The *lexicon*, the imagistic law that governed discursive structures and propagated the common sense of proper meaning, ruled an unconscious practice.[6]

The linguistic turn which had its impact on law in the 1980s and motivated much of critical legal studies suffered from the dominance of analytic linguistic philosophy and the continuing drive to science. Linguistics, but not critical linguistics or a politically motivated sociolinguistics, emerged and fairly rapidly faded in the jurisprudence syllabus.[7] The pioneering Anglophone work, Bernard Jackson's *Semiotics and Legal Theory*, appeared in 1985 and was exemplary in evincing a near complete obliviousness of rhetoric while treating semiotics as a support for positivist jurisprudence. Legal semiotics was an exercise in mapping the linguistic presuppositions of legal theory, and it was the grammar of law that Jackson expressly sought to elucidate.[8] There is no need for any lengthy account as to the limited character of this structural linguistics, and the selection of positivist legal theory as its exclusive object meant that it had little critical appeal. The book was supposed to be the first of a triptych, but no further study appeared. From the viewpoint of critical legal theory, the appeal was small not only because of the choice of structural linguistics as the primary model for analytic intervention but also because the purpose of the exercise was at least implicitly the legitimation of the extant legal order. There was little takeup, although Duncan Kennedy did publish an article titled 'A Semiotics of Legal Argument' in 1991, and Jack Balkin followed suit with a couple of pieces on legal semiotics that in the main reiterated Kennedy's point: that legal arguments were malleable and could be flipped, which is to say, inverted into their opposite – a logical point that added little to earlier realist accounts of the endless pro et contra of any juristic doctrinal debate.[9] No argument is hermetically sealed, and meanings are plural. The action wasn't here, however promising the idea.

---

[6] This is the theme of Derrida, *Of Grammatology* (Johns Hopkins University Press: 1976) who argues that discourse – law – precedes speech, and that deconstruction, attentive to the play of meanings, always undoes the exemplary sense that the jurist – the pedagogue, the filing clerk – seeks to impose and relay.

[7] There was a brief flirtation in the US legal academy, or more accurately mainly in the legal studies academy, with legal hermeneutics. See, for example, Gregory Leyh, *Legal Hermeneutics: History, Theory, Practice* (University of California Press: 1992); Austin Sarat & Thomas Kearns (eds), *The Rhetoric of Law* (Michigan University Press: 1994). In the UK there was Peter Goodrich, *Reading the Law: A Critical Introduction to Legal Method and Technique* (Blackwell: 1986); and Goodrich, *Legal Discourse: Studies in Rhetoric, Linguistics and Legal Analysis* (Macmillan: 1986).

[8] Bernard Jackson, *Semiotics and Legal Theory* (Routledge: 1985); and the collection Domenico Carzo & Bernard Jackson (eds), *Semiotics, Law and Social Science* (Gangemi: 1990).

[9] Duncan Kennedy, 'A Semiotics of Legal Argument' (1991) 42 *Syracuse Law Review* 75; Jack Balkin, 'The Promise of Legal Semiotics' (1991) 69 *Texas Law Review* 1831.

The flaw in the theory lay not simply in restricting semiotics to a linguistic model, corrosive though that was, but more in the failure to understand law as a semiotics in a full sense, replete with the plurality and plenitude of signifying relays, as intrinsically rhetorical, gestural, figurative and theatrical. The expanded concept of rhetoric as semiosis, as the theatre of signification by whatever means, needed to be embraced and enhanced, whereas a lawful linguistics unaware of its inherent normative drive had little of the rhetorical left in it. There was nothing of the body, affect, play, nor anything of the incarnadine or imagistic in these rather cardboard pages of legal theory, and so critique took other paths. For the moment, however, it is the failure of rhetoric, the demise of legal semiotics, that needs noting. The critical legal theory textbooks – there are not many of them, my task is quite easy – uniformly ignore any explicit address of the rhetorical or semiotic. Thus Lieboff and Thomas, the exemplum of a critical coursebook, now in its second edition, has no reference to either enterprise but has rather moved on into a terrain of disparate critical enterprises that acknowledge the situated and corporeal character of interpretation and the play of image and imagination that necessarily encroach upon any analysis of law.[10] By the same token, Douzinas and Gearey's graduate level text makes the same move but without linking critique in any explicit fashion to the rhetorical laws and semiotic forms that political discourse necessarily takes.[11] The collective volume *New Critical Legal Thinking* indicates that what is new is variously affective, ludic, resistant and dissenting, and the contributors play with style, express commitments, examine practices and engage in performances of the politics advocated. Reflexivity as to existential and political commitments is not, however, mirrored in any direct focus upon questions of rhetoric, semiotics or the material presence of law. In similar vein, the European treatise *Law, Order and Freedom: A History of Legal Philosophy* addresses legal hermeneutics and a variety of critical and postmodern theories of law that acknowledge the metaphoricity of legal discourse but – somewhat surprisingly, granted the historical scope of the work – does not single out either rhetoric or semiotics as domains or disciplines meriting independent attention.[12] Such an endeavour, if it were to occur, would seem to be categorized defensively as belonging to the literary study of law, to the ornamental or figurative accessories of the text, and not to doctrine or law as properly and prosaically determined.[13] And as a final example, the recent, massive tome *In Search of*

---

[10] Marett Leiboff & Mark Thomas, *Legal Theories* (Lawbook Co: 2014) although at 137 they do provide a brief reference to rhetoric, but in illustration of hermeneutic method rather than in its own right. Scott Veitch (et al), *Jurisprudence: Themes and Concepts* (Routledge: 2012, 2nd edn) also adopts an integrated approach that briefly addresses specific topics, such as deconstruction, that have rhetorical resonance, but do not adumbrate any study of rhetoric or semiotics in their own right.

[11] Costas Douzinas & Adam Gearey, *Critical Jurisprudence* (Hart: 2005). The early work, Douzinas, Warrington & McVeigh, *Postmodern Jurisprudence* (Routledge: 1991) ch. 5, by contrast, does have a chapter on the 'Rhetoric of Natural Law' and several ludic analyses and novel literary excursions.

[12] C.W. Maris & F.C.L.M. Jacobs (eds), *Law, Order and Freedom: A Historical Introduction to Legal Philosophy* (Springer: 2011).

[13] Guyora Binder & Robert Weisberg, *Literary Criticisms of Law* (Princeton University Press: 2000) is an exemplum of this trait, with a chapter on rhetorical criticisms of law that

Contemporary Legal Thought is mainly an exercise in the loss of a project – the history of a growing separation of critique from law, and semiotics from legal analysis.[14]

It is time, then, as Barthes would doubtless have commended, to return to the roots of the rhetorical tradition and to acknowledge in its dramatic and plural forms the limitless possibilities for recognizing, contesting and performing critical versions of the theatre of law. Delivery has always been the most flexible and dynamic of the rhetorical arts, and the old disciplines, of gesture, dance, chirography and choreography, of figuration, performance, delivery and enactment, press out of the rhetorical curriculum and into the present.[15] So too the uses of imagery, from the paint of Rome to the inkhorn divinity of the protestant text, also provide intriguing models, historical exempla for analysis and critique of what we are too often surprised to confront as the novelty of the present.

2. THEATROCRACY UNBOUND

The allure of rhetoric, the fact that *rectorica non moritur*, that the rhetoric of law persists and insists, is tribute to the expansive possibilities of the forensic curriculum and particularly the study of performance and delivery that traditionally travelled under the sign of *elocutio*.[16] Rhetoric was tied to the theatrical dimensions of legality, to the moving and bending of auditors, the playing to the pit that critics complained of in the numerous condemnations of the thespian, from Plato to contemporary legal positivism.[17] Those who know how to persuade and move to action, who comprehend the dynamic and relational character, the emotive undertow of communication as staged in court and now also in the varying virtual forums and relays of a mobile optimized internet, increasingly hold the key to success.[18] Rhetorical delivery, the study of performance, not only increasingly defines the active modes of *rectorica*, as an expanding field, but also hints at a theatrocracy unbound, no longer confined to the court but rather mobile, instantaneous and unwired.[19] This, as Leiboff points out in relation to 'theatre proper', takes the performance out of its theatrical space and here

---

presents a history and culminates with James Boyd White's *When Words Lose Their Meaning* (Chicago University Press: 1984), with the 'law as rhetoric trope' still binding academic rhetorical study to literary representations of law and friendship.

[14] Justin Desaults-Stein & Chris Tomlins (eds), *Searching for Contemporary Legal Thought* (Cambridge University Press: 2017).

[15] For a brief overview, see Julie Stone Peters, 'Law as Performance', in Elizabeth Anker & Bernadette Meyler, *New Directions in Law and Literature* (Oxford University Press: 2017) 193.

[16] *Rectorica* is a medieval neologism for legal or forensic rhetoric, combining rule and oratory. The Latin successfully conveys the tensions within legal discourse.

[17] For an introductory analysis of historical links, see Peter Goodrich, 'Law', in Tom Sloane (ed.), *Encyclopedia of Rhetoric* (Oxford University Press: 2001).

[18] A point made extensively and well in Richard Sherwin, *Visualizing Law in the Age of the Digital Baroque* (Routledge: 2011), and also in Desmond Manderson (ed.), *Law and the Visual: Representations, Technologies, Critique* (Toronto University Press: 2018).

[19] For this coinage, see Julie Stone Peters, 'Theatrocracy Unwired: Legal Performance in the Modern Mediasphere' (2014) 26 *Law and Literature* 31. The key source or analysis of the divergence of law in court and law filmed, between trial and tribunal, is Cornelia Vismann,

trial, legal performance proper, moves beyond its confinement to the court: 'a place of the body, a place of responsibility, and a place in which response is shared.'[20] The rules of procedure, the decorum of court, the dialogic protocols and further textual limitations upon time, action and discourse melt away in the imaginal domain, the virtual space of internet and videosphere.

At the more structural level of doctrine, the constraint of rhetoric and the restriction of the study of persuasion to the linear and static formulations of the text have their roots in the protestant slogan *sola scriptura* and the subsequent restraint not only of images but also of figures, of any ornament in the text, or any imagination of spirit and divinity in the mind. Images and picturing were alike deemed idolatrous, and while there are more antique roots to the condemnation of the theatrical and the performative it is the political philosophy of neoscholasticism, associated with Ramus and with Luther, that most indicatively and perniciously excludes the expansion of rhetorical study to the imagery and figuration, enactment and media that transmit the law.[21] There is only the text, the linear linguistic elaboration of logical propositions; image and imagination remain excluded or relegated to the literary and accessory. It is this textual repression barrier that rhetoric, and specifically the study of figuration as fabrication – of affect, body, gesture – and the moving and bending of performance that needed recovery and reintroduction into the heartland of legal studies. The *vita activa* of lawyering, the practice of persuasion, the enactment of justice and law as the proper study of an engaged curriculum is precisely the ambit and ambition of a theoretically informed critical rhetoric of law or *rectorica critica*.

The rhetorical study of delivery has dual roots in the pedagogy of law. There is first the training of the body to do the work of law, which is historically the role of the Inns of Court – the practical inculcation of character which Aristotle, in the *Rhetoric*, had insisted was the start of all 'speaking well', of arguing justly, in civil matters. The institution of the persona of the lawyer as actor was the first stage and stepping stone of practice, and as Mukherji lengthily expatiates, this training as legal player, as *dramatis persona*, continued throughout the lawyer's career, not least in the proximity of the law courts to the theatres and the fluid passage of personnel between the two venues – a correlation now supplanted by the pervasiveness of screens from cinema, to television, to mobile phone.[22] Historically, masks and revels were key to the social life internal to the Bar and also part of the lawyer's leisure pursuit, a passion that is reflected in the training of advocates from Cicero to courtroom television, from the trial of Socrates to the drama of impeachment. What matters in law are the *leges actiones*, and in common law the system of writs which bring with them the possibility of social inscription, the

---

'Tele-Tribunals: Anatomy of a Medium' (2003) 10 *Grey Room* 5, reprinted in Marit Paasche & Judy Radul (eds), *A Thousand Eyes: Media Technology, Law and Aesthetics* (Sternberg Press: 2011).

[20] Marett Leiboff, 'Theatricalizing Law' (2018) *Law and Literature* 6.

[21] That history is rehearsed in Goodrich, Oedipus Lex: *Psychoanalysis, History, Law* (University of California Press: 1995).

[22] Subha Mukherji, *Law and Representation in Early Modern Drama* (Cambridge University Press: 2006) and also Paul Raffield, *Images and Cultures of Law in Early Modern England: Justice and Political Power, 1558–1660* (Cambridge University Press: 2007).

performance of words, embodiment and public propulsion, as much as the monumentalization in perpetuity and defiance of death with which law is also popularly associated.[23] The actors have to take the public stage and manipulate what current argot terms a 'functioning legal knowledge', and 'practical legal skills' that move beyond the arbours of the academy and into the theatre and increasingly virtual staging of public life. The rush to clinical legal education – to law graduates who can walk into a courtroom trial ready to act, equipped to file briefs, ready to draft complex instruments – that now dominates the US legal academic scene is simply a confused return to the theatrics of legality, the pedagogy of character and action, which rhetorical delivery had always implied and yet had for political reasons sought to keep hidden for fear that the ludic dimension and thespian forms of legal agonistics would be too easily perceived.

Character is tied to action, and action to *ethos* or the other dimension of the theatre of contemporary law, which is the decline in legal ethics, the diminishing trust placed in law and in lawyers. The rhetorical desire to teach *idonea persona*, the right person, and specifically good character, precedes and dictates the modes of gesture and delivery that the didactic curricular manuals would teach. Ethics, according to Aristotle, is action, the path of patterns or habits of behaviour. Habit is dress and *habitus* or space of being is similarly an accoutrement or architectural costuming of being, wherein, as Gary Watt expounds in his elucubrations on the law of dress, costume is custom and clothing is a first law.[24] How we appear is key to impression and effect, a precondition of persuasion and movement to action, which are goals of successful delivery. Appearance is never simply appearance but rather, as with the image, it is more than it seems. It is this theme that rhetoric has played with and developed into the elaborate theatrical devices of juridical dissimulation which Puttenham classically defines as the first figure of *allegoria*, common to courtier and 'the gravest Counselor' that will alter the 'whole and entire meaning' of a speech. It is the figure of allegory whereby 'we speak one thing and think another, and … our words and our meanings meet not'.[25] Writing from the English Bar, Puttenham has a profound sense of the politics of legal performance and with it a corresponding appreciation of the theatrical quality of law. Insofar as a legal trial is a staging, a performance or enactment of the cause and defence, it is necessarily a fiction, a representation, rather than a reality or direct truth.[26] It is not that theatre is only false, but rather that it is a necessary dissemblance,

---

[23] On the *leges actiones*, the source is Gaius, *Institutes*, and for commentary, see Giorgio Agamben, *The Sacrament of Language: An Archaeology of the Oath* (Polity: 2010) 57–65. The theme is also an important one in Vico. See: *The New Science of Giambattista Vico* [1744] (Cornell University Press: 1994) and the prescription taken from the Twelve Tables, *uti lingua nuncupassit, ita ius esto* – as it is declared by the tongue, so shall it be binding.

[24] Gary Watt, *Dress, Law and the Naked Truth* (Bloomsbury: 2013); and also Watt, 'Law Suits: Clothing as the Image of Law', in Leif Dahlberg (ed.), *Visualizing Law and Authority: Essays on Legal Aesthetics* (De Gruyter: 2012) at 23. On habit, see Agamben, *The Highest Poverty* (Stanford University Press: 2013) 13–18; Goodrich, 'The Example of Undressing: Obnubilations on the Empty Space of the Rule' (2018) *Law and Literature* 101.

[25] George Puttenham, *The Art of English Poesie* [1559] (Cornell University Press: 2007) 270–1.

[26] For contemporary elaborations of these themes, see Alan Read, *Theatre and Law* (Palgrave: 2016).

a species of allegory or morality play that has dramatic decisional and didactic purposes. Law is staged for public consumption, for the pit and now for the media, and that performative character and quality is the covert and yet essential facet and fabrication of legality. The theatre of law is a spectacle of justice and as such it has to accede to the primary rule of rhetorical delivery, which is attention to and fashioning so as to appeal to the audience. We are witness here to what the legal tradition terms the image as *veritas falsa*, a false truth, the paradox that Puttenham also notes in the maxim *qui nescit dissimulare nescit regnare*.

The law's a play, and in that dual sense of performative and ludic or feigned, the dependence of legality upon its visibility and staging at least provides the basic tools for the orchestration and enactment of the art of judgment. Critical rhetoric addresses precisely these themes and moves of the theatrical in the legal, the medium as a substantial part of the message, through the study of the architecture, the costume, the gestures or, in more classical terminology, the *notitia dignitatum*, the symbols of office, the choreography, the chirology and chironomy of advocacy as studied in the early modern manuals and beyond.[27] The *lex gestus* or law of gesture goes back to the ancients, to Cicero and Quintilian, the theory of rhetorical action and the art of dignified mimicry in which performance mirrors thought. The danger and the interest of focus on the theatrical character of law, however, is precisely, as Puttenham points out, to track the dissimulative quality of the performance, the art of persuading the auditors being that of adapting appearance to desire and engaging the viewer in a projection of their own topics or preconceptions. The study of the theatre of rule, of theatrocracy, is thus much more than a simple scrutiny of staging. It is rather an opening up of jurisprudence to the spatiality, temporality, auricular and visual tones and scenes of law.

The entry into the courtroom as a space of performance suggests that it is the visual import and message of the theatre of law that is most pertinent to the contemporary transmission of law. Far more than the text or linear scriptural narrative of judgement, it is the memes, bytes, clips and scenes that will circulate and model the identity and role of social subjects. Just as the courts ban mobile phones and digital cameras of all sorts from the courtroom, the inevitability of capture on film, whether by appointment or by covert ripping of images, is increasingly acknowledged. Cameras are part of the life of the courts and where direct filming is effectively disallowed, the mass media, news cycles and narrative features can all relay dissimulative but realistic stagings of what has happened 'in camera' or off screen. The attention of the media, as Vismann notes so effectively, brings the world into the courtroom, and while some fear this move as a theatrocratic shift to legal populism, the scene is rather one of dramatic reorientation and rethinking of the manner and media of law's transmission: 'The camera intervenes in even the forensic ritual of coding violence and threatens to

---

[27] On *chirology* and *chironomia*, the key source is Bulwer, *Chirologia: or the Natural Language of the Hand … Whereunto is added Chironomia: or the Art of Manual Rhetoricke* (Twyford: 1644). More broadly or manually, see Goodrich, *Legal Emblems and the Art of Law* (Cambridge University Press: 2014) ch. 6 ('The Missing Hand of the Law'), and Goodrich, 'Visiocracy: On the Futures of the Fingerpost' (2013) 39 *Critical Inquiry* 498.

topple the media conversion of act to language in favor of another: act to image.'[28] Law increasingly becomes a visual communication, a material and synaesthetic atmosphere and form relayed through performance, with its capture and transmission in digital images cut and concatenated for the instantaneous circulations of diverse web platforms.

Law as a visual phenomenon is wholeheartedly and most effectively embraced by MacNeil in *Lex Populi*, a work dedicated to celebrating the modalities of the legal imaginary as portrayed in popular novels, television shows and films.[29] For MacNeil and the proponents of law and popular culture, jurisprudence can be rendered greatly more accessible and the transmission of law can be studied in much more profound detail by addressing it not through the desiccated and outmoded frame of formal texts, but in the alluring and ludic mode of *Buffy the Vampire Slayer*, *Harry Potter*, *Legally Blonde* or *The Walking Dead*.[30] Here the popular modes of narrative entertainment provide indirect but significant insight into legal personnel and institutions as perceived and appropriated by mass media. This egalitarian impetus and method of studying law signals a dissipation of the cathartic impact of legality.[31] The esoteric and closed, procedurally governed, obscure and highly formal theatre of the court is displaced by popular media and mobile relays that break the law up but also signal a huge increase in the audience and circulation of images of lawful behaviour and of normative institutions. Theatrocracy is not simply unbound and unwired but is released into virtual space as atmosphere, mobility, mood and flow. The theatrical closure of legality, in other words, is broken down and law seeps into the environment – becomes a lawscape, a series of ruptures, small spaces of encounter where it is spatial justice, the interaction of bodies and images, that forms the modality of an ambulant, virtual law in an augmenting diversity of imaginary spaces.[32]

---

[28] Vismann, 'Tele-tribunals', at 15. On the fear of the camera as populism in court, and with it the erasure of procedural rules and decorum, see also Richard Sherwin, *When Law Goes Pop: The Vanishing Line between Law and Popular Culture* (Chicago University Press: 2004).

[29] William P. MacNeil, *Lex Populi: The Jurisprudence of Popular Culture* (Stanford University Press: 2007).

[30] On the last item, see MacNeil, 'The Litigating Dead: Zombie Jurisprudence in The Walking Dead, The Rising and World War Z', in Delage et al (eds), *Law and New Media: West of Everything* (Edinburgh University Press: 2019) 138–55.

[31] On the low cathartic impact of images seen on mobile devices, small screens, in brief and partial viewings, see Gabriele Pedullà, *In Broad Daylight: Movies and Spectators after the Cinema* (Verso: 2012).

[32] I am drawing here from Andreas Philippoulos-Mihapoulos, *Spatial Justice: Body, Lawscape, Atmosphere* (Routledge: 2015). For interesting studies of Scandinavian courtrooms, see the essays collected in Kjell Modéer & Martin Sunnqvist (eds), *Legal Stagings: The Visualization, Medialization and Ritualization of Law in Language, Literature, Media, Art and Architecture* (Tusculanum Press: 2012).

3. IMAGINAL LAW

The court and trial scene are emblematic of the agon of law and the limiting instance or adversarial testing of both character and skill. What has happened since the advent of film and television's intrusion both indirectly and directly upon the trial scene is an erasure of the boundaries of the courtroom and the increasingly omnipresent image of law and lawyers in the diverse platforms and dissipating relays of the public sphere. The expanding theatrocracy, meaning the ever more visible presence of law in social space and social media, gives away the secret of law, or at the least provides accessible evidence of the theatrical character and stage rulings of the process. Law cannot any longer hide behind its forms and costumes, architecture and portraiture for the simple reason that these are now fully on display, there to be seen rather than obscured by hierophantic language, the physical distance and daunting thresholds of the traditionally ensconced modes of legal presence. The change in forms and media of visibility carries with it a series of implications for our understanding of legality, as an institution and as a social and political practice. Rhetorical study of law now expands into visual and virtual jurisprudence, into what the French mediologist Debray terms the videosphere, the realm of the eye and of circulation through new visual media. As Debray also alludes, a change in medium signals also a change in order and law.[33] This is a point also made with force by Samuel Weber, which merits recognition. Theatre and theory share the same linguistic root in the Greek word *thea*, a place from which to observe or see. While it is true that this root suggests a privileging of sight, the more interesting connotation is that a change in theatre will have effects upon, either expanding or disorienting, the theory of transmission. Thus, '[t]heatricality demonstrates its subversive power when it forsakes the confines of the *theatron* and begins to wander: when in short it separates itself from the theatre'.[34]

The concepts of a law that wanders, an itinerant law and peripatetic jurists are hardly novel, except that the mode of escape is one of rupture or disjuncture in which the rules of representation, of argument and address, are abandoned in favour of those that govern or facilitate the new media. The confines of the court exert radically restrictive rules, dress codes, formalities of placement and speech which greatly limit what can be argued as well as how such advocacy is delivered. The new forms and media do not constitute a novel space or jurisdiction over which law governs in new modes, but rather a breaking of boundaries, an intermediate space, undetermined and unconfined by the traditional restraints or, theatrically, the unities of action, time and place. The videosphere, in Debray's analysis, is global, relational and situational. Fluid sites, moods and atmospheres, transitory conjunctures and symbolic relays determine the choral apparition of norms and acclamatory modes of political decision making. In the videosphere, authority resides in the visibility of structures, personnel and messages of governance circulating as what Debord terms 'the immense accumulation of spectacles'

---

[33] Régis Debray, *Cours de médiologie générale* (Gallimard: 1991) at 387–9. See also the expansion of the classification in Debray, *Vie et mort de l'image: Une histoire du regard en Occident* (Gallimard: 1992) ch. 8, which chapter is translated as 'The Three Ages of Looking' (1995) 21 *Critical Inquiry* 529.

[34] Samuel Weber, *Theatricality as Medium* (Fordham University Press: 2004) at 37.

of rule.[35] These signs of power act as visual exempla of social relations which appropriate and commodify public space while deflecting and distracting focus from the practice of administration and the disposition of collective goods. It is in this critical sense that the spectacle is deemed an illusion, an opium, that requires for Debord a critique of human geography which triggers communal construction of alternative spaces expressive of the actual experience of production and the 'total history' of the group.[36] There is an alternative, in other words, to the passive consumption and alienated subjectivity of image relay and spectacularity.

The symbolic economy of the videosphere tends to be viewed by Debord as a one way street, a fetishistic flow of images from sovereign to subject, constituting an alienated symbolic politics of appearances disjoined from any reality. The choral and acclamatory character of political spectatorship, the politics of populism, replaces participatory democracy with a dangerous theatrocracy.[37] Against such a negative view, though not without considerable caution, a critical argument can be made for reinstituting a more plural concept of the spectator and of the dramaturgy of the social. Rancière, for instance, argues that the theatrocracy of the image allows for a democratization of what he terms 'the distribution of the sensible', the institutional order of the sayable and the visible, the law of what can be said and of what bodies can appear.[38] The spectator can be emancipated, the audience can respond, changes can be made through a plural and active sense of listening and viewing. At one level, 'the image has to become the active, disruptive power of the leap – that of the change of regime between two sensory orders', as a challenge to consensus and as a critique of the passivity attributed to spectatorship.[39] The internet offers mobility, access and opportunity for alternative spectacles and stagings, installations, interventions and events, as witnessed with the Occupy movement and the Arab Spring. The anti-apparatus of *V for Vendetta* can suddenly go viral and global, the same nonperson appearing in Brazil and in Birmingham, San Francisco and Hong Kong in a sudden pluralization and equalization of the production of spectacles – a reorientation, as Bottici argues it, that equalizes freedom.[40]

Changes in theatre signify changes in theory, the collapse and reforming of the symbolic in differing modes. The key to what is best formulated as the contemporary mediasphere, a plural sense and expansion of the videosphere, is the legitimation of governance through visibility and both verbal and visual virtual relays. For Bottici, this is the space and domain of the imaginal, the contested platform of a politics predicated upon the circulation of images, verbal, pictorial, sensory and chimerical. To the extent

---

[35] Guy Debord, *The Society of the Spectacle* [1967] (Zone Books: 1994) 12.
[36] Debord, *Society of the Spectacle*, 126.
[37] For a more recent and powerful version of this argument, applied to the 11 September 2001 attacks and their aftermath, see I.B. Retort, *Afflicted Powers: Capital and Spectacle in a New Age of War* (Verso: 2006) ch. 1.
[38] Jacques Rancière, *The Politics of Aesthetics* (Continuum: 2004); and most importantly for the legal implications of theatrocracy and police, see Mónica López & Julien Etxabe, *Rancière and Law* (Routledge: 2017).
[39] Jacques Rancière, *The Future of the Image* (Verso: 2007) 46. On the contestation of the passivity of the spectator, see Jacques Rancière, *The Emancipated Spectator* (Verso: 2009).
[40] Bottici, *Imaginal Politics*, 179.

that politics and law depend upon this internetwork of virtual and viral bytes, the circulation and recirculation of memes, grams, tweets, emojis and emoticons, the traditional, binary structures of active and passive, real and merely apparent, are deconstructed in favour of a distinct category of the imaginal, which can be both fictitious and real, passive and active, unconscious and present simultaneously. Thus 'the imaginal is not a world, but it is what makes a world possible in the first place'.[41] Extant between the sensible and the intellectual, the dominion of images suspends the real, the ontology of the image being its presence as an entity, a thought, a participation in collective life that precedes and exceeds the static formulations of the old materialism, or what used to be termed empirico-criticism. For Bottici, it is necessary to extend our concept of the imaginal to traverse both conscious and unconscious images and to recognize that part of our mental life that, to borrow from the argot of Catholicism, is 'consubstantial to images themselves and cannot be reduced to something else'.[42]

A change of theory leads to alternate methods and, in relation to law, to a reintroduction of the study of the role of the image, of emblems, costumes, pictures, visual representations, animation and videography, figures and portraits in the interior and affect of decision and law. The imaginal lies at the heart of legal policy, the key determiner of judicial voting patterns, of juristic interpretation and of attachment to law. The critical lawyer, as Kennedy points out, suffers from a hermeneutic of suspicion, a species of recidivism or holding back, standing away from and pulling down both affect and image to explanations predicated upon exterior and corrupt causes.[43] Imaginal suggests a more positive and interventionist method, an expansion of the objects and relays of legal study as well as of the methods of their transmission. The imaginal is apprehended differently, a point that the early lawyers understood in their use of the notion of proceeding, where it was a question of performance or image, *ad apparentiam*, according to the visual relay, the theatrical force and connections of the depicted, rather than simply according to analogy or linear similarity of words.[44] The eye traverses the image in a lateral and ambulatory mode, according to visual connectors with blind spots and tensors that are absent from textual scanning.[45] The imaginal is an acknowledgement of mood, of proliferating and intensive affects that challenges cynical and critical reason alike by displacing distrust, semiotic suspicion and critique as chariness, with an opening to the image as a realm of potential, of

---

[41] Bottici, *Imaginal Politics*, 61.

[42] Bottici, *Imaginal Politics*, at 71.

[43] Duncan Kennedy, 'The Hermeneutic of Suspicion in Contemporary American Legal Thought' (2014) 25 *Law and Critique* 91; and at greater length, see Rita Felski, *The Limits of Critique* (Chicago University Press: 2015), especially pp. 18–26.

[44] On the legal conception of procedure *ad apparentiam*, see Goodrich, *Legal Emblems*, 134–6, 155–645; and see also the recent volume, Desmond Manderson (ed.), *Law and the Visual: Representations, Technologies, Critique* (Toronto University Press: 2018) for expatiation of such themes in diverse contexts and jurisdictions.

[45] On the differences between reading and viewing, see Jean-François Lyotard, 'The Dream-Work Does Not Think', in Lyotard, *Discourse, Figure* (1971) (Minnesota University Press: 2011) 268–76. For a radical development of this thesis in relation to cinema, see Laurence Moinereau, *Le Générique: De la lettre à la figure* (Presses universitaires de Rennes: 2009).

possibility, of exuberance and expression in variable and contestable forms. The critical legal theorist can finally open to their role in continuing the tradition, and in creating a living law.

4. NEW MEDIA, REMEDIATION, LAW

No less a figure than William Blackstone, in a chapter on private wrongs, remarks in a discussion of points of law that 'the Judges of the Court upon testimony of their own senses, shall decide the point'.[46] It is precisely to the testimony of the senses, to the body of the judge, as also to the sensorium of the jurist, that the imaginal belongs. To address the visuality of legality, to avoid reducing the image to scripture or picture to text and word, it is necessary to resort to other disciplines and methodologies cognizant of the imaginal and unleashed from the page into the *corpus iuris* of the body. Blackstone's chance remark, invoking the body and by implication a synaesthetics of judgment, allows a point of entry into the methods of the cinematic and the concatenation of images as being also a medium and modality of law. The final phase of rhetorical analysis of delivery, the semiosis of the imaginal, takes us into the terrain of what Coccia labels the sensible life of the intrabody.[47] This is the body as flow, as a stream of images and sensations, external and internal, joined by the medium of perception and consistency over time.

For the purposes of legality, meaning here the legitimation and transmission of governmental norms and administrative practices, the imaginal opens up a world that legal positivism has long occluded. The new media as they intrude upon law undo the unities of the juridical tradition, the archive, text, court, discourse, their protocols and limits. The image is an intermediary, interior and exterior, an affect that in its mobility transports and impacts. The novelty of the cinematic was precisely in its movement, as medium or mode of transmission of life, and as affect or the possibility of impacting the subject in relation to externality and other bodies. Three ruptures with the graphosphere or scriptural world of law are key to apprehending the image as another mode of sensibility and independent medium of transmission that takes root in film. First, cinema is movement-image, what Deleuze terms *pure semiotics*, and by implication an absolute break with the unitary concept of text and language – reading – as the mode of intelligibility.[48] The movement-image of cinema is precisely the reason that a semiotics modelled on linguistics cannot but have a reductive and negative role in understanding the import of filmic images. There is no grammar or syntax of film because there are no fixed or stable entities that can form the dictionary upon which

---

[46] Sir William Blackstone, *Commentaries on the Laws of England* (1767–8) (Oxford University Press: 2016) Book 3:22, p. 218.

[47] Coccia, *Sensible Life*, at 67: 'The images that live within us make up a type of body, a particular, minor body, that we apprehend in dream.'

[48] Gilles Deleuze, *Cinema: The Movement Image* (1983) (Minnesota University Press: 1986) ch. 1. For an interesting development of Deleuzian cinema theory, see Daniel Frampton, *Filmosophy: A Manifesto for a Radically New Way of Understanding Cinema* (Wallflower Press: 2006); and for an excellent introduction to the psychoanalytic roots of film theory, see Vicky Lebeau, *Psychoanalysis and Cinema: The Play of Shadows* (Wallflower Press: 2001).

putatively univocal communication can be predicated.[49] The movement-image of film is unique and intrinsically medial, a facet that leads to a second rupture, the exodus of the law from the library and from the courtroom, and takes the juridical into the world in modes of visibility and presence that are both dissipations of the power of law, its formal communicative constraints and expansions of its practical jurisdiction.

The expansion of the image that cinema allows takes it out of the theatre and into an extensive domain of internet platforms and instantaneous web networks. For good or ill, the cinema has left the theatre and the collective and intensified experience of viewing theatrically has been largely displaced by the free circulation of images or a 'postauditorium' cinematics that creates volatile and novel combinations of viewers in virtual seriality.[50] The density and copresence of actor and audience in the theatre, replaced in cinema by the image of an absent actor, is displaced by the mobile intensification and fragmentation of spectatorship, the rapid cut and streamed flow of postcinematic narrative and imagery which predominantly takes the form of a continuous series of *intermezzi* – the classical mode of performances that took place during the main show's intermissions.[51] Now there are only *intermezzi*, moments of stolen viewing, voyeuristic entertainments peeked at in heterogeneous contexts free of any religious aura or legal *gravitas*: 'For its spectator the film unfolds in that simultaneously very close and definitively inaccessible "elsewhere" in which the child sees the amorous play of the parental couple ... In this respect the cinematic signifier is not only "psychoanalytic"; it is more precisely Oedipal in type.'[52] The image, the pure semiotic of passion without transformation, is the essential link not simply to the somatic body but also to memory and childhood, a shared, because most accessible and constant, medium. This is the *theatrum mundi*, the world as apprehended by media that precisely makes its apprehension possible in constantly changing forms.

The third facet of the movement-image is its play upon desire. We exist in and are bonded to images because the image is at root our identification with the self and its appetites. The body is image, because it is given body by the image: 'In fact every living being can be defined as that which has an essential relationship to an image, as something that holds infinite images within itself – in the form of consciousness, in the form of the species and of its own appearance and identity.'[53] Formulated in the rhetorical terms of delivery or the gestural elocution of imagery, it is precisely the capacity or more strongly the drive of imagery, the scopophilic lure of the visual, that immerses and moves the subject in a sensual experience of the imaginal world.[54] Film proffers fascination, rapture, tactile epistemologies, embodied perceptions, a haptic

---

[49] On the divorce of film and structural linguistics, see Jean Mitry, *Semiotics and the Analysis of Film* (Athlone Press: 2000) chs 1–3.

[50] Pedullà, *Broad Daylight*, 132–6.

[51] Pedullà, *Broad Daylight*, 107–8.

[52] Christian Metz, *Psychoanalysis and Cinema: The Imaginary Signifier* [1977] (Macmillan: 1982) at 64. See also Vicky Lebeau, *Childhood and Cinema* (Reaktiokn: 2008).

[53] Coccia, *Sensible Life*, 97, continuing: "Life seems to be a quality of images ... a capacity to hold images and make them emanate."

[54] Laura Mulvey, *Visual and Other Pleasures* (Macmillan: 1989) introduced these themes, although they can be found already in Walter Benjamin: on which see Laura Marks, *The Skin of Film: Intercultural Cinema, Embodiment, and the Senses* (Duke University Press: 2000) 138–45.

visuality, a genuinely incarnadine imaginal desire.[55] The image transports and in offering morphosis triggers both fear and pleasure, the abject and the sublime. What is essential is the immersion in and attachment to the medium of the image, its angelological character and quality allowing for a visceral relay that script and textual transfer cannot provide.

Returning to the juridical, the image is an exorbitant threat, a theatrocratic but also haptic challenge to law ways and legal forms and formularies. A legal semiotics of contemporary law thus needs to expand its scope and regenerate its method so as to be able to apprehend the new media of law. The future of the semiotics of law is thus one which is competent to address the three facets of the movement-image – mobility, fragmentation and desire – that legal rhetoric and semiotics has traditionally evaded. The image as memory, as mark of a past and precedent, is not a problem for law, it is the haptic and desiring image that changes the game and places an unconventional and proleptic demand upon critical legal theory and the jurisprudence of our day. Law is succumbing to remediation, it travels under different signs and diverse forms, and, as Sherwin has lengthily analysed, these are neither self-evident nor neutral.[56] A visual rhetoric of law, which is what a pure semiotics generates in the mode of movement, and affect, as also colour, sound and immersion in the narrative of desire, places novel demands upon jurisprudence to come to terms with the remediation of decision and transmission, the pictorial turn in law that now needs to focus upon the immersive performativity of an image driven administration.[57] The law does not escape such changes in mediality and the task of a future rhetoric of law is to devise the means to apprehend and analyse the changing social forms of law's presence. Such an enterprise will only succeed if there is a thoroughgoing rethinking of the purpose of such inquiry, a breaking away from law so as to return to it in the more realistic and contemporary mode of its circulation via and in the fragmentary and low-cathartic forms of new media.

---

[55] This theme can be pursued via the fine analysis in Martine Beugnet, *Cinema and Sensation: French Film and the Art of Transgression* (Edinburgh University Press: 2007).

[56] Sherwin, *Visualizing*, 38–42.

[57] The pictorial turn is coined in Volker Boehme-Neßler, *Pictorial Law: Modern Law and the Power of Pictures* (Springer: 2011). The major and commendable collection of essays in this area is Anne Wagner and Richard Sherwin (eds), *Law, Culture and Visual Studies* (Springer: 2014).

10. Law and deconstruction

Johan van der Walt

1. INTRODUCTION

Deconstruction is a mode of philosophical thinking that is principally associated with the work of the French philosopher Jacques Derrida. Considered from the perspective of the history of philosophical thinking, the crucial move Derrida made was to shift the focus of textual inquiry away from a direct engagement with the cognitive content of ideas put forward in a text in order to focus, instead, on the way in which the text produces a privileged framework of meaning while excluding and/or marginalising others. Instead of engaging in a debate with other philosophers – contemporary or past – about the ideas they articulated in their texts, Derrida launched inquiries into the way their texts relied on dominant modes of writing (and reading) to produce a certain semantic content and intent while excluding other modes of reading and, consequently, other possible meanings of the text.

By focusing on the *textuality* of texts – instead of on their *semantic content* – Derrida endeavoured to pay attention not only to that which the text does not say, but also that which it cannot say. The explanation that follows will show that the 'method' of deconstruction does not just consist in finding that other meanings of the text are possible or plausible, but, more importantly, in demonstrating that the possibility or plausibility of other meanings – supressed by the organisation of the text – alerts one to the infinite potentiality of meaning that necessarily exceeds the margins of the text and therefore remains unsayable. In other words, by pointing out the instability of the dominant meaning organised by the text, deconstruction alerts one to the unsayable as such, that is, to that which *no* text can say but on which all texts remain dependent for being able to say what they manage to say. Textual meaning accordingly only becomes possible by way of a selection of meaning from multiple possibilities of meaning. Deconstruction interrogates this selection process. It does not do so to replace this selection with another. It does so simply to show that any claim to exclusive meaning – a claim that invariably accompanies the privileged meaning of the text – is spurious. And it does so in order to 'reactivate' the infinite potentiality of meaning that the organisation of the text seeks to 'deactivate'.

Texts 'deactivate' the full potentiality of meaning by privileging one reading and marginalising and suppressing others. Deconstruction 'reactivates' the potentiality of meaning by exposing the instability and precariousness of this marginalisation and suppression. It allows the margins of the text to enter the body of the text again. It does not do so to choose the margin instead of the body, for by doing so it would itself select a meaning and 'deactivate' the unsayable, that is, 'deactivate' the infinite potentiality of saying that its very aim is to 'reactivate'. It allows the margin to re-enter the body of the text so as to put body and margin in play with one another. It arranges a 'showdown' between them. This 'showdown' is enough to precipitate an awareness in the reader that there is much more to say about what is said in the text than that which the text actually says or will ever be able to say.

What happens next, happens. The 'showdown' may end with the return and reconstruction of the meaning that was dominant from the start, or it may end with the rise to prominence or dominance of meaning that has hitherto been marginalised or suppressed. This rise to prominence or dominance of previously excluded meaning may be fortunate or unfortunate. Deconstruction is not concerned with this eventual fortune or misfortune. It is concerned solely with the precipitation of an *event* that offers an opportunity either for a dominant discourse to reassert itself firmly or for a new language to take its place. Deconstruction is not concerned with privileging one of the terms in a binary opposition, but with the *unstable interim* or *interval* that becomes manifest when the conventional settling of the tension between the oppositional terms – through privileging one at the cost of the other – becomes unsettled.[1] It is not difficult to see that this reassertion or renewal could be beneficial, and to see how it could effect a certain invigoration of a semantics that may have become stale. It is also not difficult to see how this reassertion or renewal could turn out to be calamitous. Deconstruction – *Derridean* deconstruction, in any case – is not particularly concerned about any of these outcomes. It is motivated by the poetic obsession with the infinite scope of meaning and action that opens up when texts are unsettled and multiple meanings compete for the stakes of resettlement; for it is here – in the drama of the event – that the linguistic closures of regular discourse open up to the precipice of the unsayable. It is tempting to attribute to deconstruction a laudably progressive politics because of its obvious aspiration to 'shake things up'. But if deconstruction is political, it is definitely not party or programme-political. Derrida's personal political position could be described as "left of centre" (more or less in line with that of Jürgen Habermas, as transpired from the warm relations between them during the last years of Derrida's life[2]), but he would have been the first to acknowledge and stress that one does not need deconstruction to articulate this political position.

To the extent that deconstruction can be said to be political, its politics would consist in the poetic retreat from the staleness of readily available political programmes. In times that are indeed marked by the tedious and lifeless repetition of more or less empty political slogans aimed at securing the vested interests of the status quo, this poetic politics may well offer an emancipatory potential. It is not difficult to grasp that the demise of significantly refreshing political imaginations is bound to reduce the political arena to a hollow façade that at best serves as a screen for the naked power play behind it. In this regard Derridean deconstruction may well have something significant to say in response to the dominance of the neoliberal political language of our time that is no longer spoken only by the 'conservative right', but also by (what used to be) the 'progressive left'. But any idea that this political response can be translated into any specific political programme would be misguided. The politics of deconstruction is a meta-politics. One may rely on it in the hope to revitalise a political

---

[1] See Jacques Derrida, *Positions* (Chicago: University of Chicago Press, 1981) 412.
[2] See Jürgen Habermas, *Ach Europa* (Frankfurt am Main: Suhrkamp, 2008) 40–6 for a telling testimony.

system that has fallen prey to a deadening securocracy. But one cannot co-opt it for any specific political programme without betraying its undeniably anarchic thrust and its poetic fascination with an unruly eventfulness, the consequences of which it refuses to censor or sanction in advance.

The difficulty related to co-opting deconstruction for a political programme also raises serious questions regarding its usefulness for legal theory. It is in the very nature of law to propose a closed system of norms for the resolution of conflicts that can be identified as *legal conflict*. The softening of the closed system of legal norms that constitute a legal system through recourse to rules of equity or equitable considerations does not open up that system. Nor does it unsettle it or render it unstable. Recourse to rules or principles of equity renders the system of law more applicable and more effective. It stabilises the systemic closure of the law and thus contributes to the legitimacy of a very specific normative programme. Any attempt to co-opt deconstruction for the purpose of enhancing the rules or principles of equity that stabilise law would therefore be deeply miscued. The coherence of such an attempt to make deconstruction a source of equity and better legal justice would have to depend on the extent that it can domesticate or simply ignore the radically subversive, anarchic and non-normative thrust of the mode of intellectual or philosophical inquiry that has come to be known as Derridean deconstruction.

Due regard for the spuriousness of any attempt to co-opt Derridean deconstruction for any project aimed at ameliorative law reform that would make the law 'more just' nevertheless does not mean that legal theory should not take careful notice of deconstruction. A good understanding of deconstruction and of the aims that it pursues will surely also deepen one's understanding of both the limits and limitations of law, on the one hand, and the unique achievement of a well-functioning legal system, on the other. One surely also gains sound insight into the aims and achievements of well-functioning law by developing an acute regard for the aims that it cannot and should not pursue. Law becomes law, one might argue in this regard, by turning away from deconstruction. Deconstruction is deconstruction because of the way it turns away from law. This is the elementary instruction that we received from Derrida when he equated deconstruction and justice, on the one hand, and insisted that law is not justice, on the other.[3] One can infer from this instruction that law and deconstruction move in opposite directions. Their respective trajectories take them away from one another instead of bringing them closer to one another. The best way of grasping their opposite trajectories is to maintain a due regard for the negative thrust of *de*-construction and the positive constructive thrust of law and legal theory.

As far as legal theory is concerned, deconstruction has thus far mostly been associated with the endeavour of the Critical Legal Studies movement to destabilise the key concepts and principles of 'mainstream' – that is, positivist, formalist, and conceptualist – jurisprudence (for one of the classical statements, see Unger 1986). However, seen from the vantage point of Derrida's rigorous insistence on the non-traversable divide between law and deconstruction, the question may well be raised whether the constructivism of Hans Kelsen's pure theory of law does not make it the

---

[3] See Jacques Derrida, *Force de Loi: Le 'Fondament Mystique de L'Autorité'* (Paris: Galilée, 1994) 35–8.

more appropriate legal theoretical 'counterpart' to Derridean deconstruction. Consistent Kelsenian constructivists and Derridean deconstructivists can be argued to belong together for reasons of the clarity with which both their respective theoretical orientations reflect a decisive methodological regard for the necessity to take leave of one another. And were this argument to hold water, it would of course make all of them 'theoretical opponents' of anyone – Carl Schmitt is a classic example – who, in contrast to both their orientations, entertains the idea that law is and should be considered a process that constantly deconstructs itself as new friend–enemy constellations emerge (aspects of Schmitt's work were well received by some CLS exponents for this very reason[4]).

The explanation of key aspects of Derridean deconstruction that follows seeks to facilitate a clear understanding of the nonnormative, anarchic and subversive thrust of this mode of inquiry. It is this subversive thrust of deconstruction that renders its co-option for legal theory highly implausible. The explanation that follows highlights this subversive thrust by situating it in the context of philosophical inquiry from which it emerged. It highlights in this regard the inseverable link between deconstruction and the critique of the history of Western metaphysics that Derrida and many of his contemporaries inherited from the seminal work of Martin Heidegger (section 2). It then moves on to explain why the centrality of this critique of metaphysics in Derridean deconstruction prevents one from interpreting it as a quasi-Kantian concern with normative progress (section 3). The section that follows then turns to the key role that the critique of textuality played in Derrida's thinking (section 4). This section also shows how Derrida's concern with textuality took leave of the philosophy of consciousness that was still central in Edmund Husserl's phenomenology and explains why this shift of focus from *consciousness* to *text* was crucial for his project of deconstruction. The final section then restates the claim that the legal theoretical engagement with deconstruction should focus on the way in which law and deconstruction move in opposite directions. It should accordingly avoid interpretations of deconstruction that turn it into a method that can be employed to improve the law or make the law 'more just'.

2. THE CRITIQUE OF THE METAPHYSICS OF PRESENCE

Everything that can be said within the history and traditions of philosophy belongs and will always belong, according to Derrida, to that mode of thinking which the German philosopher Martin Heidegger called *the metaphysics of presence*. Heidegger considered the whole history of Western metaphysics a mode of thinking that took the essence and truth of all forms of existence to consist in a fully realised positive identity that is amenable to present tense predication, that is, the mode of predication that conclusively asserts or states the way things really and essentially are. The history of metaphysics, Heidegger claimed, is a history of fundamental statements about existence as *present* existence. This fundamental presence of existence can also concern the past or future. Metaphysical thought often projected the fully realised truth of existence to a distant

---

[4] See Duncan Kennedy, 'A Semiotics of Critique' (2001) 22 *Cardozo Law Review* 1164.

past or future. The idea of a lost paradise or one that would be realised in the future – the fullness of wisdom to which Plato's philosopher once belonged and to which he might return again after a life of spiritual dedication to the ultimate Idea of the Good; the innocent existence of Adam and Eve before their fall into sin; the glorious existence in the presence of God to which the redeemed will return on the day of his final judgement – are typical examples of such fully 'present' pasts and futures. The influence of Heidegger's work on Derrida – and the close proximity of the former's *destruction* to the latter's *deconstruction* of metaphysics – is crucial for an incisive understanding of Derridean deconstruction. In his readings of Heidegger, Derrida nevertheless stressed that Heidegger himself repeatedly fell back into a metaphysics of presence in his own texts by asserting that the abyssal absence of a ground of existence (that his critique of metaphysics stressed ceaselessly) is the home or abode of authentic human existence (*Dasein*). Derrida's own work also stressed the abyssal groundlessness of existence that Heidegger's thinking underlined, but he understood well that this groundlessness offered human existence nothing that one could call a 'home'. This critique of Heidegger is already evident in his early essay '*Différance*'[5] and would recur often in his work.[6]

It is important to note that the notion of the fully present truth of something can also be invoked in the form of a fictional or "regulative" assumption. This is why Immanuel Kant's articulation of an ultimate reconciliation of nature and reason (and thus of natural inclination and moral duty) in terms of a *summum bonum* can be considered another chapter in the history of the metaphysics of presence. Kant conceived of the *summum bonum* as a regulative idea – that is, something that cannot be proved to exist but must be assumed to exist in order to make sense of the moral imperative to which human conduct is subject. Kant obviously did not consider the *summum bonum* a future reality that will become present one day. He considered it nothing more than a thinkable idea with reference to which the logical conclusion that any commitment to comply with moral duty is futile and therefore meaningless – considering that it involves an eternal struggle between nature and reason and an eternal failure of reason to overcome nature – can be avoided. This methodological assumption of the *summum bonum*, without which he considered his idea of moral duty incoherent, evidently has a fictional status. But that which is fictionally assumed in the process is the possibility of a moral perfection from which nothing would be absent or lacking; a moral reality, in other words, that would be fully present, were it ever to materialise.

A Derridean or deconstructive reading of Kant's text would much rather turn Kant's logic on its head. It would much rather endeavour to show that the *summum bonum* is not the thought that renders the moral imperative possible and meaningful, but exactly the idea that destroys it and renders it completely meaningless. It would consider the endeavour to comply with moral duty an option of human existence that is, quite to the contrary, conditioned by the regard for its impossibility. Derrida once observed that we

---

[5] See Jacques Derrida, *Marges de la Philosophie* (Paris: Les Éditions de Minuit, 1972) 1–29.
[6] See especially Derrida, *De l'esprit* (Paris: Galilée) 1987.

do nothing unless we do the impossible.[7] Full of paradox as it is – and deconstruction may well be considered as an obsessive concern with the paradoxes of human existence – this statement alerts one to the insight that an ethics that would always only be committed to doing that which evidently can be done, would never allow for a significant act or action. In other words, the commitment to comply with moral duty is something that becomes possible because of its irreducible impossibility. For the Derridean reader of Kant, the problem of futility that induced Kant to contemplate the *summum bonum* is the key *aporetic* moment that renders his text – his contemplation of morality – possible. In other words, for a Derridean reader of Kant's text, the *aporia* of futility renders Kantian morality possible, not impossible. From this Derridean perspective, it is, quite to the contrary, the methodological contemplation of the *summum bonum* through which Kant seeks to banish futility from his text that renders Kantian ethics impossible.

The contemplation of a possibility that renders impossible and an impossibility that renders possible goes to the heart of the deconstructive ethics that Derrida would articulate in his later works. It is to this ethics that we turn now. It is important, however, to keep in mind how this ethics ties in with the project of the critique of the metaphysics that Derrida took over from Heidegger. The key insight at stake here concerns the way in which all the founding ideas of metaphysics entertained notions of the ultimate truth of existence in terms of a full presence that lacks nothing. As such, these metaphysical conceptions of truth also signified ideas of moral perfection (among which must also be counted the Nietzschean idea of a-moral perfection) that supposedly guided human conduct and thus rendered ethics and morality possible. From the perspective of the Derridean ethics explained below, any such conception of an achievable or thinkable moral perfection – whether it arrives from an ontological or theological foundation (such as the eternal Idea of the Good or the eternal goodness of God) or a methodological assumption (such as Kant's *summum bonum*) – necessarily ruins the possibility of moral conduct or ethics, instead of sustaining it. Derrida therefore also stressed that his thought regarding the *democracy to come* (*la démocratie à venir*), which he developed in texts that are widely regarded as constitutive of the 'political turn' in his work, should not be understood in terms of a Kantian regulative idea.[8]

3. THE POSSIBILITY OF THE IMPOSSIBLE

Contemplation of the possibility of the impossible was one of the guiding thoughts in Derrida's oeuvre, as he himself observed in his acceptance address when he received the Adorno Prize in 2001.[9] This thought nevertheless remains one of the most perplexing elements of his thinking and it is important to look more closely into it in order to avoid the wide scope for misunderstanding that can easily come to burden it. It

---

[7] See Jacques Derrida, *Manifeste pour l'hospitalité* (Grigny: Éditions Paroles d'Aube, 1999) 141.
[8] See Jacques Derrida, *L'autre cap* (Paris: Les Éditions de Minuit, 1991) 125.
[9] See Jacques Derrida, *Fichus* (Paris: Galilée, 2002) 19–20.

is for instance tempting to interpret the idea of an 'impossibility that conditions the possible' as something akin to a Kantian regulative idea or an ideal of impossible perfection that allows one to persistently raise levels of moral perfection as far as human beings are capable of doing so. The key political terms to which Derrida would resort to articulate the thought of the impossible that renders possible the possible – the gift, justice, friendship, hospitality and forgiveness – can all too easily be interpreted in this way. The impossibility of justice which Derrida invoked in his essay 'Force of Law' can easily be understood in terms of an ideal of perfect law that would do justice to everyone involved. And although justice thus conceived as perfect law may then duly and quite realistically be understood as impossible because of the imperfection that burdens all human institutions, one might still want to argue that adherence to the ideal of perfect law will at least see to it that lawmakers continue to improve the law as far as humans can indeed hope to do so.

One could similarly understand the impossible gift that Derrida contemplates in his response to Marcel Mauss' 'Essay on the Gift' in terms of an unachievable generosity to which one should strive in order to sustain the highest levels of generosity of which humans are capable.[10] The impossible hospitality that he contemplated in response to the work of Emanuel Levinas could likewise be understood as an unachievable hospitality, the consciousness of which guides and inspires one to become as hospitable to others as one can possibly afford to be.[11] And the impossible forgiveness that would forgive the unforgivable could then similarly be understood as an ideal to which we should remain faithful in order to become more forgiving towards those who have wronged us. And the notion of the impossibility of real friendship could likewise be interpreted as a regulative idea that constantly requires friends to strive to become better friends.

If this were all that these key thoughts of Derrida had to offer, one surely would have had reason to wonder what all the fuss about deconstruction is or was about. One could have been forgiven for thinking that the formidable oeuvre of works that Derrida contributed to the history of philosophy contained little more than a restatement of a rather simplistic or common-sense Kantian ethics. But Derrida stressed consistently that the distinction between justice, the gift, hospitality, friendship and forgiveness, on the one hand, and law, affordable generosity, generous but affordable accommodation of strangers, generous friendship and the magnanimous willingness to pardon the understandable imperfections of those who have harmed us, on the other, concerns something more profound and significant than the perfection denoted with the former set of terms and the remaining levels of imperfection associated with the latter set. At issue for him was an unbridgeable categorical divide or heterogeneity that allowed for no translation of the former set into the latter. And this categorical divide that Derrida contemplated should rather alert one to the possibility that Kant himself may have had something more significant and incisive in mind than the facile Kantianism that is often

---

[10] See Jacques Derrida, *Donner le temps 1. La fausse monnaie* (Paris: Éditions Galilée, 1991).

[11] See for example Jacques Derrida, *Manifeste pour l'hospitalité* (Grigny: Éditions Paroles d'Aube, 1999).

associated with his thought, instead of tempting one to reduce the unique thrust of Derrida's work to such a facile Kantianism.

The categorical divide at stake here requires that one consider these key terms of Derrida's ethics of deconstruction spectral concepts that signal the need for an ethical response, without guiding that response or indicating what is demanded of it. These spectral concepts have no body or substance that offers determined criteria for the ethics they demand. They can therefore not figure as measures of ultimate perfection that may inspire persistent amelioration. They are absolutely undetermined and for this reason remain irreducibly disconnected from any determined response to them. Their complete indeterminacy renders them absolute and for this reason impossible to grasp in any positive terms, let alone positively realisable. They simply open a register of absolute impossibility that has absolutely nothing to do with the determined possibility or impossibility of any conceivable response to them, the impossibility that results, for instance, from incidental human frailties and imperfections. But the opening of this spectral register of impossibility cannot be circumvented. It demands a response (or non-response) and thus conditions the possibility of response that is worthy of the word *response* and *responsibility*. For this is the key insight on which deconstructive ethics would consistently turn: A response that responds in terms of available and determined criteria cannot be considered a response in the strict sense of the word.

The key terms of the ethics of deconstruction – justice, friendship, hospitality, forgiveness and gift – thus remain outside any determined response to them. They do not enter the response or become part of it. This is the categorical divide that is at stake in them. Their complete indeterminacy constitutes a certain 'nothingness' that comes to haunt human language and human conduct, as if from nowhere. They remain outside whatever ethical discourse they solicit, but they nevertheless remain this irreducible source of solicitation, the origin of which is indeterminable and unnameable. They haunt, as if from nowhere. They constitute, in the final analysis, the non-existing 'outside of the text' with which Derrida was already concerned in the very early stages of his career. It is this categorical nothingness 'outside the text' to which we turn now.

4. THERE IS NOTHING OUTSIDE THE TEXT

The 'categorical divide' at stake in Derrida's work can best be approached by returning to the key shift in focus from the semantic content or meaning that texts claimed to communicate, on the one hand, to the textuality of the text, on the other. The latter, argued Derrida with recourse to a vast array of deconstructive readings of philosophical and literary texts, most often rendered the former unstable. The most famous example from Derrida's early works was the exposure of the paradoxical way in which Plato's and Rousseau's arguments about the primacy and superiority of spoken language and the derivative and inferior status of written language depended on well-established traditions and codes of writing. These traditions and codes of writing, argued Derrida, produced the meaning of texts; the same was the case for oral communication. They did not just record or register meaning that was already available in a pretextual, directly or immediately cognisable format. Writing, Derrida argued in response to Plato and Rousseau, is the very source or 'origin' of meaning, not its subsequent recording and archiving.[12] Archiving precedes the archived, it does not follow in its wake, as another seminal text would claim in similar fashion.[13]

Derrida thus began to develop a philosophical argument regarding the ubiquitous textuality that organises the production of all meaning and communication, and allows for no circumvention and no immediate access to immaculate knowledge or meaning that is untouched by the textuality that conditions it. This argument would find one of its most salient expressions in the assertion that 'the text has no outside' – *il n'y pas de horse-texte*.[14] The purport of this statement – and the whole concern with a textuality that does not allow scope for a cerebral circumvention that would produce non-textual, text-free and therefore pure meaning – cannot be grasped properly without taking into account the philosophical debate and background from which they emerged. This background is well captured by Michel Foucault's phrase 'the thinking of the outside' – *la pensée de dehors*.[15] Along with Foucault and other prominent French thinkers of his generation, Derrida's work responded to an insight that especially Husserlian phenomenology and the structural linguistics of Ferdinand de Saussure made the point of departure for a significant part of twentieth century philosophy, hermeneutics and broader social theory. At issue was the regard for the *general horizon or world of meaning that conditions all specific instances of meaning.* This development severed the referential relation between language and the world of things outside language and relocated linguistic reference in the interplay between the different elements and components of language itself.

The regard for a horizon or world of meaning – more precisely, the shared intersubjectivity of a lifeworld – outside of which no meaning is possible, became the pivotal concern in Edmund Husserl's later works. This turn in Husserl's thinking was well prepared by the implicit emphasis in his early work that *consciousness has no outside*. Husserl's early works already stressed that the modern epistemological concern with immaculately objective knowledge that would not be distorted by the subjectivity of the subject of knowledge was fundamentally miscued. He insisted that the way in which phenomena appeared in the consciousness of the subject of knowledge was the only cognitive reality to which human subjects could ever have access. The aim of the search for true knowledge should therefore not be to rid knowledge of the subjectivity of the subject of knowledge, but to purify this subjectivity by ridding it of natural preconceptions that distorted the appearance of phenomena in the consciousness of the subject of knowledge. This could be done, claimed Husserl, through recourse to the rigorous phenomenological reductions – the transcendental and eidetic reductions – that he developed in his work. This was what the phenomenological method was all about: not stripping knowledge of subjectivity, but ridding consciousness of all the undue habits of perception and thinking that distorted the pure subjectivity that makes knowledge possible. Husserl never took leave of this method in his later works. What was new in his later works was only the regard for the way in which this transcendental

---

[12]   See Jacques Derrida, *De la Grammatologie* (Paris: Éditions de Minuit, 1967).
[13]   See Jacques Derrida, *Mal d'Archive* (Paris: Éditions Galilée, 1995).
[14]   Jacques Derrida, *De la Grammatologie* (Paris: Éditions de Minuit, 1967) 227.
[15]   Michel Foucault, *La pensée de dehors* (Montpellier, Fata Morgana, 1986).

subjectivity (this subject of knowledge) is always an intersubjectivity that shares a common world of meaning. His key contention was still that the phenomenological method could rid this common world of meaning – the lifeworld, as he called it – from undue distortions.

A similar transformation of the 'outside of the text' into the 'internal' structural and referential play between the linguistic components of 'the text' was underlined by developments in the field of structural linguistics in which the work of Ferdinand de Saussure played a key role. Saussure stressed that the referential relation between linguistic signs and that which they signified did not consist in the 'mirroring' of a reality outside language. That which is communicated by the linguistic sign, or signified by the signifier, he stressed, is the product of referential relations between linguistic signs. There is, in other words, no direct relation between the signifier and the signified. The signified is the 'secondary' result of the referential and differential play between signifiers. The word 'cat', for example, has its specific meaning because of the way it can be distinguished from the words 'dog' and 'mouse'. The letter 'a' becomes a functional linguistic sign because of the way it can be distinguished from the letters 'b' and 'c', and thus allows – because of these distinctions – for an interplay with 'b' and 'c'. The aim of structural linguistics was – in many respects similarly to the aim of Husserlian phenomenology – to identify the rules that govern the 'correct' interplay between linguistic signs that stabilise linguistic meaning despite the fact that it has no anchor outside language.

It should be clear from the above that both phenomenology and structural linguistics had the effect of confining the possibility of knowledge, meaning and understanding to the internal play of language, the inside of language, and thus to the 'inside' of the text. Derridean deconstruction came to be understood as part of a (broader) post-phenomenological and 'post-structuralist' development in French philosophy because of the way that it endeavoured to sustain a regard for the outside of the text, without betraying the fundamental insights of phenomenology and structuralism that precluded any invocation of such an "outside".

The 'thinking of the outside' in the case of Derrida concerned a resistance to both Husserl and Saussure. On the one hand, it concerned a resistance to the phenomenological reduction of human cognition and experience to the censored or purified interior of consciousness, or the common consciousness that Husserl in the final analysis attributed to the intersubjectivity of the life world. On the other, it entailed a resistance to the structural linguistic endeavour to stabilise the referential play of the text. Close study of texts, Derrida insisted, destabilises instead of stabilises the meaning proposed by the text, and it is via this insight – that highlighted the unruly textuality of texts – that he would also put forward his formidable critique of the philosophy of coherent consciousness that informed Husserl's phenomenology. His statement that there is 'nothing outside the text' can be understood as an ingeniously double-edged gesture that confirmed the impossibility of transgressing the boundaries of consciousness, on the one hand, and resisted it, on the other, by confronting consciousness with its irreducible textuality. The statement that the text – the common text or texts through which human societies fabricate meaning – has no outside asserts the impossibility of any transcendence or transgression that would escape from this text. This should already be clear in view of the explanation above. The statement that the confrontation of the text with its very textuality also embodies *a resistance* to the impossibility of transgression or transcendence demands further explication. Why can it be argued that the mere regard for the confining limits of textuality also offers an opportunity for some kind of resistance to those limits?

The answer to this question lies in the irrepressible "unruliness of textuality" mentioned above. An acute regard for textuality alerts one to the fault lines and seams of textuality that consciousness generally manages to erase, repress and ignore. Consciousness – especially as dominantly conceived in the wake of the Enlightenment – is generally inclined to experience itself as a fully coherent, seamless and transparent cerebral and cognitive capacity. It is most uncomfortable with the slightest contradiction, paradox or opacity that could threaten its sense of seamless coherence and full transparency. That is why it is generally inclined to repress and ignore any such threat to its sense of coherence and transparency. And because of the fluidity of its medium, it generally manages to erase the signs or marks of contradiction, paradox and opacity with a liquid forgetfulness. This cannot be done so easily in the case of written texts. Written texts generally show the marks of the fabrication that went into the *construction* of textual coherence. It only takes an acute and careful reading to expose these marks and *deconstruction* is, in the final analysis, little more than the acute reading that highlights these marks. It highlights the *traces* of the erasures and the added *supplements* that were needed to establish an adequate semblance of the seamless coherence and transparency to which the text aspires. That consciousness as such is similarly marked by these rhetorical strategies of textuality was already highlighted by Sigmund Freud. Freudian psychoanalysis illuminated the rhetorical strategies through which consciousness suppressed and rendered subconscious whatever was not reconcilable with its sense of complete coherence and self-transparency. Freud, claimed Derrida, showed well that consciousness is already a text produced by various modes of writing.[16] From a psychoanalytic perspective, the transcendental reductions from which Husserl sought to extract pure subjectivity could themselves be considered strategies of textual suppression.

What was the motive behind this deconstructive exposure of the fault lines of textuality? The exposure of the fault lines of textuality surely did not give deconstructive readings of texts access to the outside of any text. Deconstruction, we saw above, was after all itself adamantly claiming that there is nothing outside the text. The most it could do in view of its own fundamental (phenomenological or structural linguistic) point of departure was to show that the text is never as comfortably contained inside its own boundaries as it pretends to be when it presents itself as a coherent and seamless whole. The confrontation with its limits – its traces of erasures, its supplements – could at best alert the text to the exteriority of a limit that could not be named, since naming would just add more text and more textual interiority. 'Nothing' or 'nothingness', or 'absence of an outside', are of course already names or quasi-names, and Derrida would constantly sense the need to erase them again and to supplement them with other such quasi-names for purposes of sustaining the consistency of the thought that he was endeavouring to think. *Spectrality* would become another of these quasi-denotations of exteriority after the publication of *Spectres de Marx*. It can also be considered one of

---

[16] Jacques Derrida, *L'Écriture et la différence* (Paris: Éditions du Seuil, 1967) 293–340.

the most effective of the operative concepts to which Derrida took recourse over the years, given the way it accentuated the very motive of deconstruction, namely, its desire to see to it that the texts that produce the common consciousness of humanity remain haunted by their outside, haunted by the spectrality – the sheer ghostliness – of an outside that they cannot name. *Haunting* would indeed also become a key term in Derrida's work with the publication of *Spectres de Marx*.[17]

Why this deconstructive obsession to alert the consciousness of humanity – or at least of Western humanity – to a spectral exteriority that this humanity has always preferred to ignore and suppress? Very humanistic readings of Derrida's texts that would especially come to the fore in legal theoretical engagements with his work would mostly stress the potential for progressive social transformation that would be opened up by the deconstructive confrontation with hitherto excluded possibilities of meaning.[18] It is not necessary to argue here that Derrida was averse to such humanistic readings of his work, and readers who are intent on combing his work for evidence of such a concern with social progress would probably find enough material to make a forceful point in this regard.[19] Such readings of Derrida's texts could plausibly take his concerns with an impossible justice, impossible gifts, impossible hospitality and impossible forgiveness as simple concerns with more justice, more generosity, more magnanimity, and so on, as pointed out above. But in doing so they would take Derrida's work for a common sense Kantianism that fails to appreciate the deeply disruptive thrust of the deconstructive critique of Western consciousness that he developed in his works.

By focusing predominantly on the progressive social transformation that deconstructive readings of the dominant texts of Western consciousness may bring about, such Kantian or humanist engagements with Derrida's work would effectively remain concerned with the present, past or future *interiors* of this *text of the West*, this Latin-Christian text that Derrida would also come to call a global Latinisation or globalatinisation (*mondialatinisation*).[20] They would have to ignore a significant element of Derrida's work that simply disrupts and takes leave of the normative concerns of this text for purposes of contemplating the *nothingness outside the text* for its own sake, and not for the sake of improving or transforming the inside. Humanist readings of Derrida's text would have to ignore two key concepts that guided his thinking, two concepts which – unlike 'justice', 'hospitality', 'gift' and 'forgiveness' – do not lend themselves easily to humanistic reductions. They would have to ignore Derrida's deep concern with *the event*, and with it, the concern with *différance* that guided his thinking throughout his life. The concepts of *différance* and *the event* (*l'événement*) denoted for him the untameable disruptiveness that could always and at

---

[17] See Jacques Derrida, *Spectres de Marx* (Paris: Éditions Galilée, 1993) 89.
[18] See for instance Jack Balkin, 'Deconstructive practice and legal theory' (1987) 96 *Yale Law Journal* 743–86.
[19] See for instance Jacques Derrida, *Force de Loi: Le 'Fondament Mystique de L'Autorité'* (Paris: Galilée, 1994) 62.
[20] Jacques Derrida, *Foi et Savoir* (Paris: Éditions du Seuil, 1996) 48.

any time cut into the text, as if coming from the outside, to disrupt it and render it inoperative.[21]

Derrida did not *value* these eventful and differential or *différantial* disruptions of the text for reasons of their beneficial effects. He did not value them because he had no doubt that they could not be valued or evaluated. They did not themselves have any value that they could offer and they would not necessarily add value to the evaluative systems or frameworks that they would come to disrupt. They were *invaluable*, not in the sense of 'extremely valuable', in which we often understand this word, but literally and simply *invaluable*, that is, completely impervious to all evaluative endeavours. And Derrida had no doubt that they could be hugely destructive as far as existing systems of value and evaluation are concerned. Hospitality to the event, he wrote in *Spectres of Marx*, entails the willingness to risk the materialisation of evil.[22]

5. DECONSTRUCTION AND LEGAL THEORY

Legal theoretical engagements with Derrida's work have thus far made little effort to make sense of the notion of a seemingly reckless hospitality to the potentially hugely destructive eventfulness of existence. The legal theoretical engagement with his work has thus far largely focused on other key terms of his work such as justice, hospitality, forgiveness, friendship and the gift. These terms would seem to be more employable for the normative purposes of legal theory, but they only seem so as long as one ignores the fact that Derrida considered all these terms synonymous with the mad hospitality to the disruptiveness of the event. This disruptiveness of the event is evidently less amenable to co-option by the normative concerns of legal theory than the notions of justice, hospitality, friendship and forgiveness. Justice, the most legal-sounding, or the apparently most relevant among these terms as far as legal theory is concerned, is no less insane, according to Derrida, than the mad hospitality to the event that would risk the most destructive consequences for the law as we know it.[23] The conception of justice that he developed in his work suggested, as forcefully as Foucault suggested (although in terms of a "masculine" truthfulness that Derrida may well have found difficult to digest), that 'the way from man to the true man passes through the mad man' (*de l'homme à l'homme vrai le chemin passe par l'homme fou*).[24] If legal theorists were to continue to deem it important to engage seriously with Derridean *deconstruction* for purposes of distilling from it *constructive* insights for the normative concerns of legal theory, they would either have to rely on a highly tamed and domesticated understanding of Derrida's work that ignores large parts of it, or they would need to

---

[21] For a concise and telling statement of this pervasive theme that runs through most if not all of his works, see Jacques Derrida, 'The Deconstruction of Actuality', Interview with *Passages*, translated and reprinted in (1994) *Radical Philosophy* 31.

[22] Jacques Derrida, *Spectres de Marx* (Paris: Éditions Galilée, 1993) 57, 111–12.

[23] See Jacques Derrida, *Force de Loi: Le 'Fondament Mystique de L'Autorité'* (Paris: Galilée, 1994) 56.

[24] Michel Foucault, *Histoire de la Folie à l'âge classique* (Paris: Gallimard, 1972) 544.

break new ground to show what the radically disruptive potential of his work might mean for legal theory.

Neil MacCormick once responded to the 'deconstruction wave' in legal theory with some concession to its transformative and innovative potential, but insisted on the need for 'reconstruction' after 'deconstruction'.[25] It is doubtful whether MacCormick fully grasped the vertiginous depths of disruption that Derrida contemplated, for if he did, he may well not have allowed it into the vaulted halls of jurisprudence at all. But he sensed enough of the disruptiveness of deconstruction to insist that the real task of legal theory and jurisprudence would always consist in retreating from it. The task of jurisprudence would always consist in reconstructing the coherence and certainty of the law in the wake of the sense of indeterminacy and uncertainty that may have passed through it as a result of 'deconstruction'. MacCormick's response to the wave of legal theoretical 'deconstruction' taking hold in law schools around him gently, but acutely and accurately, sent out the message that the really important work of jurisprudence and legal theory lies elsewhere. Taking this response as one's cue, one may even want to go so far as to change the title of his intervention from 'Reconstruction after Deconstruction' to 'Reconstruction *and* Deconstruction', thereby severing the two terms more clearly, but also suggesting that something significant might be learned from simply juxtaposing them. Legal theory can gain from deconstruction the duly painful regard that the limits and limitations of law disqualify it from responding to the Orphic desire for that of which the visible world only offers a retreating glimpse before it vanishes into irretrievable nothingness. The law may well catch that glimpse sometimes, and may well want to turn to it and weep for it, but it cannot attempt to do so without endeavouring to become the poetry that it is not and was never meant to be.

REFERENCES

Balkin, J.M., 'Deconstructive practice and legal theory' (1987) 96 *Yale Law Journal* 743–86.
Derrida, J., 'The Deconstruction of Actuality' Interview with *Passages*, translated and reprinted in (1994) *Radical Philosophy*, 28–41.
Derrida, J., *De la Grammatologie*, Paris: Éditions de Minuit, 1967.
Derrida, J., *De l'esprit*, Paris: Galilée, 1987.
Derrida, J., *Donner le temps 1. La fausse monnaie*, Paris: Éditions Galilée, 1991.
Derrida, J., *Fichus*, Paris: Galilée, 2002.
Derrida, J., *Foi et Savoir*, Paris: Éditions du Seuil, 1996.
Derrida, J., *Force de Loi: Le 'Fondement Mystique de L'Autorité'*, Paris: Galilée, 1994.
Derrida, J., *L'autre cap*, Paris: Les Éditions de Minuit, 1991.
Derrida, J., *L'Écriture et la différence*, Paris: Éditions du Seuil, 1967.
Derrida, J., *Mal d'Archive,* Paris: Éditions Galilée, 1995.
Derrida, J., *Manifeste pour l'hospitalité*, Grigny: Éditions Paroles d'Aube, 1999.
Derrida, J., *Marges de la Philosophie*, Paris: Les Éditions de Minuit, 1972.
Derrida, J., *Positions*, Chicago: University of Chicago Press, 1981.
Derrida, J., *Spectres de Marx*, Paris: Éditions Galilée, 1993.
Derrida, J., *Voyous*, Paris: Galilée, 2003.
Foucault, M., *Histoire de la Folie à l'âge classique*, Paris: Gallimard, 1972.
Foucault, M., *La pensée de dehors*, Montpellier: Fata Morgana, 1986.

---

[25] Neil MacCormick, 'Reconstruction after Deconstruction' [1990] *Oxford Legal Studies* 539–58.

Habermas, J., *Ach Europa*, Frankfurt am Main: Suhrkamp, 2008.
Kennedy, D., 'A Semiotics of Critique' (2001) 22 *Cardozo Law Review* 1162–90.
MacCormick, N., 'Reconstruction after Deconstruction' [1990] *Oxford Legal Studies* 539–58.
Unger, R., *The Critical Legal Studies Movement*, Cambridge, MA: Harvard University Press, 1986.

11. The ethical turn in critical legal thought
Louis E. Wolcher

Gninnigeb eht ta nigeb
George Oppen, *Daybook III* (ca. 1963–4)[1]

1. RATIONAL ETHICS AND THE ETHICS OF COMPASSION

Which should come first in ethics: reason or compassion? The question seems to offer (or force) a choice between two possible foundations—the head or the heart—for the ethical treatment of others. Given that this chapter's primary purpose is to elucidate the deeply contested meanings and significance of "ethics" for law and politics, it would probably be unwise to attempt to tie down what the ethical treatment of others means at the very outset of the discussion. So, let us just say for now, in a rather anodyne fashion, that treating other people ethically means treating them in a way that is morally right (one possible philosophical criterion), and/or in a way that allows you to look at yourself in the mirror in the morning without feeling moral revulsion at the person whose reflection you see there (a plausible psychological criterion).

Once again, then: Which should come first in ethics: reason or compassion? Choosing implies the freedom to choose, of course, and here Hannah Arendt's idea of freedom provides a useful point of departure. Freedom of action, she said, is the power to initiate a "new beginning": a beginning at which we are somehow able to break free of forces from the past and found something new in the living present.[2] Seen from this standpoint, our leading question seems to presuppose the possibility of our being able to momentarily dam the flow of history during a given face to face encounter with another person, and then choose authoritatively to put our head in command of our heart, or our heart in command of our head.

If this is our definition of freedom, however, the poet George Oppen's epigram gives us reason to doubt the very intelligibility of our leading question. It suggests that it is impossible to begin to understand, let alone to decide upon, anything at the beginning. Here Oppen, whose *Daybooks* contain numerous references to Heidegger, subtly and ironically illustrates the latter's thesis of *Befindlichkeit*: the insight that at any given moment each of us finds ourselves always already inhabited by a preexisting mood (*Stimmung*) and a pretheoretical understanding (*Vorgriff*) of things before ever setting out to make the world (including ourselves) meaningful to ourselves. The basic

---

[1] George Oppen, *Selected Prose, Daybooks, and Papers*, ed. Stephen Cope (Berkeley: University of California Press, 2007), 176.
[2] Hannah Arendt, *The Human Condition* (Chicago: University of Chicago Press, 1958), 202.

existential truth of our always already having been thrown into a world (*Geworfenheit*, or "thrownness," as Heidegger called it)[3] thus indicates that the grounds for our comprehending, or failing to comprehend, anything whatsoever are already secretly underway in us before the beginning of any attempt to understand it that we might choose to initiate.

Less obviously, but more importantly for present purposes, Heidegger's thesis implies that the mood of compassion—defined as a more or less strongly felt sense of care and concern for the suffering of another person—emerges temporally as a phenomenon in pretty much the same way that a given instance of rational understanding emerges. Both get pushed above the waterline of the present atop a submerged dynamic substrate of past forces and events of which we are largely unaware. Considered as purely temporal phenomena, spontaneously feeling concern for a baby when it starts to cry, spontaneously understanding what the linguistic signs "begin at the beginning" mean without having to look up the words in the dictionary, and spontaneously feeling puzzled upon first encountering the linguistic signs "*Gninnigeb eht ta nigeb*" all belong to the same order of experience: the feeling of immediacy.

The existence of irreducible immediacy in the linguistic realm is the precise analog of an unpremeditated outburst of emotion. Linguistic immediacy is characterized by the effortless understanding of language unpreceded by anything that could rightly be called a rational "act" of understanding. Words can always be interpreted, of course, but even then—*especially* then—the act of interpretation eventually ceases, after which I just know how to go on. Or rather, I then just *do* go on in a certain way, having been prodded or pushed in that direction by certain words and their associated images. Pascal characterized the human being as "a thinking reed," a metaphor that attempts to glorify thinking while drawing attention to the relative feebleness of our physical existence. But in truth even the tip of the reed that performs the most rigorous thinking is always overwhelmed in the end by what remains exogenous to thought. That is what rationally understanding language looks and feels like, if one does not take too distant a view of it. For adopt whatever model or scheme of interpretation you may, it will eventually terminate at a level made up of still more linguistic signs; and then, as Wittgenstein says, "there will be no such thing as an interpretation of that."[4] *You just go on*, kinetically, perhaps with a piece of paper in your hand or an image in your mind, perhaps *with* nothing else at all.

The existence of irreducible immediacy in the reception of language and images is easily demonstrated by phenomenological analysis (Wittgenstein was especially adept at doing this sort of thing). It strongly suggests a thesis that is unflattering to reason's traditional pose of superiority *vis à vis* human emotion. The thesis is that reason and emotion, head and heart, *both* lie at the mercy of historical forces that they cannot, as a matter of principle, master in advance. All of which implies, in turn, that the correct phenomenological answer to the question whether reason or compassion will in fact come first in any given ethically charged situation is just this: if either one does emerge

---

[3] Martin Heidegger, *Being and Time*, trans. John Macquarrie & Edward Robinson (New York: HarperCollins, 1962), 175.

[4] Ludwig Wittgenstein, *The Blue and Brown Books* (New York: Harper & Row, 1958), 34.

first, this will be because it just happened on that *particular* occasion to win a murky underwater contest with and against all its competitors (including the feeling of indifference) to rise to the surface of our consciousness.

The predominant ethical viewpoint in mainstream Western thought sees things differently, of course. An article in the hoary Macmillan *Encyclopedia of Philosophy*, for example, defines philosophical ethics (sometimes called metaethics) as the rational inquiry into general ways of life and "rules of moral conduct."[5] As for the role of compassion in this inquiry, ever since Plato's allegory of the charioteer, in *Phaedrus* (246a–254e), traditional thinking about ethics—especially ethics in relation to law and politics—has authoritatively claimed that the only proper relationship between reason and compassion is akin to that between an intelligent teamster and an unruly horse: reason should come first, in the form of rigorous self-control, and compassion second, but only if it is harnessed and steered by reason in the morally correct direction. Over the centuries, philosophers as notable and varied as Seneca, Spinoza, and Kant have gone out of their way to scold compassion as a dangerous moral weakness that tends to cloud reason's capacity to recognize what the correct performance of moral duty requires. Its reputation was also slandered by Rousseau and Nietzsche, both of whom attempted to diminish compassion's altruistic self-image by characterizing it as just another manifestation of the desire to extend the self and exert power over others.

Traditional ethical formulas such as the Golden Rule and the Categorical Imperative neglect compassion altogether, ultimately justifying their injunctions to act with decency toward others by appealing to rational self-interest. They offer people compensation for good deeds in the present by promising a future full of law-governed normative reciprocity, thereby demoting compassionate acts from what Max Weber would have called subjectively rational ends-in-themselves to mere instrumentally rational means for making everyone better off in the long run. Even Kant's thesis that you have an unconditional duty to act according to the maxim that you would wish all other rational people to follow would lose its appeal unless the very wish of it were rooted in the prospect of reciprocity over time. In sum, ever since Hegel began touting the rational moral excellence of a people's given "ethical life" (*Sittlichkeit*),[6] conventional philosophical thought, if not common understanding, has tended to construe "ethics" as reason's willing acquiescence in a rationally justified (and usually collectively imposed and enforced) system of rules or customs designed to constrain the natural selfishness of the individual by threatening social disapproval and offering social rewards.

It is true, of course, that there have also been critics of this neo-Platonic interpretation of ethics. Schopenhauer, having noticed that reason's alleged ability to control compassion is predicated on our capacity to will this rather than that—X rather than Y—pointed out the awkward fact that the prerational causes and conditions of the will itself are as many and varied as the intensity and direction of breezes playing on a weather vane. Camus also could not have disagreed more strongly with the theory that

---

[5] Raziel Abelson & Kai Nielsen, "History of Ethics," in Paul Edwards ed., *The Encyclopedia of Philosophy* (New York: Macmillan, 1967), iii 81–117 at 81–2.

[6] G.W.F. Hegel, *Philosophy of Right*, trans. T.M. Knox (London: Oxford University Press, 1967), 319 n. 75.

ethics can or should be a rigorously rational enterprise: "I have abandoned the moral point of view," he wrote in one of his postwar *Notebooks*, because "morals lead to abstraction and to injustice—they are the mother of fanaticism and violence."[7] In a more positive vein, the philosopher Martha Nussbaum, also a critic of neo-Platonic ethics, has recently argued that compassion ("the basic social emotion," according to her)[8] should begin to play a more prominent role in philosophical ethics, not to mention in conventional legal and political thought. It is worth noting, however, that the very fact that Nussbaum had to make the argument, and also that her recent work on compassion has been received in many quarters as refreshingly original, underscores the point that heretofore compassion has only rarely played a definitive role in mainstream academic discussions of philosophical ethics.

The formal structure of the latter, just like that of everyday ethical discourse, is quite literally reactionary. It holds that the sense of compassion, when properly controlled by reason, lies (and should lie) dormant in the individual subject, who is otherwise morally free to pursue his own interests and desires in good conscience unless and until the ethical impulse to care for the other is brought to life by the "right" circumstances. The ethical impulse, when dressed in its conventional garb, is *res*ponsible in the precise etymological sense of the Latin term *respondēre*: it stands ready to "answer back" to the predicament of another person, but only *after* the ethical actor has judged the other's situation worthy of self-restraint or positive intervention. Such a view of ethical responsibility is premised on a legalistic and reciprocal conception of moral duty: I owe you the exact same moral consideration that you owe me, neither more nor less, and vice versa. All excess compassion be damned!

It is important to understand that the so-called ethical turn in *critical legal thought*, the subject of the present chapter, has nothing to do with ethics conceived as a rationally justified system of rules or customs. Still less does it pertain to what Marinos Diamantides has ironically called "the virile business of stringing together justifications for our actions."[9] Critical legal scholars, or many of them at least, have come to believe, with Derrida, that "the way we define ethics today is shaking on its lack of foundations."[10] Thus, whatever else may be said about the ethical turn in critical legal thought, its style and substance are neither legalistic nor morally symmetrical. Those who inwardly cling to the possibility of secure rational foundations for right conduct, including especially the decision to inflict "just" suffering on others in good conscience, sometimes reproach postmodernist discourse about ethics, law, and politics as dangerously immoral and irresponsible. But for those who feel themselves shaking on a lack of foundation in these spheres, it is the very decision to bestow unqualified trust

---

[7] Albert Camus, *Notebooks 1951–1959*, trans. Ryan Boom (Chicago: Ivan R. Dee, 2008), 248.

[8] Martha Nussbaum, "Compassion: The Basic Social Emotion," *Social Philosophy and Policy*, 13/1 (2009), 27–58.

[9] Marinos Diamantides, "Editor's Introduction," in id, *Levinas, Law, Politics* (New York: Routledge-Cavendish, 2007), 1–32 at 18.

[10] Jacques Derrida, Hans-Georg Gadamer, & Philippe Lacoue-Labarthe, *Heidegger, Philosophy, and Politics: The Heidelberg Conference*, ed. Mireille Calle-Gruber, trans. Jeff Fort (New York: Fordham University Press, 2016), 24.

in the traditional categories of responsibility in ethics, law, and politics that comprises the worst act of moral irresponsibility.

2. THE ETHICAL TURN IN CLS

Given that the work of any author is probably overdetermined, ethics experienced as the unmediated irruption of compassion for this or that group of oppressed human beings has probably always played *some* role in critical legal scholarship, if only as an inchoate factor motivating many radical leftwing critiques of the law. Not all of them, to be sure: Marx, whose hostility to emotionalism of all sorts is well known, was hardly a visible font of compassion for others. Nevertheless, it is a reasonable hypothesis, albeit one that would take us too far afield to pursue much farther here, that the determining motive behind most post-Marxist, postmodern attacks on conventional claims about something's "presence" in the "present" (that is, the objective reality of rights, duties, values, truths, the present moment, and so forth) is *not* the nonpragmatic or vandalistic exercise of a reason that has lost its way and, like Narcissus, fallen in love with its own reflection. Rather, Lyotard's famous definition of the postmodern as "incredulity toward metanarratives"[11] is better explained as an ethical gesture rooted in moral aversion to the baleful consequences of lending too much credulity toward grand narratives. The latter tend to explain everything by ignoring or suppressing differences, thereby preparing the way for the bureaucratic administration of what is different by what is always the same. Adorno's statement, in *Negative Dialectics*, that there can be no poetry after Auschwitz unless it is poetry about Auschwitz, indicates that critical theory's inclination to expose "the untruth of identity" in the administrative state—"the fact that a concept does not exhaust the thing conceived"[12]—rests more on a profound sense of moral alarm than it does on a pedantic desire to satisfy an intellectual itch by the clever application of neo-Hegelian logic to political problems.

Before the ethical turn, the radical critique of conventional notions of moral responsibility generally followed the same strategies as the CLS critique of the liberal legal order: bourgeois conceptions of ethics, like those of law, were condemned as ideologically suspect; logically indeterminate; predicated on a distorted, false, or selective view of subjectivity; biased against women and minorities; a tool or aspect of ruling class hegemony, and so forth. Among other things, the turn to ethics in critical legal scholarship represents a turn away from all forms of structuralism, including especially what might be called the "sociological" way of thinking. According to the latter, it is always imperative, not only first and foremost, but also lastmost and without remainder, to explain existing legal institutions and patterns of thought from the outside, so to speak, by tracing them to their hidden historical causes and conditions (class and gender relations, ideologies, economic interests, racism, colonialism, and so forth). After the turn, however, critical legal scholars began to consider the possibility

---

[11] François Lyotard, *The Postmodern Condition: A Report on Knowledge*, trans. Geoff Bennington & Brian Massumi (Minneapolis: University of Minneapolis Press, 1984), xxiv.

[12] Theodor Adorno, *Negative Dialectics*, trans. E.B. Ashton (Routledge & Kegan Paul, 1973), 5.

that the ethics of law could *also* be thought from the inside, from the point of view of the individual actors without whose active participation or passive acceptance these institutions would grind to a halt.

That said, and putting the hypothesis of hidden compassionate motives aside, a suitably comprehensive intellectual history of the critical legal studies movement would have to trace the origins of a distinctly *self-conscious* "ethical turn" in CLS to no earlier than the mid-1990s. For this was when Simon Critchley, Costas Douzinas, Ronnie Warrington, and Marinos Diamantides, among others, started writing extensively about the ideas of Emmanuel Levinas, postmodernity's philosopher of compassion *par excellence*. Levinas, who died in 1995, was not a philosopher of law in the usual sense of the term. But he was a highly accomplished Talmudist as well as a brilliant secular phenomenologist in the tradition of Husserl, Bachelard, early Heidegger, Gadamer, and Ricœur. Ethics as described in Levinas's own, uniquely phenomenological language tends to emerge experientially out of the blue, so to speak, without warning. Nowhere does it manifest itself more clearly than in the sort of unpremeditated behavior that the Russian writer Vassily Grossman, in his monumental novel *Life and Fate* (1960), called "senseless kindness."[13]

It is important to understand that Grossman, whose ethical outlook was much admired by Levinas, deployed the concept of senselessness not as a reproach—its normal usage in everyday speech—but rather as a philosophical encomium. Grossman (and with him Levinas) *lauded* the impulse to treat others with rationally unjustified (and perhaps unjustifiable) decency and humaneness. A strong hint of this phenomenon's radical potential to break up reason's traditional monopoly over philosophical ethics can be found in the following excerpt from one of Levinas's published interviews:

> [T]he "small goodness" from one person to his fellowman [of which Grossman speaks] is lost and deformed as soon as it seeks organization and universality and system, as soon as it opts for a doctrine, a treatise of politics and theology, a party, a state, and even a church. Yet it remains the sole refuge of the good in being. Unbeaten, it undergoes the violence of evil, which, as small goodness, it can neither vanquish nor drive out. A little kindness going only from man to man, not crossing distances to get to the places where events and forces unfold! A remarkable utopia of the good or the secret of its beyond.[14]

Levinas's emphasis on the affective dimension of the existentially concrete and unrepeatable face-to-face encounter between two human beings (a Self and an Other), together with his call to overthrow the traditional privileges of metaphysics and ontology in favor of "ethics as first philosophy,"[15] began to strike a responsive chord in the minds and hearts of many critical legal thinkers during the 1990s. Levinas made it possible to think about the ethics of law and politics in terms of what can be called a radically asymmetrical *pre*sponsibility, to coin a useful neologism. The notion of

---

[13] Vasily Grossman, *Life and Fate*, trans. Robert Chandler (New York: Harper & Row, 1985).

[14] Emmanuel Levinas, *On Thinking-of-the-Other Entre Nous*, trans. Michael Smith & Barbara Harshav (New York: Columbia University Press, 1998), 230.

[15] Emmanuel Levinas, "Ethics as First Philosophy," trans. Seán Hand & Michael Temple, in Seán Hand ed., *The Levinas Reader* (Oxford: Blackwell, 1989), 75–87.

presponsibility stands opposed to the previously discussed traditional Western conception of reactive responsibility. Presponsibility signifies a way of thinking about ethical responsibility that removes it from the Kantian category of a duty dependent upon rational reflection and places it, in Derrida's words, in a category that is "prior to the senses and to their performative orientation."[16] It advances the claim that each one of us always already bears a burden of guilt and responsibility because of the actual or possible suffering of the Other—*any* given other whom we face—without reference to the acknowledgment or proof of some discrete act of wrongdoing on our part.

Levinas called the impulse to presponsibility "the idea of the infinite,"[17] and said that the immediate consequence of this impulse is a burdensome but morally necessary sense of "guilt without fault."[18] For Levinas, human existence itself is without reason or basis, and therefore unjustifiable; it follows that each one of us stands in need of forgiveness merely on account of the fact that we exist: "My 'being in the world' or my 'place in the sun,' my home—are they not a usurpation of places that belong to the other man who has already been oppressed or starved by me?" Rational ethics strives to be finite or limited in advance by what it takes its linguistic norms to "mean" before they are applied. In contrast, the concept of infinite ethical responsibility to the other, before and beyond any prior judgment or rational calculation, uses the word "infinite" in the etymologically precise sense of "not-finite," that is, amorphous—lacking in any prior analytical definition or limitation. Infinite ethical responsibility in Levinas's sense should not be thought of as an infinite number of ethical acts, and still less as an inchoate moral "duty" to perform such acts. It is better characterized as the indeterminate possibility of noticing, with compassion, the many sorts of human suffering that the singleminded pursuit of rational ethics causes us to overlook. "What the eye doesn't see, the heart doesn't grieve over," said Wittgenstein.[19] If only the eye that sees can grieve (and possibly act) because of what it sees, then Levinas's gesture of drawing attention to infinite ethical responsibility represents a moral wager on the proposition that the more suffering we are able to see, the wider the circle of our actual ethical concern will become.

Purely as a matter of intellectual history, the latter idea is traceable to Schopenhauer's thesis, influenced by Buddhism, that unbounded compassion is both the origin and ultimate justification of all of ethics. Later in the nineteenth and early twentieth centuries, certain well-known critiques of traditional Western ethical discourse credibly portrayed it as but an elaborate subterfuge for hidden factors that at any given moment remain inaccessible to the ethical actor's rational understanding. Historically contingent ideologies (Marx), the will to power (Nietzsche), profound anxieties caused by a religious belief in the inscrutability of personal salvation (Weber), unconscious psychological drives (Freud): these sorts of accounts began to subvert and replace the

---

[16] Derrida et al., *supra* note 10, at 90.

[17] Emmanuel Levinas, "Transcendence and Height," in id, *Basic Philosophical Writings*, eds Adriaan Peperzak, Simon Critchley & Robert Bernasconi, trans. Simon Critchley (Bloomington: Indiana University Press, 1996), 11–31 at 19.

[18] Emmanuel Levinas, "Interview with François Poirié," in id, *Is It Righteous to Be?*, ed. Jill Robbins, trans. id. & Marcus Coelen (Stanford: Stanford University Press, 2001), 23–83 at 52.

[19] Ludwig Wittgenstein, *Remarks on the Foundations of Mathematics*, eds G.H. von Wright, R. Rhees, & G.E.M Anscombe (Cambridge: MIT Press, rev. edn., 1983), 205.

Enlightenment's appeal to the dictates of universal or transcendental human reason as the justification for conventional morality.

Eventually the rise of poststructuralist skepticism regarding the human subject made it possible for critical scholars to question the firmness of the boundary between self and other that has always undergirded the ubiquitous neo-Kantian premise that ethical responsibility can only arise between metaphysically distinct rational individuals. Various critical "turns" in the twentieth century—including Heidegger's phenomenological investigations into Dasein's being-there *before* what is called "the subject," Foucault's historical genealogies of the modern Western concept of subjectivity, Lacan's radical transformations of Freudian psychology, and Derrida's deconstructive interventions in philosophy and legal theory—had the effect of finally knocking the mainstream ethical subject off its pedestal.

Like Shelley's Ozymandias, whose empty pedestal read "Look on my works, ye Mighty, and despair," the West's ethical subject—first placed firmly on its plinth by Kant—has always made grandiose claims about the moral excellence of its procedures. It was Levinas, however, who most clearly articulated the *ethical* significance of the "hidden violence" that has always been contained in the unitary subject's relentless *conatus essendi*—that is, its destructive but ultimately futile attempt to persevere through time as an impervious egoistic unity. What makes the discourse of the "subject" a lie—a distortion and concealment of reality—is that it abstracts real human beings into what Husserl called their "formula-meaning" (*Sinnesveräusserlichung*),[20] separating them from their phenomenal origins as these are continuously and messily presented firsthand in people's day-to-day lives. For Levinas, no rational ethics of the subject, nor any humanistic ethics of "man," could ever go anywhere deep enough into the countless and infinitesimally concrete problem(s) of moral responsibility to be satisfactory.

To treat someone as an end, as Kant had advocated, is to respect them—to look back or regard them (*respicere*) as a type of being that deserves something. What is deserved in the ordinary conception of ethical respect is often summed up in anodyne phrases like "whatever it is that is essential to our humanity." This way of thinking about respect ties morality to abstractions—the "essential" attributes of an entity called "the human being"—and avoids attending to each particular other's real face, real needs, real vulnerabilities in the here and now. For Levinas, on the other hand, there is nothing even remotely abstract about ethics. The only proper subject matter for ethics, over and over again, almost to the point of exhaustion, is just *this* real human being's face in all its unrepeatable uniqueness.

"Man speaks," said Lacan, "but it is because the symbol has made him man."[21] Plucked out of context, statements like this can strike some readers as indifferent to the moral value of the one who speaks "man," as if the merely symbolic content of "man" meant that the so-called Rights of Man were even less important, less valuable, than the inscrutable nonbeing for whom they were written. Mere symbols of a symbol, so to speak, analogous to Pindar's dreams of a shadow. But Levinas, for one, never gave

---

[20] Edmund Husserl, *The Crisis of European Sciences and Transcendental Phenomenology*, trans. David Carr (Evanston: Northwestern University Press, 1970), 44.

[21] Jacques Lacan, *Écrits: The First Complete Edition in English*, trans. Bruce Fink (New York: W.W. Norton, 2006), 229.

anyone reasonable cause to doubt the deeply compassionate axiology underlying his own efforts to subvert the Kantian model: "Contesting subjectivity," he wrote, "means asserting the value of the subjectivity that does the contesting."[22] Levinasian neighborliness thus means the exact opposite of moral indifference to the plight of the Other. The close identification of ethics with compassion construes ethics experientially, as an inwardly felt inclination to put the suffering Other's interests before one's own concerns, come what may. Rather than elevating, as Plato did, philosophical reason over the ethical impulse to take charge of compassion as its wise guardian (or stern warden), the idea of unchosen, infinite ethical presponsibility for the other places a certain kind of nonphilosophical *experience* of compassion at the head of philosophical ethics as its guide.

The practical consequences for law and politics of Levinas's hypertrophied notion of ethical responsibility, rooted in "love without concupiscence,"[23] are not immediately obvious. But his discourse does suggest the rhetorical value of using certain tropes, certain ethical gestures, in discussing legal and political questions. Thus, for example, Douzinas and Warrington will write, in 1994, that the Levinasian incalculability of ethics "demands of us to calculate and to make the relation between calculation and the incalculable central to all judgment."[24] Quite a few other thinkers, in turn, have strummed the same chord in their own work, with greater or lesser intensity, ever since. For example: Amanda Loumansky has asserted that Levinas's philosophy calls on us to "whisper in [law's] ear, 'Remember the other'";[25] Matthew Stone has invoked Levinas's ideas to advocate for "a subjectivity that is politicised by its unconditional ethical orientation";[26] and Marinos Diamantides has argued that Levinasian ethical thought delivers important political lessons for the rule of law that are closely analogous to the kind of thing we can learn by watching the "theater of the absurd."[27]

The strumming has not always been harmonious, of course, and even within the CLS movement there have been many critics of Levinas. His determinations of who is "Other" in the various ethical relations that he describes can sometimes seem selective, if not biased. Thus, some have accused him of ignoring or marginalizing the perspectives of women in his work. Others have reproached him for his relative silence on the injustices committed by Israel in continuing to produce and ignore the suffering of Palestinians in the occupied territories. Still others have charged him with a dangerous sort of nostalgia for a mythical, pre-lapsarian world in which law and politics somehow have grown sweeter and gentler—"more knowing in the name, the memory, of the original kindness of man toward the other"[28]—than any known legal or

---

[22] Emmanuel Levinas, *Humanism of the Other*, trans. Nidra Poller (Evanston: University of Illinois Press, 2003), 46.
[23] Hand, *supra* note 15, at 131.
[24] Costas Douzinas & Ronnie Warrington, *Justice Miscarried: Ethics, Aesthetics and the Law* (Hemel Hempstead: Harvester Wheatscheaf, 1995), 184.
[25] Amanda Loumansky, "Me Voici, Here I am, Here I Stand, I Can Do No Other," *Law and Critique*, 11/3 (2000), 287–300 at 300.
[26] Matthew Stone, *Levinas, Ethics and Law* (Edinburgh: Edinburgh University Press, 2016), 156.
[27] Diamantides, *supra* note 9, at 27.
[28] Levinas, *supra* note 14, at 229.

political institution, at least those interested in succeeding and persisting *as* "institutions," has ever been before.

More generally, critics and supporters alike cannot help wondering whether Levinas's exaggerated sense of ethics and its possibilities—we should all strive to perfect legal justice "against its own harshness," he once said[29]—is compatible with *any* sort of progressive action in the legal and political spheres. They wonder this because the infliction of pain on *someone*, even lots of someone*s*, according to an economy of "necessary suffering" that cares about accomplishing its ends seems to be an inevitable consequence of acting purposefully at all.

Derrida once said that the ethical event as such is "menaced by its own rigor"[30] in Levinas's thought—a trenchant observation which points toward a difficulty for critical theory that is less theoretical than it is practical and motivational. Politics accomplishes many or most of its goals through law; and once law is created, its métier is to threaten the infliction of legitimate violence, or what Benjamin called "law-preserving violence."[31] When Derrida issued a "very cautious" call, at the outset of the second Gulf War, for actual progress toward a justice-to-come (*à venir*) that would break with traditional political categories ("a messianicity without messianism"), he advocated for some form of nameless but nonetheless *real* political action that would, as he put it, "give force and form to this messianicity."[32] Given the basic reality that those unwilling to acknowledge either messiahs or messianism must always be coerced or destroyed if progress toward messianic justice is to be made, it is hard to see how anyone who sincerely remains, with Levinas, "troubled at the prospect of committing violence—albeit necessary for the logical unfolding of history"[33] could ever remain an unqualifiedly effective agent of radical political change for very long. Notwithstanding several credible disclaimers in Levinas's work, one can be forgiven for wondering if the extreme squeamishness that he displayed toward the infliction of suffering on others, again and again in his books and interviews, is not more than a little conducive to political quietism, if not conservatism.

3. THE THIRD PERSON, OR ETHICS MEETS JUSTICE

On the other hand, historical experience also gives us ample reason to sympathize with Camus' observation that "Whoever is virtuous must cut off heads."[34] Like Camus,

---

[29] Id.

[30] Jill Robbins, "Introduction: 'Après Vous, Monsieur!,'" in Levinas, *Is It Righteous to Be?*, *supra* note 19, at 8.

[31] Walter Benjamin, "Critique of Violence," trans. Edmund Jephcott, in Peter Demetz ed., *Walter Benjamin, Reflections: Essays, Aphorisms, Autobiographical Writings* (New York: Schocken Books, 1978), 277–300 at 300.

[32] Jacques Derrida & Lieven De Cauter, "For a Justice to Come: An Interview with Jacques Derrida," in Lasse Thomassen ed., *The Derrida-Habermas Reader* (Chicago: University of Chicago Press, 2006), 259–69 at 268–9.

[33] Emmanuel Levinas, "Peace and Proximity," in id, *Basic Philosophical Writings*, *supra* note 17, 161–9 at 164.

[34] Camus, *supra* note 7, at 248.

Levinas was fully aware of the apparent incompatibility between political and legal justice, which perforce always ends in the use or threat of violence against the unwilling, and the radically asymmetrical kindness that characterizes the ethical relationship as he describes it. He knew that the social world is not just composed of two human beings alone—one called "myself" and the other called "the Other"—but rather contains millions and billions of other Others who do not happen to be facing the self in the instant of any given face-to-face encounter between the self and just *one* Other. Each one of these other Others also demands some sort of ethical recognition, and this creates a menace that presses upon Levinas's notion of ethical responsibility even more perilously than its own excessiveness: a menace that he called "the hour of inevitable justice."[35]

Always already present virtually, if not actually, alongside the Other's face is the face of what Levinas calls the *third person* (as well as the faces of the fourth, the fifth, and so on almost *ad infinitum*). The copresence of other human beings disturbs the original intimacy of the binary ethical relation between an *I* and a *you* because the third person is another Other whose existence potentially asserts an equal claim on the *I*'s ethical responsibility. The "third person" in Levinas's writings represents the entire society or world of other human beings, any one of whom could gratuitously step forward at any moment to become the *I*'s Other in the face-to-face encounter that is, for Levinas, the origin of all ethics.

Given that one's time, resources, and motility are always finite, how is one to choose (assuming choice has anything to do with it) where and how to discharge one's ethical responsibility for "the" Other among such a formidable plenitude of Others? Since Levinas wanted to interpret human sociality as independent of the lost unity represented by being-as-a-whole, these other Others cannot be conceived collectively, but must each be viewed as singularities that are just as unique, ineffable, and needy as the original Other. Toward whose face, then, should I turn my face? Although injustice can be annulled by forgiveness within the circle of the binary ethical relationship, it demands redress when the entrance of the third person turns two into three. "Hence," Levinas will conclude, "it is important to me *to know* which of the two [Others] takes precedence."[36]

"In order to be just, it is necessary to know," Levinas says; "to objectify, compare, judge, form concepts, generalise, etc."[37] Hence the for-the-other of the ethical relationship between self and Other must recede or be suppressed so that a knowing judgment can be made between multiple others. The immanence of knowledge that is required to establish justice gives affront to the unique alterity of the Other by leaving him "de-faced" (*dé-visagés*).[38] That is because the one who aspires to become an agent of *justice*, precisely—and not just some helter-skelter kind of anarchy—must form rational concepts of all Others who stand before it, and because it cannot allow itself to be ethically affected ("biased") by any particular Other while it is trying to do justice

---

[35] Hand, *supra* note 15, at 229.
[36] Id. at 104.
[37] Id. at 204.
[38] Emmanuel Levinas, *Alterity and Transcendence*, trans. Michael Smith (New York: Columbia University Press, 1999), 170.

among them. The de-facing and masking accomplished by the work of justice is indeed the very meaning of the blindfold in conventional representations of the Goddess of Justice: *Dikē* wants neither to *see* the Other's face nor to *feel* compassion for its suffering. Instead, she desires merely to *know* about the Other's situation, so she can judge it in relation to the claims of other Others.

What I have elsewhere called the "problem of the passage"[39] between ethics and justice goes from an intimate relation without reciprocity to a structured relation in which reciprocity—conceived politically as the formal equality of all citizens—characterizes the justice-seeking *I*'s new attitude and comportment toward others. "My search for justice," says Levinas, "presupposes just such a new relation, in which all the excess of generosity that I must have toward the other is subordinated to a question of justice."[40] Paradoxically, the ethical *I* must somehow manage to deny and efface its own essence (that is, unqualified compassion) before it can metamorphose—or *become* metamorphosed against its will, like Gregor Samsa in Kafka's famous story about a man who turned into a gigantic insect[41]—into a responsible agent of justice.

Strangely enough, the impossible demand that the existence of this paradox places on the one who would become an agent of justice is made palpable by the record of a macabre legal case that apparently arose in Genoa, Italy, during the early 1600s. In his rambling and eclectic history of Paris, the seventeenth century French historian Henri Sauval gives an account of a man that was murdered—stabbed in the neck—by one of a pair of conjoined twins. The murderer, Lazarus Colloredo, was the healthier of the two twins, and wore a cloak to conceal the protruding upper body of his brother, Johannes Baptista, who was blind, deaf, and mute. The two had been joined together at the stomach since birth, and we are told that the feebler twin had nothing whatsoever to do with the killing, other than having had the inevitable misfortune of just being there when it happened.

As was required by the principles of law and justice operative at that time and place, the healthy twin was prosecuted, convicted of murder, and sentenced to death. Sauval reports that the sentence was not carried out, however: "But there was no execution [of the guilty twin] because of his brother, who played no part in the murder; it being impossible to kill the one without killing the other at the same time."[42] Sauval goes on to describe the details of the twins' physical condition at some length, and notes that the doctors at the time believed that it was medically impossible to separate them. He does not say what the law did to the twins after the sentence of death was negated, but he does claim to have played a game of handball with them in Paris, where they were said to be living openly as late as 1638, at the mutual age of 21.

In his lectures on the genealogy of the concept of abnormality, Foucault refers to the case of the Colloredo twins to illustrate how the notion of the "monster" developed in

---

[39] Louis Wolcher, *Beyond Transcendence in Law and Philosophy* (London: Birkbeck Law Press, 2005), 121.

[40] Levinas, *supra* note 38, at 102.

[41] Franz Kafka, "The Metamorphosis," in id, *The Complete Stories*, ed. Nahum Glazer, trans. Willa & Edwin Muir (New York: Schocken Books, 1983), 89-139.

[42] Henri Sauval, *Histoire et Recherches des Antiquités de la Ville de Paris* (Paris: Moette & Chardon, 1724), ii 564.

The ethical turn in critical legal thought 193

the eighteenth century as essentially a legal category defined by a sort of double illegality: "its existence and form is not only a violation of the laws of society but also a violation of the laws of nature."[43] But the case also seems to me to evoke a much larger theme: namely, the disturbing possibility that a certain inescapable monstrosity is inherent in the very concepts of law and justice themselves. More precisely, Sauval's account helps to show why the idea of justice has lost its nimbus for those critical scholars who find themselves strongly attracted to the work of Levinas and his followers. For the inescapable principle of the Colloredo case is just this: It was not possible to do justice in the case of the guilty twin without doing an injustice to the innocent one; or, more broadly still, justice for one would, pari passu, have been an injustice to the other, and vice versa.

The fact that the Genoese legal system chose to spare the innocent man instead of executing the guilty one is understandable and even predictable, given that Blackstone's famous ten-to-one ratio expresses a sentiment that most people would probably agree with: "it is better that ten guilty persons escape, than that one innocent suffer."[44] Indeed, "guiltiness" itself in this context is a legal concept, not an ethical one: whether justly imposed or not, it is the product of the kind of rational judgment according to legal categories that Levinas characterized as the antithesis of ethics. For Levinas, rational thought *about* the Other is a rupture of the ethical *I*'s unconditional compassion *for* the Other, as if the ethical relation that preceded the moment of justice were not the "beginning of society, but its negation." To paraphrase Vladimir Jankélévich, thinkers such as Levinas are burdened by the nagging realization that every real person we collectively or individually condemn and punish today infinitely exceeds the sin in which our sense of injustice (or *ressentiment*) wants to imprison him.[45] Levinas knew that the minute we begin to think of *any* human being as less than this—as exactly equivalent to his legal categorization, for example—we are lost.

If legal guilt, and even the kind of moral guilt that is adjudged according to categorical reason, both fail as a matter of principle to wholly exclude the condemned from the sphere of innocence, and if the punishment of the guilty always produces unforeseen or unintended harm to the nonguilty, then it follows that the very idea of human justice entails the certainty that innocents will suffer along with the guilty. This Levinasian syllogism leads one to ask a profoundly depressing question: What if historical violence, whatever its pedigree or claim to justness, can never be redeemed, but only endured in sadness? Walter Benjamin's famous distinction between mythical (human) violence and divine violence—much discussed in CLS circles—certainly points in this direction.[46] But this much is certain: the more decisively and acutely one has made the ethical turn in critical legal thought, the more *all* possible instances of justice according to law can show themselves as like the case of the Colloredo twins.

---

[43] Michel Foucault, *Abnormal: Lectures at the Collège de France 1974–1975*, trans. Graham Burchell (New York: Picador, 2003), 55–6, 65.

[44] William Blackstone, *Commentaries on the Laws of England* (1st edn., London, 1769; facs. edn. Chicago: University of Chicago Press, 1979) iv 352.

[45] Vladimir Jankélévitch, *Forgiveness*, trans. Andrew Kelley (Chicago: University of Chicago Press, 2005), 19.

[46] Benjamin, *supra* note 31, at 297.

Consider the troubling liminal case of a Nazi guilty of genocide. While such a one is doing the bloody deed, Levinas has no problem saying that the idea of justice calls for the use of violence against the Nazi, who "no longer has a Face."[47] But what about after the deed is done, and presumably even before it is done if one is not certain that it will be done? One of the most revealing, if not shocking, remarks ever made by Levinas was in response to an interviewer's question about whether literally every other person is an ethical Other, including especially the face of a "brute." His response:

> Jean-Toussaint Desanti asked a young Japanese who was commenting on my works during a thesis defense if an SS man has what I mean by a face. A very disturbing question which calls, in my opinion, for an affirmative answer. An affirmative answer that is painful each time! During the [Klaus] Barbie [aka "the butcher of Lyon"] trial, I could say: Honor to the West! Even with regard to those whose "cruelty" has never stood trial, justice continues to be exercised. The defendant, deemed innocent, has the right to a defense, to consideration. It is admirable that justice worked in that way, despite the apocalyptic atmosphere [of the trial]. It must also be said that in my way of expressing myself the word *face* must not be understood in a narrow way. This possibility for the human of signifying in its uniqueness, in the humility of its nakedness and mortality, the Lordship of its recall—word of God—of my responsibility for it, and my choseness *qua* unique to this responsibility, can come from a bare arm sculpted by Rodin.[48]

By his own lights, Levinas is right to suggest—indeed, must suggest—that a bare arm sculpted by Rodin could be modeled on the real arm of a saint *or* a brute, and that this does not matter, ethically speaking. The infinite presponsibility owing to the face of the Other in Levinasian ethics would collapse in on itself—would show itself to be a mere variation, albeit floridly expressed, of conventional philosophical ethics—if it attempted to draw lines in advance about who "legitimately" is Other and who is *a priori* unentitled to that status.

Ethics for Nazis! The first three sentences of the above quoted passage are completely consistent with Levinas's ethical thinking in general. And although the remaining sentences uncharacteristically confuse or elide his own distinction between ethics and justice, it still seems to me that to affirm the proposition that "an SS man has what I mean by a face" is to cross an ethical Rubicon. No longer would it be possible for those who crossed this Rubicon with Levinas to pretend that the violence entailed by any imaginable instance of human justice is not always deeply, profoundly problematic from the standpoint of an ethics grounded in infinite compassion.

Derrida, who made a similar ethical crossing himself, once defended those who practice a deconstructive discourse against the charge that it leads to "a politics of neutrality, indifference, [and] indecision," by affirming exactly the contrary: given that deconstruction is always characterized by a moment of logical undecidability between opposing terms, he said, "there is no possible responsibility that does not undergo the ordeal of this undecidability."[49] Ethically speaking, anything less is merely the mindlessly tranquil and irresponsible unfolding of a program: "The program can be Nazi, democratic, or something else, but if one does not traverse this terrifying ordeal

---

[47] Hand, *supra* note 15, at 105.
[48] Id. at 231.
[49] Derrida, et al., *supra* note 10, at 68.

of undecidability, there is no responsibility."[50] The psychological toll taken by the terrifying ordeal that Derrida mentions is obvious. For the ethical turn in critical legal thought is a turn away from the confident construction of remedies for injustice and toward the preparation of a consciousness that is constantly, agonizingly attuned to human suffering in all its many forms.

4. A TURN, BUT WHAT KIND OF TURN?

The attraction of Levinasian ethics to poststructuralist thought is an almost inevitable consequence of a strange kind of background knowledge: the knowledge that claiming to know the secure foundations for what law, morality, and politics require is always a contingent social act—an element of the knower's conscious or unconscious assertion of power over others. Seen from the point of view of such a paradoxical background "knowledge," power is always delivered by history, not logic; it comes "crowned by Fate," as Benjamin put it,[51] rather than in the form of transcendently objective necessity. Derrida's critique of "logocentrism" in ethics, law, and politics ultimately goes back to this fundamental insight,[52] as does Levinas's call for a "break-up in the omnipotence of the logos."[53] Both critiques of the ubiquity of hyperrational discourse in these spheres are concerned with the differences that metaphysical language attempts to cover up.

More importantly, both Derrida and Levinas took especial care to expose the ethical meaning (and peril) of those differences for the very individual who covers up the differences in any given case. This includes, for example, the flesh and blood official (judge, lawyer, police officer, civil servant, and so on) who, though he perhaps thinks of himself as an ethical person, is nonetheless prepared to perform a quasi-religious kind of logocentric ceremony. Like a lump of bread somehow becoming the body of Christ during the Eucharist, the logocentric ceremony of justice transubstantiates what is always uniquely other—just *this* situation, here and now—into what is just another iteration of the same; that is, it becomes a determinate "case" indistinguishable from others of its type.

It should be clear by now that what this chapter calls the ethical turn in critical legal thought is not about compassion and ethics in any conventional sense of these words. It is not even about using some suitably progressive ethical theory or discourse as a useful argument in this or that leftwing, feminist, or otherwise radical critique of law and politics. For even the most original critical thinkers, like everybody else, harbor precritical orthodoxies of their own. And they have reason to realize, perhaps more acutely than more traditional thinkers, that these orthodoxies can prevent them from noticing the inhumane tendencies of their very own theories—tendencies which lie

---

[50] Id. at 68–9.
[51] Benjamin, *supra* note 31, at 286.
[52] Jacques Derrida, *Of Grammatology*, trans. Gayatri Charkravorty Spivak (Baltimore: Johns Hopkins University Press, 1976), 3.
[53] Emmanuel Levinas, "God and Philosophy," in id., *Basic Philosophical Writings*, *supra* note 17, 129–48 at 152.

concealed, like dandelion spores in a well-tended garden, inside the cracks and fissures of even the most excellent of critiques.

Rather than describing or offering yet another theory of how the law or politics can or cannot, should or should not, "be made more knowing in the name, the memory, of the original kindness of man towards his other," to quote Levinas,[54] I would like to end this chapter by taking the metaphor of a "turn" in critical thought extremely seriously. To paraphrase a remark of Derrida's, my goal is not to think by means of metaphor but to think the metaphor as such. It is to bring to language, in as intimate and personal a way as possible, what the ambiguities of the ethical turn as a social phenomenon have to say about the current situation of critical legal thought, or rather, about the intellectual and emotional predicament that the turn has created for the ethical "Me myself" of the conscientious individual critical legal thinker.

The metaphor of a turn in the critical orientation of a thinker is most famously associated with the philosophy of Martin Heidegger, who referred to it in his own case as *die Kehre* ("the turn") in the 1947 essay "A Letter on Humanism."[55] Of course, it can be dangerously misleading to apply to a collectivity a category that acquires its primary meaning from a supposed change in a historical individual's way of thinking, especially if the collectivity is as disorganized and intellectually heterogenous as the one called "critical legal studies." Nevertheless, there are enough productive affinities between Heidegger's case and what my title calls the ethical turn in critical legal thought to let a brief exegesis of the former serve as a useful trope for my conclusion, not least because Levinas himself was so heavily influenced by Heidegger's philosophy.

The question of Being as such (*das Sein*), as opposed to scientific or metaphysical questions about the existence and nature of mere beings (*die Seiende*), remained *the* question for Heidegger throughout his life. For him, Leibniz's basic question—why anything at all is there, rather than nothing—eclipsed in importance all other philosophical questions that have ever been asked. Heidegger's first and best known book, *Being and Time*, approached that question through a phenomenological analysis of the everyday experience of "*Dasein*" (literally, "being-there"), that is, the only kind of being, conventionally called the "human being," whose very Being is an issue for it. However, Heidegger later came to believe that the language of metaphysics used in *Being and Time* to expose Dasein's "fundamental experience of the oblivion of Being" still retained too much of the taint of the traditional subject/object dichotomy, and therefore had failed as an adequate saying of Being.[56]

Now, a "turn" can mean a change of direction of a moving body, as when a ship suddenly turns towards east, west, or south after a period spent sailing north, *or* it can mean a change in the direction toward which an otherwise stationary body points, as when a weathervane turns on a pivot in response to a change in the direction of the wind. In "A Letter on Humanism," Heidegger said that Sartre and the so-called French existentialists had all too eagerly heeded the call in *Being and Time* for a destruction (*Destruktion*) of the Western metaphysical tradition through a phenomenological

---

[54] Hand, *supra* note 15, at 229.
[55] Martin Heidegger, "Letter on Humanism," trans. Frank Capuzi, in id, *Pathmarks* (Cambridge: Cambridge University Press, 1998), 239–76 at 250.
[56] Id.

analysis of Dasein, but they had utterly failed to understand the primary *raison d'être* for that analysis. The existentialists had interpreted the book's hermeneutic approach to Dasein as a kind of end in itself: they believed it *privileged* existence over essence because "existence precedes essence," as Sartre put it,[57] thereby paving the way for human beings to live more freely and authentically; whereas in fact Heidegger had intended his analysis of Dasein to serve as a necessary but preliminary philosophical means, so to speak, that would clear away centuries of dense metaphysical underbrush to prepare the ground for a more primordial thinking and saying of Being as such. That is why Heidegger insisted, in the "Letter on Humanism," that "This turning is not a change of standpoint from *Being and Time*."[58] Whatever else can be said about Heidegger's subsequent work, including his more "poetic" and experimental writings, it was not like a change in direction of a moving body. It was instead a pivot around the same old axis that had always transfixed his philosophical attention: Being as such.

The postmodern effort to subvert the glorification of traditional forms of knowledge glorifies in turn its own counterthesis that truth is always relative to historical context, thereby leading to a kind of return of the repressed in the mind of any critic who grows overly attached to the superiority of his own insights. To paraphrase the philosopher Eugen Fink, the resulting postmodern predicament is the task of finding a concept or language to express perceiving, knowing, and understanding that, on the one hand, does not implicitly refer to active building or constructing by an "I" (idealism), and, on the other hand, does not implicitly refer to a merely passive receiving of what is already constituted (realism). The acuteness of the dilemma created by this task cannot be overstated. On the one hand, a critique of conventionally accepted categories of law *based* on someone's theory of ethics is always possible, as the existence for more than two millennia of various forms of natural law reasoning can attest. In a post-Heideggerian world, however, every general theory, however original, shows itself as having been built with the bricks of old concepts, just as every confident assertion that we should follow this or that moral norm can always be interpreted as indeterminate at best, or an instance of special pleading at worst.

And yet, on the other hand, an ethical discourse such as Levinas's that is inclined to disparage the redemptive powers of reason threatens to weaponize ethics against the possibility of justice, and even threatens to transform critique itself into a fellow traveler of injustice. Thus, it is probably right and good that political theorists continue to remind us of the Levinasian existential truism that "only the individual can see the tears of the other, the tears that even the just regime cannot see."[59] But what then? To go further—to advocate, say, for an "anarchic disturbance of politics" by ethics based on Levinas's insights (Miguel Abensour and Simon Critchley[60])—does not offer a *program* of action that can or should be welcomed without hesitation. Or so it seems to me. After all, the case could be made in 2018, at the time of writing, that we have all

---

[57] Jean-Paul Sartre, *Existentialism Is a Humanism*, trans. Carol Macomber (New Haven: Yale University Press, 2007), 20.
[58] Heidegger, *supra* note 55, at 250.
[59] Diamantides, *supra* note 9, at 22.
[60] Simon Critchley, *The Ethics of Deconstruction: Derrida and Levinas*, 3rd edn. (Edinburgh: Edinburgh University Press, 2014), 314.

been obliged to endure Brexit, Donald Trump, and the resurgence of rightwing European populism because of a worldwide anarchic disturbance of politics on the part of white, working-class voters whose care for their own suffering—and compassion for the suffering of others who look and think enough like them—is utterly uninformed by any rational understanding of that suffering's real causes and conditions in the overall context of global capitalism.

The uneasy relationship between ethics and justice is the well-known Achilles' heel of Levinas's thought, and hence too of the ethical turn in critical legal thought. Levinas once implied that his main difference of opinion with Heidegger had to do with the ethical consequences of the latter's chosen pivot point, Being as such: "I don't think [Heidegger] thinks that giving, feeding the hungry and clothing the naked is the meaning of being or that it is above the task of being."[61] From the Being of beings to the Other ineffable human being whose face I perceive; from fundamental ontology to ethics as first philosophy; from the strategic use of nomos and logos for political ends to promoting the compassionately anarchic disruption of all systemic conceptions of justice. It seems to me that the ethical turn in critical legal thought resembles a change in direction of a moving body more than it does a turn in the direction of a gaze that remains confidently affixed to the selfsame standpoint.

Since a complete account of the reasons for all the developments in CLS that go under the name "the ethical turn" would have to be as complex and varied as the biographies of the many individuals who have been responsible for it, such a project lies beyond the scope of the present chapter. Instead, from here on out we will examine the ethical turn in critical legal scholarship in the context of what seems to me to be at once a deep paradox at its heart *and* the intellectual and psychological condition of its possibility. The ethical turn is the consequence of, on the one hand, a profound loss of faith in "reason" interpreted as an *impersonal faculty of intuition* that can correctly "see" abstract things like essences and universal truths in the spheres of law and morality; and yet, on the other hand, it is also the consequence of an inability to let go of faith in "reason" interpreted as a *discursive faculty of reasoning* from premises to conclusions according to the principle of sufficient reason. For the latter holds, among other things, that nothing whatsoever—be it good, bad, or indifferent—can exist without some reason for giving us grounds to hope that it will arrive someday.

The idea that a belief can continue to produce powerful effects even after people cease believing it is most closely associated with Max Weber's thesis that duty in one's calling remains the fundamental basis of capitalism's social ethic even though belief in the Calvinist foundation of worldly asceticism that gave rise to it has largely disappeared. "The idea of duty in one's calling prowls about in our lives like the ghost of dead religious beliefs," remarked Weber, so much so that "the [modern] individual generally abandons the attempt to justify it at all."[62] It seems to me that something like this has happened in CLS. Faith in reason *qua* the rational intuition of universal essences is dead; but the use of reason *qua* the faculty of reason*ing* goes on and on, for without it nothing whatever could ever be made intelligible. Even the sort of

---

[61] Hand, *supra* note 15, at 116.
[62] Max Weber, *The Protestant Ethic and the Spirit of Capitalism*, trans. Talcott Parsons (New York: Charles Scribner's Sons, 1976), 182.

deconstructive practice that allows language to show itself to the reader as always already multivocal with respect to its own possibilities needs the discursive faculty of reasoning according to the principle of sufficient reason to demonstrate the many paths that *can* be taken from a given premise.

The motivation to criticize the established, taken for granted order of things generally comes from two sources: the desire to *change* the way things are, and the desire to *understand* the way things are. Call the first the "revolutionary impulse," and the second the "truth impulse." Marx's famous 11th thesis on Feuerbach expresses the revolutionary impulse quite succinctly: "The philosophers have only *interpreted* the world differently; the point is to *change* it."[63] Embedded in this quotation is an unconscious subversion of the ground of the truth impulse. The belief that one can describe the world the way it really is, Marx's words suggest, is not just ineffectual in itself—such a belief also fails to comprehend that any mere description of the way things are is already just another "interpretation" standing beside all the other interpretations that people give of the world. Interpretations alone, even true interpretations, *do* nothing on their own, and Marx is saying that although they may be a means to the end of doing, they are not ends in their own right. It is changing the world that is the proper end of the revolutionary impulse, and not just interpreting it.

But what if the revolutionary impulse cannot emerge in a person without the truth impulse preparing the way? What if believing that one has understood the world correctly (including all its unjust oppressions, together with their causes and conditions) is a necessary condition for the revolutionary impulse to become kindled in the first place? In that case a kind of paradox would emerge. The impulse to change, grounded in the undeniable truth of the need for change, would cut itself adrift from the task of bearing witness to suffering by beginning to *enact* revolutionary change; and in cutting itself loose, it would lose the ability or the will to bear witness to all that is happening as it changes the world. As Mannheim noted in *Ideology and Utopia*, it would become invested in "not seeing" facts that would undermine its own existence as a revolutionary impulse.[64]

The truth impulse says, "slow down—not so fast—maybe you're doing more harm than good," whereas the revolutionary impulse says, "forward now to change the bad things in the world!" The revolutionary impulse, if it needs the truth impulse as its necessary ground, also does not need—indeed, may be killed by—subsequent irruptions of the truth impulse in the form, say, of the desire to see the tears that a civil servant cannot see. Kant famously said, "Thoughts without intuitions are empty, intuitions without concepts are blind."[65] It seems to me that something similar can be said about the ethical turn in critical legal thought: criticism of the established order that is not informed by the desire to bear witness to human suffering is blind, but

---

[63] Karl Marx, "Theses on Feuerbach," in id. & Friedrich Engels, *Basic Writings on Politics and Philosophy*, ed. Lewis Feuer (Garden City (NY): Anchor Books, 1959), 243–5 at 245.

[64] Karl Mannheim, *Ideology and Utopia: An Introduction to the Sociology of Knowledge*, trans. Louis Worth & Edward Shils (San Diego: Harcourt Brace Jovanovich, 1985), 40.

[65] Immanuel Kant, *Critique of Pure Reason*, eds & trans. Paul Guyer & Allen Wood (Cambridge: Cambridge University Press, 1998), B75 at 193–4.

criticism that answers only to the impulse to discover and recognize such suffering is ineffectual.

SELECT BIBLIOGRAPHY

Critchley, Simon 2014, *The Ethics of Deconstruction: Derrida and Deconstruction*, 3rd ed., Edinburgh University Press, Edinburgh.
Critchley, Simon 2012, *Infinitely Demanding: Ethics of Commitment, Politics of Resistance*, Verso, London.
Diamantides, Marinos, ed. 2007, *Levinas, Law, Politics*, Routledge-Cavendish, Milton Park.
Douzinas, Costas & Ronnie Warrington 1994, *Justice Miscarried: Ethics, Aesthetics and the Law*, Harvester Wheatsheaf, Hemel Hempstead.
Levinas, Emmanuel 1998, *On Thinking-of-the-Other Entre Nous*, trans. Michael Smith & Barbara Harshav, Columbia University Press, New York.
Levinas, Emmanuel 1996, *Basic Philosophical Writings*, eds Adriaan Peperzak, Simon Critchley & Robert Bernasconi, Indiana University Press, Bloomington, IN.
Lindroos-Hovinheimo, Susanna 2012, *Justice and the Ethics of Legal Interpretation*, Routledge, Milton Park.
Moyn, Samuel 2005, *Origins of the Other: Emmanuel Levinas between Revelation and Ethics*, Cornell University Press, Ithaca, NY.
Nussbaum, Martha 1996, "Compassion: The Social Emotion," *Social Philosophy and Policy*, vol. 13, no. 1, pp. 27–58.
Stone, Matthew 2016, *Levinas, Ethics and Law*, Edinburgh University Press, Edinburgh.
Wolcher, Louis 2016, *The Ethics of Justice without Illusions*, Routledge, Milton Park, Abingdon, Oxon.
Wood, David 2006, *The Step Back: Ethics and Politics after Deconstruction*, State University of New York Press, Albany, NY.

12. Law is a stage: from aesthetics to affective aestheses
Andreas Philippopoulos-Mihalopoulos*

1. INTRODUCTION

Legal aesthetics is undergoing a major transformation. What used to be a quest for definition of the law (with, through and along aesthetics) has now become, as I will be arguing here, a quest for presentation or *staging* of the law. Indeed, the main aesthetic question for law nowadays can be summed up as 'how should law present itself in order to be accepted as law?' or, to put it differently, 'how is law to stage itself in order to prove itself relevant?' This set of questions, which, as I suggest in section 4 of this chapter, has replaced some of the fundamental aesthetic questions of modernity, is indicative of a law as image-conscious and volatile as media or politics, relying more and more on its ability to 'show off' (rather than actually to prove through its actions) its relevance. This of course is not an isolated legal phenomenon. It is largely due to the fact that aesthetics on the whole is shifting, from the ontology of definition (beauty, art, sublime) to the new ontology of apparition and staging.

The need is not purely declaratory: it is not enough for law to say that it is law. Law has to *show* itself as law, and must communicate to the world that itself and none other *is* the law. It has to stage itself in a consumer-oriented way, to market itself in a socially engaging way, and to package itself in a media-appetising way. This is similar to what Terry Eagleton finds in the context of Burke's aesthetics: 'the aesthetic was the way power, or the Law, would be carried into the minutest crevices of lived experience, inscribing the very gestures and affections of the body with its decrees.'[1] In order for the law to inscribe itself in the various bodies, it turns into an affect. As an affect, the law constitutes atmospheres of legality, fairness, universality, justice and other such values, while at the same time hiding behind them and dissimulating itself as nonlaw, as I explain in sections 6 and 7. These atmospheres are both politically suspect and

---

* With thanks to Dan Matthews, Swastee Ranjan and the editors of the volume for their comments.
[1] Terry Eagleton, 'Aesthetics and Politics in Edmund Burke' (1989) *History Workshop Journal* 28(1), 53–62, 54. And while in the eighteenth century this resulted in the concept of manners, nowadays it results in the practice of staging, 'so that the laws which govern subjects [are] to be felt as directly pleasurable, intuitively enjoyable, aesthetically appropriate'. At 54–5.

necessary. It is through them that the law establishes its relevance. It is important to note that the term 'atmosphere' here is not a metaphor. As I show in section 5 of the chapter, law, just as everything else, has succumbed to the embrace of atmospherics that demand a differentiated behaviour, one that matches the expectations of a consumerist, immunised and segregated society.

The aesthetic question for law has thus shifted. From the modern aesthetic quest for definition, the question has now become how the law orchestrates its appearance. From law's 'nature' to law's selfie, as it were, this shift has remarkable political and ontological consequences. One of the most important consequences is the bypassing of such foundational questions as what the law is, what its function and what its connection to justice. In modernity, aesthetic considerations for law meant the quest for an ontological, definitional purity – and the above questions were attempting to cover exactly that. Law followed and to some extent solidified this classic modern questioning with its consequent boundary-setting between disciplines, concepts, systems and so on. So, although law was following the definitional attempts of art, it was at the same time carving its own differential space: law might have been borrowing the (aesthetic) method from art, but only in order to differentiate itself from it. The modern aesthetic quest has traditionally been an ontological probing on questions of being.[2]

A direct follow up to this definitional attempt is the question of the origin of the violence of law as defined by Derrida, himself following Benjamin's work.[3] In late modernity, law was simply what can be legitimised (by recourse to violence or otherwise) as law. Law's origin became the main legal definitional aesthetics: law is law because it can claim its mystical foundation. Thus, the aesthetic question for law became one of legitimation.[4] This paved the way for what I argue is the current aesthetic focus of the law: its legitimation nowadays arises not so much from its use of the origin of violence but rather from the way it incorporates it and dissimulates it as affective desire on behalf of its subjects. From the society of discipline (Foucault) to that of control (Deleuze), and now to that of self-staging, the law deals with the need for legitimation by marketing itself as desirable.

---

[2] Jacques Ranciere, *The Politics of Aesthetics: The Distribution of the Sensible*, trans. G. Rockhill (Continuum, 2004).

[3] Jacques Derrida, 'Force of Law: The "Mystical Foundation of Authority"', trans. M. Quaintance, in D. Cornell, M. Rosenfeld and D. Gray Carlson (eds), *Deconstruction and the Possibility of Justice* (Routledge, 1992).

[4] See also Niklas Luhmann, *Legitimation durch Verfahren* (Suhrkamp, 2006).

The above is, of course, intimately related to an understanding of law as commodity value.[5] The most widely recognisable forms of law (state law, private law, corporation law and so on) have always been associated with an economic value, which would sit, albeit with some unease, next to both the functional value of the law as the order provider in society, and its ideal value as provider of justice. Law is needed for society to function, and as such forms part of the economy of exchange. These days, however, things are slightly different: law's commodity value is, if not superseded, at least strongly complemented by law's staging value, namely its ability to communicate to the world that itself and none other *is* the law. Remarkably, this is not an abandonment of the ontological definitional quest of the law, namely, what the law is. Rather, it is an epiphenomenon of a seismic shift across disciplines, of an emergent ontology of staging, atmospheric dissimulation and constructed desire. Despite its strong roots in English aesthetic theory as I show below, this is a specifically contemporary, as opposed to modern, issue. The tools to tackle the shift and its consequences are to be found in the passage from aesthetics to *aestheses*, namely the preponderance of the sensorial and the emotional in the aesthetic staging of law.

In what follows, I first look at the connection between law and art/aesthetics. In section 3, I engage with the shift from aesthetics of definition to aestheses of immersion, namely immersion into affects that involve sensorial and emotional responses. I argue that law is in practice deeply involved with the affective turn, despite the fact that only a few sections of legal theory have explicitly caught up with it; this is because, as I show in section 4, law is called to stage itself affectively, namely sensorially and emotionally, in order to prove its legality and social relevance. I have called this 'atmospherics', which can be defined as the excess of legal affect that is directed in a certain way in order to produce planned outcomes. In an atmosphere, law can stage its relevance more easily. This is because, if an atmosphere is engineered correctly, it becomes a self-perpetuating emergence, and law becomes an integral part of it. What is most dramatic, though, is that law often needs to dissimulate itself as nonlaw and withdraw from the atmosphere. Naturally this is just a staged vanishing act, which, however, has serious consequences in terms of the way that law can be used. Finally, in the last section of the chapter, I examine legal atmospherics empirically through an experimental performance dealing with issues of atmosphere engineering, distinction as aesthetic choice and legal withdrawal that took place in London in 2015.

---

[5] Evgeny Pashukanis, *The General Theory of law and Marxism* (Pluto Press, 1987); see also Dragan Milovanovic, 'The Commodity-Exchange Theory of Law: In Search of a Perspective' (1981) *Crime and Social Justice* 16, 41–9.

2. LEGAL AESTHETICS

A plethora of literature deals with issues of legal aesthetics, whether these are law and art,[6] the visual,[7] street art,[8] photography,[9] film,[10] music and sound production,[11] sculpture,[12] literature,[13] poetry,[14] or photography, theatre and performance;[15] or they

---

[6] For a relatively recent collection see Oren Ben Dor (ed.), *Law and Art: Justice, Ethics and Aesthetics* (Routledge, 2011). See also Merima Bruncevic, *Law, Art and the Commons* (Routledge, 2016); Andreas Philippopoulos-Mihalopoulos, 'Beauty and the Beast: Art and Law in the Hall of Mirrors' (2004) *Entertainment Law* 2(3), 1–34.

[7] E.g. Peter Goodrich and Valérie Hayert (eds) *Genealogies of Legal Vision* (Routledge, 2015); Leif Dahlberg (ed.), *Visualizing Law and Authority: Essays on Legal Aesthetics* (de Gruyter, 2012); Costas Douzinas and Lynda Nead (eds), *Law and the Image: The Authority of Art and the Aesthetics of Law* (University of Chicago Press, 1999); Zenon Bankowski and Geoff Maugham, *Images of Law* (Routledge, 1976); Andreas Philippopoulos-Mihalopoulos, 'Repetition or the Awnings of Justice', in O. Ben-Dor (ed.), *Law and Art: Justice, Ethics and Aesthetics* (Routledge, 2011).

[8] Alison Young, *Street Art, Public City* (Routledge, 2013); Marta Iljadica, *Copyright beyond Law: Regulating Creativity in the Graffiti Subculture* (Hart, 2016).

[9] Connal Parsley, 'The Exceptional Image: Torture Photographs from Guantánamo Bay and Abu Ghraib as Foucault's Spectacle of Punishment', in D. Manderson (ed.) *Law and the Visual: Transitions and Transformations* (Toronto University Press, 2016).

[10] Nathan Moore and Anne Bottomley, 'Law, Diagram, Film: Critique Exhausted' (2012) *Law and Critique* 23(2), 163–82; Steve Greenfield, Guy Osborn and Peter Robson, *Film and the Law: The Cinema of Justice* (Hart Publishing, 2010); Austin Sarat et al, *Law on the Screen* (Stanford University Press, 2005); Leslie Moran, Christie Sandon and Elena Loizidou (eds) *Law's Moving Image* (Cavendish, 2004); Leslie Moran, 'Law's Diabolical Romance: Reflections on the New Jurisprudence of the Sublime' (2004) *Current Legal Issues* 7.

[11] E.g. James Parker, 'Towards an Acoustic Jurisprudence: Law and the Long Range Acoustic Device' (2015) *Law, Culture and the Humanities* 14(4); Desmond Manderson, *Songs without Music: Aesthetic Dimensions of Law and Justice* (University of California Press, 2000); M.J. Grant and Férdia J. Stone-Davis, 'The Soundscape of Justice' (2011) *Griffith Law Review* 20, 962; Danilo Mandic, 'Listening to the World: Sounding Out the Surrounding of Environmental Law with Michel Serres', in Andreas Philippopoulos-Mihalopoulos and Victoria Brooks (eds) *Research Methods in Environmental Law: A Handbook* (Edward Elgar, 2018).

[12] Andrea Pavoni, *Controlling Urban Events: Law, Ethics and the Material* (Routledge, 2018); Marta Iljadica, 'Is a Sculpture "Land"?' (2016) *Conveyancer & Property Lawyer* 3, 242–50.

[13] E.g. Maria Aristodemou, *Law & Literature: Journeys from Her to Eternity* (Oxford University Press, 2000); Desmond Manderson and Honni van Rijswijk, 'Introduction to Littoral Readings: Representations of Land and Sea in Law, Literature, and Geography' (2015) *Law & Literature* 27(2), 167–77.

[14] E.g. Adam Gearey, *Law and Aesthetics* (Hart, 2001); Peter Fitzpatrick, 'Taking Place: Westphalia and the Poetics of Law' (2014) *London Review of International Law* 2(1), 155–65; Peter Fitzpatrick, 'Law like Poetry – Burnt Norton' (2001) *Liverpool Law Review* 23(3), 285–8.

[15] E.g. Marett Leiboff, 'Theatricalizing Law' (2018) *Law & Literature*, DOI: 10.1080/ 1535685X.2017.1415051; Panu Minkkinen and Ari Hirvonen, '"The Uneasy Spring in 1988": A Theatrical Presentation in Five Acts with a Prologue and an Epilogue' (1987) *Crime, Law and Social Change* 11(3), 303; Honni van Rijswijk, 'Towards a Feminist Aesthetic of Justice: Sarah Kane's Blasted as Theorisation of the Representation of Sexual Violence in International Law' (2012) *Australian Feminist Law Journal* 36, 107–24.

look at law and aesthetics as a whole to flesh out the connection between law and aesthetic judgement;[16] or they deal with the sociology of legal aesthetics,[17] or with law as an aesthetic practice, therefore focusing on rituals,[18] architecture,[19] signs and emblemata,[20] or museums as loci of political and legal community formation;[21] or finally they perform the common space between aesthetics and law.[22] Without wishing to ignore the body of literature that has dealt with isolated instances of legal aesthetics in the past,[23] I would argue that it was the advent of critical legal theory and more recently what we can call critical sociolegal theory that encouraged thinking of law and aesthetics together in an easier, unforced manner.[24] Since then, law and aesthetics have been at the forefront of a critical interdisciplinary study of law, and an almost natural

---

[16] Melanie Williams, 'Euthanasia and the Ethics of Trees: Law and Ethics through Aesthetics' (1998) *The Australian Feminist Law Journal* 10, 109; Angus McDonald, 'The New Beauty of a Sum of Possibilities' (1997) *Law and Critique* 8, 141; Roberta Kevelson (ed.), *Law and Aesthetics* (Peter Lang, 1992); George Karavokyris, 'The Art of Law' (2014) *Law & Critique* 25, 67; Oren Ben-Dor (ed.), *Law and Art: Justice, Ethics and Aesthetics* (Routledge, 2011); Peter Goodrich, 'On the Relational Aesthetics of International Law' (2008) *Journal of the History of International Law* 10, 321–41; Karin van Marle, 'Liminal Landscape', in Karin van Marle and Stewart Motha (eds), *Genres of Critique: Law, Aesthetics and Liminality* (Sun Press, 2013); Andreas Philippopoulos-Mihalopoulos, 'Flesh of the Law: Material Metaphors' (2016) *Journal of Law and Society* 43(1), 45–65; Ari Hirvonen, 'Body Politics: Normative Gaze, Carnal Intimacy and Touching Pain in Vanessa Beecroft's Art', in Leif Dahlberg (ed.) *Visualizing Law and Authority: Essays on Legal Aesthetics* (de Gruyter, 2012); Marty Slaughter, 'Black and White or Technicolor' (2007) *Law and Critique* 18(2), 143–69; Marcílio Franca, 'The Blindness of Justice: An Iconographic Dialogue between Art and Law', in Andrea Pavoni et al (eds), *Law and the Senses: SEE* (Westminster University Press, 2018); Roy Kreitner, Anat Rosenberg and Christopher Tomlins, 'Arts and the Aesthetic in Legal History' (2015) *Critical Analysis of Law* 2, 314–22.
[17] Andreas Fischer-Lescano, 'Sociological Aesthetics of Law' (2016) *Law, Culture and the Humanities* 1–26, DOI: 10.1177/1743872116656777.
[18] E.g. David Marrani, *Space, Time, Justice: From Archaic Rituals to Contemporary Perspectives* (Routledge, 2017).
[19] E.g. Linda Mulcahy, *Legal Architecture: Justice, Due Process and the Place of Law* (Routledge, 2011); Jonathan Simon, Nicholas Temple and Renée Tobe (eds), *Architecture and Justice: Judicial Meanings in the Public Realm* (Ashgate, 2013).
[20] E.g. Peter Goodrich, *Legal Emblems and the Art of Law: Obiter Depicta as the Vision of Governance* (Cambridge University Press, 2014); Nathan Moore, 'Icons of Control: Deleuze, Signs, Law' (2007) *International Journal for the Semiotics of Law* 20, 33–54; Piyel Haldar, 'The Function of Ornament in Quintillian, Alberti and Court Architecture', in Douzinas and Nead, *Law and the Image*.
[21] Stacey Douglas, *Curating Community: Museums, Constitutionalism, and the Taming of the Political* (University of Michigan Press, 2017).
[22] E.g. Carey Young, 'Justice Must Be Seen to Be Done', March 2016, brooklynrail.org/2016/03/criticspage/justice-must-be-seen-to-be-done; picpoet, 'The Florence Picpoems', in Pavoni et al (eds), *Law and the Senses*.
[23] E.g., Jerome Frank, 'Words and Music: Some Remarks on Statutory Interpretation' (1947) *Columbia Law Review* 47, 1259; Richard F. Wolfson, 'Aesthetics in and about the Law' (1944–5) *Kentucky Law Journal* 33, 33.
[24] The trend-setting work being Costas Douzinas and Ronnie Warrington, *Justice Miscarried: Ethics and Aesthetics in Law* (Edinburgh University Press, 1994).

choice for those of us who work with continental philosophy. This is because continental philosophy often takes recourse to art in order to explain philosophical thought or indeed other disciplines such as politics and law, but it might also be attributed to the fact that art has always represented an escape from law, much more so than, say, politics or economics.

Art, and aesthetics in general, are often thought of (mostly be legal scholars) as providing law's antilogos, another way of worlding that feels more creative and therefore freer; more 'feminine' and therefore less law-masculine; more spontaneous and therefore less restrictive than legal command-and-control. And no doubt, there are many differences between art and law. Art represents a different causality to that of law. It is not about a linear, casuistic thinking (if A has happened, then the court will take B decision) but about a placing-together in some sort of way that might or might not work. Art follows a different temporality, more related to the practice of art production than the need to reproduce a social temporality. Finally, art is not wedded to a moment of judgement, as the law is. Artistic projects are often open-ended with a less directional engagement with the world than law.

But all these are largely romanticising, if not essentialising, ideas about art, often found when art is approached as a whole (already an issue), or when processes of art production and the art world in general are seen from the outside and in the abstract. Art production across modernity, however, has mostly been a cutthroat process, steeped in economic and political considerations, siding with power in order to be promoted, relying on religion or politics and their need for propaganda in order to come to the light.[25] To disengage art as practice from the art market and considerations of exchange value is problematic because such a separation does not take into account how demand for art affects art production. Sidestepping this and focusing only on idealised aspects of art, places art and law in a dialectics of transcendence versus mundanity, where the law ought to learn from art but hardly the other way around (not unlike Edmund Burke's inclusion of Beauty in Power in order to soften it, but never the other way round, thus leading Terry Eagleton to talk about the possibility of a 'transvestite law'[26]). The emphasis on the supposed transcendent nature of art is problematic because it makes art appear mendaciously free, and respectively law to appear uncreative and in need of escape – or, as Peter Goodrich begins his chapter in this volume, 'the principal impetus of contemporary critical legal theory is toward an exit from law'.[27] Thinking of art as the desired transcendental avenue for law is doing a disservice to both, essentialising them respectively in a fixed state of permanent creativity and sterility.

The reality of law, however, is increasingly understood to be more complex than the more traditionally critical theoretical approaches would have it.[28] Law's creativity is manifest in the way it combines the materialities of various epistemes and disciplines in

---

[25] Evelyn Welch, *Art in Renaissance Italy 1350–1500* (Oxford University Press, 1997).
[26] Eagleton, 'Aesthetics and Poltics', 60.
[27] Peter Goodrich, 'Critical Legal Theory: Rhetoric, Semiotics, Synaesthetics', in this volume.
[28] See for example A. Philippopoulos-Mihalopoulos (ed.), *Routledge Handbook of Law and Theory* (Routledge, 2018).

order to construct a legal narrative. Likewise, creativity is evident in the way law reproduces itself as a necessity (staging itself, as I show below) despite often adverse conditions that try to politicise, financialise or otherwise alter law beyond recognition. It is also spread to such a degree spatially and temporally, in short materially, that any attempt at escaping from law is met with yet another law or perhaps an extension of the existing law. In some ways, therefore, transcendence is already provided within legal immanence.[29]

3. FROM AESTHETICS TO AESTHESES

Rather than thinking of law and aesthetics as separate or even antithetical practices, it might be more relevant to think of how aesthetics emerges within law, and the kind of legal aesthetics it gives rise to.[30] Naturally, similar analyses can take place from an aesthetic point of view in relation to law,[31] but here I am concentrating on law and legal aesthetics. This is an ontological quest on the level of the law: it comes from within law and addresses the law. It is not about law's references to art and aesthetics; nor is it about law *as* art; rather, as I mentioned earlier, it is about law in its shift from aesthetics to aestheses.

Legal aesthetics at present is at a crossing, from the traditional aesthetic question of definition of law (what is law as an aesthetic question) to the *aesthesic*, namely the sensorial and emotional,[32] or in short, as I show below, the affective aspect of law. Jacques Rancière has intimated this shift with his work on the term *aesthesis*, which for him signifies 'the mode of experience according to which, for two centuries, we perceive very diverse things ... as all belonging to art'.[33] Yet his understanding of the shift, although perspicacious, remains rooted in a phenomenological theory of perception, and his use of senses, while in theory moving away from Western understandings of aesthetic appreciation, seems to end up reiterating the same historically anthropocentric, text-focused, male-centred and colonial conception of aesthetics as art.[34] What

---

[29] On this see my argument in 'Repetition or the Awnings of Justice', in Oren Ben-Dor (ed.), *Law and Art* (Routledge, 2011).

[30] As has happened already both in law and in politics. E.g., Fischer-Lescano, 'Sociological Aesthetics of Law'; Jacques Rancière, *The Politics of Aesthetics* (Bloomsbury, 2004).

[31] And to some extent, it already has: see special issue 'Imagine Law', *Oncurating* 28 (2016), ed. Avi Feldman.

[32] E.g. José Manuel Barreto, 'Ethics of Emotions as Ethics of Human Rights. A Jurisprudence of Sympathy in Adorno, Horkheimer and Rorty' (2006) *Law and Critique* 17, 73; Lionel Bently and Leo Flynn (eds), *Law and the Senses: Sensational Jurisprudence* (Pluto, 1996); Andrea Pavoni et al (eds), *Law and the Senses Book Series* (Westminster University Press, 2018–20); see also S. Shaviro, *The Universe of Things: On Whitehead and Speculative Realism* (University of Minnesota Press, 2014).

[33] Jacques Rancière, *Aisthesis: Scenes from the Aesthetic Regime of Art*, trans. Zakir Paul (Verso, 2013).

[34] The only reference to art created by women is the *Folies Bergère*, seen through the male gaze of Mallarmé's writing on them; there is no reference to anything but Western art; and there are only scant references to anything but the visual in terms of senses, making this essentially a classic ocularcentric piece of research. See also Rolando Vazquez and Walter Mignolo, 'Decolonial

I aim to do here is move from the phenomenological to the ontological through the employment of affects, which, as I show below, can be thought in terms of senses and emotions.

In some respects, this aesthesic focus is a return to the origins of aesthetics. Aristotle referred to the senses and sense perception ('aestheses') as the basis of judgement, allowing aesthetics to be thought in its intimate connection to the sensorial.[35] A departure took place in late modernity, when aesthetics was linked to issues of form and beauty, thus externalising the focus from the inner mechanisms of senses to the working out of our connection to the world and ultimately to the transcendental horizon needed for the operations of reason.[36] In Aristotle, sensorial involvement is an integral part of acting in a virtuous way, making virtuous judgements about what is good (*kalon*) and what is not. The important thing in this process is that, unlike Kantian aesthetics that understands beauty as a moral category that ultimately leads to reason,[37] in Aristotle reason is not part of the process of aesthetic appreciation and judgement:

> The virtuous agent steps back and sees, not the embodiment of a principle of reason, but an instance of aesthetic perfection. He is moved not by the reasonableness of the act, but by its beauty. The noble is fundamentally an aesthetic concept. By this I mean it is a matter of perception and not one of calculation.[38]

While for us, nourished by late modern aesthetics and moral theory, the good is not necessarily the beautiful but rather something at which one arrives after some sort of formulaic calculation (similar to what we think of law), for Aristotle the term *kalon* encompasses both external and internal beauty.

This must be coupled with the role of emotions in Aristotle, and especially the joy that one draws from having chosen the *kalon*. Again, the emotional element of judgement seems irrelevant to a Kantian aesthetic understanding, where the agent is (expected to be) disinterested and her judgement geared towards universality: 'This is something calculated, almost deductive, that we figure out. In the same way that our emotions are not relevant to solving math problems, so [for Kant] they are of no help in ethics either.'[39] While not beyond controversy,[40] this reading of Aristotle in relation to

---

AestheSis: Colonial Wounds/Decolonial Healings' (2013) *Social Text-Periscope*, 2013, socialtextjournal.org/periscope_article/decolonial-aesthesis-colonial-woundsdecolonial-healings/.

[35] Another mode of arriving perhaps at similar arguments in terms of the affective is through Platonic beauty and desire. See Claire Colebrook, 'Queer Aesthetics', in E.L. McCallum and Mikko Tuhkanen (eds) *Queer Times, Queer Becomings* (SUNY Press, 2011).

[36] Costas Douzinas, 'A Legal Phenomenology of Images', in Oren Ben Dor (ed.) *Law and Art: Justice, Ethics and Aesthetics* (Routledge, 2011) 255.

[37] Immanuel Kant, *The Critique of Pure Reason*, ed. and trans. Paul Guyer and Allen W. Wood (Cambridge University Press, 1998); Ruth Ronen, *Art before the Law* (University of Toronto Press, 2014) 12–13.

[38] John Milliken, 'Aristotle's Aesthetic Ethics' (2006) *The Southern Journal of Philosophy* 44(2), 319–39, 327. This is not uncontroversial, and at various points the aesthetic has been separated from the moral in Aristotle. Milliken however makes a compelling argument, confirmed also by the etymology of *kalon*.

[39] Ibid, 334; see also Martha Nussbaum, *Political Emotions: Why Love Matters for Justice* (Harvard University Press, 2013).

Kant is instructive.[41] It allows us to think of aesthetics and aesthetic judgement in particular in a way that includes the sensorial and the emotional, not just as conditions of judgement but also as outcomes: the joy at having chosen the *kalon* is circularly reinforced by the need to carry on the sensorial quest for aesthetic perfection.

The return of senses and emotions has been pioneered by feminist aesthetics, which regularly critiques the male bias of existing aesthetics. Some of the literature employs a deeply personal affective engagement with art. Ann Cahill's work on female beautification, for example, fleshes out the personal and embodied practice of aesthetics, replete with ethnographic sensorial and emotional references.[42] This kind of focused thinking is in the core of the shift to affective aesthetics: no longer grand definitional pronouncements but specific events with which bodies are engaged. This is inevitable in view of the knowledge, ripe by the early 1990s when some of the most important feminist writing on aesthetics emerges,[43] that femininity and womanhood cannot be forced into unitary definitions, as Hilde Hein finds.[44] An important consequence of this is also the shift of focus from the individual subject (usually as male artistic genius[45]) to the emergence of aesthetic production from within the social/temporal/spatial parameters of the event – what we could call an ontological rather than a phenomenological understanding.

Similar moves are being made in various minoritarian aesthetics,[46] with one of the most important taking place in decolonial literature. Rolando Vasquez and Walter Mignolo have written about decolonial *aestheSis* (with a capitalised S) as 'processes of thinking and doing, of sensing and existing, in which the modern distinction between

---

[40] See Terence Irwin, 'Aristotle's Conception of Morality' in John J. Cleary (ed.), *Proceedings of the Boston Area Colloquium in Ancient Philosophy* (University Press of America, 1986).

[41] See also Gilles Deleuze, *Kant's Critical Philosophy: The Doctrine of the Faculties*, trans. Hugh Tomlinson and Barbara Habberjam (University of Minnesota Press, 1984).

[42] Ann Cahill, 'Feminist Pleasure and Feminine Beautification' (2003) *Hypatia* 18(4), 42–64, and the whole issue that is dedicated to feminist aesthetics and how it has evolved in that last decade.

[43] See for example the whole special issues of *Hypatia* 5(2) (1990) on Feminism and Aesthetics, edited by Hilde Hein and Carolyn Korsmeyer; also the special issue on Feminism and Traditional Aesthetics of the *Journal of Aesthetics and Art Criticism* 48(4) (1990).

[44] Hilde Hein, 'Refining Feminist Theory: Lessons from Aesthetics', in Hilde Hein and Carolyn Korsmeyer (eds), *Aesthetics in Feminist Perspective* (Indiana University Press, 1993). See also Christine Battersby, *Gender and Genius: Towards a Feminist Aesthetics* (Indiana University Press, 1994). Feminist aesthetics have been working their way in law as well: see Mark Rose, 'Mothers and Authors: Johnson v. Calvert and the New Children of Our Imaginations' (1996) *Critical Inquiry* 22, 613.

[45] In relation to law, see Carys Craig, 'Reconstructing the Author-Self: Some Feminist Lessons for Copyright Law' (2007) *American University Journal of Gender, Social Policy & the Law* 15, 207.

[46] See for example queer aesthetics as an ethical Deleuzian position in Colebrook, 'Queer Aesthetics'; or as 'promiscuous' substitutability of art in Daniel Williford, 'Queer Aesthetics' (2009) *Borderlands* 8, 2; or black queer aesthetics in Ana-Maurine Lara, 'Of Unexplained Presences, Flying Ife Heads, Vampires, Sweat, Zombies, and Legbas: A Meditation on Black Queer Aesthetics' (2012) *GLQ: A Journal of Lesbian and Gay Studies*, 18(2–3), 347–59.

theory and practice has no purchase'.[47] In the context of decolonialism, aesthesis acquires a polemic character that challenges the predominance of colonial aesthetic canons:

> Decolonial aestheSis starts from the consciousness that the modern/colonial project has implied not only control of the economy, the political, and knowledge, but also control over the senses and perception. Modern aestheTics have played a key role in configuring a canon, a normativity that enabled the disdain and the rejection of other forms of aesthetic practices, or, more precisely, other forms of aestheSis, of sensing and perceiving.[48]

Transposing this onto legal aesthetics, the colonial norm of determining Western law as *the* law has been and still is in the core of the definitional aesthetics of law. In their attempt at defining law, legal aesthetics have regularly marginalised other forms of law, and especially law that emerges from the colonised.

Senses and emotions have an increasing role in prefiguring and determining non-Western, nonexclusively male, decolonial aesthetics. In their turn, these minoritarian aesthetics are changing aesthetics as a whole. A way to contextualise this shift is to think of aestheses in terms of affects.[49] Affects have been fleshed out by Spinoza and then incorporated in contemporary theory by Deleuze and Guattari.[50] For the purposes of this analysis, affects include the emotions and senses generated in a body, human or nonhuman, that however exceed the very body of emergence, leading thus to understanding of affects as posthuman manifestations of excess that link up bodies.[51] The affective challenge is multiple: first, to understand affect as an indistinguishable emergence of emotions and senses; second, to take affects not as human-originating qualities but as posthuman, acentral, excessive attributes that, as I show below, often coalesce into an atmosphere. Thus, affect is posthuman in the sense that it neither originates nor ends necessarily in humans; acentral, in that it floats about rather than causally originating in one source; and excessive of its body of origin.

The affective turn brings a renewed interest in understanding the law aesthetically. At the same time, the affective turn encourages us to depart from the foundational aesthetics of definition and move instead into the aesthetics of aesthesic, affective staging of law. The difference between the two has been described by the German philosopher Gernot Böhme: 'Aesthetics in the modern age has two sources: one in German rationalism, the other in English sensualism. The former is generally privileged in the history of aesthetics because it is the one which culminates in aesthetics as the theory of the work of art.' Böhme continues:

---

[47] Rolando Vazquez and Walter Mignolo, 'Decolonial AestheSis: Colonial Wounds/Decolonial Healings' (2013) *Social Text-Periscope*, 2013, socialtextjournal.org/periscope_article/decolonial-aesthesis-colonial-woundsdecolonial-healings/.

[48] Ibid. See also transnationaldecolonialinstitute.wordpress.com/decolonial-aesthetics/.

[49] E.g., see my work on affect and law in *Spatial Justice*; James E. Fleming (ed.), *Passions and Emotions* (NYU Press, 2013).

[50] Giles Deleuze and Félix Guattari, *A Thousand Plateaus: Capitalism and Schizophrenia*, trans. B. Massumi (Athlone Press, 1988).

[51] For more details, see Andreas Philippopoulos-Mihalopoulos, *Spatial Justice: Body Lawscape Atmosphere* (Routledge, 2015).

while aesthetics as a theory of the work of art was substantially responsible for creating a canon of great or authentic works – to use Adorno's terms – the aesthetics of taste [the second type of aesthetics] was much more concerned with aesthetic education ... Taste, after all, serves not only to judge objects or works of art adequately, but is rather the ability to make distinctions of all kinds.[52]

It would not be out of place, therefore, to consider English aesthetics the aesthetic theory behind the affective turn. Works by Edmund Burke, for example, on the sublime and the beautiful have managed to infiltrate and to some extent alter the understanding of not just art but aesthetics, without being invested in establishing a modus operandi of appreciating art per se, but rather concerned with discerning the beautiful.[53] Likewise, Joseph Addison's definition of taste decidedly brings together senses and emotions, in a gesture that prefaces contemporary affective theory.[54] Transposing this to law, we see how from the grand questioning of the law *qua* law, legal aesthetics is moving to the formation of taste, and specifically the contextualisation of the drawing of legal distinctions (as expressions of taste): for some time now, in terms of legal theory, law's universality has been ceding priority to the particularity of the context of the legal judgment.[55] This aesthetic move, largely brought in by critical legal theory, is complemented, as I have mentioned, by decolonial, feminist and queer aesthetic practices which aim at subverting the aesthetic norm, as well as by the more materiality-oriented parts of the critical and critical sociolegal literature. The latter is influenced by Spinozan understandings of ethics which oppose universal morality and focus on the particular conditions of the assemblage, and in particular the spatial and temporal distribution of the bodies in relation to which a decision is taken and a distinction of distance or propinquity is made.[56] This is signalling another passage which can be considered parallel to that between aesthetics and aestheses: the passage from legal morality as a blanket universaliser, to ethics as a case by case and assemblage by assemblage decision making process.

While this shift from aesthetic to aestheses and from morality to ethics therefore allows us to become more aware of other aesthetics, it is important not to overestimate the possibilities for positive action that come from such a shift. Just as we move away from the grand question of the definition of law and the role of morality, we also move away from the possibility of securing, however illusionarily or arbitrarily, a priori values. This means that a shift towards affects and ethics necessitates the acknowledgement that we can no longer prescribe in advance how the law ought to be (and even when we carry on, we are hardly heeded), but rather we can only focus on the matter

---

[52] Gernot Böhme, *Critique of Aesthetic Capitalism*, trans. Edmund Jephcott (Mimesis International, 2016) 55.

[53] Edmund Burke, *A Philosophical Enquiry into the Origin of our Ideas of the Sublime and Beautiful*, A. Phillips (ed.) (Oxford University Press, 1998).

[54] '[T]hat faculty of soul, which discerns the beauties of an author with pleasure, and the imperfections with dislike.' Joseph Addison and R. Steele, *The Spectator*, A. Chalmers (ed.), New York: Appleton, 1879, no. 409 – although Addison relies more on imagination than the pure inner senses reliance of someone like Shaftesbury

[55] See Douzinas and Warrington, *Justice Miscarried*.

[56] Baruch Spinoza, *Ethics*, trans. G.H.R. Parkinson (Oxford University Press, 2000).

in hand, namely the particular situation in which the law is called upon every time. This is undoubtedly positive and moves in the direction of a law responsive to the particular; a law that listens and understands the specific conditions since it is always part of the assemblage of these conditions;[57] and finally, a law that gives up universalising pronouncements without however succumbing to cultural or in this case ethical relativism. Still, this renewed focus on the particular in the form of aestheses has also some potentially negative consequences in terms of the way it is formed. First, law can no longer rely on its assumed functional value or even legitimate violence in order to remain relevant to society, but has to stage itself in a convincing and appealing way – in other words, it must constantly prove itself, and the means are not necessarily those of justice and fairness but more often than not market values. Second, and connected to the above, in its staging, law often has to dissimulate itself as nonlaw. I will be dealing with these two consequences below.

4. STAGING LAW

In his work on law and aesthetics, Costas Douzinas has looked into the phenomenological connection between the visual and the legal. According to Douzinas, the law mediates between beings and images by capturing that space in-between: 'by reconciling us to radical alterity and by introducing us to difference, the law helps the imagistic staging of the world for the subject.'[58] Yet by staging the world, the law does not reconcile us exclusively to radical alterity and difference. This would occur if law were thought of as an a priori force for the good, objective and unsullied by the contingent. But law cannot seriously be thought of in this theological way. Douzinas is aware of this when he writes:

> Let us take the example of the market model which has become dominant in neo-liberal capitalism. We increasingly see our relations with others and the world through a contractual imagery. A fictional frame of promises, agreements and contracts filters the way we see a large part of relations with others. This contractual framework is replacing other ways of seeing human relations, such as sympathy, care and love. It operates both as a mise-en-scène, a staging of human relations, and as a screen which approaches relations, encounters and emotions according to a model of offer, acceptance and consideration. While such an economic model is staged and artificial, it relies on the naturalising ability of the legal institution.[59]

I will return to the point of contractual staging below. Before that, however, a short critical digression is needed in order to link staging with the passage to aestheses. There is little doubt that from a phenomenological point of view, law stages the world for us. We are the prized audience for such a staging, the honoured guest, but also, and

---

[57] Kirsty Keywood, 'My Body and Other Stories: Anorexia Nervosa and the Legal Politics of Embodiment' (2000) *Social & Legal Studies* 9(4), 495.
[58] Costas Douzinas, 'A Legal Phenomenology of Images', in Oren Ben-Dor (ed.) *Law and Art: Justice, Ethics and Aesthetics* (Routledge, 2011) 256–7.
[59] Ibid, 257.

this is where the phenomenological illusion comes in, the ones who can change that if they so wish. We are the subjects in a world full of objects waiting to be apprehended. Our dispositifs of visibility, one of them also law, encourage and reinforce this unidirectionality. What is more, the connection between us and the world, as mediated by legal intentionality, retains the illusion of control. This is a human gaze, after all, and can be differently directed.[60]

Yet, with the move from aesthetics to aestheses, such anthropocentric illusions as perpetuated by phenomenology can no longer be easily entertained. Something much more grounding occurs. In the above example, law is not only staging the world for us as mainly or even exclusively contractual, and therefore neoliberal. Rather, law is staging *itself* as contractual, thus feeding into a desire for contracts, this most illusionary guarantor of legal freedom. Law no longer mediates between us and whatever else, but itself becomes this whatever else, ontologically becoming a body beyond direct human control.[61] By staging itself as contractual, law meddles not just with the phenomenological mediation between subjects and world, but with the very ontology of the world and the taken for granted category of subjects. Law staging itself means that the world becomes absorbed in law's representation of the world: the only possible world is the one offered by the staged law. This is not simply a question of epistemology, namely a phenomenological perspective on the world that can change if the subject, in whose perception the world also falls, changes. On the contrary, this is an intervention on the level of ontology: *by staging itself, law alters not just the representation of the world but the world itself*. And because law is no longer thought a priori but only situationally, it can import nothing of its supposed ideals of equity, fairness and justice in that staging, unless of course this is what is needed in that particular staging.

In most cases, however, what is 'needed' is a perpetuation of the neoliberal model. This is what Böhme calls aesthetic economics,[62] namely, the way in which commodities are staged:

> to increase their exchange value, commodities are now presented in a special way, they are given a look, they are aestheticized and are put on show in the exchange sphere … to the extent that use is now made of their attractiveness, their glow, their atmosphere: they themselves contribute to the staging, the dressing up and enhancement of life.[63]

---

[60] See my critique of phenomenology in 'Withdrawing from Atmosphere: An Ontology of Air Partitioning and Affective Engineering' (2016) *Environment and Planning D: Society and Space* 34(1), 150–67.

[61] Yet always part of an assemblage in which human and nonhuman bodies converge. See my work on 'Lively Agency: Life and Law in the Anthropocene', in Irus Braverman (ed.), *Animals, Biopolitics, Law: Lively Legalities* (Routledge, 2016). In that sense, law needs to be rethought in the manner of the posthumanism of Niklas Luhmann (e.g. *Law as a Social System*, trans. K. Ziegert, ed. F. Kastner, R. Nobles, D. Schiff and R. Ziegert (Oxford University Press, 2004)) as an autopoietic body whose connection to human conscience is only a matter of contingency.

[62] Gernot Böhme, *Atmosphären: Essays zur neuen Ästhetik* (Suhrkamp, 2013).

[63] Gernot Böhme, *Critique of Aesthetic Capitalism*, trans. Edmund Jephcott (Mimesis, 2016) 20.

Just like every other commodity, law is packaged in order to become attractive, to the point that its 'staging value'[64] becomes much more important than its initial commodity exchange value. Law stages itself through media, both traditional and social, by becoming spectacular, Twitter-based and responsive to social pressures, sacrificing its supposed myth of neutrality for another myth, that of popular value. It stages itself in support of traditional and conservative regimes of property, and aesthetically sides with the old 'art canon' of high art, while failing to recognise street art as art.[65] It stages itself with the help of technology, by becoming a service product given to entrepreneurship and innovation, computerised and binarised, standardised rather than contingent. It finally stages itself pedagogically so as to become a mechanical degree that leads to good exam results and even better career prospects, bypassing much needed spaces of open thought and critique. 'The aesthetic quality of the commodity, the commodity aesthetic, acts to put life on show. Capitalism is to be defined as the aesthetic economy in so far as it produces primarily aesthetic values, that is, commodities that act as the staging of life.'[66] Life is, therefore, mediated by law and its aesthetic value, put on show via law.

But, as I mentioned earlier, this is just the first step. The most important development is that the ontology of law, and consequently life and the world, changes because of law's aestheticisation. To put it more simply, law's staging *is* the law. Law is nothing but the *enunciation* of its mode of enunciation, to paraphrase Latour.[67] There is no other law behind this stage, no better or grander, more universal or more sovereign law that directs the staging and ultimately remains solid, reliable, valuable per se, in touch with its social function and necessity.

The stage is all there is: a scraggy immanence, brittle and unhinged, unable to entertain even the illusion of transcendence, of a better law to come.

5. ATMOSPHERICS

A way for law to stage itself is through the construction of a legal atmosphere. Building on the affective turn in law and staying within an ontological take that does not regard senses and emotions as phenomenological and human-centred attributes but rather as ontological emergences,[68] I would like to suggest that law is an institutional affect, namely, an affect that becomes directed by the atmosphere it generates. For, although an affect is excessive, acentral and posthuman, it is regularly manipulated or at least smoothed in an institutionalised direction. In *Libidinal Economy*, Jean-François Lyotard

---

[64] Ibid, 68.
[65] Young, *Street Art*; Lucy Finchett-Maddock, 'In Vacuums of Law We Find – Outsider Poiesis in Street Art and Graffiti', in Duncan Chappell and Saskia Hufnagel (eds), *Art Crime Handbook* (Palgrave Macmillan, forthcoming).
[66] Böhme, *Critique*, 68.
[67] Bruno Latour, *The Making of Law: An Ethnography of the Conseil D'État* (Polity Press, 2009).
[68] Philippopoulos-Mihalopoulos, *Spatial Justice*.

describes affects as the libidinal intensities that allow a system to direct desire.[69] In that sense, affects are regularly exploited and channelled to serve consumerist needs, capitalist abstractions, legal obedience and political placation.

The collective affect is the constituent element of an atmosphere. I have previously defined an atmosphere as the ontology of affective excess that emerges by, through and against human and nonhuman bodies.[70] If affect is the intercorporeal element that keeps bodies together, an atmosphere is the excess of affects emerging as an order of sorts. An atmosphere is often put in the service of consumerist, religious, political and other purposes. Above all, however, an atmosphere is engineered in order to promote its own perpetuation. This means that, upon the atmospheric emergence, the various affects are instrumentalised in order to feed and preserve the atmosphere.

Thus, in an atmosphere of legal and political oppression, affects between, say, neighbours, or between humans and property, will be put in the service of the oppressive atmosphere, reinforcing it from within. Diverging affects, such as resistance or disobedience, sometimes have the effect of breaking the oppressive atmosphere and moving on; however, as often as not, they are coopted and anticipated by the atmosphere and used as a way of reinforcing the atmosphere (say, by demonising the resistance movement as anarchists, and so on).

For law to keep on proving itself, it needs to engineer an atmosphere of legality, fairness, universality, justice and other such values. While these values are integral to legal delivery, they need to be spectacularised in order for law to be relevant. As I have mentioned, the spectacularisation of law becomes *the* law. Rancière writes that the mise-en-scene was 'an art born out of the reversal by which the auxiliary art that was supposed to put drama in tableaux and in movement proved to be the means of renewing it, of giving thought fixed in words the spatial form that suits it'.[71] Ironically, this reversal has now become ontological, and has taken up all available space. Law invests in 'an *appearance* or *look*, endowing [it] with a *radiance* or *glow*, an atmosphere'.[72] A legal atmosphere is the perfect set for law's staging itself: once set up, the atmosphere perpetuates itself. It does so by converting into 'needs' the desires of the participating bodies.

Continuing with the neoliberal theme, law creates an atmosphere of contractual freedom, in which bodies simply cannot see the imbalance of power, because they are blinded by the apparent fairness and equality of opportunity that is in the core of a contractualised law. This desire is individualistic and neoliberal par excellence, and has to do with illusionary notions of achieving personal freedom through mortgages, promotions, new gadgets, sports shoes, trendier handbags and so on. This is not about

---

[69] Jean-François Lyotard, *Libidinal Economy*, trans. Iain Hamilton Grant (Athlone Press, 1993).
[70] Philippopoulos-Mihalopoulos, *Spatial Justice*.
[71] Rancière, *Aisthesis*, 89.
[72] Böhme, *Critique*, 20.

survival or covering of actual needs. This is pure surplus consumption which 'is seldom referred to today as *luxury* or *extravagance*, because it is no longer bound up with certain privileges or limited to certain classes, but is now taken for granted as a universal standard of living'[73] – or at least the universally aspired to standard of living, even when basic needs are not covered. In generating and acting through an atmosphere, law matches the expectations of a consumerist society, while continuing to nurture these expectations so that more of the same is needed. An atmosphere generates a cycle of addiction where, once the supposed desires are converted into 'real needs', more of the same is offered continuously and in excess.[74]

On a different level, law is fed by and in turn feeds the ever increasing 'need' for security, immunisation, segregation and distancing from risk. There are multiple examples: gated communities that exclude everything that does not belong to the aesthetics of the class they are promoting while creating artificial spaces of risk-free ludic pleasures; shopping malls that prohibit all spontaneous street activity while imitating street culture; 'fortress Europe' that professes tolerance and respect for human rights while failing spectacularly to deal with the refugee issues of the early twenty-first century: all these are legal atmospheres that are engineered with the recourse of media, economy, politics, religion and so on. These atmospheres are naturalised because in a circular, simultaneous manner, they both create and nourish the supposed need for security and immunisation. The Western world is its own glasshouse of atmospheric partitioning, with immigration policies that control the use of elements such as water and land in terms of spatial approaches to jurisdictional utopias, or the boundary that separates the occident from the orient, constructing both exteriors and interiors through the bent glass of religion, economy, culture and so on. Frantz Fanon writes that 'the colonial world is a world divided into compartments'.[75] Racial violence has often been at the core of atmospheric engineering, in the form of racial threat (when in white atmospheres) or racial discrimination and oppression (when in nonwhite atmospheres). Tayyab Mahmud's work on postcolonial spaces of oppression shows this amply. Slums are atmospheric constructions where 'surplus humanity' is piled up and kept inside through atmospheric techniques of accumulation through dispossession and primitive accumulation (namely, Marx's concept of deprivation of the means of subsistence).[76] These techniques define the

---

[73] Ibid 10. This is the point of Sloterdijk's analysis in the *World Interior of Capital: Towards a Philosophical Theory of Globalization* (Polity Press, 2013) 170, as 'a climatized luxury shell in which there would be an eternal spring of consensus'. The affectivity of luxury finds its most prominent form in the Grand Installation of the glasshouse of capitalism, that 'interior-creating violence of contemporary traffic and communication media': 198.

[74] Böhme points out that 'desires cannot be permanently satisfied, but only temporarily appeased, since they are actually intensified by being fulfilled' (*Critique* at 11). While this is true for the kind of desires that we could identify as false desires, and that form part of an economy of desire that is indeed inexhaustible, they have to be contrasted with the kind of desire that emerges from a body's movement and pause, namely the conative desire of a body that is ethically situated in relation to other bodies.

[75] Frantz Fanon, *The Wretched of the Earth*, trans. C. Farrington (Grove Press, 1963) 37.

[76] Tayyab Mahmud, '"Surplus Humanity" and Margins of Law: Slums, Slumdogs, and Accumulation by Dispossession' (2010) 14(1) *Chapman Law Review*.

exterior of the slum as a nonpossibility, thus strengthening what can be described as negative belonging, that is, belonging because of the impossibility of belonging anywhere else.

Atmosphere relies on the circumvention of rationality. Although of course rationality is not always a guarantee of sound solutions, it can and does shatter the atmospheric glass bubble when employed (although again in a convincing and appealing manner, so in a way still within the confines of atmospheric aesthetics). But the move to aestheses means that atmospheric engineering relies precisely on this bypassing of consciousness and the appeal instead to sensorial and emotional responses. Atmospherics mobilises the full sensorium and its connection to the emotional,[77] and often reaches the point of synaesthetic disorientation of the kind that makes a body an even more pliable participant.[78] Again, this does not make atmospherics any more or less worthy or, conversely, risky. It only means that this kind of reaction can be manipulated more easily and put in the service of atmospheric perpetuation.

Perhaps the main point about atmospherics is that it relies on the desire of the participating bodies, often to an extreme degree, to preserve the atmospheric status quo. Foucaultian power welling up from everywhere means that law is not just top-down state law but an institutional affect in and between bodies. These bodies control each other and themselves even in the absence of a top-down state law. Individual self-policing vies with collective behavioural pressures to fit in, and the fundamental desire to belong becomes exploited by atmospherics. An atmosphere presents itself as an ontological singularity, quite apart from the rest of the world assemblage but safe, insular, community-like and, what is more, emerging rather than engineered. In other words, just as law needs to stage itself, so does an atmosphere: it needs to dissimulate the fact that it is engineered for a specific purpose, and rather appear as spontaneous, emergent and even inevitable.

6. DISSIMULATION AND WITHDRAWAL

The greatest conjuring effect of an atmosphere is its ability to appear emergent rather than engineered. The irony of this should be made explicit: even an engineered atmosphere operates within the broader atmosphere of packaging, glowing, staging oneself in order to become appealing – in short, within an atmosphere. An engineered atmosphere risks appearing forced and therefore unappealing. A naturalised atmosphere, namely one that dissimulates its engineering and dons instead the cloak of

---

[77] See for example my work ('Atmospheres of Law: Senses, Affects, Lawscapes' (2013) 7 *Emotion, Space and Society* 1(7), 35–44) on intellectual property law and the sensory depletion brought about by copyrighting and patenting of colours, odours, textures and so on. See also Andrea Pavoni, 'Disenchanting Senses: Law and the Taste of the Real', in A. Philippopoulos-Mihalopoulos, *Routledge Handbook on Law and Theory* (Routledge, 2018).

[78] E.g. see Ummni Khan, 'An Incitement to Rapey Discourse: Blurred Lines and the Erotics of Protest', in Sarah Marusek (ed.), *Synesthetic Legalities* (Routledge, 2016), and generally the whole volume.

emergence, stages itself successfully. Atmospheric self-dissimulation means that an atmosphere dissimulates itself (as well as its origin and its non-top-down, rhizomatic, intercorporeal controlling nature) as non-atmosphere. In a self-dissimulating atmosphere, that most accomplished of atmospheres, there is nothing to go against: the atmosphere has converted itself into Quixotic windmills.

But what is there beyond the atmosphere? What lies behind the glass walls of an atmospheric stage, or indeed once these walls have been ruptured following successful resistance? There lies what I have called the *lawscape*, namely the ontological and epistemological tautology of law and matter. Briefly put, there is no law that is immaterial, namely aspatial and not embodied; likewise, there is no piece of matter that is not emanating and partaking of a legal regime of material (spatial and temporal) order. The main characteristic of the lawscape is that it can play with its degrees of visibilisation, making itself fully visible when needed (for example, an airport control where space, time and human and nonhuman bodies operate in a heightened lawscaping mode that aims at conveying bodies on the other side) and withdrawing from visibility when a softer, less obviously legal space is needed (for example, a café with tables available to sit at, provided that one orders something). This means that, depending on the degree of visibilisation, a body is more or less able to manoeuvre the lawscape, namely to act lawfully or unlawfully, to ignore ethical and more strictly legal commands, to embark on unscripted lines of flight, excesses, conflicts or revolts.

In an atmosphere, however, a body is somnambulistically, as Gabriel Tarde would put it,[79] following not so much a leader or supposed authority as its own desire to be part of the atmospherics. Since a body is tied up sensorially and emotionally, and the atmospheric addresses a body's preconscious state, there is hardly any space for manoeuvring, negotiating and essentially using the law (as one would do in the lawscape) and its potentially transformative effect in order to position oneself better in the wider assemblage. An atmosphere *feels* like the City of God, where justice reigns supreme, everything has found its perfect emplacement and there is no reason to move. But this is exactly the freezing effect of an atmosphere, where bodies are paralysed in an all-embracing aestheses of fake belonging. What is more, if a legal atmosphere is successfully staged, the absence of legal possibilities is not felt. This is because of yet another grand dissimulation: the lawscape has withdrawn from the atmosphere, leaving in its place a supposedly anomic utopia where no law is needed except for the foundational atmospheric distinction between the belonging inside the atmosphere and the exclusion outside.

With this, we have touched on the most important movement of legal aesthetics: law dissimulating as nonlaw, withdrawing from itself in order to remain relevant. The aesthetics of withdrawal is the ultimate demand of a law that stages itself to annihilation. In order to be appealing, law has to vanish, to become thin air, atmospheric. It needs to not appear as law but to dissimulate itself specifically as anomic comfort or security, health and safety, common sense, media morality, the right choice. It has to be replaced by an atmosphere of law in absentia, where everything is

---

[79] Gabriel Tarde, *The Laws of Imitation*, trans. Elsie Clews Parsons (H. Holt, 1903).

saturated by a law of direction and exclusion, in exclusion of law's transformative, positive potential. The aesthetics of withdrawal for law is the ultimate capitalist aesthetics.

7. DO YOU LIKE ANCHOVIES?

In May and June 2015, the experimental performance group No Feedback staged an immersive production at the London Theatre Delicatessen that transposed the concepts of atmospherics onto the stage. I was asked to get involved from the beginning, thinking along the various stages and trying to construct an immersive, participatory piece of theatre, where the audience would follow instructions, use their senses to create distinctions between inside and outside, invest these distinctions with emotions of belonging and not belonging, explore their desire to belong and similarly the desire to not belong where they actually belonged, and so forth. The ultimate aim of the performance was to trace the steps that prepare a society for genocide – and preparation meant active involvement and participation in genocide despite the fact that, a priori, most would oppose it.

In what follows, I draw inspiration from some of the feedback that the performance received (appearing below in italic) in anonymous audience feedback sheets that were distributed after each performance. I am using this as a brief case study in which to reflect further on what I have explained so far in terms of legal aesthetics.

it began innocently and got pulled in by it

A simple question that usually gets a simple answer: do you like anchovies? This is the first distinction, the one that carves the universe into two: anchovy eaters and noneaters. The theatre performance begins deceptively innocently. The question hides nothing behind it. It is served on a platter of smiles and gentle but firm gestures. One chooses, hand on heart or perfectly flippantly, and is directed to one of the two opposite ends of the space, one end for anchovy eaters, the other for non-anchovy eaters. The question appears as random and irrelevant as several other random events in our lives, such as where one was born, what skin colour one has, in what religion one was brought up. But every distinction can call itself the first distinction.[80] Aryans versus Jews, Jews versus Arabs, Christians versus others, ISIS versus others: we are all, at any point in time, part of multiple distinctions. Yet we are, at any one point, dwellers on only one side. You cannot both eat and not eat anchovies. To dwell on one side is natural, expected, legitimate, human – it is acceptable. To want to belong is acceptable. To want a safe place, an atmosphere of comfort, is also acceptable. The question is: what do you do about the other side?

a sense of inevitability

---

[80] George Spencer Brown, *Laws of Form* (George Allen and Unwin, 1969).

A curtain is drawn. Anchovy eaters are a lower breed of people. Convincing arguments about vitamin deficiency, body strength over mind capacity, natural skills and higher ability to work with one's body are deemed better suited to anchovy eaters: they are all aired with the levity of factual information and a chillingly familiar pattern starts to become discernible. When science is talking, the rest of us remain silent. Please do not take it personally. You need our help, and we can help. We create this world for you (and for us), for your benefit (and for ours), for your wellbeing (and for ours). This world is the distinction. There is an inside and an outside, and nothing else. Nowhere else to go. There is no real outside: there are just two places, either side of the distinction, small bleeding universes of one asphyxiating atmosphere, brimming with affects that are in the service of the distinction.

The 'choice' was not a choice. Affect aesthetics are aethesic. The 'choice' was based on taste and smell, on sensorial distinctions for which rationality often comes secondary. The anchovy eaters were asked to wear a sparkling little badge on their lapel, which turned out to be a real anchovy, taxidermically elaborated but still carrying its full affect of fish smell. Affect aesthetics are symbolic: you on this side of the room, we on the other; distance please, no crossings; kneel down, return to the floor where you belong. Affect aesthetics are emotions: do not pity them, you are superior; do not feel hard done by, you are simply not good enough and you need to be helped. Affect aesthetics are directed towards specific goals: we want you to see the other side for what it is. Anchovy eaters: wallow in your inferiority, do not move beyond your assigned territory, do not remove your badge. Non-anchovy eaters: why would you want to cross? You have everything you need here. You belong here, among your peers. Look at that sorry lot and feel fortunate in your destiny. The affects are centripetally directed towards that all-devouring distinction. This is the inevitable distinction of the atmosphere.

they deprived me of the opportunity to think for myself

The atmosphere at No Feedback is keeping the bodies together (on either side of the distinction) and separate (through the distinction) by engineering the excess of affect in a desired direction. Atmosphere attracts but also excludes: it burns everything that crosses into its periphery unless designated to be part of the atmosphere. If accepted in this atmosphere we have set up for you, you will be safe, cared for, helped: you will find your rightful, just position, whether anchovy eater or not. An atmosphere is engineered in order to allocate and maintain predetermined positions for each body. Every body knows its place and is expected to maintain it. Even if you second guess, you remain. As one reviewer wrote:

> what also disturbs me is that no one tries to rebel. No one refuses to do anything and everyone follows instructions. I am inclined to go again now that I know what happens, but to behave differently and really challenge the structure of the show. There seems to be a lot of scope for audience individuality and within our groups, we can interact. If the production is robust enough, it should be able to deal with however the audience chooses to behave.[81]

---

[81] Laura Kressly, 'No Feedback, Theatre Delicatessen – Review', in *Everything Theatre*, 2015, http://everything-theatre.co.uk/2015/05/no-feedback-theatre-delicatessen-review.html

Members of the production were prepared for rebellious behaviour, expecting or even hoping for it. Yet, it was a rare occurrence. This attests to the power of atmospherics where regular lawscaping mechanisms do not work: the law imprisons in its staging by withdrawing from it. The law is nowhere to be seen or felt. Yes, there are instructions, but they come from people like us, nothing different. Law emerges from within us, in the space of and between bodies, and keeps us in place, numbed into the distinction.

Atmospheric engineering often starts as simple distinctions in terms of taste, origin, class, neighbourhood, sexuality, gender, race, religion. At their most innocent, they remain everyday distinctions of which each one of us tries to make sense, hesitating to accept them yet often indulging them. At their most brutal, they become genocidal atmospheres, where the other side *must* perish. There is a sense of threat coming from the other side, always perpetrated within by letting the door ajar, the curtain half-drawn, the screen translucent, the bodies in relief: we need to be reminded of the blacks outside our gated community/the refugees outside our European borders/the poor outside our tennis clubs. And there is a sense of wholeness perpetrated inside, a sticking together in the face of the threat from the outside. Boundaries become more important than ever, exclusion becomes the only mechanism of self-preservation, and the world is ravaged once again with multiple distinctions lacerating its skin. We are victims of our own desires. We think we can think for ourselves but instead we have deferred our thinking to the atmosphere.

although the barrier was removed, it felt like a barrier was still there

Atmosphere builds on your and my desire to feed the atmosphere. Its greatest triumph is the fact that it uses our affects and our desires in order to maintain itself. A perfect thing, striving for its own perseverance, a perverse Spinozan *conatus* that aspires to become One, God, Nature: the Whole all-ingesting sphere of holy perfection, where all bodies are assigned positions in an inescapable theological pyramid. An atmosphere exists because we maintain it. A successfully engineered atmosphere fortifies itself by including conflict, gestures of going against it, even its own disruption. This is the total atmosphere: there is no outside and no real way out. Even when the atmosphere withdraws, like the barrier between our bodies, the barrier remains, folded in our desires. We are all, eaters and noneaters, part of the atmosphere, serving it through our desire to remain. We are the atmosphere.

Yet an atmosphere is a fragile thing, difficult to engineer fully, brittle to the touch, unpredictable. The mere fact that it is engineered by the bodies of its emergence makes it a contingent event. As Andreas Fischer-Lescano, quoting Teubner, notes, 'ultimately it is a matter of activating self-healing forces against collective anxieties, forces that encourage "dissent, protest, opposition, and civic courage against the paralyzing atmosphere of ... hierarchies and against pressures to conform"'.[82] Here is the hope: the affective excess of an atmosphere haunts the atmosphere and breaks it from the

---

[82] Fischer-Lescano, 'Sociological Aesthetics of Law', 22, quoting from Gunther Teubner, 'Whistleblowing gegen den Herdentrieb?', in Dirk Becker et al (eds), *Ökonomie der Werte* (Metropolis, 2013), 39.

inside. Affective excess creates contingency and opens up a space that ends up being used precisely in the way it was *not* supposed to be used when engineered. Resistance visibilises the law within the atmosphere, exposes false desires and supposed needs, and allows a return to a manageable lawscape, where staging is no longer the only ontology in town.

13. The responsibilities of the critic: law, politics and the Critical Legal Conference

Costas Douzinas

When I started my academic career in 1981, colleagues from other disciplines had no interest in law unless they were buying a house or getting a divorce. This represented a major cultural and epistemic change. The knowledge and study of law and legality, whether religious, moral or positive, has been a mainstay of intellectual life. The great philosophers and social scientists, from Plato to Aristotle, Thomas Aquinas, Thomas Hobbes, Immanuel Kant, Georg Hegel, Karl Marx, Max Weber, Niklas Luhmann, Jürgen Habermas, Michel Foucault, Jacques Derrida and Jean-Luc Nancy, had a detailed understanding of the law. They either wrote treatises about law and legality or turned to legal matters as evidence of the wider philosophical or epistemic claims of their theory. Aristotle's Constitution of Athens, Hegel's Philosophy of Right and Derrida's Force of Law use the law to examine the social bond, to discover what attaches the body to the soul and links them to social reproduction. They were mostly critical of what passed as official or 'positive' law in their time but they all understood that imperatives, commands, prohibitions and norms are part of what makes us human. By the 1980s, however, legal scholarship had become peripheral and parochial, a vocational study of skills. 'Reading law-books is like eating sawdust', wrote Kafka to a friend. We have all experienced the taste. Law teachers have been transmitting a formulaic knowledge, to be memorized and repeated by the students. As Friedrich Nietzsche said of his own studies, when the only organ addressed by the professor is the ear, it grows disproportionately by eating away at the brain. It was the intervention of the critical and sociolegal tradition in the latter part of the twentieth century that saved law for scholarship. But what is critique, and why has it made such a grand entry into legal scholarship and pedagogy?

Law and its contestation, orthodoxy and heresy were born together; critique has always followed the law, as its twin, shadow or ghost. It could not be otherwise. The law divides the lawful from the unlawful, the inside from the outside. The gesture that instantiates what is permitted posits also the forbidden, law's and legality's inescapable companions. Borderlines keep being breached, however, and border guards always come under attack. If law finds its destiny in its contestation, critique is bound constantly to become law. The impasse follows both critique and the mainstream. The melancholia of the lawyer, often commented upon, must be partly attributed to a certain schizophrenia that characterizes the legal thinker as critic.[1] We are caught in a dance

---

[1] Peter Goodrich, *Oedipus Lex* (University of California Press, 1995); 'The Critic's Love of the Law' (1999) 10 *Law and Critique* 3, 343–60.

between the justice of the institution and the dream of higher justice, which transcend the injustices of the present.

This seesaw between law and critique started early. The oldest surviving Western text, a fragment by Greek philosopher Anaximander, reads: 'but where things have their origin, there too their passing away occurs according to necessity; for they are judged and make reparation (*didonai diken*) to one another for their *adikia* (disjointure, dislocation, injustice) according to the ordinance of time.' An archaic injustice, *adikia*, imposes a debt on beings and opens history as its repayment. The theory of justice or the redress of injustice is the oldest Western theme, maintained from the Old Testament and Plato to Marx and Rawls. However, it has been the greatest failure too. While some of the best minds and most fiery hearts have worked on the theme of justice, we don't know where justice lies. We feel injustice, we are moved to protest and resist, to change policies, laws and constitutions. The search for justice has failed but resistance to injustice has created our political and legal systems. If the repayment for an originary injustice unravels history, the law is the record, the archive of the eternally repeated and forever failing attempt to redress injustice.

Critique is the modern rationalist expression of this eternal quest. Reinhart Koselleck wrote that

> the link between law and in critique is a central feature of modernity. In the eighteenth century, history as a whole was unwittingly transformed into a sort of legal process ... the tribunal of reason, with whose natural members the rising elite confidently ranked itself, involved all spheres of activity in varying stages of its development. Theology, art, history, the law, the State and politics, eventually reason itself – sooner or later all were called upon to answer for themselves.[2]

Kant's Critiques, the foundational document of modernity, start by posing the question *quid iuris? – by what legal right*?[3] Critique brought reason to a tribunal of law to ask reason and its faculties to justify themselves according to legal protocols. In the original Kantian sense, critique means the exploration of the transcendental presuppositions, the inescapable conditions of possibility of a discourse or practice. Critique sets limitations to speculative reason, imposing strict borders that reason cannot cross without losing its explanatory power and legitimacy.

But *krinein* also means to cut: critique is a diacritical or cutting force. In its Kantian form, the grandmother of all critical attitudes, it aims to distinguish between right or true manifestations of a phenomenon and their inauthentic counterparts. Marx's critique undercut 'bourgeois' philosophy, arguing that its categories and suppositions concealed how social relations operate. The key to understanding and changing the social world is its mode of production and reproduction. What matters is who controls the means of production; this is what determines material wellbeing but also the political and intellectual structure of a society or epoch. The critical gaze thus sees operations of inequality and power where philosophy saw only logic or the unproblematic development of ideas. To use human rights as an example, an examination of their conditions

---

[2] Reinhart Koselleck, *Critique and Crisis* (MIT Press, 1988) 9–10.
[3] Immanuel Kant, *Critique of Practical Reason* (Macmillan, 1956); Jacqueline Rose, *The Dialectics of Nihilism* (Blackwell, 1984) 11–49.

of emergence requires a critical appreciation of humanism and of the concept of right as it develops from the Western legal tradition. More importantly, it requires a socioeconomic examination of the emergence of the subject of rights: the legal person and right as the necessary forms for the rise of capitalism. The classical Marxist tradition would see these ideas as a fiction that works: they are key aspects of a socioeconomic and political order that attempts to preserve its hold on power by offering minor concessions, or blinding people with promises of the 'rights of man'. The rights of man however include the rights of some to live in luxury, and the rights of the many to starve. The key to just social organization was imagined not as catalogues of rights, but as the masses' control over the tools of production and the state mechanisms that had been used to oppress them.

In post-Marxist theory, the critic places great importance on social fantasies and the gaping cleavage between the real and its idealized, ideological representations. This type of critique was developed first by the Frankfurt School. Max Horkheimer proposed an immanent, dialectical approach and emphasized that 'true theory in a period of crisis is more critical than affirmative'.[4] Critique investigates the whole society through the dialectical tool of political economy. For Horkheimer, critical theory tries to 'take seriously the ideas by which the bourgeoisie explains its own order – free exchange, free competition, harmony of interests and so on – and to follow them to their logical conclusion [a process which will] manifest their inner contradiction and therewith their real opposition to the bourgeois order'.[5] For this type of critical theory there is no outside, no factors that remain external to the production of knowledge. While traditional theorists separate their scholarship from their life, the critical approach rejects the division between 'value and research, knowledge and action' and unites theory, politics and action.[6] Critique has therefore the whole of society as its object and emancipation as its aim. Otherwise the critic becomes a victim of ideology:

> The thinking subject is not the place where knowledge and object coincide or consequently the starting point for attaining absolute knowledge. Such an illusion about the thinking subject under which idealism since Descartes has lived, is ideology in the strict sense, for in it the limited freedom of the bourgeois individual puts on the illusory form of perfect freedom and autonomy.[7]

If we replace the 'thinking subject' with the 'legal person', Horkheimer's axiom could become the defining motto of a critical legal ontology upon which the radical critique of society could be based.

Critique therefore fights on two fronts: it demands that the law delivers the few protections for the workers, the oppressed and the poor that it fraudulently promises; at the same time, it confronts the law with a different legality. The communism of Marx, Bloch's 'spirit of utopia', Benjamin's 'angel of history', Derrida's 'democracy to come'

---

[4] Max Horkheimer, 'Traditional and Critical Theory' in *Critical Theory: Selected Essays* (Continuum, 1995) 218.
[5] Ibid 215.
[6] Ibid 208.
[7] Ibid 211.

are portents of such a transcendent justice that challenges the extant legality. Disobedience, resistance and rupture are the critic's tools for injecting traces of the transcendent into the existing.

1. THE CRITIQUE OF JURISPRUDENCE

Jurisprudence has not escaped the woody taste of the law textbook and has closely matched the three positions: first we have the nomophiliacs, positivism and the hermeneutical jurisprudence of right and principle; then the paranomic or antinomian critics; and finally the anomic followers of systemic or functionalist sociology, the economists, sociologists and anthropologists of law. Yet jurisprudence is the prudence of juris, the phronesis of the law, its consciousness and conscience. Understanding the law, its consciousness, cannot be separated from an exploration of law's justice or of an ideal law or equity, its conscience, at the bar of which law is always judged. Plato's *Republic* is the first complete search for the meaning of justice, and his Laws the most complete guide to legislation anticipating Bentham. Whenever philosophy examined the meaning of the social bond, it turned to law and became legal philosophy, the great womb from which first political economy and later the disciplines emerged in the seventeenth and nineteenth centuries respectively.

But the birth of the disciplines impoverished legal study. Modern liberalism banned the 'moral temptation' and delegitimized the search for the good. Law founded its empire on the metaphysics of subjectivity and the strict separation between subject and object reproduced in the legal dichotomies between public and private, facts and norms, rules and discretion. Law is put forward as the answer to the irreconcilability of values and as the most perfect embodiment of human reason. The rule of law is nothing but the law of rules, and not 'men' – a value neutral enterprise. Social conflict can be pacified if translated into legal rules and entrusted to rule technicians, lawyers and judges. It is delusion. Positive law promotes the values of the order it upholds. Legal interpretation not only takes place in a terrain of 'pain and suffering', as Robert Cover memorably put it; it is also imbued with the dominant beliefs of the time. If we define ideology, with Louis Althusser, as the imaginary relationship of individuals to their real conditions of existence, ideology is not 'false consciousness'. It is a constellation of beliefs, practices and values that define ways of living, give meaning to experience and define and uphold our place in the world. Law is first and foremost an ideological practice, a way of understanding the world. The claim that the law is value free is perhaps the strongest ideological ruse of our time.

The bizarre idea that the law has no morality was confirmed by its repeated failures and miscarriages of justice. At this point, the new hermeneutics of principles and rights insisted that the law is not just a system of rules but a thesaurus of meanings, values and principles. We can abandon the Grundnorm and the rule of recognition for the meaning of meaning; we can approach the texts of law through the law of text. But there is a catch. To take Ronald Dworkin's popular theory, the operation of law is presented as necessarily embodying and following moral values and principles. Legal texts must be read as a single and coherent scheme animated by the principles of 'justice and fairness and procedural process in the right relation'.[8] A similar position can be found in the work of James Boyd White, the most prominent representative of the 'law and literature' movement. Justice must be approached as translation between the values of a community and their institutional expression in its legal texts.[9] Brutal positivism had no interest in ethics; the rights and literary scholars, on the contrary, claim that law is all morality, and judicial interpretation an exercise in ethical reading. Undoubtedly, the law is about interpretation, and interpretation is in part the life of the law. But in contrast to moral hermeneutics, positivism's claims that law is about sovereign power and its nature is imperative and coercive are more realistic.

Both schools can be called restricted or 'ontological' jurisprudence. They revolve around the question 'what is law?', and law 'is', variably, commands or procedures, principles or rights, institutions or actions. The business of jurisprudence is to create an identity checklist for what is legal and what not and to use it to police the boundaries of legality. Kelsen's 'pure' theory of law represents this approach in extremis: the law is presented as a body that must be purified from all nonnormative content that does not belong to it, contaminating its austere existence. As a result, a limited number of institutions, practices and actors will be considered relevant to jurisprudential inquiry and a large number of questions will go unanswered. The presentation of law as a unified and coherent body of norms or principles is rooted in the metaphysics of truth rather than the politics and ethics of justice. The truth of justice is justice as truth. From this it follows that law is the form of power and power should be exercised in the form of law. Power is legitimate if it follows law, *nomos*, and if *nomos* follows *logos*, reason. This peculiar combination of the descriptive and prescriptive, of *logos* and *nomos*, lies at the heart of modernist jurisprudence. The task of critical and general jurisprudence is to deconstruct this logonomocentrism in the texts and operations of law.

General jurisprudence, the type of thinking about law and the social bond developed by British critical legal scholars, returns to the classical concerns of (legal) philosophy and adopts a wider concept of legality.[10] It examines the legal aspects of social reproduction both inside and outside state law. Posited law is a part only of wider legality. Interdictions, commands and norms have played a central role in social life from Moses' Decalogue to Freud's superego and Foucault's repressive hypothesis. They organize religion and animate the ethics and aesthetics of existence. General jurisprudence addresses all those issues that classical philosophy examined under the titles of *nomos* and *dike* and the Roman maxim that *jus vitam institutet*. A general jurisprudence brings back to the centre of the aesthetic, ethical and material aspects of legality. It reminds us that poets and artists have legislated, while philosophers and lawyers operate an aesthetics of life in order to bring together the main ingredients of life: the biological, the social, the unconscious. General jurisprudence includes the political economy of law, the legal constructions of subjectivity and the ways in which gender, race or sexuality create forms of identity which both discipline bodies and offer sites of resistance.

---

[8] Ronald Dworkin, *Law's Empire* (Fontana, 1986) 404.
[9] James Boyd White, *Justice as Translation* (University of Chicago Press, 1990).
[10] Costas Douzinas and Adam Gearey, *Critical Jurisprudence* (Hart, 2005), chapter 1.

2. STRATEGIES OF THE BRITCRITS

The British Critical Legal Conference (CLC) represents a school of thought committed to a plurality of theoretical approaches to law and to radical politics. The first CLC took place at the University of Kent in 1985. Conferences have taken place annually without interruption since. The conference has no officers or posts, chairpersons or secretaries, committees or delegates. It was and remains just a conference, an 'inoperative community', a broad church that lives for three days once a year and goes into abeyance once it is over. Each year the conference decides the place for the next meeting, leaving it to its organizer to put together the programme. The conference mostly takes place in the United Kingdom but has also been held in South Africa, India, Finland, the Netherlands and Sweden. People turn out every year because they love ideas and are concerned about the role of law in society and their own role within the institution.

Over the past 40 years, the CLC has introduced a number of themes, approaches and strategies unknown to or dismissed by mainstream scholarship. Semiotics, rhetoric, literature, aesthetics and psychoanalysis have helped create a much wider conception of legality, of which state law is only one part. A variety of critical schools, such as postmodernism, phenomenology, postcolonialism, critical race, feminism, queer theory, art theory and history, the ethics of otherness, the ontology of plural singularity, the critique of biopolitics and postpolitics have been pioneered in the CLC, creating a new and stronger link between theory and practice. For many years, before they became respectable and entered the mainstream, these conferences were the only academic venues in which such themes were discussed. In the 1980s an article written by myself and Ronnie Warrington was rejected by a learned journal because it included some ten words which could not be found in the Oxford English Dictionary. They included 'deconstruction', 'logocentrism' and 'logonomocentrism'. This striking parochialism has now changed. Legal scholarship has experienced a renaissance in the past 30 years and the CLC has been at the forefront. Nowadays most issues of mainstream legal journals will contain articles on the deconstruction of this or that doctrine or the legal aesthetics of drama, poetry or the Constitution.

If we turn to politics, the European critics did not aspire or attempt to take over academic institutions. The university has a diverse set of missions, aspirations and tasks. Its legitimacy relies on its commitment to foster critical thinking and on its unconditional search for truth. No institution, grouping or theory survives without continuous and critical reflection on its premises, assumptions and practices. The intellectual and moral duty of academics is precisely to protect the integrity of the university and the discipline from privatization, commodification and the stifling audit culture. This responsibility of all scholars has been a main commitment of the critics, who act as the conscience of the profession. Outside the university, the political commitments of the critics have varied from radical lawyering and social movements to political campaigns and acts of resistance.

We can identify three phases in the intellectual development of European critical legal thinking. The first, coinciding broadly with the 1980s and early 1990s, was the epoch of aesthetics; the second, in the 1990s and early 2000s, was the period of ethics; ours is the age of politics and resistance. Like all periodizations, this is broad and openended. The dominant approaches of each period coexisted with other theoretical perspectives and their concerns and strategies overlapped. The contemporary concept of politics and the political, for example, is heavily influenced by aesthetic and ethical considerations.

2.1 Aesthetics

The fifth CLC took place at the University of Newcastle in 1989. It was something of a watershed. Peter Rush gave a performance: without speaking, he walked around and danced to a prerecorded set of comments and music. Ronnie Warrington, Shaun McVeigh, Peter Goodrich and myself performed a play entitled 'Suspended Sentences'.[11] Kate Green and Hilary Lim organised an open debate with the audience about women and law; someone played the bagpipes. It was the high point of what can be called the 'aesthetic turn' in critical legal theory. The timing can be explained.

When the Berlin Wall came down, it fell mainly on the heads of the Left. Old radical certainties, Marxist dogmas, the aspirations of radical sociology and criminology were partly abandoned. The early British critics came from post-Marxist and poststructuralist backgrounds and were versed more in philosophy than sociology, more in psychoanalysis than criminology and more in aesthetics than economics. We had spent much time in the previous period looking at the contextual characteristics of the legal system – inputs and outputs – but injustice had not been redressed as was apparent by the stream of miscarriages of justice exposed in the 1980s. Unlike our American brothers, we did not place much trust in 'trashing' doctrine or exposing law's 'fundamental contradiction'. It is not particularly hard to show that a text, any text – the Bible, Aristotle or the latest decision of the House of Lords – is full of contradictions and inconsistencies. It is much harder to work out what practices, procedures and ruses make texts authoritative and coherent despite their inner inconsistencies. It was clear that evidence of textual discrepancies does not undermine law's legitimacy. Pursuing a radical agenda after the defeat of a type of radical politics meant returning to the text and opening it through the use of rhetoric, hermeneutics, deconstruction, semiotics and psychoanalysis. If there is racism, sexism or injustice in the law, we should pursue it in the legal text: in its tropes, semiotic arrangements and intertextual connections.

Jacques Derrida's statement in 'The Force of Law' that while the law is deconstructible, deconstruction is justice, became our motto.[12] We approached the law as a textual web rather than a system of norms or a depository of principles. Traditional normativism was replaced by a joyful textuality and systemic approaches by literary theory. Largely abandoning doctrine, we addressed the concepts, argumentative strategies and discursive organization of legal texts. Legal concepts are never simple or sovereign. They are constituted within conceptual networks, which disallow closure and self-consistency. Basic principles such as free speech are defined and structured by their presumed exceptions such as police powers, obscenity, privacy, and so on. At the level of argumentation, contradictions intervene between the premises and aims of an

---

[11] Costas Douzinas and Ronnie Warrington, *Postmodern Jurisprudence* (Routledge, 1990), chapter 12.
[12] Jacques Derrida, 'The Force of Law' (1990) 11 *Cardozo Law Review* 5–6, 919.

argument and its actual operation, as when the freedom and autonomy that contract law allegedly promotes is shown to lead to its exact opposite. Finally, textual arrangement: the transplants, grafts and quotations from other discourses reveal semiotic and rhetorical dependencies and adoptions. They undermine the legal text's surface semantic aspirations and unhinge the most rigorous argument. The early deconstruction rejected epistemological foundations and considered them contingent, while normative values were replaced by situated historical genealogies. *Différance*, writing and the trace replaced binary oppositions such as public/private, fact/value, rule/policy.

The critics read legal texts not just for their coherence but also for their omissions, repressions and distortions, signs of the oppressive power and symptoms of the traumas created by the institution. If there is racism, patriarchy or economic exploitation, it will be traced in the text, in its rhetoric and images, in certainties and omissions, which will then be followed outside of the text in the lives of people and the history of domination. For critical theory, the textual and institutional organization of the law are deeply intertwined: the law as a system of signs and part of the symbolic order is both necessary and fictitious. But law's fictions operate and change the world; they help establish the subject as free and/because subjected to the logic of the institution.

2.2 Ethics

The 'new world order' was announced after the fall of communism in 1989. It marked a global 'ethical turn'. Globalized capitalism united the world economically, while political, legal and economic strategies started constructing a common symbolic, ideological and institutional framework. Its signs were everywhere. In humanitarian wars, military force was placed in the service of humanity. Economic sanctions were repeatedly imposed to protect nations and people from their evil governments. Human rights and good governance clauses were routinely imposed on developing countries as a precondition for trade and aid agreements. Renewed emphasis on international law and institutions, NGOs and INGOs and global civil society accelerated the trend. Human rights became the fate of postmodernity, the ideology after the end, the defeat of ideologies, the 'last' utopia after the end of history.[13] In the absence of a political blueprint for this new economic, social and political configuration, cosmopolitanism, an ancient philosophical idea, was promoted as the Kantian promise of perpetual peace. Globalization and cosmopolitanism were presented as capitalism with a human face.[14] In Britain, the adoption of the Human Rights Act and the rhetorical emphasis on civil participation completed the picture. Politics bent the knee to ethics, the law became the official arbiter of morality; Kant's, Kelsen's and Habermas' dream of a world order of peace and rights was finally on the horizon. Criticisms of the blind spots of human rights and the dysfunctions of the emerging 'cosmopolitan civil society' were evidence of moral deficiency.

The new emphasis on moral politics influenced jurisprudence. The 'rights' and 'morality of law' approaches replaced old, honest positivism. Positivism had excluded morality from the law in order to offer a supposedly neutral arbiter for the modern

---

[13] Costas Douzinas, *The End of Human Rights* (Hart, 2000).
[14] Costas Douzinas, *Human Rights and Empire* (Routledge, 2007).

pluralism and relativism of values and its natural conclusion, nihilism. Now morality reentered the law, presenting it as the perfect narrative of a community at peace with itself. All law is moral; with the help of moral philosophy 'right answers' can be found to all legal questions. Morality, the nightmare of positivism, turned into the noble dream of the hermeneuticians.[15] The critics, adopting a maxim from Leo Strauss, argued that 'when knowledge and reason are subjected to authority they are called "theology" or "legal learning" but they cannot be philosophy'.[16] Liberal jurisprudence, they claimed, is implicated in the very relations it claims to judge. Acts of power cannot be used to criticize power. The internal critic remains the mirror image and companion of the judge; the values espoused are those that lead to structural unemployment and the greatest equality gap in human history.

The fake moralism of the period turned ethics into a terrain of struggle. Many critics were seduced and reluctantly accepted that the ethical turn was irreversible. The critics tried to challenge the dominant non-Kantian theories of morality and justice. Then theoretical failures and political defeats of the Left, exacerbated by the fall of the Berlin Wall, turned the 1990s and 2000s into a period of defence and introspection. Some turned to systems theory and other social scientific marvels that put a premium on description and exegesis. Others retreated to aestheticism, creating a late type of the formalism that has always followed legal theory. For most, emphasis was placed on the utopian moment of law and legality, with its intrinsic moral element, in order to confront the dominant understandings on their terrain.[17] As the critic must remain a foreigner to the mainstream, a degree of incomprehension entered her description and vision. The emerging strong ethical position mobilized the quasi-transcendental or transcendent concept of the 'Other' and the associated gambits of incalculable justice, infinite hospitality or the democracy to come. Pushed theoretically by the new moralists and politically by the new world order, the critics adopted the position of the legislator who speaks in the place, or, better, in the name of the 'Other'. There are two types of justice, we argued, using historical sources from the common law as well as the philosophies of Emmanuel Levinas and Jacques Derrida, Walter Benjamin and Ernst Bloch. The first immanent conception helps redress and redirect the law when it forgets its own promises. But justice proper, both inside and outside the law, judges the whole of legality in the name of a transcendent other-based order. We need to imagine a law or society in which people are no longer despised or degraded, oppressed or dominated, and, from that impossible but necessary standpoint, to judge the here and now. But this dream was marginally connected with politics. We were reclaiming conscience but losing our radical consciousness.

---

[15] Nicola Lacey, *A Life of H.L.A Hart: The Nightmare and the Noble Dream* (Oxford University Press, 2006).

[16] Leo Strauss, *Natural Law and History* (Chicago University Press, 1965) 92.

[17] Drucilla Cornell, *The Philosophy of the Limit* (Routledge, 1992); Costas Douzinas and Ronnie Warrington, *Just Miscarried: Ethics and Aesthetics in Law* (Harvester Wheatsheaf, 1994); Michel Rosenfeld and David Gray Carlson eds, *Deconstruction and the Possibility of Justice* (Routledge, 1992); Louis Wolcher, *Beyond Transcendence in Law and Philosophy* (Birkbeck Law Press, 2004); Marinos Diamantides ed., *Levinas, Law and Politics* (Routledge, 2009).

The welcoming of the 'Other', the emphasis on a justice transcendent in immanence, the preparation for the event, appeared at the point when the political preconditions were in retreat. The acceptance of ethics as the key critical position was an admission of defeat. The hope for a just law and society was transferred into some unpredictable future. With hindsight, this explicit turn to morality was too big a concession to the dominant ideology of the time. It did not always avoid a slide into moralism and left the critics exposed to accusations of hypocrisy. Significantly, the turn to morals introduced an emphasis on the treatment of the individual – a direction that critical theory, committed to class and collectivity, had consistently resisted. Politics was sidelined, the critique of capitalism marginalized; form won over content. As Fredric Jameson commented apropos of the flourishing catastrophe movie genre, we are more prepared to accept that the end of the world is nigh than that the end of capitalism is.

2.3 Politics

Our North American comrades followed a parallel but separate route. The last American Critical Legal Studies conference in Georgetown in 1994 ended in acrimony. The old Marxist guard, which had promoted a legal politics of class, departed, protesting their marginalization by the new critique of difference. This divide did not develop in the CLC. The theoretical and methodological resources of poststructuralism had been integral to the movement from the start. The Europeans had turned to Freud, Derrida or Foucault not as replacements for Marx or alternatives to politics, but as the most advanced theoretical approaches that could help fill the lack left by the defeat of the more traditional radicalism.

When the American critical community reassembled in the 2000s it was no longer as critical legal studies but as 'law and humanities'. The early law and literature strategies were somewhat problematic. Teaching morsels of law in Sophocles, Shakespeare or Kafka is not a particularly critical enterprise. It offers a cultural gloss to future corporate lawyers. But as the new movement of law and the humanities matured, the early humanism was sidelined and a more interesting law as literature approach emerged, influenced by postcolonialism, psychoanalysis, art and queer theory. It is strongly represented in the review *Law, Culture and Humanities*. Law and the humanities cannot fully replace critical legal studies, however. A majority of conference participants and contributors to the review are not legal academics. As a result, specifically legal themes have not been extensively addressed. Additionally, a certain formalism characteristic of literary criticism migrated from literature to law. But perhaps the most important shortcoming of the new school was a relative indifference towards political themes and campaigns.

This was not the road taken by the European CLC. The new world order announced in 1989 was the shortest in history. It came to an end first with the attacks in the United States on 11 September 2001 and then with the collapse of Lehman Brothers and the bursting of the financial bubble in 2008. The protests, insurrections and revolts that broke out all over the world after 2010 have made our epoch the age of resistance. For the BritCrits, aesthetic and ethical concerns remained methodologically strong. But the collapse of the new world order led to a distinct turn to a politics of resistance. The theoretical realization that law is no longer the form, instrument or restraint of power, but is becoming an integral part of its operation, seemed confirmed by experience. Biopolitical governance and neoliberal economics undermine legal form. They privatize public areas of activity and deliver them to the logic of profit while at the same time legalizing and controlling domains of private action.

Biopolitical law is a sad remnant of the rule of law tradition. This great achievement of European civilization has been 'reduced to an ensemble of rules and no other basis than the daily proof of its smooth functioning'.[18] As law is disseminated throughout society, its form becomes detailed and inconsistent, its sources multiple and diffused, its aims unclear, unknown or contradictory, its effects unpredictable, variable and uneven. All major aspects of legality have been weakened. Rule is replaced by regulation, normativity by normalization, legislation by executive action, principle by discretion, legal personality by administratively assigned roles and competencies. Regulation and normalization are ubiquitous and invisible; they come from everywhere and nowhere. They mobilize nonpunitive tactics, deferrals and delays, appeals and counterappeals, media solicitations and ensnarings. They both assume and engender acceptable corruptions and forgivable transgressions as an integral component of politics, business and finance. The biopolitical order normalizes and corrupts, and corruption is part of its normality.

Detailed regulation emanating from local, national, supranational and international sources penetrates all areas and aspects of life. From the most intimate and domestic relations to global economic and communication processes, no area is immune from state or market intervention. Everything, from the composition of tinned food to torture, has found its way into (public or private) law. The law expands inexorably at the price of assuming the characteristics of contemporary society, becoming decentred, fragmented, nebulous. The claim that the legal system forms a consistent system of norms was always unrealistic. It now looks extravagant as the law starts resembling an experimental machine 'full of parts that came from elsewhere, strange couplings, chance relations, cogs and levers that aren't connected, that don't work, and yet somehow produce judgments, prisoners, sanctions and so on'.[19] Outside the trappings of central power, law is increasingly law because it calls itself law. The legitimacy of routine legality depends on law's ability to mobilize the symbols of power and the force of the police with little reference to justice, morality or democratic legitimacy. This omnivorous – public or private – regulatory activity means that some legal statements take a normative – 'ought' – form; most are just descriptive of procedures, techniques and regularities. In this sense, law is well on the way to replicating life in its annals. Modern law tries to regulate the world; late modern law just mimics it.

The mission of modern law (and of the metaphysics of modernity) was to open a distance, occasionally imperceptible, between itself and the order of the world. Law was a form of the ideal next to religion, nationalism or socialism. It aimed to correct reality. Now this distance is fast disappearing in the vast expanse of law-life. This is a law with force but with little value or normative weight, a law that constitutes and

---

[18] Jean-Marie Guehenno, *The End of the Nation-State* (Victoria Elliott trans.) (University of Minnesota Press, 1995) 99.

[19] Michel Foucault quoted in Colin Gordon, 'Afterword' in *Power/Knowledge* (Harvester, 1980) 257.

constrains but does not signify. In the past, lawmaking and interpretation were domains of great political struggle. Now, only efficiency matters. Validity, modern law's mark of identification, is discussed in law textbooks as a relic from the past not dissimilar to natural law. Proliferating individual rights increasingly adopt and legalize the claims of individuals and identity groups reproducing society's 'natural' order. Rights have replaced right, individual interest the collective good.[20] Human rights have become an integral part of power relations, preceding, accompanying and legitimizing the penetration of all parts of the world by the new order.[21] 'Nothing is more dismal', writes Giorgio Agamben, 'than this unconditional being-in-force of juridical categories in a world in which they no longer mirror any comprehensive ethical content: their being-in-force is truly meaningless'.[22] Law is autopoetically reproduced, as the systems theorists insist, in a loop of endless validity without much value or significance.

Michel Foucault, commenting on Kant, argued that critique must be transformed into a 'possible crossing over'.[23] It is *'l'art de n'être pas tellement gouverné'*.[24] He associates critique with resistance to governance and with acts of de- and resubjectification, of relative detachment from the demands of biopolitical power. This is how Foucault put it:

> The role of the one who speaks [the intellectual, in our context] is not that of legislator or the philosopher between camps, the figure of peace and armistice ... To establish oneself between adversaries at the centre and above them, to impose a general law on each and to found an order that reconciles: this is not what is at issue. At issue is the positing of a right marked by dissymetry, the founding of a truth linked to a relation of force, a weapon truth and a singular right. The subject that speaks is a warring – I won't even say a polemical – subject.[25]

The subject is warring, placed on a battlefield, surrounded by enemies, out to attain a particular victory and with a perspectival view of truth. The intent of moralism and cosmopolitanism was to relieve us of the anxiety of conflict under universalizing claims, which include both human rights and the grossest capitalist exploitation and cultural misery. The semiotics and ethics of the era renamed conflict as economic competition, domination as market penetration and war as humanitarian liberation. The Foucauldian critic revives the tradition of (class) struggle in acts of fashioning different selves and confronting the power or governance with the potentiality of praxis. The realization of the redundancy of moralistic critique led the European critics to adopt a

---

[20] Costas Douzinas, 'The Poverty of (Rights) Jurisprudence', in Conor Gearty and Costas Douzinas eds, *The Cambridge Companion to Human Rights Law* (Cambridge University Press, 2012).

[21] Costas Douzinas, 'Postmodern Just Wars' in John Strawson ed., *Law after Ground Zero* (Glasshouse, 2002).

[22] Giorgio Agamben, Means without Ends: Notes on Politics (Minneapolis, University of Minnesota Press, 2000), 133.

[23] Michel Foucault, 'What Is Enlightenment', in Paul Rabinow ed., *Ethics* (New Press, 1997) 315.

[24] Michel Foucault, 'Qu'est que ce la critique Critique et *Aufklärung*', *Bulletin de la société française de philosophie*, 84ème année, n°2, Avril-Juin 1990.

[25] Michel Foucault, *Society Must Be Defended* (Penguin, 2004).

politics of resistance in the 2010s. The protests that broke out all over the world and the deep economic austerity and political crisis that followed in Southern Europe helped resituate our theoretical and political stance. In periods of tension and crisis, the dormant radical potential of rights and law emerges again. The law treats disobedience, resistance or revolution as degraded, criminal activity. Yet, without the dissidents and revolutionaries, the law becomes sclerotic, atrophies, loses its ability to adapt and therefore generate its own legitimacy.[26] Let us turn to a brief examination of the inner link and confrontation between law and resistance.

3. LAW AND RESISTANCE

Legal right, whether private or public, the right to property or the right to vote, appears as one, individual, undivided and indivisible. It claims a single source, the subject's will; a single justification, law's recognition; a single effect, the will's ability to act and shape the world. The modelling of political rights on property however contaminated their operation. A yawning gap separates the will from its effects, the ideal from the actual, the normative weight from empirical operation. Formal right, the legal subject's capacity to will, is theoretically limitless. But real people are embedded in the world: class, gender or colour inequalities condition them, prevent formal rights from becoming effective. We are all legally free and nominally equal, unless of course we are improper men, in other words men of no property, women, colonials, or of the wrong colour, religion or belonging.

This was partly the reason why will, the first source of right, soon diversified into a second, adopted by the dominated and the oppressed. For the wretched of the earth, right is not about law and judges, a game they can scarcely play. It is a battlecry, the subjective factor in a struggle, which asks to be raised to the level of the universal. Right is the demand not to be treated as an object or as nobody. It is the claim of the dissident against the abuses of power or the revolutionary against the existing order. As Ernst Bloch, the messianic Marxist, argued, individual rights were initially created for the protection of the creditor and 'adopted in a quite different way by the exploited and oppressed, the humiliated and degraded. It is precisely this that appears in its incomparable second sense as the subjective catchword of the revolutionary struggle and actively as the subjective factor in the struggle'.[27] The legally created rights call for obedience – the right to insubordination, as Maurice Blanchot put it – expresses the exercise of freedom:

> Where there is a duty, we merely have to close the eyes and blindly accomplish it; then everything is simple. A right, on the contrary refers only to itself and to the exercise of freedom of which it is the expression; a right is a free power for which everyone is

---

[26] Costas Douzinas, *Philosophy and Resistance in the Crisis* (Polity, 2013); '"The Right to the Event": The Legality and Morality of Revolution and Resistance' (2014) 2(1) *Metodo: International Studies in Phenomenology and Philosophy*, 151–67.
[27] Ernst Bloch, *Natural Law and Human Dignity* (MIT Press, 1988) 217.

responsible, by himself, in relation to himself, and which completely and freely engages him: nothing is stronger, nothing is more serious.[28]

This second right is the exercise of free will, a justified free power which draws its force from morality instead of legality.

Right therefore has two metaphysical sources. As a claim accepted or seeking admission to the law, right is a publicly recognized will, which finds itself at peace with the world, a world made in its image and for its service. But, second, right is a will that wills what does not exist, a will that finds its force in itself and its effect in a world not yet determined all the way to the end. This second right is founded *contra fatum*, in the perspective of an open cosmos and the belief that it cannot be fully determined by (financial, political or military) might. It eventually confronts domination and oppression, including those instituted and tolerated by the first legalized will. 'The second origin of the facultas agendi enters here in a thoroughly decisive way, as an origin conforming more than ever before to the hegemony in men (according to a Stoic expression) that lets men walk with their head held high.'[29]

Two conceptions of right or the universal are in conflict. On one side is an acceptance of the order of things raised to the dignity of general will. It dresses the dominant particular with the mantle of the universal. On the other side, the second universality is founded on a will created by a diagonal division of the social world that separates rulers from the ruled and the excluded. This dimension of truth does not rest on the existing order but on its negation. It forms an agonistic universality; it does not emerge from neo-Kantian philosophical texts but from the struggle of the excluded from social distribution and political representation. The excluded, the contemporary 'rabble', are the only universal today in a legal and social system that incessantly proclaims its egalitarian credentials. Legal right enforces individual will. The second type of will starts as individual disobedience and matures into collective resistance and perhaps revolution. It confronts the formalism of law and has motivated the struggles for group economic and social rights. The will to change the world and create a society of equality, freedom and justice has taken various historical forms. It appeared as the republican idea in the great eighteenth century revolutions and as the socialist idea in the nineteenth century; it became linked with the Communist Party and state in the twentieth century and suffered as a result of the betrayal of the revolution. Today this will brings together the ideas of radical equality, resistance and democracy – democracy not just as a system of parliamentary representation and elections, but as a form of life that extends into all aspects of the social fabric, from home to work to social and cultural life. The resistances, insurrections and revolts of the past few years precisely combined popular will with ideas of social justice and democracy, which initiated autonomous collective political action and direct, unmediated democratic forms.

Radical change results from the dialectical relationship between ideal and necessity accelerated by will. Will and idea come together in a dialectical voluntarism, as Peter

---

[28] Maurice Blanchot, 'Declaration of the Right to Insubordination in the Algerian War (Manifesto of the 121)' in Maurice Blancot, *Political Writings*, Zakir Paul trans. (Fordham University Press, 2010) 33–4.

[29] Bloch, *Natural Law* 219.

Hallward puts it.[30] When this happens, will no longer gives passive consent to power; it becomes an active force that changes the world. History is full of such confrontations, eternally condemned and eternally returning. Disobedience is the first step. It manifests a rift between the normatively guided will and the existing political and legal reality. Dissident will does not disobey the law. The obligation to obey the law is absolute only when accompanied by the judgement that the law is morally just and democratically legitimate. Disobedience is the beginning. Protests mostly challenge law's conserving violence, breaking public order regulations in order to highlight greater injustices.[31] As long as the protesters ask for this or that reform, this or that concession, the state can accommodate them. When will no longer recognizes itself in existing social relations and their legal codification, disobedience becomes a collective emancipatory will. What the state fears is the fundamental challenge by a force that can transform the relations of power and present itself as having a 'right to law'.

Despite the reservations of the liberal philosophers, revolution has become a normative principle, the modern expression of free action when the order of the world decays and suffocates.[32] 'The ultimate subjective right would be the license to produce according to one's capabilities, to consume according to one's needs; this license is guaranteed by means of the ultimate norm of subjective right: solidarity.'[33] The normative weight of this right is felt every time a Bastille is taken, or a Tahrir, Syntagma or Taksim Square filled. In the same way that the psychoanalytical real, a void in human existence, is both impossible and banned but sustains subjectivity, the right to revolution is the void that sustains the legal system. Without it, the law becomes sclerotic, moribund. Paraphrasing Alain Badiou, we can say that rights are about recognition and distribution among individuals and communities, except that, additionally, there is an indelible right to resistance.

---

[30] Peter Hallward, 'Communism of the Intellect, Communism of the Will', in C. Douzinas and S. Žižek, *The Idea of Communism* (Verso, 2009) 117.

[31] Walter Benjamin, 'Critique of Violence', in *Reflections*, Edmund Jephcott trans. (Schocken Books, 1978) 277–300.

[32] Costas Douzinas, 'Adikia. On Communism and Rights' in Douzinas and Žižek, *The Idea of Communism* 81–100.

[33] Bloch, *Natural Law* 221 (italics in original).

14. Law in the mirror of critique: a report to an academy

Kyle McGee

1. HORIZON

How we think about law says a great deal about how we understand our attachment to the world: law is itself a critical mode of attachment to the world. Legal constructs, and the forms of thought and practice and the bodily habits or normative exchanges they both presuppose and engender, are caught up in dense networks that not only coerce, compel, and normalize but also shape environments, structure interactions, fabricate identities, bind communities, and invent possible worlds. It falls to legal theory to flesh out how and under what conditions and constraints they do so, on what grounds and with what effects, in conjunction with which other modes of thought and practice.

I take the general problem of *critique*, and of *legal critique* in particular, in this register of attachments to worlds. Critique confronts its object with its own conditions, demanding a rational accounting capable of establishing its legitimacy: constituting itself as judge, it divides the rational from the irrational, the clear and distinct from the obscure and confused, the scientific from the superstitious, the real from the illusory. It does so to challenge the necessity of what is given, the fanaticism of belief, and, perhaps, to welcome a new world yet in the making. Its tests of legitimacy are varied, its specific means far too heterogeneous to yield a general formula, but they are never strictly those of the object of critique: as Koselleck showed long ago, there is something irreducibly utopian in critique insofar as the standards it employs to decide on the question of legitimacy differ from those that would be selected by the actors immersed in the everyday controversies of, as relevant here, matters of law and state.[1] Even so-called immanent critique must mobilize standards of legitimacy (coherence, consistency, or noncontradiction, and one or more ideological or sociological criteria that are inferred from the historical, material, or intellectual "context" of the object) that set its processes off from those of the object, which need not submit itself to such standards.[2] It is sometimes said of legal critique that, as a purposive movement, as a front in an intellectual or institutional *Kampfplatz*, it died off because it could offer no viable alternative to the juridical order of things; a subtler understanding reveals that this diagnosis would apply to *every* historical form of critique, including those at the root of the modern secular liberal order. So its death sentence is at once necessary and

---

[1] Koselleck (1988).
[2] Christodoulidis (2009) offers a compelling immanent critique of legality hinging on the *tu quoque* form of argumentation.

permanently suspended. The world to which critique is attached is always a world yet to come, yet its interventions are resolutely fixed on the present order.

Legal critique has been pronounced dead often enough to recognize that this gesture is no more than a pretext for the easy dismissal of its practical and utopian aspirations. The other chapters in this volume should dispel any suggestion that legal critique has met its demise.[3] If anything, critique has become commonplace to a fault—not merely in that the repertoire of critical strategies, edges appropriately softened, has been more or less successfully integrated with more orthodox sociological and theoretical approaches to legal issues, but in the more problematic sense that critique itself has become at once too habitual or formulaic, and too self-concerned to notice. As a result, its practitioners too often forget that their standards are unstable fabrications constituted by and bound to specific chains of nonlegal associations, that their reports too are local, transient, and inexorably subject to the power of their successors, and that critique enjoys no real distance from its objects but rather lives in their midst. And so, if conditions have changed—if the liberal political economy or the modern naturalist cosmology have vanished, if entirely new distributions of agency and sensibility have come into being as a result of technoscientific, aesthetic, political, or other innovations, if the problem of the transcendent Form of Law has given way to a proliferation of fragile jurimorphs—we could be forgiven for asking whether existing models of legal critique remain relevant.

2. AN INVITATION

Although all of the influential traditions of modern legal thought have fallen under the critical guillotine at various times, the object of legal critique has never been any one school; it has been the form of law itself. Most famously, the early ("first wave") American critical legal studies movement sought to expose the ineradicable conceptual and normative indeterminacy of the form of legality as such. As a tool for the critic, this object has the advantage of being rather opentextured, affording the cheap and easy ascription of a wide range of metaphysical qualities that the law is supposed to possess: stability, self-identity, transparency, coherence, neutrality, objectivity, and so on. When the critic detects a lapse, she pounces. Here, the court is dissembling, speaking from a moral or political position, merely enforcing her symptom, her preference, her fear or aversion; there, the structure of the norms resist closure, vacua must be eliminated if a judgment is to be reached, and ideological investments prioritizing either individualism or altruism, Self or Other, liberty or coercion, lurk beneath the surface. Making explicit the contradictions implicit in the form of law would debunk the key qualities and values attributed to the legal institution in the popular and professional imagination, demonstrating the prevalence of the politics of class, sex, and race concealed within the ostensibly apolitical law.

The critic's form-of-law construct is not pure makebelieve. The dominant line of modern liberal legal thought has long championed a largely instrumental view of law as an organic order or system of positive, known (or knowable) rules, an evolving

---

[3] See also Stone, Wall, & Douzinas (2012); Douzinas (2014); Douzinas (2016).

institution establishing conclusively the legitimate legal relations that are valid within the boundaries of a political territory, which impartially carries out objectives formulated in other institutional quarters, chiefly politics and economics. No one school of legal thought can claim ownership or authorship of all of these elements; they together represent a miscellany of jurisprudential, theological, political, scientific, and other sources traversing the fractured histories of what is still speciously described as the Western legal tradition. This commonsense image of modern law draws a line between properly legal operations (norms, interpretative techniques, procedures) supposed to be free of nonlegal interferences, on one hand, and, on the other, the contingent material and symbolic circumstances in which those operations are necessarily situated, which are the proper subject matter of the social sciences. It is an image that can be found in many orthodox theoretical accounts of law and it appears regularly, if implicitly, in the nontheoretical accounts of judges and lawyers and the popular understanding of the rule of law. It is the image at work in the background of everyday life, where the scope of lawfulness is assumed to be stable, certain, neutral, and fair. Like Heidegger's broken hammer, it becomes visible in concrete experiences of injustice, as well as in minor crises, such as in the experience of uneasiness that accompanies learning, for example, that corporations spend millions of dollars to influence US state judicial elections or that there is a well-defined pipeline for federal judicial appointees that passes directly through rightwing lobbyist and influence-peddler networks, by way of elite law schools and learned societies: such facts blur the line on which depends the integrity, impartiality, and autonomy of the modern legal institution.[4] Obviously, examples could be multiplied.

And yet the device of the legal form is highly suspect. The reason has less to do with any deficiency in correspondence—as noted, it is strategically vague, so it resists most direct challenges—and more to do with the presumption that what law is, and is made of, is known in advance. The purpose of the form, considered as the critic's resource rather than as a real thing in the world, is to maximize critical flexibility while *at the same time* limiting what passes as legitimate. The form will be used against itself to debunk the law's pretensions to neutrality, equality, stability, and the rest. And the critic can show that the legal form is indeterminate and, consequently, that the law is nonneutral, nonobjective, and so on, only if she posits in advance that the legal form possesses the specific qualities she will find lacking in the phenomena studied. On a smaller scale, the same thing is true of moral critics and many (American) legal realists objecting that legal phenomena exhibit qualities they ought not, containing or encoding moral preferences, class or ethnic interests, and other kinds of political domination.

Another influential mode of legal critique, associated more closely with deconstruction, psychoanalysis, and "second wave" CLS, moves beyond ideology critique to contest not only the purity, stability, or objectivity of law but even its claim to existence as an organic order irreducible to the forces of language or rhetoric, which ceaselessly deliver the law's disavowed contingencies to the heart of its purportedly enclosed operational sphere. This current—which includes the "aesthetic turn" or the "rhetorical turn" in legal studies—is roughly the incarnation in legal thought of the broader semiotic or linguistic turn in the humanities and social sciences. In what is now

---

[4] Along these lines, see Kennedy (1982).

recognizable as its penumbra arose a multiplicity of critical approaches deploying similar strategies but directed in a more self-aware manner toward the ethical domain—in the Lyotardian or Lévinasian senses—as well as sustained calls to renew the political critique of law. These latter approaches generally seek to develop accounts of law in its deep and extensive connections with processes of globalization, neoliberalism, austerity politics, the security state, and biopolitics. (To be sure, there are too many deviations and interstitial moments in this arc to expect it to bear much weight, but it suffices as a quick overview.)

Both "waves" of legal critique remain tethered to the conventional image from which they dissent. The ideological unmasking of the first and the rhetorical dissolution of the second require the dominant conception of law in order to produce their critical effects. They require it not only as a touchstone or reference point but as an operative construct, because the transgressions they identify (or enact) only matter if the law/nonlaw boundary that they stake out matters.

These critical paths will never lead to the realization that that form or boundary is drawn elsewhere, or drawn differently, because it remains the implicit regulator of the critical discourse. For the same reason, they cannot detect variations in the properties of legal beings as compared to, say, scientific or political or religious beings—for instance, in the forms of objectivity or personhood they construct, or how they represent or gather entities. Law may possess a kind of objectivity that is not found in the sciences, or a logic of representation foreign to political assemblies, or an anthropology quite distinct from that of religious discourse. And if any of the standard liberal elements normally incorporated in the form-of-law construct, like the requirement of legitimacy, really have no place at all in the making of law, legal critique will not let us know. It will proceed instead to debunk the ontology of law *as such*, satisfied to demonstrate the contradiction between appearance and reality. After all, legal critique does not leave things untouched, but instead of a better, more realistic, more complicated, or richer account of what law is, it yields but a dim reflection of its own theoretical commitments and resources. And insofar as current work on law and the political self-consciously prolongs the work of CLS and the aesthetic turn, reorienting the inquiry without reinventing the critique of law as such, what was said of the other forms of critique is applicable to these approaches as well. This would account for the ready invocation in contemporary critical legal thought of "the law" as something already known, a term with a stable or at least uncontroversial referent—an epistemological and rhetorical strategy facilitating the necessary totalizing work of critique, as we will see.

Indeed, critics sometimes denounce the law as such for expropriating social relations: doctrinal categories, practices of legal reasoning, and formal procedures translate and thus transform sociopolitical conflicts, domesticating them and submitting them to a logic that neuters their radical potentiality or potential radicalism. So, a class conflict is neutralized and masked as a mere landlord–tenant dispute, or a question of the efficient allocation of risks and resources. But from another point of view, the real gesture of denunciation is in critique's expropriation of law *in the name of* social relations. It is this other point of view that many "postcritical" forms of legal theory adopt, if in immensely different ways. If the expression "postcritical" means anything—and I am not sure that it does—it would not necessarily signal a rejection of the ethical or political dimensions of critique. Instead, it would demand a different orientation toward law altogether, in part with the purpose of inviting new, noninstrumental, nonreductive forms of conjugation among law, politics, and ethics (to say nothing of religion and the sciences). Nor would it oppose the function of selection, discernment, and judgment integral to the work of critique (*krinein*). However, it may find that critique troublingly *rushes* to judgment before it can assemble the relevant agencies, resulting in a distorted picture of its object and ultimately in its substitution by a mere repetition of critique's own assumptions. By raising anew the question of the composition of law, it would relocate the place of critique, perhaps, but would not eliminate it. In that sense, as I have argued elsewhere, it may be preferable to refer not to a *post*critical but to an *ante*critical mode of thought.[5] The aim of this chapter is to shed a bit of light on what that might look like.

3. BRANCHES

If critique is many things, so too is the patchwork of tendencies, dispositions, and practices gathered under the unavoidable term "postcritique." As a turn away from what it often scorns as an unjustly hostile force of eliminative negativity, "postcritique" is a doubly ironic expression: it names only a rejection, declining to take the risk of instituting any of the affirmative modes of thought it champions, and it suggests a deterministic project or at least a linear sense of succession as intellectual progress. What is more, it objects to critique's tendency to unify or totalize its object while readily engaging in the same tactic as its own founding gesture: the very proposition of a *postcritical theory* is a kind of performative contradiction, because it requires the application to critique of what is supposed to be offensive about the practice of critique. Writers taken as its proponents—for example, Bruno Latour, in his well-known piece on how critique has "run out of steam"—have lamented the ready cooptation of critical theory's social-constructionist resources by its avowed ideological enemies, such as ExxonMobil and Fox News (and now, the Trump administration), which peddle disinformation, pseudoscientific skepticism, rehearsed ignorance, and fantastical conspiracy theories by mobilizing the fact of scientific controversy and dissent within research communities or gaps and lacunae in the scientific record as evidence of falsity.[6] But the turn of such writers from the dark depths of power to the shallow surface of things, from deep structure to fleshy texture, may seem to render them complacent, if not complicit, with an unjust status quo. In that sense, postcritique is like the tone-deaf patrician capitalist promoting the fundamental equality of markets and can-do entrepreneurialism to the impoverished masses, who for their part seem intent on refusing to help themselves. Or, alternatively, by rejecting the reality of power and its overbearing structures—capitalism and neoliberalism chief among them—do postcritical theorists not more closely resemble the Chechen president Ramzan Kadyrov, who baldly proclaims that there are no homosexuals in Chechnya?

---

[5] McGee (2018a).
[6] Latour (2004).

Postcritique is not a unified school or approach or method organized on common principles. The empty label is an attempt to welcome misfits of all sorts who have, for one reason or another, become fatigued by the persistence of the negative,[7] the symptomatic readings and the unforgiving suspicion of the text, the sanctimonious oneupmanship, and the militant certainty that the critic, situated above the fray, knows best. As usual, however, the "big tent" approach fosters inconsistency and controversy, ultimately throwing the utility of the label into doubt. For example, modes of thought with a social-scientific pedigree, such as perspectivist anthropology, actor-network theory, and the pragmatic sociology of critique, inconsistent even among themselves, talk at utter crosspurposes with what are arguably, from a certain perspective, their closest counterparts embracing roots in the theoretical humanities, object-oriented ontology, process philosophy, and assemblage theory.[8] Even within the "materialist" wing, the posthumanists, neopragmatists, vitalists, and other new materialists studying the adventures, entanglements, and becomings of complex, worldly, relational material agencies and biosemiological couplings seem to share little common ground, beyond mere aversion to anthropocentrism, with the speculative materialists and nonphilosophers attached to the Absolute, mathematical ontology, and nonrelational Being or, *a fortiori*, the extinctionist/eliminativist materialism growing out of these constructs.[9] (Admittedly, some of these currents fall outside the scope of what many writers have in mind when they mention postcritique, but that only reinforces the point that the big tent nomenclature is problematic: there is undoubtedly a case to be made for their distinction from critical theory, but they distinguish themselves from it in different ways.)

It is clear that these approaches have inflected the course of disciplines as diverse as philosophy, science and technology studies, environmental humanities, anthropology, media studies, literature, sociology, theology, political theory, management studies, architecture, and art history, among others, but it remains unclear what, if anything, draws them together and what durable effect, if any, they will have on the organization of knowledge. These questions—too broad for a full inquiry in this chapter—will linger in the background as I address a more immediate, manageable problem: to assess the challenge that these forms of "postcritical" thought address to the tradition of critical legal theory, and what possibilities they may afford to lawyers for whom critique has run out of steam.

---

[7] A nod to Noys (2010), one of the earliest sustained studies of postcritical thought.

[8] On perspectivist anthropology, see Viveiros de Castro (2014); Viveiros de Castro (2015). On actor-network theory, see Latour (2005). On the pragmatic sociology of critique, see Boltanski & Thévenot (2006); Boltanski (2011). On object-oriented ontology, see Harman (2005); Harman (2009). On process philosophy, see Shaviro (2014); Debaise (2017). On assemblage theory, see DeLanda (2016).

[9] On posthumanism, see Braidotti (2013). On neopragmatism, see Massumi (2013); Manning (2013). On vitalism, see Bennett (2010). For other articulations of new materialism, see Barad (2007); Alaimo (2010); Coole & Frost (2010). On speculative materialism, see Meillassoux (2008). On nonphilosophy, see Laruelle (2011). On extinctionist/eliminativist materialism, see Brassier (2007).

4. DETACHMENT

For many attempting to move beyond or outside of the strictures of critique, the model of critique is fundamentally Kantian. Kant's transcendental idealism stands as the single most important watershed in the historical elaboration of critique, but it is not sufficient to merely take issue with its postulates. Coarsely, no one is actually a Kantian—even if in some respects, nearly everyone is. Actually-existing critique is, like Kantianism, about diagnosing limits and debunking dogmatic illusions, but also demonstrating the work such illusions perform in safeguarding the status quo and tracing their grounds in existing social structures. The point is not only to show that there are illusions, but that the social order generates and must generate those illusions to perpetuate itself, including by directing or determining the thoughts and actions of nominally free subjects.

Kant showed that all experience is structured by universal *a priori* forms and categories operative solely in the constitution of the subject, displacing ontology by epistemology and outlawing philosophical inquiry into the nature of things (and of the world, the soul, and God). The proper domain for critical thought is the set of conditions of possibility of knowledge about the nature of things, the limits of which critique is alone capable of establishing, and not the nature of things in themselves. (Put aside the obvious rejoinder, not fully articulated in philosophy until William James and Henri Bergson, that of course knowledge is itself a thing.) Because critique alone can—and must—account for its own possibility, it is situated at the edge of the possible. It must constantly assure itself that it is not crossing those limits, but also that it is not ("uncritically") adopting concepts untethered to their conditions of possibility: neither over the edge (which would be madness or fanaticism) nor comfortably immersed in everyday doxa (mere dogmatism or naivete). This accounts for critique's self-reflexive drive to continually, some might say obsessively, mark the boundaries of its own activity, which seem to shift in place every time they are interrogated. This "tendency for critique to transmute into self-critique"[10] is both a property of what Didier Fassin recently called the *endurance* of critique,[11] and a caesura that merits further inquiry. Critique *must* encounter conditions that destabilize its own operations (crises) in order to endure and evolve, but those conditions *must* arise out of those operations.[12] As a result, the endurance of critique demands the augmentation of its own inner rationality, the ever tighter closure of its circuits. But as Kant intuited, and as others, from Hegel to Derrida, would demonstrate more decisively, the practice of critique turns on a kind of self-displacement, so that the subject and the object of critique are never self-identical. As Stathis Gourgouris explains, "the one who

---

[10] Anker & Felski (2017), 9.

[11] Fassin (2017). For Fassin, endurance here "means that critique repeatedly undergoes ordeals, that it bears them with patience and that it continues to exist beyond them." I would add that critique *requires* these ordeals because they stimulate the transformations necessary to sustain the practice (and tradition) of critique.

[12] This may seem obscure. It means that the crises on which critique thrives must *be seen to* or *be made to* arise out of its own totalizing conditions. It is not to say that a series of market crashes or works of art or rapturous experiences are themselves results of critical operations, only that their phenomenal apparitions, or the ways they appear, are.

differentiates is also the one who differs," so "critique falters if it is not simultaneously self-critique." And this essential "doubling back" means that the "self" is displaced, dethroned, decentered, destabilized, ruling out structural coincidence or mere circularity.[13] Critique is self-critique, in other words, but the tautology remains essentially incomplete: as a limit case, a permanent crisis in itself, the shifting conditions of possibility of critique necessarily inform the conditions of any other phenomenon. The meager foothold this noncoincidence affords at once prevents critique from dissolving into illusion (as a mere symptom of the social order or system of domination under scrutiny) and opens it onto possible (emancipatory) futures.

It is this internally fissured or fractured logic of critique that must be engaged, not a sterile Kantian version. While it resists the allegation of pure narcissistic self-regard, it succumbs to a related charge: that it has nevertheless substituted its own epistemological limits for what Gourgouris calls "the limits of this world."[14] For critique, the limits of this world *are* the limits of critique, which is always on the edge of the possible. This move is required if critique is to systematically oppose the necessity of the factual: it can break out of the merely mundane world of domination to reach what is presently impossible—thus opposing all reactionary discourse—only if it takes its own differentiation from itself, its own dialectical movement, to correspond to a latent, concealed, structural disjuncture in its object or the world. How this move is authorized varies from tradition to tradition or even thinker to thinker, but it seems to be a morphological constant in the argumentative structure of post-Kantian critical theory.

To enact this logic of substitution and thus to get beyond ideological deceptions that willfully or otherwise consecrate the presently existing order of things, critique relentlessly interrogates its object for traces of what it has, by virtue of what was said above, already posed as its own operational presupposition: for instance, fissures in a chain of legal reasoning disclose the indeterminacy of legal form, which in turn attests to the "fundamental contradiction of self and other" for early CLS writers. For them, the legal form is woven into the fabric of modern legal culture, itself a component of the liberal social order. The movement is from the given to the hidden ground, the conditioned to the condition, in succession: from a particular legal phenomenon to a formal construct it both requires and violates, to the structural tensions in the culture that explains the form, to the organization of power in the social order sustaining the culture. In post-CLS critique, deep structures of language, unconscious formations, *habiti*, forms of governmentality, logics of sexuation, and other figures perform functions analogous to the fundamental contradiction of ideology: virtually any legal phenomenon can be explained by deftly invoking these skeleton keys, whose inclusion in the construct of the social totality of domination is the primal but unstated critical-theoretical gesture. In other words, the indeterminacy of the legal form, or more radically its impossibility, is no longer a product of ideological conflict but of the structure of writing (*écriture*), the symbolic order, and other synthetic constructs beyond the grasp of any actual participants in legal controversies, who are constrained to reproduce them.

---

[13] Gourgouris (2013), 17.
[14] Ibid, 26.

The form of law, and so law as such, quickly—too quickly—comes to stand in for the social order itself. Overcoding the law's whole distribution of agency, the form serves to reduce out of existence its every complexity in order to render law an undifferentiated dispatcher of oppression: an inversion of the liberal legal form. It is necessary not to accumulate but to sever as many ties as possible in order to evoke its Cause, which is as a rule concealed from the perceptions of mere mortals caught up in webs of naïve belief. Things become traces or ciphers of something deeper, more nefarious than meets the eye—something that, if it remains hidden, may succeed in legitimating the given or even in guaranteeing the natural or necessary character of what is, protecting the totalizing machine.[15] So critique must clear the brush. Critique *de-cides*, in the etymological sense of making a cut in the given, and what it finds beneath the surface never fails to upset our dopey empirical expectations, to destabilize certainties we carelessly took for granted, or to explain with supreme confidence the *real* chain of social causality we had previously overlooked.[16]

5. AMIDST

This is not to say that the reflexive loops of self-critique are all-consuming. But like Red Peter in Kafka's story ("A Report to an Academy"), those feeling caged cannot simply choose freedom; they must invent a way out, they must "beat the bushes" (*sich in die Büsche schlagen*, also translated as "steal away secretly" or "disappear in the thicket"—that is, adapt, transform oneself and one's environment in the same movement). Critique has powerful transcendental, dialectical, interpretative, genealogical, and deconstructive tools at its disposal. To become postcritical would mean not simply abandoning these, as though that were possible, but submitting them to tests that dramatically *weaken* them, reorienting and subordinating them to the multiple forms of agency disclosed in what they formerly overtook with too much ease.

However, I am not satisfied to respond to critique as some avowed "postcritical" writers do: by insisting that, sometimes, a pipe is really just a pipe. What is needed is not a louder, prouder brand of naïve realism or commonsense empiricism. What is needed is an empiricism of attachments that shows why a pipe is never really just a pipe, but is a motley assemblage of things visible and invisible, proximate and remote: decades old Portuguese briar root, much older agricultural and husbandry techniques; technologies and instruments for extracting, hauling, processing, and shaping wood; markets; retailers; administrative regulations; contracts; tobacco. None

---

[15] A totalizing machine that is, of course, a product of critique's own totalizing operation as applied to law, consisting of the reduction of legal technicality, historicity, aesthetics, materiality, and other dimensions to a homogenous instrument of oppression.

[16] Incidentally, aversion to this characteristic of critique above all else—of critique as a brand of what Paul Ricoeur called the "hermeneutics of suspicion," the model of the critic-as-detective—seems to lie at the heart of postcritical literary studies. It has important predecessors in interactionist sociology (Erving Goffman) and ethnomethodology (Harold Garfinkel), which often go unmentioned, as well as the political theory of Jacques Rancière, which gets far more airtime. Recent collections of work on post-critique in literature include Anker & Felski (2017) and Di Leo (2014); see also Felski (2015).

of those things stands alone and none can plausibly claim to have caused the pipe to exist. To individualize *this* pipe requires *more*, not *fewer*, connections.

Crucially, "stealing away" from critique would mean recognizing, with Luc Boltanski, that the scholarly critic is no more detached from the affair confronting her than the participant whose actions and utterances constitute it. From this it follows that the critic patiently undoing argumentative threads, revealing the contingent forces concealed in necessitarian logics, and reimagining the discourses that entrench dominant interests, all at a distance from the claims of the actors ensnared in the affair and subjected to its local conditioning effects, is herself a participant in the affair that she objectifies and *prolongs* in her critical report. This is a basic tenet of the pragmatic sociology of critique,[17] as well as actor-network theory. Indeed, Boltanski writes:

> When we compare a researcher's reports to those of actors ... we can only be struck by their similarities, in form and content alike. Like research reports, actors' reports include a claim of validity based on manoeuvres designed to establish proof. They offer interpretations, deploy arguments and single out facts by selecting the elements that can either be retained as necessary or rejected as contingent in the context of the affair; they invalidate objections, justify actions, engage in critiques, and so on.[18]

What the scholarly critic may add—other than her substantive reasoning, which may well differ from that offered by the other actors—is an intellectually coherent account of the principles or premises on which the affair turns and which ground the critiques and justifications of the other actors. Such an account is possible not because the actors are dupes who cannot see through the ideological veil, but because the scholarly critic usually has access to a broader range of actors' reports and more time with which to synthesize them as a result of her position in a specific professional organization, typically an academic institution. But this account, too, is essentially transient: as soon as it is uttered, it may be seized by the other actors, translated, misconstrued, renewed, expanded, cut back, and contested and mobilized in myriad unforeseen ways. It is not a whole synthesizing parts, but one corridor among many others in a complex ongoing affair. (That the immediate controversy has abated by the time the critic arrives on the scene does not mean the affair is no longer ongoing; the critic's report extends it into new localities.) The scholarly critic's exteriority is not durably different than the lay critic's interiority; both are destined to deepen the immanence of the affair to which they belong in common.

6. SHARDS

Postcritical legal studies differ widely in approach, theme, style, and vocabulary. In this section, I discuss a few exemplary reports with an eye toward what they share in common. It turns out they do not share much. I take this as an index of the lack of utility of "postcritical" as a descriptive term and as an encouraging sign that there are, in fact, a multitude of ways of adapting, or "stealing away" in Kafka's sense, to do

---

[17] See Boltanski & Thévenot (2006).
[18] Boltanski (2012), 23.

innovative, generative legal theory without being caught in the mirror of critique. It goes without saying that these examples do not exhaust the terrain and that none are beyond reproach. My intention here is merely to illustrate.

What can be said for commonality is that the concepts, languages, and dispositions at work in such studies vary according to the matter at hand. Consider a few reports on the production of legal doctrine. In a justly celebrated article, Annelise Riles makes an erudite plea directed to humanistic (or cultural) legal scholars—read, critics—to "take on the technicalities" of law.[19] Legal technique and technicality are the obvious sacrificial victims of legal critique: they are good only for providing a way into the elusive form of legality and the social order it crystallizes. Her argument is not merely that the devils of politics, culture, and meaning are actually located in the details of arcane legal doctrine—though that is part of it[20]—but that doctrine, as *mere* technicality, results from a contentious set of transformations redefining law as technology, legal knowledge as technical knowledge, and the legal specialist as a kind of engineer or technician. Following the thread of the "revolution" in American conflict of laws jurisprudence (one of several historical narratives about the triumph of realism over formalism), she complicates familiar accounts of the overcoming of the "classical" or "formalist" approach to the question of which forum's law governs in multijurisdictional disputes by a "modern" or "realist" approach by, first, foregrounding a cascade of displacements that cumulatively reimagine law as technical means rather than scientific or logical end, and second, demonstrating that the new regime of legal technoscientificity prevailed not by force of reason or its qualitative properties but by strategically blackboxing its statements and preferred metaphors. Taking her cue from Latour's argument that the credibility or certainty associated with a statement depends not on its inherent qualities but on the successive transformations to which it is put by later statements,[21] she shows how the realist metaphor of law as tool was itself transformed, from within the realist epistemology, into a "tool of legal knowledge,"[22] or "literalized," by mid-century conflict of law specialists who devised a formulaic and portable step by step analytic template. When transmuted into a mere problem solving technique operated by a modest judge-technician, however, Riles shows how the legal tool acquires a dramatic new ontological capacity: rather than neutrally securing an extralegal end (a social policy, a political choice, and so on), the tool—which is to say the metaphor of law as tool, a metaphor that here serves as an obvious and uncontroversial tool itself—"define[s], limit[s], and even constitutes" those ends.[23] The transformative gambit succeeds, in Riles' telling, because of its modesty and the familiar understanding of law work as a kind of problem solving exercise—a

---

[19] Riles (2005).

[20] The claim that legal technique or technicality embeds political choices or projects political effects—a bulwark of first wave CLS—is neither rejected nor offered as a basis for denunciation, but is rather enthusiastically embraced by some contemporary writers. Within the domain of conflicts, see Michaels (2015), which argues that conflicts doctrine is a "fictional" language into which political relations are translated; see also Knop, Michaels, & Riles (2012).

[21] Latour (1987).

[22] Riles (2005), 1009.

[23] Ibid, 1020. Riles adds: "Legal knowledge defines its own outside from the point of view of the inside even as it is presented as a 'function' of other interests."

familiarity that derives from the very practice of the deductive "formalist" mode of reasoning that the realist revolution was supposed to have displaced. But it derives as well from a more elemental feature of legal knowledge and practice, which Riles calls an "aesthetic of instrumentality" characterized by, here, a poverty of expressiveness, as well as reductiveness, hermeticism, and closure. If there is today a crisis in conflict of laws thinking, she suggests, it is a result of professional fatigue or lawyerly detachment from the aesthetic interest compelled by the existing forms, a state produced not by the failure but by the success of this mechanized form of jurisprudence. By mapping controversies and epistemological transformations in the production of doctrine, Riles shows that legal technicality is a specific empirical achievement of situated practices rather than a property of legal form.

From the tool of law-as-tool in conflicts jurisprudence, we can move to the law-machine in patent law. Alain Pottage has shown that the "material rhetoric" of scale models played a fundamental role in shaping nineteenth century American patent law: "[m]echanical form was the medium in which texts, testimony, and doctrinal categories were made legible, articulated, communicated, interpreted and disputed,"[24] notably as judges and juries were generally incapable of appreciating the technical engineering drawings and documents representing the patented article. If Riles tells a crucial story about the mechanization of law, Pottage reveals a countercurrent in his account of the juridification of mechanism. The forensic models did not merely reproduce a particular mechanistic structure; if they signified in the courtroom, they did so by mediating a doctrinal construct. Pottage argues, in effect, that such models are a kind of abstract machine—understood as a machine for eliminating the indexicality associated with the real-world functions or effects of the actual device corresponding to the invention, and for abstracting a "principle" or "mode of operation" from an arrangement of matter without allowing it to be reduced to the order of ideas. This *tertium* which is neither matter nor idea is precisely legal doctrine. The doctrinal categories of patent law—invention, principle of the machine, mode of operation—were figured or fabricated in and through the material rhetorics of such models. Even after significant developments in the sociolegal regime of patent jurisprudence and practice—the declining importance of adjudication, changes in administrative and procedural forms, rejection of certain doctrinal categories, the rise of "immaterial," informatic, and biological inventions—the story Pottage tells matters, if only because the vestiges of these material rhetorics resound in the very paradigmatic image of invention that reigns to this day: the figure of the machine. Indeed, although their stories are very different, if Pottage's account is put into dialogue with that of Riles, one can glimpse how the recursive instrumentalization charted by the latter depends deeply on the juridical or doctrinal transformations revealed by the former. Diffracted by the agency of the scale model, the material traces of the machine gradually coalesce to become a blackboxed legal actor capable of remaking doctrine in its mechanized image.

In addition to studies, such as those of Riles and Pottage, bringing STS resources to bear, in different ways and toward different if complementary ends, on legal history and doctrine, ethnomethodological studies of legal practice represent another key genre of

---

[24] Pottage (2011). This account is also developed in Pottage & Sherman (2010).

postcritical legal studies. Ethnomethodology is also a common resource in STS, of course, but it preceded and enabled the latter, whereas the approaches exhibited by Riles and Pottage take advantage of anthropological methods developed within the field of STS.

Some of the core principles—if they are in fact principles, which is not clear—of ethnomethodology were forged in the fires of legal phenomena. Garfinkel notes that its roots lie in his classic study of juror deliberation in personal injury cases showing how, among other things, cases are decided without formal or doctrinal grounds supporting the decision, which only come later.[25] Interactions producing witnessable forms of local order are plentiful in empirical legal practices, which perhaps accounts for their attraction as objects of sociological inquiry for ethnomethodologists, conversation analysts, and organizational theorists. Indeed, ethnomethodology is today one of the most significant currents in legal sociology generally, having accumulated over several decades a relatively vast corpus of texts joyfully but rigorously puncturing inflated expectations about law.[26] How, though, does it qualify as a key "postcritical" form of "legal theory"?

It is true that ethnomethodology resists assimilation with theory, legal or otherwise. Its interest lies in the ordinary practices, improvised methods, and observable techniques people use to interactionally construct orders as local and fleeting achievements. And it is in exactly that sense that it can be understood as postcritical theory: if critical theory always returns to a hidden Cause, a fatal Schism in the order of the world, ethnomethodology makes that move difficult or at least unsatisfying by constantly resubmerging the matter in the local reflexivity of everyday interactions and events, complicating any generic causal or explanatory scheme. Its "theory" is disposable, one-time-use theory valid only for *this* encounter in *this* interactional milieu.[27]

Which is not to say that it cannot shed light on basic, enduring jurisprudential problems. For instance, Tim Berard's recent study of hate crime law raises fundamental questions about the ontological processes that law and legislative politics depend upon and modify.[28] Instead of presuming, as many theorists do, that there is a fatal contradiction between ontological naturalism (that legal categories or relations are natural kinds with a form of existence exceeding their institutional representation) and constructionism (that such categories or relations have existence only within an institutional discourse), Berard shows how legal actors constantly shift between naturalist and constructionist registers. Where a critical view of these shifting grounds of legal speech would condemn the inconsistency and seek an explanatory faultline, ethnomethodology admits their pragmatic irreducibility. They are aspects of the

---

[25] Garfinkel (1974).

[26] Sadly, ethnomethodologists report that graduate students and early career researchers declaring an interest in ethnomethodology are on the decline. This was surprising news to me because the field seems so obviously useful for the study of legal and nonlegal matters alike.

[27] Lynch (2017) is a compelling example of the advantages of studying the interactional techniques of lawyers and witnesses in constructing evidentiary statements through testimonial and documentary practices. Conversation-analytic tools have similarly been brought to bear on empirical legal phenomena, with powerful results. See Cooren (2015).

[28] Berard (2017).

practical achievement of the law. Regarding hate crime law in particular, the zigzagging movement between naturalism and constructionism is essential to both the maintenance and the transformation of the sphere of acts recognized as hate crimes. Such crimes are labels or constructs in the important sense that they capture a mode of deviance subject to enhanced punishment and symbolic, moral, and political condemnation, which may alter the "social identity" or matrix of relations in which one subject to the label is bound. Unrecognized acts of violence or discrimination are not hate crimes until they are formally criminalized, but they cannot be criminalized if they are unrecognized, so it is necessary to address such acts *as* crimes in order to accomplish their legal recognition. In other words, proponents adopt the constructionist ontology of hate crimes to preserve the efficacy of the label, yet are constrained to deploy naturalist strategies (the violent act is a hate crime *not yet* recognized by the criminal code) in order to construct the act as a recognized legal offense. If there is a legal form at work here, it differs from occasion to occasion in response to the shifting ontological grounds of ordinary legal interaction.

The highly situated ethnomethodological inquiry complements another current, which moves still further from the historicodoctrinal analyses of Riles, Pottage, and other STS-grounded approaches: where the relative anarchy of law-in-action introduces a challenge that only a versatile approach like ethnomethodology can adequately address, that approach can be seen to run aground when confronted with the circulation of legal beings outside of the legal institution. That law is not (only) a specialist or expert discourse, or even (only) a discourse, is a foundational insight for both new materialist legal studies and at least one other alternative mode of legal thought (which, however, lacks a stable identifier). I will address each in turn.

Law is an important component in new materialist thinking. Although many strands of postcritical materialism pursue a politics of entanglement with self-organizing processes and human/nonhuman agents acting on multiple scales, traversing a bewildering range of fields, institutions, and disciplines with little concern for the specificity of any single one, several writers have explored the landscape with law in mind.[29] It is not uncommon to find particles of evolutionary biology laced with Augustinian theology, the sociology of mass movements, and Western and indigenous legal practices, to say nothing of quantum physics, geology, modernist literature, Earth systems science (or its predecessors[30]), the history of chemistry, postcolonial theory, animal ethology, radical democratic politics, and so on, in materialist tracts. The point, we may surmise, is to find the zones of interaction, joint articulation, and productive flourishing in these strange couplings—not to annul their differences, but to grasp their mutuality in extension. The risk, however, is that new materialist legal studies may go too far and lose the thread of law in a flood of other forces, depriving it of any ontological specificity.

In *Law Unlimited*, Margaret Davies unpacks a new materialist account of law that is premised expressly on the notion that law should be seen as *unlimited*, in the sense of ubiquitous or omnipresent. Where we think law is not, law has merely engineered its

---

[29] E.g. Davies (2017); Lay (2016); Philippopoulos-Mihalopoulos (2014).
[30] Hamilton (2017) is immensely critical of philosophical and political theories that engage only with "ecology" as distinguished from Earth systems science.

own invisibility.[31] Davies flatly rejects any notion that law is a unique "agential thing" or reality with "its own persona and agency": she explains that "[l]aw does not *do* anything or *say* anything itself, and it is not even an identifiable thing—all of these are shorthands for the actions of human beings enmeshed in material contexts who use an imaginary of law to relate and engage."[32] Law and norms materialize in spatial relations, social intercourse, human bodies—even in the gradual formation of neural pathways in the brain, according to a logic of emergence that Davies repeatedly indicates without quite unraveling. Through a wide-ranging engagement with sociolegal and feminist scholarship, analytical jurisprudence, critical legal thought, legal geography, and recent work in materialism (especially that of Karen Barad), Davies offers an account of a thick, densely interconnected, culturally variable and radically plural, materially and physically constituted law that pivots on the notion of performativity. For Davies, lived legality surfaces in performance and interaction (or intra-action), emerging from the intersection of multiple discourses and places, histories and imagined futures, humans and nonhumans—in short, the entire undifferentiated continuum of "natureculture." But while Davies resists the identification of any singular source or distinctive means of authorization as antithetical to her materialist questioning of law's emergence, it is the scripted or unscripted performances of subjects embedded in that plenitude that does the crucial work of generating and mingling different modalities of law and other norms. Indeed, she suggests that the figure of the boundary—so integral to the Western statist conception of law and self—be replaced in legal studies by the figure of the pathway (or "complex of pathways"[33]), a metaphor chosen in part for its denotation of repetition, iteration, habit. As a complex of pathways, law has no outside (or inside), only multiple trajectories of entangled matters and meanings. In the end, law has the same kind of existence as God: a necessary presupposition for certain kinds of human institutions, meanings, aspirations, and practices, which is, in the last analysis, indistinguishable from those very practices.[34]

An alternative approach that shares many preoccupations with new materialist inquiry has been developed in my work, which relies more heavily on actor-network theory. I too have argued that legality is a question of performances well beyond the courthouse or assembly hall, of interactions and hybridizations rather than rules, policies, or discourses about rules and policies, of conventionally nonlegal mediations of legal normativity. But if I have extended the scope of legal phenomena, it is to better specify the distributions of agency comprising law. Unlike materialists, I do not reject the notion of legal form; I reject its causal efficacy, the assumption that it grounds legal force and normativity, that it endures or diffuses itself, that it preexists and is impervious to its material and corporeal expression, and so on, but not the claim that law differs from other modes of existence. I have occasionally referred to these studies of legal materiality as components not of a *materialist* inquiry but of a *materiological* inquiry. The difference is crucial but ill understood. Briefly, a materialism—new or old—is a theoretical doctrine while a materiology is a dimension or attribute of what is

---

[31] A point made with greater theoretical nuance in Philippopoulis-Mihalopoulos (2014).
[32] Davies (2017), 29–30.
[33] Ibid, 151.
[34] Ibid, 156.

theorized. It is nonsensical to claim that law *has* a materialism, because a materialism is an assemblage of concepts and models that may be used to understand or explain, for example, law. But it is meaningful to claim that law has a materiology, because a materiology is a set of parameters helping to define a practical ontology; it is implicated in and *immanent* to the ontology of law, and must be made explicit to be understood. If it is made more explicit than it was, the effect is to *increase* the differentiation of law from other ontologies, even as it becomes more apparent that such differentiation consists in more, not less, heterogeneity, entanglement, and interference. Law's materiology resists materialism.

To draw the dividing line between new materialism and this alternative approach more sharply, it should be noted that law's immanent materiology is but one dimension of the ontology of law: to it are added an immanent anthropology and an immanent sociology of action. These three dimensions differ starkly and each is grounded in assumptions delegated to the others. Law's anthropology fabricates *personae* and corresponding durable legal identities through specific techniques of personation, for instance, but has no concern for the production or circulation of powers, liabilities, obligations, and rights. The latter is a core element of law's materiology, which deploys a logic of expression to create bonds in a variety of media ecologies—the sort of media ecologies new materialism also studies, hence its proximity at times to the problem of materiology—but those bonds are transient events. They do not durably attach to persons because persons do not durably exist for law's materiology. This is the site of multiple *forces of law* generated through the promiscuous exchange of properties among law and its media: technological artifacts, market devices, cinematic images, political statements, and so on.[35] Law's sociology of action brings the disparate dimensions of anthropology and materiology together, but in such a way that neither gets precisely what it wants: neither pure fixity nor pure transience. If a bond attaches, it attaches locally and provisionally in an *ordeal*—the privileged site of law's sociology of action—which can include formal proceedings in courts or tribunals as well as informal encounters in everyday life. What is achieved in an ordeal, even a formal one, is local stabilization. The mirage of a stable legal system or institutional normative order or organic body of law emerges only through the theoretical act of neglecting the essential labor necessary to *connect* ordeals. They do not connect or resonate unless *made* to do so.[36]

With this, we return to the notion that postcritique is, perhaps, better understood as *ante*-critique. If there is a thread running through these divergent modes of thought, it may be that each is impelled to collect anew the elements of legality rather than accept (and then debunk) a problematic self-image. Their alternative constructions would then operate as *propositions* that could serve as experimental conditions for engaging law critically, in the sense of discerning and judging where to make cuts in response to other phenomena that exceed law. For instance, from the perspective I adopt, the law's anthropology, materiology, and sociology of action each engender modes of legal relation that are seriously deficient if examined not by their own lights but in the shadow of the Anthropocene. But it is only *after* drawing up the proposition—here, the

---

[35] For discussion, see McGee (2014), ch. 3.
[36] On this point, see McGee (2018b).

description of the ontology or "practical metalanguage" of law—that it is really possible to reimagine that ontology in ways that take account of the new climatic regime and its politics, disturbing certainties embedded in legal phenomena such as the linear, univocal models of causation and imputation that law's anthropology establishes (but which its materiology constantly undermines). Both the need for *and* the possibility of constructs of, for example, multiple or distributed imputation, or entirely new legal bonds not reducible to the familiar set of rights, powers, duties, and so on, or new legal rituals not reducible to the oath, trial, or other familiar artifices of truth, or indeed new models of legal truth, presuppose a robust account of law's *existing* distribution of agency. If the thesis that law—via the legal form—replicates broader social orders or systems of domination has lost its charge, perhaps it is because it requires abandoning law as a potential site of resistance to the present.

There is yet another technique for "stealing away" from legal critique that, in important respects, precedes it—but it is, frankly, difficult to pull off. What might be called *critical postcritical* thought hangs tightly to the thread of critique in full cognizance of its impossibility. It tells of law as life, as visibilities, surfaces, events, encounters, attachments: the whole "realm of actual governance, the formation of subjects, the organization of visible spaces and faces, and the normative lens of quotidian interaction ... is the proper object of post-critical legal hermeneutics," Peter Goodrich observes.[37] Goodrich has long argued that critique, in its indifference to legal doctrine, conceals "a certain affection or love for the obscure object or enigma of substantive law,"[38] a love dissimulated in the aggressivity of denunciation and the critic's very recourse to legal form. The conceptual architectures and idiolects of Lacanian psychoanalysis, Bourdieusian sociology, and deconstruction, just like the ancient common law, the Roman law, and the enigmas of political theology, remain quite visible, central even, but somehow disabled: all emblems of a profane law without force.[39] Goodrich—whose every text is a work of literature proceeding from detour to erudite detour until we discover at last that *la loi, c'est moi*—can be said to have taken (and instigated) the "aesthetic turn" several times over, arriving latterly in the uncharted spaces of a law that propagates and transmits but does not rule. The rule itself does not rule; rather, the manifestation, or the apparition, or the image governs.[40] The "nomogram" positions us, subjects us, elicits an affective investment in the authority it mediates before doctrines, policies, principles, or norms enjoy efficacy.[41] If this modality is difficult to execute, it is because it deploys the tools of critique to disrupt the flow of critique, a kind of inverted self-critique disabling its own tendency to denounce and its constitutive utopianism, animated not by a desire to judge but by a desire to amass the doctrinal and imagistic transformations that judgment presupposes. What it will do with them is anyone's guess.

---

[37] Goodrich (2010), 610.
[38] Goodrich (1999), 348.
[39] In Agamben's (2005) terms.
[40] Goodrich (2010), 624.
[41] Goodrich (2006). This argument owes much to Pierre Legendre's thinking on law and the image. See generally Legendre (1997).

7. HORIZON

Let us conclude not on the question of legality but on politics: although critique is a quintessentially juridical technique, it knows itself as a political mode of thought. So what are the politics of postcritique? Consistent with my skepticism about the coherence and unity of postcritique, that question has not one but many answers. Those answers are organized around different centers of gravity: *oikonomia*, technocracy, neoliberalism, Anthropocene. Above all, it is important to recognize that modes of thought situated in the midst of these aggregates, rather than above them, are not merely entrenching them: their wager is that closer attention to their constituent processes and relations can generate richer accounts and novel perspectives that can alter the political stakes of critique. In other words, postcritique is not necessarily the reconstruction-after-deconstruction it is often thought to be; the postcritical retains a close connection or attachment to critique.

On one (broadly Latourian) account, postcritical politics turn on the *insufficiency of the old settlement*, of the modern division of labor crystallized in the bounded institutions of Science, Literature, Law, Politics, Economy, Technology, Religion, and so on.[42] The modern settlement can no longer contain the overflow of its own productivity: its excess is evident in virtually all domains. The critical strategy of reducing or eliminating this overflow, of ceaselessly redrawing the limits of the world in the image of the limits of critique, is inadequate in light of the disorienting vertigo of placelessness associated with the abstract Globe and the catastrophic vertigo of landlessness associated with the new climatic regime, which are radically annulling those limits.[43] If there is a need for postcritical thought, it is in part because critique tends to renew the pernicious logics at the core of the modernization front. That is not to blame critique for the dizzying expansion of global capital, or the perpetuation of injustice and inequality, or global warming, or the Sixth Mass Extinction Event. It is to say that critique has chosen one path—that of modernization, reduction, distance, explanation—when another—that of ecologization, entanglement, proximity, uncertainty—seems to be called for. But even if critique had a hand in eroding public and scholarly confidence in institutions such as Science, Law, and Religion, it is not enough to say that postcritique seeks to restore that trust. If restoration is part of its project, it is only under the sign of *composition*, precisely the composition of a common world that does not yet exist. Does critique not forcefully reemerge here as necessary to discern the laws of compossibility and to decide how to coexist, how to reinvent values, how to redesign or reconfigure practices, institutions, and forms of life?

If it is not sufficient to say that postcritique works for the restoration of trust in institutions, neither is it sufficient to say that it responds to the new "postnormative" condition of neoliberal governmentality, taken as the extension of a market rationality to every facet of life and the earth itself, an all-encompassing canopy hanging over both

---

[42] See especially Latour (2013).
[43] McGee (2017); Latour (2017).

Nature and Society.[44] This is, despite appearances, a conventional critical-theoretical statement of the problem since it makes neoliberalism a distant totalizing agent. With this formulation, how that extension and that rationality are enacted remains obscure. It is not that events or practices that may be leveraged as signs or manifestations of neoliberalism are hard to come by; on the contrary, they abound. The question is whether the putative dispatching agency of neoliberalism itself ever discloses anything like the kind of identity ascribed to it. If not, "neoliberalism" is just another absent Cause comforting the afflicted with the conviction that all injustice is traceable to some Author, some logic of capitalist necessity that can and must be opposed. That it really does not perform any action at all, however, does not in turn mean that neoliberalism is pure fantasy. What it means is that neoliberalism cannot be allowed to circulate so freely unless and until the scope of the practices and forms of agency belonging to it have been circumscribed. Instead of generic or universal forms of *market rationality*, for example, it would be preferable to examine *market devices* in their indexicality and positivity. That is not merely a task for economic sociologists; market devices proliferate, after all, creeping into literature, the sciences, law, politics, and so on. An understanding of the aggregation that is neoliberalism may develop *after* and *as a result of* a more sustained inquiry into the migrations of market devices and an accounting of the *local* ways in which they totalize other things. This is another opportunity to clarify that what is called postcritique need not uncritically reentrench the necessity of the given, but rather, by inventing new theoretical dispositions that are generative rather than explanatory, may create entirely new modalities of rupture with the present.

If it is preferable to speak of *antecritique*, it is because we do not know in advance what the law is or is made of, and it is necessary to collect the agencies it organizes using diverse techniques, none of which will predominate over the others. And this may in turn suggest what it would mean to be *post*critical: to have done with the purification and hierarchization of method, without becoming indifferent to or otherwise losing touch with the critical. In that sense, too, postcritique would remain to be invented.

BIBLIOGRAPHY

Agamben, Giorgio. 2005. *State of Exception*, trans. Kevin Attell. Chicago: University of Chicago Press.
Alaimo, Stacey. 2010. *Bodily Natures: Science, Environment, and the Material Self*. Bloomington, IN: Indiana University Press.
Anker, Elizabeth & Rita Felski (eds). 2017. *Critique and Postcritique*. Durham, NC: Duke University Press.
Barad, Karen. 2007. *Meeting the Universe Halfway: Quantum Physics and the Entanglement of Matter and Meaning*. Durham, NC: Duke University Press.
Bennett, Jane. 2010. *Vibrant Matter: A Political Ecology of Things*. Durham, NC: Duke University Press.
Berard, Tim. 2017. "Hate crimes, labels, and accounts: Pragmatic reflections on hate crime law in the USA." In Baudouin Dupret, Michael Lynch, & Tim Berard (eds), *Law at Work: Studies in Legal Ethnomethods*. Oxford: Oxford University Press, 223–39.
Boltanski, Luc. 2011. *On Critique: A Sociology of Emancipation*, trans. Gregory Elliott. Cambridge: Polity.
Boltanski, Luc. 2012. *Love and Justice as Competences: Three Essays on the Sociology of Action*, trans. Catherine Porter. Cambridge: Polity.

---

[44] This is a line pursued in Huehls (2016), an inventive study of contemporary American literature.

Boltanski, Luc & Laurent Thèvenot. 2006. *On Justification: Economies of Worth*, trans. Catherine Porter. Princeton: Princeton University Press.
Braidotti, Rosi. 2013. *The Posthuman*. Cambridge: Polity.
Brassier, Ray. 2007. *Nihil Unbound: Enlightenment and Extinction*. New York: Palgrave Macmillan.
Christodoulidis, Emilios. 2009. "Strategies of rupture." *Law & Critique* 20: 3–26.
Coole, Diana & Samantha Frost (eds). 2010. *New Materialisms: Ontology, Agency, and Politics*. Durham, NC: Duke University Press.
Cooren, François. 2015. "In the name of the law: Ventriloquism and juridical matters." In Kyle McGee (ed.), *Latour and the Passage of Law*, Edinburgh: Edinburgh University Press, 235–72.
Davies, Margaret. 2017. *Law Unlimited: Materialism, Pluralism, and Legal Theory*. Oxon: Routledge.
Debaise, Didier. 2017. *Speculative Empiricism: Revisiting Whitehead*, trans. Tomas Weber. Edinburgh: Edinburgh University Press.
DeLanda, Manuel. 2016. *Assemblage Theory*. Edinburgh: Edinburgh University Press.
Di Leo, Jeffrey (ed.). 2014. *Criticism after Critique: Aesthetics, Literature, and the Political*. New York: Palgrave Macmillan.
Douzinas, Costas. 2014. "A short history of the British Critical Legal Conference or, the responsibility of the critic." *Law & Critique* 25(2): 187–98.
Douzinas, Costas. 2016. "On a recent change of tone in politics and law." In Rafal Manko, Cosmin Cercel, & Adam Sulikowski (eds), *Law and Critique in Central Europe: Questioning the Past, Resisting the Present*, Oxford: Counterpress, xii–xvi.
Fassin, Didier. 2017. "The endurance of critique." *Anthropological Theory* 17(1): 4–29.
Felski, Rita. 2015. *The Limits of Critique*. Chicago: University of Chicago Press.
Garfinkel, Harold. 1974. "On the origins of the term 'ethnomethodology.'" In Roy Turner (ed.), *Ethnomethodology*, Harmondsworth: Penguin, 15–18.
Goodrich, Peter. 1999. "The critic's love of the law: Intimate observations on an insular jurisdiction." *Law & Critique* 10: 343–60.
Goodrich, Peter. 2006. "A theory of the nomogram." In Lior Barshack, Peter Goodrich, & Anton Schütz, *Law, Text, Terror: Essays for Pierre Legendre*, New York: Routledge, 13–34.
Goodrich, Peter. 2010. "The empty tomb: Post-critical legal hermeneutics." *Nevada Law Review* 10: 607–29.
Gourgouris, Stathis. 2013. *Lessons in Secular Criticism*. New York: Fordham University Press.
Hamilton, Clive. 2017. *Defiant Earth: The Fate of Humans in the Anthropocene*. Cambridge: Polity.
Harman, Graham. 2005. *Guerrilla Metaphysics: Phenomenology and the Carpentry of Things*. Peru, IL: Open Court.
Harman, Graham. 2009. *Prince of Networks: Bruno Latour and Metaphysics*. Melbourne: re.press.
Huehls, Mitchum. 2016. *After Critique: Twenty-First-Century Fiction in a Neoliberal Age*. Oxford: Oxford University Press.
Kennedy, Duncan. 1982. "Legal education and the reproduction of hierarchy." *Journal of Legal Education* 32: 591–615.
Knop, Karen, Ralf Michaels, & Annelise Riles. 2012. "From multiculturalism to technique: Feminism, culture and the conflict of laws style." *Stanford Law Review* 64: 589–656.
Koselleck, Reinhart. 1988. *Critique and Crisis: Enlightenment and the Pathogenesis of Modern Society*. Cambridge, MA: MIT Press.
Laruelle, François. 2011. *Philosophies of Difference: A Critical Introduction to Non-Philosophy*, trans. Rocco Gangle. London: Continuum.
Latour, Bruno. 1987. *Science in Action: How to Follow Scientists and Engineers through Society*. Cambridge, MA: Harvard University Press.
Latour, Bruno. 2004. "Why has critique run out of steam? From matters of fact to matters of concern." *Critical Inquiry* 30: 225–48.
Latour, Bruno. 2005. *Reassembling the Social: An Introduction to Actor-Network-Theory*. Oxford: Oxford University Press.
Latour, Bruno. 2013. *An Inquiry into Modes of Existence: Anthropology of the Moderns*, trans. Catherine Porter. Cambridge, MA: Harvard University Press.
Latour, Bruno. 2017. *Facing Gaia: Eight Lectures on the New Climatic Regime*, trans. Catherine Porter. Cambridge: Polity.
Lay, Bronwyn. 2016. *Juris Materiarum: Empires of Earth, Soil and Dirt*. New York: Atropos.
Legendre, Pierre. 1997. *Law and the Unconscious: A Legendre Reader*, trans. Peter Goodrich with Alain Pottage & Anton Schütz, New York: St. Martin's Press.

Lynch, Michael. 2017. "Turning a witness: The textual and interactional production of a statement in adversarial testimony." In Baudouin Dupret, Michael Lynch, & Tim Berard (eds), *Law at Work: Studies in Legal Ethnomethods*, Oxford: Oxford University Press, 163–89.
Manning, Erin. 2013. *Always More than One: Individuation's Dance*. Durham, NC: Duke University Press.
Massumi, Brian. 2013. *Semblance and Event: Activist Philosophy and the Occurrent Arts*. Cambridge, MA: MIT Press.
McGee, Kyle. 2014. *Bruno Latour: The Normativity of Networks*. Oxon: Routledge.
McGee, Kyle. 2017. *Heathen Earth: Trumpism and Political Ecology*. Earth: Punctum Books.
McGee, Kyle. 2018a. "Actor-network theory and the critique of law." In Thanos Zartaloudis (ed.), *Law and Philosophical Theory: Critical Intersections*. London: Rowman & Littlefield, 45-62.
McGee, Kyle. 2018b. "Hybrid legalities: On obligation and law's immanent materiology." In Scott Veitch & Daniel Matthews (eds), *Law, Obligation, Community*. Oxon: Routledge, 163-182.
Meillassoux, Quentin. 2008. *After Finitude: An Essay on the Necessity of Contingency*, trans. Ray Brassier. London: Continuum.
Michaels, Ralf. 2015. "Post-critical private international law: From politics to technique." In Horatia Muir Watt & Diego P. Fernandez-Arroyo (eds), *Private International Law and Global Governance*, Oxford: Oxford University Press, 54–67.
Noys, Benjamin. 2010. *The Persistence of the Negative: A Critique of Contemporary Continental Theory*. Edinburgh: Edinburgh University Press.
Philippopoulos-Mihalopoulos, Andreas. 2014. *Spatial Justice: Body, Lawscape, Atmosphere*. Oxon: Routledge.
Pottage, Alain. 2011. "Law machines: Scale models, forensic materiality and the making of modern patent law." *Social Studies of Science* 41(5): 621–43.
Pottage, Alain & Brad Sherman. 2010. *Figures of Invention: A History of Modern Patent Law*. Oxford: Oxford University Press.
Riles, Annelise. 2005. "A new agenda for the cultural study of law: Taking on the technicalities." *Buffalo Law Review* 53: 973–1033.
Shaviro, Steven. 2014. *The Universe of Things: On Speculative Realism*. Minneapolis: University of Minnesota Press.
Stone, Matthew, Ilian rua Wall & Costas Douzinas. 2012. "Law, politics and the political." In Stone, Wall, & Douzinas (eds), *New Critical Legal Thinking: Law and the Political*, Oxon: Routledge, 1–7.
Viveiros de Castro, Eduardo. 2014. *Cannibal Metaphysics*, trans. Peter Skafish. Minneapolis: Univocal.
Viveiros de Castro, Eduardo. 2015. *The Relative Native: Essays on Indigenous Conceptual Worlds*. Chicago: HAU Books/University of Chicago Press.

PART III

15. Property law
Paddy Ireland

1. INTRODUCTION: PROPERTY AS THING-OWNERSHIP

Every spring since 1989, *The Sunday Times* has published a list of the 1,000 wealthiest people or families resident in the UK. It mirrors the American business magazine *Forbes*' annual ranking of the world's billionaires, first compiled in 1987. Both rank people by their net wealth – in other words, by reference to the value of the *property* they own: their financial and nonfinancial assets, minus liabilities. The lists are striking for various reasons. Most obviously, they highlight the extraordinary wealth of the richest members of our society. But they also highlight the often rapid and dramatic shifts, upwards and downwards, in the net wealth of these elites: annual rises or falls of billions of pounds are commonplace. What do these lists tell us about the nature of property in general, and the nature of property in contemporary capitalist societies in particular?

There is no doubt that in common sense 'property' is associated with 'things'. 'Most people, including most specialists in their unprofessional moments', writes Thomas C. Grey, 'conceive of property as *things* that are *owned* by *persons*'. To own property, he explains, is 'to have exclusive control of something – to be able to use it as one wishes, to sell it, give it away, leave it idle, or destroy it'.[1] This common sense idea of property in terms of *thing-ownership* identifies property with what William Blackstone famously referred to as the 'sole and despotic dominion which one man claims and exercises over the external things of the world, in total exclusion of the right of any other individual'.[2] In other words, it is a 'physicalist' conception that tends to associate property with tangible things ('the external things of the world'). It also identifies property with *private* property – 'sole and despotic dominion [by] one man', with what has been called 'full liberal ownership'.[3] It thus conjures up notions of *meum* and *teum*, of *my* car, *your* house, *her* jacket. Indeed, the term 'property' is often used to refer to the 'things' themselves, and the term 'property rights' to refer to the rights held over them.

By the eighteenth century, when Blackstone was writing, the idea of property as absolute dominion over physical objects had emerged as 'one of the central tropes of

---

[1] Thomas C. Grey, 'The Disintegration of Property' in J.R. Pennock and J.W. Chapman (eds) *Property* (Nomos XXII, 1980) 69.

[2] William Blackstone, *Commentaries on the Laws of England*, Book II (first published 1766, Oxford edition, ed. Wilfrid Prest, 2016) 1.

[3] See Tony Honoré, 'Ownership' in A.G. Guest (ed.), *Oxford Essays in Jurisprudence* (Oxford University Press, 1961).

... public discourse'.[4] Indeed, Blackstone himself argued that there was 'nothing which so generally strikes the imagination, and engages the affections of mankind as the right of property'.[5] And yet, his detailed account of 'the law of things' in Book II of the *Commentaries* is curiously at odds with his depiction of property in terms of 'sole and despotic dominion' and 'the external things of the world'. Moreover, despite his assertions about the 'affection' for (private) property and his claims about its social value and utility, Blackstone was clearly anxious about its nature, status and legitimacy. Having extolled the positive feelings felt towards private property rights, Blackstone observed that 'very few ... give themselves the trouble to consider the origi[n] and foundation' of these rights, 'not caring to reflect that (accurately and strictly speaking) there is no foundation in nature or in natural law' for many of them. This was to be welcomed: it would be better, he concluded, 'if the mass of mankind ... obey[ed] the laws when made, without scrutinizing too nicely into the reason for making them'.[6] Blackstone didn't want people digging too deep.

Since then, his description of property in terms of 'sole and despotic dominion' and 'the external things of the world' has become even more problematic. And yet, as Carol Rose observes, although Blackstone's 'exclusivity axiom' is 'a trope, a rhetorical figure describing an extreme or ideal type rather than reality', the idea of absolute dominion remains 'powerfully suggestive ... [and] still molds our thinking about property'.[7] Indeed, recently, after a period in which in academic circles, if not in common sense, the conception of property as thing-ownership had been largely superseded by an alternative conception of property as a 'bundle of rights', the thing-ownership conception has undergone something of an academic revival. Not insignificantly, perhaps, since the 1990s there has been a marked increase in the number of references in law journal articles to Blackstone's 'sole and despotic dominion'.[8]

This chapter uses the continuing appeal of Blackstone's thing-ownership conception of property as a jumping off point for a critical and historically and contextually informed exploration of the nature of property and property rights in contemporary capitalism. It argues that history reveals the public, contested and contingent nature of property and property rights, and their lack of an essence which transcends temporal

---

[4] Robert W. Gordon, 'Paradoxical Property', in John Brewer & Susan Staves (eds), *Early Modern Conceptions of Property* (Routledge, 1996) 95.

[5] Blackstone (n 2) 1. By 'mankind', Blackstone meant above all else the 'gentlemen of independent estates and fortune' who were his main audience and who he described as 'the most useful as well as considerable body of men in the nation'. One of the reasons they should read his book was that 'the understanding of a few leading principles, relating to estates and conveyancing, may form some check and guard upon a gentleman's inferior agents, and preserve him at least from gross and notorious imposition': see William Blackstone, *Commentaries on the Laws of England*, Book II (first published 1765, Chicago University Press 1979) 2.

[6] Blackstone (n 2) 1.

[7] Carol Rose, 'Canons of Property Talk, or, Blackstone's Anxiety' (1998) 108 *Yale Law Journal* 601 at 603–4.

[8] See David Schorr, 'How Blackstone Became a Blackstonian' (2009) 10(1) *Theoretical Inquiries in Law* 103.

and spatial specificities: property and property rights are contextually bound.[9] They are also important sources of power and sites of class struggle, particularly when they relate to productive resources. The simple thing-ownership conception of property, it argues, tends to underplay and conceal these social–relational dimensions. The chapter concludes by suggesting that developing a proper understanding of property and property rights in contemporary capitalism requires us to recognise that there are important senses in which property is simultaneously a thing, a bundle of rights and a relationship between people.

2. 'HEROIC REIFICATION': CREATING PROPERTY

In Book II of the *Commentaries* Blackstone focused mainly on land, the most important productive resource in a still predominantly agrarian society. Notwithstanding his rhetorical flourishes about 'sole and despotic dominion', Blackstone made it abundantly clear in his detailed analysis that absolute private property in land (what he referred to as 'property in its highest degree') was far from the norm. As David Schorr says, 'at every turn, on every page, less-than-absolute property rights are explicated, delimited and qualified', with 'several hundreds of pages of counterexamples' to sole and despotic dominion.[10] Not only was there much land in which lesser interests were vested in persons other than the fee simple holder, but much land was commonly owned, and many members of the labouring classes had specific use rights – rights to gather and glean, to graze, to cut turves, and so on – over much otherwise 'privately' owned land. In Blackstone, 'the typical *lack* of an owner with sole and despotic dominion over an external thing' is placed 'front and centre'.[11]

It wasn't, however, only the idea of property as 'sole and despotic dominion' that was belied by the positive laws described by Blackstone. So too was the 'physicalist' conception of property implied in the idea of dominion over 'external things'. Blackstone's 'physicalist' conception of property might have 'mirror[ed] economic reality to a much greater extent than it did before or has since',[12] but even when he was writing it was problematic, as his coverage of incorporeal hereditaments and advowsons, tithes, rights of chase and other esoterica showed. Moreover, new forms of *intangible* property were emerging. Indeed, Blackstone was centrally involved in the legal struggles surrounding the constitution of one of these new forms: copyright, or, as it was referred to at the time, literary property.

Aimed primarily at securing the 'continuing production of useful books' and at balancing private interests with the public good,[13] the Statute of Anne (or Copyright

---

[9] On the idea of 'essence', see Joanne Conaghan, 'The Essence of Rape' (2019) *Oxford Journal of Legal Studies* (forthcoming).
[10] Schorr (n 8) 107, 114.
[11] Schorr (n 8) 107.
[12] Grey (n 1) 783; see also Kenneth Vandevelde, 'The New Property of the Nineteenth Century: The Development of the New Concept of Property' (1980) 29 *Buffalo Law Review* 325.
[13] Ronan Deazley, 'The Myth of Copyright at Common Law' (2003) 62 *Cambridge Law Journal* 106 at 108.

Act)[14] 1709 granted authors a time limited but exclusive right to control copying of their books (an 'ad hoc discretionary monopoly grant'[15]), after which works would enter the public domain. In the 1730s, when the statutory copyrights began to expire, publishers began to seek statutory extensions. When Parliament refused to oblige, the publishers turned to the courts. Many of the resulting disputes centred on whether the rights of authors were created by (and dependent on) the statute or whether they already existed at common law as 'property' rights, and whether, as such, they were perpetual.

Some argued that, in the absence of a tangible object, copyright lacked the required qualities of 'property'.[16] Thus in *Tonson v Collins* (1761), counsel for the defendant, Joseph Yates, working from what he called the 'essential conditions' of property, argued that 'all property ... begins and ends with manual possession' and that 'the subject of property'[17] had to be 'something susceptible to possession'. By contrast, Blackstone, representing the plaintiff, sought to detach 'property' from physical objects, arguing that 'the one essential requisite of every subject of property, [was] that it must be a thing of value', by which he meant exchange value – the 'capacity of being exchanged for other valuable things'. Whatever 'hath a value is the subject of property'.[18] According to Blackstone, in insisting that property had to have as 'its subject [something] substantial, palpable and visible', Yates had failed to grasp the distinction between corporeal and incorporeal rights, and the ability of the latter to form the basis of property.[19] Contrary to the idea of property as involving 'external things', Blackstone urged the rejection of a physicalist conception of property in favour of a new abstract model of property as exchange value.[20] So much for 'sole and despotic dominion ... over the external things of the world'.

Although the court did not render judgment in *Tonson,* the case proved to be a rehearsal for *Millar v Taylor* in 1769. In *Millar*, the court upheld by a majority the existence of common law copyright. Two of the majority judges, Mansfield and Willes, largely avoided abstract discussion of the nature of property, but the third, Aston, adopted a position very similar to Blackstone's in *Tonson*. The physicalist notion of 'property', he argued, was now 'very inadequate to the object of property at this day'. The 'objects of property' had been 'much enlarged by discovery, invention and art', and 'the rules attending property must keep pace with its increase and improvement'. What was required for property was 'a distinguishable existence in the thing claimed as property' and 'actual value', interpreted to mean exchange value. Property was 'anything merchandizable and valuable'. Yates, by now on the bench, dissented,

---

[14] 8 Ann. c. 21 or 8 Ann. c.19.

[15] Stuart Banner, *American Property: A History of How, Why and What We Own* (Harvard University Press 2011) 24.

[16] See Oren Bracha, *Owning Ideas: A History of Anglo-American Intellectual Property* (JD thesis, Harvard 2005) 203.

[17] We would now use 'object' rather than 'subject': see Andreas Rahmatian, 'The Property Theory of Lord Kames' (2006) 2 *International Journal of Law in Context* 177 at 179.

[18] *Tonson v Collins* (1761), 96 ER 180 at 185.

[19] Ibid at 188. In the event, the court did not render judgment, having discovered that the action had been brought by collusion, with a nominal defendant: *Tonson* (in n 18) 191.

[20] Bracha (n 16) 208.

restating his physicalist conception of property. Could, he asked, 'any-thing ... be the object of a proprietary right, which is not the object of corporeal substance'? He answered emphatically in the negative, arguing that it was 'a well-known and established maxim, which ... holds as true now as it did 2000 years ago, that nothing can be an object of property, which has not a corporeal existence'.[21]

Yates was well aware that property rights seemed to exist in intangibles, but argued that at the end of every incorporeal property right there was a piece of land or tangible object that was the real, physical object of the right: all property rights required, ultimately, 'a substance to sustain them'. He was well aware that in business practice intangibles were commonly treated as business assets to be bought and sold, but the fact that they were treated as if they were 'property' by people did not render them such in the eyes of the law.[22] Yates sought to retain an objective, physical essence for property and property rights which distinguished them from other rights. In the event, the existence of perpetual common law copyright was later rejected, first by the Scottish Court of Session in *Hinton v Donaldson* in 1773,[23] and then by the House of Lords in *Donaldson v Beckett* the following year: copyright in published works was 'property' but it was not perpetual; rather, it was subject to statutory limits.[24]

Copyrights were not the only rights beginning to be recognised as property rights despite their lack of any direct relation to a tangible 'thing'. The growth in commercial relations – the rise of capitalism – saw the rapid expansion and development of the credit system and rapid growth of rights to receive revenues such as interest payments on debts and dividends on joint stock company shares. Originally, these rights were classified at common law as *choses in action*, a category which by the eighteenth century encompassed instruments as diverse as bills, notes, cheques, government stock and shares. Choses in action involved *personal* rights against specific persons, enforceable only by action, not by taking physical possession of a tangible object.[25] Conceptualised as rooted in contract and as *personal* to the parties bound by the obligation, one of their main characteristics was their nonassignability.[26] Thus, if, for example, shareholders in joint stock companies wished the company's shares to be transferable, they had to acquire corporate status and ensure that the instrument of incorporation specifically provided for it. It followed that shares in unincorporated companies were unassignable: it was legally impossible for the assignee to take the place, and assume all the rights and liabilities, of the assignor.[27]

Gradually, however, the nature of (some of) these choses in action began to change. In response to changing business practices in an increasingly market-based society,

---

[21] *Millar v Taylor* (1769), 98 ER 201 at 221, 229.
[22] *Millar* (n 21) 232, 237; see also Bracha (n 16) 216.
[23] (1773) 5 Brn 508.
[24] (1774) 98 ER 257; 98 ER 837.
[25] W.S. Holdsworth, *A History of English Law*, Vol 7 (Methuen 1925) 516.
[26] W.S. Holdsworth, 'The History of the Treatment of *Choses* in Action by the Common Law' (1920) 33 *Harvard Law Review*, 997 at 1016. So prominent a characteristic was this that 'lawyers were inclined to place any right permanently or temporarily unassignable in the category of *choses* in action': ibid 1016.
[27] Holdsworth (n 25) 531–2. On the non-assignability of shares in unincorporated joint stock companies, see *Duvergier v Fellows* (1828) 5 Bing 248, per Best CJ.

equity, in particular, began to 'recognise the validity of the assignment both of debts and of other things recognised by the common law as *choses in action*'.[28] Although some contractual rights continued to be considered 'too personal' in nature to permit assignment, very soon the common law, while maintaining in theory that a chose in action was unassignable, began to abandon this principle too, in practice, in the case of debts. The motivation was 'mercantile convenience or necessity'.[29] As Robert Gordon says, 'property in contracts, property in hopes and expectations, was becoming the prevalent form of commercial property'.[30] The result was that some of these rights 'changed their original character, and [became] very much less like merely personal rights of action and very much more like rights of property'.[31]

Crucially, transferability not only gave these rights market value, but made them look less like personal obligations and more like 'things' and, therefore, more like 'property'. It turned them into 'usable wealth'.[32] As Gordon says, however, making these contractual rights 'fit into the picture of the proprietor standing majestically alone upon his "thing"' required 'heroic acts of reification'. In similar vein, in the landed context, the 'deviations between absolute dominion ideology and the unruly pluralism of much lesser rights recognised in legal practice' were dealt with 'by reification': 'each lesser form of right [was redefined] as an "estate" or as a "thing" in itself, so that even if one only held the lesser right, one held it absolutely'.[33] In the context of joint stock companies, the rise of the railways spurred similar changes. Before this, there was no developed market for company shares and shares in both incorporated and unincorporated companies were legally regarded as equitable interests in the company's assets. The rise of the railways generated a dramatic increase in the number of joint stock company shares and the rapid rise of a developed share market, rendering shares much more easily transferable, liquid assets. With this, shares acquired a market value of their own, quite independent of the value of the company's assets. In response, the courts reconceptualised the legal nature of shares, deeming them not to confer any direct proprietary interest in the assets of companies but to be property in their own right, quite separate from and autonomous of those assets – property in the form of a right to profit.[34]

---

[28] Holdsworth (n 26) 1020.
[29] Holdsworth (n 26) 1021–2.
[30] Gordon (n 4) 99.
[31] Holdsworth (n 26) 543; Holdsworth (n 26) 1029.
[32] See Sarah Worthington, *Equity* (2nd ed., Oxford University Press 2006) 58.
[33] Gordon (n 4) 99–100.
[34] See Paddy Ireland, 'Capitalism without the Capitalist: The Joint Stock Company Share and the Emergence of the Modern Doctrine of Separate Corporate Personality' (1996) 17 *Journal of Legal History* 40.

3. VANISHING INTO THIN AIR: PROPERTY AS A BUNDLE OF RIGHTS

It was quickly recognised that these developments had rendered the thing-ownership conception of property problematic. In his lectures on jurisprudence, delivered in the 1820s and 1830s, John Austin explored the different meanings – some 'extensive', others 'more circumscribed' – attached by lawyers to the word 'things'. Blackstone, he observed, initially confined the term 'to things properly so called', meaning 'permanent external objects'. As he proceeded, however, he incorporated into the term 'the whole class of rights which may be styled obligations: that is to say, rights arising directly from contracts and quasi-contracts, together with the rights to redress which arise from civil injuries'. This 'extension of the term thing', Austin concluded, rendered the meaning of the term 'extremely uncertain'.[35]

For Austin, the same was true of 'property'. Even when defined simply as 'every right in and over a thing', it was still a 'most ambiguous word' with 'various meanings'. In its 'strict sense', he argued, 'property' referred to something resembling Blackstone's 'sole and despotic dominion' over 'a determinate thing'. Indeed, it was often 'taken in a loose and vulgar acceptation to denote not the right of property or dominion, but the *subject* of such a right; as when a horse or a piece of land is called my property'. Austin noted, however, that, as with the word 'thing', Blackstone began with a narrow concept of 'property' linked to tangible, external objects, but eventually extended it to encompass 'whole classes of rights arising directly from contracts and quasi-contracts, which are not rights over things at all, but rights to acts and forbearances to be done and observed by determinate persons'. This wider conception of 'property', Austin suggested, although 'vague, vulgar and unscientific', accorded with common sense. Thus, when we spoke of 'a man of property, meaning a wealthy man, we seem chiefly to contemplate the value of his rights in external things, or of the debts due to him; the most conspicuous portion of his rights'. Austin concluded that it is 'most difficult to get on with [the term 'property'] intelligibly and without endless circumlocution'.[36]

This 'vague, vulgar and unscientific' use of the terms 'thing' and 'property' continues to underpin the thing-ownership conception of property. It has been long and widely recognised, however, that the extension of the concept of 'property' to these intangibles creates conceptual problems. For Sarah Worthington, for example, the growing recognition of certain rights, such as those based on debt obligations, as property rights, despite their lack of any direct connection to 'the external objects of the world', has undermined the boundaries between property and obligation. By 'acceding to persistent commercial pressure', she argues, '[equity] has effectively eliminated the divide between property and obligation, or between property rights and personal rights'. This change has been 'supported and reinforced' by the common law and statute. The result is that, gradually, more and more obligations, or personal rights, have come to be

---

[35] John Austin, *Lectures on Jurisprudence*, Volume II (4th ed., Robert Campbell ed., 1873) 802–3. Austin, a Benthamite, was no fan of Blackstone.

[36] Austin ibid 817–21. The ambiguities of the words 'thing' and 'property' had already been noted by eighteenth century commentators. See Rahmatian (n 17) 180.

treated as property. Indeed, she argues, not only has the 'notion of property ... dramatically expanded', 'rights that continue to be labelled as "personal" are receiving "proprietary" protection'.[37]

For others, however, these developments have rendered simply untenable the conception of property as simple thing-ownership. This has been reflected in the emergence and widespread adoption of the idea that property is not a 'thing' but a 'bundle of rights' with certain qualities, most notably excludability and transferability.[38] The emergence of the 'bundle of rights' view of property is often linked to the work of Wesley Hohfeld and the American legal realists in the late nineteenth and early twentieth centuries, but it has 'a pedigree that long antedates the rise of Progressive thought'.[39] Some suggest that Blackstone himself was a forerunner of 'bundle of rights' thinking about property,[40] and the phrase itself seems to have first appeared in the mid-nineteenth century.[41] However, Hohfeld's analysis not only helped to establish the 'bundle of rights' conception of property but gave it an added, radical twist. Hohfeld argued that what we loosely refer to as 'rights' are in fact a number of distinct legal capacities or entitlements, which he broke down into a complex typology of jural correlatives in which each legal capacity of a rights holder is defined by a corresponding noncapacity among non-rights holders. Influenced by the growing detachment of the concept of property from tangible objects, he then applied this typology to a range of legal relations, including the rights to things (rights *in rem*) thought of as property rights. Properly conceptualised, Hohfeld suggested, property rights were not rights to things (even when tangible things were involved) but rights against persons, any right over a thing entailing a duty owed by someone else to the rightsholder which the state would enforce. This suggested that property rights 'establish[ed] not vertical relationships between people and things ... [but] a series of horizontal relationships among people'.[42] In other words, property is not (or not only) a thing but a *social relation*.[43]

---

[37] Sarah Worthington, 'The Disappearing Divide between Property and Obligation' (2007) 42 *Texas International Law Journal* 917 at 917, 919.

[38] '[O]ne of the important attributes of property', Sarah Worthington writes, 'is that it is transferable: it is not just wealth; it is *usable* wealth. Without this attribute, however tightly circumscribed, a right is unlikely to be classed as property': Worthington (n 32) 58 (her emphasis). Transferability is important also because it gives these bundles of rights thinglike qualities, making possible their reification. Other commentators, such as Kevin Gray (see n 45), lay greater emphasis on excludability as property's key characteristic.

[39] Richard Epstein, 'Bundle-of-Rights Theory as a Bulwark against Statist Conceptions of Private Property' (2011) 8(3) *Econ Journal Watch* 223 at 225.

[40] Schorr (n 8) 108.

[41] Banner (n 15) ch. 3.

[42] Barbara Fried, *The Progressive Assault on Laissez-Faire: Robert Lee Hale and the First Law and Economics Movement* (Harvard University Press 1998) 52–3. Wesley Hohfeld, 'Some Fundamental Legal Conceptions as Applied in Judicial Reasoning' (1913) 23 *Yale Law Journal* 16; 'Fundamental Judicial Conceptions as Applied in Judicial Reasoning' (1917) 26 *Yale Law Journal* 710.

[43] More precisely, property clearly does not *only* describe a relationship between a person and a *tangible* thing. Most of those who defend the idea that 'property relations all involve a juridical relation between a person or group and a "thing"', extending the meaning of 'thing' to

For some property theorists, then, the effect of the rise and proliferation of these new intangible property forms – shares, bonds, intellectual property and so on – and of the resulting emergence of 'bundle of rights' and social relation conceptions of property has been far more radical than the mere undermining of boundaries between property and obligation. For Thomas Grey, for example, it has led not only to the erosion of the view of property as (tangible) thing-ownership, but to the 'disintegration of property' as a concept with an identifiable and stable essence. This disintegration, Grey argues, was 'not a result of attacks on capitalism by socialists' but the product of 'a process internal to the development of capitalism itself'.[44] In similar vein, Kevin Gray has argued that, on close analysis, 'the concept of "property" vanishes into thin air'. It may appear to be an 'objective reality which embodies our intuitions and needs', but in reality it is a 'gross [and] systematic deception', an 'illusion', a 'fraud, a concept 'of curiously limited content', 'a conceptual mirage', which on closer analysis 'dissolves into a formless void'. 'Perhaps more accurately than any other legal notion', Gray writes, property 'deserve[s] the Benthamite epithet, "rhetorical nonsense – nonsense upon stilts"'. This leads him to the view that 'Proudhon got it wrong. Property is not theft – it is fraud'. It 'does not really exist: it is mere illusion'.[45]

4. THE CONTESTED NATURE OF PROPERTY RIGHTS

The historically changing nature of property and property rights not only highlights their legally and socially constructed nature and their lack of an essence which transcends historical specificities, but also helps us to understand Blackstone's anxieties.[46] So too does the context in which he was writing. The eighteenth century was marked by fierce class struggles over property rights, particularly in land. At the beginning of the sixteenth century, a large proportion of English farming was undertaken by farmers working within a complex system of open fields and common rights. Two centuries later, much of this land still remained commonly held and in many parts of the country it was still the case that 'no one landowner enjoyed exclusive rights to the use of particular tracts of land'. Rather, numerous people enjoyed rights, recognised in custom and law, to use land for certain purposes.[47] These use rights were critical to the livelihoods of many people, enabling self-sufficiency or partial self-sufficiency and reducing dependence on wage labour and market-purchased goods.

At this time, then, property and property rights in land were embedded not only in customary practices but in a complex and hierarchical social whole. The conception of property which resulted found expression in Blackstone's detailed exposition of the law, where he described, often in painstaking detail, property rights that were not only

---

include reified intangibles: see, for example, Tony Honore, 'Property and Ownership: Marginal Comments', in Timothy Endicott et al (eds), *Properties of Law: Essays in Honour of Jim Harris* (Oxford University Press 2006) 129 at 131.

[44] Grey (n 1) 74.
[45] Kevin Gray, 'Property in Thin Air' (1991) 50 *Cambridge Law Journal* 252 at 252, 305–6.
[46] See Rose (n 7).
[47] Robert Malcolmson, *Life and Labour in England, 1700–80* (Hutchinson 1981) 24–5.

fragmented and divided, but bound up in intricate and visible social relations between people occupying different places in a complex, hierarchically organised and interconnected social whole. Property carried public responsibilities; it was bound up in hierarchical webs of mutual social and political obligation.[48]

Beginning in the fifteenth and sixteenth centuries, however, social relations in rural England began gradually to be transformed. Enclosures saw previously commonly held land converted into private property: between 1760 and 1780 alone, Parliament passed 700 enclosure acts.[49] At the same time, hard-won customary rights to use 'private' land in particular ways (to graze, glean, gather firewood and turves, and so on) were extinguished, turning land into pure private property. Activities which had previously involved the legitimate exercise of rights were criminalised and land increasingly became less subject to regulation by custom and the community. The effect was to undermine the self-sufficiency of many members of the labouring class, rendering them dependent on wage labour and on markets. These processes frequently involved violent expropriation.[50]

The gradual emergence of these increasingly market-based, capitalist social relations underpinned the emergence of a new conception of property. Enclosure made possible the development of an idealised conception of property in land in terms of 'sole and despotic dominion' and 'total exclusion'. Under this new conception, property and property rights in 'things' (like land) were, ideally, absolute and also fundamentally private and individual in nature. The ideal was never realised in reality because, notwithstanding the elimination of many of the use rights described by Blackstone, less than absolute private property rights in land persisted. They still do today, though not because of old-style use rights, but because of the restrictions placed on landowners by planning laws, environmental laws and the like. But the idealised conception became, and remains, a powerfully suggestive trope which still shapes thinking about property.

Under this new idealised conception, property rights described a relationship between a person and a 'thing' rather than describing complex social relations between (hierarchically organised) people. Property increasingly implied a domain of 'complete mastery, complete self-direction, and complete protection from the whims of others' – a domain in which there was no need to have regard to others in respect of the things you owned.[51] In short, it was a conception of property as pure thing-ownership, of property and property rights relieved of social obligation and of their social–relational aspects. It was a conception of property which helped to constitute and reflected the emergence of an increasingly liberal, market-based, capitalist society, composed, at least in theory, of formally equal, solitary, autonomous individual private property owners engaging in acts of exchange but owing one another, in principle, nothing. It

---

[48] On recognition by the wealthy that they were dependent on labour of the poor, and the idea that poverty was socially necessary, see Malcolmson ibid 12–17.

[49] Hannibal Travis, 'Pirates of the Information Infrastructure: Blackstonian Copyright and the First Amendment' (2000) 15 *Berkeley Technology Law Journal* 777 at 789.

[50] See E.P. Thompson's account of the Black Act 1723: *Whigs and Hunters* (Allen Lane 1975).

[51] Rose (n 7) 604. There were, of course, restraints on the use of property, but as Thomas Grey says, these restraints on the free use of one's property were, and still are, 'conceived as departures from an ideal conception of full ownership': Grey (n 1) 69.

was a society in which private property and the invisible hand of Adam Smith's market was replacing civic virtue and obligation as the guarantor of the public good.

Blackstone was, then, living through an era in which property and property rights were both being created (increasingly absolute private property rights in land, debts, intellectual property) and destroyed (commons, use rights over land), and in which conceptions of property were changing. In these circumstances, it was difficult to deny the socially constructed, contingent, and contested nature of property and property rights. This was manifested in Blackstone's reluctance to rest his case for specifically *private* property on natural rights arguments, notwithstanding the tendency of the major English theorists of property, Hobbes and Locke, to do so. Despite occasional rhetorical flourishes suggesting otherwise, Blackstone recognised that, 'accurately and strictly speaking', there was 'no foundation in nature or in natural law' for many property rights; while private property was 'probably founded in nature', he conceded, many existing 'modifications' of it were 'entirely derived from society' and rooted in positive law.[52]

It was for this reason that Blackstone felt it necessary to 'examine more deeply the rudiments and grounds of these positive constitutions of society'[53] and to offer utilitarian, consequentialist explanations and justifications for the emergence and extension of private property rights, particularly in land. The creation of private property rights, he argued, not only promoted 'peace and security', but also encouraged the more intensive and productive exploitation of land as a resource. In other words, it furthered agricultural 'improvement'.[54] What we find in Blackstone, therefore, is a mix of rather hesitant natural rights-inspired rhetoric and utilitarian arguments – what one commentator calls a 'charmed convergence of scared rights and utilitarian progress'. He 'weaves together natural rights and utilitarian rhetoric into a seamless argument for enclosure and against the continued exercise by the peasantry of their rights in the commons'.[55] Ideas of civic humanism are 'promiscuously intermingle[d]' with ideas about property as 'absolute individual right, the legally guaranteed security of private possession, disposition, and alienation required for individual happiness, self-government, political stability, and economic improvement'.[56] Blackstone urged steady pursuit of 'that wise and orderly maxim, of assigning to every thing capable of ownership a legal and determinate owner'.[57]

Little has changed. In recent decades, it is precisely consequentialist arguments of this sort that have been deployed in support of neoliberal ideas about economic development (the 'Washington consensus') and the creation of new private property rights through the privatisation of productive resources and activities – processes which often entail dispossessions and enclosures of one kind or another. Privatisation, it is argued, not only creates incentives for people to work hard and for producers to

---

[52] Blackstone (n 2) 2; Blackstone (n 5) 134–5. See also Albert Alschuler, 'Rediscovering Blackstone' (1996) 145 *University of Pennsylvania Law Review* 1 at 29.

[53] Blackstone (n 5) chapter 1.

[54] In this respect, Blackstone was echoing the work of Hobbes and especially Locke, who also deployed the idea of improvement.

[55] Travis (n 49) 784, 798.

[56] Gordon (n 4) 95.

[57] Blackstone (n 5) ch. 1.

innovate but also facilitates the operation of the market mechanisms which ensure that resources are allocated efficiently so that growth and social welfare are maximised. In property scholarship, this argument underpins the recent attempts, associated with people like Thomas Merrill and Henry Smith, to revitalise the thing-ownership idea of property by conceptualising it in terms of the right to exclude others and justifying it in terms of exclusion's economic efficiency.[58]

There are other noteworthy similarities between Blackstone's arguments and those of contemporary neoliberals. Underpinning Blackstone's analysis of the rise of private property is a 'staged' account of historical and social development drawn from enlightenment thinkers like Hume and Smith, for whom history was characterised by various social stages, culminating in 'commercial society' (or capitalism). According to Blackstone, 'in the beginning of the world' God made all things 'the general property of all'. Initially, 'these general notions of property' were 'sufficient to answer all the purposes of mankind'. However, as mankind increased in 'number, craft and ambition', new conceptions of property were required and ideas of private property began to emerge, first in relation to 'houses and home-stalls' and 'movables of every kind', and later in relation to key productive resources such as land. 'Had not ... a separate property in lands, as well as movables, been vested in some individuals', human progress would have been impeded. 'Necessity', Blackstone concluded, 'begat property'.[59] Again, there are similarities between these kinds of arguments and economically determinist arguments suggesting that liberal capitalism represents 'the end of history' and that 'there is no alternative' to a social order based predominantly on private property and markets.[60] Economic determinism of this sort has also been a prominent feature of certain versions of Marxism, the difference being, of course, that communism, rather than liberal capitalism, is seen as representing 'the end of history'. One of the dangers of determinisms of this sort is that the belief that history (or law and economics 'efficiency') is on your side can be, and is, used to justify changes involving forced dispossessions, rights reallocations and hardships in the alleged service of the longer term social good.[61]

---

[58] Thomas Merrill & Henry Smith, *Property: Principles and Policies* (Foundation Press 2007): 'Property at its core entails the right to exclude others from some discrete thing', at v.

[59] Blackstone (n 2) 1–6. 'Property' here clearly meant private property.

[60] Francis Fukuyama, *The End of History and the Last Man* (Free Press 1992).

[61] A striking example of this is provided by the mindset of Fabrice Tourre, a Goldman Sachs trader responsible for inventing one of the instruments involved in the great financial crash. In private emails he confessed (to his girlfriend) that he didn't understand all the implications of the 'monstrosities' (the 'complex, highly leveraged, exotic trades') he had created. He knew the 'poor little subprime borrowers [wouldn't] last long' but continued to sell bonds 'to widows and orphans'. He didn't 'fee[l] too guilty about this', though, because, after all, 'the real purpose of [the] job is to make capital markets more efficient': see Cedric Durand, *Fictitious Capital* (Verso 2017) 12.

5. PROFITING FROM 'THE EFFORTS OF OTHERS': PROPERTY AS POWER

Conflicts and struggles over property are, of course, to be expected because property rights confer power on their holders. Much of this power derives from the legal right of property owners to *exclude* others from resources, both tangible (personal possessions and productive resources) and intangible (intellectual property). It is this – Carol Rose's 'exclusivity axiom' – that gives the right(s) in the property bundle exchange (market) value. As Kevin Gray says, property 'is a power-relation constituted by legally sanctioned control over access to the benefits of excludable resources'. From this perspective, property is not so much a 'thing' or a resource but 'a legally endorsed concentration of power over things and resources'; it is 'not a thing but a power-relationship'. Moreover, it is a power relationship which is, by definition, publicly constituted and enforced. As Gray says, the state plays a key role in constituting and defining property and property rights, and in determining the protections given to them. All property, including private property, thus has 'a public law character'; 'it is never truly private'.[62] It is, as Robert Hale pointed out, a form of delegated *private* government.[63] More fully, private property is a state-constituted and state-enforced form of private power which appears to be separate from the state.[64]

In this context, the distinction between property rights in personal possessions and property rights in productive resources is critically important. Put simply, property rights in the means of production, in particular, and property rights derived from them (like corporate shares) enable their holders, in different and varied ways, to appropriate part of the product of the labour of others. Indeed, this has been implicitly recognised by the United States Supreme Court. In *Securities and Exchange Commission v W.J. Howey Co.*, the Supreme Court had to decide whether a particular investment was within the definition of 'security' for the purposes of federal securities law. The test, Justice Murphy held, writing the majority opinion, was 'whether the scheme involves an investment of money in a common enterprise with profits to come *solely from the efforts of others*'.[65]

In a range of different ways, property and property rights in the means of production (or derived from them, like shares and corporate bonds) enable their holders to benefit

---

[62] Gray (n 45) 252, 294–5, 299.
[63] Robert Hale, 'Law-Making by Unofficial Minorities' (1920) 20 *Columbia Law Review* 451 at 453.
[64] On this, see Ellen Meiksins Wood, *Liberty and Property* (Verso, 2012).
[65] 328 U.S. 293 (1946), emphasis added. Since *Howey*, discussion has centred not so much on the correctness of the test but on the specific meaning of one or other of its component parts. Since then, the '*Howey* test', as it has come to be known, has been consistently affirmed, although the requirement that the profits come 'solely' from the efforts of others has been relaxed. In *United Housing Foundation Inc. v Forman*, for example, the Supreme Court argued that 'the essential attributes that run through all the Court's decisions defining a security ... is the presence of an investment in a common venture premised on a reasonable expectation of profits to be derived from the entrepreneurial or managerial efforts of others': 421 U.S. 837 (1975) at 852, per Powell J. See Miriam Albert, 'The *Howey* Test Turns 64' (2011) 2 *William & Mary Business Law Review* 1.

'from the efforts of others'. In Blackstone's day, for example, enclosures enhanced the rights and power of landowners, while simultaneously reducing the rights and power of many labouring people. Denied access to land and thus to a crucial means of subsistence, the latter were increasingly compelled to sell their labour for a wage to earn a living. Henceforth, landowners were not only able to appropriate part of the product of the 'efforts of others' in money form through the levying of rents, but were better placed (as were all owners of the means of production) to appropriate part of the product of the efforts of the growing number of propertyless wage labourers through employment contracts. Indeed, this was one of the key tenets of John Locke's theory that property originates in labour. Under Locke's theory, the labour which gave a 'master' a right to property included the labour of his 'servants'. In master–servant relationships, which for Locke encompassed what we would now call wage labour, some created wealth for others by working for them.[66]

Over time, of course, with industrialisation and technological advance, the nature of the means of production has changed, as, with the rise of the large joint stock corporation and institutional investment, have forms of ownership. Land, while still important, is now only one of many key productive resources. More and more of these resources have come to be directly owned by large corporations, or indirectly controlled by them through the power they wield over the smaller firms in their supply chains. In law, the property of the corporation, tangible and intangible, is owned not by the corporation's shareholders but by the corporations as separate legal entities. Corporate shareholders, the great majority of whom are pure *rentier* investors (money capitalists), do not have any direct proprietary interest in the corporate assets. Rather, they own shares, quite separate pieces of *financial* property – property in the form of a right to receive revenues (dividends) drawn from the corporation's productive activities. Like bondholders, they receive their revenues in the form, if not at the level, of interest.[67] The returns accruing to shares, like the returns accruing to the owners of other forms of financial property, appear to derive from money's magical ability to grow; from its seeming ability to generate more money by itself.[68] But, in reality, as the court in *Howey* recognised, money is not autonomously productive: the returns that accrue to financial property (to investments of money) inevitably derive from 'the efforts of others'. They entail transfers, in money form, of part of the product of one person's labour to another.

In recent decades, the volume and importance of intangible financial property has grown. Since the 1980s, there has been a steady and continuous rise in levels of debt – both private (households, corporations) and public (states) – and a corresponding growth in the volume of property (securities) based in some way on it. Alongside this, there has emerged a vast array of exotic contract-based financial instruments, such as derivatives, whose precise legal nature and status remains rather opaque. The English courts have recognised the commercial value of these instruments, and, in that sense, implicitly recognised that they have, like some other choses in action, some of the key

---

[66] On Locke, see Ellen Meiksins Wood & Neal Wood, *A Trumpet of Sedition* (Pluto 1997).
[67] The returns on bonds are usually fixed in advance; those on shares vary with profitability.
[68] 'It becomes a property of money to generate value and yield interest, much as it is an attribute of pear-trees to bear pears.' Marx, *Capital* Vol 3 (Lawrence and Wishart 1973) 392.

qualities of 'property'. However, the courts find it hard not to see derivatives, even when there is a genuine hedging element, as, ultimately, contracts involving speculation for profit. Others have gone further, calling them 'naked bets' akin to gaming contracts.[69] The rapid growth of speculative financial instruments of this sort is one of the defining features of contemporary neoliberal capitalism and of what has been called 'financialisation'.

So too is the growth of debt. Unlike in Blackstone's time, when wealth was closely tied to property rights in tangible things (and especially in land), much of the wealth of those at the top of the *Sunday Times* Rich List now takes the form of ownership of intangible financial property – of revenue rights such as shares and bonds. Indeed, as Thomas Piketty and others have shown, financial property is the form of wealth that is most heavily concentrated among those at the very top of the wealth pyramid.[70] Crucially, in the past four decades, the erosion of the constraints imposed on finance by the postwar settlement (the dismantling of Bretton Woods), the gradual liberalisation of financial flows, the enhancement of investor protections (the 'new constitutionalism') and the declining power of labour have seen a dramatic increase in the rights and power of these (financial) property-owning, *rentier* elites.[71] Put simply, their bundles of rights – their property rights – have been significantly enhanced, and this, together with the declining legal rights and economic power of labour, has had major (and predictable) distributional consequences, underpinning the sharp increases in inequality.

The financial element of the property owned by members of the Rich List also helps us to understand the often rapid shifts, upwards and downwards, in their wealth. Financial property is property in the form of a right to receive a revenue *in the future*. Much of the property of those at the top of the Rich List thus takes the form of the right to draw on wealth that has yet to be produced; they possess multiple claims on the future 'efforts of others'. As this suggests, the value of financial property is determined not by the value of any particular tangible object, but by *expectations* about future returns. Assessing the value of financial property is, therefore, inherently speculative. And, as we have seen only too clearly in recent years, expectations can be wrong – either absurdly overoptimistic (as with bubbles) and/or fraudulently manipulated (Enron, Carillion and countless others). As a result, the value of financial property can rapidly rise and equally rapidly fall. As Robert Gordon observes, writing about the eighteenth century, the 'intangible and speculative nature of the new contract property deprived it of any fixity or solidity'. The value of these contractual revenue rights was 'dependent on ... economic conditions, on the vagaries of public policy, on the surface

---

[69] Lynn Stout, 'Uncertainty, Dangerous Optimism and Speculations' (2012) 97 *Cornell Law Review* 1177. One of the things that militates against seeing them as 'property' is the uncertainty about their value.

[70] See Thomas Piketty, *Capital in the Twenty-First Century* (Belknap 2014); Paddy Ireland, 'The Corporation and the New Aristocracy of Finance', in Robe, Lyon-Caen & Vernac (eds), *Multinationals and the Constitutionalization of the World-Power System* (Routledge 2016) 53 at 85–7.

[71] Their power was, of course, exemplified after the crash, when bailing out the banks and preserving the financial system (and financial property) more generally was given the highest priority, whatever the consequences – one of which was austerity.

tension of speculative bubbles, and on sudden shifts in the business cycle'.[72] This is especially true of corporate shares, the value of which can move up and down with astonishing rapidity. In many cases, it is fluctuations in the value of the intangible financial assets of the Rich List, and in particular in the value of their corporate shareholdings, that underlie their changing fortunes.

A further manifestation of the ever greater importance of these property forms in today's highly financialised capitalism, and of the growing economic and political power of the elites that own such a large proportion of this form of property, is the increasing policy prioritisation of 'investor protection' over other social goals and interests. Because its value is not derived from tangible objects but is dependent on future production, financial property is unusually vulnerable. Protecting it involves exerting as much control as possible over the future to ensure that the income streams continue to flow. This explains the rise of the 'new constitutionalism', whereby the property interests of investors have been given quasi-constitutional protections from state actions, such as enhanced environmental or labour standards, that might diminish the size of the future revenue streams or, worse still, increase the risk of nonpayment. One of the goals of the new constitutionalism is to try to protect investors and their property from states and democracy.[73]

Financial property is interesting and instructive in other ways too, because its social–relational dimensions are sometimes closer to the surface. Debt, after all, involves one person owing another person something. Indeed, it was precisely because of its character as a personal obligation that, historically, there was reluctance to characterise debts as property. The social content of different forms of debt-based financial property varies, however, highlighting the need for specific, contextual analysis to properly grasp their underlying social nature. Thus, household debt often has a certain resemblance to old-fashioned usury and involves a preemption of future income from labour. Corporate debt, on the other hand, has a different character: here interest is drawn directly from productive activities and surpluses (corporate profits). Public debt, which has burgeoned in the years since the great financial crash, is different again. With states finding it increasingly difficult to raise from tax-avoiding multinational corporations and the globally mobile super-rich the taxes they need to maintain public services, they have to borrow money – and to borrow it from the very people who are avoiding taxes. In the United States, the share of government bonds held by the richest 1 per cent had risen to 40 per cent by 2010.[74] In what amounts to a major transfer of income, this elite receives interest payments funded out of the taxes levied on the general population – by 'the efforts of others'.[75]

---

[72] Gordon (n 4) 99.
[73] David Schneiderman, *Constitutionalizing Economic Globalization* (Cambridge University Press 2008).
[74] Durand (n 61) 89.
[75] See Wolfgang Streeck, *Buying Time* (Verso 2014).

6. NEOLIBERALISM AND THE SECOND ENCLOSURE MOVEMENT

Nor is the conversion of key productive resources into private property a purely historical phenomenon. Land enclosures continue to occur around the world, encompassing straightforward uncompensated fencing of land as well as so-called land grabs involving largescale land acquisitions by corporations, states and individuals. In Britain the biggest privatisation has been the privatisation of public land. Brett Christophers calculates that since the advent of Margaret Thatcher's government an eyewatering two million hectares of public land, meaning land held by local and central government, has been privatised – around 10 per cent of the entire British land mass.[76] This important dimension of privatisation has gone largely unnoticed, hidden behind the higher profile privatisations of public utilities and services.

In similar vein, recent decades have seen fierce struggles over intellectual property. Intellectual property rights enable their holders to prevent others from using the products of the mind – ideas, inventions, knowledge, artistic creations and so on – without their consent, meaning, in most cases, without the payment of money. Because of the analogies with the land enclosure movement in England, some have dubbed the extension of intellectual property rights and the erosion of the limits on them a 'second enclosure movement'. This movement, headed by large corporations, involves 'an expansion of property rights over the intangible commons, the world of the public domain, the world of expression and invention'. As James Boyle points out, the second enclosure movement has also 'quite frequently … involved introducing property rights over subject matter – such as unoriginal compilations of facts, ideas about doing business, or gene sequences – that were previously [thought] to be outside the property system' because they were considered either uncommodifiable or part of the commons.[77] Once again, the creation of intellectual property rights, with their right to exclude, enables their corporate holders to extract revenues – such as licence payments – and once again, indirectly, to benefit from the 'efforts of others'. Corporations have developed a formidable legal arsenal to establish, extend and protect their intellectual rights and to prevent the free use of resources which are not depleted by this use. Corporate intellectual property rights also, of course, render the resources less often subject to collective community regulation.

In 1991, Kevin Gray argued that 'the role of property is not simply to guarantee the private ownership of certain goods, but also to stop others more powerful than ourselves from propertising all the goods of life and thereby precluding general access'.[78] Since then, new privatisations have seen the range of resources over which

---

[76] Brett Christophers, *The New Enclosure: The Appropriation of Public Land in Neoliberal Britain* (Verso 2018). The selloffs have been greatest under Tory and Tory-led administrations, but they did not stop under Blair's New Labour: the NHS estate, in particular, was ravaged during his administration.

[77] James Boyle, 'Enclosing the Genome: What the Squabbles over Genetic Patents Could Teach Us', in Herman Tavani (ed.), *Ethics, Computing and Genomics* (Jones & Bartlett 2005) 255.

[78] Gray (n 45) 305.

private property rights are claimed venture into new territory. For Gray, 'this is the source of both the greatest challenge and the greatest danger confronting the law of property in the twenty-first century'. As he observes, the limits on property are 'fixed, not by the "thinglikeness" of particular resources but by the physical, legal and moral criteria of excludability. By lending the support of the state to the assertion of control over access to the benefits of particular resources, legislatures and courts have it in their power to create "property"'[79] and, in so doing, to exclude some and empower others. Because of the power conferred by property rights, particularly property rights in key productive resources, privatisation has had significant distributional consequences, as the work of Thomas Piketty, Tony Atkinson and others has shown. As Charles Reich observed in the early 1990s, 'new property has been used more and more openly as a way for one group to enrich itself at the expense of others … [it] is a powerful way to redistribute wealth, often upward'.[80]

The arguments made in support of these extensions of private property echo those made in Blackstone's time. The conversion of land into private property, it is argued, encourages economic development and investment. It also, the argument runs, prevents the overuse of resources associated with the so-called tragedy of the commons. More generally, it is claimed that extending the reach of private property also extends the reach of market mechanisms and the 'efficiency' benefits they bring. In similar vein, the extension and expansion of intellectual property rights is also commonly justified in terms of creating incentives for investment, research and the development of new socially beneficial technologies. There is no doubt that constructing property rights structures that create appropriate incentives is socially important. There is, however, considerable evidence that in many contexts the commodification of knowledge through patents inhibits both investment and innovation.[81] Moreover, as Mariana Mazzucato has noted, while innovation does often depend on bold entrepreneurship, the entity which frequently takes the boldest risks is the state, not the private sector.[82] Put bluntly, the extension of intellectual property rights has often been the product not of legitimate attempts to maintain much needed incentives but of the political power of vested corporate interests.

7. THE IDEOLOGICAL ATTRACTIONS OF PROPERTY AS THING-OWNERSHIP

Despite its seeming conceptual inadequacies, recent years have seen some academic lawyers attempt to revive the notion that the concept of property is inextricably linked

---

[79] Gray (n 45) 299.
[80] Charles Reich, 'The New Property after 25 Years', 24 *University of San Francisco Law Review* (1989–90) 223 at 224.
[81] See, for example, Ugo Pagano, 'The Crisis of Intellectual Monopoly Capitalism' (2014) 38 *Cambridge Journal of Economics* 1409.
[82] Mariana Mazzucato, *The Entrepreneurial State* (Anthem 2013).

to 'things'.[83] This has been motivated in part by their desire to find a 'definable essence' to property which transcends time and place,[84] and by their fear that if the link between property and 'things' is dissolved, the very concept of property threatens to 'disintegrate' or to 'vanish into thin air'. The revival of the thing-ownership conception of property can be seen, then, at least in part, as part of a search for some kind of transhistorical, universal essence to property – a search for something that identifies what is distinctive about property and property rights, and that gives property greater coherence as a distinctive legal category.

In this context, the belief that property and property rights are in some way 'special' is important. Although, as Kevin Gray says, conceptually property is 'not all it is cracked up to be',[85] this does not mean that acquiring 'property' status for rights is not economically and politically significant. As John Austin observed in his discussion of the different meanings of 'property', 'in [its] largest possible meaning', that 'very ambiguous word … means legal rights or faculties of any kind … legal rights in the largest sense'.[86] Indeed, the lack of clarity about the essential distinction between property rights and rights in general leads Kevin Gray to suggest that the idea that property is a bundle of rights rather than a thing does not resolve the conceptual problems thrown up by the 'unattainable quality inherent in the notion of private property'. Even the bundle of rights approach doesn't tell us what exactly distinguishes property rights from other (bundles of) rights. 'Wherein lies the "property" character of the rights in the bundle?', Gray asks: 'What constitutes the "propertiness" of property'?[87]

What is clear is that having rights labelled *property* rights and perceived in terms of thing-ownership brings benefits to their holders. In our society property rights – and *private* property rights, in particular – are widely regarded and experienced as 'special', as 'keystone rights', and, as such, as deserving greater, and often constitutional, protection.[88] As Gray says, property may be 'a conceptual mirage', but it still 'exerts a powerful … moral leverage'. The notions of *meum* and *teum* have 'deep resonance' and while claims based on them 'do not protect rights of any sacrosanct or a priori nature', they add 'with varying degrees of sophistication … moral legitimacy to the assertion of self-interest in the beneficial control of valued resources'.[89]

---

[83] See, for example, Merrill & Smith (n 58); Henry Smith, 'Property Is Not Just a Bundle of Rights' (2011) 8 Econ Journal Watch 279.

[84] Epstein (n 39) 223. In the words of Barry Hoffmaster, 'a strategy that begins by defining the essence of property and then applies this definition to the facts … is fallacious because if there any essentialist concepts at all, property is not one of them': 'Between the Sacred and the Profane: Bodies, Property, and Patents in the Moore Case' (1992) 7 *Intellectual Property Journal* 115 at 130.

[85] Gray (n 45) 303.

[86] Austin (n 35) 819–20.

[87] Gray (n 45) 252, 259. Gray emphasises the criterion of 'excludability' as 'the core' of 'property'; others emphasise the transferability of the rights bundles and their potential market value; still others emphasise both: Worthington (n 32) ch. 3.

[88] Carol Rose, 'Property as the Keystone Rights?' (1996) 71 *Notre Dame Law Review* 329; Laura Underkuffler, 'Property: A Special Right' (1996) 71 *Notre Dame Law Review* 1033.

[89] Gray (n 45) 305–7.

There are various reasons for this. First, in our society, private property, particularly in productive resources, is seen as a prerequisite for the operation of the free market and the material benefits that come from its 'invisible hand' and alleged ability to allocate resources 'efficiently'. Private property, the argument runs, creates the incentives and security that underpin wealth creation and prosperity at both the personal and social levels, hence the desirability of continued privatisation. Private property is also seen as the political and social basis for individual independence, autonomy and self-governance, and as central to civility, social stability and democracy. Private property, particularly in personal possessions, is thus regarded as an expression of personality, individuality, autonomy and liberty; human beings 'naturally' come to regard some objects as, in some way, important extensions of themselves.[90]

It is for these reasons that private property rights have tended to be able to command (and demand) special legal protection, both from other individuals and from the state. Unlike many other rights which are seen as being within the gift of the state and thus capable of being withdrawn without compensation, property rights tend to be seen as 'special' – as rights that should not be taken away or infringed without due process and the payment of appropriate compensation.[91] It was the special nature of property rights that in the 1960s led Charles Reich to try to extend the category of 'property' to welfare entitlements. Traditionally, the latter had been regarded as politically determined entitlements – akin to charity – which could be withdrawn at any time by the state without compensation. Aware of the special procedural and substantive protections that property rights could command, Reich sought to recharacterise welfare entitlements as 'new property' – and, as such, as 'things' that could not easily be taken away.[92] In a similar vein, though coming from a very different direction, Richard Epstein has sought to revive an older, nineteenth century use of the bundle of rights approach to extend the idea of 'takings' to get the special protections afforded property and property rights for every single stick in every particular property rights bundle.[93] This is especially significant in the context of intangible financial property forms, where changes in things such as government environmental and labour protection policies can impact on investment returns and the value of financial property. Under the 'new constitutionalism', it is possible to characterise such policies as 'regulatory takings' and violations of investors' property rights.

The renewed promotion of the thing-ownership conception of property is not, however, motivated only by conceptual concerns: it is also motivated by ideological considerations. The bundle of rights approach to property is seen as 'appeal[ing] especially to statists', by which is meant that by underlining the fact that property and

---

[90] Grey (n 1) 77.
[91] In the well-known US case of *Goldberg v Kelly* (397 U.S. 254, 1970), for example, the question was whether it was constitutional to terminate the welfare benefits of the those who already had them without something resembling an adversarial trial. The majority, adopting a framework derived from Charles Reich's idea of 'new property', in effect constitutionalised a judicial-like procedure for deciding these cases.
[92] Charles Reich, 'The New Property' (1964) 73 *Yale Law Journal* 733.
[93] See Epstein (n 39) 223. On this older use of the bundle of rights approach, see Banner (n 15) 45. It is clear that Epstein thinks that, at root, the bundle of rights view of property is potentially politically dangerous.

property rights are social/legal/political (state) constructs, it also underlines that property and property rights can be politically and legally reconstructed. 'When we deal with property rights', Epstein writes, 'the fear' that is generated by the bundle of rights conception 'is that the people who put the bundle together are public authorities'.[94] Similarly, Merrill and Smith object to what they see as the political agenda of the legal realists who promoted the bundle of rights approach, 'namely dethroning the sanctity of private property and the private ordering it enables in order to enhance levels of collective control and redistribution'.[95] As Grey says, 'the concept of property as thing-ownership serve[s] important ideological functions' in that it helps to legitimate both a liberal individualist view of human beings and capitalist social relations.[96]

The fear is that the bundle of rights conception of property threatens to lay uncomfortably bare the power and political/public dimensions of property, not least its *ad hoc* nature, undermining existing private property rights, particularly in productive resources, and endangering the status quo and a liberal individualist conception of property and society. Hence the desire to reestablish an essentialist – and, as these commentators see it, a more robust – view of (private) property able to resist what Epstein refers to as the 'shadowy collective presence' hovering over it.[97] Given the obviously public dimensions to the constitution and maintenance of the 'things' deemed 'property', however, the objections to 'statism' seem rather odd, an example of politics taking precedence over analytical depth and honesty. What would have happened to the intangible financial property of the wealthy if the state hadn't stepped in after the great financial crash?

8. CONCLUSION: PROPERTY AND SOCIAL RELATIONS

Property and property rights are not as straightforward as the common sense thing-ownership conception suggests. This is not to say that there aren't important senses in which property and property rights *are* about tangible things and need to be understood as such. On the contrary, it is essential to recognise this, not least because of the power that flows from possession of property rights over productive resources. But it is clear that property and property rights are not always about 'the external things of the world', but often about reified bundles of rights, not least revenue rights, with no direct connection to physical objects. It is, of course, tempting to simply extend the term 'thing' to these reified, intangible rights bundles. After all, as a result of being bought, sold, licensed, and so on, they have acquired thinglike qualities; they *appear* to be 'things'. Moreover, accepting their reified existence at face value makes it possible to maintain a conception of 'property' that distinguishes property rights from other rights:

---

[94] Epstein (n 39) 225.
[95] See Robert Ellickson, 'Two Cheers for the Bundle-of-Sticks Metaphor, Three Cheers for Merrill and Smith' (2011) 8(3) *Econ Journal Watch* 215 at 216.
[96] Grey (n 1) 73.
[97] Epstein (n 39) 226.

it seems to give property a definable essence. It also, of course, helps the bundles of rights concerned to secure the special status and treatment accorded to 'property'.

But this focus on appearances is inevitably superficial: thinking about property and property rights in terms only of a simple, extended idea of thing-ownership leaves us at the surface. It conceals as much as it reveals, and impedes rather than enriches our understanding of property and property rights. History shows that trying to conceptualise property and property rights, in the liberal manner, in abstraction from their particular social contexts – as though they have a static, universal essence – generates only a very partial and incomplete understanding of them. J.W. Harris hints at this when he says that 'all attempts in the history of theorizing about property to provide a univocal explanation of the concept of ownership, applicable within all societies and to all resources, have failed'.[98]

History reveals property and property rights to be contextually bound and deeply contested. What is needed, then, is an approach to property which focuses less on abstract enquiries into what property (universally) is and more on its historical and cultural specificities, on situated engagements with the way in which property and property rights have been, and are, constructed and embedded in particular societies and contexts; and which is sensitive to, and recognises, the political struggles surrounding them. Property and property rights, particularly in productive resources, are about power, and about power not only over things but over other people – over 'the efforts of others'.

In undertaking this contextualisation, it is also important to remember that property and property rights are about social relations in the widest sense; property and property rights in the means of production, in particular, are about power not only at an individual micro level, but at a wider societal macro level – at the level of the social formation (or, if you prefer, mode of production) as a whole. This is crucial if we are to begin to understand the role and nature of property in today's highly financialised capitalism. As Thomas Grey says, the disintegration of the thing-ownership conception of property was the result of processes internal to the development of capitalism. In a similar vein, the rise of new property forms and dramatic growth in financial property and financialisation are largely the products of processes internal to capitalism. Indeed, the specific ways in which property and property rights are constructed do much to shape these processes and the dynamics, logic and struggles that contribute to their own transformation.[99]

In the context of today's financialised capitalism, the thing-ownership conception of property, even when stretched to cover intangibles, can go but a little way to help us to understand contemporary property and property rights. At times its use is nakedly ideological, deployed to promote a person-thing understanding of property that suppresses its social–relational dimensions and any suggestion that property rights might carry social obligations. At other times, it seems nostalgic, harkening back to a world that passed long ago, if it ever existed. Either way, used alone, the thing-ownership conception of property conceals as much as it reveals. There are important senses in which property in contemporary capitalism is simultaneously a thing, a

---

[98] J.W. Harris, *Property and Justice* (Oxford University Press 1996) 5.
[99] See Ellen Meiksins Wood, *The Origin of Capitalism* (Verso 2002).

bundle of rights and a social relation. On the surface it appears as a thing; dig down and it emerges as a bundle of rights; dig deeper still, and its social–relational aspects come into focus. Get out your spades.

16. Ideology and argument construction in contract law

*Richard Michael Fischl**

1. INTRODUCTION

I've been invited to write about contract law and critical theory, a task that takes me back to my initial encounter with each in Duncan Kennedy's Contracts class a million years ago. Critical legal studies wasn't even a thing yet, and—at least to hear Grant Gilmore tell it—contract law hadn't been a thing for all that long either.[1] Kennedy was likewise new to the scene, up for tenure the year we had him. But the intersection in question was a central preoccupation of that extraordinary class and the focus as well of what was soon to emerge as one of the original critical legal studies, provoking several generations of work on ideology and argument construction in contract law and beyond.[2]

Much of that work has taken place in the law school classroom, where it all began for many of us. Indeed, the robust connection between pedagogy and legal theory was a staple of first generation cls scholarship,[3] and those who followed mentors into the legal academy continued the effort with great enthusiasm.[4] There is obviously a politics to foregrounding the classroom in one's scholarly work. Treating students as collaborators in the enterprise—taking their confusion or opposition seriously and recognizing their Emperor's New Clothes moments as potential sources of insight—reflects a

---

* Many thanks to Karl Klare for a generous and uncommonly insightful critique of an earlier draft; to the editors for including me in this important and engaging volume; and to Wolters Kluwer for graciously authorizing the use of considerable material from Richard Michael Fischl, Teaching Law as a Vocation: Local 1330, Promissory Estoppel, and the Critical Tradition in Labour Scholarship, 33 International Journal of Comparative Labour Law and Industrial Relations 145 (2017).

[1] Grant Gilmore, *Death of Contract* (1974).

[2] Duncan Kennedy, Form and Substance in Private Law Adjudication, 89 Harvard Law Review 1685 (1976).

[3] Classics of the genre include Karl Klare, Contracts Jurisprudence and the First-Year Casebook, 54 New York University Law Review 876 (1979); Duncan Kennedy, The Political Significance of the Structure of the Law School Curriculum, 14 Seton Hall Law Review 1 (1983); Jay M. Feinman, Critical Approaches to Contract Law, 30 UCLA Law Review 829 (1983); Mary Joe Frug, Re-Reading Contracts: A Feminist Analysis of a Contracts Casebook, 34 American University Law Review 1065 (1985).

[4] *See* James Boyle, The Anatomy of a Torts Class, 34 American University Law Review 1003 (1985); Jennifer Jaff, Frame-Shifting: An Empowering Methodology for Teaching and Learning Legal Reasoning, 36 Journal of Legal Education 249 (1986); Jeremy Paul, A Bedtime Story, 74 Virginia Law Review 915 (1988).

commitment to "eliminating illegitimate hierarchy" in the academic workplace (bet you haven't heard *that* expression in a while) and offers a critique by example of the use of the Socratic method to lord professorial expertise over charges who've been studying law for all of ten minutes. But it seems to me that the central link between pedagogy and theoretical work in the critical tradition lies in the relentless focus on the recurring rhetorical structures of legal justification, a "demystification" project that produced enormously effective classroom teaching tools and at the same time exposed to a broader academic and professional audience the revealing patterns of thought lurking in the nooks and crannies of legal reasoning.

I will offer an extended illustration of the demystification link here and will focus on promissory estoppel, a doctrine that receives sustained attention in the typical US Contracts class and has been the focus of a great deal of scholarship, critical and otherwise, for decades. Following this introduction, the chapter proceeds in two parts. In section 2, I introduce promissory estoppel in the same way I do in my classes, contrasting mainstream, legal realist, and critical "stories" about the history and role of the doctrine in American contract law. I warn my students—as I am warning readers here—that the contrasting accounts are to some extent caricatures, for surely no self-respecting legal academic would actually admit to being "mainstream," and I gather from what I read in the casebooks as well as from discussions with others teaching the course that most of us bring insights from a mix of realist, critical, and other schools of thought to our classroom work. But the point of proceeding in this fashion is to attempt to highlight the contributions of the critical tradition to pedagogy as well as legal theory, and in section 3 I'll bring those contributions to bear on a critical study of the *Local 1330* case, a storied challenge to the closing of a pair of aging steel plants in the industrial Midwest nearly four decades ago.

2. CONTRACTS STORIES

2.1 The Mainstream Account

The mainstream story of promissory estoppel goes something like this. In the bad old days, promises were unenforceable unless supported by consideration, and under the so-called bargain theory of consideration—developed in the latter part of the nineteenth century along with so many other heartless and cruel common law doctrines—a promise wasn't legally enforceable unless it was part of an exchange transaction. Thus, if you promised me a barrel of widgets and reneged on that promise, I had no legal recourse against you. Your promise was "gratuitous," and the point of bargain theory was to render such promises unenforceable. But if you promised me that same barrel of widgets in exchange for something I gave or committed to give in return—that is, for some sort of quid pro quo for the widgets—then your failure to make good on the promise was an actionable breach of contract.

Now most of the time the requirement of bargained-for consideration was not a problem, for in the commercial world the vast majority of transactions involve giving and getting on both sides: I work and for my efforts receive a salary and benefits; you sell a house and accept payment in return; and so on. But in some commercial contexts, and in many familial, social, and charitable settings, people make promises with no expectation of receiving anything in return—apart, perhaps, from the pleasure of giving itself. So what happens if I make a promise—say I promise my sister-in-law a safe place to raise her family after the untimely death of her spouse, to take a not quite random example—but extract no "price for the promise" in return?[5]

Far more often than not, what happens is that the promising party will make good on the commitment; fortunately for familial and other forms of social harmony, most people seem to keep most of their promises most of the time. And even if the promising party has second thoughts—where, for example, an ill-considered promise is made in a state of momentary exuberance or extreme grief—there may be no lasting problem if the second thoughts follow upon the first quickly enough.

But if the promising party reneges after the would-be beneficiary has pursued some costly course of action on the faith of the promise—say the grieving widow abandons her former home and moves her family many miles through dangerous terrain in order to take advantage of the promised place to live, only to find herself and her children out on the street a short while later—then the requirement of bargained-for consideration has bite, and the one who gets bitten is the widow or, more generally, the party seeking the law's assistance in holding the promising party to his word. The promise is gratuitous, the court would say; you gave nothing in return, so your mere reliance on the promise—no matter how much that reliance hurt—will not secure its enforcement.

In the mainstream account of American contract law, the requirement of bargained-for consideration was the "majority rule" in the late nineteenth century, seemingly just another example of the preference for commerce over caring during an era very much in the thrall of social Darwinism and laissez-faire. But in our enlightened modernity, along to the rescue came promissory estoppel, the knight in shining armor sprung thus from the First Restatement of Contracts: "A promise which the promisor should reasonably expect to induce action or forbearance of a definite and substantial character on the part of the promisee and which does induce such action or forbearance is binding if injustice can be avoided only by enforcement of the promise."[6] The notion of enforcing promises on the basis of reliance was of a piece with a broader movement toward the liberalization of contract law—as often as not in the service of widows, workers, and other vulnerable parties—and, during the ensuing half century, promissory estoppel smote the cold-hearted bargain theory in jurisdiction after jurisdiction, soon becoming a majority rule all of its own.

2.2 The Realist Account

The legal realist version of the promissory estoppel story is a little different. Instead of a knight in shining armor, we get Dorothy Gale from Kansas, and she's had the ruby slippers all along. And in place of the mainstream account of liberalizing progress, it's a story of conflict between black-letter judicial pronouncements and the law "on the ground." In this account, we focus on the debates over the First Restatement, when the

---

[5] Readers who've been subjected to a first-year Contracts course in the US will no doubt recognize the reference to the facts of Kirksey v. Kirksey, 8 Ala. 131 (1845).
[6] Restatement (First) of Contracts § 90 (1932).

drafters—led by Samuel Williston, aka Oz the Great and Powerful—were busy making the bargain theory of consideration the doctrinal centerpiece of their black letter masterwork. They were not only enshrining it as an invariant requirement for the enforcement of promises but also using it to rationalize a host of other hoary doctrines, including the rules governing "past" consideration (which infamously permitted a father to renege on a promise to pay for nursing care previously provided to his son by a good Samaritan[7]) as well as those governing midterm contractual modifications (which likewise infamously permitted a ship's captain to renege on a promised raise for sailors forced to work with assertedly unserviceable fishing nets[8]).

And then along came Arthur Corbin, in the role of Toto pulling back the curtain to expose the Wizard's humbug. As legend has it, Corbin announced to his fellow Restaters that he'd found hundreds of American decisions in which courts had enforced promises with no bargain in sight—an intervention made all the more impressive by the absence in those days of photocopy machines, let alone online research tools.[9] Some of the cases hailed from jurisdictions that had yet to adopt bargain theory and continued instead to embrace the antecedent English "benefit/detriment" test for consideration. Under that test, either a benefit to the promisor or a detriment to the promisee would do the trick,[10] and thus the widow's move or other reliance suffered on the faith of even a concededly gratuitous promise might well have secured legal protection by establishing consideration via the required detriment. In other cases Corbin brought to the debate, courts expanded longstanding legal doctrines in order to enforce gratuitous promises that induced detrimental reliance. Foremost among those was equitable estoppel, a device available then as well as now to protect a party's reliance on a misrepresentation of existing fact by "holding the perp to his lie"—preventing (or "estopping"), for example, a minor from pleading youth as a basis for avoiding contractual liability where he has misrepresented his age to a merchant. For some courts, it was a short leap from "holding the perp to his lie" to "holding the perp to his broken promise," when it was a promise of future conduct—rather than a misrepresentation of existing fact—that had induced reliance by its would-be beneficiary.[11]

Corbin's demonstration of a yawning gap between black-letter rules and "the law on the ground" was part of a larger realist project that called into question the extent to which judges actually do what they say they are doing when they decide cases. That project was perhaps exemplified most dramatically by Karl Llewellyn's iconic analysis of the "canons of construction," which presented a lengthy list of frequently encountered and utterly noncontroversial judicial pronouncements about how courts should

---

[7] Mills v. Wyman, 20 Mass. (3 Pick.) 207 (1825).
[8] Alaska Packers Ass'n v. Domenico, 117 F. 99 (9th Cir. 1902).
[9] The account offered here of the respective roles played by Corbin and Williston follows the narrative made famous in Gilmore, supra note 1, at 62–3. Subsequent scholarship has called aspects of Gilmore's narrative into question, but even those critiques credit Corbin's work with exposing the considerable gap between bargain theory and then-existing caselaw. *See* James Gordley, Enforcing Promises, 83 California Law Review 547, 565–8 (1995); E. Allan Farnsworth, Contracts Scholarship in the Age of the Anthology, 85 Michigan Law Review 1406, 1454–62 (1986–7).
[10] *See* Hamer v. Sidway, 27 N.E. 256 (N.Y. 1891).
[11] *See* Ricketts v. Scothorn, 77 N.W. 365 (Neb. 1898).

interpret statutes, each of them paired with a likewise frequently encountered and utterly noncontroversial trope that completely contradicted its twin. (Compare, for example, "statutes in derogation of the common law shall be strictly construed" with "remedial statutes shall be liberally construed"—bearing in mind that "remedial" statutes almost invariably "derogate" the very common law they are designed to "remedy."[12])

As the realist story continues, Williston and his fellow drafters—who were committed, after all, to "restating" the law of contracts—had no choice after Corbin's demonstration but to include a doctrinal mechanism for enforcing promises on the basis of reliance. As a result, in the First Restatement promissory estoppel took its place alongside consideration doctrine with no effort on the part of the drafters to explain how to square the bargain requirement with its seeming negation—at least where "injustice can be avoided only by enforcement of the promise"—a few short provisions later. So the lesson we're to draw from the realist account is this: Don't take all those confident black-letter pronouncements too seriously, for we should pay as much attention to what courts actually do as we do to what they say. And what they do turns out to be messy and complicated, often more responsive to facts, equities, and social policies than to solemn professions of doctrinal entailment. In other words, we should pay a lot more attention to the actions of the man behind the curtain and a bit less to his sound and fury.

2.3 The Critical Account

2.3.1 Form and substance in contract law

And what's the critical version of the story? In a nutshell, critical scholars found order in all that decisional messiness, contending that the man behind the curtain wasn't just randomly contradicting himself; rather, they argued, he was contradicting himself in recurring and hence revealing ways. And what the scholarship brought to the surface was the profoundly *ideological* dimension of legal analysis and argument. While most critical scholars would have wholeheartedly agreed with the realist insight that judicial professions of doctrinal entailment promise a bit more than they deliver, they nevertheless took the content of those professions seriously, mining the doctrinal material for hints, suggestions, and (with surprising frequency) forthright declarations of ideologically loaded assumptions and commitments. A principal critical lesson is thus that what courts say is very much a part of what courts do and that careful attention ought therefore be paid to the justificatory rhetoric of legal decisions as well as to decisional results.

Turning to promissory estoppel, Duncan Kennedy's seminal critical study unearthed a persistent conflict between individualism and altruism in American law—individualism characterized by an ethic of private autonomy and a legal system devoted to the facilitation of self-interested exchange versus altruism characterized by an ethic of solidarity and judges at the ready to protect the vulnerable and powerless.[13] On this account, the tension between bargain theory and promissory estoppel is neither a

---

[12] Karl Llewellyn, *The Common Law Tradition: Deciding Appeals* 521–35 (1960).
[13] Kennedy, supra note 2.

drafting anomaly nor a transitional stage in the steady march to enlightened liberalization, but instead merely an instance—albeit a telling and central instance—of a larger and abiding conflict. Thus, under bargain theory, private autonomy and self-interest prevail, and the reneging promisor needn't continue to provide the widow with a place to live since there's nothing in it for him. But under promissory estoppel, solidarity rules the roost, and we'll hold the cad to his word in order to protect the widow and family made vulnerable by reliance on his promise.

Focusing principally on contract law, Kennedy revealed this conflict at work in an extraordinary number of doctrinal contexts. But of even greater significance to our story was his further claim that there is a politics of legal form that corresponds to the politics of substantive conflict: a connection between individualism and a preference for governance via rigid rules (as in "a party is free to exit a contract without further obligation if his trading partner's performance deviates in any respect from the terms of the parties' agreement"), and a corresponding connection between altruism and a preference for flexible, fact-sensitive standards (as in "contractual exit isn't permitted once the trading partner has substantially performed"). Kennedy located the link between form and substance in the rhetorical conventions of legal contestation, noting for example the focus on self-reliance in the arguments for both rigid rules and individualist outcomes ("don't expect the state to rescue you from your own improvidence!") and the focus on sharing and sacrifice in the arguments for standards as well as altruist outcomes ("don't expect the state to permit you to enjoy a windfall at your trading partner's expense simply because her performance was imperfect in some minor respect!").

It is no coincidence, then, that bargain theory takes the form of a rule (a promise is binding if and only if there's a quid pro quo) and that promissory estoppel is the poster child for a flexible standard (a promise is binding if the promisor should "reasonably" expect reliance by the promisee and "injustice can be avoided only by its enforcement"). But the larger payoff is that the careful study of legal rhetoric—dismissed by many realists as the after the fact rationalization of results reached on unconscious or undisclosed grounds—could offer valuable insight into the role of ideological conflict in American law.

2.3.2 Taking argument seriously

And what were students to make of all this? My own experience—as a student of Kennedy and other first generation cls scholars—was that critical teaching marked a vast improvement on what was going on in most of our other law school classes. And by the mid-1970s that was decidedly not legal realism, the lessons of which were typically reduced to sound bites about the occasional role of policy in judicial decisions but otherwise ignored or dismissed with a glib reference to the contents of a judge's breakfast. Indeed, critical scholars revived and revitalized realist insights about the gap between the rhetoric of reasoning and decisional results, unearthing ideological contestation not only in legal doctrine but also in the analysis of facts, equities, and social policies that realists had offered in their effort to explain the law "on the ground."

For those of us who entered the legal academy during that heady time, exploring patterned conflict in every darkened corner of legal analysis became a principal frame for the use of theory in the classroom, a practice some of us continue to this day. We offer it not for its own sake nor in order to demonstrate our chops with fancy philosophical concepts and jargon—great fun though that may be—but instead as a tool of demystification, of unveiling the law's politics while at the same time recasting those otherwise seemingly random invocations of fact sensitivity, situational equities, and social policy as an integral part of the law rather than as the occasional handiwork of a rogue or dyspeptic judge.

2.3.2.1 Paired arguments In my own classes, for example, we explore the ways in which ideological conflict frames not only the choice of legal rules but also the application of rules in particular cases. To continue the widow's saga, let's say the governing jurisdiction has a robust body of case law embracing the use of promissory estoppel in situations involving unbargained-for reliance, so there's not much doubt that a court will apply promissory estoppel instead of bargain theory in the widow's case. But as any victim of the Socratic method will tell you, this doesn't mean a sure win for the widow, for the lawyers on each side still have plenty to argue about.

Thus, familiar conflicts will likely emerge over how to interpret the facts, with one side emphasizing the "four corners" of the brother-in-law's promise (he never said the widow could stay "forever") and the other emphasizing the widow's "reasonable expectations" (but the promising party is her deceased husband's brother whom she should surely be able to trust, and he's offered the widowed mother of his brother's children "a place to raise her family"); how to balance the equities, with one side emphasizing the point of view of the put-upon promisor (he's doing all the giving and getting nothing in return) and the other emphasizing the plight of the relying promisee (but the widow and her children moved many miles over difficult terrain on the faith of his promise, and they no longer have a home to return to if the eviction stands); and how to further sound social policy, with one side contending that promises should be narrowly construed lest folks be reluctant to make them and the other contending that promises should be broadly construed lest folks be reluctant to rely on them.

2.3.2.2 Nesting If I'm doing my job well, my students soon learn to recognize and even anticipate these and many other "paired arguments" on their own.[14] With the aid of some Socratic prodding, my students may also begin to discern the outlines of a larger pattern that frequently frames the deployment of the argument pairs they encounter: Conflict over the application of a legal rule often recapitulates the conflict attending the choice of that rule in the first place. To continue with the widow's case, bargain theory may have "lost" out as the governing rule of the jurisdiction in cases involving unbargained-for reliance, but it lives to fight another day as lawyers and judges contend over the application of promissory estoppel to particular facts. Thus, note that each of the "against the widow" arguments rehearsed in the previous

---

[14] Most of them eventually figure out that a book on legal reasoning and law exams co-authored and shamelessly promoted by their professor can be of considerable assistance in this endeavor. See Richard Michael Fischl and Jeremy Paul, *Getting to Maybe: How to Excel on Law School Exams* (1999), which builds on the cls "legal semiotics" work cited supra at notes 3 and 4.

paragraph emphasizes the threat to the brother-in-law's freedom and/or the absence of an exchange relation and thus draws on the individualistic underpinnings of bargain theory itself. Likewise, each of the "pro-widow" arguments highlights the vulnerability that results from her reliance on her brother-in-law's promise and thus draws on the solidaristic underpinnings of promissory estoppel. The fancy name for this pattern—in which seemingly settled arguments re-emerge again and again at other levels of analysis—is "nesting," a phenomenon that is as familiar in contemporary political stalemates as it is in American legal reasoning.

2.3.2.3 Framing But the ideological character of law doesn't stop there. A further insight of critical scholarship is that ideology not only organizes and permeates the arguments that lawyers and judges routinely deploy but also helps to shape the way legal decisionmakers think about and come to understand legal issues and disputes. Consider one more time the widow's case and yet another rhetorical pattern that is evident in the arguments posed on each side. Note that the arguments against the widow focus intensely on the brother-in-law's promise, carefully delimiting its precise terms and emphasizing the absence of anything sought in return. By contrast, the arguments in the widow's favor treat the promise as merely a starting point for analysis and focus more broadly on the context of the promise-making and on the events that follow.

In class, I describe these contrasting approaches as "the snapshot vs. the film," and it's easy to see how they might emerge from the competing world-views associated respectively with individualism and bargain theory (on the one hand) versus altruism and promissory estoppel (on the other). To someone in the thrall of the former, virtually everything a legal decisionmaker needs to know can be captured at the moment of promising—either something is sought in exchange for the promise or it's not, and at all events any restriction on a promisor's freedom is strictly limited by the precise terms of his freely made promise. To someone of the opposing bent, the analysis certainly takes the promise into account but treats it as simply one event occurring within a larger narrative of the promisee's susceptibility to the promisor's lure and the life decisions she proceeds to take on the faith of his assurances.

Of course, these competing approaches to the framing of facts can be deployed instrumentally. If you're a lawyer representing the brother-in-law—or a judge inclined to rule in his favor—you would be wise to emphasize "the snapshot" (since those are the facts that favor his case) rather than "the film" (since those facts tug the other way), and the reverse is naturally true of the widow's lawyer or a judge sympathetic to her cause. But the argument here is that these competing conceptions of contractual obligation can also influence and shape the way a dispute is understood by legal actors, operating as a powerful heuristic through which lawyers arguing a case—and judges deciding it—may come to decide what counts as a legally relevant fact and what feels like a compelling story.

2.3.2.4 Flipping One might assume from the discussion thus far that the critical take follows the mainstream and realist accounts in treating promissory estoppel as the "hero" and bargained-for consideration as the "villain," and that is indeed often the case: promissory estoppel has frequently come to the rescue of widows, workers, and other vulnerable parties left out in the cold by bargain theory. But in much the same way that "wins" at the choice of rule level can turn into "losses" during rule application, the choice of rule can itself have unintended consequences, and advocates should be careful what they wish for. If today consideration doctrine thwarts the effort of workers to modify their employment contracts to secure additional pay for unexpectedly difficult work,[15] tomorrow they might deploy the doctrine in their favor and resist contractual modifications by an employer seeking to eliminate previously promised job security.[16] And if today promissory estoppel might come to the aid of the widow Kirksey in her efforts to house her children, tomorrow it might be deployed in an effort to force her to give up a child she has brought to term.[17] We call this "flipping"—using a rule against its seemingly natural beneficiary—and lawyers who succeed in the maneuver are likely to enjoy the double entendre almost as much as the win.

2.3.2.5 Form and substance redux: individualism and formalism reloaded So how has the larger conflict between solidarity and self-regard fared in the intervening decades? The individualism Kennedy described in the mid-1970s was a chastened one, bloodied and even bowed a bit by the realist critique. Reluctant to proclaim the moral primacy of naked self-interest—a heavy lift in a culture venerating Mother Teresa as the paragon of virtue—its partisans hedged their bets by invoking the invisible hand ("selfishness in service of the public good") or defending individualism with "clenched teeth," acknowledging its moral deficiencies but contending that efforts to suppress it via the legal system would lead to greater evils still.[18]

Needless to say, contemporary individualism seems to have "gotten over" realism as well as apologetics, exuding a muscular moral confidence and worshiping at the neo-liberal altar of freedom of choice. (Workers of the world unite: we are all consumers now.) By contrast, altruism has been humbled by an extended encounter with law and economics, frequently reduced to the role of addressing market imperfections—instances of market access and information barriers, collective action problems, toxic externalities, transaction costs, and the like—in order to fend off a nigh hegemonic deregulatory agenda with a pitch for modest "win–win" interventions and "regulation lite."[19]

Against this backdrop, it's no surprise that promissory estoppel has been taken down a notch, with partisans of individualism proclaiming "the death of reliance" and the relegation of the doctrine to a market serving role.[20] To be sure, the celebration may be somewhat premature. As a distinguished defender of the older order demonstrated in a

---

[15] See Alaska Packers Ass'n v. Domenico, 117 F. 99 (9th Cir. 1902) (the "sorry about the fishing nets but kidding about that raise" case).
[16] See Torosyan v. Boehringer Ingelhein Pharmacy, 234 Conn. 1, 13–7 (1995).
[17] See Brown C. Lewis, Due Date: Enforcing Surrogacy Promises in the Best Interests of the Child, 87 St. John's Law Review 899, 940–2 (2013).
[18] Kennedy, supra note 2, at 1716.
[19] See Richard Michael Fischl, Efficiency and Its Discontents, 9 Jurisprudence: An International Journal of Legal and Political Thought 408–12 (2018).
[20] See Randy Barnett, The Death of Reliance, 46 Journal of Legal Education 518 (1996); Nathan B. Oman, *The Dignity of Commerce* (2017).

careful study of what American courts are actually doing in promissory estoppel cases, reliance remains crucial to recovery; yet even he conceded that estoppel claims face an uphill battle in most courts.[21]

A similar development is evident in the contemporary politics of rules and standards, the neo-formalist dimension of this neo-liberal moment. In Kennedy's account—and as the realists demonstrated—formalism was often a mug's game as rules promised more predictability and constraint than they could deliver, partly a result of proliferating counterrules and exceptions and partly because judges were unwilling to "bite the bullet" when a particular rule's under- or over-inclusion would lead to manifest unfairness.[22] But today the shoe is on the other foot, and it is extraordinary how often standards crafted to post-realist tastes get "rule-i-fied" into a rigid repertoire of constituent elements.

Promissory estoppel is again a case in point. Virtually any analysis of the doctrine's application to a particular dispute is likely to begin with a rote recitation of "elements" that must be satisfied for a claim to succeed: (1) a promise; (2) a reasonable expectation of reliance on the part of the promisor; (3) reliance-in-fact by the promisee; and (4) a showing that injustice can be avoided only by enforcement of the promise.[23] Predictably, this has prompted many courts to adopt a "checklist" approach to decisionmaking—examining each of the elements in isolation and thus ignoring the forest in a search for individual trees—though once again there are cases and commentary to the contrary.[24]

2.3.3 The taken-for-granted, the Trump, and the "tells"
The argumentative techniques described in the previous section suggest a great deal of "play in the joints" in legal reasoning. The fancy term for this is "indeterminacy," the notion that (some, many, most, all?) cases might be decided "either way" despite the ritual declarations of doctrinal constraint by American judges. Yet there is a competing tradition of critical work that takes those declarations seriously, searching them for hints of what is "taken for granted" by decisionmakers, assumptions so deeply ingrained in American legal thinking that they may trump more conventional sources of law in what passes for reasoning and analysis. Examples abound, and seasoned observers learn to recognize the "tells": when, for example, a court introduces a proposition reeking of race, gender, or class bias with an "of course," a "clearly," or similar language designed to assure the reader that what follows is so incredibly obvious it needs neither authoritative nor evidentiary support;[25] or bases the resolution

---

[21] Robert A. Hillman, Questioning the "New Consensus" on Promissory Estoppel: An Empirical and Theoretical Study, 98 Columbia Law Review 580, 619 (1998).
[22] Kennedy, supra note 2, at 1700–1.
[23] See E. Allan Farnsworth, Contracts § 2.19 (4th ed. 2004).
[24] See Jay M. Feinman, The Last Promissory Estoppel Article, 61 Fordham Law Review 303 (1992) (critiquing judicial and scholarly treatment of promise and reliance as discrete elements detached from the context of the parties' relationship); for contrasting cases illustrating the point, see footnotes 42–3 infra and accompanying text.
[25] See Teamsters v. Daniel, 439 U.S. 551, 560 (1979) (emphasis added), rejecting the argument that employee pension plans are investments protected by federal securities law: "Only in the most abstract sense may it be said that an employee 'exchanges' some portion of his labor

of a factual dispute on a cringeworthy economic analysis parading as a dispassionate evaluation of the evidence;[26] or runs roughshod over statutory text, legislative history, and precedent as it confidently reaffirms existing relations of power (merchants over consumers, capital over labor, racial domination, patriarchy, heteronormativity, and so on).[27] In such cases, the reader can be forgiven for suspecting that something other than random error is at work and that ideological commitments are shaping what passes for "common sense" among legal thinkers. You could fill books and book-length articles with tales of ideologically charged assumptions exerting their influence on various areas of American law, and critical scholars have been developing a rich body of work doing just that since the dawn of the movement.[28]

2.4 Critical Theory and the Classroom Experience

So what did the insights of critical legal studies mean to those of us who came to law school eager to use the law for social justice work? That depended a lot on what you wanted from the law. If you were looking for a sure bet in the service of progressive transformation, you were in serious trouble. In Dorothy's immortal words, there was nothing in that little black bag for you—no invincible argument in the Constitution, the common law, or anywhere else you could count on to get you where you wanted to go.

---

in return for [his pension plan] … His decision to accept and retain covered employment may have only an attenuated relationship, if any, to perceived investment possibilities of a future pension. Looking at the economic realities, *it seems clear that an employee is selling his labor primarily to obtain a livelihood, not making an investment.*"

[26] *See* Domenico v. Alaska Packers Ass'n, 112 F. 554, 556 (N.D. Cal. 1901), aff'd, 117 F. 99 (9th Cir. 1902) (once again the "sorry about the fishing nets but kidding about that raise" case): "The contention of [the sailors] that the nets provided them were rotten and unserviceable is not sustained by the evidence. The [employer's] interest required that [the sailors] should be provided with every facility necessary to their success as fishermen, for on such success depended the profits [the employer] would be able to realize that season from its packing plant, and the large capital invested therein. In view of this self-evident fact, it is highly improbable that the [employer] gave [the sailors] rotten and unserviceable nets with which to fish."

[27] Compare Hill v. Gateway 2000, Inc., 105 F.3d 1147 (7th Cir. 1997) (enforcing fine print terms of document first encountered by consumer upon opening a shrink-wrapped shipping carton containing goods consumer had already paid for) with the express language of U.C.C. § 2-206(1)(b) (under which the deal would have been closed—and the contract fully formed—no later than the moment the merchant shipped the goods); the express language of U.C.C. § 2-207(2) (under which the fine-print terms of the merchant's "late hit" would have constituted mere 'proposals' that the consumer was free to reject); and Official Comment # 1 to the latter provision (which states that § 2-207 governs transactions involving a single form, contrary to the court's citation-free assertion that the provision is "irrelevant" to shrink-wrap transactions since "there is only one form").

[28] For classics of the genre, see Karl Klare, The Judicial Deradicalization of the Wagner Act and the Origins of Modern Legal Consciousness, 1937–1941, 62 Minnesota Law Review 265 (1978); Alan Freeman, Legitimizing Racial Discrimination Through Antidiscrimination Law: A Critical Review of Supreme Court Doctrine, 62 Minnesota Law Review 1049 (1978); Fran Olsen, The Family and the Market: A Study of Ideology and Legal Reform, 96 Harvard Law Review 1497 (1983).

But if you wanted to understand the law—to move beyond the mainstream myths of liberalizing progress and "just doin' my job, ma'am" doctrine-crunching—it seemed like you'd come to the right place. As you prepared for law practice, the relentless revelation of argument pairs and larger structures of ideological conflict went some distance to diminish the sense that the law was hopelessly stacked against the good and the true. You learned that there was a lot of "deviant" doctrine out there—that hidden in the maze of legal argument there was solidarity as well as self-regard, a legacy of regulation as well as laissez-faire. There was, in other words, the thrill of mastering the master's tools and sometimes the master himself, for it was often possible—with the help of hard work, creative energy, and a wee bit of luck—to develop a counterargument that might find some purchase and do some good.

Developing a keen eye for the "taken for granted" and an appreciation for its influence was enormously useful as well, offering more than occasional glimpses of the law's otherwise hidden argumentative terrain. To be sure, an extended encounter with that terrain was seldom a cause for celebration. But to recall the mantra of untenured critical scholars during the anti-cls backlash of the 1980s, at least it meant you would "never underestimate the danger you are in." Yet a clear-eyed understanding of the law's politics was not inevitably a downer, for there were emancipatory possibilities as well. For one thing, it was liberating (even sanity preserving) to vindicate the intuition that law had a politics, countering the persistent mainstream myth that law and politics were distinct and dichotomous phenomena. For another, there was the prospect that exposing the exercise of power behind the pretensions of constraint and necessity— much as Toto tugged back the curtain to reveal the Wizard as an ordinary man—might embarrass power's apologists into a day of reckoning or even a change of course.

3. PROMISSORY ESTOPPEL AND *LOCAL 1330*: A CRITICAL STUDY

3.1 The Case

The value of critical methodology is best assessed by seeing it in action, and thus I'll conclude the chapter with an examination of an illustrative case: *Local 1330 v U.S. Steel*, a tragically unsuccessful effort in the late 1970s to prevent the closing of two aging steel plants in the industrial Midwest.[29] I've chosen the case for a number of reasons. For one thing, inspired by a most engaging conference a few years back, I have resumed teaching the case in my courses and had recent occasion to put some thoughts about it to writing.[30] For another, the case represents a nodal point in American history, a harbinger of late twentieth century deindustrialization as well as of the declining fortunes of labor unions and the "rust belt" workers they represented,

---

[29] Steelworkers Union, Local No. 1330 v. U.S. Steel Corp., 492 F. Supp. 1 (N.D. Ohio E.D. 1980), *aff'd* Local 1330, Steelworkers Union v. U.S. Steel Corp., 631 F.2d 1264 (6th Cir. 1980).

[30] *See* Local 1330 v. U.S. Steel: 30 Years Later (Harvard Law School, Feb. 25, 2011), proceedings available at http://legalleft.org/conferences/local-1330-conference/; Fischl, Teaching Law as a Vocation, supra note *.

developments explored with alarm by progressive economists and legal scholars several decades before the 2016 US presidential election brought them forcefully to the forefront of American politics.[31] And for still another, the case turns out to have been an early symptom of the neo-liberal/neo-formalist turn described earlier.

The case was filed against U.S. Steel, the plants' owner, by union locals ("the union," for ease of expression) representing some 3,500 affected employees. The action sought to enjoin the threatened closure via promissory estoppel, contending that the employer had broken its promise to keep the plants open if the workers redoubled their production efforts and succeeded in making the plants "profitable." In the litigation that ensued, there was little dispute that the workers had accomplished and indeed sacrificed a great deal on the faith of that promise, but in the end the courts rejected their claim on the basis of a finding that the effort had fallen short of the "profitability" benchmark.[32]

The profitability issue was hotly disputed by the parties. For its part, the union took its evidence straight from the horse's mouth, citing repeated representations by company officials—from the superintendent of the doomed plants to the chair of the company's board of directors—that profitability had indeed been achieved at the plants, and establishing that company representatives made this point repeatedly in communications to the workers as well as in various statements to the press.[33] At trial, the company argued that the profitability claim was accurate only with respect to the fixed costs of operating the plants and did not take into account a fair allocation of company-wide purchasing, sales, and management expenses. When the latter were included in the calculus, officials claimed, the plants were operating at a loss despite the many contemporaneous public declarations to the contrary.[34]

In the end, both the district court and the court of appeals embraced the definition of profitability that U.S. Steel asserted at trial, though the courts offered differing rationales for doing so. The district court treated the profitability benchmark as a "condition precedent" to liability under promissory estoppel and concluded that the union had failed to overcome the company's showing.[35] The appellate court steered clear of the lower court's "condition precedent" analysis, reasoning instead that it was unreasonable for the workers to read the union's version of profitability into the company's promise.[36] But the courts were very much on the same page with respect to the tragedy at hand, the district court lamenting that U.S. Steel "should not be permitted to leave the Youngstown area devastated after drawing from the lifeblood of the community for so many years,"[37] and the appellate court describing the situation as

---

[31] *See* Barry Bluestone & Bennett Harrison, *The Deindustrialization of America* (1984); Joseph William Singer, The Reliance Interest in Property Law, 40 Stanford Law Review 611 (1988).
[32] 492 F. Supp. at 3–8; 631 F.2d at 1269–79.
[33] 631 F.2d at 1272–4.
[34] Ibid at 1279.
[35] 492 F. Supp. at 7.
[36] 631 F.2d at 1279.
[37] 492 F. Supp. at 9.

an "an economic tragedy of major proportion" and a "devastating blow" to the employees as well as the Youngstown community.[38]

3.2 Critique

3.2.1 The path not taken

A central lesson of the "critical legal history" of promissory estoppel is the tension between the ethic of solidarity and mutual dependence reflected in that doctrine (on the one hand) and the ethic of private autonomy and individual self-interest reflected in the bargain theory of consideration (on the other). Thus, when a court treats promissory estoppel as the governing rule—as did both the district court and the court of appeals in *Local 1330*—solidarity has seemingly won the day. But if the union thus enjoyed the legal equivalent of the "home field advantage," why didn't it go on to succeed with its claim? As suggested earlier, an important insight of critical work is that the choice of the governing rule frequently marks just the beginning rather than the end of conflict and that the application of the chosen rule to the facts of a particular case presents an occasion to fight that fight again. As it happens, *Local 1330* offers a striking example of this phenomenon.

Let's begin with a close examination of the reasoning offered by the courts in support of the result, and at this point we'll focus on the court of appeals since it had the final and authoritative say. Thus, the appellate court began its analysis by asserting that "the profitability issue in the case depends in large part upon definition" and went on to critique the union's version for failing to account for company-wide expenses fairly allocable to the Youngstown operation.[39] "Obviously," the court observed, "any multiplant corporation could quickly go bankrupt if such a definition of profit was employed generally and over any period of time."[40] The court's analysis continued:

> Plaintiffs point out, however, that this version of Youngstown profitability was employed by the Youngstown management in setting a goal for its employees and in statements which described achieving that goal. The standard of Restatement (Second) of Contracts § 90, upon which plaintiffs-appellants rely, however, is one of *reasonable expectability of the "promise" detrimentally relied upon*. The District Judge did not find, nor can we, that reliance upon a promise to keep these plants open on the basis of coverage of plant fixed costs was within reasonable expectability. We cannot hold that the District Judge erred legally or was "clearly erroneous" in his fact finding when he held that the "promise" to keep the plants open had to be read in the context of normal corporate profit accounting and that profitability had not been achieved.[41]

The court thus acknowledged that the union's definition of profitability was the version embraced by U.S. Steel in contemporaneous public statements but dismissed that fact as irrelevant to its "reasonable expectability of the 'promise'" test. Exactly why the statements of company officials to the workers had no bearing on "reasonable

---

[38] 631 F.2d at 1265.
[39] Ibid at 1279.
[40] Ibid.
[41] Ibid (emphasis added).

expectability" is not explained, though the clumsy formulation is notable for its erasure of speaker and spoken to alike. The court thus evidently viewed "expectability" as a quality inhering in "the 'promise',," and, together with those scare quotes, this suggests a focus on the promise in and of itself. There is case law supporting this approach, which is consistent with what I described earlier as the neo-formalist tendency to "rule-i-fy" standards by analyzing the constituent elements in isolation from one another.[42] And when the inquiry is framed that way—severed from parties and context—it is no surprise that "profitability" might be read through the lens of "normal corporate profit accounting" and that events extrinsic to its making (like the repeated assurances that the benchmark had been met) would be ignored as beside the point.

Students who have begun to master the hunt for "paired arguments" will recognize the move the court has made here—focusing like a laser beam on the "four corners" of the promise—and begin the search for its missing rhetorical twin, the "reasonable expectations" of the parties, as we saw during our imagined relitigation of *Kirksey* ("I didn't promise she could stay forever!" versus "He's my dead husband's brother, and he assured me of a place to 'raise my family'!"). As it happens, the twin can without much difficulty be found in the relevant legal materials. The court's "reasonable expectability" formulation offers a nod in that direction, though it is (again) treated as a quality of the promise, while the text of §90 focuses instead on the "reasonable expectations" of the parties and specifically on the expectations of the promising party regarding the likely effect of the promise on the promisee. The language of the provision can thus be read to ask not how the promise should be read in isolation and by some disinterested third party—let alone by a "corporate accountant," normal or otherwise—but instead how the real-world promisor should reasonably expect the real-world promisees to understand it and respond.

Turning back to our case, once we bring our particular promisor's expectations about likely reliance into the picture, it is hard to dispute that U.S. Steel should have expected its workers to believe precisely what company officials had repeatedly told them to believe—that the plants were once again profitable—right up to the moment the parties headed for court. Nor is there any suggestion in the text of §90 that inquiry should be limited to the promisor's expectations at the moment the promise is made, and there is case law on this side of the issue as well.[43]

Note that the "four corners of the promise" versus "reasonable expectations" standoff presents a classic example of argument "nesting" as well. If bargain theory lost the "choice of governing rule" debate with promissory estoppel, it nevertheless lived to fight another day in the application of the supposed winner to the facts of *Local 1330*. Thus, if the union's argument was all about the reliance generated by the company's promises, the company focused instead on the price it exacted for the continued

---

[42] *See* Prenger v. Baumhoer, 939 S.W. 2d 23, 27–8 (Mo. App. 1997) (rejecting argument that promissory estoppel claim should focus primarily on "how the promise relates to 'its ability to provoke reliance' rather than just the promise in isolation" and basing the analysis instead "on the alleged promise itself").

[43] *See* Ulrich v. Goodyear Tire Co., 792 F. Supp. 1074, 1081–2 (N.D. Ohio 1991) (post-promise events relevant to reasonableness of promisee reliance).

operation of the mill and resisted enforcement because it did not in the end get what it sought in return (dare we say "bargained for"?): profitability.

We can likewise see how these opposed legal theories "framed" the parties' contrasting presentations of the case. The company's pitch enabled it to "stop the action" at the moment of promising and offer a "closeup" of the promise itself. If this sounds a bit like what we described earlier as the "snapshot," then the union's contrasting account offers "the film," bringing the story of the workers' reliance into sharp relief and revealing the role that the company's assurances of profitability played in its sustained effort to induce its workers to rely on it to the hilt.

To put it another way, the union's "film" focused on what the word "profitable" *did*, whereas the company's "snapshot" focused on what the word "profitable" *meant*. Thus, the court took a "deep dive" into the language of the company's promise, and, in the abstract, it is difficult to argue with the logic that "any multiplant corporation could quickly go bankrupt" if apportioned companywide expenses were not taken into account in determining the profitability of an individual plant.

But it demeans the Youngstown workers to suggest—as did the court of appeals, the company, and not a few contemporaneous commentators—that their expectations were the product of a naïve and homespun failure to come to grips with the rules of "normal corporate profit accounting" when those expectations were in fact shaped by the public proclamations of company officials that the redoubled productivity effort was succeeding and that the plants were once again profitable. The assurances of profitability were thus an integral part of the promising, deployed for precisely the same purpose, and to precisely the same effect, as the initial round of promises: As part of a calculated effort to boost the workers' morale and induce them to continue their sacrifices and redoubled efforts right up to the last possible moment.

3.2.2 Here Be Dragons

If cogent legal arguments might thus have justified an outcome in the union's favor, why did those arguments fail to persuade judges otherwise so seemingly sympathetic to the workers' plight? We have been focusing thus far on the opinion of the court of appeals, but a close look at the district court's handiwork may be revealing in this respect. It will be recalled that the lower court treated the profitability benchmark as a "condition precedent" to promissory estoppel liability and that the appellate court took a different approach, treating profitability as a part of the company's promise under §90. The appellate court nevertheless affirmed the lower court's finding that the company's definition of the term, rather than the union's, established the applicable productivity target, quoting with approval the following passage from the lower court opinion:

> This Court is loathe to exchange its own view of the parameters of profitability for that of the corporation. It is clear that there is little argument as to the production figures for the Youngstown mills—the controversy surrounds the interpretation of those figures … Perhaps if this Court were being asked to interpret the word "profit" in a written contract between plaintiffs and defendant, some choice would have to be made. Given the oral nature of the alleged promises in the case at bar and the obvious ambiguity of the statements made, this Court finds that there is a very reasonable basis on which it can be said that Youngstown facilities were not profitable. Further, plaintiffs have made no showing of bad faith on the part

Ideology and argument construction in contract law 299

of the Board of Directors in the Board's determination of profitability, nor have they given any grounds to suggest that defendant's definition of profitability is an unrealistic or unreasonable one.[44]

In sum, the district court found that there was "a very reasonable basis" for the company's interpretation of "profitability" and further found that the union had failed to counter that position by showing it to be "unrealistic or unreasonable" or offered in "bad faith." But the court did not explain why the union bore a burden that the company did not. Perhaps its thinking was influenced by the view that profitability was a "condition precedent" to company liability, prompting it to assume that the union bore the burden of proving the condition's fulfillment. Yet the court didn't *say* that and focused instead on the "oral nature of the alleged promises," suggesting somewhat cryptically that it might have reached a different conclusion if a "written contract" were at stake. (Because we construe writings against the drafter but oral statements against the listener?) Less cryptic is the opening sentence of the analysis: "This Court is loathe to exchange its own view of the parameters of profitability for that of the corporation." The sentiment is expressed with an air of conviction that is otherwise notably absent in the passage and may go a long way to explain why the court viewed the union's challenge to the company's version as an uphill and ultimately unsuccessful battle.

A seasoned labor lawyer would have smelled trouble the moment she encountered the quoted phrase, for it is a ritual incantation in cases challenging an employer's right to close a business and decided under (if not exactly in accord with) the National Labor Relations Act. Thus, the NLRA prohibits all manner of retaliation against employees who decide to unionize, but there is a judicial carve-out for business closure in retaliation for a pro-union vote, despite the Supreme Court's candid acknowledgment that such closure "is encompassed within the literal language" of the governing provision.[45] The NLRA likewise requires an employer to bargain with a union representing its employees over "wages, hours, and other terms and conditions of employment," but there is a judicially created exception for an employer's decision to close a plant despite the Court's candid acknowledgment that the quoted statutory language "plainly cover[s] termination of employment which … necessarily results from closing an operation."[46] To appreciate the vigor with which this particular American exceptionalism is policed, consider the following passage quoted with approval by the Supreme Court in the retaliatory closing case (the italics are mine):

> But none of this can be taken to mean that an employer does not have the *absolute* right, at *all* times, to *permanently* close and go out of business, or to actually dispose of his business to another, for *whatever reason* he may choose, whether union animosity or *anything else*, and without his being thereby left subject to a remedial liability under the Labor Management Relations Act.[47]

---

[44] 631 F.2d at 1278–9, quoting 492 F. Supp. at 7.
[45] Textile Workers v. Darlington Manufacturing Co., 380 U.S. 263, 269 (1965).
[46] First National Maintenance Corp. v. NLRB, 452 U.S. 666, 681 (1981) (internal quotation marks omitted).
[47] *Darlington*, 380 U.S. at 271 (quoting NLRB v. New Madrid Manufacturing Co., 215 F.2d 908, 914 (8th Cir. 1954)).

Who *talks* like that? Certainly not American judges in any other setting, and especially not in labor law cases when they are ruling in favor of employee rights, which are invariably described in apologetic and oh-so-carefully hedged terms.

If the unambiguous provisions of a federal statute can't resist a business closure override, a "mere" state-based common law doctrine like promissory estoppel isn't likely to fare much better. But what is even more telling about the deployment of the "won't exchange our own views for the company's" trope in *Local 1330* is its utter inapplicability to the facts at hand. The union was not, after all, asking the court to substitute the court's "own views" of profitability for the views of responsible officials at U.S. Steel. It was asking instead that the court hold the company to the meaning of "profitability" repeatedly and publicly proclaimed by its officers and agents, and prevent its lawyers from substituting an entirely different meaning of the term despite the extensive and intended reliance of the workers on those earlier pronouncements.

There is a name for holding a party to out-of-court representations designed to mislead in this manner: equitable estoppel, the tried and true common law doctrine that, as noted earlier, was an important historical precursor to estoppel of the promissory variety. In its application, the court's "own views" of the meaning of profitability would have been no more relevant than the court's own view of the "real" age of a minor who passed a fake ID to a merchant and then attempted to invoke his youth to disaffirm the contract thus procured. Yet an American court hears the words "plant closure" and finds itself chanting a robotic mantra ("Must … Not … Substitute … My … Views …!"), drawn irresistibly to an all too predictable result, never mind the facts, let alone the consequences.

17. Critical copyright law and the politics of "IP"
Carys J. Craig

1. INTRODUCTION: MAKING "THINGS"

The conceptual task of intellectual property law is to construct commercially valuable intangibles into propertylike "things" that can be legally recognized as the proper subject matter of private rights, commodification, and commercial exchange. If the law always depends on the functional embrace of legal fictions for its operation and legitimacy,[1] perhaps nowhere is this more obvious than in the realm of intellectual property law, which thrives on a combination of metaphor, analogy, abstraction, and universalization in the invention of its subjects and objects. The shifting and ephemeral nature of intellectual property law's object—"IP"—is under ever more strain to sustain its façade of "thingness" as it becomes a central focus of our technological age, and a prime locus of wealth creation in our information economy. Regarded critically, the law is irretrievably wedded to power. When the law ascribes rights and protects privileges in relation to valuable resources, it plays a key role in both allocating power and controlling its flow. IP law performs this role by granting rights and regulating behavior in relation to what many consider to be today's most valuable resource—information itself—whether residing in technological innovations (the subject of patent law), trade source signifiers (the subject of trademark law), or original authored expression (the subject of copyright law). IP law writes legal fictions that naturalize the private capture and control of information, communications, and cultural content. Perhaps it is not surprising, then, that it has emerged as a vibrant site for critical legal theorizing. Indeed, some have even suggested that IP scholarship has effectively generated a resurgence or "second wave" of critical legal studies (CLS) critique and activism, at least in substance if not in name.[2]

From today's vantage point, it seems clear that the field of IP scholarship, as it now exists, was born out of a sudden need, in the latter decades of the twentieth century, for a radical critique of the rapidly expanding protections offered to commercially valuable intangibles. As such, the field blossomed from the beginning on a foundation of critical legal realism and rights skepticism. While the CLS intervention in the late 1970s and

---

[1] cf Lon L. Fuller, *Legal Fictions* (Stanford University Press 1967) 1; cited by Craig Allen Nard, "Legal Fictions and the Role of Information in Patent Law" (2016) 69 Vand. L. Rev. 1517, 1521.

[2] See Victoria Smith Ekstrand, Andrew Famiglietti, and Cynthia Nicole, "The Intensification of Copyright: Critical Legal Activism in the Age of Digital Copyright" (2013) 53 IDEA 291, 291. See also Sonia K. Katyal and Peter Goodrich, "Commentary, Critical Legal Theory in Intellectual Property and Information Law Scholarship" (2013) 31 Cardozo Arts & Ent. L.J. 597, 599.

1980s had been directed mostly at the stalled civil rights movement, from the mid-1990s onward the CLS position was channeled, perhaps most effectively, toward IP law and the new realm of internet regulation.[3] Many of the most prominent IP scholars in US legal scholarship during this period either were critical legal scholars or were clearly influenced by CLS methodologies.[4] Moreover, many leading IP scholars became remarkably active participants in the public debate around IP through test cases, advocacy, public education, and political engagement.[5] For critical legal theorists, the partition between law and politics is falsely erected—axiomatically, law *is* politics. In the field of IP, the partition between legal scholarship and political action has always been porous, to good effect. IP scholars bringing a critical lens to the law have been instrumental in giving voice to public interests in the political arena.

The aim of this chapter is to give the reader a sense of how the field of IP law scholarship has been influenced and shaped, over four decades or so, by the currents of critical legal theory, while also pointing to what particular critical approaches—from deconstructionism and CLS to feminism and critical race theory—can reveal about the nature (and ongoing nurture) of modern IP systems. There is no attempt made here to offer a unifying definition of critical legal theory or critical perspectives, and nor is there any pretense at offering a comprehensive account of the myriad critical contributions to legal scholarship in the vast field of IP law. I am not approaching the task of writing about critical approaches to IP law as an exercise in mapping a body of scholarship (though others have made important efforts to do so),[6] or even as an exercise in identifying familial resemblances between various critical strands of IP scholarship.[7] Rather, I approach it as an opportunity to probe particular dimensions of the critical IP project to demonstrate how some of the basic insights of critical legal theory have been brought to bear to radically upset some of the core assumptions—and to reveal some of the central contradictions—upon which this body of law is built.

---

[3] cf Sonia Katyal in Sonia Katyal, Peter Goodrich, and Rebecca Tushnet, "Critical Legal Studies in Intellectual Property and Information Law Scholarship (Symposium)" (2013) Cardozo Arts & Ent. L.J. 601, 614.

[4] While by no means a comprehensive list (and no doubt a contestable one), I am thinking here of figures such as Jack Balkin, James Boyle, Yochai Benkler, Margaret Chon, Julie Cohen, Rosemary Coombe, Peter Drahos, Niva Elkin-Koren, Peter Jaszi, David Lange, Lawrence Lessig, and Carol Rose.

[5] Prominent examples include, for example, Michael Carrol, Michael Geist, Peter Jaszi, Lawrence Lessig, and Pamela Samuelson.

[6] See Margaret Chon, "IP and Critical Theories" in Irene Calboli and Lillà Montagnani (eds), *Handbook on Intellectual Property Research* (Edward Elgar, forthcoming 2019); K.J. Greene, "Intellectual Property at the Intersection of Race and Gender: Lady Sings the Blues" (2008) 16 Am. U.J. Gender Soc. Pol'y & L. 365; Kara Swanson, "Intellectual Property and Gender: Reflections on Accomplishments and Methodology" (2016) 24 Am. U.J. Gender Soc. Pol'y & L. 175; John Tehranian, "Towards a Critical IP Theory: Copyright, Consecration, and Control" (2012) 4 BYU L. Rev. 1233; Anjali Vats and Deirdré Keller, "Critical Race IP" (2018) 36 Cardozo Arts & Ent. L.J. 735. See generally, Sonia K. Katyal and Peter Goodrich, "Symposium: Commentary, Critical Legal Theory in Intellectual Property and Information Law Scholarship" (2013) 31 Cardozo Arts & Ent. L.J. 601.

[7] cf Brenna Bhandar, "Critical Legal Studies and the Politics of Property" (2014) 3 Prop. L. Rev 186, 188.

Section 2 will offer a brief account of some of these basic insights and their evolution within the dynamic school of critical legal thought, identifying particular themes that resurface throughout the chapter. Then, as a point of entry for thinking specifically about critical theories of IP, I will take up what is perhaps the most obvious, but also the most foundational, abstract legal concept at play in the field: the idea of "intellectual property" as such, around which all concepts of ownership, rights, and exploitation necessarily gravitate. Section 3 begins this process with a backward glance to legal realism and the use of legal categories to naturalize intellectual propertization. Focusing on copyright law, section 4 then pivots to explore the political construction of the public domain—copyright's "other"—in the production and perpetuation of value, privilege, and subordination among particular actors and expressive activities as seen through the critical lenses of race and colonialism, sex and gender. The chapter concludes by identifying the many other points of entry at which critical legal perspectives have made inroads into copyright structures, breaking down false binaries, and creating space for radical reimaginings. Ultimately it is suggested that only critical legal theories have the transformative and emancipatory potential required to effectively resist the power-legitimizing logic of IP law.

2. COMMON CHARACTERISTICS OF CRITICAL LEGAL THEORY

While there is no single encompassing definition that can embrace the many versions and variations of critical legal theory, there are certain common characteristics that, alone or in some combination, can serve to help identify and distinguish critical approaches to law. This chapter proceeds with four broadly defined characteristics in view.[8] First, a critical theory of law recognizes and resists law's *reification*, by which is meant not only the "making real" of law, but also law's power to reify its constructions, its fictions and presumptions. As Jack Balkin observes, "[l]aw proliferates power by making itself true in the world."[9] Second, a related critique targets legal *rhetoric*, with its capacity (by design) to both mystify and legitimize the operation of law. Connected to this is a third common theme in critical theorizing: an insistence upon law's inherent *indeterminacy*, or at least its open texture and inevitable plasticity, which allow for it to be molded in service of powerful interests while legal conclusions are presented as necessary or "correct." Fourth, an overarching and arguably defining characteristic of critical legal theories is the claim that law is therefore *political* and so complicit in the self-interested perpetuation of privilege, subordination, and injustice. Law is an instrument wielded in service of power, albeit concealed behind legal processes, claimed impartiality, and perceived neutrality.

---

[8] See Jack M. Balkin, "Critical Legal Theory Today" in Francis J. Mootz III (ed.), *On Philosophy in American Law* (Cambridge University Press 2009) 64–72.
[9] ibid 64. See also Jack M. Balkin, "The Proliferation of Legal Truth" (2003) 26 Harv. J.L. & Pub. Pol'y 5.

In combination, these characteristics of critical legal theory can produce what Balkin calls a "pejorative" conception of law.[10] It is this vision of law as fundamentally and irretrievably defective that is commonly associated with the critical legal studies movement as such. And it is this CLS version of critical theory that many, particularly in North America, seem now to regard as a failed intellectual movement—a radical, nihilistic effort to deconstruct legal institutions and legal rationality, which ultimately had no compelling alternative to offer. Balkin reminds us, however, that the CLS conception of law was not purely pejorative; in some variations, at least, the law was viewed more ambivalently. If law is a method for legitimating the exercise of power in society, then it poses both threat and promise: "Even if law is a supple tool of power, law also serves as a discourse of ideas and ideals that can limit, channel, and transform the interests of the powerful."[11] For some critical theorists—critical race and feminist theorists, in particular—legal discourse was therefore recognized as both oppressive and potentially emancipatory. When it is understood that law is not autonomous from politics, and that legal culture, institutions, and discourse serve political values, law is revealed to be a way of "doing politics"—a way of exercising, shaping, and restraining power.

Balkin's insights paint a picture of the evolution of CLS rather than a story of its demise. Critical movements are necessarily products of their time, and their targets will change as different elements of law become newly salient.[12] This in itself reflects a critical process of deconstruction and reconstruction. Along similar lines, Peter Goodrich muses that, if CLS was killed, it was thereby immortalized; if it failed, its failure was productive, sowing the seeds for other political, theoretical, and social justice movements to carry forward its methodological DNA.[13] (CLS is dead! Long live CLS!) This allows us to perceive the influence of critical theorizing, over the course of its evolution, in the IP scholarship that emerged and blossomed over the same place and time: the foundational CLS-infused critique of IP law that took root in the 1980s and 1990s (targeting IP law's reification, indeterminacy, mystification, and legitimation), which sowed the seeds, in this century, for a flourishing body of feminist, critical race, and postcolonial critique (emphasizing IP law's complicity in social inequality and injustice, as well as exploring its potential promise as a tool of agency and empowerment).

IP scholarship has long been a field rich with critical theoretical insights. Critical legal theory has consistently offered an essential counterbalance and alternative (some might say antidote) to rights- and utility-based critiques of IP law, and it appears once again to be resurgent. What follows, I hope, offers a sense of why this should be—and why it matters.

---

[10] Balkin (n 8) 68.
[11] ibid 67.
[12] ibid 71.
[13] Peter Goodrich in Katyal, Goodrich, and Tushnet (n 3) 601–2.

3. (DE)CONSTRUCTING "INTELLECTUAL PROPERTY"

3.1 Legal Realism and Transcendental Nonsense

Building on the intellectual legacy of legal realism, a core concern of CLS is the constitutive and inherently political nature of legal categories, with their capacity to import unexamined values and precipitous conclusions—a capacity on full display in the realm of IP law. In his foundational attack on legal formalism as "transcendental nonsense," Felix Cohen, a central figure in the American legal realist movement, identified this phenomenon at work in respect of the ever expanding protections offered to trade names. Exposing the logical fallacy inherent in the justifications for these new powers, Cohen described a "vicious circle, which accepts the fact that courts do protect private exploitation of a given word as a reason why private exploitation of that word should be protected."[14] He continued:

> The circularity of legal reasoning ... is veiled by the "thingification" of property. Legal language portrays courts as examining commercial words and finding, somewhere inhering in them, property rights. According to the recognized authorities ... courts are not *creating* property, but are merely *recognizing* a pre-existent Something ... [L]egal reasoning on the subject of trade names is simply economic prejudice masquerading in the cloak of legal logic ... It will not be recognized or formulated so long as the hypostatization of "property rights" conceals the circularity of legal reasoning.[15]

The legal construct is reified and the rationalizations uncritically accepted because the nature of the thing designated "property," and the rights and duties thus attached to it, are presented—and widely perceived—as preexistent and self-evident. The realist critique of propertization is thus directed at the law's capacity to conceal underlying motivations, to disguise loaded assertions as mere truisms, and so to foreclose the kinds of questions that ought to be raised when such rights are created and allocated. When one scrapes away the façade, a newly political picture emerges in which inequalities loom large and the role of law in the distribution of wealth and power becomes readily apparent. In Cohen's terms:

> Courts, then, in *establishing inequality* in the commercial exploitation of language are creating economic wealth and property ... not, of course, ex nihilo, but out of the materials of social fact, commercial custom, and popular moral faiths or prejudices. It does not follow, except by the fallacy of composition, that in creating new private property courts are benefiting society. Whether they are benefiting society depends upon a series of questions which courts and scholars dealing with this field of law have not seriously considered.[16]

Whether, how, and to what extent private rights over the intangible products of human creativity actually benefit society are fundamental questions that now pervade IP scholarship, and feature (increasingly, but not sufficiently) in government policymaking

---

[14] Felix Cohen, "Transcendental Nonsense and the Functional Approach" (1935) 35(6) Colum. L. Rev. 809, 815.
[15] ibid 816–17.
[16] ibid.

and judicial decisionmaking. Such questions are brought into sharp relief by the US Constitution, which explicitly ties Congress' power to create copyright and patent rights to the advancement of "progress of science and the useful arts,"[17] explaining at least in part why US scholars have largely led the way in both making and challenging the utilitarian claims and economic rationality of the IP system.[18] The social goals of encouraging learning and innovation in the name of the public good have, however, been at the heart of the justifications offered for copyright and patent laws since their inception.[19] Such teleology would seem to demand empirically informed consideration of the social benefits and costs of private ownership over particular kinds of subject matter in specific contexts—but the legal category of "property," with its presuppositions and deontological ethics, has impeded critical engagement with the logic of the law and the consequentialist claims that are made on its behalf. If it is true that "we are all legal realists now,"[20] then we should agree that legal rules cannot be adequately understood or justified simply by appealing to the abstract concept of property. And so the first point of entrance for a critical approach to copyright law must be the deconstruction of the legal category of "intellectual property" to which it belongs.

3.2 Mesmerizing Metaphors and IP Rhetoric

"Intellectual property" is now the umbrella term commonly used to capture a variety of different but somewhat related and sometimes overlapping protections granted by the laws of copyright, patent, trademark, industrial design or design patent, trade secret, and unfair competition. The very idea of intellectual property as such is, of course, a metaphorical construct—and a relatively recent one at that. Emerging in Europe in the late nineteenth century,[21] this terminology was taken up by defenders of the patent system in response to a growing patent-abolitionist movement, with the political aim of equating the inventor's right with the author's right as protected by the (less controversial) law of copyright. The label "intellectual property" was strategically employed in this context to unite, in the public imagination, the results of intellectual creativity, whether literary or scientific, into a single conceptual category containing analogous

---

[17] US Const art. 1, §8.
[18] See e.g. William M. Landes and Richard A. Posner, *The Economic Structure of Intellectual Property Law* (Belknap Press 2003); Mark Lemley, "Property, IP and Free Riding" (2005) 83 Tex. L. Rev. 1031; Brett Frischmann and Mark Lemley, "Spillovers" (2007) Colum. L. Rev. 257; Glynn Lunney Jr, "Reexamining Copyright's Incentives-Access Paradigm" (1996) 49 Vand. L. Rev. 483.
[19] See Ronan Deazley, *On the Origin of the Right to Copy* (Hart 2004) 31–50. See also Brad Sherman and Lionel Bently, *The Making of Modern Intellectual Property Law* (Cambridge University Press 1999) 11–42.
[20] See Joseph William Singer, "Legal Realism Now" (1988) 76 Cal. L. Rev. 465, 467–8, 503–16.
[21] First adopted by the North German Confederation in Article 4(6) of its 1867 ("der Schutz des geistigen Eigenthums") the term was embraced in 1893 with the naming of the United International Bureaux for the Protection of Intellectual Property (subsequently the World Intellectual Property Organization).

things over which natural rights of ownership could be claimed.[22] Analogizing across categories of human creativity through the lens of intellectual property continued, over the following century, to offer readymade rationalizations for the expansion of the IP system and the development of new propertylike controls over an increasing array of intangibles, from software code to trade secrets, and from public personalities to private databases.[23] Lamenting the rise of "intellectual property" terminology in the late twentieth century, Richard Stallman, a prominent "Copyleft" activist, explained: "It leads people to focus on the meager commonality in form that these disparate laws have—that they create artificial privileges for certain parties—and to disregard the details which form their substance: the specific restrictions each law places on the public, and the consequences that result."[24] The seeming immutability of IP structures facilitates their continual creep, unchallenged, into new spheres of human activity.

Not only has the legal category of "intellectual property" performed the political function of uniting a variety of essentially different intangible outputs of human creativity under a single rationalizing roof, but it has also succeeded in conceptually conjoining that category of intangibles with the physical world of real property. Just as Britain's eighteenth century literary property debates were fought through analogies to real property, modern proponents of strong IP frequently present it as "analogous to the home or the castle of the landowner, and thus ... present the IP owner as the legitimate recipient of far-reaching rights to control the use of their property."[25] This is the legitimizing function of legal rhetoric at work. The IP metaphor informs our intuitions around entitlement, exclusion, and infringement (commonly referred to as "theft," "piracy," or "misappropriation" in testament to the traction of the metaphor) in a way that misrecognizes both the nature of the subject matter at play and the public interest at stake. Mark Rose, a literature scholar who has written extensively on IP's metaphors, reminds us that "[m]etaphors are not just ornamental; they structure the way we think about matters and they have consequences."[26] William St Clair, whose legal historical work charts the subtle shifting of IP's property metaphors over time, from piracy to landed property to moveable property, captures their epistemological power:

> Metaphors have been intrinsic to the way in which intellectual property has historically been analysed, understood, presented, and enforced, not only by authors, publishers ... and other participants in the book industry, but by governments, parliaments, lawyers, judges, and

---

[22] Adrian Johns, *Piracy: The Intellectual Property Wars from Gutenburg to Gates* (University of Chicago Press 2009) 276–7. See also Oren Bracha, *Owning Ideas: The Intellectual Origins of American Intellectual Property 1790–1909* (Cambridge University Press 2016).

[23] See Siva Vaidhyanathan, *Copyrights and Copywrongs: The Rise of Intellectual Property and How It Threatens Creativity* (NYU Press 2003) 18.

[24] Richard Stallman, "Did You Say 'Intellectual Property'? It's a Seductive Mirage" (*GNU Operating System*) www.gnu.org/philosophy/not-ipr.html accessed 4 May 2018.

[25] Helena R. Howe and Jonathan Griffiths, *Concepts of Property in Intellectual Property Law* (Cambridge University Press 2013) 2.

[26] Mark Rose, "Copyright and Its Metaphors" (2002) 50 UCLA L. Rev. 1, 3.

courts ... They are part of the history of the nexus of ideas that have historically surrounded and shaped both law and practice through to the present day.[27]

Many IP scholars writing from a variety of different theoretical perspectives have decried the prevalence of the property metaphor, pointing to the problematic infusion of real property reasoning into IP rules notwithstanding critical differences between the physical and intellectual realm.[28] As Mark Lemley warned, however, the shorthand of property has made "the move from rhetoric to rationale ... almost irresistible,"[29] and IP protection has increasingly expanded to exhibit, in effect, many of the characteristics of the real property to which it is inaptly compared.[30]

It might reasonably be contested, at this point, that "property" itself is merely a legal construct—a metaphor that similarly inscribes an inevitable but false "thingness" to what is better understood as a manufactured relationship of occupation and exclusion, advantage and disadvantage, established and enforced by law. Indeed, a critical view reveals that, "when all is said and done ... property is a social construction and a product of law."[31] But the problem with the IP conceit is that it relies on "heuristics derived in relation to *physical* property, which is rivalrous and excludable."[32] While the property metaphor naturalizes rules that could be said (if only for the sake of argument) to be efficient or necessary (if not necessarily fair) in relation to scarce, depletable, and rivalrous physical property, it mobilizes the same intuitions within the realm of IP, where the public goods in question are nonrivalrous and nonexcludable. The problem is not that intellectual property is a metaphor, then, but that the metaphor is inapposite. Regarded evenly through a critical or realist lens, property and copyright are revealed to be fundamentally different in both their social and political ends and the means by which they purport to achieve them.[33] The nature of *intellectual* property alters the practical and economic equation, as well as the distributional impact and experienced effects, of granting exclusivity through law.[34] As St Clair writes, "[w]hat none of the property metaphors has been able to accommodate is the fact that the

---

[27] William St. Clair, "Metaphors of Intellectual Property" in Ronan Deazley, Martin Kretschmer, and Lionel Bently, eds, *Privilege and Property: Essays on the History of Copyright* (Open Book Publishers 2010) 374.

[28] See e.g. Shyamkrishna Balganesh, "Debunking Blackstonian Copyright" (2009) 118 Yale L.J. 1126; Dan Hunter, "Cyberspace as Place and the Tragedy of the Digital Anticommons" (2003) 91 Cal. L. Rev. 439; Mark Lemley, "Property, Intellectual Property, and Free Riding" (2005) 83 Tex. L. Rev. 1031; Neil W Netanel, "Why Has Copyright Expanded? Analysis and Critique," in Fiona Macmillan (ed.), *New Directions In Copyright Law* (vol. 7, Edward Elgar Publishing 2007) 3.

[29] See Lemley (n 18) 1032.

[30] Howe and Griffiths (n 25) 2.

[31] Carol M. Rose, "Canons of Property Talk, or, Blackstone's Anxiety" (1999) 108 Yale L.J. 601 at 639 (citing Mark Kelman, *A Guide To Critical Legal Studies* 258 (1987)).

[32] Brian Frye, "IP as Metaphor" (2015) 18 Chapman L. Rev. 735, 757.

[33] Shubha Ghosh, "Deprivatizing Copyright" (2003) 54 Case W. Res. L. Rev 387, 389.

[34] See e.g. Tom Bell, "Author's Welfare: Copyright as a Statutory Mechanism for Distributing Rights" (2003) 69 Brook. L. Rev. 229.

differences between 'property' and 'intellectual property' are not contingent or superficial but essential, inescapable, and unignorable."[35] So too, then, are the implications for the legal structures that define and regulate them. Even if we resist the reification of property and employ Carol Rose's elegant conception of property as storytelling, we can see that the possession of *intellectual* property tells a very different story.[36] In the absence of any natural scarcity in the realm of knowledge and ideas, IP laws manufacture artificial scarcity—and they make that scarcity real in the world. In respect of a subject matter that could be shared infinitely without depletion, the law intervenes precisely to restrict its free flow.

Baseline assumptions inform how we perceive the law and the demands that should be made of it in the name of fairness or equality. If one begins with the premise that information, ideas, and expression are, but for law's intervention, part of a shared public domain, then the state's creation of private, proprietary rights demands justification—a normative rationalization grounded not in the protection of the owner's property as a matter of private right, but in service of society's interests. By lifting the veil of property, as Felix Cohen suggested, our focus can shift to the social benefits that the system should bring, and its success (or lack thereof) in doing so. Of course, how we might understand and pursue those social benefits opens up yet more ground for debate: whether we are committed to a certain vision of economic efficiency, social progress, or democratic participation, for example, or the extent to which we are convinced by the role of the market, economic incentives, or financial or other rewards in the attainment of that vision. But again, this is precisely the point: to reject IP law's property metaphor is to open the doors to what is necessarily a political debate, allowing light to be shed on the economic and social realities of intellectual and cultural production, consumption, and exchange, and demanding greater accountability in respect of the law and its consequences. Here, critical theorists would insist that the key to generating consensus is not reliance upon metaphors and legal formulae, but normative argument that "encompass[es] the creation and elaboration both of competing social visions and forms of moral persuasion," with people who hold different views engaging in honest dialogue and recognizing competing perspectives.[37]

If, as it is widely claimed, IP law grants exclusive rights over nonrivalrous intangibles with the aim of producing certain beneficial outcomes for society as a whole, property rhetoric has made us complacent about evaluating copyright's practical effects and guarding against the obvious risks of a system that permits the "monopolisation of knowledge, ideas, education and the means by which they are made available."[38] In any attempt to justify the copyright system teleologically, the legitimizing label of "intellectual property" obscures more than it illuminates. As we will see, in doing so it also supports a variety of assumptions about what and who should reap the

---

[35] William St. Clair, "Metaphors of Intellectual Property" in Ronan Deazley, Martin Kretschmer, and Lionel Bently (eds), *Privilege and Property: Essays on the History of Copyright* (Open Book Publishers 2010).

[36] See Carol M. Rose, "Property as Storytelling: Perspectives from Game Theory, Narrative Theory, Feminist Theory," (1990) 2 Yale J.L. & Human. 37.

[37] Singer (n 20) 533.

[38] St. Clair (n 27) 395.

benefits of the rights that it accords. Alert to the politics of the law, a critical theory of copyright scrapes away IP's property façade to reveal the interests that it privileges, and the power structures that it perpetuates, when it chooses private property over the public domain—and, as we will see, vice versa.

4. THE POLITICS OF THE "PUBLIC DOMAIN"

The real property analogy and the impression of solidity that it conveys can be sustained only by virtue of accompanying metaphors such as the "public domain," and gatekeeping fictions like copyright law's "originality" threshold and "the idea-expression dichotomy." Taken together, these constructs reify the boundaries of the "work"—the thing over which ownership is claimed—giving its ephemeral essence sufficient shape, substance, and stability that it can perform its assigned role as the object of ownership. At the same time, through these conceptual mechanisms, the law limits the scope of the owner's claim "by erecting presumptively omniscient sentries around the [public] domain's perimeter."[39] Jessica Litman's groundbreaking article, "The Public Domain," was part of a wave of critical US copyright scholarship that built rapidly over the final decades of the twentieth century, challenging the perceived inevitability of copyright law's core constructs. Litman persuasively argued that the idea of the public domain—the unowned intellectual commons on which all are free to draw—is essential to the operation of the copyright system, and to sustaining the myth of original, creative authorship on which it depends:

> The public domain should be understood not as the realm of material that is undeserving of protection, but as a device that permits the rest of the system to work by leaving the raw material of authorship available for authors to use ... The public domain ... makes it possible to tolerate the imprecision of these property grants.[40]

The public domain is perceived not just as the legal term of art for unowned intangibles, but as a legal *device* employed to sustain the legitimacy of the law in the face of its disconnect with reality. This bold assertion bears the hallmarks of critical legal thinking. The gulf between the actual processes of authorship and the law's construction of human creativity, Litman argued, would render the copyright system unworkable were it not for the construct of the public domain, which "protects the copyright system by freeing it from the burden of deciding questions of ownership that it has no capacity to answer."[41]

4.1 The Politics of Doctrinal Line Drawing

The inherent imprecision of copyright law's grant of exclusivity reflects both the malleable nature of its subject and the messy realities of the human creative process. Copyright protects only "original expression" that results from an author exercising her

---

[39] Nard (n 1) 1521.
[40] Jessica Litman, "The Public Domain" (1990) 39 Emory L.J. 965, 968.
[41] ibid 969.

skill, labour, judgment, and/or creative capacities. Ideas, facts, and information are not protected, nor are systems, methods or principles, or unoriginal (copied) or common stock elements. Both the legal definition of originality and the delineation of protectable from unprotectable elements vary from jurisdiction to jurisdiction—and indeed from case to case—depending largely on the underlying philosophy and politics of IP ownership that are brought to bear by lawmakers and courts. But in any copyright case, the line between public and private traverses the work, separating it into pieces that are privately owned and pieces that belong in the public domain. This line is always shifting and subjective, dependent on a decisionmaker's interpretation of doctrine, of course, but also on her impression of the equities at play, the scope of the author's rightful claim, and the degree of moral dis/approbation evoked by the defendant's use. In a moment striking for its ostensible legal realism, Justice Learned Hand famously proclaimed, when finding that a defendant's movie copied only unprotected ideas from the plaintiff's play:

> [T]he whole matter is necessarily at large … We have to decide how much [of the play's content went into the public domain], and while we are as aware as any one that the line, wherever it is drawn, will seem arbitrary, that is no excuse for not drawing it; it is a question such as courts must answer in nearly all cases.[42]

The seemingly arbitrary lines that courts and the law must draw, in copyright as elsewhere, are not dictated or even determined by the simple application of legal doctrine to specific circumstances. There is no legal formula that can produce a definitively "right" answer to the question of how much of a plaintiff's work constitutes protectable "original" "expression," or how "substantially similar" a defendant's work must be in order to "reproduce" it. Most courts are less transparent in their deliberations, however, presenting the lines they draw—between abstract idea and detailed expression, original features and common stock devices, protectable elements and the public domain—as somehow predetermined or self-evident. They purport to discover the lines, rather than to draw them.

The reality, of course, is that these lines do not exist until they are drawn. Even the most detailed expression resides in the realm of ideas, and even the most original expression borrows and builds on what has gone before. Nothing is created out of a vacuum, Litman reminded us, and no one can see inside the human mind (not even the human whose mind it is!) to parse the original and generative from the copied, derived, or inspired. Yet the law requires the results of creativity to be so categorized in order to produce a legal conclusion. It is by virtue of the impossible nature of this challenge that copyright law provides an unusually transparent window onto the internal operations of legal logic. It does not take the critical eye of a radical deconstructionist to see that, whatever side of the public/private binary the court ultimately privileges, an alternative conclusion was available to it. Any semblance of determinacy in a court's application of these legal concepts to a particular work in fact depends on a slew of structural factors and subjective impressions, value-laden commitments, and contentious beliefs.

---

[42] *Nichols v Universal Pictures Corporation et al.* 45 F.2d 119 (2d Cir. 1930).

Whatever meaning is privileged, whatever outcome favored, depends less on the internal logic of the law than on the inescapable politics of legal reasoning.

Critical race and feminist theories, building on the insights of critical legal studies, take aim at the law's claimed neutrality, not only for masking its politics, but specifically for its complicity in the construction and ongoing legitimation of racial and gender hierarchies. Adding a feminist frame to the critique would highlight that such seemingly "arbitrary" line-drawing exercises predictably produce gendered results. Certainly, it is striking that many of the groundbreaking copyright rulings that initially defined the limits of copyright and the importance of the public domain in the late nineteenth and early twentieth centuries involved the unusual scenario of female plaintiffs seeking to enforce rights against male alleged infringers. While hardly a systematic study, it could reasonably be contended that courts were uncharacteristically keen, in such cases, to earn their pedigree as defenders of the public domain. In *Nichols*, it was the female playwright who sought protection against male movie producers. In the landmark Privy Council case of *Deeks v Wells* (ruling that no one can own the facts of history or their chronological order) it was a female "spinster" historian who sought protection against copying by the venerated author H.G. Wells.[43] Even in *Baker v Selden*, which established copyright's merger doctrine and its rule against monopolizing systems or methods, the litigation was pursued by the widow of the deceased accountant against his (male) competitor.[44] Such patterns come as no surprise to critical theorists of copyright law. As Ann Bartow writes, "Men have defined key copyright concepts such as 'authorship,' 'protectability,' 'infringement,' and all of the other precepts, terms, and conditions of copyright law. It is highly probable that there are gendered differences in the ways that copyright laws benefit and burden everyone affected by copyright laws and practices."[45]

Similar observations have been made about the gendered nature of decisions regarding "fair use"—the doctrine that permits otherwise infringing uses for purposes such as criticism and review.[46] Requiring an inherently flexible and contextual analysis of the fairness of the use, courts have been more inclined, it seems, to favor fairness and to carefully circumscribe copyright control in cases where the works feature women used in a sexualized way (such that criticism of women's bodies is practically "the prototypical fair use").[47] Based on a comprehensive review of relevant cases, critical IP scholar Andrew Gilden concludes that US courts are most comfortable relegating the plaintiff's work to "raw materials" freely available for the defendant's

---

[43] *Deeks v Wells* [1932] UKPC 66. See A.B. McKillop, *The Spinster and the Prophet: H.G. Wells, Florence Deeks, and the Case of the Plagiarized Text* (Da Capo Press 2000).

[44] *Baker v Selden* (1879) 101 U.S. 99. See Pamela Samuelson, "The Story of *Baker v. Selden*: Sharpening the Distinction Between Authorship and Invention" in Jane Ginsburg and Rochelle Dreyfuss (eds), *Intellectual Property Stories* (Foundation Press 2005).

[45] Ann Bartow, "Fair Use and the Fairer Sex: Gender, Feminism, and Copyright Law" (2006) 14 Am. U.J. Gender. Soc. Pol'y & L. 551, 558.

[46] Fair uses are "outside the public domain in theory, but ... inside in effect." Pamela Samuelson, "Mapping the Digital Public Domain: Threats and Opportunities" (2003) 66 L. & Contemp. Prob. 147, 149.

[47] Rebecca Tushnet, "My Fair Ladies: Sex, Gender, and Fair Use in Copyright" (2007) 15 Am. U.J. Gender, Soc. Pol'y & L. 273.

fair use in cases where those "raw materials" consist of, for example, visual representations of "'anonymous' women's body parts, 'generic' black men, and Jamaican men in their 'natural habitat.'"[48] Whether someone is in the privileged position of lawfully mining culture for "raw materials," as opposed to producing or even becoming those "raw materials," is a determination that quite consistently appears to turn on social status, race, and gender.

To be clear, the point of such observations is not to baldly assert that "win" rates in copyright cases are irrationally determined by the gender, race, or sexual orientation of litigants. The point, rather, is that the stories we tell about the logic and limits of IP are essentially narratives about entitlement and exclusion. By retelling the stories from different perspectives, we can see more clearly what alternative endings were available, which characters were pushed to the margins, and what other tales could have been told. This critical approach insists that seemingly basic legal conclusions about what is in—and what is out—of copyright's protective sphere in any particular case are neither predetermined nor arbitrary, but are constructed around gendered, racialized, and other assumptions about entitlement and value, and so function to perpetuate existing social hierarchies. The constructed and malleable nature of IP allows it to be readily allocated or withheld in service of power. On this reasoning, of course, a decision to privilege the public side of the public/private binary and so to allow free use of a work is no less political than a decision to stringently enforce copyright and so to protect the private rights of IP "owners."

4.2 The Making (and Unmaking) of the Public Domain

We considered, in section 3, the political power of IP as a metaphorical construct that reifies and legitimizes the private capture of the intangible commons. Let us now turn, then, to consider the politics of its opposite, the "public domain," as a metaphorical construct in its own right. In this respect, IP scholars have been particularly deliberate in their politicization of public domain discourse, with important implications. Like "intellectual property," the term "public domain" dates back to the late nineteenth century;[49] but the "affirmative discourse" of a public domain—the deliberate "construction of a legal language to talk about public rights"[50] and so to conceptually conjure up "copyright's constraining counterpart"[51]—is a more recent development, coming about a century later. In a 1981 essay criticising the emergence of publicity rights, David Lange urged that proprietary claims for new IP interests should be offset by an "equally deliberate recognition of individual rights in the public domain."[52] Over the next 20 years, a body of scholarship developed that sought to define, map, conceptualize, and deploy the concept of the public domain as a positive entity capable of confining

---

[48] Andrew Gilden, "Raw Materials and the Creative Process" (2016) 104 Geo. L.J. 355, 357.

[49] Jane C. Ginsburg, "Une 'Chose Publique'? The Author's Domain and the Public Domain in Early British, French and US Copyright Law" (2006) 65(3) C.L.J. 636, 637.

[50] Mark Rose, "Nine-Tenths of the Law: The English Copyright Debates and the Rhetoric of the Public Domain" (2003) 66 L. & Contemp. Prob. 75, 77.

[51] Ginsburg (n 49) 636.

[52] David Lange, "Recognizing the Public Domain" (1981) 44 L. & Contemp. Prob. 147.

copyright's private domain. Singer's insight seems particularly apt here: whereas liberal theorists purport to "find" metaphors, critical theorists hope to rely more on "making" them.[53] Playing off the same landed property metaphor as its opposite, "IP," James Boyle called for the strategic reimagination of the public domain as an "environment," with the aspiration of mobilizing an "environmental movement" in its name.[54] Public domain activists' efforts to protect—and even to contractually construct—an intellectual and cultural commons did indeed take root and bear fruit over the course of the following decades.[55]

As Boyle explained, how we define the substance and scope of the public domain depends on why we care about the public domain, for what vision of freedom or creativity we think it stands, and what danger it protects against. This is legal realism for the public domain,[56] which is overtly hailed as "a social-legal construct,"[57] imagined to assist us "in thinking of a complex issue, to organize our thoughts, to serve as a 'short cut' to denote a mindset, a view, a perception."[58] Moreover, because "the private domain of copyright and copyright's public domain necessarily share the same boundary,"[59] this effort underscores the indeterminacy of copyright itself. It becomes apparent that energies spent debating doctrinal niceties at the borders of IP might be better spent articulating political goals and identifying the legal tools with which to advance them.[60]

As for those political goals, however, critical legal perspectives have not been uniformly brought to bear in service of the protection and expansion of the public domain. In a powerful intervention in the scholarly conversation, Madhavi Sunder and Anupam Chander drew attention to the manner in which the escalating "romance of the public domain"[61] among progressive IP scholars had itself privileged one position (free) over another (owned), thereby embracing a kind of libertarianism that elided equality concerns and perpetuated global hierarchies of dominance and subordination. Regarded through a critical postcolonial lens, the public domain was increasingly performing as a discursive vehicle capable of justifying the continued devaluation of knowledge and cultural outputs of the global South, indigenous populations, and other racialized and culturally marginalized "Others." Masquerading as the romantic realm of free, equal, and unrestrained access, the public domain was simultaneously a metaphor

---

[53] Singer (n 20) 533.

[54] James Boyle, "A Politics of Intellectual Property: Environmentalism for the Net" (1997) 47 Duke L.J. 87.

[55] See Lawrence Lessig, *Free Culture: How Big Media Uses Technology and the Law to Lock Down Culture and Control Creativity* (Penguin 2004); http://creativecommons.org.

[56] Boyle, "The Second Enclosure Movement and the Construction of the Public Domain" (2003) 66 L. & Contemp. Prob. 33, 62, and 67.

[57] Pamela Samuelson, "Enriching Discourse on Public Domains" (2006) 55 Duke L.J. 783, 816.

[58] Email from Michael Birnhack to Pamela Samuelson (October 28, 2005), quoted ibid 145.

[59] Ronan Deazley, *Rethinking Copyright* (Edward Elgar 2006) 131.

[60] See Carys Craig, "The Canadian Public Domain: What, Where and to What End?" (2010) 7 C.J.L.T. 221.

[61] Anupam Chander and Madhavi Sunder, "The Romance of the Public Domain" (2004) 92 Cal. L. Rev. 1331.

employed to exclude—as though inevitably and necessarily—certain products, people, and voices from the value and power that intellectual propertization confers.

One component of a CLS methodology is to identify the binary oppositions at work in the law as sites of fundamental contradiction, and, by uncovering the previously suppressed sides of such binaries, unveil the myth of law's neutrality.[62] If we take copyright's binaries—owned/unowned, created/discovered, authored/unauthored, private/public—and regard them through a critical lens, we can perceive the politics behind the choice to designate something as owned, created, authored, and private. By the same token, however, this reveals as political any choice to privilege the category of unowned, discovered, unauthored, and public.[63] As with any legal concept—and just like "intellectual property"—the "public domain" can work to suppress and to oppress, rationalizing as legal necessities outcomes that in fact reflect and perpetuate established inequalities on a global scale.

4.3 Race, Gender, and IP's Public/Private Divide

A significant body of critical race and feminist scholarship in the IP field has now developed, which explores not only how IP's protections exclude people from monopolized cultural resources, but also how IP's exclusions preclude people (and *peoples*) from enjoying equal access to the power of IP. Boatema Boetang has been a compelling voice calling out the global politics of intellectual property and the public domain. Cultural products flow freely from the global South to the global North courtesy of the "public domain," she observes, while cultural products flow from North to South prepackaged in the trappings of intellectual property. As a result, "the law has different consequences for groups that vary not only in the nature of their cultural production, but also in their race, ethnicity, nationality, and class. It also affects groups and people within them differently on the basis of gender."[64] Through her work on the gendered nature of cloth production in Ghana, for example, Boateng weaves a complex picture of the ways in which gender interacts with race and class through state, institutional, and legal structures to produce sites of domination, victimization, and, potentially, empowerment. The treatment of indigenous cultural production as "traditional," she argues, renders it "feminized" in its encounter with "masculinized modernity, including IP law."[65] Western IP laws, built on patriarchal knowledge systems and imposed through colonial regimes, reproduce gender biases and operate as a space of continued subordination and exploitation. Ruth Okediji has also been vocal in her criticism of the public domain as "a rhetorical tool used by transnational actors" to justify what she regards as misappropriation of traditional knowledge and cultural resources of the

---

[62] See Duncan Kennedy, "The Structure of Blackstone's Commentaries" (1979) 28 Buff. L. Rev 205, 211–12.
[63] See Chander and Sunder (n 61) 1334–5.
[64] Boatema Boeteng, "Walking the Tradition-Modernity Tightrope: Gender Contradictions in Textile Production and Intellectual Property Law in Ghana" (2007) 15 Am. U.J. Gender, Soc. Pol'y & L. 341, 345; citing James Boyle, *Shamans, Software, and Spleens: Law And The Construction of the Information Society* (Harvard University Press 1997) 141–2.
[65] ibid 349.

global South.[66] Pointing to the plasticity of the public domain as political construct, Okediji caustically concludes: "asserting the public domain appears to be principally about protecting *existing* beneficiaries of the IP system."[67]

The racialization of particular kinds of cultural production—coded public, unowned, and free for the taking—has also been the subject of critical inquiry in a body of IP scholarship focused on the unequal treatment of African American music in the development of the modern US music industry. K.J. Greene describes how the early music industry was "built on the back of black cultural production from the era of slave songs and spirituals to the period of black-face minstrelsy" through to ragtime and blues.[68] Repeated patterns of black innovation followed by white imitation demonstrate how deeply and racially coded are the concepts of authorship and appropriation. Poking at the interstices of IP, race, and gender in American society, Greene invokes the idea of intersectionality to emphasize the extent to which black women's contributions to the nascent music industry were both vital and invisibilized. Pointing to commonalities between the treatment of early blues artists and native peoples in the United States—and noting, specifically, the similarly group-focused, collective, and often oral nature of Indigenous and African American creative and cultural practices—Greene condemns IP law for its failure (indeed, refusal) to adequately capture the cultural and economic significance of their works. The potent combination of colonial power asymmetries and colonizing discourses of possessive individualism has consistently ensured that works of the colonized and subordinated have been deemed to be freely appropriable resources residing in the public domain.[69] This is no accident of oversight, nor the necessary outcome of neutral legal rules; from a critical perspective, it is plainly the exercise of power to secure privilege and domination through the political structures of law.

Racialized binaries of owned/unowned (authored/unauthored) have been the target of similarly blistering critique in the context of choreographic copyright, with works by Caroline Picart and Andrea Kraut charting the vagaries of propertization as applied to traditional European ballet (with its whitened aesthetic)[70] and the jazz, tap, and other improvised dance forms performed by racialized black bodies. Picart insists, "[i]t is not surprising that intellectual property law, in general, tends to privilege 'whitened' dance forms, such as ballet, because there are clear choreographers who author ... using the bodies of dancers ... as 'raw material.'"[71] Charting the ebbs and flows, successes and failures, of copyright claims in choreographic works, Kraut demonstrates that the

---

[66] Ruth L Okediji, "Traditional Knowledge and the Public Domain," *CIGI Papers* No 176 (June 2018) 3–4.

[67] ibid 15.

[68] Greene (n 6) 372.

[69] See Greene (n 6) 383, quoting Rosemary Coombe, *The Cultural Life of Intellectual Properties: Authorship, Appropriation and the Law* (Duke University Press 1998) 209. See also Olufunmilayo B. Arewa, "From J.C. Bach to Hip Hop: Musical Borrowing, Copyright and Cultural Context" (2006) 84 N.C.L. Rev. 547.

[70] Caroline Joan S. Picart, *Critical Race Theory and Copyright in American Dance: Whiteness as Status Property* (Palgrave Macmillan 2013).

[71] ibid 64.

recognition or denial of copyright has always depended on the dancer or choreographer's "position in a raced, gendered and classed hierarchy, and on the historical conditions in which they made, and made claims on, their dances."[72] She argues that choreographic copyright emerged out of, and so retains, the same "racialized logic of property that has persistently treated some bodies as fungible commodities and others as possessive individuals."[73]

Feminist IP scholars have also worked to make visible, particularly over the past 15 years, the "underlying masculine assumptions existing in our construction of intellectual property as well as highlight[ing] a political economy of intellectual property that has historically benefited men more than women."[74] On the theme of IP's exclusions, Rebecca Tushnet has pointedly observed that "when we compare fields that get intellectual property protection (software, sculpture) with fields that do not (fashion, cooking, sewing) it becomes uncomfortably obvious that our cultural policy has expected women's endeavors to generate surplus creativity but has assumed that men's endeavors require compensation."[75] Malla Pollack is even more frank in her assessment that "[t]he choice not to protect food and clothing under copyright law is gendered and anti-feminine."[76] Collaborative and collective projects, whether based on relationships of care or born of functional necessity, have been marginalized or problematized by the defining model of individual, commodified intellectual production at the core of copyright law—usually with both gendered and racialized implications.[77]

Without a critical lens, it might be argued that such exclusions simply reflect the appropriate boundaries of copyright as a system that protects original expression—works that appeal to the aesthetic senses rather than functional creations that fulfill practical human needs. A critical perspective reveals that copyright's distinctions turn on established cultural hierarchies that purport to distinguish between "high" and "low" art.[78] Copyright law is, of course, widely claimed to be aesthetically neutral. Alfred Yen has argued, with a distinctly critical bent, that the judicial insistence upon avoiding aesthetic judgment seeks to sustain a distinction between aesthetic reasoning (presumed to be subjective and indeterminate) and legal reasoning (purported to be objective and rigorous). Not only is this distinction entirely illusory, but in copyright cases, Yen argues, "judges necessarily show a preference for certain aesthetic perspectives when

---

[72] Anthea Kraut, *Choreographing Copyright: Race, Gender, and Intellectual Property Rights in American Dance* (Oxford University Press 2016) xiii.

[73] ibid xviii.

[74] Debora Halbert, "Feminist Interpretations of Intellectual Property" (2006) 14 Am. U.J. Gender Soc. Pol'y & L. 431, 433. See e.g. Shelley Wright, "A Feminist Exploration of the Legal Protection of Art" (1994) 7 Can. J. Women & L. 59; Caren Irr, *Pink Pirates: Contemporary American Women Writers and Copyright* (University of Iowa Press 2010).

[75] Tushnet (n 47) 557 (quoted in K.J. Greene (n 6) 379).

[76] Malla Pollack, "Toward a Feminist Theory of the Public Domain, or Rejecting the Gendered Scope of United States Copyrightable and Patentable Subject Matter" (2006) 12 Wm. & Mary J. Women & L. 603, 608.

[77] See Peter Jaszi & Martha Woodmansee, "The Ethical Reaches of Authorship" (1996) 95(4) S. Atl. Q. 947, 967–8.

[78] See Christopher Buccafusco, "On the Legal Consequences of Sauces: Should Thomas Keller's Recipes Be Per Se Copyrightable?" (2007) 24 Cardozo Arts & Ent. L.J. 1121; Rebecca Tushnet, "Worth a Thousand Words" (2012) 125 Harv. L. Rev. 683.

they decide cases."[79] I have argued elsewhere that, underlying copyright law, a Romantic aesthetic invokes a strongly gendered vision of the autonomous self and the author "genius."[80] Building on Yen's observations, John Tehranian explains that copyright's aesthetic adjudications

> [i]nextricably affect the type of works we, as a society, receive from our artists ... Even more fundamentally, however, aesthetic judgments can serve to both maintain and preserve existing power structures. The seemingly neutral laws of copyright, therefore, have the potential to create a hierarchy of culture that serves hegemonic interests.[81]

In doing so, these laws create and maintain inequalities of property and wealth, but also inequalities in social, cultural, and communicative power. The past few decades have seen astounding advances in information and communication technologies, bringing new possibilities for collaboration and dissent, knowledge sharing and social transformation. The relative "freedom of cyberspace," as Sonia Katyal has argued, "has particular significant for 'outsider' groups, particularly women and minorities," shedding new light on the "relationship between gender, sexuality and intellectual property."[82] The emancipatory promise of digital technologies has, however, been compromised by an architecture of control justified by the protection of IP rights. Given the escalating significance of copyright's regulatory mechanisms in our daily activities, copyright laws are equipped to produce enormous economic (dis)advantage but also, and more insidiously, to thwart social participation, control cultural protest, limit knowledge flows, and punish expressive disobedience.

A critical approach offers a methodology by which to examine IP law, but it also reflects a shared commitment to a political end goal: resisting exploitative power structures that are reinforced by IP law.[83] It might seem, from this survey of copyright's private/public contradictions that we are therefore faced with the political choice of either adopting or rejecting IP structures: seeking either to expand IP to include that which it has wrongfully excluded; or to eradicate it in order to free that which it has wrongfully enclosed. But even this is a false binary. Because critical theories perceive law's embeddedness in (and *as*) culture,[84] strategies of resistance to exploitative power structures can productively include the adaptation of prevailing legal categories. It is sometimes suggested that critical theories run themselves aground on the shores of their own critique: if the law is irretrievably crippled by fundamental contradictions, inescapably political, and therefore always subject to the whims and predilections of

---

[79] Alfred C. Yen, "Copyright Opinions and Aesthetic Theory" (1998) 71 S. Cal. L. Rev. 247, 250.

[80] See Carys J. Craig, "Feminist Aesthetics and Copyright Law: Genius, Value, and Gendered Visions of the Creative Self" in I. Calboli and S. Ragavan (eds), *Protecting and Promoting Diversity with Intellectual Property Law* (Cambridge University Press 2015), 273–93.

[81] Tehranian (n 6) 1280. See also Arewa (n 69) 585.

[82] Sonia K. Katyal, "Performance, Property, and the Slashing of Gender in Fan Fiction" (2006) 14 Am. U.J. Gender Soc. Pol'y & L. 461, 466.

[83] See Katyal and Goodrich (n 2) 599.

[84] See Caroline Joan "Kay" S. Picart, *Law In and As Culture: Intellectual Property, Minority Rights, and the Rights of Indigenous Peoples* (Farleigh Dickinson University Press 2016).

those in power, can critical theories promise any truly emancipatory effect *within* the legal system and society in which they are advanced? Indeed they can. Feminist and critical race theorists, in particular, have shown that it is possible to disrupt the hegemony of the law from within its contradictions, formulating normative arguments that use its tools while knowingly inhabiting its tensions.[85]

The law, we know, is not autonomous from politics; but appreciating its *relative* autonomy permits us to be strategically ambivalent about its institutions and arguments.[86] It becomes possible to see, in the politics of IP, the capacity to harness IP discourse and the rhetoric of rights in order to advance social justice and equality. Drawing lessons from feminist and critical race scholarship, I have argued, for example, in favor of embracing the discourse of "user rights" as a political tool to restrain copyright, while also cautioning against the blind embrace of individual rights-based reasoning.[87] Scholarship emerging around the racialized dynamics of musical borrowing acknowledges the inadequacy of copyright's boundary-drawing doctrines while applauding copyright infringement rulings that recognize the marginalized contributions of musicians of color, thereby *shifting* the benefits that flow through our albeit flawed copyright system.[88] Ongoing efforts to protect and preserve traditional knowledge and cultural heritage have walked similarly delicate lines between the rejection and redirection of modern IP/public domain discourse.[89] As Lateef Mtima explains, by turning to extrinsic disciplines such as critical legal theory, the growing IP and social justice movement aims to "socially rehabilitate" IP norms and to "infuse the IP system with a progressive social consciousness."[90] Similar strategies are being employed in efforts to reorient the international IP regime away from trade and toward international development goals.[91] IP talk, for all its frailties and falsities, carries important symbolic freight in the redistribution and equality projects with which critical theorists are engaged.[92]

Recognizing the dynamic circulation of power through law illuminates the counter-hegemonic potential of both claiming and contesting the law's symbolic forms, inviting

---

[85] Angela P. Harris, "The Jurisprudence of Reconstruction" (1994) 82 Cal. L. Rev. 741, 744. See also Patricia Williams, "Alchemical Notes: Reconstructing Ideals from Deconstructed Rights" (1987) 22 Harv. C.R.-C.L. Law. Rev. 401.

[86] Balkin (n 8).

[87] Carys J. Craig, "Globalizing User Rights-Talk: On Copyright Limits and Rhetorical Risks" (2017) 33 Am. U. Int'l L. Rev. 1.

[88] See e.g. Sean O'Connor, Lateef Mtima, and Lita Rosario, "Overdue legal recognition for African-American artists in 'Blurred Lines' copyright case," *The Seattle Times* (May 20, 2015). See also *Williams v. Gaye*, No. 15-56880 (9th Cir. 2018).

[89] See e.g. Jane Anderson, "Indigenous Cultural Knowledge and Intellectual Property" (2010) Issues Paper Prepared for the Centre for the Public Domain, online at https://law.duke.edu/cspd/itkpaper/.

[90] Lateef Mtima, "From Swords to Ploughshares: Towards a Unified Theory of Intellectual Property Social Justice" in Lateef Mtima, *Intellectual Property, Entrepreneurship and Social Justice: From Swords to Ploughshares* (Edward Elgar 2015) 265, 265–6.

[91] See e.g. Margaret Chon, "Intellectual Property Equality" (2010) 9 Seattle J. Soc. Just. 259.

[92] cf Rose, "Blackstone's Anxiety" (n 31) 630.

activities that both resist and rework the meanings that accrue to them.[93] The accusations commonly leveled against critical legal theory's deconstructive appetite too readily overlook this reconstructive enterprise. As much of the IP scholarship over the past decades has demonstrated, critical theories illuminate not only channels of critique but also a multiplicity of avenues for action through dialogic engagement with the law, its structures, and its normative discourses.

5. CONCLUSION: CRITICAL RESISTANCE

This chapter has offered just a small sample of the many ways in which a critical legal lens can be brought to bear in the field of intellectual property law to challenge core assumptions about the nature of IP, what it protects and excludes, why and to what end. I have taken, as a point of entry, the metaphor of IP as "intellectual property," and the politics at play in the construction of its opposite, "the public domain." Lurking underneath these ideas are many other features of our IP system that, when probed, open doors to similar insights about the power dynamics, knowledge hierarchies, and patterns of subordination that pervade the system.

Within the field of copyright scholarship alone, critical perspectives have been productively employed to challenge and reimagine all of copyright's core constructs, from its object (the "work") to its subjects (the "author" and its opposite, the "user"/"pirate") and the nature of the "rights" that they (respectively) claim. Thus, for example, copyright's concept of the "work" as an original and stable text has been critically examined by scholars drawing on poststructuralist ideas about language and text, as well as insights from continental aesthetics and literary theory, invoking notions of dialogism and intertextuality that reveal fundamental contradictions within the copyright scheme.[94] The work of feminist literary theorists has been brought to bear to recast and reclaim the authorial contributions of women, as well as to reimagine the empowering potential of authorship as relational and community-oriented, rather than monologic and independent.[95] The idea of the original "author" has been critically

---

[93] See ibid 97–8, citing Rosemary J. Coombe, "Contingent Articulations: A Critical Cultural Studies of Law" in Austin Sarat and Thomas R. Kearns (eds), *Law in the Domains of Culture* (University of Michigan Press 1998) 37.

[94] See e.g. Robert Rotstein, "Beyond Metaphor: Copyright Infringement and the Fiction of the Work" (1993) 68 Chi-Kent L. Rev. 725; Anne Barron, "Copyright Law and the Claims of Art" (2002) 4 I.P.Q. 368; David Lange, "At Play in the Field of the Fields of the Word: Copyright and the Construction of Authorship in the Post-Literate Millennium" (1992) 55 L. & Contemp. Prob. 139; Michael Madison, "The End of the Work as We Know It" (2012) 19 J. Intell. Prop. L. 1. See also Annemarie Bridy, "Fearless Girl Meets Charging Bull: Copyright and the Regulation of Intertextuality" (2019) 9 UC Irvine L. Rev. 293.

[95] See e.g. Andrea Lunsford, "Rhetoric, Feminism, and the Politics of Textual Ownership" (1999) 61 Coll. Engl. 529; Deborah Halbert, "Poaching and Plagiarizing: Property, Plagiarism, and Feminist Futures" in Lise Buranen & Alice M. Roy (eds), *Perspectives on Plagiarism and Intellectual Property in a Postmodern World* (Suny Press 1999) 111; Carys J. Craig, *Copyright, Communication and Culture: Towards a Relational Theory of Copyright Law* (Edward Elgar 2011).

examined as a relic of romanticism and a mythic ideal, belying the collaborative processes of creativity and celebrating a patriarchal, westernized conception of selfhood.[96] Critical feminist conceptions of the self as, at once, socially constituted and creative, interdependent and autonomous, have been advanced to break down the self/other and agent/dependent dichotomies, injecting into copyright discourse an enriched vision of the author-self.[97] Postcolonial perspectives and indigenous ways of knowing have challenged copyright's individual/community dichotomy as well as the past/present temporal linearity in which it situates its subjects and objects.[98] Critical rights-skeptics have contested the rhetoric of authorial rights within the copyright scheme, and the individuated subject that it assumes.[99] By problematizing copyright's construction of its subjects, and its inherited enlightenment legacies, these critical perspectives create space for new voices and new creative forms. At the same time, these perspectives break down the dichotomy between author/audience, owner/user, and so open up new versions of the user who has resided, until now, on the wrong side of copyright's false creator/copier binary.

As I claimed at the outset, a vast swathe of the intellectual property scholarship that has bloomed over the past few decades, as IP itself has expanded in its reach and relevance, builds implicitly or explicitly on insights gleaned from legal realism, critical legal studies, and their political and intellectual progeny. IP scholarship has, for decades, been preoccupied with exposing the reification of IP law's constructs, its mystifying rhetoric, its inherent indeterminacy, and its inescapably political nature. There are, of course, significant exceptions to be noted. Scholarship rooted in law and economics is still dominant in the US literature and thriving around the world, buoyed by the linkages between IP, trade, and the modern economy, and the ascendency of neoliberal economics. There is also a strong current of traditional liberal rights

---

[96] See e.g. Keith Aoki, "(Intellectual) Property and Sovereignty: Notes Toward a Cultural Geography of Authorship" (1996) 48 Stan. L. Rev. 1293; Boyle, *Shamans, Software, and Spleens* (n 64); Marilyn Randall, *Pragmatic Plagiarism: Authorship, Profit and Power* (University of Toronto Press 2001); Mark Rose, *Authors and Owners: The Invention of Copyright* (Harvard University Press 1993); Martha Woodmansee and Peter Jaszi (eds) *The Construction of Authorship: Textual Appropriation in Law and Literature* (Duke University Press 1994).

[97] See e.g. Julie E. Cohen, "The Place of the User in Copyright Law" (2005) 74 Fordham L. Rev. 347; Carys J. Craig, "Reconstructing the Author-Self: Some Feminist Lessons for Copyright Law" (2007) 15(2) Am. U.J. Gender Soc. Pol'y & L. 207; Katyal (n 82); James Meese, *Authors, Users, and Pirates* (MIT Press 2018); Betsy Rosenblatt & Rebecca Tushnet, "Transformative Works: Young Women's Voices on Fandom and Fair Use" in *Egirls, Ecitizens: Putting Technology, Theory and Policy into Dialogue With Girls' and Young Women's Voices* (Ottawa University Press 2015); Betsy Rosenblatt, "Belonging as Intellectual Creation" (2017) 82 Mo. L. Rev. 91.

[98] See e.g. Boatema Boateng, *The Copyright Thing Doesn't Work Here: Adinkra and Kente Cloth and Intellectual Property in Ghana* (University of Minnesota Press 2011); Boateng, "The Hand of the Ancestors: Time, Cultural Production, and Intellectual Property Law" (2013) 47 L. & Soc'y Rev. 943.

[99] See e.g. Julie Cohen, "Creativity and Culture in Copyright Theory" (2007) 40 U.C. Davis. L. Rev. 1151; Haochen Sun, "Copyright and Responsibility" (2013) 4 Harv. J. Sports. & Ent. L. 263.

theorizing in the field, which finds its roots in continental and enlightenment philosophies of natural justice and deontological ethics.[100] Theoretical perspectives informed by liberal conceptions of equality and progress can effectively challenge some disparities in the allocation and enforcement of rights, no doubt; but critical perspectives perceive the ways in which the inequalities flow through the inherited legal constructs, and so demand a more fundamental reimagination of legal norms and institutions, always with a view to disrupting prevailing power structures.[101] To my mind, then, it is these critical approaches—with the new voices they empower and the political activism they propel—that offer the most challenging and promising route by which to understand, situate, and reshape modern IP structures (and so to resist their rapid and seemingly irrepressible growth). Both law and economics and liberal rights-based theorizing offer routes by which to formulate effective internal critiques of IP and its logic—but the IP system requires an immanent critique that transcends its disturbed framework, its contradictions and injustices, rather than couching critique within its terms.[102] Regarded through the lens of critical theory, it is clear to see that IP law now resides "in a cultural battleground of hegemony, social dominance, and resistance."[103] Resistance, by definition, must be capable of registering "without being absorbed, integrated or co-opted into the system against which it stands."[104]

SELECT BIBLIOGRAPHY

Bartow, Ann, "Fair Use and the Fairer Sex: Gender, Feminism, and Copyright Law" (2006) 14 Am. U.J. Gender Soc. Pol'y & L. 551, 558

Boateng, Boatema, *The Copyright Thing Doesn't Work Here: Adinkra and Kente Cloth and Intellectual Property in Ghana* (University of Minnesota Press 2011)

Boyle, James, "The Second Enclosure Movement and the Construction of the Public Domain" (2003) 66 Law and Contemp. Probs 33

Chon, Margaret, "IP and Critical Theories" in Irene Calboli and Lillà Montagnani (eds), *Handbook on Intellectual Property Research* (Edward Elgar, forthcoming 2019)

Coombe, Rosemary, *The Cultural Life of Intellectual Properties: Authorship, Appropriation and the Law* (Duke University Press 1998)

Craig, Carys, *Copyright, Communication and Culture: Towards a Relational Theory of Copyright Law* (Edward Elgar 2011)

Greene, K.J., "Intellectual Property at the Intersection of Race and Gender: Lady Sings the Blues" (2008) 16 Am. U.J. Gender Soc. Pol'y & L. 365

---

[100] See e.g. Abraham Drassinower, *What's Wrong with Copying* (Harvard University Press 2015); Robert P. Merges, *Justifying Intellectual Property* (Harvard University Press 2011); Richard A. Spinello & Maria Bottis, *A Defense of Intellectual Property Rights* (Edward Elgar 2009).

[101] Both modern rights theory and law and economics can be understood as heirs to legal realism, but part company with critical theories in their embrace of elements of formalism or formalistic reasoning. See Singer (n 20). See also Cohen, "Creativity and Culture" (n 99) 155–62.

[102] cf Emilios Christodoulidis, "Strategies of Rupture" (2008) 20(1) Law & Crit. 3, 6.

[103] Greene (n 6) 378, citing Rosemary J. Coombe, "Critical Cultural Legal Studies" (1998) 10(2) Yale J.L. & Human. 463, 481.

[104] Christodoulidis (n 102) 5.

Halbert, Debora, "Feminist Interpretations of Intellectual Property" (2006) 14 J. Gender Soc. Pol'y & L. 431
Irr, Caren, *Pink Pirates: Contemporary American Women Writers and Copyright* (University of Iowa Press 2010)
Chander, Anupam and Madhavi Sunder, "The Romance of the Public Domain" (2004) 92 Cal. L. Rev. 1331
Katyal, Sonia K., Peter Goodrich, and Rebecca L. Tushnet, "Symposium: Commentary, Critical Legal Theory in Intellectual Property and Information Law Scholarship" (2013) 31 Cardozo Arts & Ent. L.J. 601
Kraut, Anthea, *Choreographing Copyright: Race, Gender, and Intellectual Property Rights in American Dance* (Oxford University Press 2016)
Picart, Caroline Joan S., *Critical Race Theory and Copyright in American Dance: Whiteness as Status Property* (Palgrave Macmillan 2013)
Picart, Caroline Joan "Kay" S., *Law In and As Culture: Intellectual Property, Minority Rights, and the Rights of Indigenous Peoples* (Farleigh Dickinson University Press 2016)
Pollack, Malla, "Toward a Feminist Theory of the Public Domain, or Rejecting the Gendered Scope of United States Copyrightable and Patentable Subject Matter" (2006) 12 Wm. & Mary J. Women & L. 603
Rose, Mark, *Authors and Owners: The Invention of Copyright* (Harvard University Press 1993)
Swanson, Kara, "Intellectual Property and Gender: Reflections on Accomplishments and Methodology" (2016) 24 Am. U.J. Gender Soc. Pol'y & L. 175
Tehranian, John, "Towards a Critical IP Theory: Copyright, Consecration, and Control" (2012) 2012(4) BYU L. Rev. 1233
Vats, Anjali and Deirdré Keller, "Critical Race IP" (2018) 36 Cardozo Arts & Ent. L.J. 735

18. A different kind of 'end of history' for corporate law

Lilian Moncrieff

In the opening piece for a recently published handbook on corporate law, US corporate law scholar Ronald Gilson gives his readers something like a birth story for corporate governance.[1] In the 1960s and 1970s, Gilson says, corporate law scholars realised that their discipline was not doing a very good job of explaining how corporations were structured and performed. Gilson cites Yale and Stanford law professor Bayless Manning as having described corporation statutes in 1962 as 'empty' and as 'towering skyscrapers of rusted girders ... containing nothing but wind'.[2] Corporate statutes generated only minimal legal requirements (such as the requirement to appoint one or two directors and to hold an annual general meeting) and papers rarely read or referred to as evidence for the company's existence (such as the certificate of incorporation and share certificates). They did not speak to the day to day nature of how companies operated, or explain how the different contributions of managers, shareholders, labour, creditors, suppliers, communities and so on combined. Gilson goes on to describe the rising power of corporations in the 1970s and beyond, suggesting that this power was to become at odds with the minimal kinds of knowledge available about companies. The company's social relations, material dimensions and informational processes increasingly began to present themselves as essential components for lawyers, policy-makers and scholars interested in learning about companies and their impact in operational terms.

Coincidentally, a similar realisation was surfacing in financial economics. Michael Jensen and William Meckling were to describe the firm in the late 1970s as an 'empty' or 'black box', and to regret the absence of theoretical engagements to explain how the differing interests of individual participants and stakeholders might be thought through and organised.[3] This 'black box' was the instigator for their now famous economic theories about the firm, which sought to explain the structure and operations of the corporation in efficiency terms. They set out the 'agency' of managers for shareholders as the main feature of this company and correlated its purpose (to maximise returns for shareholders). A contractarian view of the firm accompanied the thesis, and understood it (the company) as a 'nexus' or 'hub' around which individuals contract and bargain

---

[1] See Ronald Gilson, 'From Corporate Law to Corporate Governance' in Jeffrey Gordon and Wolfe-Georg Ringe (eds), *The Oxford Handbook of Corporate Law and Governance* (Oxford University Press 2016).

[2] Ibid 2.

[3] Ibid, discussing Michael Jensen and William Meckling, 'Theory of the Firm: Managerial Behavior, Agency Costs and Ownership Structure' (1976) 3(4) *Journal of Financial Economics*, 305–60.

with each other in exchange for economic rewards (wages, dividends, price, and so on). 'The result', says Gilson of Jensen and Meckling's 'seminal *reframing of* corporate law into something far broader than disputes over statutory interpretation', was that '*both* Manning's empty skyscrapers and Jensen and Meckling's empty box began to be filled' (emphasis added). Corporate practitioners began to shift their attention 'from legal rules standing alone to legal rules interacting with non-legal processes and institutions,' with law and economics in mind.[4] They increased their engagement with the company's decisionmaking and informational processes, social relations and the financial determinants of corporate projects. 'It was', Gilson says of this engagement, 'no coincidence that the term "corporate governance" appeared about this time'.

That time was the 1990s, and there was an explosion of interest in the company and its governance processes. A search for the 'organisational Holy Grail' proceeded, which is often told to corporate governance students as a kind of 'growing up' by code and committee.[5] A first milestone was reached with the UK Cadbury Code in 1992, which developed the 'financial aspects of corporate governance'. The Greenbury Report in 1995 added recommendations in the UK to do with remuneration committees and disclosure. The Hampel Report in 1998, and a meeting of ministers at the OECD, preceded the consolidation of emerging principles into a new 'Combined Code' in the UK and the OECD 'Corporate Governance Principles'. Higgs and Smith, in the UK, added recommendations about nonexecutive directors (NEDs) and external auditing firms in 2003. The Walker Report, the US Senate and the Basel Committee produced more guidance on corporate risk management, disclosure and the responsibilities of NEDs around 2009. More recent reviews in the UK in 2016 and 2017 added recommendations and requirements on stakeholder consultation, corporate culture and pay and social reporting. Recommendations from the different stages and committees are reflected in corporate governance codes, such as the UK Corporate Governance Code, the G20/OECD Principles for Corporate Governance and the NYSE Corporate Governance Standards, and in a spread of governance instruments across Europe since 2000.[6] These codes set out standards of good practice for (primarily) listed companies, mainly on board structure and composition, executive pay, shareholder relations, accountability and audit.

Just under the surface of this history by code and committee, however, there lies another story that is probably more familiar to critical legal scholars. Signs of it creep out from under the many committees and codes that make up the field, such as the Cadbury Committee, the Walker Report, the OECD Corporate Governance Principles, and so on – for as well as enacting a new field, each committee also marks the site of considerable *turbulence*, *crisis*, and *social antagonism* to do with companies and their governance processes. Cadbury, for example, was formed in the wake of major accounting scandals and corporate insolvencies at Robert Maxwell's companies, at

---

[4] Both quotes ibid 3.

[5] See Christine Mallin, *Corporate Governance* (3rd edition, Oxford University Press 2010), chapter 3 and David Kershaw, *Company Law in Context: Texts and Materials* (2nd edition, Oxford University Press 2012), chapter 7.

[6] See European Corporate Governance Institute (ECGI), 'Codes' at www.ecgi.global/content/codes accessed 15 October 2018.

Polly Peck and at the Bank of Credit and Commerce International (BCCI). The Greenbury Report was prompted by concern about excessive director remuneration, mainly in respect of the newly privatised utilities companies. The Higgs and Smith Committees and comparable Senate Committee reviews in the US took place as a response to major accounting scandals at Enron, WorldCom and Parmalat. The Walker Review, Senate, Basel and EU interventions in 2009 were prompted by the financial crisis and the global economic slowdown that followed it in 2007 and 2008. Recent consultations and reports on corporate governance in the UK in 2016 and 2017 were prompted by 'poor corporate practices', including at British Home Stores (BHS), Carillion and retail giant Sports Direct.[7] Much has been made by the current UK government (and the Opposition) of their intention to address the 'unacceptable face of capitalism' by renovating a corporate governance culture that has shown signs of being engulfed by 'short-termism' and 'City excess'.[8]

Committees, of course, perform something *like* an intervention on this antagonism when they try to understand what has gone wrong and make suggestions for reform. But, by themselves, they also might be said to serve a mainstream narrative that tends mainly to consolidate belief in the social *responsiveness* of corporate laws, codes and institutions in their current form; the committees and codes approach rarely contains any new analysis of the corporate form and structure itself. In this chapter about the contribution of *critical legal scholars* to corporate governance, by contrast, the intention is to track a very different kind of intervention in the field. Critics are defined in this chapter by their use of company law theory and legal analysis to get *under the antagonism* caused by companies, seeing this antagonism as a sign of wider peril and social strain. They provide a social context and a critical framework for the understanding of how the company governs itself, and situate the history of corporate governance in the history of political economy and law. The lines of antagonism tend to multiply in their analyses, rather than resolve (after a committee). Peril often extends to governance and responsibility issues right across financial institutions, tech companies, energy companies, procurement and PFI, and to corporate networks and supply chains that leave trails of social and environmental turmoil behind them. A very different picture of the company emerges compared to the financial economists'. The critics' engagements tend to say less (or in many cases nothing) about how the company measures up to abstract values like 'efficiency' or 'agency costs', and more about the 'social' constitution of the company, its power and autonomy, and 'institutional' effects. They draw out the social causes and consequences of decisionmaking power within business organisations, focusing particularly on those that are large enough and/or transnational enough to be socially significant in their impact.

This chapter looks closely at the character and significance of the critical legal project within corporate governance in three parts. It starts from the idea that the continued antagonisms presented by corporate projects underscore the presence of real strains in the mainstream narrative for the field, and suggest the need for alternative

---

[7] Department for Business, Energy and Industrial Strategy (BEIS), 'Corporate governance reform: Government response' (2017) BEIS/16/56 at www.gov.uk/government/consultations/corporate-governance-reform accessed 15 October 2018.

[8] 'Teresa May attacks "unacceptable face" of capitalism', BBC News, 27 August 2017.

ways of understanding the company. The chapter looks at how critical legal scholars have taken up this argument over the years. Section 1 begins with Marx's estimations of the company at a time of great antagonism (the industrial era) and around the birth of the modern-day company. It then looks at more recent disputes about company law and theory through which today's critical legal scholars make out their consciously critical attitude. Central throughout is the insistence of critical legal scholars on the 'social' character of productive activities and on the 'antisocial' nature of financialised corporate governance, which for them is tolerated, if not driven, by the mainstream narrative. Section 2 looks at the 'seminal reframing of corporate law' that Gilson underscores, and at the crucial entrenchment of shareholder-orientated corporate governance from the 1970s (after financial economics). It explores the difficulties that this particular 'end of history' creates for critics' *legal* projects, and at alternative possibilities for 'socialising' companies presented by 'regulatory governance' and 'reflexive law'. Section 3 concludes with the summation, however, that both approaches are struggling to realise their 'prosocial' ambitions amid global functional systems (for capital, debt, work, commodities, science, culture, technology and so on) that reinforce the demand for shareholder-dominated systems (that can 'cope' with complexity). An impasse is identified that raises difficult questions, highlighted by the author, about the future of the critical legal and social projects in corporate governance.

The chapter explores a 'different' pathway for critical legal scholarship in the final part. It focuses on reconceptualising *antagonism* (rather than the company and its governance modalities) as a way to open up new organisational possibilities for a world that is not *just* complex but also (on the brink of environmental catastrophe) 'unhinged' at best.[9] This analysis/sense of possibility finds its feet in a 'pre-/ante-' critical engagement with the political history of capitalism, as told by Albert Hirschman. Hirschman's narrative about the promises of early modern capitalism and 'doux commerce' is used here to recontextualise the powerful efficiency demands that attend corporate governance systems after the 'end of history'. But it also tries to make space from the difficult problems identified in section 2 by creating a meaningfully different pathway for critics' 'evaluations' of or 'complaints' about corporate structures and operations. This pathway invites and encourages critical legal scholars to basically stay with the antagonism (that creeps out from under the history by code and committee) and to look for new certainties within this matter (that could be seen or experienced or talked to). The aim is to cultivate a different kind of subversive and emancipatory learning about corporate legacy and affect, which wants to undo a coupling between normative thinking and global corporate systems that has become problematic amid ruin and planetary-scale threats. It sets critical scholarship on a path which is different but also complementary to the long held ambition of carving out a different 'end of history' and finding new ways to take up the normative problems that companies iteratively spurn.

---

[9] Ulrich Beck, *The Metamorphoses of the World* (Polity Press 2018).

1. THE CRITICAL LEGAL PROJECT AND CORPORATE GOVERNANCE

In seeking an understanding of the turbulence and antagonisms that might be associated with the corporate economy, Karl Marx is the obvious starting point for many critical legal scholars. Marx wrote in the century in which the corporate form came to life in statute (around the middle of the nineteenth century) and in practice (enterprises commonly took up the corporate form by the end of the nineteenth century). Marx's departure point, in Part V of Volume III of *Capital: A Critique of Political Economy*, is also the same one that Gilson alludes to above: namely, the worldly or social character of the relations that the productive process engages, including those engaged by the 'enormous expansion' of enterprise that took place under the stock company after the 1860s.[10]

For Marx, the relations inherent in commodities, commodity production and circulation concern the *social* labour of individuals and groups of individuals in the exchange economy. He talks about the corporate legal form as a form of 'social enterprise' and a 'coming together', which is distinguishable from the individual and entrepreneur.[11] The investment of labour and resources in the separate legal personality of the company allows for the emergence of the company as a distinct unit of social action, devolved from the laws of individual private property and ownership. This unit – the corporation – carries its social potential all the way through for Marx, as 'the ultimate development of capitalist production' and as a 'necessary transitional phase towards the reconversion of capital into the property of the producers ... as outright social property'.[12] However, antagonism persists in the industrial era for him, due to the continued commodification of social relations within the corporate paradigm and the entrenchment of a system that is basically class exploitative.[13] A surplus is extracted from the social labour of the many to pay for the lifestyles of managers and 'money capitalists', who convene within the company as 'owners'.[14] Various other antagonisms flow from the first, according to Marx's analysis, including the growth of monopolies, a new aristocracy of finance, bubbles of speculation and 'stock jobbing', a squeeze on labour amid falling profits and technologisation, and the growth of credit markets.[15]

Plenty about the present circumstances of the corporate economy corroborates aspects of Marx's account. One list of indicative events might include different

---

[10] See Karl Marx, *Capital: A Critique of Political Economy, Volume III: The Process of Capitalist Production as a Whole*, edited by Frederick Engels (Three volumes written 1863–1883; first published 1894; online version transcribed in 1996 by Hinrich Kuhls, Dave Walters and Zodiac and in 1999 by Tim Delaney and M. Griffin) at http://marxists.org accessed 15 October 2018. Chapter 27, 'The Role of Credit in Capitalist Production'. 'Enormous expansion' at 315.

[11] Ibid 315–16.

[12] Ibid 316.

[13] Ibid 317: 'ensnared in the trammels of capitalism'.

[14] Ibid 317: 'the little fish are swallowed by the sharks and the lambs by the stock-exchange wolves'.

[15] Ibid.

speculative bubbles (dot.com, subprime), corporate failures and mass redundancies, precarity among workers and squeezes in pay, and growing levels of public and private indebtedness pre and post financial crisis. Another list, more focused on corporate social responsibility issues (CSR), might add largescale corporate tax evasion and avoidance, environmental impacts from the extractive industries and intensive agriculture and breaches of human rights in global supply chains (GSCs) to the patterns of exploitation that Marx highlights.[16] Shareholders mainly convene, still, in their companies as 'owners', despite the changing narratives in company law in recent decades.[17] This convention is still widely believed to make for elite and exclusive decisionmaking forums, detached from the social realities of the productive process, particularly amid the concentrations of voting power that have been able to form among financial institutions and asset managers in recent decades.[18] Critics trying to explain and overcome these situations routinely highlight crucial breaches of the law (LIBOR, misselling, tax evasion, breaches of fiduciary duty, accounting malpractice and so on). However, many will also encounter unnerving combinations of legal and unsanctionable activities among the largescale problems to which companies contribute (including waste, warming atmospheres, inequality, social exposure, and so on). This suggests, again after Marx, law's alignment in places 'with domination'.

Critical observations of this order (for example, big picture or planetary) often sit slightly behind engagement with the corporate legal form in critical legal scholarship. Critical company law tends not to pursue largescale social forces such as (primitive) accumulation, commodification and commercialisation (after Marx), or to make up organisations from the actions and experiences of their constituent parts (as the economists did). They engage, as their starting point, the very definite juridical features of the company, for example separate legal personality, limited liability, delegated management and transferable shares, as established by the 'legal revolution' that accompanied expansion of the railways and industrialisation in the nineteenth century.[19] These (rusty) frames carry critically controversial forces, such as gain, capital, speculation and responsibility and liability free privileges as a matter of course.[20] Their

---

[16] The literatures on these lists are extensive. There is an attempt to gather some of the discussion together in Lilian Moncrieff, 'On the Company's Bounded Sense of Social Obligation' in Scott Veitch and Daniel Matthews (eds), *Law, Obligation, Community* (Routledge 2018).

[17] See Andrew Johnston, 'The Shrinking Scope of CSR in UK Corporate Law' (2017) 74 *Washington and Lee Law Review*, 1001; see the references to shareholders as 'owners' in BEIS (n 7).

[18] See Ewan McGaughey, 'Do corporations increase inequality?' (2015) Kings Law School, SSRN Paper: https://papers.ssrn.com/abstract=2697188 accessed 15 October 2018.

[19] See Paddy Ireland, 'Finance and the Origins of Modern Company Law' in Grietje Baars and Andre Spicer (eds), *The Corporation: A Critical, Multi-Disciplinary Handbook* (Cambridge University Press 2017) 238–46; Lorraine Talbot, *Critical Company Law* (Routledge 2018).

[20] Ireland (n 19); Lorraine Talbot, *Progressive Corporate Governance: Governance for the Twenty First Century* (Routledge 2013). Talbot underlines the strength of these 'capital' histories when she details how enterprises shifted from the use of partnerships to companies amid the Great Depression of 1873–96. It was amid falling rates of profit from industrial activities that the company limited by shares became attractive for meeting *investors' demand* for taking on more risk and merger activity, and limiting (investors') liabilities for loss or harm (30–40).

history is entwined with longrange extractive, colonial and environmental transformations across the globe, and with the broad-based defeat of corporate responsibility and liability for the same.[21] As such, the challenge facing critical company law scholars would seem to be significant. It is to 'socialise' and 'repurpose' companies limited by shares against the thrust of their commodified and capital and extractive histories, to achieve equitable and progressive outcomes (defined by Lorraine Talbot as 'promoting the interests of people as a whole').[22]

There are a number of interesting ways in which critical legal scholars seek to do this, working with theory and critical readings of company law. Central to their combined efforts is the foundational insistence on the 'social' (rather than purely economic) character of productive activity, carrying the theme forward from Marx. Critical legal scholars commonly give definition to their works by characterising the company as a 'social actor' or 'social-economic institution'.[23] Companies draw on the participation and potential of many actors and things (employees, consumers, investors, suppliers, communities, natural resources, technologies, infrastructure), and exist within a social context in terms of both their activities and their impacts.[24] Progressive scholars have fleshed this out over the years by highlighting the role that labour plays in the creation of firm value and how this participation lends itself to enhancing corporate governance, as in the case of German codetermination.[25] 'Stakeholder theories', 'team production' and 'commons' theories of the company have flourished in a similar vein. Each has become an ideal, in the field, for conceptualising a wider variety of stakeholder contributions (than only shareholders).[26] Also (theorywise), the historically and conceptually distinct 'entity theory' of the corporate enterprise makes a highlight of the company's separate legal personality (from shareholders and other interested parties) and the 'public' and 'institutional' character of corporate actions and autonomy, particularly in respect of powerful (or socially significant) multinational corporations.[27] The European Parliament recently reignited this debate about the 'institutional' and 'quasi-public' dimensions of how socially significant companies

---

[21] Anna Grear, 'Deconstructing Anthropos: A Critical Legal Reflection on "Anthropocentric" Law and Anthropocene "Humanity"' (2015) 26(3) *Law and Critique*, 225–49.

[22] Talbot (n 20) xx.

[23] See Eric Orts, *Business Persons: A Legal Theory of the Firm* (Oxford University Press 2013).

[24] John Parkinson, *Corporate Power and Responsibility: Issues in the Theory of Company Law* (Oxford University Press 1995).

[25] Ewan McGaughey, 'The Codetermination Bargains: The History of German Corporate and Labor Law' (2016) 23 *Journal of European Law* 135; Marc Moore and Martin Petrin, *Corporate Governance: Law, Regulation and Theory* (Palgrave 2016) chapter 6.

[26] John Kay, 'The Stakeholder Corporation' in G. Kelly, D. Kelly and A. Gamble (eds) *Stakeholder Capitalism* (Macmillan 1997); Margaret Blair and Lynn Stout, 'A Team Production Theory of Corporate Law' (1999) 85 *Virginia Law Review* 247; Simon Deakin, 'The Corporation as Commons: Rethinking Property Rights, Governance and Sustainability in the Business Enterprise' (2012) 37(2) *Queens Law Journal* 339–81.

[27] Adolf Berle, 'The Theory of Enterprise Entity' (1947) 47(3) *Columbia Law Review* 343; the debate on this extends to Otto von Gierke (1841–1921) and Walter Rathenau (1876–1922) and their highlight of the 'real-existence' and 'autonomy' of the 'enterprise as such'.

operate when it endorsed the link between companies and their 'social licence to operate' in its policy statements on corporate responsibility.[28]

'Social' and 'institutional' accounts of the company carry governance implications, which critical legal scholars are keen to highlight. 'Companies are private forums or contexts in which social planning is carried on', says John Parkinson; 'their decisions constitute exercises of significant social power'.[29] A modern kind of management involving 'economic statesmanship' and 'responsibility for the world that they [directors] were helping to create' is the corollary of this view, according to early twentieth century company law scholars Adolf Berle and Gardiner Means and scholar/statesperson Walter Rathenau.[30] Today's critical legal scholars point to the law's anticipation of this, too, in statutes that require directors to promote the success of the *company* (rather than shareholders' interests), and in provisions that suggest directors are expected to look to 'long-term' stability and the success of the enterprise as a whole.[31] Critical scholars highlight the different varieties of capitalism (Germany, Japan) and a 'progressive' period in Anglo-American corporate governance in the postwar era as evidence of places and times when a more 'social' consciousness of this kind was in evidence.[32] Even without specific directions in law, they say, managers have shown themselves to be willing and able to balance the interests of a variety of constituents and to transcend purely financial interests. They did so with an eye to the stability and reputation of the company insofar as shareholders were confined, by force of regulation, to 'conventionally adequate' returns.[33]

This emphasis in critical legal scholarship on shareholders' *enforced* modesty is, of course, more than incidental. Relating corporate governance to the 'social' character of production and public interest critically depends on dealing with the status and claims of financial constituents over company assets and cash surpluses. This task defines critical legal scholars' most fundamental battle line with financial economists, who elevate highly naturalised claims about shareholders when they conceptualise the firm – for example, that investors are 'owners' of the company or 'risk bearers' and 'residual claimants' on its profits. But a careful reading of the history of corporate and securities law, says Paddy Ireland, suggests that shareholders do not really 'own' publicly held

---

[28] European Parliament, 'Corporate Social Responsibility: promoting society's interests and a route to sustainable and inclusive recovery' 2012/2097(INI), 17.

[29] Parkinson (n 24) at 2.

[30] Adolf Berle and Gardiner Means, *The Modern Corporation and Private Property* (7th edition, Transaction Publishers 2005), 357; Blanche Segrestin, 'When Innovation Implied Corporate Reform: A Historical Perspective through the Writings of Walter Rathenau' (2017) *Gérer et Comprendre. Annales des Mines, Les Annales des Mines* (English version), 6 (citing Rathenau).

[31] Beate Sjåfjell, 'Redefining the Corporation for a Sustainable New Economy' (2018) 45(1) *Journal of Law and Society* 29–45; Barnali Choudhury, 'Serving Two Masters: Incorporating Social Responsibility into the Corporate Paradigm' (2008) 11(3) *University of Pennsylvania Journal of Business Law* 631; John Parkinson, 'The Legal Context of Corporate Social Responsibility' (1994) 3(1) *Business Ethics* 16.

[32] Paddy Ireland, 'Corporate Schizophrenia: The Institutional Origins of Corporate Social Irresponsibility', in N. Boeger and C. Villiers (eds) *Shaping the Corporate Landscape* (Hart 2018); Talbot (n 20) 41–70.

[33] Ireland (n 32) 41.

companies in this way.[34] Shareholders 'own' merely their shares and the right to dividends and to assign their shares for value, as established in law since the middle part of the nineteenth century. Ireland identifies a 'schizophrenic' dimension within company law, which concerns the ability of shareholders to hide behind the 'real entity' that is the company when it comes to liability for losses and harms, but to convene in the company as 'owners' when it comes to shaping strategy and claiming profits.[35] US corporate law scholar Lynn Stout, collaboratively, queries the legal, normative and empirical validity of the alternative claim that shareholders are residual claimants and 'risk-bearers'.[36] The proposition is not generally reflective of company law, argues Stout. The company is basically its own residual claimant other than in liquidation. The combination of limited liability and superliquid capital markets also means that shareholders are no longer the 'risk bearers' that financial economists assume them to be in an empirical (and normative) sense.

Critical legal scholars challenge, with this, the notion that companies and their assets are exclusively *shareholder property*. They mark out the possibilities for attending wider social and environmental purposes in existing company law, while suggesting legal reforms that can state these purposes more explicitly. Beate Sjåfjell, echoing the ambitions of many in the field, suggests writing the company's wider purposes into law, as creating value for 'shareholders and other stakeholders' (this goal might be implemented on a 'voluntary' basis during a transitional phase, Sjåfjell adds).[37] Simon Deakin broadens the ambitions for public finalities further in his much discussed article that propositions the company as a 'commons'.[38] This prospect takes us back to Marx (although Marx is not mentioned) and the 'distinct unit for social action' that is admitted as the defining feature of 'modern' companies.[39] This company (as a social unit) might be 'devolved' from the 'norm' of shareholder primacy,[40] says Deakin, and operationalised through legal reforms as a 'shared resource' or 'commons'. Shareholder primacy is for him but a social norm, not a legal requirement, and therefore should be

---

[34] Ireland (n 32).
[35] Ireland (n 32). He suggests fully 'depersonalizing' the company (treating it as a separate and real entity) and downgrading the status of shareholder rights to close off this channel for exploitation.
[36] Lynn Stout, *The Shareholder Value Myth: How Putting Shareholders First Harms Investors, Corporations, and the Public* (Berrett-Koehler Publishers 2012).
[37] Sjåfjell (n 31): she cites from the European Commission's statement in 2011 that businesses 'should have a process in place to integrate social, environmental, ethical, human rights, and consumer concerns into their business operations and core strategy in close collaboration with their stakeholders, with the aim of maximizing the creation of shared value for their owners/shareholders *and for their other stakeholders and society at large*'. Reflecting the ambitions of many in the field, see Jeroen Veldman and Lynn Stout et al, 'The modern corporation statement on company law' SSRN Paper, www.ssrn.com/abstract=2848833 accessed 16 October 2018.
[38] Deakin (n 26).
[39] Also, of course, observed by legal scholars apart from Marx: see for example Adolf Berle and Gardiner Means (n 30) and their emphasis on separate legal personality and separation of ownership and control in 1932, and Rathenau in 1918 and his '*Unternhemen an sich*' (the enterprise as such) (in Segrestin n 30).
[40] Deakin (n 26) at 355–60. See also Stout and Veldman (n 37).

relativised within the industrial and economic apparatus for social and sustainability purposes. The commons model 'better describes the legal structure of the business enterprise than the shareholder primacy model' for Deakin, due to the emphasis that company law places on 'the autonomy granted to managers via the board to organize the business'.[41] Thinking about stakeholders in terms of their overlapping property rights (rights to access, withdrawal, management, exclusion and alienation, and so on) and closing the gap between the institutional dimensions of how a company and a commons operate offers an opportunity, for Deakin, to consolidate a large part of the critical company law tradition. His thesis fills the company from the bottom up with the possibility of participation, redistribution and creating 'benefits for society as a whole'.

Importantly, though, Deakin's and the other critics' reform proposals still concern the legal persona and history that is the company limited by shares, and not alternative business organisations such as workers' cooperatives or mutuals. Alternative organisational forms, Deakin explains, 'do not have a strong association with business enterprise' or with the 'functional needs of private sector business firms', which for him include transferable shares, separate legal personality, limited liability and so on.[42] This is interesting because it continues the hardest part of the work for critics: adapting the Victorian apparatus of the company and its world building (and world suppressing) capacity for progressive purposes, and trying to *defuse* the 'rusty' or 'windy' frames that have been responsible for much of the (abrasive) history of capitalism since the nineteenth century. Added now is the insistence that companies are not just 'empty' forms awaiting efficiency claims, but defined pieces of legal apparatus with an institutional and (in some places) progressive history. But hints remain that those 'rusty' or 'windy' frames that Manning talked about are also more steellike than rusty, and full of crosscutting histories and arguments that can make critical progress difficult. For example, for a while now, the European Union has agreed with critics that shareholders are *not* the 'owners' of the company, but the adjustment to talking about 'equity ownership' instead has caused little real change in the distribution of rewards (or social impact). More needs to be said, then, about some of these steelier frames and their purposes for the company, and how hard it is to overcome some ends in history.

2. THE CRITICAL LEGAL PROJECT AND THE 'END OF HISTORY'

It was the turn of the millennium when US corporate law scholars Henry Hansmann and Reiner Kraakman published their now infamous proposition for twenty-first century corporate law, 'the end of history for corporate law'.[43] Like other end of history theses before it, the article sets out a destination and endpoint for the sociocultural evolution of (in this case) corporate law. This destination and endpoint concerns

---

[41] Deakin (n 26) 339.
[42] Ibid 354.
[43] Henry Hansmann and Reinier Kraakman, 'The End of History for Corporate Law' (2001) 89(2) *Georgetown Law Journal* 439–68.

'efficiency' and the mode of promoting efficiency that is known as shareholder primacy: the proposition that shareholders are the party to whom managers are accountable and the party in whose interests the company is chiefly run. Certain benefits to mankind are contemplated by the authors, such as increases to the overall value and receipts of the company, which portend the maximisation of stakeholder interests and social welfare overall. But key to the deployment of the 'end of history' motif is a culmination that points beyond welfare arguments to the completion of the logic and normative propulsions of corporate law as such. By the 1990s, say Hansmann and Kraakman, a consensus had emerged among academic, business and governmental elites that control of the company *should* lie with the shareholder class. Their expectation is that corporate legal 'history ends' when this normative consensus or belief produces 'substantial convergence', the world over, in corporate law.

The events that make up corporate capitalism did not actually come to an end in the decade following the publication of the article. Nor did history actually stand still for long enough for the shareholder-orientated model to assume the position of a *celebrated* triumph or destination to the course of corporate law. On the contrary, the thesis of the 'end of history' for corporate law (and 'endism' more generally) came under immense pressure throughout the first decade of the new century. Major accounting scandals (at Enron, WorldCom, and Parmalat, for example) highlighted the potential for shareholder demands to fundamentally corrupt the company's sense of purpose. The global financial crisis that followed this led to widespread condemnation of shareholder-led corporate governance and its amplification by a network of financial intermediaries, now associated with myopic short-termism, mass bankruptcy and the destabilisation of public budgets on a massive scale.[44] The following decade, Thomas Piketty published his hardhitting contradiction of the proposition that maximising the return on investment was always the same thing as improving social welfare for all.[45] Other political and labour economists joined him, to suggest that shareholder-led capitalism is tilted not towards better overall welfare but towards the concentration of wealth and other benefits among the top 10 per cent and 1 per cent.[46] Further, and bringing the analysis back to the critical legal scholarship above, lots happened after 2001 in the *legal narratives* surrounding corporate governance, which highlighted not the 'completion' of the company's decisional logic but the legally and normatively contestable nature of the propositions involved.[47]

It has been considerably more difficult, with all of this turbulence and social antagonism in clear sight again, to continue to talk of how the shareholder-orientated model outperforms all competing models for the governance of companies. Organisations from the OECD to the European Commission have become the unexpected advocates of an openly critical attitude in policy debates that acknowledge how (in the words of the Commission) 'confidence in the model of the shareholder-owner who

---

[44] Deakin (n 26) outlines the literature linking shareholder-led governance to the weak governance of companies. See also Wolfgang Streeck, *Buying Time: The Delayed Crisis of Democratic Capitalism* (Verso 2014).
[45] Thomas Piketty, *Capital in the Twenty-First Century* (Harvard University Press 2014).
[46] Discussing corporate governance aspects: McGaughey (n 18).
[47] Sjafjell (n 31); Deakin (n 26); Stout (n 36); Ireland (n 32); Talbot (n 19 and n 20).

contributes to the company's long term viability has been severely shaken'.[48] Yet 'the end of history' thesis for corporate law is still compelling in 2018 because of its ability to endure and outlive many of the crises and antagonisms that bubble and blister around it. Shareholder-based forms of accountability have endured, and even strengthened, in many company law quarters since the financial crisis as a technique for overcoming shareholder passivity and increasing board accountability. In the UK and Europe, for example, concern about executive pay and mismanagement produced 'say on pay' regulations that extended the only advisory vote on pay (or 'say') at the yearly meeting to shareholders.[49] Revisions to corporate governance codes in the wake of the crisis and beyond have placed more emphasis on shareholder engagement and 'stewardship', and on the availability of nonexecutive directors (NEDs) to investors with 'issues and concerns'.[50] (NEDs were invited to 'challenge' managers more frequently, with the suggestion given of being 'terrier like'.) Investor status and power would seem to agglomerate rather than retract, in this context, as part of the overriding ambition of public policymakers to attain 'real shareholder democracy' and to make 'stewards' of formerly egotistical members.

The shareholder orientation for corporate governance remains normatively forceful in this, because '[i]t is not just external factors that promote shareholder value', as Talbot says; '*it is also the law*' (emphasis added).[51] Talbot's detailed work on the 'financialisation' of corporate governance takes its readers back to the nineteenth century again, to highlight the capital and 'investor-oriented' ambitions behind the establishment of the company. This investor orientation was interrupted amid a political and regulatory shift to the left in the postwar era, in Talbot's analysis (echoing Ireland above), before advancing again in the 1970s. Policymakers in the deregulatory, or neoliberal, era reaffirmed shareholder-led corporate governance as part and parcel of the desire to promote financial services and ensure that markets were 'self-regulating'. One pinnacle of these developments, for Talbot and also Andrew Johnston, is the direct requirement to represent shareholders' interests set out in the UK Companies Act 2006 ('CA 2006'). 'Section 172', says Johnston, 'explicitly fixes shareholder primacy as the goal of companies, restricting managerial discretion and legitimating the wider social norm that managers should maximize shareholder value'.[52] And: 'Decisions that do not contribute to short-term shareholder value and that directors cannot justify in dialogue with shareholders either informally or in general meeting will be sanctioned by declining share prices, resulting in foregone bonuses and the threat of hostile takeover.'[53] Key in

---

[48] European Commission. 2010. 'Green Paper: Corporate governance in financial institutions and remuneration policies' *COM* 284 final, 3.5.

[49] Enterprise and Regulatory Reform Act 2013 (c24); see also amendments to the Shareholder Rights Directive (Directive 2007/36/EC), which are due to take effect in 2019.

[50] Corporate Governance Code 2016, Section E, download at www.frc.org.uk/directors/corporate-governance-and-stewardship/uk-corporate-governance-code accessed 15 October 2018 (a new version of the CG Code takes effect from 2018); Stewardship Code 2012, download at www.frc.org.uk/investors/uk-stewardship-code accessed 15 October 2018.

[51] L. Talbot, 'Trying to Save the World with Company Law? Some Problems' (2016) 36(3) *Legal Studies* 513–34, at 513.

[52] Johnston (n 17).

[53] Johnston (n 17) at 1034.

critics' work here is an emerging outline of the law and policy choices taken over the years to advance investors' claims (by legislators, governments and organisations that represent the international economic order). But the emphasis on *law's entanglement with domination and maldistribution* also places something of a question mark over the near future of the critical *legal* project, and the effort to retrieve a more progressive approach to corporate governance from *within* corporate law. 'The law as it stands is not a source of resistance', says Talbot, pointing to the need for initiatives that can combine reform with more widespread social and political transformation ('concerning the future of capitalism itself').[54] Johnston, similarly, highlights Brexit and recent scandals that have undermined public trust in companies as signs that the problems exceed law and that politically 'the status quo is unlikely to persist'.[55]

But what of the many fragmented parts of company law and governance that open onto nonfinancial considerations, and that try to make something 'social' or 'progressive' out of this seemingly matted situation (the company is locked into gain and financial markets amid surging global functionality)? These parts include recent amendments to the UK Corporate Governance Code, which encourage wider stakeholder engagement, policies for the establishment of a 'healthy' corporate culture and remuneration for directors that supports 'long-term success'.[56] They include directors' duties in section 172 Companies Act 2006 (CA 2006) to have 'regard for' wider interests (labour, community, environment, suppliers, and so on), and new UK regulations (from January 2019) that require directors to set out how this wider 'regard' is practically attended by directors in the Strategic Report.[57] Social and environmental reporting requirements for large and listed companies widely mirror this need for directors' to be 'reflexive' about social and environmental risks, and to increase the flow of nonfinancial information to investors and other stakeholders.[58] Companies and investors are encouraged to think ever more broadly about their social role and responsibility. They increasingly respond by implementing, on an organisation-led basis, policies to do with board diversity, human rights, environment and corporate social responsibility (CSR).[59] Guidelines, recommendations and codes concerning CSR continue to proliferate at national, regional, supranational and international levels in support of this developing corporate 'social' reflexivity.

---

[54] Talbot (n 51) 533.
[55] Johnston (n 17) 1041.
[56] Corporate Governance Code (n 50). This reform includes a new and much discussed requirement in Part 1, Provision 5 of the 2018 Corporate Governance Code that the 'board should understand the views of the company's other key stakeholders', and a requirement (on a comply or explain basis) that directors adopt a mechanism for engaging with the workforce from the following options: a director appointed from the workforce; a formal workforce advisory panel; a designated nonexecutive director to represent workers. See Department for Business, Enterprise and Industrial Strategy (BEIS) (n 7) for a discussion and review of consultation responses.
[57] See section 172 (1) (a)–(f), Companies Act 2006 (c46) and the Companies (Miscellaneous Reporting) Regulations 2018.
[58] See ss414A–D Companies Act 2006 (c46); Directive 2014/95/EU.
[59] European Parliament (n 28).

Significant numbers of policymakers, legislators and governments, and also scholars working with new inflections of the 'critical spirit' in company law, have turned to these fragmented parts and social references in company law, to deny the possibility of ending legal history with a *fait accompli* for shareholder primacy. The move, conceptually speaking, draws on influential debates from the 1980s and 1990s about the rise (and necessity) of 'new governance' and 'reflexive law' amid globally functioning systems and rising nonstate power.[60] It finds joy in the *discursive processes* that support the company's coordination of economic activity and promote reflexivity about the company's performance *and* social functions.[61] Companies are presented as exposed to a plurality of normative perspectives and learning pressures in the course of their economic activities (the 'social' nature of productive activities again). The external pressures emanate from a mix of industry actors, consumers, investors, activists, scholars and community organisations, and find their point of interaction within companies' decisionmaking processes and outward-looking legal duties (such as directors' duties, social disclosure, and so on). Emerging global legal phenomena capture the resultant waves of normative interaction between companies and the affected, for example in corporate codes of conduct, CSR policies and statements and protocols, audit and third party monitoring, standard setting within contracts and GSCs (some of which engage transnational private law, consumer law, and so on). 'Corporate codes', says leading proponent, Gunther Teubner, 'juridify fundamental principles of the social order and seek to overcome the primacy of shareholder value in favour of a stakeholder orientation as well as to realise self-restraint in the areas of labour, product quality, environment, and human rights'.[62]

Teubner, however, also talks about 'overall configurations' of enterprises (such as networks, connected contracts, supply chains, franchising chains, and so on) as more adequate to the 'multiple orientation' for reflexive law than the corporate entity itself.[63] This is, he says, because the necessary acts of legal balancing which reflexive law imputes conflict with company law rules that entrench value maximisation as the company's main purpose.[64] In the UK, for example, directors are duty bound to promote the success of the company for the benefit of their members while also – that is, at the same time as – having 'regard' to wider interests (section 172, CA 2006). But several factors, including the subjective nature of the duty (the extent of regard is up to

---

[60] David Sciulli, *Corporate Power in Civil Society: An Application of Societal Constitutionalism* (NYU Press 2001).

[61] Gunther Teubner, '"Corporate Responsibility" als Problem der Unternehmensverfassung' (1983) 12(1) *Zeitschrift für Unternehmens und Gesellschaftsrecht* 34; Colin Scott, 'Reflexive Governance, Meta-Regulation and Corporate Social Responsibility: The Heineken Effect' in Nina Boeger, Rachel Murray and Charlotte Villiers, *Perspectives on Corporate Social Responsibility* (Edward Elgar 2008).

[62] Gunther Teubner, 'Self-Constitutionalizing TNCs? On the Linkage of "Private" and "Public" Corporate Codes of Conduct' (2011) 18(2) *Indiana Journal of Global Legal Studies* 617–38 at 623.

[63] Gunther Teubner, 'Law and Social Theory: Three Problems' (2014) 1(2) *Asian Journal of Law and Society* 235–54.

[64] Ibid 242.

directors), the enforcement mechanisms (there is no right for social stakeholders, only shareholders) and the insistence on blending 'social regard' with 'the business case' considerably reduce the space for social reflexivity (i.e., for directors to do justice to the plurality of rationalities to which they are exposed). Considerable *uncertainty* follows about the legibility of the critical and social project in this (blended, matted) context. It is hard to know whether 'social pacting' and 'social learning' are really developing in an impactful way when the claims that companies make are simultaneously pegged to instrumental horizons, or when most of the available modes for testing the company's social performance also rely on the company's own words (reports, audits, disclosures, and so on). The communicative journeys that concerned citizens must make through corporate reports, audits, slavery statements and so on become ever more strange as the world is thrown into the most physical and affective of ruins – in the oceans, forests, soils, atmosphere; years after Rana Plaza, at the Aral Sea, and so on.[65]

The normatively diminutive conditions for regulatory governance and responsibility are confirmed in *R (People & Planet) v HM Treasury* in 2009.[66] This English juridical review case concerns an NGO's objections to the adoption by the UK government of a 'commercial approach' to the management of its majority shareholding (83 per cent) in a bank taken into public ownership during the financial crisis. Rejecting the claimant's case, the court cited matching obligations for directors and investors not to 'skew the performance' of companies 'in an anti-competitive way'. Only if a company's CSR policies were 'worse than at other banks, such that they have a negative effect on the value of the company and its shares' would directors be justified in acting to extend the environmental accommodations at issue (climate change) and only in order to protect the value of shares.[67] The case confirms the legal orientation of the public company towards investors and globally integrated financial markets, and makes it difficult for even the willing to break out of the mould and to pluralise the company's sense of purpose if such a move is at odds with investor gains. Corporate managers and other constituents (communities, workers, and so on) that rationally anticipate the outcome (must) similarly cultivate their service to the cause of shareholder value if they want to be accommodated within corporate plans. The ruling is, of course, specific to the UK, where a history among the drivers of industrialism and financialisation might suggest elements of particularity. But, then, this is also the point about hyperconnected markets, which is captured so prophetically in Hansmann and Kraakman's thesis as well as by the critics: the demands that global functionalism and integrated financial markets make on the societies and natures around them mean that 'continued convergence' is likely.

---

[65] This argument is more fully discussed in Lilian Moncrieff, 'Karl Polanyi and the Problem of Corporate Social Responsibility' (2015) 42(3) *Journal of Law and Society* 435–59.

[66] *R (People & Planet) v HM Treasury*, Queen's Bench Division, Administrative Court, 2009.

[67] Ibid at 12.

3. A DIFFERENT KIND OF HISTORY

Critical legal scholars have done important work in this chapter in making connections between the social antagonisms that surround big business and the corporate legal infrastructure that is in place. Yet it is apparent that changing the legal frameworks to reflect critics' 'social' ambitions (wider corporate purposes, commoning, subversive learning) remains challenging, due to global functionalism, the domination of financial constituents (Talbot and Johnston) and the overdetermination of the company's systems for 'responsiveness' in regulatory governance (*R (People & Planet) v HM Treasury*). Insightful critical company law scholars increasingly speak to the need for bigger (societal level) changes when faced with this impasse. Governance scholars, in a relatable but opposing move, speak to the necessity of working harder within the existing juridical processes to change social attitudes and behaviour. In this final section, the chapter looks for a different kind of history that can help to re*contextualise* these different but opposing moves. The aim is to set critics on a different but complementary path to the (shared) objective of attending a different 'end of history' for corporate law and overcoming the potential for neutralisation that lies in the combined interactions of the two sides to the critical project.

For this contextualisation, the chapter needs to return to some of the 'big picture' questions that were briefly raised in section 1 (in the discussion of Marx). It helps to return to the bigger *expectations* surrounding companies and markets, further to Talbot and Johnston's suggestion that the critical impasse surrounding mainstream corporate governance is part of a bigger framing exercise and 'belief in the great moderation and the self-regulatory capacity of markets'.[68] A starting point for assessing this 'belief' is Karl Polanyi's *The Great Transformation*, where he discusses the restraints that an economically liberal government is expected to show towards markets and economic ordering.[69] The practical obligation on liberal governments by the end of the nineteenth century, says Polanyi, was to create conditions that encouraged the development of markets for 'all elements of industry', and to ensure that markets formed the only or main organising force in the economic sphere.[70] Self-regulating markets were the objects of legal and *political pursuits* as well as economic doctrines, in this analysis, amid the modes of association that were quickly forming around industrialisation. This political characterisation is evident, for Polanyi, in the 'uniformity of institutional arrangements' that evolved around this time, and in the 'utopian' character of the momentum for self-regulating markets.[71] The latter tended to advance market imaginations and self-interest, and (crucially) the propulsions of *homo economicus*, while repressing news of the antagonism and protectionism that (actually) followed their advance (the famous 'counter movement').

---

[68] Johnston (n 17) 1006. See also Teubner's contrasting suggestions about understanding the context for self-governance (as the only option) after 'functional differentiation' (n 63).
[69] Karl Polanyi, *The Great Transformation: The Political and Economic Origins of Our Time* (Beacon Press 2002).
[70] Ibid 72.
[71] Ibid 218.

Polanyi traces this rise of marketisation and *homo economicus* in *The Great Transformation* to Adam Smith, and his insistence on the 'propensity to barter, truck and exchange one thing for another'. He describes the figure as a 'mis-reading of the past', having 'hardly shown up on any considerable scale in the life of any observed community'.[72] However, Albert Hirschman, in his 1977 book *The Passions and the Interests: Political Arguments for Capitalism before Its Triumph,* identifies much longer-range fascinations with self-interest, discipline and economic rationality, which extend to well before Smith and the modern arguments for (and against) capitalism concerning property.[73] This historically preceding argument, Hirschman says, speaks to the *political* genesis of the 'spirit of capitalism' and to the notion of 'doux commerce' (famously ridiculed by Marx). It concerns a basically positive attitude to economic activities, traced by Hirschman to eighteenth century thinkers and political economists, who proposed that the pursuit of interests could 'repress and atrophy' the destructive sides to human personalities, the passions. Economic expansion, and the preoccupation with individual gain and improvement that went with it, were forces for the strengthening of global political order, in this view, and for 'taming' of the passions of the powerful and corrupt. 'The diffusion of capitalist forms', Hirschman observes, 'owed much to the search for a 'less multifaceted, less unpredictable and more "one-dimensional" human personality', and to the revolutionary (for the time) notion that 'honour' was the preserve of the pecuniary.[74]

The long (long) shadow of this political and economic history brings us back, *but using a meaningfully different pathway*, to the atmospheric cool of financial economics and shareholder-orientated corporate governance. The ability of financial economists to bring modern scientific rationality together with the pursuit of 'interests' finds collaboration in a history that extends to the era of Montesquieu (writing in 1748 about the modest manners of commerce in *L'esprit de Lois*) and James Steuart (writing in the mid 1700s about the operation of 'interests' in politics, long before these became a matter of doctrine in economics). Interests, for these early thinkers, could 'divert man from "striving for honour and preferment"',[75] and professed a kind of cool detachment from emotion that is not a million miles away from more contemporary ambitions for the evolution of market technologies.[76] Importantly, however, Hirschman also sees new tones to capitalism (property, political freedom) in these contemporary developments. 'By the middle of the nineteenth century,' he says, 'the experience with capitalism was such that the argument about the benign effects of *le doux commerce* on human nature had totally changed'.[77] The 'reality of capitalist development' came into view, giving

---

[72] Ibid 45.
[73] See Albert Hirschman, *The Passions and the Interests: Political Arguments for Capitalism Before Its Triumph* (first published in 1977; Princeton University Press 2013).
[74] Ibid 132.
[75] Ibid 126.
[76] See Fredriech von Hayek, *Law, Legislation and Liberty: A New Statement of the Liberal Principles of Justice and Political Economy* (Routledge 1982); on the corporate dimension to market order and social reflexivity, see Fredriech von Hayek, 'The Corporation in a Democratic Society: In Whose Interests Ought It and Will It Be Run?' in Fredriech von Hayek, *Studies in Philosophy, Politics and Economics* (UCP 1980).
[77] Hirschman (n 73) 126.

birth to landmark sociologies of alienation (Marx, Weber, Freud) as well as to new and more 'modern' political doctrines in support of capitalism (property, freedom). Yet, Hirschman insists that this earlier history and political doctrine are still 'worth reconstructing', where they suggested a more complicated and also arrested view of political development. 'In all of these explicit or implicit critiques of Capitalism,' Hirschman says of Marx et al, 'there was little recognition that to an earlier age, the world of "full human personality," replete with diverse passions, appeared as a menace that needed to be exorcized to the greatest possible extent'.[78] And finally: 'capitalism was supposed to accomplish what was soon to be denounced as its worst feature'.[79]

This *history of expectations* matters to the present enquiry for a couple of reasons, which need to be highlighted. These reasons are important, if difficult to grasp because they fall beyond the usual critical tradition and also seek a different resolution to reflexive law and corporate socialization. To begin with, the emphasis on expectations offers a frame through which critical legal scholars might engage more closely with the *political pursuits* that underlie the 'end of history' for corporate law. Hirschman's book speaks to the 'schizophrenic' dimensions of capitalism that critics highlighted in section 1 (for example in the work of Ireland). He helps to explain why trying to transform the company by contesting its social and property dimensions (shareholders as 'owners' and so on) is difficult. It is difficult, that is, because the company and capitalist institutions command their validity from more than one set of histories or values. That there are *unmet expectations* built into both sets of plans (overcoming despotism, growing property and welfare) is highlighted by the long list of social antagonisms attended to throughout this chapter and throughout critical scholars' work. These antagonisms are a horizon, clearly, for the continuation of the critical project, and for identifying the places where corporate governance fails to deliver on the intelligibility that it claims. Yet moving along this horizon could involve also doing something apart from the classic efforts at socialisation, which tend to *move quickly* between the observation of socially harmful consequences and changes to the modalities of corporate governance (in the effort to socialise corporate property and gains and so on). Hirschman opens up another pathway, however, when he talks about evaluating capitalism in a (rarely attempted, he says) critique of '*intended but unrealized effects*'.[80] Perhaps it is talking to these 'unrealised effects' that can put a reflective pause on the effort to fit the social world *into* the company and its historically abrasive frames, when we are not really sure what the prospects or impact of that will be – or when we are sure because the dynamic of corporate systems is limited by the higher order terms of financialisation (in *R (People & Planet) v HM Treasury*).

What does this involve or mean? It brings us back again to Hirschman's largely forgotten history and counterintuitive formula for critique: that rationalisation and even alienation *were always intended in capitalism* but peace or better welfare *did not result* (for example at sites where turbulence, crisis and social antagonism are clearly in evidence). 'Illusory expectations' about commerce or calculation that are not displaced or denaturalised by being linked to their real world effects go on to inform and

---

[78] Ibid 133.
[79] Ibid 132.
[80] Ibid 131.

facilitate more decisions and commercialisation in Hirschman's analysis (hence Hirschman's interest in clarifying *what* precisely these expectations were). This happens for the company in the *R (People & Planet) v HM Treasury* case, where the justice looks over and beyond the company to the interests of financial markets when faced with problems at the level of the company or board (subprime, environmental protection, and so on). This 'looking over' brings us back to the somewhat mythical progress of financial economics that Gilson alludes to at the start of this chapter (a 'seminal reframing', their opening up of the 'black box') and the steeliness of their higher order frames. It installs other kinds of counterfactualities that make critique hard to move forward with. This includes (most worryingly) the possibility that the attendant claims about alienation present on some level as banal or unremarkable, having been somewhere intended in the first place (such as the alienation that 'capitalism was supposed to accomplish'). If this is hard to process, most trips to a low-cost retailer, a supermarket or other arenas for the widespread casualisation of harms in the UK can confirm that something like this subversion of intention could be in place. Ditto the morally disorientating debates about ruinous practices, such as sweatshops, being 'good' for the poor.

Critical scholars faced with this totally unwanted set of perplexities – where arguments for corporate socialisation get caught up in crosscutting political and theological arguments about capitalism and interests – could do with another approach. Highlighting more alienation as part of a formula that hopes for a change in the company's outlook is an uncertain strategy when the fundamental expectations (to do with calculation) have *not* been displaced. It can open onto the deepening of corporate power and financialisation (as complexity surges and the search for order becomes intense), and uncertainty (as the real extent of instrumentalisation becomes difficult to track and contend). A different trajectory is needed, which *stays with* the antagonism that stretches around companies and looks for the defeated expectations *within this matter* that might be seen or heard or talked to. The aim here is not immediately to add more to the causes for advancing 'social' reflexivity at companies, or adding more participants to the list of *the company's* stakeholders (emphasis added to possessive).[81] The aim, rather, is to cultivate a different kind of subversive and emancipatory exchange about corporate materiality, processes and affect, which wants to hold onto the antagonism so that it might undo a coupling between normative thinking and global corporate systems that has become uncertain and blindsighted and threatening amid planetary-scale threats. There is a meaningful difference, this chapter suggests, between what learning about social theory could *do for* socialising the corporation (which locks the company and also shareholders in as respondents) and what learning about the societies and environments touched by companies could *do to* normative and political

---

[81] This sounds counterintuitive, but there is evidence that being added to the list of corporate consultees does not always advance communities' claims, and sometimes actually carries its own containments and harms: see the work of Subhabrata Bobby Banerjee, 'Corporate Social Responsibility: The Good, the Bad and the Ugly' (2012) 34(1) *Critical Sociology* 51–79 on 'stakeholder colonialism' in stakeholder consultation and CSR.

expectations around the systems that make up corporate governance (for the defeat or 'metamorphosis' of calculative expectations).[82]

What then for corporate law and governance? What of 'commoning' the company, depersonalising it, and installing better social reflexivity on the board of the 'social unit' that Marx identified so long ago? The critical scholars' plans have come to depend, in this analysis, on a different set of 'social' investigations concerned with how corporate matter stretches across time and space; how legacies are built and maintained, and the range of constituents' (known and unknown) experience of this. These investigations are necessary for formulating the social and normative demands of projects like 'commoning' and 'stakeholding' in the economy, and for allowing the *communities of interest* and *experience* that form around corporate organisations to acquire their own dynamic sensibility. Without it (this sensibility), critics' reform ambitions (for commoning, socialising corporate horizons, and so on) are hard to get off the ground (for example, they routinely face charges of vagueness, slowness and impracticability),[83] and risk becoming an empty reference point for expanding commercialisation. Calculative expectations, in fact, routinely invert energetic socialising agendas that try to argue with *homo economicus* in a normative desert (for example, around widespread subjection). This inversion occurs where the very signs of fragmentation and pluralisation, which critics would normally seek to catalyse and transform, can also double as signs of the very hazards and unknowns that *steely* corporate management systems are *intended* to order, marshal and suppress.

4. END THOUGHTS

The chapter has sought to lay bare the disorientating set of circumstances that face critical scholars in the field of corporate governance, where the arguments of critical scholars risk falling between the different histories and commitments outlined. Stakeholder and commons theories and more 'social' enactments of corporate purposes are all seemingly logical propositions against 'antisocial' and financialised corporate governance, which seems to 'bracket' much of what economic activities are actually about. But the options for reforming the classic shareholder orientation in corporate governance also seem thin after the 'end of history', as financialisation speaks not just to property but also to an urgent search for certainties in a globally functioning world. Certainly, in corporate governance classrooms it is this pursuit of a calculative 'hold' from something chaotic that tends to make the stronger impression on students, as the

---

[82] Beck (n 9) at xxii: 'metamorphosis implies a much more radical transformation in which the old certainties of modern society are falling away and something quite new is emerging'. Beck opposes this to 'change' or 'transformation', terms that imply that some things change but other things remain the same – 'capitalism changes but some aspects remain as they always have been'.

[83] See Gilson (n 1), highlighting speed and responsiveness as the measure of the 'right' systems for corporate government in the twenty-first century; Hayek (n 76), making arguments about complex social worlds and the need to constrain director discretion and have certainty.

enduring justification for efficient corporate governance (rather than the more contested claims to do with property).

That antagonism persists, and sometimes in extremis, in and around corporate networks is an indication of certain compositional and likely behavioural errors concerning the company's kinship with certainty and order in its present guise (early modern *homo economicus*). Can critical legal scholars overcome this by working within the field of corporate governance and company law? This would (still) seem to be the important question. The answer would seem to be first: that, yes, the critical legal project is broadly 'correct' that a major 'barrier' to addressing the social antagonisms created by companies is shareholder primacy. But this barrier needs to be approached not just at the level of domination and (corporate) socialisation, but also at the level of the political pursuits that allow companies to manage and act over society and to stretch their gaze. Critical company lawyers could do more work on this latter front by staying with the antagonism that companies generate, and using what they learn about the relationality that underpins it to bring the expectations about corporations back 'down to Earth'. It is with this different sense of critical inquiry that a new pretext for normative and legacy bound engagement is opened up in the company's case.

19. Critical labour law: then and now
Ruth Dukes[1]

1. INTRODUCTION

Labour law is unusual among legal disciplines in that its mainstream tradition is critical (Klare 2002). It was conceived originally as an intervention in a mode of production in which, for structural reasons, the worker was in a position of weakness relative to his employer, and consequently vulnerable to ill or unfair treatment. The purpose of labour law was widely understood in terms of addressing the imbalance of power in the employment relationship so as to protect and emancipate the vulnerable worker. Early scholars in the field observed that law could achieve this goal in two ways: either directly – by way, for example, of minimum wage or health and safety legislation – or indirectly, by providing for the collectivisation of workers and the collective regulation of workers' terms and conditions of employment. In either case, the desired result of legal intervention was that the freedom of the employer to impose terms unilaterally should be limited and the freedom of the worker correspondingly augmented.

The mainstream tradition in labour law scholarship could not rightly be called Marxist, but it was heavily influenced in its original conception by Marx's writings; above all, perhaps, in its insistence on the human quality of labour – 'this peculiar commodity, which has no other repository than human flesh and blood' (Marx 1849). From the essential fact of labour's humanity followed the concern with the worker's welfare and dignity; the injunction not to treat him as a commodity like any other but somehow to shelter him from exposure to raw market forces. Labour law scholars followed Marx, too, in their comprehension of the defining features of relations of production under capitalism: the existence of distinct social classes (the owners and nonowners of capital) with oppositional political interests, and the subordination of the working class to the capitalist class, the worker to his employer. A second rationale for labour law was often located with the need to establish means of resolving conflicts of interest between capital and labour, management and the workforce, in a way that avoided unconscionable disruptions to production.

In what follows, the mainstream critical tradition in labour law is further elaborated by way of the identification and discussion of four key elements of that tradition, in addition to those already mentioned. These are: (a) a (partial) rejection of the public/private divide in law; (b) a commitment to legal pluralism; (c) legal scepticism;

---

[1] The project leading to this publication has received funding from the European Research Council (ERC) under the European Union's Horizon 2020 research and innovation programme (grant agreement No 757395). I'm grateful to Karl Klare for very helpful comments on an earlier draft.

and (d) the adoption of sociolegal methods. Throughout, reference is made primarily to the two 'founding fathers' of the field with whose work I am most familiar, the German-Jewish scholars Hugo Sinzheimer (1875–1945) and Otto Kahn-Freund (1900–79), and to examples drawn from UK and German law. My suggestion is nonetheless that these four elements were common to mainstream labour law scholarship on both sides of the Atlantic, in the Antipodes and in other jurisdictions which modelled their labour laws on those of European or Anglo-American nations. In section 3 of the chapter, I explain the threat posed in recent decades to the continued viability of systems of labour law that are broadly speaking protective of workers' interests, and emancipatory of workers, by myriad pressures associated with globalisation and deindustrialisation. Again, the discussion proceeds by way of consideration of the four key elements of the critical tradition identified in section 2. The main question addressed is how scholars have sought to adapt their approaches and methods so as to continue to make interventions that are critical in nature and concerned, still, with the transformative potential of labour law.

Especially in a contribution to a volume on critical legal theory, it is important to clarify at the outset the precise sense in which I use the term *critical* in connection with the mainstream tradition in labour law. As is developed in what follows, my point is that labour law scholarship was critical primarily of the substance of laws and legal systems which placed workers in a situation of vulnerability and subordination relative to their employers. Against laws and regimes which entrenched hierarchy and domination, leading scholars in the field argued for the protection and the empowerment of workers, and for the spread of democracy from the public to the private sphere, primarily through the institution of collective bargaining and other forms of collective representation. For the most part, they did not take a critical view of law, legal discourses and legal practices in a manner that would have warranted their designation as *critical legal scholars*. In the postwar decades, moreover, and allowing for some variation across jurisdictions, it is probably fair to say that the critical edge of labour law scholarship became blunted. In some cases, in the 1970s and 1980s, mainstream scholars found themselves denounced from the left for their conservative legitimation – even glorification – of established industrial relations institutions; for cloaking what were argued to be, in fact, repressive practices and regimes with fulsome expressions of approbation (Hyman 1978); for overlooking or obscuring the extent to which trade unions failed to serve the interests of particular categories of workers, including categories that were predominantly or wholly populated by women and by racial and ethnic minorities (Conaghan 1986). In the USA, prominently, such criticism was internal to the field of labour law, so that a gap opened up between two schools: the liberal mainstream and an identifiable 'left' that was *critical* in both senses identified above – on substantive issues, and on jurisprudential questions (Klare 1982b; Fischl, this volume). In other jurisdictions, leftist objections were raised primarily from the sidelines of labour law, by scholars of industrial relations or sociology (e.g. Hyman 1978; Streeck 1984). While the main aim of this chapter is to characterise mainstream approaches *as* criticism, I also refer throughout to such criticisms *of* the mainstream approaches, insofar as space allows. In section 2, I demonstrate how the space for critical interventions of a kind that was originally typical of the mainstream has been narrowed in recent decades, their force weakened, their substance hollowed out. The consequent search for new critical approaches must encompass a root and branch reconsideration of the whole outlook and methodology of scholarship in the field.

2. THE CRITICAL TRADITION IN LABOUR LAW SCHOLARSHIP

Labour law first emerged as a distinct field of scholarship around the beginning of the twentieth century. Of course, by then, laws had long been in force which we might today categorise as labour laws: laws which sought to regulate aspects of relations between workers and those for whom they worked, such as pay; to permit the creation of associations of workers and the taking by them of industrial action; to create mandatory safety standards in mines and factories; and to provide for pensions and welfare for unemployed workers. It was not until the beginning of the last century, however, that – in Germany first of all – anyone thought to consider such laws together, as a single, coherent body of law. What lent the otherwise apparently disparate collection of laws the requisite *sense of coherence* was precisely the notion of intervention, or 'vocation', referred to above: labour laws were those laws which sought, directly or indirectly, to right the imbalance of power in the worker/employer relation, to address the subordination of the working to the capitalist class, and so to protect the otherwise vulnerable worker from ill or unfair treatment (Collins 1989). Also fundamental to labour law scholarship, as it developed across jurisdictions during the course of the following decades, were an at least partial rejection of the public/private divide in law; a recognition of, or commitment to, legal pluralism; a degree of legal scepticism; and the adoption of sociolegal methods.

2.1 Rejection of the Public/Private Divide

Writing in the 1920s on the political significance of labour law in the Weimar Republic, Ernst Fraenkel highlighted as a precondition of the emergence of labour law the 'preparatory work' of developing socialist legal concepts and modes of legal reasoning (Fraenkel 1932). 'There have long been legal relations which we would now characterise as institutions of labour law. But it was not until the peculiarity of labour law relations was recognised, not until the employment relationship was disconnected from the abstract rules of the law of obligations … that labour law as such was discovered' (Fraenkel 1932). As Fraenkel explained, the need for new 'socialist legal concepts' resulted from the inadequacy of the existing institutions of private law when it came to the task of reflecting the economic and social reality of employment relations, and of regulating those relations justly. The individual employment relationship, for example, was only formally a legal contract; substantively it was a relation of dictatorship of the economically strong employer over the economically weak employee. In bargaining collectively, employers and trade unions did not enter into *contractual* relations but, rather, engaged in the autonomous creation of norms governing the relations of third parties (Fraenkel 1932).

The legal scholar and practitioner Hugo Sinzheimer was in no small part responsible for undertaking this 'preparatory work' of analysing employment relations and inventing appropriate legal concepts. In common with other theorists in the late nineteenth and early twentieth centuries, Sinzheimer conceived of labour law, in essence, as a corrective to private law. In doing so, he was directly influenced by Marx and Karl Renner, and above all, perhaps, by Otto von Gierke (Sinzheimer 1922). Writing towards the end of the nineteenth century, Gierke argued in favour of the creation of a body of law to be known as 'social law', which would address the inequities arising from the formalistic separation of private and public law that was embodied in the German Civil Code (Seifert 2011). Social law would protect the economically weak by ensuring a greater degree of 'balance' in private law transactions, tempering the power of the economically stronger party.

In the work of Sinzheimer, as in that of Beatrice and Sidney Webb before him, the imbalance of power in the employment relation was understood to merit the drawing of an analogy with the sovereign and subject, or state and citizen. In this way, again, the public/private divide was disputed, and the case made instead for the necessary application of 'public law' concepts – democracy, participation – to the economic sphere. To wage labourers, wrote the Webbs,

> the uncontrolled power wielded by the owners of the means of production, able to withhold from the manual worker all chance of subsistence unless he accepted their terms, meant a far more genuine loss of liberty, and a far keener sense of personal subjection, than the ... far-off, impalpable rule of the king. (Webb and Webb 1897)

In demanding freedom of association and factory legislation, workers demanded, in effect, a 'constitution' in the industrial realm. The legal recognition of collective bargaining and the gradual elaboration of a labour code signified the concession of a 'Magna Carta' to the entire wage-earning class, and the extension of the values of liberty and equality from the political into the industrial sphere. For Sinzheimer, as for the Webbs, it was important that the state – as representative of the common interest – should be recognised as the ultimate guardian and architect of the system of collective bargaining and labour law: the economic constitution ought to be subordinate, in other words, to the political constitution. As a matter of principle, and as prescribed by law, economic actors should be autonomous from the state but at the same time dependent upon it as the ultimate source of their legislative powers (Sinzheimer 1927). For Kahn-Freund, Sinzheimer's onetime student, in contrast, collective bargaining was a process decidedly private to the collective parties engaged in it. The parties should enjoy the freedom to decide on the content of negotiated agreements, and on the methods of their negotiation and enforcement, without undue 'interference' from government. But this did not alter the perception that what was being brought to the economic sphere through the spread of collective bargaining was a measure of *democracy* (Davies and Freedland 1983). Indeed, this was a commonly held view in the postwar decades, not only among scholars of labour law, of course, but also those sociologists and social and political theorists who advocated economic or industrial democracy and industrial or social citizenship.

Whether and to what extent these 'public law' ideas – democracy, citizenship – were also accepted and utilised by governments and policymakers as a means of understanding and justifying labour laws and collective bargaining no doubt varied from jurisdiction to jurisdiction. Insofar as relations between workers and their employers continued to be conceived of as essentially *contractual* in nature, however, and employers to be thought of still as the *owners* of the employing organisation or workplace in question, private law concepts and principles remained highly relevant, even central, to the interpretation of labour law. In the common law courts of Anglo-American jurisdictions, they were used (still are used) quite routinely to justify the imposition of limits on workers' collective rights, and narrow interpretations of their statutory employment rights (Wedderburn 1986). In 1982, Karl Klare famously analysed such tendencies on the part of the judiciary with direct reference to the 'public/private distinction in labor law':

> The essence of the public/private distinction is the conviction that it is possible to conceive of social and economic life apart from government and law, indeed that it is impossible or dangerous to conceive of it any other way. The core ideological function served by the public/private distinction is to deny that the practices comprising the private sphere of life – the worlds of business, education and culture, the community and the family – are inextricably linked to and at least partially constituted by politics and law (Klare 1982a).

In truth, argued Klare, there was no 'public/private distinction', but instead 'a series of ways of thinking about public and private that are constantly undergoing revisions, reformulations, and refinement'. The distinction posed as an analytical tool in labour law but functioned instead 'as a form of political rhetoric used to justify particular results' (Klare 1982a).

2.2 Legal Pluralism

In conceiving of collective bargaining as a *regulatory* process – of terms of collective agreements as *norms* having application to third parties – scholars of labour law claimed, or assumed, the legitimacy of the involvement of nonstate actors in law creation and law enforcement. Often, the notion of 'industrial pluralism' was used to describe and analyse systems of collective bargaining, implying, again, a set of analogies with democratic institutions from the political sphere.

> The collective bargaining process is said to function like a legislature in which management and labour, both sides representing their separate constituencies, engage in debate and compromise, and together legislate the rules under which the workplace will be governed. The set of rules that results is alternatively called a statute or a constitution – the basic industrial pluralist metaphors for the collective bargaining agreement (Van Wezel Stone 1981).

The characterisation of collective bargaining as regulation was underpinned by the fact that – in a variety of ways, depending on the jurisdiction in question – the normative terms of collective agreements were accorded the force of law. Relying quite directly on Sinzheimer's analysis of collective agreements, for example, a provision was enacted in Germany in 1918 which accorded such terms 'automatic compulsory normative effect' in respect of all workers and employers bound by the agreement. Under UK law, the normative terms of collective agreements were understood to be implied terms of the relevant contracts of employment, and binding, as such, on the parties to those contracts. Moreover, it was not only the terms of collective agreements which were recognised to have legal force, but also, in certain circumstances, norms originating from the 'custom and practice' of a particular trade, from the rulebook at a factory or plant, or from the constitution, or rule book, of a trade union. Used descriptively, or analytically, then, the terms 'pluralism' or 'industrial pluralism' were intended to capture something of the 'complexity, heterogeneity and internal diversity', as Harry Arthurs put it, of the regulation of working relations:

> the inability of overarching normative regimes to penetrate and transform all contexts, such as places of work, and the persistent tendency of such contexts themselves to generate and enforce distinctive norms expressing values which are, at least in some respects, different from those of the encompassing society. (Arthurs 1985)

Used normatively rather than descriptively, the notion of industrial pluralism tended to imply or explain the user's approval of systems of collective bargaining. Writing about British society in the first half of the twentieth century, for example, Kahn-Freund famously described with admiration what he understood to be the tendency for interest groups to participate increasingly in a variety of 'governmental' functions – 'the "pressure" of the pressure groups has been so organised as to work inside the legislative, administrative, judicial and policy making processes' – a tendency which had been of particular significance, he observed, for the development of collective bargaining (Kahn-Freund 1959). Arriving in London in 1933 from Germany, Kahn-Freund believed himself to have encountered in Great Britain 'an inherited political and social culture in which everyone participated, including the workers in the unions' (Kahn-Freund 1981). This was the type of democracy which was furthered, in the pluralist's vision, by the institution of collective bargaining.

Developed in response to the fascism of the Nazis, and informed by the writings of Harold Laski, Kahn-Freund's pluralism was of a firmly social democratic variety. It drew criticism, nonetheless, from the left as resting on a set of highly questionable assumptions: that through the unionisation of workers a balance of power was achieved between labour and capital; that the 'legitimate' interests of labour were only those that could be accommodated through the process of collective bargaining; that workers valued trade unions first and foremost as a means of participating in the regulation of jobs, and not as a means of securing improvements in their working and living conditions (Hyman 1978). Similar objections were raised elsewhere to US scholars' use of the 'industrial pluralism' label, in their case not as a refutation of Nazism, but rather as a celebration of the superiority of the American way over the 'totalitarianism' of the USSR (Van Wezel Stone 1981; Hyman 1978).

2.3 Legal Scepticism

In its original conception, as we have seen, the very idea of labour *law* inferred a belief in the transformative potential of new legislation, of new legal concepts and principles. At the end of the First World War and in the early days of Weimar social democracy,

Sinzheimer's writings were striking for the extent to which their argument relied upon the presumed ability of the people to construct a better and fairer way of life for themselves, harnessing the power of the state, and the law, in order to do so. In the 1930s, mass unemployment and the ensuing 'crisis in labour law' led him to question what he had previously taken for granted: the capacity of law to mould or transform social life (Sinzheimer 1933). In the first years of the Republic, as Sinzheimer saw it, labour rights and collective institutions had been introduced in the belief that these could achieve the resolution of conflicts of interest between the social classes, allowing for the regulation of production and work in the interests of all. Bringing with it steeply declining wages and catastrophic levels of unemployment, the economic crisis of the early 1930s cast doubt on the capacity of labour law to function as intended within a capitalist – 'private law' – economy. A renewal of labour law no longer appeared possible without the renewal of the entire economic order.

Influenced by his own experiences of the decline of the Weimar Republic, Kahn-Freund later developed a theory of labour law in the UK that was premised on a very marked degree of scepticism regarding the capacity of law to influence social behaviour. 'In labour relations', he wrote, 'legal norms cannot often be effective unless they are backed by social sanctions as well, that is by the countervailing power of trade unions and of the organised workers asserted through consultation and negotiation with the employer and ultimately, if this fails, through withholding their labour' (Kahn-Freund 1972). For Kahn-Freund, it was a mark of the comparative maturity of trade union organisation and collective labour management relations in the UK that these functioned with little need for *legal* sanctions (Kahn-Freund 1954). 'British industrial relations have, in the main, developed by way of industrial autonomy ... [E]mployers and employees have formulated their own codes of conduct and devised their own machinery for enforcing them' (Kahn-Freund 1954).

While remaining more sanguine about the potential of legislation to effect change, others directed their scepticism more specifically at the involvement of the *courts* in labour law. Pointing, in the first instance, to the essentially political nature of employment relations, courts were argued to be fundamentally unsuited to the task of deciding work-related disputes and interpreting labour law. 'It is not good for trade unions that they should be brought in contact with the courts', commented no less a figure than Winston Churchill in 1911, 'and it is not good for the courts' (Kahn-Freund 1959). Even if outright class bias on the part of the judiciary could be discounted, it was elsewhere argued, it remained the case that judges were trained first and foremost in the *common, or civil, law*. To them, then, labour law – and especially perhaps the branch of it pertaining to trade unions and collective bargaining – appeared to consist of a set of 'artificially' imposed and essentially inequitable contraventions of common (civil) law rules and principles. That being the case, it was argued further, justice in the sphere of labour law could only be achieved through the creation of specialist labour courts or tribunals to hear labour disputes. Only by removing labour law from the purview of the ordinary courts could the necessary *autonomy* of labour law from private law be secured (Bogg, Costello et al 2015).

2.4 Sociolegal Method

The perceptions that private law was not up to the task of regulating working relationships; that concepts drawn from the public sphere – democracy, constitution – could rightly be applied to the organisation of work and production; that the common or civil law courts had better not be entrusted with that task – all of this followed from the apprehension of a few essential truths about working relations: that labour was human, and not a commodity like any other; that it was inherent to capitalism that the interests of the social classes should conflict; and that the worker was subordinate to the employer, as labour was subordinate to capital. For some scholars writing at the beginning of the twentieth century, these truths had little direct relevance to the discipline of labour law. In line with the notion of *law as science*, it was argued that scholarship in the field should limit itself quite decidedly to treating in depth the *legal* aspects of the material at hand (Nogler 1996). Sinzheimer and his followers differed from these scholars most decidedly in their adoption of a sociological approach to the study of the law. For them, it was of fundamental importance that 'the law' (that which was embodied in legislation and court judgements) should be recognised to differ in its nature from 'legal reality' (the norms which governed social action). Laws did not always take effect as intended by the legislature or the courts; moreover, norms could develop in the course of economic and social interactions that were not always recognised by the legal order. Analysis of the law had then to look beyond the law books at 'concrete' legal forms and arrangements, and to analyse these and their relationship to formal law. It had to consider 'the social effect of the norm ... the way in which it appears in society and ... its social function' (Kahn-Freund 1981). Where discrepancies could be identified between the formal law and social actors' understandings of the norms which governed their behaviour, these could be used to inform policy formation.

In his work on English labour law, Kahn-Freund employed an approach similar to Sinzheimer's, drawing a distinction habitually between 'the law' and a separately identifiable social reality: 'the actual state of affairs' (Kahn-Freund 1954). While the former could be read from the statute books and case reports, the latter, it seemed to be assumed, was a question of 'the facts' as revealed through observation or empirical investigation. In seeking to ascertain the relevant facts, in England in the 1950s and 1960s, Kahn-Freund found that he was unable to rely on the work of fellow legal scholars. Most legal scholarship at the time was 'positivistic, setting out and analysing the conceptual detail of legal rules, with scant recognition of history or sociology' (Hepple 2013). Instead, he turned to academics working in the field of industrial relations, especially the 'Oxford School' led by Allan Flanders and Hugh Clegg. Normatively, these scholars shared with Kahn-Freund a pluralist outlook that was rooted in a traditional liberal distrust of power (Hyman 1978). Broadly speaking, their preferred methodology was sociological, or 'multidisciplinary'; it was characterised above all by a preference for empirical methods and by a degree of scepticism regarding the usefulness of 'grand theory' (Brown and Wright 1994). The priority, as Richard Hyman once wrote of Clegg, was 'to get the facts right' (Hyman 1994).

During the course of the 1950s, 1960s and 1970s, the collaboration between Kahn-Freund and members of the Oxford School extended beyond those particular individuals to encompass a whole generation of British and Irish labour law scholars and 'industrial relations scholars with a legal bent', chief among them Bill Wedderburn, Paul O'Higgins, Roy Lewis, Jon Clark and Bob Hepple (Davies and Freedland 2002). When Wedderburn published the first edition of his famous textbook *The Worker and the Law* in 1965, he quite consciously emulated Kahn-Freund's method, placing the institution of collective bargaining at the heart of the analysis rather than any statute or body of case law, and referring throughout the text to the work of historians and other social scientists, as well as to primary and secondary legal materials (Hepple 2013). In 1983 he continued to advocate this approach, writing, with Lewis and Clark, that 'the lawyer who ignores the insights into the problems of industrial relations offered by colleagues in the social sciences will never make, by the standards which Kahn-Freund set, a labour lawyer worthy of the name' (Wedderburn, Lewis et al 1983). He also defined the purpose of labour law scholarship in a way that echoed Sinzheimer's identification of a concern with policy as inherent to the field: the role of the scholar, in Wedderburn's opinion, was to assess the consequences for workers of particular laws and social arrangements with a view to influencing the formation of legal policy, legislation and legal precedent. 'Projects for new labour laws must be tested in concrete terms by their effect upon real people, the condition and quality of their lives, their prosperity and their – real, not theoretical – liberty' (Wedderburn 1986).

Reflecting the extent to which this kind of sociolegal or 'law in context' approach became mainstream not only in the UK but throughout western Europe, a similar method was adopted and elaborated by a group of leading scholars embarking on a major comparative research project in the 1970s (Hepple 1986a). For these scholars, it was of fundamental importance that labour law should be recognised to be part of an historical process, and not as a relatively static and neutral set of rules and institutions intended to regulate employment: 'the rules and institutions are shaped by the historically given possibilities within which various sectional groups pursue their often-conflicting objectives. Labour law is made by men and women in a society not of their own making' (Hepple 1986b).

Resisting any suggestion that the development of labour law within capitalist societies was *universal* – that in all jurisdictions it would develop along the same lines for the same reasons – the authors sought instead to address the question of how particular measures came to be introduced within each country at particular points in time. The crucial element in the making of labour law, they believed, was power. Labour legislation was best understood as the outcome of a process of struggle between different social groups – monarchy, bureaucracy and middle class; bourgeoisie and working class; townspeople and countryfolk – and of competing ideologies of conservatives, liberals and socialists, as well as religious and secular groups. What any particular group of people got from the struggle was not just a matter of what they chose or wanted, however, but of what they could 'force or persuade other groups to let them have' (Hepple 1986b).

3. LABOUR LAW TODAY

The mainstream tradition in labour law scholarship was influenced very profoundly by the political economy of the time. This was an era in which Fordist methods of production predominated, with stable, full-time employment for male breadwinners, managerial hierarchies in vertically integrated firms and high levels of trade union membership. Employer-producers and worker-consumers alike were largely nationally based and confined, as were the labour and product markets within which they operated. During the course of the past half century, the organisation of work and production has been transformed as part of broader trends associated with deindustrialisation and globalisation. A particular brand of neoclassical economic thinking about working relationships and labour law has asserted itself as orthodox, shaping the policy and legislation of governments of both the centre right and centre left, and even, over time, workers' own perceptions of the world of work – increasingly, we have come to self-identify as entrepreneurs of ourselves, entering the labour market (rather than looking for a job), making ourselves 'marketable'. Each of these developments has posed significant challenges to traditional ways of thinking about labour law, occasioning much soul-searching on the part of scholars in the field. The dominant discourse in recent decades has been one of *crisis*: old ways of thinking about the subject, of describing and analysing it, have seemed increasingly inadequate, but new ways have yet to be found (Davidov and Langille 2011).

3.1 Reassertion and Shifting of the Public/Private Divide

It is definitive of the new economic orthodoxy that the desirable role of the state in the economy generally, and in the regulation of work more specifically, should be recast in primarily negative terms. In order to ensure economic growth and job creation, so the line of reasoning goes, governments should take steps to maximise entrepreneurial freedom, liberating business from the unnecessary and damaging 'red tape' of worker-protective laws and institutions. Previously state-owned industries (in which unions were traditionally strong) should be sold off, and in the remaining rump of a public sector the logic of competition should be forcibly introduced, with services (and therefore jobs) contracted out to whomever can promise to provide them most cheaply. If support is to be given at all, any more, to trade unions and other forms of worker representation, then this should be done not in the name of furthering industrial democracy, but with reference instead to the economic benefits of facilitating (strictly limited and neutered) expressions of employee 'voice'. If rights are to be accorded, still, to individual employees – rights to a minimum wage or to parental leave – then these should be tailored to ensure that the burden on employers is not too great, the benefit to 'the economy as a whole' sufficiently well established.

Insofar as national governments accept and adopt the appealingly simple logic of such arguments – and most of them do – the implications for the labour law of the country in question will likely be severe. Where there is opposition from the electorate to the dismantling of hard-won labour rights and protections, reference may be made by government to the stark realities of the globalised world: the increased mobility of capital and the intensification of global competition that result from the liberalisation of trade (Klare 2002). Because capital is free to threaten or choose relocation, thereby resisting or circumventing the strictures of national laws and institutions, national governments are under significant pressure to lower labour standards and corporate taxes as a means of retaining or attracting capital investment. The liberalisation and integration of finance, meanwhile, create a new source of discipline for national governments, which must now either tow the orthodox economic line or face the – potentially devastating – prospect of capital flight, or an increase in the rate of interest charged on government bonds. As the example of the European Union illustrates, governments might choose to enter into multilateral or bilateral trade agreements which place further limits on their capacity to retain or enact labour rights and standards, as such rights and standards come to figure as prohibited breaches of the contract, or property, or free trade rights enjoyed by private actors under the terms of the trade agreements (Dukes 2017). States in need of financial aid from international organisations such as the World Bank or IMF, meanwhile, may quite routinely be required to agree to programmes of deregulation or 'flexibilisation' of their labour markets as conditions of loan agreements (Adams and Deakin 2015).

With reference to the public/private divide, these developments may be apprehended as the recolonisation of the public by the private, the political by the economic; the extension of markets and economic rationalities into spheres which were previously ordered according to alternative logics. Scholars of labour law have criticised governments for the political use they've sought to make of the 'globalisation' narrative – our hands are tied! – but while they have emphasised the extent to which nation states are themselves the authors of that narrative, they have not, for the most part, contested its essentials. On the part of scholars too, then, the language of industrial democracy is rarely used any more, unless it is to mourn all that has been lost. Across the field, a fairly widespread change in approach has been discernible from the study of labour law understood as the law of work, to the analysis of those laws (including social welfare, immigration) which regulate labour markets. Utilising economic methods and modes of analysis, some scholars have turned their attentions to constructing a defence of what were originally understood to be – *celebrated as* – market-correcting institutions, on the basis, now, of their putative – or even demonstrable – economic benefits: labour laws are beneficial because they address negative externalities, provide solutions to collective action problems, minimise transaction costs. Others have used a 'market' framing of the field to call into question matters which, traditionally, were taken as read: for example, the treatment in law of some work (jobs) as paid employment and other work (domestic and reproductive labour) as an unpaid and untaxed contribution to the household (Fudge 2011). More generally, questions have been directed at the constitution of labour markets by law and other social norms: not only labour law, but also social welfare, immigration and – of course – private law. In contrast to scholars in the postwar decades, at least some of those working in the field today have placed a rather clearer emphasis on the contingency of private law as well as labour law rules, treating the former not as a preexisting field in which labour law then intervenes, but as themselves embodying contestable political judgements regarding the definition and attribution of privileges, powers and entitlements (Klare 2002). An important task for critical scholars is then to identify the distributive consequences of *all* market-constituting rules – private law, labour law, social welfare law – and to consider their variation as a potential route to achieving particular goals (Klare 1982).

3.2 Legal Pluralism Continued

As a result of the lowering of labour standards and the weakening and marginalisation of trade unions – the recommodification of labour – the contract is emerging as the primary source of legal norms in the organisation of work. As systems of collective industrial relations are replaced by professionalised human resource management, it is more and more often the case, moreover, that the choice of form of work contract, and the drafting of specific terms, is in the power of the employing organisation alone. On the part of the worker there is very little, if any, scope for negotiating improved terms and conditions. Motivated in particular by a desire to maximise 'flexibility', employers have made ever greater use of a variety of forms that do not fall within the legal category of 'contract of employment'. Throughout the developed world, there has been a significant rise in the number of workers hired through agencies, or as part-time, or casual, or zero hours workers, or as formally self-employed 'entrepreneurs', paid by 'clients' for the performance of discrete tasks or 'gigs' (Stone and Arthurs 2013). By workers, this has been experienced first and foremost as a loss of security in employment; as the substitution of *precariousness* for security. Because they are not 'employees' in the eyes of the law, employment protection laws do not apply.

Notwithstanding this resurgence of the contract as the primary means of regulating working relationships, legal pluralist perspectives remain important to the study of labour law. The terms of collective agreements are after all still legally binding and still significant in substance, albeit for a shrinking proportion of the workforce. In the face of the retreat of the state from the economic sphere, meanwhile, there has been a proliferation of private orderings of working relations and labour standards, not only by means of contract but also, significantly, corporate codes, multilateral 'accords' or 'alliances', and – rather less frequently – supranational collective agreements. At the supranational level, too, labour standards are now routinely addressed by trade agreements, or 'side agreements' appended thereto. In an influential study of 2007, Bob Hepple surveyed these developments and inferred from them the emergence of a 'spider's web' of hard and soft transnational labour standards regulation, woven around domestic labour laws and influencing them profoundly (Hepple 2007). Less optimistic accounts have criticised corporate codes, accords and alliances as 'vague, horatory, and not well suited to compelling compliance' (Arthurs 2004), and labour side agreements for being soft in nature and thin in substance, especially when compared with the trade agreements to which they are appended (Church Albertson and Compa 2015). In such circumstances, the existence of a plurality of regimes and orderings has been identified by some as itself a threat rather than a boon to the maintenance of labour standards (Alston 2004). Absent a body capable of exercising statelike powers of coordination and enforcement at the supranational level, who will decide which rules apply in a case of 'conflict of laws', other than the employing organisation itself?

3.3 Legal Scepticism of a Different Sort

In the current political context, where the word is with Friedman and Hayek and not with Keynes, scholars of labour law do not always view the courts with the same degree of suspicion that they once did. Instead, many look to the judiciary as a potential force for good when it comes to the furtherance of workers' interests: as a potential brake on the deregulatory impulses of legislatures. In exercising such powers of control, or review, courts should have reference, it is argued, to the human rights or fundamental rights guaranteed in one or other of a wide range of international, regional or national charters and treaties, and even by the common law (Bogg 2018). Whereas Wedderburn once observed a pendulum of statutory rules swinging between the progressive intentions of Parliament and the reactionary interpretations of the judiciary, today we should rather expect a similar kind of motion, but with a reversal of the poles (Wedderburn 1986). Scholars frequently engage in the important work of analysing the extent of the constraints posed by human rights on the freedom of action of a legislature; of identifying the fundamental rights and principles inherent or emergent in the common law and pointing the way to their future development (Bogg 2016). In doing so, they may hope to assist courts or potential litigants, but also perhaps to strengthen political arguments for legislative change or – where deregulation is threatened – more modestly for maintenance of the status quo.

Of course, many voices continue to be raised warning of the likely limits of a 'human rights strategy' when it comes to the furtherance of workers' interests. In an oft cited paper, Kevin Kolben identified a problematic lack of fit between labour rights and human rights which, in his opinion, threatened a 'weakening commitment to the economic justice and workplace democracy principles that have long underpinned labor rights thought and practice' (Kolben 2010). Others have given renewed emphasis to lessons learned long ago regarding the inherent conservatism of the courts, and the ineffectiveness of individual litigation as a means of furthering the interests of a whole class (Arthurs 2007). Case studies have been developed demonstrating that, on the part of legislatures, the notion of human rights breaches can tend more easily to criminalisation of the worst kinds of abuses, rather than to the raising of standards across the board (Fudge 2018). It is quite possible, on the other hand, to be cognisant of the limitations and stumbling blocks in the way of advocating for workers' human rights, and nonetheless to seek to do so – partly, perhaps, because other strategies and courses of action appear, in particular contexts, even less likely to succeed (Klare 2014). In the field of labour law, as elsewhere, moreover, and in the face of the apparent futility today of arguments which speak to workplace democracy and social citizenship, human rights discourse provides an alternative – and widely understood – language with which to insist upon limits to the otherwise inexorable spread of markets and market thinking (Ewing 2010). It follows that a sizeable proportion of labour law scholarship now includes at least an invocation of human or fundamental rights, if not a detailed consideration of their relevance to the question at hand.

3.4 Methodological Innovation?

Together with the turn to human rights, on the one hand, and to labour markets, on the other, there has been a growing perception among scholars of labour law of the need for methodological innovation in the field. Seeking a firmer basis for the normative claims inherent in any argument for the protection of workers' rights, some have looked to philosophy and political theory – mostly of the liberal variety, but sometimes also socialist or social democratic in persuasion (Collins, Lester et al 2018; K.D. Ewing 1995). On the part of those who have sought directly to refute the orthodox position that labour standards inhibit economic growth – that, at best, they benefit a few 'insiders' to the cost of all 'outsiders' – there has been greater recourse to economic methods and modes of reasoning. Microeconomic models, game theory, econometrics, new institutionalism – all have been used to garner evidence that labour laws can help to improve productivity levels, reduce unit labour costs and increase the profitability of businesses and the competitiveness of whole sectors and national economies (Estlund and Wachter 2012).

Acknowledging the importance of labour markets as elements of the field of study, but finding the critical potential of even heterodox economic approaches to the analysis of 'labour market regulation' to be limited, others have identified the challenge of identifying or developing methods which might better allow for the analysis of the role of law in constituting markets and, at the same time, for recognition of the inherently *political* nature of the manner of such constitution: of the questions of how markets are combined with or constrained by 'nonmarket' institutions and modes of action and interaction; of who falls to benefit and who to be disadvantaged by particular market configurations and orderings (Chapman, Landau et al 2017; Fenwick and Marshall 2016). Of course, this is not a challenge that is particular to the field of labour law. Right across the social sciences, the colonisation of the public by the private, as it was termed above – the 'interpenetration of the social and the market' (Rittich 2014) – has called into question the well-established practice, in both economics and sociology, of treating the economy as a social domain differentiated from the rest of society and subject to its own rules (Beckert and Streeck 2008). If the dividing line between the economy and society has broken down in practice then it also, it has been argued, needs to be broken down in theory. An approach or set of approaches is needed which will allow researchers to explore the social logic and the social nature of the economy – of economic institutions and economic action – and to revisit the question of the essential relationship between economy and society. A promising first step might be to return to the classical traditions of sociology and political economy represented in the work of Durkheim, Weber and the institutional economists of the early twentieth century (Beckert and Streeck 2008; Coutu 2011; Stone 2014).

From the point of view of the analysis of labour law, political economy approaches are useful for the attention which they draw to the role of the state, and to legislation and public policy as expressions of struggles between different actors over political influence (Menz 2015). Using such approaches, scholars can analyse labour markets as they are configured within particular economies and not as ahistorical, apolitical entities with their own 'natural' logics. They can assess the impact of particular laws and policies over a period of real time and not only in the 'snapshot' view presented by economic modelling (Robinson 1980); and they can again utilise the kind of comparative and historical methodologies that have long been typical of mainstream labour law (Marshall 2014). Economic sociology, meanwhile, seeks to understand behaviour that is economically motivated but configured, at the same time, by social norms, institutions and understandings, so that the fit with working relationships and the behaviour of parties to those relationships is clear (Swedberg 1998; Bandelj 2009). Scholars of labour *law* are, of course, also concerned to understand how (economic and social) behaviour is shaped – directly and indirectly – by applicable laws and regulations; and, at the same time, how human agency pervades the construction of social and legal orders (Klare 1982b). Methods are required that will allow for the investigation of actors' perceptions of the law and the ways in which those perceptions shape their behaviour in the world of work, while taking account also of their economic interests and motivations, and of social norms and shared understandings of what is standard or fair in any given situation.

4. CONCLUSION

My principal objective in this chapter has been to present the mainstream tradition in labour law as critical, and, in section 3, to demonstrate how, in the course of deindustrialisation and globalisation, changing practices, procedures and perceptions have rendered traditional lines of argumentation increasingly redundant or unlikely to be heard. Highlighting four central elements of labour law scholarship, I suggested that the mainstream tradition was critical, primarily, of the *substance* of law and legal regimes which placed the worker in a situation of subordination and vulnerability relative to the employer. In the Weimar Republic, scholars called for the democratisation of the economy as a means of emancipating workers and securing greater substantive quality between the social classes. In the postwar decades, scholars used a similar language of industrial democracy or industrial pluralism to express and explain their support for collective bargaining, and other mechanisms for the collective representation of workers. If the Weimar scholars understood – albeit too late – the ways in which the 'social' rationality of labour law would forever be undermined by the 'individualistic' rationality of private law and the capitalist economic order (Sinzheimer 1933; Fraenkel 1932), a central shortcoming of mainstream labour law scholarship in the postwar era was its partial blindness in this respect: its assumption that an effective system of labour law could be rigged on top of systems of private law and corporate law that were otherwise essentially unchanged (Klare 1982b). Building on the work of current scholars of labour law, but also on critical approaches in legal theory, political economy and economic sociology, a renewed and reimagined critical labour law today must grapple more comprehensively with questions of the legal construction of labour markets, of relations of work and of production.

REFERENCES

Adams, Z. and S. Deakin, 'Structural Adjustment, Social Policy and Social Policy in a Regional Context: The Case of the Eurozone Crisis' in A Blackett and A Trebilcock (eds), Research Handbook on Transnational Labour Law (Edward Elgar 2015)
Alston, P. '"Core Labour Standards" and the Transformation of the International Labour Rights Regime' (2004) 15(3) European Journal of International Law 457–521
Arthurs, H. 'Understanding Labour Law: The Debate over "Industrial Pluralism"' (1985) 38(1) Current Legal Problems 83–116
Arthurs, H. 'Private Ordering and Workers' Rights in the Global Economy' in J. Conaghan, M. Fischl and K. Klare (eds), Labour Law in an Era of Globalization (Oxford University Press 2004)
Arthurs, H. 'Labour and the "Real" Constitution' (2007) 48(1/2) Les Cahiers du Droit 43–64
Ashiagbor, D. 'Theorising the Relationship between Social Law and Markets in Regional Integration Projects' (2018) 27(4) Social & Legal Studies 435–55
Bandelj, N. (ed), Towards an Economic Sociology of Work (Emerald 2009)
Beckert, J. and W. Streeck, 'Economic Sociology and Political Economy: A Programmatic Perspective' (2008) MPIfG Working Paper 08/4
Bogg, A. 'Common Law and Statute in the Law of Employment' (2016) 69(1) Current Legal Problems 67–113
Bogg, A. 'The Common Law Constitution at Work: R (on the application of UNISON) v Lord Chancellor' (2018) 81(3) Modern Law Review 509–26
Bogg, A., C. Costello, A.C.L. Davies and J. Prassl (eds), The Autonomy of Labour Law (Hart 2015)
Brown, W. and M. Wright, 'The Empirical Tradition in Workplace Bargaining Research' (1994) 32(2) British Journal of Industrial Relations 153–64
Chapman, I., I. Landau and J. Howe (eds), The Evolving Project of Labour Law: Foundations, Development and Future Research Directions (Federation Press 2017)
Church Albertson, P. and L. Compa, 'Labour Rights and Trade Agreements in the Americas' in A. Blackett and A. Trebilcock (eds), Research Handbook on Transnational Labour Law (Edward Elgar 2015)
Collins, H. 'Labour Law as a Vocation' (1989) 105 Law Quarterly Review 468–84
Collins, H., G. Lester and V. Mantouvalou (eds), The Philosophical Foundations of Labour Law (Oxford University Press 2018)
Conaghan, J. 'The Invisibility of Women in Labour Law: Gender Neutrality in Model Building' (1986) 14 International Journal of Sociology of Law 377–92
Coutu, M. 'John R. Commons and Max Weber: The Foundations of an Economic Sociology of Law' (2011) 38(4) Journal of Law and Society 469–95
Davidov, G. and B. Langille (eds), The Idea of Labour Law (Oxford University Press 2011)
Davies, P. and M. Freedland (eds), Kahn-Freund's Labour and the Law (Stevens 1983)
Davies, P. and M. Freedland, 'National Styles in Labor Law Scholarship: The United Kingdom' (2002) 23 Comparative Labor Law and Policy Journal 765–87
Dukes, R. The Labour Constitution: The Enduring Idea of Labour Law (Oxford University Press 2014)
Dukes, R. 'International Labour Rights: Legitimising the International Legal Order?' (2017) 67(4) University of Toronto Law Journal 544–68.
Estlund, C.L. and M.L. Wachter, Research Handbook on the Economics of Labor and Employment Law (Edward Elgar 2012)
Ewing, K.D. 'Democratic Socialism and Labour Law' (1995) 24(2) Industrial Law Journal 103–32
Ewing, K.D. 'Foreword' in T. Novitz and C. Fenwick (eds), Human Rights at Work (Hart 2010)
Fenwick, C. and S. Marshall (eds), Labour Regulation and Development: Socio-Legal Perspectives (Edward Elgar 2016)
Fraenkel, E. 'Die politische Bedeutung des Arbeitsrechts' (1932) in T. Ramm (ed.), Arbeitsrecht und Politik: Quellentexte 1918–1933 (Luchterhand 1966).
Fudge, J. 'Labour as a "Fictive Commodity": Radically Reconceptualizing Labour Law' in G. Davidov and B. Langille (eds), The Idea of Labour Law (Oxford University Press 2011)
Fudge, J. 'Modern Slavery, Unfree Labour and the Labour Market: The Social Dynamics of Legal Characterization' (2018) 27(4) Social & Legal Studies 414–34
Hepple, B. (ed.), The Making of Labour Law in Europe: A Comparative Study of Nine Countries up to 1945 (Mansell 1986)

Hepple, B. 'Introduction' in B. Hepple (ed.), *The Making of Labour Law in Europe: A Comparative Study of Nine Countries up to 1945* (Mansell 1986)
Hepple, B. *Labour Laws and Global Trade* (Hart 2007)
Hepple, B. 'Wedderburn's The Worker and the Law: An Appreciation' (2013) 34 Historical Studies in Industrial Relations 215–27
Hyman, R. 'Pluralism, Procedural Consensus, Collective Bargaining' (1978) 16(1) British Journal of Industrial Relations 16–40
Hyman, R. 'Theory and Industrial Relations' (1994) 32(2) British Journal of Industrial Relations 165–80, 165
Kahn-Freund, O. 'Legal Framework' in A. Flanders and H.A. Clegg, *The System of Industrial Relations in Great Britain* (Blackwell 1954)
Kahn-Freund, O. 'Labour Law' in M. Ginsberg (ed.), *Law and Opinion in England in the 20th Century* (Stevens 1959)
Kahn-Freund, O. *Labour and the Law* (Stevens 1972)
Kahn-Freund, O. 'Hugo Sinzheimer' in R. Lewis and J. Clark (eds) *Labour Law and Politics in the Weimar Republic* (Oxford 1981) 98
Kahn-Freund, O. 'Postscript' in R. Lewis and J. Clark (ed.), *Labour Law and Politics in the Weimar Republic* (Oxford 1981) 199
Klare, K. 'The Public/Private Distinction in Labor Law' (1982) 130(6) University of Pennsylvania Law Review 1358–1422
Klare, K. 'Critical Theory and Labor Relations Law' in D. Kairys (ed.), *The Politics of Law: A Progressive Critique* (3rd ed, Basic Books 1982)
Klare, K. 'Horizons of Transformative Labour Law' in J. Conaghan, R.M. Fischl, K. Klare (eds), *Labour Law in an Era of Globalisation: Transformative Practices and Possibilities* (Oxford University Press 2002)
Klare, K. 'Critical Perspectives on Social and Economic Rights, Democracy and Separation of Powers' in H. Alviar García, K. Klare and L. Williams (eds), *Social and Economic Rights in Theory and Practice* (Routledge 2014)
Kolben, K. 'Labor Rights as Human Rights?' (2010) 50 Virginia Journal of International Law 449–84
Marshall, S. 'How Does Institutional Change Occur? Two Strategies for Reforming the Scope of Labour Law' (2014) 43(4) Industrial Law Journal 286–318
Marx, K. 'Wage Labour and Capital' (1849) *Neue Rheinische Zeitung*, April, 5–8 and 11 www.marxists.org/archive/marx/works/download/pdf/wage-labour-capital.pdf
Menz, G. 'Employers and Migrant Legality: Liberalization of Service Provision, Transnational Posting, and the Bifurcation of the European Labour Market' in C. Costello and M. Freedland (eds), *Migrants at Work* (Oxford University Press 2015)
Nogler, L. 'In Memory of Hugo Sinzheimer (1875–1945): Remarks on the Methodenstreit in Labour Law' (1996) Vol. 2 Cardozo Law Bulletin, www.jus.unitn.it/cardozo/review/laborlaw/nogler-1996/nogler.htm
Rittich, K. 'Making Natural Markets: Flexibility as Labour Market Truth' (2014) 65(3) Northern Ireland Legal Quarterly 323–44
Robinson, J. 'Time in Economic Theory' (1980) 33 Kyklos 219
Seifert, A. '"Von der Person zum Menschen im Recht" – zum Begriff des sozialen Rechts bei Hugo Sinzheimer' (2011) 2 Soziales Recht 62–73
Sinzheimer, H. 'Die Krisis des Arbeitsrechts' (1933) in Hugo Sinzheimer, *Arbeitsrecht und Rechtssoziologie: gesammelte Aufsätze und Reden* (Europäische Verlagsanstalt 1976)
Sinzheimer, H. Grundzüge des Arbeits Rechts (2nd ed., Verlag von Gustav Fischer 1927)
Sinzheimer, H. 'Otto Gierke's Bedeutung für das Arbeitsrecht: Ein Nachruf' (1922) 9 Arbeitsrecht 1–6
Stone, K. 'A Right to Work in the United States: Historical Antecedents and Contemporary Possibilities' in V. Mantouvalou (ed.), *The Right to Work* (Hart 2014)
Stone, K. and H. Arthurs (eds), *Rethinking Workplace Regulation: Beyond the Standard Contract of Employment* (Russell Sage Foundation 2013)
Streeck, W. *Industrial Relations in West Germany: A Case Study of the Car Industry* (Heinemann 1984)
Swedberg, R. *Max Weber and the Idea of Economic Sociology* (Princeton University Press 1998)
van Wezel Stone, K. 'The Post-War Paradigm in American Labor Law' (1981) 90(7) Yale Law Journal 1509–80
Webb, S. and B. Webb, *Industrial Democracy* (London 1897)

Wedderburn, K.W. *The Worker and the Law* (3rd ed, Hammond 1986)
Wedderburn, K.W., R. Lewis and J. Clark, 'Preface' in K.W. Wedderburn, R. Lewis and J. Clark (eds), *Labour Law and Industrial Relations: Building on Kahn-Freund* (Blackwell 1983)

20. Social rights
Fernando Atria and Constanza Salgado

1. INTRODUCTION: SOCIAL RIGHTS IN A NEOLIBERAL AGE

Neoliberalism is the form adopted today by capitalism – a capitalism that has freed itself from the constraints imposed by democracy after the Second World War.[1] Neoliberalism not only refers to a way to organize production and distribution; it is also a rationality. As a rationality that has achieved hegemony, it reinterprets most political concepts. Thus reinterpreted, social rights are minimums, that is, benefits that constitute a safety net for the poor and unfortunate, for those who are not able to get what they need in the market. Just as it would be self-defeating for a safety net to interfere with the acrobatics of trapeze artists, those benefits should operate through the market or in ways compatible with it. Social rights, then, do not challenge but instead legitimize markets, to the extent that they prevent the most brutal consequences of market operations.

This chapter defends an alternative (though not novel) understanding of social rights, in which social rights aim to emancipate us from neoliberalism.[2]

---

[1] Austerity has strengthened neoliberalism. Put differently, many Western governments have been using the economic crisis of 2008 as a means for further entrenchment of neoliberalism. In this sense, austerity can be understood as neoliberalism's third phase. As Hendrikse and Sidaway assert, 'phase 1 comprised the emergence and implementation of proto- and rollback neoliberalism. Proto-neoliberalism was the intellectual project shaped by Hayek and Friedman (Mirowski and Plehwe, 2009) which then underwrote rollback, via austerity, monetarism, and privatization, undertaken by Pinochet (through force of arms), Thatcher, Reagan, and Lange. Subsequently, during phase 2 of rollout, neoliberalism 'gradually metamorphosed into more socially interventionist and ameliorative forms, epitomized by the Third-Way contortions of the Clinton and Blair administrations ... in which new forms of institution-building and governmental intervention have been licensed within the (broadly defined) neoliberal project.' Reijer Hendrikse and James Sidaway, 'Neoliberalism 3.0' *Environment and Planning A* 2010, volume 42, 2037–8. The third phase would be a return to a neoliberalism *without human face*.

[2] See further Fernando Atria, 'Social Rights, Social Contract, Socialism' *Social and Legal Studies* 2015, volume 24, 598–613, and Fernando Atria, *Derechos Sociales y Educación: un Nuevo paradigm de lo publico* (Santiago de Chile, Lom, 2014).

2. WHAT WE CAN LEARN FROM THE LEFTIST CRITIQUE OF RIGHTS

2.1 The Critique of Rights

The emancipatory value of both constitutional and human rights is not uncontroversial. Here we will revisit three important critiques of rights. Only by considering and taking them seriously will we be able to regard social rights in a way that permits the deployment of their emancipatory potential.

The first is the critique posed by Karl Marx. In 'On the Jewish Question', Marx takes issue with Bruno Bauer's view of what it is for Jews to achieve political emancipation. According to Bauer, Jews can only be politically emancipated if they abandon Judaism, and, more generally, to achieve emancipation, mankind must renounce religion. But Bauer's answer, claimed Marx, failed to understand what political emancipation means, and failed to notice the difference between political emancipation and human emancipation. Political emancipation leaves religion in existence because political emancipation is freedom *of* religion, not freedom *from* religion.

Political emancipation, through civil and political rights, eliminates the political character of civil society. However, the removal of political constraints 'meant at the same time throwing off the bonds which restrained the egoistic spirit of civil society'.[3] Thus, on the one hand, the achievement of political emancipation means the removal of property qualifications for the right to elect or to be elected and the abolishment of distinctions of birth, social rank, education and occupation. But on the other hand, such abolishment 'allows private property, education, occupation, *to act in their way* – i.e., as private property, as education, as occupation, and to *exert the influence of their special nature*'.[4] Hence, inequality, unfreedom and oppression persist in the civil State through material differences rather than legal status differences. Although civil society achieves emancipation from its political constraints, it does so within the particularity of its material existence.

The problem with rights – 'rights of man', as Marx puts it – is not only that they are the rights of an egoistic man, that is, the rights of a particular individual who is left free but alone in the pursuit of her aims, but also that they *empower each individual differently*, depending on material circumstances. Rights consider individuals as equals, blurring the differences that exist in civil society, the differences that are produced by unequal social power. Material inequalities are irrelevant before the law, but at the same time, they are irrelevant *for* the law. Rights, therefore, are not instruments that can emancipate the oppressed. On the contrary, they entrench such oppression by *reaffirming and naturalizing the social powers of civil society*.

Following some of Marx's insights and Foucault's ideas about power, Wendy Brown develops a penetrating critique of rights.[5] Brown tries to answer a crucial question:

---

[3] Karl Marx, 'On the Jewish Question'.
[4] Ibid.
[5] Wendy Brown, *States of Injury: Power and Freedom in Late Modernity* (Princeton University Press 1995); Wendy Brown, 'Revaluing Critique: A Response to Kenneth Baynes' *Political Theory* 2000, volume 28, 4; Wendy Brown, "Suffering the Paradoxes of Rights", in W.

what is the emancipatory power of rights claims (or rights discourse) for the oppressed? Note that the question is not whether rights *as such* are emancipatory but whether *some* articulations of them are or are not.

Brown's account follows from her Foucaultian understanding of power. Power does not exist in opposition to freedom and rights, as is the standard view. On the contrary, power is ubiquitous – it is everywhere and all the time. Power produces subjects and disciplines them through different mechanisms, including rights. Rights, then, might become the instruments of regulation and domination even when they confer recognition or redress of subject-specific injuries.[6] Given this framework, the emancipatory potential of rights claims needs to be assessed historically and contextually. It is through contextual analysis of rights that Brown asserts, following Marx, that 'rights emerged in modernity both as a vehicle of emancipation from political disenfranchisement or institutionalized servitude and as a mean of privileging an emerging bourgeois class within a discourse of formal egalitarianism and universal citizenship'.[7]

Rights, then, can both emancipate and dominate. The question is when and whether rights 'are formulated in such a way as to enable the escape of the subordinated from the site of that violation, and when and whether they build a fence around us at that site, regulating rather than challenging the conditions within'.[8] One of the ways in which rights dominate or regulate is by depoliticizing the conditions that give rise to them. Note here that the claim that rights may produce depoliticization does not mean that rights remove particular issues from public debate because they are 'trumps', as in the standard liberal view. This would be depoliticization in a narrow sense. Consider the case of abortion. According to Brown, the fact that access to abortion has been both discussed and formulated in the United States as a matter of the right to privacy has not resulted in greater visibility of women's subordination. To the contrary, privacy tends to conceal domestic subordination and abuse of women. Brown says the appropriate question to ask, if we want to assess whether rights claims open paths of emancipation or close them, is: 'Given the historical privatization of women and reproduction, how has the framing of the abortion issue in terms of privacy rights contributed to the invisibility of women's economic and social subordination through child bearing in an inegalitarian sexual and reproductive order?'[9] Why not frame women's right to abortion instead as a matter of liberty or equality? The value of rights language, then, is not univocal. It can be either politically emancipatory or regressive.

Brown's view regarding human rights is even more sceptical.[10] Human rights are indeed a defence against political power's ability to inflict pain, indignity, cruelty and death. According to Brown, however, 'there is no such thing as mere reduction of suffering or protection from abuse – the nature of the reduction or protection is itself

---

Brown and J. Halley (eds), *Left Legalism/Left Critique* (Duke University Press 2002); Wendy Brown, '"The Most We Can Hope For ...": Human Rights and the Politics of Fatalism', *The South Atlantic Quarterly* 2004, volume 103, number 2/3.
[6] Brown (2000) 477.
[7] Brown (1995) 99.
[8] Brown (2002) 422.
[9] Brown (2002) 422.
[10] Brown (2004).

productive of political subjects and *political possibilities*'.[11] Human rights, as a project of protection against pain inflicted by the State, carry a particular image of justice, and they therefore compete and displace other political projects that also aim for justice. Is the international project of justice articulated through the notion of human rights 'the most we can hope for'? This is the question that Brown ultimately poses.

Less critical than Brown, but equally compelling, is Samuel Moyn's account of human rights. According to Moyn, there is a clear difference between early rights and human rights.[12] Early rights, such as those declared in United States in 1776 and in France in 1789, were rights belonging to a political community, while human rights promoted a politics against human suffering. What is crucial is that *constitutional rights emerged through the construction of spaces of citizenship*, and 'these spaces not only provided ways to contest the denial of already established rights; just as crucially, they were also zones of struggle over the meaning of that citizenship, and the place where defenses of old rights, like campaigns for new ones, were fought'.[13] Human rights, by contrast, are vested in humanity, rather than within a space of citizenship.

Although human rights appear on the scene in 1940s, with the Universal Declaration of Human Rights of 1948, Moyn shows they were marginal at the time. They were not considered the annunciation of a new age. At that time the human rights discourse was not the hegemonic discourse it would become by the end of the 1970s. It is in the 1970s that human rights gained prominence in the global sphere. Human rights become prominent as maximalist utopias declined, emerging 'as the last utopia – one that became powerful and prominent because other visions imploded'.[14] However, for Moyn, human rights gained and still have precedence because of their *minimalism*.

They offer, in fact, a global but *minimalist utopia*. Unlike social rights under the Welfare States, human rights do not aim at producing distributive equality. Indeed, human rights, even perfectly realized, are compatible with radical inequality.[15] According to Moyn, 'precisely because the human rights revolution has focused so intently on state abuses and has, at its most ambitious, dedicated itself to establishing a guarantee of sufficient provision, it has failed to respond to – or even much recognize – neoliberalism's obliteration of any constraints on inequality'.[16] Moyn, however, takes issue with more radical critiques of human rights which assert that human rights are a neoliberal phenomenon, that there is a causal interdependence between them. According to Moyn, a better way to frame the relationship between neoliberalism and human rights 'is in terms of parallel trajectories, with the tragic consequence that (as some of Marx's own brilliant work implies) structural insight into the root causes of social suffering went missing at the time that it was badly needed'[17] (more on this later).

---

[11] Brown (2004) 460.
[12] Samuel Moyn, *The Last Utopia* (The Belknap Press of Harvard University Press 2010).
[13] Ibid 13.
[14] Ibid 4.
[15] Samuel Moyn, 'Are Human Rights Enough?' *Vikerkaar* 10–11/2017 (Estonian version)/ *Eurozine* (English version) (2017).
[16] Ibid 6.
[17] Samuel Moyn, 'A Powerless Companion: Human Rights in the Age of Neoliberalism' *Law and Contemporary Problems* 2014, volume 77, 159.

2.2 Can Social Rights Be Emancipatory?

Should we abandon the language of rights? Are we making a mistake when articulating our claims of justice in the language of social rights, by using a language that undercuts the very claims we are making?

A negative answer to these questions cannot ignore the critiques we have seen. We cannot simply ignore that civil rights empower, through property rights, those already powerful, naturalizing their power and its effects. That is why, if they are to be emancipatory, rights have to provide a basis to contest that power and its operation. They have to challenge, in other words, the oppressive power of neoliberal capitalism.

Constitutional social rights can ground this challenge as human rights cannot. This is because, while the latter are based on a politics of suffering that offers no basis to any challenge of neoliberalism,[18] the former are based on citizenship. This implies a more ambitious project, as we will see in the next sections: citizenship both contains an egalitarian principle and provides a space to struggle for its realization. Social rights, therefore, have the emancipatory potential that is missing in the idea of human rights.

However, such potential has been neutralized by the same powers that social rights aim to challenge. This is due to the fact that the hegemonic rationality of neoliberalism understands them as rights to minimal provisions that, instead of challenging neoliberalism, provide its legitimation discourse. Unlike Moyn, who sees the relationship between human rights and neoliberalism as a matter of 'parallel trajectories', we can say that human rights are neoliberalism's utopia. Human rights do not only displace other utopias; the point is more radical than that: human rights discourse is the legitimation discourse of neoliberalism, because it provides a discourse that legitimates the minimal justice that neoliberalism can offer. This discourse accommodates the social justice that neoliberalism can deliver, because its natural space is not the political, but courts of law.

Contrary to what happens with human rights, the locus of social rights is citizenship, and therefore the political. Thus, *political power* can be used to challenge *social power*.

3. TWO UNDERSTANDINGS OF SOCIAL RIGHTS

3.1 Social Rights as Challenges

The emancipatory potential of social rights unfolds when social rights are understood as challenges aimed at transforming the oppressive forces of the extant system – today, the oppressive forces of neoliberalism.

In this understanding, there is a progressive continuity between civil, political and social rights. Here, social rights are not less important than civil and political rights, as the hegemonic view of social rights states, but its realization. They are 'more

---

[18] The low baseline that human rights provide, at least from the point of view of social justice, has encouraged scholars to engage, for example, in more ambitious subjects such as 'global justice'.

important' because they entail a more developed principle of justice, a principle already contained in civil rights but not yet fully developed.

The idea that there is a continuity, in which each category of rights displays a more developed notion of freedom, is better explained by looking to T.H. Marshall's seminal *Citizenship and Social Class*.[19] As is well known, Marshall argues that the emergence of civil, political and social rights has to be understood as successive waves that expand the reach of citizenship, thus aiming to overcome the injustices of social class. In his view, this slow but persistent progress would eventually remove the most important differences of social class, and therefore the most important source of social conflict.

This movement was possible because rights were linked to citizenship. In Marshall's view each type of rights, that is, civil, political and social rights, corresponds to a different type of citizenship – civil, political and social citizenship. As Marshall noted, citizenship is not only a distinctive property of modern status systems whose most important feature is the egalitarian principle it contains, but also a structure and ideology that provide the main source of whatever solidarity modern societies possess.[20]

Although civil citizenship contained a principle of equality, it was a formal equality, and therefore it was compatible with capitalism, which 'is a system, not of equality, but of inequality'.[21] Civil rights understood citizenship as a formal status and liberty as equal liberty before the law. Because of this, such rights were indispensable to capitalism, a crucial condition for the development of markets. Here it is important to see the transition between feudal and modern societies as articulated through the notion of civil rights. In feudalism the legal situation of individuals depended on their social status in a hierarchical system. Individuals' social and legal relations, and therefore their rights and obligations, were derived from the status each one had in this hierarchy.[22] Civil rights implied the abolition of a feudal order in which property determined social obligations and in which the existence of noncontractual relations entailed mutual obligations. In this sense, the emergence of civil rights was indeed a movement 'from status to contract'.[23] Because feudalism was the hostis and the bourgeoisie the agent of change, civil rights mainly meant freedom of contract and absolute property rights. Even though individuals were now equal before the law, their unequal economic and social power would determine their social relations.

According to Marshall, since the latter part of the nineteenth century a more substantive principle of equality became relevant. Thus, although citizenship 'had done little to reduce social inequality, it had helped to guide progress into the path which led

---

[19] Thomas H. Marshall, *Citizenship and Social Class* (Cambridge University Press 1950).
[20] David Lockwood, 'For T.H. Marshall', *Sociology* 1974, volume 8, number 3, 364–5. According to Lockwood, with the concept of citizenship Marshall provides 'the clearest and most cogent answer to the question which was posed but never satisfactorily posed by Durkheim: namely, what is the basis of the "organic solidarity" of modern societies?' (p.365).
[21] Marshall (n 19) 29.
[22] Manfred Rehbindert, 'Status, Contract, and the Welfare State' *Stanford Law Review* 1971, 23.
[23] Henry Sumner Maine, *Ancient Law: Its Connection with the Early History of Society, and its Relation to Modern Ideas* (Cambridge University Press 2012) (1st ed. 1861) 170.

directly to the egalitarian policies of the twentieth century'.[24] The twentieth century was the moment of social citizenship. Before, what we would call today 'social provisions' was no more than 'poor relief', and its goal, as Marshall claims, 'was to abate the nuisance of poverty *without disturbing the pattern of inequality* of which poverty was the most obviously unpleasant consequence'.[25] Poor relief, by its very nature, was not for citizens and did not aim to challenge social class.[26]

It was during the twentieth century that the idea of social rights became available. Now they are rights and not just 'social provisions' because they are incorporated as part of the status of citizenship. This changed their goal: they now aimed not only to eliminate poverty, but also to *modify the whole pattern of social inequality*. Social rights are able to achieve that goal 'by a progressive divorce between *real* and *money incomes*' which is seen in the main social services such as health and education.[27] What Marshall meant by this distinction is that inequality of monetary income should not have any effect on the essential spheres of human wellbeing. The differential ability to pay (the inequality of monetary incomes) would not have distributive consequences because the sphere of social rights would not be organized according to the market principle. In these spheres it would be as if all had the same income (real income), because the ability to pay would cease to be a criterion of distribution of social provisions. For Marshall, universality of social provisions was the way in which inequality (of monetary incomes) could be abolished in some specific spheres.

In this understanding, social rights decommodify (some) human needs, which occurs when their satisfaction does not depend on the market principle and therefore on the unequal economic power of individuals.[28]

3.2 Social Rights as Minimums

Today, instead, the hegemonic view understands social rights as no more than a safety net, that is, as a net that aims to protect individuals from poverty. Social rights are understood as rights that provide a minimal floor of welfare protection. In this conception, social rights are guided by market forces.

As we saw, social rights imply decommodification because they replace money, and therefore they break the inequality of income characteristic of neoliberal societies. Rights – not money – are what everyone has in these spheres. If, however, social provisions adopt the form of means-tested benefits which aim only to prevent poverty, they do not replace money; rather, they act as a functional equivalent to it, and

---

[24] Marshall (n 19) 40.
[25] Ibid 46.
[26] As Marshall explains, the social provisions contained in the Poor Law of England 'treated the claims of the poor, not as an integral part of the rights of the citizen, but as an alternative to them – as claims which could be met only if the claimants ceased to be citizens in any true sense of the word ... The stigma which clung to poor relief expressed the deep feelings of a people who understood that those who accepted relief must cross the road that separated the community of citizens from the outcast company of the destitute': Ibid 24.
[27] Ibid 81.
[28] Gosta Esping Andersen, *The Three Worlds of Welfare Capitalism* (Polity Press 1990).

therefore perpetuate the consequences of its unequal distribution. Here social rights join civil rights as (part of) the legal architecture of inequality.

It is important to note how this understanding of social rights is built upon an inversion. From a conception that challenges neoliberalism and the market principle by emphasizing the political nature of certain spheres, in which monetary income is different from real income, they are transformed into a notion that ratifies commodification, by providing those who have no access to the market the means to do so. Rights, then, become 'benefits', and benefits do not make markets irrelevant. If social services are meant to provide means-tested benefits, they have to be compatible with the market principle for those who are not entitled to such benefits. This implies that there must be a noticeable difference between benefits that are provided 'for free', and commodities that are bought in the market by those who can afford them. This completes the radical inversion: in neoliberalism, those who receive benefits are 'privileged', in the sense that they receive free of charge what others must pay for. The *privilege* of those who can use their monetary income to access better healthcare, education and pension plans becomes their burden. Thus, the claim to introduce or maintain universal provisions is dubbed a 'regressive' reform, a case of making (through taxes) the poor pay for services to the rich.

In this understanding, social rights are reinterpreted as promoting rather than challenging neoliberalism.

3.3 Social Rights' Neutralization and Progressivism

The irony is that this reinterpretation of social rights has not been the work of the Cato Institute and other neoliberal thinkers or institutions, but of lawyers and jurists of a 'progressive' self-understanding. This is not anomalous; it is in fact what 'hegemony' is about: to the extent that a neoliberal rationality is hegemonic, the neutralization comes not only from the right, but also from 'progressive' views.

These 'progressive' lawyers and jurists begin by denouncing a significant asymmetry between civil and social constitutional rights: while the former are recognized to have the full consequences that legal thought assigns to rights (in particular judicial enforceability), social rights are treated as nonbinding 'promises'. This denunciation contains a programme: that of showing that there is nothing in the concept of social rights that warrants this differential treatment, which has to be recognized, therefore, as purely 'ideological'. A true commitment to social rights would imply the abolition of this differential treatment; its measure of success is then the (judicial) enforceability of social rights.

This is a three-step programme. The first step is to show that civil and political rights have (or used to have) a significantly different legal status vis-à-vis social rights: only the former could ground legal action against the government in a court of law. The second step attempts to show that this differential treatment is not justified by any 'structural' differences between rights. The conclusion, then, is that the lack of judicial enforceability is the consequence of (an ideologically motivated) devaluation of social rights, which must be rectified by recognizing judicial remedies against infringements of social rights. Progressive legal thought, therefore, understands that the cause of social rights can be promoted by insisting on the 'no-difference' thesis. And in this regard, it has been remarkably successful.

But if there are no differences between civil and social rights, then social rights lack any emancipatory content. In this sense, as a *progressive* programme, its success is its failure: the more this point is established, the more the aptitude of social rights to challenge neoliberalism is lost.

In what follows we will take a closer look at the last two steps of this programme.

3.4 All Rights Have Some Positive Content, All Rights Have Costs

Conservative critiques of social rights used to claim that social rights are structurally different from civil rights in that civil rights ground negative duties or duties of noninterference, while social rights ground positive duties, that is, duties to act. And 'positive' rights 'are subjected to a problem that defensive rights do not have: scarcity'.[29] Since the defining feature of social rights as opposed to civil and political rights is that they are 'positive' rights, their judicial enforceability would give courts power to decide on the best way to use public funds – that is, on issues of public policy that ought to be the realm of legislative and administrative authorities and process. On the other hand, since civil rights are said to be 'negative', that is, a set of prohibitions directed against State action, their judicial enforceability would imply no such interference, but only that legislative and administrative decisions are constrained by law.

The second step of the progressive programme identified above was to deny such 'structural' differences. In recent decades a growing body of work by progressive legal scholars has successfully argued that civil and social rights have negative as well as positive aspects, given that both categories imply the use of public resources. In this view, *all rights are positive and all rights have costs*, as Stephen Holmes and Cass Sunstein have famously claimed.[30] All rights require the action of the State to protect them. All rights assume the existence of a whole set of institutions to realize them. Even property rights require title registries, police and judicial structures to sanction or provide some remedy when they are breached. The operation of these institutions depends on allocation of significant resources, typically obtained through taxation. Thus, scarcity is a problem faced not only by social rights but also by civil and political rights because *all rights have costs*. Although there is a difference in the amount of resources that civil and social rights demand, this would be a *quantitative* and not a *qualitative* difference.

This progressive view, however, ignores the crucial political difference between civil and social rights, a difference that changes the meaning of the correlative duties they entail. It is of course undeniable that civil and political rights require adequately funded institutions. However, the mobilization of resources required by the protection of property and formal freedom (freedom of contract) is qualitatively different than that

---

[29] Otfried Hoffe, *Democracy in an Age of Globalization* (Springer 2007) 47.
[30] Stephen Holmes and Cass Sunstein, *The Cost of Rights: Why Liberty Depends on Taxes* (W.W. Norton 1999). Also see David Garland, "On the Concept of 'Social Rights'", in 24 Social and Legal Studies (2015).

required by social rights. The point here is not that civil and political rights do not 'have costs' and do not need resources for their realization but rather that there is a difference in the interests for which these resources are mobilized.

Civil and social rights entail two different understandings of taxes. In the case of civil rights, taxes are tantamount to prices and therefore they do not break with the market principle. Thus owners can contribute to the funding of a title registry by paying a registration fee to that effect. In this understanding, the burden of taxation is allocated in proportion to the services received by the State. Taxes, then, are the payment each individual makes for the different benefits provided by the State. This is a view of taxes according to the market principle, because it maintains at least the idea of an equivalence between benefit and payment. The reason why taxation and not the market is the instrument for financing these benefits is simple: markets are not able to provide benefits as a consequence of 'market failures'. Such failures are, in turn, to be explained because institutions such as the police, courts, external defence and the like are 'public goods', in other words, goods that the market is unable to provide because they are either nonrival or nonexclusionary (or, indeed, both). Therefore, its financing through taxes is the only way to ensure its provision. But, if the market were able to provide them, taxation would not be needed.

Social rights, instead, require not only more abundant resources, but resources whose justification is different. With social rights taxes are not prices because they break the link between what each contributes and what each receives from the State. When it comes to universal social rights, each contributes according to ability, and each receives according to need. Taxes are no longer justified by reference to the individual interest of the person who pays them, because they deny, even in principle, the equivalence between benefit and payment. Taxes now become justified because they make social rights possible.

Here we can see Marshall's argument, as appropriated above, at work: once universal social rights are recognized, and the public, decommodified space of citizenship has expanded beyond the market (formal status of equality before the law: civil rights) and the political process (universal franchise: political rights), we can use this understanding of citizenship, social rights and taxes retrospectively to reassess the idea of civil and political rights. But the progressive move we are considering now goes in the opposite direction: it aims to understand social rights by making them analogous to civil and political rights, to interpret the political content of social rights through the lens of civil and political rights.

To the extent that social rights are challenges to neoliberalism, there is no equivalence between the resources these rights demand and the services they fund. Social rights are not simply 'more expensive'. Their claim is to counteract the power of money that, through markets, neoliberalism has extended almost to every sphere of human life.

3.5 Judicialization of Social Rights

'Social rights are actionable rights', claim progressive legal scholars.[31] Especially in Latin America, for these scholars, the judicial enforcement of social rights is seen as the most important battle to be waged. But this is a mistake.

The reason is that judicial enforcement transforms social rights, neutralizing them. Judicial institutions are unable to articulate the transformative content of social rights. This is because they are claims based on distributive justice, and therefore they cannot be contained by the structure of adjudication, as determined by the logic of corrective justice.[32] Since the transformative content of social rights cannot be articulated through adjudication, they can only be enforced if they are transformed, deprived of their transformative content. This is why 'the institutions most directly associated with civil rights are the courts of justice'.[33] It is a mistake to think of courts as instruments to protect whatever one wants to protect. They serve to protect what they are capable of protecting. When a plaintiff claims her right to healthcare, the original idea of healthcare as a decommodified sphere, located in the realm of citizenship rather than that of the market, disappears and must be reformulated into a claim that can be grasped by a court of law. It then becomes a particular plaintiff's claim against the State, seeking a particular benefit.[34] Social rights do not get to see their day in court; what does is an individual's claim that her interest be served, even at the cost of everyone else's interests. Courts, then, are not the most appropriate forum for addressing matters of distributive justice.

Additionally, decades of litigation have shown that social rights adjudication does not bring with it any deep social transformation. Indeed, there is a clear disconnection between what the enforceability of social rights is supposed to achieve and what it has in reality achieved.[35] Judicial enforceability is supposed to favour the most disadvantaged members of society. However, the empirical reality shows that ultimately it does not favour disadvantaged groups, but rather the middle and upper classes.[36]

Perhaps for this reason, authors such as Tushnet and Sunstein argue in favour of a weaker role for courts regarding social rights.[37] Judicial enforceability here is important not on account of its potential for securing results in a particular case. Rather, it helps to identify and highlight problems and shortcomings in the way in which social rights are fulfilled, leaving policy decisions to political and administrative bodies. This 'weak

---

[31] See, for example, Víctor Abramovich and Christian Courtis, *Los Derechos Sociales como Derechos Exigibles* (Trotta 2002).
[32] Claudio Michelon, 'Introducción: derechos sociales y la dignidad de la igualdad' *Discusiones* 2004, volume 4, 12.
[33] Marshall (n 19) 11.
[34] Fernando Atria, '¿Existen derechos sociales?' *Discusiones* 2004, volume 4, 45.
[35] David Landau, 'The Reality of Social Rights Enforcement' *Harvard International Law Journal* 2012, volume 53, number 1, 403.
[36] Octavio Motta Ferraz, 'Harming the Poor through Social Rights Litigation: Lessons from Brazil' *Texas Law Review* 2011, volume 89, number 7; Jeff King, *Judging Social Rights* (Cambridge University Press 2012) 83 and 84.
[37] Cass Sunstein, *Designing Democracy: What Constitutions Do* (Oxford University Press 2001); Mark Tushnet, *Weak Courts, Strong Rights* (Princeton University Press 2008).

form' of justiciability, a 'dialogical' form as they call it, would be the best way to balance the enforcement of social rights with the lack of both democratic legitimacy and institutional capacity of courts. Enthused by the decisions of the Constitutional Court of South Africa (especially in the case *South Africa v. Grootboom*), Tushnet, Sunstein and others have seen these rulings as a form of enforcement appropriate for social rights. However, as Landau points out, this weak form of judicial enforcement has not really been used outside of South Africa, and even there has not been entirely effective.[38] The hopes that both Tushnet and Sunstein have for this form of justiciability do not seem well founded in light of its minor transformative consequences. This stems from the fact that institutional forms are not totally pliable. Consequently, it appears difficult to escape from the classic model of justiciability, in other words, a contest between plaintiff and defendant as to the legitimacy of the claim of the former against the latter. The reason is that, as we saw, this is the paradigmatic form in which courts discharge their function and for which they are institutionally better prepared.

But the judicialization of social rights also juridifies social rights language, narrowing its horizon. To see how this is the case it is useful to consider Robert Alexy's theory of constitutional rights, possibly the most influential and best known theory in Latin America.[39] In Alexy's theory, the content of rights is always approached from the point of view of judicial control. In this account, courts only have power to control social rights policies when they are below the minimum. For Alexy this minimum results from balancing all the possible values that could be involved. On the one hand, such policies are required by the principle of freedom; on the other, both the democratic principle and the opposing principles (such as property rights) must be affected 'in a relatively small extent'.[40] Such conditions are met, we are told, 'in the case of minimum social rights, that is, in the case of a vital minimum, a simple house, scholar education, vocational training and a minimum standard of medical assistance'.[41] Notice how form becomes substance: the methodological approach that underlies Alexy's theory of constitutional rights determines his understanding of social rights. What social rights demand is what is legally required; what is legally required has to be judicially enforceable; what is judicially enforceable is the minimum standard, otherwise the opposing principles are violated. Hence, what social rights demand is a minimum provision. Social rights become rights to minimum provisions not because of any substantive argument about their true political content, but only because it is necessary for them to be judicially enforceable.

3.6 Social Rights' Utopia?

The fact that the neutralization of social rights arises from the progressive side is illustrative of our current political predicament. Today, indeed, social rights as challenges to neoliberalism are deemed utopian. Certainly, they 'can function as ideals,

---

[38] Landau (n 35).
[39] Robert Alexy, *Teoría de los Derechos Fundamentales* (Centro de Estudios Constitucionales 2008).
[40] Ibid 454.
[41] Ibid 455.

as symbolic weapons, and as mobilization devices, and "history-on-our-side" teleologies – such as Marshall's – may help shape values, create convictions and build public support'.[42] But social rights as challenges would not be 'real' social rights. Once we acknowledge that the advent of neoliberalism showed that history was not, after all, on our side, so the argument goes, we must abandon any maximalist understanding of social rights.

But Marshall's understanding of social rights, or at least our interpretation of it, did not imply a teleology, and thus it was not proven wrong by the fact that the crisis of the welfare state was followed by neoliberalism. Social rights as challenges are deemed utopian because neoliberalism has weakened the political. With a toothless democracy, social rights as minimums seem to be the best game in town. Its alternative seems not to be universal social services, but rather, no social provisions at all.

4. CITIZENSHIP, DEMOCRACY AND NEOLIBERALISM

4.1 Retrospective Self-Understanding

Neoliberalism has not proven Marshall wrong – or at least, not in our interpretation. We do not take his idea of waves of rights, or more precisely of a certain continuity between civil, political and social rights, as proposing a sort of teleology (a 'history-on-our-side' teleology).

The importance of our appropriation of Marshall's argument is to be found in the idea of movement – a movement where there is neither a predefined direction nor a final point driving it. And it is the idea of citizenship what makes this movement possible. It provides both a principle of justice, a principle of equality and a space – the political space – to claim for the realization of such principle in different spheres. Marshall shows what is necessary for a principle of equality (or, what is the same, of equal freedom), a principle that was already contained in the idea of civil rights, to develop. That is why, according to Marshall, civil, political and social citizenship do not contain three different and independent principles/ideas, but one that each time is more fully realized.

Marshall does not articulate this realization theoretically; rather, his aim is to show that this is a better way to understand how citizenship, in fact, developed. 'The limit of my ambition has been to regroup familiar facts in a pattern which may make them appear … in a *new light*', says Marshall in explaining how political and subsequently social citizenship was built from the scaffoldings that previous rights made possible.[43]

Equality, or, more precisely, equal freedom, is what civil, political and social citizenship make possible. Civil rights contains a *formal* and *individual* conception of equal freedom: freedom means that individuals have no obligation to each other beyond those obligations they assume through contracts. Modern markets are the institutional framework in which this freedom unfolds. But contractual obligations do not suffice to make common life possible; some legal rights and duties are also necessary. However,

---

[42] Garland (n 30) 33.
[43] Marshall (n 19) 45.

now that equal freedom protects us from imposed obligations, for law to be legitimate, it must contain everybody's will. Political rights and democratic institutions expand freedom by making political freedom a legitimatory principle of law, and therefore a legitimatory principle of power. But both freedom of contract and freedom to partake in the formation of the common will are still *formal*, to the extent that they are secured by legal rules that equally distribute a given status. From the point of view of political rights, however, freedom can no longer be understood as individual: the democratic principle implies a *collective* understanding of freedom. Social rights, in turn, challenge the formal conception of freedom, securing the material conditions for autonomy. If autonomy (freedom) requires certain material conditions, then equal freedom cannot be understood as equal formal freedom. Rather, it must be understood as securing equally and for all these material conditions.

The movement that Marshall described allows for retrospective self-understanding rather than a predictable fixed path. Today, when it is easier to imagine the end of the world than the end of capitalism, as Fredric Jameson once said,[44] it is extremely important to think of Marshall's movement as a movement that is pushed by resistance to commodification rather than pulled from an articulable image of a postcapitalist ideal.[45] Now that we can no longer describe such an ideal, what is relevant is the idea that drives the movement, controlling, to a certain extent, its direction.

4.2 The Tension between Private Property and Citizenship

Upon closer examination, we can see that Marshall's movement towards social rights contains a tension.[46] This movement, then, is better described as a movement in constant tension, which translates into a permanent struggle between capitalism and citizenship. That Marshall saw this tension is evident in his statement that 'in the twentieth century citizenship and the capitalist class system have been at war'.[47]

Aneurin Bevan, the founder of the NHS, explained this tension by saying:

> society presented itself as an arena of conflicting social forces and not as a plexus of individual striving. These forces are in the main three: private property, poverty and democracy. They are forces in the strict sense of the term, for they are active and positive. Among them no rest is possible. The issue therefore in a capitalist democracy resolves itself into this: either poverty will use democracy to win the struggle against property, or property, in fear of poverty, will destroy democracy.[48]

---

[44] Fredric Jameson, 'Future City', *New Left Review* 2003, volume 21, 76.

[45] In fact, it is perfectly possible that there is progress in some sense without a predefined direction. Such is the case with Darwinian evolution, in which there is progress without teleology. Here there is a process pushed from the starting point rather than pulled towards a final point.

[46] In Emilios Christodoulidis' words, 'for the radicalized Marshall, then, continuity is understood as antinomic or not at all'. 'Social Rights Constitutionalism: An Antagonistic Endorsement', *Journal of Law and Society* 2017, volume 44, number 1, 147.

[47] Marshall (n 19) 29. The same statement is repeated at 68.

[48] Aneurin Bevan, *In Place of Fear* (Heinemann 1952) 2–3.

Bevan's idea is better expressed by using the term 'citizenship' instead of 'poverty'. With this in mind, Bevan's passage gives us a clue if we understand it in the sense that either citizenship will use democracy to win the struggle against property, or property, in fear of citizenship, will destroy democracy.

A segment of the left always thought that winning the struggle against property meant doing away with private property, that is, expropriation. But there was an alternative: attacking the unequal power that property accords owners. In this case, the solution to the tension between citizenship and private property is not expropriation but rather social rights.

One of the main ways in which the unequal power deriving from private property deploys is in action in the market, because the market is a space in which each agent is expected to use whatever power she possesses in her own benefit. Social rights as a challenge to neoliberalism offer a solution to the tension between citizenship and private property by decommodifying spheres of life, so that in these spheres the unequal power of private property will no longer imply inequality. We have already seen that Marshall understood the aim of social rights to be

> a progressive divorce between real and money incomes. This is, of course, explicit in the major social services, such as health and education, which give benefits in kind without any *ad hoc* payment ... The advantages obtained by having a larger money income do not disappear, but they are confined to a limited area of consumption.[49]

Simply put, the opposition between the equality principle that citizenship contains and the unequal power of private property (of 'monetary income') is faced not through the abolition of private property, but through forms of decommodification of some spheres of common life, so that the unequal distribution of private property does not manifest itself in these spheres. Inequalities do not disappear, but they are restricted to a limited area of consumption.

It is important to note here that the issue at hand is not strict equality but the unequal power that property gives.[50] The expansion of markets is one measure of that inequality. Social rights challenge that inequality by creating decommodified spheres. Thus, although social rights do not abolish wage labour markets, as they expand they are able to counteract, to some extent, not only neoliberalism, but also capitalism (witness the current discussion on universal basic income).

In brief, social rights as challenges aim to create spheres of equality through the exercise of political power against the social power of private property.

---

[49] Marshall (n 19) 81.
[50] Social rights are not concerned with what we might call 'brute' equality, that is, equality of monetary income. The fundamental problem we face is not inequality of material goods, but rather the power that property gives, which turns freedom into privilege and makes the many dependent on the few. Equating the idea of equal freedom that underpins social rights to some desiderata of brute equality is usually the first move of an argument designed to discard it as 'utopian'. For this reason, neoliberal authors discuss inequality of monetary income, ignoring inequalities of power (freedom). This can be seen in their curious fixation with the justification of fortunes made by sportsmen/women rather than those made by corporate fat cats.

4.3 Neoliberalism against Democracy: What Is Left for the Left

We saw that the movement towards social rights relies on a tension, on a struggle between 'conflicting *social forces*'. Thus citizenship is not only an egalitarian *idea* but also an *agent* (the citizenry) that struggles for the realization of this idea. Likewise, private property and more specifically, capital is also an agent that struggles for its own interests.

Bevan said that this tension is resolved, on the side of capital, by destroying democracy ('property, in fear of poverty, will destroy democracy').[51] But destroying democracy could mean destroying it either by violence (as in Chile in 1973) or by weakening it until it becomes powerless vis-à-vis capital. Today it is difficult to deny that this latter possibility is the one chosen by capital. As Wolfgang Streek explains, in the early 1970s, capital began to seek to release itself from the 'chains' imposed after the Second World War, by citizens through democracy. What is striking is that, as Streeck notes, 'it was not the masses that refused allegiance to post-war capitalism and thereby put an end to it, but rather capital in the shape of its organization, its organizers and its owners'.[52] However, not even capitalism's critics were able to see that neoliberal capitalism was coming. According to Streeck, critics underestimated capital both as a political actor and as a factual power capable of generating strategies for its liberation. And they also overrated the capacity of democracy to counteract the power of capital. Much of that error lies, for Streeck, in having understood capital as an object rather than as an agent, as a means of production rather than as a class with power and interests.[53]

Neoliberalism is capital gaining the upper hand in the struggle against citizenship. This implies a weakening of democracy. The progressive reinterpretation of social rights that we criticize can be explained as the consequence of the fact that the strength of democracy has been weakened to the point that it is unable to prevail against capital. Since capital cannot be politically opposed, court-centred legal action is what is left for the left. But this is like waving a white flag.

The alternative is to devise creative forms of political action to advance the cause of social rights. Social citizenship and democracy have interconnected trajectories.

---

[51] Bevan (n 48) 3.

[52] Wolfgang Streeck, *Buying Time: The Delayed Crisis of Democratic Capitalism* (Verso 2014) 16.

[53] One of the most important conclusions of Streeck's book *Buying Time* is that it is no longer possible to theorize about democracy without considering capital as a fundamental actor. Today it is not possible to make democratic theory without understanding that the economy, especially in its capitalist configuration, is a space of power. As Streeck points out, 'unless the sociology of social crises and the political theory of democracy learn to conceive of the economy as a field of social-political activity, they inevitably fall wide of the mark': ibid xv.

21. Between persecution and reconciliation: criminal justice, legal form and human emancipation

Craig Reeves, Alan Norrie and Henrique Carvalho

> The difficult thing is for each individual to take full responsibility for the destructiveness that is personal, and that inherently belongs to a relationship to an object that is felt to be good; in other words that is related to loving.[1]

> It is, however, a grave mistake to assume that the law itself and men's attitudes toward it can exist *in abstracto* ... It is ... a fundamental error, for all emotional attitudes—and even respect for law and a sense of responsibility are emotional attitudes—arise in response to concrete impulses ... We have no sense of responsibility as such.[2]

1. INTRODUCTION

1.1 Criminal Justice and Emancipation

In a recent review of critical criminal justice scholarship,[3] two of the three present authors noted the emphasis placed on how law operates as a mode of social control, often in ways that are hidden behind the stated goals and purposes of criminal justice systems. Law is seen as a form of social or political governmentality, and insofar as criminal justice in the liberal view sees itself as representing a sphere of liberties, law's nature as a means of repression through the forms of freedom is an important critical theme. The review found that critical writers deployed various 'hermeneutics of suspicion'[4] to interrogate critically law's claims and self-understanding as a virtuous institution reflecting themes of freedom.

Despite the negative critical standpoint, there was also, however, a *leitmotif* of reflection on an underlying, immanent, relationship between law and emancipation. If the critic could show how law works formally to express freedom, but in practice or substance to repress it, *and* she could show the mechanisms that produce these relations of form and substance, then the critique had got closer to understanding how repression works, what might be the conditions for its possibility, and what might be the conditions that needed to be removed for repression to stop. Further, in investigating

---

[1] D. Winnicott (1984) 'Aggression, Guilt and Reparation', in C. Winnicott, R. Shepherd and M. Davis (eds) *Deprivation and Delinquency* (London: Tavistock), p. 137.

[2] G.H. Mead (1918) 'The Psychology of Punitive Justice', 23(5) *American Journal of Sociology*, 577, 584.

[3] H. Carvalho and A. Norrie (2017) '"In This Interregnum": Dialectical Themes in the Critique of Criminal Justice', 26(6) *Social & Legal Studies*, 716–34.

[4] H-G. Gadamer (1984) 'The Hermeneutics of Suspicion', 17 *Man and World*, 313–23.

the law, scholars might also find contained within it something like a utopian promise, or trace of something better, that might come into being. Forms of control that operate behind actors' backs, abstract universalisations of freedom which ignore and repress concrete forms of unfreedom, unacknowledged discriminations grounding violations: all these suggest different possibilities in differently made worlds as to how lives could be lived better. In these settings, the formal symbols of freedom might mark a space where substantive emancipation might later emerge. Understandings, for example, of abstract and formal senses of autonomy might expand into deeper, grounded, senses of what it means to act autonomously, with the richer moral and psychological substance thereby invoked. Formal freedom betokens something richer and deeper, the possibility of a fuller flourishing held in check under present arrangements.

This emancipatory promise does not alleviate the tension in modern criminal law and justice; rather, it makes it more acute, because the liberal promise of individual freedom and responsibility is directly pitted against the coercion of political authority and the structural inequalities and violence it defends. That violence is real and ongoing, so that it sometimes seems like vanity or narcissism to point to criminal law as a harbinger of emancipation. No doubt, we glimpse the better future to which criminal justice points 'through a glass, darkly'. Yet, our view is that it is necessary to engage critically with this future. We take our line from Antonio Gramsci, who wrote that 'the old is dying and the new cannot be born; in this interregnum a great variety of morbid symptoms appear'.[5] We see 'the old' as a world governed by the broken promises of the liberal Enlightenment and 'the new' as one that would be emancipated across a variety of social registers; but the new would still draw upon the values of humanity that modern society renders in a particular, more formal than substantive, way, while generating a variety of morbid symptoms in the dystopic present.

Liberal theorists might view such a characterisation as overly critical of the role and forms of law, while poststructuralists might see it as overly generous and idealistic. Nonetheless, we think that a view of criminal justice as placed in a confused and confusing historical world where law masks and is not always what it seems, where circumstances are bad and may be getting worse, where the need for change is urgent but not easy to achieve, and where emancipation might nonetheless find some guidance through law: such a view may orient us towards redeveloping critique in this field of scholarship. This would, however, raise an immediate question. What would be the precise connection between emancipation and criminal justice, and how can we get from one to the other?

Emancipation involves a freeing of the self, throwing off the things that hold us back. In its original meaning, emancipation involved the freeing of the slave from the master. In modern times, it is linked to ideas of political self-determination, social freedom for exploited classes, the liberation of women and subjected races and peoples. Always tied in with these different meanings is the way in which people may free themselves not only in terms of their material conditions but also from the mental ties that bind. Emancipation involves the full development of human freedom. The theory of criminal

---

[5] A. Gramsci (1971/1999) *Selections from the Prison Notebooks*, Translated and Edited by Quintin Hoare and Geoffrey Nowell Smith (London: ElecBook), 556.

justice is also, ultimately, a theory of human freedom, of how it is given up by criminal actors in return for punishment. However, this involves a sense of freedom that is limited and problematic, one that is very partially linked to ideas of emancipation. It is in between an account of mental and moral freedom in the broad sense of human emancipation and the account of those same things as they are expressed in criminal justice theory that we find a gap that needs to be filled. How, beyond the terms of the problematic of law and liberal theory, might we be free?

1.2 Political Theory and Moral Psychology

Liberal political theory typically, but incorrectly, fuses two types of question: those around the legitimacy of state punishment, and those concerning a moral psychology appropriate to a setting of violation of another's lived being (feelings of guilt, forgiveness, blame and reconciliation). It focuses on the first kind of question and has less to say about the second, not generally seeing it as a question in need of an answer.[6] Critical criminal justice theory, in responding to the liberal model, has made the same mistake, and also primarily addressed the first type of question. It has done so mainly by taking the form of an historical critique based on the social structure that underlies, and the social functions that accordingly shape, a criminal justice system.[7] Showing how the system reflects particular social interests in a setting of structural violence undermines political legitimations based on contractarian or other abstract rationalist grounds. Showing the historicity of the legal subject challenges the view that legal subjectivity and its responsibility forms are ahistorical and inevitable. Such work is important, but it is not enough.

We can show this quite simply. In the liberal model, an unjust social system cannot sustain the legitimacy of its control processes, so that the right to punish – to find a person *guilty* – is placed under question. The responsible subject that is hypostatised by extracting it from the criminogenic context is revealed in its decontextualisation. Yet even in an unjust system, a person may feel psychological guilt at her actions and a victim may feel violated. Accordingly, there are questions of moral psychology that are not properly addressed by a model that conflates them with questions of normative

---

[6] H. Morris (1976) *On Guilt and Innocence: Essays in Legal Philosophy and Moral Psychology* (Berkeley: University of California Press, viii). Though written some time ago, we do not think the overall focus of legal and philosophical thought has changed much. Jeffrie Murphy (2012) *Punishment and the Moral Emotions* (Oxford: Oxford University Press) raises questions. We discuss the work of Antony Duff in the text. We think Bernard Williams's assessment is correct, that liberal philosophy generally thinks the second question should be seen as an extension of the first: B. Williams (1993) *Shame and Necessity* (Berkeley: University of California Press), ch. 3.

[7] Cf C. Wells and O. Quick (2010) *Lacey, Wells and Quick: Reconstructing Criminal Law* (4th edition, Cambridge: Cambridge University Press); A. Norrie (2014) C*rime, Reason and History: A Critical Introduction to Criminal Law* (3rd edition, Cambridge: Cambridge University Press); N. Lacey (2016) *In Search of Criminal Responsibility: Ideas, Interests, and Institution*s (Oxford: Oxford University Press); L. Farmer (2016) *Making the Modern Criminal Law: Criminalization and Civil Order* (Oxford: Oxford University Press).

political theory. This is the area that both critical criminal justice and liberal theory need to address if they are to get at questions of human freedom and emancipation.

The idea of a moral psychology points in two directions: towards the moral and towards the psychological. This is appropriate in that we are interested in how we understand concepts that are ethically significant for actors, but also, at a deeper level, in how these are embedded in the psychological experience of a certain kind of being, the human being. Because we are interested in this as a general phenomenon concerning questions of guilt, forgiveness, blame, and so on, we think it important to take these concepts out of the orbit of concepts with similar names that are governed by the gravitational pull of legal and liberal philosophical categories. We want to think about these things separately from political and normative theory, which is concerned with law and legal relations, in order to better understand how the findings of a moral psychology might ultimately relate to law.

In pursuing the idea of a moral psychology, we have drawn on a psychoanalytic understanding of human being to help us understand the moral categories in play around conceptions of violation, blame, guilt and victimhood. Here our thinking has been informed primarily by psychoanalysis in the object relations tradition, and the emphasis there on the evolution of human identity through love and loving relations, which can, of course, go wrong. This tradition includes psychoanalytic thinkers and practitioners such as Melanie Klein, Hans Loewald, Donald Winnicott, Jessica Benjamin and Jonathan Lear. This is not to discount the significance or contributions of other psychoanalytic traditions – classical Freudian, Lacanian, or feminist psychoanalysis – but, in our view, the object relations tradition is a rich source of insight that has thus far received virtually no serious attention in critical criminal justice scholarship and promises to reward careful engagement.

Our premise, then, is that one way to address the ethical lacuna in both liberal theory and the social and historical critique of criminal justice is to pursue object relations-based psychoanalytic perspectives on the moral psychology of guilt, violation and wrongdoing, responsibility and judgement, and blame and forgiveness. Moral psychology seeks to account for ethical experience, which here includes the moral emotions, and what we might think of as their cognitive experience and expression, such as the moral duties or obligations possessed or owed to another. Moral psychological inquiry tries to make sense of such phenomena, the moral grammars in which we articulate fundamental feelings or emotions, as they arise from the resources of our psychology.

Of course, what it means to 'account for' or 'make sense of' ethical phenomena in psychological terms needs clarifying, and while this is not the place to give a detailed answer to that question, suffice it to say that two possibilities are ruled out from the start. First, we may well think that what is needed is in some sense a 'naturalistic' account, but that cannot mean that we are reductively to analyse ethical phenomena into organisations of more basic or 'natural' mental states. For one thing, it is not clear that we have any means of knowing in advance what the more 'natural' items to which ethical phenomena should be reduced are, and if we are not simply to beg the question as to what ethical possibilities are really grounded in our psychological nature, we must remain openminded. Second, a naturalistic moral psychology is incompatible with a Panglossian moralism that simply writes back into our psychology, and thus affirms, whatever ethical experiences and intuitions we are familiar with as if they were anthropological constants. That is, we will want a genuinely moral psychology rather than 'a moralizing psychology, one that simply assumes the very categories it seeks to vindicate'.[8]

In the Western tradition, moral psychology has tended to fall into one or the other of these two reductive traps: a moral*ising* psychology that takes for granted the moral emotions, intuitions and attitudes of the form of life and seeks to vindicate them simply by writing them back into the fabric of our psychological nature, as perhaps we find in Aristotle's account of virtues and vices; or a sceptical project that seeks to deflate moral emotions and intuitions in narrow, behavioural science, terms or as the obscure expression of altogether seamier impulses, as we find – at least at times – in both Nietzsche and Freud.[9] The aim, as we see it, would be for a moral psychology of wrongdoing and responses to it that would not blindly seek to rationalise whatever people happen to think and do in a particular historical period. Nor would it blithely dismiss the ethical substance of such phenomena *tout court* as reducible fluff, but would rather be able to offer real grounds for distinctions among putative ethical experiences.

The basic suggestion is that an adequate moral psychology might allow us to distinguish nonarbitrarily between *supposedly* ethical experiences that are really expressions of psychological distortions or fabulations, and those ethical possibilities that are more securely grounded in valuable psychological potentials, even if such potentials are at present only sporadically realised. Moral psychology could then come of age and pull its normative weight in the division of labour within ethical and legal theory, leading to a better understanding of what it would mean for human beings to be free and emancipated and to have real autonomy. On this basis, it would also be possible, more particularly, to think about what it means to blame, to feel guilt, to be responsible. Such an approach would take us through and beyond a mere 'hermeneutics of suspicion' to an investigation of the real ethical possibilities grounded in human psychological powers which conduce to emancipation.

---

[8] J. Lear, *Wisdom Won from Illness* (Cambridge, MA: Harvard University Press, 2017), p. 33.

[9] Williams seems to think that Nietzsche and Freud provide genuine cases of moral, but neither moralising nor reductive, psychology. Both seem to us to tread at times very close to, if not over, the line of reductionism. Freud, we think, is appropriately read in reductionist terms on the face of his ethical texts, but opens the door to better, nonreductionist, readings which ground ethical experience in his later structural approach to psychic development. Though we draw on Klein's metapsychology in this essay to identify persecutory and reconciliative forms of guilt, we think a parallel route to conflicting forms can be developed by contrasting Freud's account of guilt as repressive, fear, and anger-based with an alternative view implicit in his later structural theory that sees guilt as based on love and the desire to atone to, to be 'at one' with, another: A. Norrie (2018) 'Animals Who Think and Love: Law, Identification and the Moral Psychology of Guilt' *Criminal Law and Philosophy* DOI 10.1007/s11572-018-9483-8. Here, we draw upon J. Lear (1990) *Love and Its Place in Nature: A Philosophical Interpretation of Freudian Psychoanalysis* (New Haven: Yale University Press); (1998) *Open Minded* (Cambridge: Harvard University Press); (2015) *Freud* (2nd edition) (Abingdon: Routledge); and on Hans Loewald (1980) *Papers on Psychoanalysis* (New Haven: Yale University Press).

1.3 Moral Psychology and Blaming Practices

In what follows we seek to build a moral psychology of criminal justice, on the basis of a dialogue between two perspectives. The first perspective takes up the key positions, the 'paranoid-schizoid' and the 'depressive', identified by Melanie Klein in her account of the pre-Oedipal phase of infant development. The second considers Jessica Benjamin's relational psychoanalytic account of recognition and domination. We think Klein can shed significant light on modern punitive practices, in the following three ways.

1.3.1 A critique of retributive blaming

The first draws upon Klein's identification of the paranoid-schizoid position in infant development, in which a phantasy of omnipotence prevails, and in which the world is split, in Manichean terms, into all good and all bad objects. This is a world that lacks proper bearing in relation to the reality of others, where appreciation of the mixture of good and bad qualities and the interconnection between the self and the other (I am what I am because you are what you are) are not grasped. This is also Benjamin's world of the doer and the done to, where 'only one can live'.[10] It is possible to see this phantasy as lying at the heart of forms of retributive punishment which seek to banish or permanently 'hurt' the offender, as is often reflected in law and order politics. There is a sense here of the intrinsic pleasure in punishment, but it is based on a negative phantasy. In this view, guilt and punishment are essentially persecutory in their form.

1.3.2 Guilt and reparation

A second route follows Klein's view of the so-called depressive position, which suggests a feeling of guilt and a desire to repair in relation to a loved one that one fears one has damaged in phantasy through one's anger. This can be put together with Benjamin's argument that intersubjective mutual recognition, based on love, struggles with interpersonal relations of domination and submission. Linking these, it can be argued that guilt is the unhappy state of one whose act towards another is one of domination, but who has sufficient upbringing in relations of mutual recognition to experience a conflict between what she does and who she is. Here, guilt and its outcomes are essentially reconciliatory in form. We will seek to interpret current criminal justice problems in light of the interplay between these two psychological positions.

1.3.3 Holding responsible and taking responsibility

A third view comes from the difference between the two accounts of responsibility drawn from the above. The first involves an actualist, momentary and individualistic account of responsibility, which is associated with law, which identifies a voluntary act and accompanying cognitive state and holds an actor responsible for that act. We think this compatible with Klein's schizoid and persecutory position in the critique of retributive blaming. The second is a holistic account of agency which relates acts to the underlying psychological conditions and surrounding contextual setting of action,

---

[10] J. Benjamin (2017) *Beyond Doer and Done To: Recognition Theory, Intersubjectivity and the Third* (Oxon: Routledge), p. 232.

including the understandings, distortions and phantasies under which it occurs. It is consistent with Klein's depressive and reconciliatory position. Taking responsibility is being committed to understanding and addressing the unconscious mental processes and the social contexts that mesh with conscious agency to produce action.

In section 2 of this chapter we develop Klein's account of the two psychic positions just sketched, and in section 3 we relate them to practices of guilt and blame. Finally, in section 4, we relate these findings about the nature of guilt to the way in which legal practices relate to issues of guilt and blame in modern social settings.

1.3.4 The moral, the legal and the broken third
This draws upon Benjamin's recent work on the moral third, which is the form taken by the relationship of mutual recognition at the core of identity formation as it moves out from infants and parents, and beyond the analyst–patient relationship and into broader social relations. It takes wrongdoing and its repair out of the split position of 'doer' and 'done to' and offers the possibility of the repair of violation in legal settings. The moral third is in line with Klein's depressive, reconciliatory position. It is a relationship that embodies mutual recognition, and which serves in settings of violation to permit witnessing and acknowledgement of what has happened. It raises questions, however, as to how the moral third could link to law – does law for example reflect aspects of the *moral* third as a *legal* third? Here we note that modern law is located on sites of structural violence, and this undercuts its ability to reflect positions of moral thirdness: law may be seen accordingly as a site of the broken third. More broadly, structural violence is the basis for law's relationship to persecutory trends in the human psyche and in social practices. Accordingly, here we see criminal justice practices as sitting between the persecutory and the reconciliatory, and we see the abstract nature of legal form as the means whereby law can be utilised both regressively to persecute and, to a certain extent, progressively, to reconcile. Here we move back from the sphere of moral psychology to that of political theory.

2. MELANIE KLEIN'S MORAL PSYCHOLOGY

In this section, we provide a brief outline of the two positions developed by Melanie Klein in her understanding of infantile development in the pre-Oedipal phase.[11] In respect of the deep ethical issues with which criminal justice attempts to deal – those of wrongdoing and violation, responsibility and judgement, blame and guilt – one avenue that seems most promising is that established by her development and transformation of Freud's psychoanalytic research programme. Freud's account of guilt is certainly less onesided than it has sometimes been thought to be. The stock interpretation is that guilt is the feeling of anxiety about retaliation or punishment from the internalised father figure in respect of the infant's possessive desires towards the mother figure. The infant internalises the father figure and thus takes inside itself an imagined vengeful or

---

[11] For a more detailed discussion of Klein's work, and its application to punishment scholarship, see C. Reeves (2019) 'What Punishment Expresses', 28(1) *Social and Legal Studies* 31–57.

punishing authority who is also omnipotent (as the parents are imagined to be), such that violations of the father figure's *diktats* will provoke dreadful retaliation.

Such a story might be thought to offer a more developmentally grounded and less speculative fleshing out of Nietzsche's genealogy of guilt in *On the Genealogy of Morality*,[12] though both might be thought to reduce unacceptably the ethical dimensions of guilt to base narcissism and resentment. Yet already in *Civilization and Its Discontents* the internalised figure is not *only* hated and feared,[13] but *also* loved, and Freud's seemingly reductive account appears to eat its own tail. There, Freud indulges his own Nietzschean impulse for a speculative historical anthropology. The guilt associated with the infant's hateful, destructive wishes towards his frustrating father is traced to the original patricidal act of the primal band of brothers, but he then makes a startling U-turn. Since the band of brothers story is supposed to explain the taboo on patricide, it must not presuppose it. It is supposed to precede the development of the internalisation of the father as an internal punishing figure, and since they have actually killed him, they cannot have grounds to actually fear his retaliation. Yet, apparently, they feel guilty and set up the taboo on patricide, and in turn that on incest, as a response. The question then arises: *why did they feel guilty* about killing the father in the first place? Freud's answer: because they not only hated and feared him but also loved him and *felt remorse at having destroyed one whom they loved*.[14]

The psychological account of guilt that Melanie Klein eventually developed can fruitfully be seen as a systematic exposition and clarification of the insights which Freud touched upon but was unable to articulate otherwise than aporetically. The irony that Freud had, in attempting to trace guilt to narcissistic impulses, eventually been led to the genealogical ground state of a basic, irreducibly ethical, impulse of care for a loved other and remorse at having harmed him is what Klein, by reversing the developmental order, turned into a paradigm shift. This was not a systematic undertaking on Klein's part, but was nevertheless one of her key achievements. One of the crucial innovations flowing from her pioneering work with child psychoanalysis was the development of an account of pre-Oedipal phantasy structures (and an increased understanding of the blurriness and gradualness of the Oedipal/pre-Oedipal distinction itself).[15] She claimed to identify two distinct developmental phases or 'positions', both of which in essence preceded Freud's triangular Oedipal position. In their different ways, both address the questions of love and hate that remained unresolved in Freud's account.

The first phase is the originary psychic situation for the infant – one could say the diachronic starting point of its conditions of experience. The basic feature, conceptually

---

[12] See F. Nietzsche (1887/2017) 'Second Essay', in *On the Genealogy of Morality*, edited by K. Ansell-Pearson, translated by C. Diethe (3rd edition, Cambridge: Cambridge University Press).

[13] S. Freud (1930/2010) *Civilization and Its Discontents* (Mansfield: Martino Publishing).

[14] See also Norrie, 'Animals Who Think and Love: Law, Identification and the Moral Psychology of Guilt'.

[15] Not all of which, of course, exactly showered her in ethical glory. She famously analysed her own five-year-old boy, publishing the case study as the analysis of 'a friend's son', a practice which – particularly in light of her experimental methods – is hardly a model of best practice today (nor was it even then).

speaking, is that the infant as yet lacks the capacity to experience whole objects outside itself that persist through time and that may have different and conflicting qualities manifested at different times. In metaphysical terms (not Klein's), it lacks the category of substance.[16] The consequence is that the world, and the figures in it – at this point, primarily the 'mother', that is, primary caregiver – do not appear as complex persisting wholes. Rather, the infant's experience is organised around fleeting, transient experiences of figures that possess one or another quality, depending on how it feels towards them. Basically, the figures that populate its world are onesided, experienced as either very good or very bad. The frustrating mother is one, bad, figure; the satisfying mother is a different, unrelated, very good figure. Hence, Klein described this early organisational form of experience as 'schizoid', or pervasively *split*. But because momentary frustration is bound to be more common than instant gratification, this world is also predominated by bad figures.[17] At this point one of the most controversial aspects of Klein's theory arises: she hypothesises first that the infant's rage at being frustrated is projected onto the bad, frustrating figures, transmogrifying them into horrific persecutors, and second, that the infant expresses anger and frustration by phantasising vicious attacks – of an oral, biting and chewing nature – on those persecutors in retaliation for their hostility. And the consequence of these biting and chewing phantasies is that the persecutors are phantasised to be taken inside the infant as part of its psychic formation.

This early experiential world is what we might call an age of extremes: the infant's experience (Klein speculates) oscillates between engulfment in the loveliness and perfection of the idealised loved object/mother, enraptured in what Richard Wollheim calls 'archaic bliss',[18] and suffocation by the terror and dread of a world populated by a multitude of entirely bad persecutors who are not just outside, but have been taken in by, the infant. We should not forget the importance in this phase of idealised love, but, since frustration is bound to predominate over gratification, Klein emphasises the latter – calling this position the 'paranoid-schizoid position'. We will refer to it more simply as *the persecutory*, its main features being fear and rage.

Developmentally, this position gives way to a second, the 'depressive position', within the first year. The crucial advance here is that the infant begins to acquire the intellectual and emotional capacity to experience whole, complex objects, and thus to begin to put together the good and bad figures – which now come to be seen, retrospectively, as merely part-objects – into the wholes of which they were merely momentary glimpses. The major step now – ideally, at least – is that the infant becomes able to recognise that the loved and hated, treasured and attacked, objects are actually not separate objects but aspects of the same, complex, ambiguous, loved whole person. The frustrating mother and the comforting mother are one and the same person, at different moments.[19] Klein calls this the depressive position because this realisation

---

[16] See R. Wollheim (1985) *The Thread of Life* (Cambridge: Harvard University Press).
[17] M. Klein (1946/1975) 'Notes on Some Schizoid Mechanisms', in *Envy and Gratitude, and Other Works 1946–1963* (London: Hogarth).
[18] Ibid.
[19] M. Klein (1935/1975) 'A Contribution to the Psychogenesis of Manic-Depressive States', in *Love, Guilt and Reparation, and Other Works 1921–1945* (London: Hogarth).

that the loved person and the hated person are simply aspects of the one whole person ushers in a period of despair, which Klein interprets as a basic, irreducible, though developmentally and diachronically secondary, ethical experience: remorse or real guilt arising out of love and concern for the other and out of the realisation of the true nature of one's own destructive impulses, wishes and (phantasised[20]) actions regarding them. The phantastic fear is that the infant has harmed the loved object. This depressive realisation presents to the infant the most crucial developmental challenge they will encounter.

There are two basic possibilities at this juncture. First, the infant may turn away in hopelessness from the realisation, reverting to the splitting of the persecutory position as a defence against it. In that case, the parts are kept apart and the confrontation with despair is avoided but at the cost of substituting for it the dreadful anxiety of the persecutory world. The second is that the infant begins to work through the depressive position instead of fleeing from it altogether. Now, this depends essentially on the infant's capacity for hope – both in the loved object's (the real parent's) capacity to withstand and survive the infant's attacks, and in the infant's own capacity for love and care and the hope that it cannot undo the harm done, but can repair it and make amends. The depressive phase is in its essence reconciliatory. The drive for reparation is crucial at this juncture and is tied to creative capacities to rebuild, repair, cure, mend; to make anew and whole again. Of course, as Klein was aware – but as Winnicott emphasised more forcefully[21] – hope depends in part on the input of the caregiver, both to reassure the infant that their attacks haven't in fact destroyed the loved parent, and in providing opportunities for and recognition of – and thus confirmation of – the infant's attempts at reparative activity. Whereas the turn back to persecutory splitting marks an inability to tolerate the self's own ambivalence, the working through of the depressive position marks the growth of the capacity to do so and to develop the infant's own psychic reality. The consequence is a growth in the capacity to experience the world as it is, rather than defensively fragmenting and dissimulating it.

Now, crucially, these positions are by no means *merely* developmental stages, but are rather claimed to be persistent *unconscious phantasy structures of experience*. We may think of them as competing categorial and hermeneutic *a priori* emotional frames of reference. They organise actual experience, providing the categories, roles and narratives into which we must interpellate the experienced world, which indeed arrange that world and so both make possible and constrain (in various ways) our experience. The two basic frameworks sit alongside one another, as if vying for prominence. Ordinary psychic life, beyond the early developmental phases in which they arise, is structured by the negotiation of the tension and oscillation between these two great emotional paradigms, under the constantly changing pressures of real life. The fluctuation between these positions, as Klein is thinking of it, might be thought of along the lines

---

[20] At this point, the infant has not acquired the distinction between real world actions and phantasised ones; indeed, they are still only negotiating the distinction between 'inside' and 'outside'. See D. Winnicott (1960/1965) 'Ego Distortion in Terms of True and False Self', in *The Maturational Process and the Facilitating Environment* (London: Hogarth).

[21] D.W. Winnicott (1965) *The Maturational Processes and the Facilitating Environment: Studies in the Theory of Emotional Development* (Madison: International Universities Press).

of a paradigm or *gestalt* shift, whereby a whole framework for understanding experience can be suddenly displaced by, or is in competition with, another. Klein's claim is that at least one very important aspect of how adult life is organised is in terms of such a paradigm struggle, with the possibilities of fluctuation and shift.

Klein's revolutionary distinction between the two distinct phantasy positions – the competing, oscillating, emotional *a priori* categorically organising experience – makes possible a moral psychology that is neither reductive nor moralising. For it suggests a way of accounting for, or making sense of, our putative ethical experience, not in an undifferentiated way which opts either for rationalisation or elimination, but in a way which offers to explain the whole range of the phenomena involved in that experience. And this distinction is in no way question-beggingly reliant on prior ethical judgements of what is or is not preferable. It is not rooted in moral intuitions but in morally uncontentious psychological distinctions, that is, in distinctions not grounded in moral claims but in real psychological states – which then represent the source of emergent moral attitudes. The depressive position may then be preferred morally, to be sure, but this is on the basis that realistic apprehension of the world and of the self, as against distortion and delusion, represents a preferable mindset. Essentially, the persecutory phantasy world organises experience into falsely split off, onesided objects and prevents the apprehension of whole substances, while the depressive position generates an agentive and interactional space in which, through hope, psychic reality can be realistically tolerated and outer reality can be realistically apprehended. These are positive and preferable mental positions not because a moral theory says they are, but because realistic experience is preferable to paranoia at the level of rational health.[22]

3. DIFFERENT SIDES OF PUNISHMENT: ANGER, GUILT AND RESPONSIBILITY

What might all this imply for a realistic psychology of wrongdoing and violation, blame and guilt, responsibility, judgement and justice? There are, we think, initially three fruitful directions in which this analysis leads us. The first and second concern two competing accounts of guilt as a case of persecutory anxiety, or a form of concern related to reconciliatory efforts to regain wholeness through making good a harm done. A third aspect concerns our understanding of what modern responsibility practices involve and how ethical potentials are mediated by them.

---

[22] This argument chimes with Lear's account of psychoanalytic truthfulness as a foundational virtue for ethics, aligning the possibility of human flourishing with a self-understanding that is both psychoanalytic and Socratic: 'Psychoanalysis is not directly a training in familiar ethical virtues, but it is a training in the truthfulness that such virtues require' (Lear, *Freud*, p. 18).

3.1 Retributive Blame and Persecutory Anxiety

First, Klein furnishes us with the resources to make critical sense of retributive blaming emotions in a way that avoids simple reduction (to something else, such as Nietzschean *ressentiment*[23]), but which at the same time offers an explanatory-critical challenge to those emotions rather than simply accepting them. It is sometimes said in the criminological literature that psychoanalytic explanations of punitive attitudes cannot possibly have normative implications since nonpunitive attitudes must also have psychoanalytic explanations,[24] but that is to assume that psychoanalytic moral psychology must be reductive in just the bad sense that we have rejected. A Kleinian moral psychology makes it possible to offer explanatory interpretations of retributive blaming that avoid such pitfalls, for Klein's is not simply a 'hermeneutics of suspicion'; it is a hermeneutic rooted in a realistic moral psychology. In brief, while on the Nietzschean–Freudian view retributive attitudes and emotions are to be denounced as based on narcissistic or dominatory drives *just like everything else in ethical experience*, a Kleinian view makes possible a differentiated interpretation of them as primarily arising from defensive regressions to persecutory ways of experiencing the world.

Such a line of inquiry might begin from the observation that retributive blame presupposes, or at least often involves, a partial view of the person being blamed as a formally free wrongdoer abstracted from an experience of their concrete wholeness as a real person. The categorial framework of criminal law and the philosophical justification of retributive punishment are agreed in excluding from view the concrete reality of the person. In the persecutory mindset, aggressive, punitive, retaliatory, destructive, or even annihilating, impulses make emotional sense, insofar as the other person is being conceived not as a whole person but merely as a bad, persecuting fragment, a part object, that possesses no goodness. The abstract individualist conceptualisation of the criminal in both legal theory and retributive philosophy is at least open to being read as an intrinsically bad, dangerous person, since that person has (a) performed a harmful act and (b) been evacuated of any preexisting moral contextualisation linked to the person's actual social and psychological formation.[25] The way is open through legal–philosophical abstraction to persecutory condemnation on the basis of paranoid-schizoid thinking.

Moreover, the forms of punishment as they have evolved in the modern period might be susceptible to an interpretation in terms of persecutory anxieties: they centre, after all, first on violence, then exclusion, then containment and control – characteristic phantasies of the persecutory period. And the much explored new popular punitiveness seems fairly undeniably to marry together wider anxieties of a narcissistic, self-directed

---

[23] Nietzsche, 'Second Essay'.
[24] Cf S. Maruna, A. Matravers and A. King (2004) 'Disowning Our Shadow: A Psychoanalytic Approach to Understanding Punitive Public Attitudes' 25(3) *Deviant Behavior*, 277–99.
[25] For critical accounts of this problem, cf A. Norrie (2000) *Punishment, Responsibility, and Justice: A Relational Critique* (Oxford: Oxford University Press); H. Carvalho (2017) *The Preventive Turn in Criminal Law* (Oxford: Oxford University Press).

nature,[26] linked to feelings of subjective and ontological insecurity, and phantasies about possible or actual persecutors and imagined threats that are at least out of proportion to reality.[27] The two key elements – splitting and paranoia – of the persecutory position seem to be in evidence in the punitive complex. Since persecutory experience is characterised by distortion rather than realistic apprehension, these suggestions should give us pause for thought. For they would suggest, on moral psychological grounds, that retributive blaming is corrupted by paranoid-schizoid, persecutory, thinking.

Such a judgement would not depend on the sui generis value judgement that there is something wrong with retributive blaming, but would flow from the normative implications of the naturalistic moral psychology that Klein presents, and which suggests that persecutory mentation is 'bad' in the precise sense that it is unrealistic, based on motivated cognitive distortion. This is not to suggest that guilt and blame have no proper place within human responses to harmful behaviour. Rather, it is to suggest that the blaming emotions may be, and often are, embedded within a black and white, simplistic categorial frame of experience in which good and bad are kept separate. This is not a world of beings who comprise a basic, flawed, and vulnerable humanity, but a world in which there is a split between a 'doer' and a 'done to', in Benjamin's terms.[28] This may be quite independent of the fact that we know rationally that this is not the case. Indeed, one of the striking features of the philosophical discourse of criminal justice is that the persecutory view of the offender as a free rational person electing to do wrong and the rational understanding of offending as socially conditioned are kept rigorously apart. To 'understand less and blame more', as British voters were once advised, is a classical splitting along persecutory lines.[29]

The question that Klein's moral psychology ultimately raises is whether there might be possible forms of anger that are not split off from love in a doer/done to formation, but are rather *integrated with love*. As we will now suggest, Klein's work also provides the basis for a moral psychology that can ground judgements of this kind, and work in this direction is a second promising avenue which we think should be explored.

3.2 Guilt, Remorse and Reparation: Reconciliatory Desire

A second avenue for exploration is the inquiry into the role of guilt as remorse in contexts of violation and wrongdoing. Klein's account can be interpreted as differentiating two distinct species of guilt, or anyway two distinct emotional kinds that are

---

[26] D. Garland (2001) *The Culture of Control: Crime and Social Order in Contemporary Society* (Chicago: Chicago University Press); J. Pratt, D. Brown, M. Brown, S. Hallsworth and W. Morrison (eds) (2005) *The New Punitiveness: Trends, Theories, Perspectives* (Cullompton: Willan Publishing).
[27] P. Ramsay (2009) *The Insecurity State* (Oxford: Oxford University Press).
[28] Benjamin, *Beyond Doer and Done To*.
[29] Norrie, *Punishment, Responsibility and Justice*, pp. 219–20. It should be said that the alternative counterslogan in the same campaign, 'tough on crime, tough on the causes of crime', was, by creating an analytical separation between the two forms of toughness, equally aimed at maintaining persecutory splitting at the level of penal policy.

commonly collapsed together under the concept of guilt.[30] The advance that Klein makes possible is to hold in view the possibility of a narcissistic, *ressentiment*-fuelled, form of guilt such as that which Nietzsche and Freud had identified – persecutory guilt rooted in anxiety for the self – while insisting that this is not all there is to guilt by discriminating a deeper form of *depressive guilt*, real remorse for the harming of the loved object that is independent of self-regarding anxiety. This is the irreducibly naturalistic, ethical, form of guilt that gets lost on a Nietzschean view, and to which Freud eventually appealed when he spoke of love in the band of brothers story. Klein's distinction between persecutory and depressive guilt opens up several directions for promising future research.

Moral retributivists have often appealed to guilt in their arguments. Michael Moore,[31] for example, builds an argument for the truth of retributivism along Nietzschean lines upon the supposed results of thought experiments concerning how we would feel, and what we would want to do or undergo, were we to commit a horrific crime. His answer is that we would feel guilty, and the desire that would flow from this is that we would want to be punished. Now quite aside from the obscurities involved in the setup of this supposedly maximally intuition-pumping thought experiment, Moore seems to be appealing to one kind of guilt at the expense of another. It has been shown in empirical test situations where subjects are invited to undertake thought experiments concerning how they would feel if they did something that hurt a valued other, that while there are those who feel 'guilt' and desire to be punished, many feel 'guilt' but desire to undertake reparative actions to try to mend or heal the harm done.[32]

Such findings can be made ready sense of by Klein's moral psychology: we are encountering two different kinds of guilt. One kind of guilt brings in its train the desire to be punished, but this is the persecutory kind. For the subject of persecutory guilt, punishment may be desired because it is imagined that it will provide relief. They feel internally threatened by vengeful persecutors, and the desire for actual punishment might be a form of acting out, in which the subject's desires are governed by the

---

[30] Klein herself later decides to call only depressive guilt 'guilt', and to treat persecutory guilt simply as 'anxiety', distinct from guilt: M. Klein (1948/1975) 'On the Theory of Anxiety and Guilt', in *Envy and Gratitude, and Other Works 1946–1963* (London: Hogarth Press). This could make sense as an attempt to privilege depressive guilt as a more fully realised form of guilt, but little is gained by insisting that the privative persecutory case is not guilt at all. We should rather say simply that it is guilt, but a privative case of it.

[31] M. Moore (1997) *Placing Blame: A Theory of the Criminal Law* (Oxford: Oxford University Press).

[32] The prominence of reparative impulses has been extensively recorded, albeit often in contexts where it was assumed rather than tested for: see J.P. Tangney, 'Moral Affect: The Good, the Bad and the Ugly', (1991) *Journal of Personality and Social Psychology* 61(4), 598–607, p. 600; S. Carnì et al, 'Intrapsychic and Interpersonal Guilt' (2013) *Cognitive Processing* 14(4), 333–46; J.P. Tangney and R.L. Dearing, *Shame and Guilt* (New York: Guilford Press, 2003); and see R. Rodogno (2010) 'Guilt, Anger and Retribution', *Legal Theory* 16(1), 59–76. This literature has tended to minimise the prevalence of persecutory guilt, but it is clearly evidenced in the founding studies, such as J. Lindsay-Hartz (1984) 'Contrasting Experiences of Shame and Guilt', *American Behavioral Scientist*, 27, 689–704 at 691; and F.W. Wicker, G.C. Payne and R.D. Morgan (1983) 'Participant Descriptions of Guilt and Shame', 7 *Motivation and Emotion*, 25–39.

impulse to arrange the real world to conform with their phantasy and the actual punishment might provide relief by exacting in a determinate, external, way the internal retaliation that otherwise would seem interminable.[33] This is often how things seem phenomenologically: people talk of the feeling that they would be eaten up by guilt unless they are punished. Punishment may also provide a sadomasochistic satisfaction. Nietzsche may have exaggerated the centrality of sadism in human nature, but sadistic pleasure is clearly a possibility for us, and insofar as the person identifies with the punishing figure, and draws through this identification pleasure from the punishing that is exacted on themselves, they may find gratification in their own punishment. But what of those who do not share Moore's intuition, those who respond to the thought experiment with guilt that leads them to the desire not to be punished but to make reparation?

This is precisely what Klein claims is the content and motivational direction of depressive, or reconciliatory, guilt. Whereas persecutory guilt is preoccupied with the anticipated retaliatory attacks on the self, depressive guilt is preoccupied with the harm done to the other. This is why persecutory guilt leads to the desire *to be punished* – a self-directed and passive desire – while depressive, reconciliatory guilt leads to the desire for reparation – an other-directed and active desire. Once this distinction is drawn, a critical response to the retributivist appeal to guilt can be developed: appeals to guilt only support retributive punishment insofar as we limit our attention to persecutory guilt and exclude reconciliatory guilt from consideration. Once we think of guilt in terms of reconciliation with a harmed other, the retributive urge turns into something else.

A second role for guilt in retributivism has long been defended by those who see punishment as a moral endeavour whose aim should be to inspire guilt in the offender. Anthony Duff,[34] for example, has defended the view of criminal punishment as a moral dialogue, in which the offender's part is that of secular penance, and where the aim of the whole enterprise is to provoke guilt in the offender so that they come to see the wrongfulness of what they have done and resolve to act differently in the future. Unlike Moore, Duff recognises that there is a distinction between the 'unhealthy, unproductive kind of guilt'[35] and the healthy, constructive kind, but he says nothing more about what this distinction might amount to, nor whether criminal justice is well equipped to bring out the one rather than the other. Klein's moral psychology suggests a realistic, grounded, way to elaborate this distinction.

When the fullness of this distinction is in view, we may well be able to make more sense of Duff's intuition and to delineate what the potentials are for unhealthy, unproductive, persecutory guilt and healthy, productive, depressive guilt. Depressive,

---

[33] R. Wollheim (1988) 'Crime, Punishment and Pale Criminality', 8(1) *Oxford Journal of Legal Studies*, 1–16. There may be other motives involved as well. Perhaps being punished is the only recognition someone can aim for or imagine when they are in a persecutory mode. Perhaps punishment is the only formal recognition of their agency they can imagine in a social world that ignores them. And it should at this point be remembered that to invoke persecutory phantasy is in no way to imply that there isn't also real, actual persecution going on.

[34] R.A. Duff (2001) *Punishment, Communication, and Community* (New York: Oxford University Press).

[35] Ibid, 108.

reconciliatory guilt is, for Klein, bound up with the capacity to tolerate psychic reality, and that is dependent on the capacity for hope – both in oneself, and in the world and the objects one has harmed. While hope that one possesses enough goodness to persevere can come through reparative activity, such reparative activity must be recognised by the other to have emotional reality. This at least is what we learn from the work of Winnicott.[36] And for the person to have any hope in themselves and their capacity to do good in the world, and in turn to be accepted, welcomed, in the community rather than simply rejected, both the individual's capacity for remorse and the community's capacity to facilitate that remorse will be essential.

Recently, Lacey and Pickard have gone further in arguing for the cultivation of reconciliatory guilt, acknowledging that such guilt is not furthered by advancing a condemnatory narrative; a more hopeful 'redemption script' is crucial for offenders who change.[37] Their account implicitly recognises the distinction between a persecutory, destructive, 'condemnatory' kind of guilt and a distinct kind of guilt that is reparative, creative and reconciliatory. Yet they note that such reconciliatory guilt is linked to a contextual self-appraisal on the offender's side that is incompatible with the decontextualised attributions of culpability and responsibility at the core of criminal law. This raises the question of the extent to which criminal law's formal morality can accommodate and nurture reconciliatory guilt, but this is a question Lacey and Pickard sidestep, accepting the nature of criminal law's judgement and recommending that we resign ourselves to the fact that offenders in the criminal process will, insofar as they are to experience productive, reconciliatory guilt, not acknowledge 'the entirety of their culpability'[38] – a conclusion that seems anathema to the spirit of ethical truthfulness and self-knowledge that informs reconciliatory guilt.

The initial impression, then, is that Kleinian 'depressive guilt' lies at the heart of recent attempts to retheorise criminal law as a rational and dialogic moral practice, but that the form of that practice as those same theorists defend it rules out the nurturing of that sort of guilt. If that is indeed the case, further work is needed both to develop in more detail an account of the kind of real guilt that is inherent in violation and a possibility within our ethical form of life, but that may well be blocked off by criminal law's categories. But the underlying question lingers: if there is a potentially progressive core to guilt through restorative and reconciliative forms, can it be that the state, through its convictions and punishments, can represent a mechanism to deliver reconciliative guilt? While law's abstraction may leave it open to move in the direction of reconciliation, its operation in the medium of the punitive, class-based state and its penal system must radically circumscribe, without doing away with, reconciliative possibilities.[39]

---

[36] D. Winnicott (1984) 'The Depressive Position in Normal Emotional Development', in *From Paediatrics to Psychoanalysis: Collected Papers* (London: Karnac).

[37] N. Lacey and H. Pickard (2015) 'To Blame or to Forgive? Reconciling Punishment and Forgiveness in Criminal Justice', 35(4) *Oxford Journal of Legal Studies*, 665–96, 690.

[38] Ibid, 690.

[39] Here, we point to the range of reconciliative projects that operate in the margin and the shadow of the prison and the penal system, and the possibility that individuals within that system will find moral assistance, come to regret acts of violation and change their moral outlook. See for example some of the dialogues between victims and perpetrators found in M. Cantacuzino

In the light of Klein's identification of two forms of guilt, the persecutory and the reconciliatory, we suggest two hypotheses for consideration. The first is that modern criminal justice systems operate on a persecutory model in which social anxieties are focused on 'getting' wrongdoers and making them suffer. Within that system it is possible for agents to inflect and temper practice with reconciliatory intentions and actions, but these are inevitably caught up in the broader persecutory framework. The second is that philosophies of punishment based on retributive grounds can take up either a persecutory or a reconciliatory approach. The persecutory approach fills out the abstract rationality of the philosophical subject with a negative emotional reaction that portrays the perpetrator of a wrongdoing as a part object, different from normal humanity and subject to retaliation for their badness. The reconciliatory approach takes the same abstract rationality and seeks to supplement it with emotionally restorative and reintegrative purposes. In the former, retributive punishment is the rigorous application of a persecutory psychological mindset given philosophical expression. In the latter, such punishment is at most a way of gaining the attention of a person who has done wrongful acts, so that they may embark on restorative work for themselves and their victim. But the question that remains unanswered in this latter situation is whether the institution of punishment as it is structurally positioned can play the role of a trigger for reconciliation when it is, at its core, part and parcel of a persecutory penal system in a social world based on structural violence (see below, section 4.3).

3.3 Holding Responsible and Taking Responsibility

A third avenue drawing on reconciliatory guilt concerns the possibility for radically rethinking the conceptual structure of our responsibility practices. Criminal theorists often say that the point of holding someone responsible is to get them to *take* responsibility, but what the latter might actually involve is left unexplored. It seems usually to be assumed that taking responsibility is simply holding oneself responsible, but that seems to be too hasty. The moral psychology of responsibility suggests a different conclusion. The language of holding responsible and taking responsibility may thus be seen to be further apart than we normally suppose, with the former related to Klein's persecutory complex and the latter to her depressive standpoint. While holding responsible might be thought to be bound up with persecutory phantasies, vindicating Nietzschean scepticism about retributivism, the reconciliatory phantasy world of the depressive may imply a fundamentally different sort of responsibility practice.

(2015) *The Forgiveness Project* (Jessica Kingsley: London and Philadelphia), and a recent book by a former prisoner, E. James (2016) *Redeemable: A Memoir of Darkness and Hope* (Bloomsbury: London). On the ethics brought out by the Forgiveness Project, see A. Norrie (2018) 'Love Actually: Law and the Moral Psychology of Forgiveness', *Journal of Critical Realism*, doi.org/10.1080/14767430.2018.1472409. It has to be said that the young Hegel was already on to moral reconciliation two centuries ago, in his early theological writings, though his mature work is more lawminded and points to the persecutory, albeit within a framework that is formally reconciliative: A. Norrie (2018) 'Love in Law's Shadow: Political Theory, Moral Psychology and Young Hegel's Critique of Punishment' *Social and Legal Studies* doi.org/10.1177/0964663918758512.

Criminal justice theorists often suggest we are faced with two irreconcilable alternatives, where one is plainly unacceptable. These are based on free will and determinism, so that we must accept free will in one form or another, because the practical and logical outcome of accepting determinism – that humans are only capable of behaviour modification and therapy – is morally and phenomenologically unacceptable. However, the responsibility practice that stems from taking responsibility would neither conspire with the asceticism of existing retributive norms and the failed aspirations of the so-called justice model, nor lurch towards a reifying treatment model that apprehends offenders as mere things or animals and fails to allot them respect as persons.[40] The moral grammar of taking responsibility, we suggest, is what is implicit in the psychological structures of the depressive position, and it is very different from the practice of holding someone responsible as a free agent in a punitive, blaming way. It corresponds to depressive, that is, whole-object-oriented, forms of anger and guilt. These offer the starting point for concrete utopian exercises in thinking about what radically different, alternative, responsibility practices might be. Such practices as the grammar of taking responsibility presages would, far from being morally unserious, be much more morally serious about human possibilities than our existing ones.[41]

The practice of holding responsible, tied to free will and other retributive thoughts, embodies a distancing of the person and an abstract, decontextualised, sense of personal autonomy leading to the attribution of blameworthiness. Asking someone to take responsibility per contra may actively acknowledge unfreedom and heteronomy in the person and their past actions, while still resisting simply ignoring the reality of the wrongs they have done. The latter approach is processual rather than static, inviting an active engagement in an undertaking that takes time and involves real change. It is also dialogical in a genuine sense, opening itself up to the impetus of the conversation in which the agency or community which asks the offender to take responsibility must at the same time also be prepared to take appropriate responsibility itself for its part in the situation. Kleinian moral psychology thus offers guidance as to radical alternatives to our existing responsibility practices which would be rooted in, and answerable to, the ethical potentials and needs in our real human nature, and such lines of inquiry are an important third avenue for critical criminal justice research to explore.

4. LOCATING LAW BETWEEN THE PERSECUTORY AND THE RECONCILIATORY

The ideas of responsibility used in law and legal theory have often been criticised as thin and impoverished. The semiotician Roland Barthes spoke of law's universal language lending 'a new strength to the psychology of the masters' by dealing only in adjectives and epithets, 'ignorant of everything about the actions themselves, save the

---

[40] Cf C. Reeves (2016) 'Adorno, Freedom, and Criminal Law: The 'Determinist Challenge' Revitalised', 27(3) *Law and Critique*, 323–48.

[41] See C. Reeves, 'Responsibility beyond Blame', in C. Lemestedt and M. Matravers (eds) *Criminal Law's Person* (Oxford: Hart, forthcoming).

guilty category into which they are forced to fit'.[42] The philosopher Bernard Williams described legal responsibility as 'governed by a certain political theory of freedom in the modern state, not by a moral refinement of the very conception of responsibility'.[43] Norrie characterised legal morality as a 'morality of form', one that is abstract and universal, and removed from the real experiences of what it means to be responsible and human while living in a structurally divided and violent world.[44] These views either discount or, at least, leave unanswered the question of law's ultimate relationship to underlying moral issues, despite its particular forms.

How should the moral experiences of what it means to be responsible be understood? What, equally, would 'a moral refinement of the very conception of responsibility' look like? At the end of *Shame and Necessity*, tucked away in an appendix, Williams wrote in psychoanalytic terms of the 'primitive basis [of guilt] in an internalised figure [of] a victim or an enforcer ... [an] internalised figure [of] anger' that is 'progressively more structured by social, ethical, or moral notions'.[45] This is not much more than a gesture in the direction of psychoanalysis as the ground on which moral theory should be built, in a way that would take it away from political encipherment and towards a fuller appraisal of the human ethical condition. Williams's description of the psychological basis of guilt is unclear. It looks pretty much like Freud's account in *Civilization and Its Discontents*, though it could be related to Klein's account of the paranoid-schizoid position and persecutory guilt. In this chapter, we have sought to give a fuller account of the psychological elements that may underpin an understanding of guilt, and to show how these may be more complex than Williams's sketch might suggest. In particular, we have outlined two accounts of guilt that go in different directions, one persecutory, the other restorative and reconciliatory. We think both are not only eminently identifiable in modern moral experience, but also can be related to the workings of the criminal justice system, in line with the two hypotheses that we outlined above (section 3.2).

In this final section, we wish to consider how we might develop an account of how persecutory and reconciliatory trends bear on criminal justice practice. We want to be clear that our intention in identifying these two broad moral psychological thrusts within practice is not reductive. We do not wish, for example, to replace an historical understanding of the emergence of modern criminal justice with a psychoanalytic understanding. Rather, we think an understanding of the moral psychology of persecution and reconciliation as positions within the criminal justice system must be related to social, historical, political and economic dimensions over time. The persecutory and the reconciliatory are embedded in structural developments in a complex way and are pushed one way and another as the criminal justice system develops in line with other major developments in society.

In line with this, we equally do not wish to align law with either persecution or reconciliation. We mentioned above the criticism of legal form as abstract and thin, and, in its abstraction and thinness, as usable for a purpose beyond the form itself. Thus

---

[42] R. Barthes (1973) *Mythologies* (St Albans: Paladin), 45.
[43] B. Williams (2008) *Shame and Necessity* (Berkeley: University of California Press), 66.
[44] Norrie, *Punishment, Responsibility, and Justice*.
[45] Williams, *Shame and Necessity*, p. 219.

Barthes's suggestion that law's universal language becomes an aid to the psychology of mastery in modern society. This seems to us an important way to approach legal abstraction in relation to persecutory or reconciliatory trends in the human psyche and in modern society as a whole. As we have noted, law's abstract form lends itself to persecutory application, since an abstract person who has done a bad thing may quite easily be interpreted as a bad person. Equally, however, a free legal subject able to act autonomously in a rational compact with other citizens might become *in substance* one who finds real agreement with other human beings and acts accordingly. The formal requital of harm in the retributive exchange of equivalents might become a concrete making of amends, leading to genuine emotional change.

The question then would be: if law in its abstraction can move regressively towards the persecutory or progressively towards the reconciliatory, how do we see this happening in criminal justice practice? In this section, we consider these two directions of legal travel, first in relation to how law might assist in moral and emotional healing. Here, we consider Jessica Benjamin and the place of law in relation to the possibility of social transition. Then, second, we consider how law is generally situated in connection with structural violence and how its effects generally establish a persecutory shadow over criminal justice practice.

4.1 Towards Reconciliation: Benjamin's Moral Third

Jessica Benjamin's work is an excellent opportunity for engagement between law and psychoanalysis both because of its sustained long term treatment of critical themes in political theory from a psychoanalytic perspective and, in its most recent form, because it deals with issues that are in effect in the law's domain. It is on the latter that we focus here.[46]

At the beginning of *Beyond Doer and Done To*, Benjamin talks about the importance of the lawful world as a central category of human experience. By this she means a world in which 'the other's behaviour is not simply always predictable but more importantly confirms when the unexpected or painful wrongness occurs as well as the need to put things right'.[47] She adds that the idea of the lawful world 'refers not to juridical law, but to a belief in the value and possibility of intelligible, responsive and respectful behaviour as a condition of mental sanity and interpersonal bonds'.[48] Many lawyers and legal theorists in the liberal tradition would say that the values Benjamin associates with the lawful world are precisely those that they associate with the juridical world. We agree with Benjamin that there is a distinction to be made between law in the juridical sense and the idea of lawfulness, and her work is helpful in developing it. What is the nature of legal (especially criminal) justice, and to what

---

[46] Benjamin, *Beyond Doer and Done To*. A full treatment of her work must also take in the account of recognition and domination in J. Benjamin (1988) *The Bonds of Love* (Pantheon: New York) and her engagements with feminist and poststructuralist theory in J. Benjamin (1998) *Shadow of the Other* (Routledge: New York). See A. Norrie, 'The Moral Grammar of Guilt: Perspectives in Political Theory and Moral Psychology', in K. Lernestedt and M. Matravers (eds), Criminal Law's Person (Oxford: Hart, forthcoming).

[47] Ibid, 6.

[48] Ibid.

extent can it be compared with the process of what she calls 'moral thirding' that make the world a lawful place in her terms?

Benjamin's interest is to move from considering the dynamics of child development and therapy to the role that such an understanding can perform at the level of society, politics and law, in particular in situations of traumatisation and transitional justice. The lawful world is a way of speaking about the moral third, an overall setting of assumptions and practices that can hold together the relationship between a 'first' and a 'second', and render their relationship appropriately respectful and loving. In the parent/child dyad, or in the analyst/patient setting, thirdness is a negotiated set of asymmetrical relations which holds the parties together. This starts with a sense of bodily co-understanding in the parent/child setting (the 'rhythmic third' – the 'One in the Third'), and progresses to moral or lawful thirdness (the 'Third in the One') as a relationship progresses. Allowing for obvious differences, the psychotherapeutic relationship reflects what evolves in the parent–child relation. The parenting process of recognising, sharing and emotional holding, when applied mutatis mutandis in the therapeutic context, provides a moral setting in which a patient can articulate her concerns, learn from her actions and identify new ways to proceed.

4.2 The Moral Third as Broken in Modern Sociopolitical Settings

Moving from these existing settings of moral thirdness to the social and political settings of traumatisation and transitional justice, moral thirdness takes on its own forms: such thirdness may be, as in the other settings, 'embodied', as in processes of shared empathic feeling in truth processes; but it may also be 'public', and here a political and legal process acts to publicise but also to state authoritatively that some things did happen, and in that sense to stand for a generalised statement of truthfulness. And it may be universal in the sense of affirming the value of all lives: 'the principle that we are all human, that vulnerability and suffering must be honoured.'[49] Law is linked to much of this. Hence we can extend the idea of moral thirdness to include co-related ideas of the 'public', the 'legal' and the 'universal' third. This extension of thirdness to the sociopolitical, the public, and the legal and ethical levels must however be treated with caution: where public witnessing fails, for example, thirdness cannot happen, and we are in the place of what Benjamin refers to as the 'failed' or the 'dead' third.[50] More broadly, we live in a social and political world in which nationalism and imperialism prevail, and this inculcates the phantasy that opposes moral thirdness at all levels, the phantastic split between the doer and the done to, the claim that 'only one can live'.[51] This is paranoid-schizoid, persecutory, territory, emerging out of modern social and political contexts, and it too must be a significant element in public settings. If so, how will it affect claims of public, legal and universal thirdness?

---

[49] Ibid, 240.
[50] Ibid, 288, following S. Gerson (2009) 'When the Third is Dead: Memory, Mourning and Witnessing in the Aftermath of the Holocaust', *International Journal of Psychoanalysis* 90(6), 1341–57. Cf J. Améry (1980) *At the Mind's Limits* (Bloomington: Indiana University Press).
[51] Benjamin, ibid, 232.

An interesting interlocutor here might be Robert Meister's *After Evil*,[52] in which the author adopts the critical view that the human rights and transitional justice movement in the post-1989 unipolar world is a way of providing victims with the appearance of resolution to their traumatic suffering. However, what is really happening is that a merely *symbolic* recognition of victims is provided as a means of ensuring that the beneficiaries of violation retain their status and wealth in the transitioning community. Relating this to Benjamin's terms, we might speak here of a superficial, or perhaps a 'hollow', third. Against this, it would be a mistake to think that 'moral thirding' does not remain a central element in what is happening, even if its potentialities are significantly limited by social, political and economic considerations in the emerging, transitional, polity. To examine critically the limits of the processes we see occurring in countries such as Chile, South Africa, Colombia and Northern Ireland cannot be to deny the hard emotional and moral work involved in addressing past traumatisation. That work is real and invested with a true spirit of moral thirdness. It should be honoured. But equally, to fail to acknowledge the systematic limitations and the structural violence operating against the possibility of the public third, often with bitter outcomes for those involved, would be untrue to the situation. Note, however, that the moral untruth that has to be charted would lie in the failure to represent the fate of the human drive to moral thirdness in a political world structured against it. Acknowledging the real limits of transitional processes in practice thus occurs *in the name of* the moral third.[53]

One possible way of exploring the gap between the theory and the practice of moral thirdness in the legal and political arena would be to speak of it as establishing a position of partial or *broken* thirdness. In a recent book, *Justice and the Slaughter Bench*, Norrie refers to the 'broken dialectic' that is present in legal justice to indicate something of the same phenomenon.[54] There, the idea is that legal justice must be valued at the same time as we understand its social and historical limits under modern political and economic conditions. The book's title refers to Hegel's description of history as a 'slaughter bench': if this is the terrain on which law operates, then law and violence must be connected and co-related. If that is so, then the projected dialectical resolution of conflicts that Hegel claims to foresee will not occur, and the dialectic will be shown to be unresolved and broken under modern conditions. From this perspective, it is possible to think of Benjamin's account of moral thirdness in the 'nationalist and imperialist' world we inhabit as entailing, equally, a third that is *both* valid *and* broken.

---

[52] R. Meister (2011) *After Evil* (New York: Columbia University Press).

[53] A good illustration here is the enduring search of family members for the bodies of their loved ones decades after their murder in countries such as Chile. Patricio Guzman's film *Nostalgia for the Light* (2010) is a moving depiction of the relentless commitment to moral thirdness in private and public settings, as well as its limits and vulnerabilities, in that country post-Pinochet. See A. Norrie (forthcoming) 'Identification, Atonement and the Moral Psychology of Violation: On Patricio Guzman's *Nostalgia For The Light*' Journal of Critical Realism.

[54] A. Norrie (2017) *Justice and the Slaughter Bench: Essays on Law's Broken Dialectic* (Abingdon: Routledge).

4.3 Criminal Justice and Structural Violence

This brings us to the issue of structural violence in modern societies. In a social reality where state institutions actively work to preserve a social order marred by pervasive structural inequality and violence, the normative framework underpinning the juridical world should be understood as being shaped not only by what it expresses and defines in terms of lawful and unlawful conditions and behaviours, but equally also by the aspects of social experience that it does not concretely address, and thus inherently conceals or represses. At its heart, the notion of a broken third suggests that the moral claims advanced by the law can be seen as inherently paradoxical: the law makes promises and furnishes aspirations that, upon closer scrutiny, not only remain perennially unfulfilled, but also ultimately turn out to be in direct opposition to much of what the law promotes and accomplishes in practice. Awareness of this contradictory nature of the workings of the law evidences that there is something in the juridical world that is kept hidden from view, but which is nevertheless intrinsic to it.

In criminal justice, evidence of this phenomenon abounds. Scholarship has pointed to a paradox in the very notion of individual liberty, one of the cornerstones of liberal law, in that the very exercise of political and juridical power that is supposed to protect and promote freedom ends up posing a threat to it.[55] One of the primary expressions of this paradox lies in the framework of punishment, where its practice seems to betray every one of its normative[56] and political justifications;[57] that is, while punishment is often justified as a modern institution aimed at respecting the wellbeing and rational agency of individuals, in reality the state's penal power is experienced primarily as a hostile and exclusionary instrument of social control. Another manifestation of this paradox can be found in the notion of criminal responsibility, where the proposition that individuals should be respected as responsible agents leads the criminal law to regulate an ever increasing proportion of individuals' social agency.[58] The criminal law has been shown to both limit and embody authoritarianism,[59] its subject to be at the same time responsible and dangerous,[60] and punishment to express fear and aggression as much as

---

[55] Cf A. Ashworth and L. Zedner (2014) *Preventive Justice* (Oxford: Oxford University Press); L. Zedner and A. Ashworth (2018) 'The Rise and Restraint of the Preventive State', 2(1) *Annual Review of Criminology*, 1.1–1.22.

[56] Cf T. Mathiesen (2005) *Prison on Trial* (Winchester: Waterside Press); H. Carvalho and A. Chamberlen (2016) 'Punishment, Justice, and Emotions', in M. Tonry (ed.), *Oxford Handbooks Online: Criminology and Criminal Justice* (Oxford: Oxford University Press).

[57] Cf A. Norrie (1991) *Law, Ideology and Punishment* (Dordrecht: Kluwer); L. Farmer (1997) *Criminal Law, Tradition and Legal Order: Crime and the Genius of Scots Law 1747 to the Present* (Cambridge: Cambridge University Press); H. Carvalho and A. Chamberlen (2018) 'Why Punishment Pleases: Punitive Feelings in a World of Hostile Solidarity', 20(2) *Punishment and Society*, 217–34; D. Fassin (2018) *The Will to Punish* (Oxford: Oxford University Press). On the last of these, see A. Norrie (2019) 'Beyond Persecutory Impulse and Humanising Trace: On Didier Fassin's *The Will to Punish*' in *Criminal Law and Philosophy* (online first) https://doi.org/10.1007/s11572-019-09491-y.

[58] Farmer, *Making the Modern Criminal Law*.

[59] Norrie, *Justice and the Slaughter Bench*.

[60] Carvalho, *The Preventive Turn in Criminal Law*.

it does respect for individual freedom.[61] The persecutory nature of modern criminal justice is real and practical.

To explore fully the morality of criminal justice in a manner that takes its normative claims seriously, it is fundamental to critically engage with the tensions and contradictions which permeate its institutional structure and practice. Here, the lessons taken from critical, sociolegal, criminal justice scholarship are many and invaluable.[62] However, while many of these contributions expertly reveal and examine the broken character of the juridical world of criminal justice, it is much less common to find comprehensive attempts to examine how such engagement can move beyond exposing or acknowledging the existence of this broken character, towards an effort to directly face it and work through it.

4.4 Under the Shadow of Liberal Law

Directly and critically engaging with the paradoxical character of criminal justice has the potential not only to shed light on its darker side, but also to reveal that these two poles of the juridical world – light and dark, the expression and the repression of human freedom – are two sides of the same coin, and as such, they are inextricably related.[63] Understandably, the temptation to focus predominantly on the authoritarian, exclusionary and violent aspects of the law – to see it 'through a glass, darkly' – is an inherent aspect of critical criminal justice scholarship, since this is the side that is neglected and concealed from most mainstream scholarship. However, this tendency also runs the risk of presenting a similarly polarised, and thus ultimately skewed, picture of criminal justice practices. Instead, the focus on relationality invoked by the notion of thirdness suggests that considerable attention must be dedicated to the dynamics and the interaction between liberal law and its dark shadow.

This image of a shadow is very useful for understanding the relation between the two contradictory poles of criminal justice, especially when this relation is scrutinised from a psychoanalytical perspective. The psychoanalytic shadow has been conceptualised as the part of an individual's self that exists mostly in the unconscious, away from the individual's self-consciousness and self-perception. However, the shadow nevertheless has a significant role in shaping that individual's personality, the more so since the individual is unaware of the shadow's influence. Indeed, besides being neglected, the influence of the shadow over the self's personality is inherently uncomfortable, since it undermines the strongly held ideas around the autonomy and self-control of the conscious self. In addition, the shadow is often taken to represent those aspects of personality that are considered inferior, that are feared or despised. As a result, instead of being actively recognised and assimilated into the individual's conscious self, the shadow is almost always repressed, and its most active traits are often projected externally, so that the conscious self sees them as reflections of other subjects and

---

[61] Reeves, 'Adorno, Freedom and Criminal Law'; C. Reeves (2018) 'What Punishment Expresses', *Social & Legal Studies* (Online First).
[62] Cf Carvalho and Norrie, 'In This Interregnum'.
[63] A. Norrie (2014) *Crime Reason and History* (Cambridge: Cambridge University Press), ch 13.

objects instead of its own personality and comes to interpret them as a result of the outside world – therefore justifying its own limitations.[64] The negative aspects of criminal justice can be seen to operate within the framework of the juridical world much in the same way as the shadow works within the self, as an obfuscated dimension of the law that is nevertheless intrinsic to its constitution, and which significantly influences its role and practice.

The juridical world appears to deal with its own shadow in much the same way as the unreflexive self. The paradoxes within law and justice point to the existence of a 'social shadow',[65] at the core of which lies the problem of structural violence. In this sense, the broken third constituted by the juridical world is largely characterised not only by the existence and the effects of structural inequality, social marginalisation and exclusion, but also by an active (if unconscious) effort to repress this darker side of the law, to project it externally onto others – in the case of criminal justice, others who are deemed to be dangerous, and whose dangerousness is deemed to be the source of law's problems and limitations. Reluctance and resistance to deal with this shadow is perhaps one of the main reasons why it is so difficult to engage with the problems in criminal justice, and why the persecutory position grounding the need for punishment as a form of justice appears to be so socially alluring,[66] and so difficult to overcome.[67]

The recognition of liberal law's inability to come to terms with its own complicity in the preservation and promotion of structural violence can add another level of depth to the critique of criminal justice, by turning our attention to the processes through which the two terms in the various paradoxes contained within the law shape and condition each other. This approach can potentially enable us, for instance, to explore the ideological and authoritarian elements within criminal responsibility and punishment, without completely dismissing or losing sight of the real moral demands that are embedded within such concepts and institutions – even while recognising that these demands are posed in an abstract, often significantly distorted manner, which ultimately prevents them from being concretely realisable. In other words, the paradoxical nature of the law, when taken seriously, can suggest and sometimes reveal something deeper about human relations and desires, which needs to be a part of any critical analysis of the law.[68]

4.5 Moving beyond the Broken Third

How, then, can an engagement with the relation between the law and structural violence help us to move beyond the broken third of the juridical world? At its core, the idea of moral thirdness implies the pursuit of a social condition which enables mutual

---

[64] For a discussion of the psychoanalytic role of the shadow, cf C.G. Jung (1959) *Aion: Researches into the Phenomenology of the Self* (London: Routledge).
[65] A. Matravers and S. Maruna (2005) 'Contemporary Penality and Psychoanalysis' in M. Matravers (ed.), *Managing Modernity: Politics and the Culture of Control* (New York: Routledge), 118–44, 123. Cf also Carvalho and Chamberlen, 'Why Punishment Pleases'.
[66] Cf A. Chamberlen and H. Carvalho (2018) 'The Thrill of the Chase: Punishment, Hostility, and the Prison Crisis', *Social & Legal Studies* (Online First).
[67] Cf Reeves, 'What Punishment Expresses'.
[68] Cf Norrie, *Justice and the Slaughter Bench*.

recognition. This is an assumption that is often identified with the higher aspirations of liberal law.[69] However, the very existence of structural violence in liberal societies, together with law's role in maintaining the conditions for such violence, betrays such aspirations.[70] This paradoxical state within the law inevitably generates a tension, which the law attempts to resolve through repression. But in repressing its shadow, and projecting it so that the responsible agency of law-abiding citizens is protected by being distinguished from the dangerousness of criminals, criminal justice replaces its ideal of mutual recognition with a condition of domination, in which only the subjectivity of some is fully recognised.

In her earlier work, Jessica Benjamin suggested that at the heart of human relations there is an inherent tension between self-assertion and recognition – between the need to be recognised and the need to recognise, to acknowledge our dependence upon others.[71] We seem to be constantly tempted to try and resolve this tension, either by dominating one another, and thus being fully recognised without recognising, or by submitting to the other, recognising without being properly recognised in return. Both approaches are inadequate, however, as they both only lead to the satisfaction of one need at the sacrifice of the other, and therefore to an unequal and partial relationship.[72] Instead, Benjamin suggests, we need to acknowledge, accept and maintain this tension between self-assertion and recognition, and to work through it. Doing so requires us to acknowledge the value and importance of relationships, as not only constituted by those taking part in it but also constituting and going beyond them, in the shape of a moral third.

Regarding criminal justice, this perspective is rather damning. This is so because the very kind of moral judgement that is embedded within punishment seems to imply an intrinsic (persecutory) aggressiveness that forecloses communication, which fails to reach out to those against whom such judgements are made. Instead, to preserve the tension, it is perhaps necessary to resist the 'righteous law-mindedness'[73] that is inherent to retributive justice, and to see justice in these cases as an ongoing and inextricably interrelational process. Such acknowledgment would build on the core Kleinian idea of the depressive position and the possibility that humans can take responsibility for their being in the world.

---

[69] For example, cf Duff, *Punishment, Communication, and Community*.
[70] Cf Carvalho, *The Preventive Turn in Criminal Law* and Norrie, *Crime, Reason and History*.
[71] J. Benjamin (1988) *The Bonds of Love: Psychoanalysis, Feminism, and the Problem of Domination* (New York: Random House).
[72] This is an insight taken from Hegel. Cf G.W.F. Hegel (1807/2018) *The Phenomenology of Spirit* (Cambridge: Cambridge University Press).
[73] A. Norrie (2018) 'Love in Law's Shadow: Political Theory, Moral Psychology and Young Hegel's Critique of Punishment', *Social & Legal Studies* (Online First).

5. CONCLUSION: VIEWING CRIMINAL JUSTICE IN AN EMANCIPATORY FRAME

This chapter has explored a potential avenue for present and future scholarship in criminal justice theory, grounded in a concrete engagement with issues of moral psychology. It started by deploying an analysis of Melanie Klein's work as a basis for a serious and critical account of the moral categories underpinning criminal justice, such as guilt, blame and responsibility. This analysis explored the problems and limitations inherent in retributive justice, and the need to move from a 'persecutory' to a 'reconciliatory' framework which can ground the conditions for emancipation. Then the chapter shifted its attention to a discussion of Jessica Benjamin's work, framing the ambivalent character of the normative framework of law and criminal justice within its institutional and sociopolitical context. Here, criminal justice is exposed as inherently paradoxical, and consequently espousing a broken ethical condition.

The question this analysis leaves would be: how do we, as legal scholars, strive to move beyond the broken third in the social, political and legal settings that exist today? An answer to this question might have at least three elements. One would be to relate the failures of moral thirding as legal and public thirding in the sociopolitical world to the forms of structural (economic, ideological, institutional) violence, and the systematic limitations in public practices that these generate – and to expose and explore these relationships through critical legal scholarship. Here, attention to the persecutory dimensions of an abstract moral psychology embedded within legal categories is particularly important.

Second would be to strive to recognise instances of justice practice where there is more or less scope for more concrete, reconciliatory forms of moral thirding. For instance, if we examine transitional justice settings as diverse as Chile, South Africa, Colombia and Northern Ireland, it is possible to distinguish transitions according to how they are related differentially to structural violence and systematic limitation in different contexts, and thus how they relate differently to each other. Here, it is also fundamental to acknowledge how similar concerns can take substantially differentiated expressions and generate unique outcomes in particular contexts; it cannot be a question of one size fits all.

This process of identifying the differently conditioned processes of legal and public thirding, in their limited and broken forms, involves examining moral thirding in particular social totalities. It is a step that is committed to the claims of moral thirdness in concrete terms, and that thus seeks a sociohistorical understanding of how, when, why, and to what extent emancipation could be made possible. This totalising viewpoint might be regarded as an additional move that respects the importance of moral thirding and thinks about how it is undermined, and how it might be supported in practice.

Finally, a third point would involve insisting on the underlying psychoanalytic significance of that which moral thirding is directed against: the persecutory splitting of doer and done to, the assumption that 'only one can live'. Benjamin's recent work identifies the underlying existence of a powerful conflictive alternative to moral thirdness in psychoanalytic understanding. She draws on Melanie Klein's identification of the paranoid-schizoid position as a basis for hostile splitting.[74] From a legal point of view, we would propose that law's push in the direction of reconciliation and public reparation clashes with a world in which persecutory and paranoid-schizoid forms are also present, if not predominant. Law inevitably reflects and embodies *both* sides: think for example of the turn to authoritarian forms of criminal justice in the US and the UK. Accordingly, an overall view of the co-constitution of law is necessary, involving claims to moral thirding and alternative, hostile, paranoid-schizoid, reflexes under modern social–historical conditions. Law's abstract universality is open to both persecutory and reconciliative moves, both of which are embedded as potentials in the nature of the human psyche. The progressive, reconciliatory, drive can ground the possibility of human emancipation, but in order to get to it, it would be necessary to address the regressive, persecutory, element in human psychology, especially as it is given encouragement by modern social, economic, and political conditions.

---

[74] Cf Benjamin, *Beyond Doer and Done To*, 5.

22. Facticity as validity: the misplaced revolutionary praxis of European law

Michelle Everson and Christian Joerges

1. INTRODUCTION

If, writing in 2018, the EU and its law can be said to be in crisis, it is tempting to lay the blame for contemporary malaise firmly at the door of financial crisis, dating from the collapse of Lehman Brothers in 2008. A cascade of further threats followed. Our focus, however, will remain the financial crisis and its impact. Exogenous to the workings and to the competences of the EU, the near breakdown of global capital markets nevertheless precipitated a series of very European happenings, which culminated most strikingly in the very visible, dual disintegration of the European rule of law in sovereign debt crisis. On the one hand, the rapid assertion of *ersatz* or 'crisis law' throughout the Union undid the already strained democratic legitimacy of the fragile European constitutional compromise, as national budgetary autonomy became subject to the discretionary oversight of the economically functionalist, supranational executive,[1] on the other, primary European law, in its self-assumed character as constitutional guardian of the Union, also disappointed as the CJEU rushed to condone the appearance of extra-legal structures of crisis law within the European legal map, drawing legitimating references from dominant economic theories of fiscal restraint and monetary conditionality.[2]

Yet, important as these and other legal manifestations of current crisis are, a review of the *longue durée* of European law similarly reveals the inevitability of the normative collapse within European law. Bedevilled by history, or a series of factual happenings which have buffeted the European telos this way and that in a maelstrom of creeping economic realignment and unforeseen geopolitical upheaval, European law has been called upon to be a revolutionary, but has never had the luxury of room and space to enunciate a coherent revolutionary philosophy of self-legitimation. Keeping the show on the road, European law will always reach for an 'empty' functionalism, uproarious in its rejection of formalism, but minus any vision beyond the tautology of ever closer Union.

Taking Joseph Weiler's seminal reconstruction of the 'Transformation of Europe' as our starting point,[3] in section 2.1 we distinguish between a formative period ranging from 1958 up to the Single European Act and the move from the 'Common' to the

---

[1] 'Executive federalism' is the much cited notion coined by Habermas 2012.
[2] See Everson & Joerges 2014; 2017 and the discussion in section 4 below.
[3] Weiler 1991.

'Internal' Market as projected by the Commission White Paper of 1985,[4] accompanied by new regulatory policies and further consolidated following the upheavals of the late 1980s by the Maastricht Treaty of 1992 (section 2.2). Thereafter, in section 2.3 we discuss the renewed integration impetus sparked by the need to master eastward enlargement and given functional form by the Commission's 2001 White Paper on governance and the advent of the 'open method of coordination'.[5]

As indicated in our introductory remarks, we do not subscribe to the normative logic and aspirations which are so widely assigned to these developments. We nevertheless argue that in all of its evolutionary potency, the structures of European law have normalised, and continue to normalise, the political and economic facts of European integration, in equal measure imposing, and failing to impose, any credible *ex post* rationalisation upon the *de facto* progression of the EU. This type of 'normalisation' operates as legalisation, albeit one, which is under-theorised and devoid of renewed normative vision.

2. THE INHERITED WISDOM: A LAW OF ITS OWN INVENTION

The integration process has been shaped by events and political facts which have formed and reformed the European body politic, but have done so outside the normal process of constitution. Lacking an '*acte constituant*', European law has had no choice but to learn and to adapt, and has done so within its own claim to 'constitutionalism'. This constitutes the revolutionary *praxis* of European law. At the same time, however, where European legal constitutionalism establishes a *de facto* revolutionary character for European law, it also emerges as its greatest problem: hovering in the indistinct space between facts and norms, legal adaptation has never been, and can never be, a guarantee of its own success. Though changing in its *gestalt*, the challenge has remained constant, as has the 'instructive' futility of all attempts to address it.

2.1 The 'Integration through Law' Project

Tucked away in the fairyland Duchy of Luxembourg and blessed, until recently, with benign neglect by the powers that be and the mass media, the Court of Justice of the European Communities has fashioned a constitutional framework for a federal-type Europe.[6]

The history of the ECJ is one that has long fascinated, since it seems to confirm the existence of a legal culture of argumentation that is accepted over and above national legal systems. The revolutionary ability of European law to assert its norms outside traditional structures of legal power lays the basis for its claim to be a law *sui generis*, but also leaves the observer with a tantalising question: can it really be that, like Baron von Münchhausen, European law pulled itself out of a swamp by its own hair,

---

[4] Commission of the EC 1985.
[5] Commission of the EC 2001.
[6] Stein 1981, 1.

achieving, unlike international law, a status far greater than that of intergovernmental politics, and imposing its validity on sovereign states?

2.1.1 The legal narrative of spontaneous (hierarchical) constitutionalisation, and the misplaced critical moment

The self-narratives of European lawyers leave little room for doubt. The interpretation of the European system as a supranational legal community was an ingenious ECJ invention. Its jurisprudence has found such widespread support, in the legal system and beyond, that it can be regarded as the dominant orthodoxy of Community law. By contrast, it took considerable effort on the part of legal historiography to remind us that the constitutionalisation of the EEC Treaty was an audacious exercise,[7] and meticulous sociological inquiry to reveal the intensive lobbying by legal elites which encouraged the creation of this ideational edifice.[8]

The extraordinary success story of the 'integration through law' orthodoxy continues to amaze. Joseph Weiler, the project's most important protagonist, had underlined early on in his writings that the supremacy of European law was anything other than self-sustaining.[9] Yet, a later, much cited, 1990 essay downplays the constitutional element of legitimation within the saga, laying renewed emphasis upon the integrationist impetus: law, we are told, could and should operate as 'the object and the agent of integration'.[10]

The flaws within this defining expression of the 'integration through law movement' are many, but may be summarised in three interrelated points. First, the integrationist trend suggests that legal diversity is bad *per se* and that legal uniformity is a defining feature of Europe's 'constitutional charter' – a command mode of law that must surely be questioned in its claim to bypass the validity claims of constitutional democracies. Second, methodologically speaking, the 'integration through law' movement assigns a mysterious strength to the 'law as such' and seems unhealthily fixated with the strictly legal operations of the judiciary and administrative bodies. Third, perhaps the most intriguing flaw within the 'integration through law movement' is the camouflage which it has provided for an agenda that has at times been out of step with the post-war European welfare state consensus.[11] Where Community law contained no competences in the fields of labour law and social policy,[12] this consensus might be argued to have been confirmed: the integration of formerly national economies was not designed to dismantle the various national 'social acquis'. Implicit within the 'law through

---

[7] See, e.g., Borger & Rasmussen 2010.
[8] See Vauchez 2013; Schepel & Wesseling 1997.
[9] Weiler 1981.
[10] Dehousse & Weiler 1990, 243.
[11] As documented in the seminal work of Milward 2000, in particular at 21 ff.
[12] Cf Giubboni 2006 who argues: '[T]he apparent flimsiness of the social provisions of the Treaty of Rome (and of the slightly less meagre ones of the Treaty of Paris) was in reality consistent with the intention, imbued with the embedded liberalism compromise, not only to preserve but hopefully to expand and strengthen the Member States' powers of economic intervention and social governance: *i.e.*, their ability to keep the promise of protection underlying the new social contract signed by their own citizens at the end of the war' (16).

integration' movement was the destruction of the protective 'embeddedness' of postwar liberalism,[13] an agenda which had to be hidden.

2.1.2 Ordoliberal economic constitutionalism: Europe as 'market without state'

This latter point is now a common wisdom: the combined research of the Cologne Max Planck Institute for the Study of Society, in particular,[14] has documented the close affinities between the dominant doctrines of European law and the neoliberal political economy of the 1980s which informed much Western economic and social policy just as the European project entered into its second stage. Anglo-Saxon neoliberalism, however, also finds a close relation in a German variety of economic liberalism that had its roots in the Weimar Republic and its heyday at the founding of the Federal Republic.[15]

To briefly outline their commonality:[16] with a theory of self-limiting liberal government designed to foster markets at their core, various ordoliberal proponents engaged enthusiastically with the early processes of European integration, bringing their ideas successfully to bear there. Conceptually, ordoliberalism was particularly suited to the European realm, justifying, in its self-limiting liberal mode, the theorem of the primacy of European law and further detailing the precise and similarly self-limiting 'economic constitutional' content of European integration: individual economic freedoms guaranteed by the founding Treaty, the opening up of national economies, non-discrimination principles and competition rules were all easily represented as a collective decision in favour of an economic constitution that mirrored and matched the ordoliberal framework conditions for establishment of a market economic system. In this way, ordoliberalism sought to answer the question about the legitimacy of the project of integration more conclusively than the prevailing orthodoxy.

Today, German ordoliberalism has attained a striking prominence – albeit one with deeply irritating qualities,[17] which have prompted many to assert that German influence within European crisis politics equates with the 'ordoliberalisation' of Europe.[18] We will return to the ordoliberal project of economic constitutionalism in the context of the Maastricht Treaty (in section 2.3) and discuss the ordoliberalisation thesis critically in section 4. Here, we note only that the affinities between the 'integration through law' movement and ordoliberalism do not equate with the ordoliberalisation of the integration project in its formative stage. The normative ordoliberal vision of an autonomous transnational economic constitution was hardly noticed outside of Europe. Within Germany itself, there was little concord about ordoliberal views between the Ministry for Economic Affairs and the Federal Foreign Office.[19] As Giandomenico Majone adds soberly and soberingly:[20] in the 1950s, *planification* and interventionist practices were commonplace within the founding states. How could defeated Germany, of all states,

---

[13] On the concept, see famously Ruggie 1982.
[14] Pathbreaking: Scharpf 2002.
[15] See Hien & Joerges 2018, 214 ff.
[16] Cf, already, Joerges 1996.
[17] Hien & Joerges 2018.
[18] See, e.g., Blyth 2013, 142; Biebricher & Vogelmann 2017, 9 ff.
[19] Abelshauser 2016, 537 ff.
[20] Majone 2014, 90 ff.

have prevailed at European level with an *Ordnungspolitik* that could not even claim domestic consensus?

2.2 Moderate Functionalism: A Road Not Taken

If one thing unites the 'integration through law' movement and the ordoliberal vision of a transnational economic constitution, it is the failure of both to understand the *factum brutum* that dominant practice was always functionalistic and technocratic. In stark contrast, this phenomenon was captured as a conceptual legal orientation early on in the integration process by Hans Peter Ipsen in his characterisation of the (three) European Communities as 'purposive associations for functional integration' (*Zweckverbände funktioneller Integration*). Fully aware of American neofunctionalist integration theory, Ipsen rejected federal integration concepts and early interpretations of the Community as an international organization. For him, Community law constituted a *tertium quid* between (federal) national law and international law that was adequately legitimated through its 'specialized tasks'.[21]

Two decades later, Giandomenico Majone acknowledged the affinities between Ipsen's conceptualisation of the integration project and his own renewal of the technocratic legacy in his reconceptualisation of the Community as a 'fourth branch of government'[22] and as a 'regulatory state'.[23] While Ipsen's 'objective tasks' correspond to Majone's 'regulatory policies', each viewpoint asserts that problems can only be solved through application of a body of expert knowledge, which is itself to be shielded from political influence.

There are affinities; there are also differences: Ipsen's technocratic 'purposive association' is functionalist *per se*, designed simply to ensure the infiltration of the state and its administration into society. Majone's regulatory state, by contrast, is concerned with market failure, but has a normative basis within the effort to maximise the economically defined welfare of consumers and citizens. In Majone's view, the nonmajoritarian institutions of European regulatory politics and the majoritarian institutions of the Member States are complementary to one another. In particular, distributive politics (the welfare/social state) are held to be dependent on majoritarian legitimation and must accordingly remain the domain of the nation state. European regulatory action must be confined to the politically neutral realm of welfare maximisation within the market.

Did these conceptualisations contain a legitimacy-generating potential? The answer is depressing: certainly, where the translation of facticity into validity is sought, each theory held its own promise. Nevertheless, each conception found itself at odds with two competing forces, namely, the constant striving of European politics for 'more Europe' on the one hand, and the neoliberal drive for 'more market' on the other.[24]

---

[21] Ipsen 1972, 176 ff.
[22] See Majone 1994.
[23] Starting with Majone 1989.
[24] Isiksel, 2016 underlines convincingly throughout her study on European functionalism that the integration project has from early on, and continuously so, strengthened the European

2.3 On the Way to Maastricht 1992: 'Ever Closer Union' and/or Economic Constitutionalism

Following the geopolitical upheaval of the late 1980s, European integration returned to type as two competing development paths were pursued simultaneously. 'More Europe' was a seemingly logical follow-up to the steady, if cumbersome, growth and deepening of the European system. 'More market' was in line with the logic established by the *de facto* alliance between the 'integration through law' movement and economic constitutionalism. It is also a characteristic of European politics that such perspectives are not articulated openly so that European citizens can make up their minds. 'More Europe' could have been presented as the federalist option. Commission President Delors however, felt that he should instead present a modernisation package.

2.3.1 'Ever closer union'

This he did very successfully. European law continued its steady constitutionalisation project, but, overall, the Community was mired in political crisis. In the 1980s, however, the by now legendary internal market initiative enabled a breakthrough.[25] Different explanations for this renewed impetus abound across the disciplines. Economists point to the shift in opinion at national level, and an underlying upswing in approval for economic rationality patterns: efficiency and competitiveness through deregulation ('negative integration'), supplemented by 'regulatory competition', could and should give impetus to market evolution and keep welfare state policies in check. Or was it a matter of the 'political cunning' personified by Jacques Delors, which made use of a neofunctionalist logic to bind together different economic interests within a new European programme? For lawyers, however, the legal principles developed by the ECJ were still assumed to provide the most compelling integration impetus.

As ever within European law, revolution derived from a seemingly trivial happening: the *Cassis de Dijon* case that saw the Court declare a German ban on the marketing of a French liqueur lower in alcohol content than its German counterparts to be incompatible with the principle of free movement of goods.[26] From its convincing but trifling observation that German consumer confusion could be avoided by disclosure of alcoholic content, the Court derived its far-reaching doctrine of 'mutual recognition', and adopted a constitutional competence for itself to set aside national legislation in order to enable market integration on the basis of primary law alone. In turn, the Commission adopted the ECJ's decision as the legal basis for the new harmonisation policy that it developed in its White Paper on internal market policy.

Delors' Internal Market programme might have been rooted in the effort to promote economic rationality. It nevertheless also began the process of the evolution of a more multifaceted European polity: the objective of 'ever closer union' was enshrined in the Preamble to the 1992 Maastricht Treaty and the notion of a 'social Europe' was given

---

level of governance without providing for the kind of reflexive mechanisms built into constitutions in the domestic context.

[25] Commission of the EC 1985.
[26] Case 120/78, ECR [1979] 649 – *Cassis de Dijon*.

an air of constitutionalisation within the social dialogue.[27] New competences were conferred on the Union, in particular, in the new Title on industrial policy (Article 157 TEU; now Article 173 TFEU). This went hand in hand with the strengthening of social regulation (consumer, environmental and safety at work protection). A precursor of subsequent efforts attempted within the Constitutional Treaty saga, the multidimensional European polity nevertheless did not work out as envisaged, given the dead end of the overt constitutionalisation process in the Lisbon Treaty.

2.3.2 The 'Stability Union'

A 'second generation' of ordoliberal scholars had attentively followed the development of the integration project. Aware of the steadily growing influence of Anglo-Saxon economic theorising, they were deeply concerned by the displacement of their commitment to 'free competition' by the principle of 'economic efficiency' within European competition law and policy,[28] and by the broadening of community competences in the Maastricht Treaty to include industrial policy.[29] They were nevertheless welcoming of the *Cassis* judgment,[30] and the new emphasis on the principle of mutual recognition, which, the Advisory Board of the German Ministry of the Economics explained,[31] would further processes of regulatory competition among the Member States, exposing national legislation to economic rationality tests.[32] Equally, the ECJ repeatedly proved its readiness to supervise 'anticompetitive' regulation and state aid. Yet, expectations that further deregulation and privatisation would follow were to be thwarted. Instead, and far faster than either supporters or critics of the internal market programme had foreseen, new regulatory and juridification trends evolved: intense regulation; new forms of cooperation among governmental and nongovernmental actors; and a range of participation entitlements.

Regulatory interventions were intense, and most particularly so in relation to consumer and health interests, which often also comprised safety at work and environmental concerns, where the provisions of the Single European Acts and the rights of Member States with high regulatory aspirations to 'go it alone' ensured that the opening of markets was to come about only at the cost of a thoroughly modernised regulatory machinery.[33]

Lacking sufficient resources and administrative powers to generate standards and apply them at national level, the Commission was forced to promote and coordinate national certification bodies and European standardisation organisations. Further, it was forced to operate through a dense network of committees in which national administrative experts, independent scientists and representatives of economic and social interests collaborate.

---

[27] See Dukes 2014, 125 ff.
[28] See Hien & Joerges 2018, section 5b; on the critique of the American efficiency mantra see Mestmäcker 2007.
[29] Mussler 1998, 125 ff.
[30] Case 120/78, ECR [1979] 649 – *Cassis de Dijon*.
[31] Wissenschaftlicher Beirat 1986.
[32] See the critique in Joerges 2019.
[33] See Joerges 1994, 41 ff.

All of this was incompatible with the vision of a European economic constitution. Intense regulatory activity documented mistrust in the self-regulatory potential of markets, and a quest for ever more coordination. This much is undisputed: as much as national and Member State interests may have coalesced around the internal market programme, the intense juridification and reregulation that followed in its wake was not simply unloved but also intensified demand for the legitimation and control of Europe's burgeoning administrative structures. An initial answer to this demand was proffered by the theory of the regulatory state to which we referred in section 2.2. We will return to this issue in the section 2.4 on the new modes of governance. As an interim conclusion, however, we note that the internal market initiative did anything but breathe life into economic constitutionalism – certainly not in the spheres which Klaus and Kaarlo Tuori conceptualise as the microeconomic layer of the economic constitution.[34]

The prospects for an 'ordoliberalisation' of the Union did not look too promising. But then the proponents of a 'Stability Union' were aided by a powerful judicial actor. The Maastricht Treaty had met with the approval of the German government and the *Bundestag*, but was thereafter the subject of a constitutional complaint made before the German Constitutional Court. The complaint was rejected.[35] Nevertheless, the Constitutional Court's Judgment, delivered on 12 October 1993, has gone down as a milestone in European legal history, as national constitutional judges rebelled against the empty methodologies of the hierarchical constitutionalisation of Europe effected by the ECJ, and sought to limit European integration.

The judgment contained two clear shocks for European legal orthodoxy. First, the German justices appeared to deny the supranational nature of Europe, denoting it 'less than a Federation – even less than a Community' and deciding to describe it instead as an 'association of states' (*Staatenverbund*) – an association, moreover which must pay due regard to the 'national identity' of the Member States, or the 'Masters of the Treaties'. However, second, the Constitutional Court distanced itself from the principles of direct effect and the supremacy of European law. Certainly, the Court accepted majority decisionmaking (the area of application of which the Maastricht Treaty had enlarged) as a functional necessity of integration, but it still sought to counter it with reference to a principle of 'mutual respect' for the 'constitutional principles and fundamental interests of the Member States'.[36] The rub in this construction came in the fact that the interests that are of 'fundamental interest' to Germany could and should only be determined by Germany itself: the German Court reserved for itself a specific, non-transferable right of adjudicating on the assignment of competences. Should the Community ever misuse the power to extend its competences unilaterally when a Treaty revision is required, this process will not have a binding effect on the Republic.[37] The natural cohesion of Community law which was furnished by the principle of supremacy was thus broken down into a 'disordered' heterarchical relationship between national and European orders, albeit that the German Court also

---

[34] Tuori, Kaarlo and Klaus 2014, 13 ff.
[35] *Bundesverfassungsgericht*, judgment of 12 October 1993, 2 BvR 2134/92 and 2 BvR 2159/92, 89 BVerfGE 155 [*Brunner* v *European Union Treaty*, (1994) 57 *CMLR* 1].
[36] Para. 184.
[37] Para. 210.

attempted to lessen dangers of legal anarchy by emphasising its desire to establish a 'cooperative relationship' with the European Court.

At the time, the German Court's judgment was the cause of significant disquiet on the part of the European legal commentariat,[38] appearing to herald a significant renationalisation of the European integration process, especially with regard to its stated understanding of the primacy of national democratic process:

> If the peoples of the individual states (as is true at present) convey democratic legitimation via the national parliaments, then limits are imposed, by the principle of democracy, on the extension of the EC's functions and powers. State power in each of the states emanates from the people of that state. The states require sufficient areas of significant responsibility of their own, areas in which the *Staatsvolk* ['we the people'] concerned may develop and express itself within a process of forming political will which it legitimizes and controls.[39]

In a final analysis, however, European legal response to communitarian German democratic recidivism has proven, with time, to be a mere distraction from the core problem created and left to European legal posterity by the Maastricht judgment, or its renewed reliance upon the underpinning constitutional norms of ordoliberalism, even though the facts of integration had moved Europe far beyond the self-limiting liberal government envisaged by its founding fathers. European Monetary Union (EMU) was held to be in full accord with the provisions of the German Constitution. Its stability philosophy was even treated as a condition *sine qua non* of the German approval. The Court suggested that, should EMU not follow 'the agreed stability mandate', the German ratification law would no longer be valid. The core paradox in the Court's reasoning is readily apparent. First, it seeks to preserve the powers of the nation state. However, economic integration is perceived as an apolitical phenomenon occurring autonomously outside the states, and EMU as a project given functional legitimacy by its commitment to a politically neutral notion of price stability. Economic integration, in this reading, would never be subject to ongoing constitutional review for its democratic qualities. Europe would become a 'market without a state' and the so-called Masters of the Treaties would be left as 'states without markets' – a prescription that came to haunt Europe during financial and sovereign debt crisis, as discussed in section 4.

3. A EUROPEAN UNION OF INCOMPLETE INNOVATION AND FALSE PROMISES

In his speech of 15 February 2000 delivered to the European Parliament at Strasbourg, President of the Commission Romano Prodi announced far-reaching and ambitious reforms to European governance.[40] This was a message spoken in a new vocabulary, with a fresh reform agenda and a novel working method. He proposed an original division of labour between political actors and civil society, and a more democratic

---

[38] Weiler 1995.
[39] Para. 186.
[40] http://europa.eu/rapid/press-release_SPEECH-00-41_en.htm (last accessed 30/9/2018).

form of partnership between layers of governance in Europe. It was a package of innovation launched strategically into a legally nondefined space located somewhere between constitutional and administrative reform.

Nor was Prodi's speech mere rhetoric: at the turn of the millennium, plagued continuously by ongoing (traditional) Member State concern about the creeping competences of a reregulated European market, faced with the organisational bombshell of eastward enlargement and confronted with the complaints of an increasingly Eurosceptic European public, the demand for meaningful reform was unmistakable, and the programme adopted suitably millennial in depth and character.

3.1 The Commission White Paper on Governance in Europe: A Symptom of Unmastered Crisis

'Governance' has become such a commonplace term at all levels of private and public organisation that it is all too easy to forget its particular meaning and promise within the governing system of the EU. Long in vogue within international relations theory, governance was adopted by European political scientists to describe the decisionmaking processes formed within the EU system from the 1990s onwards;[41] above all, the institutions and procedures developed during and after the completion of the internal market in the awareness that the internal market programme called for proactive initiatives across all sectors, and acknowledged that permanent management of market integration was necessary in order to master its unforeseen economic and social implications. As such, the term governance, as deployed within the European context, is characterised by its own analytical vagueness, or openness to the evolving institutions and modes of governing the expanding competences of the Union. Equally, it does not equate with a normative project, or the need to 'charter' governance or to frame it in line with a law-mediated (constitutionalised) legitimacy.[42]

This is not to reject the notion of governance, however. As Philippe Schmitter convincingly argues,[43] the 'oversell and vagueness' of the concept notwithstanding, it usefully designates 'a distinctive method/mechanism for resolving conflicts and solving problems that reflects some profound characteristics of the exercise of authority that are emerging in almost all contemporary societies and economies'. It is a virtue of the concept that it captures actor configurations and problem solving activities which have emerged as responses to functional exigencies. Modern governance depends on, and similarly builds on, expert knowledge and the management capacities of enterprises and organisations. It cannot confine itself to law production and law application operating with the binary code of legal and illegal events and practices. It cannot be organised hierarchically. Seen in this light, the 'formalised' adoption of governance within European politics, as Romano Prodi announced a White Paper within which the Commission would present new perspectives for a democratically reformed 'European governance', seemed an act full of promise and innovation. For years the Union had played host to extra-legal developments and institutional innovations that had widened

---

[41] Jachtenfuchs 2002.
[42] On this concern see Joerges 2008.
[43] Schmitter 2001, 83 ff.

the discrepancies between the EU's activities and its formal legal structures. Where governance is a concept that also helps us to discover and to explain tensions between function and form, the Commission's Working Programme, drawing on the expertise and experiences of actors both within and without the Commission, was a platform for constructive debate.

Yet debate disappointed, perhaps inevitably so: 'governance' rather than 'government and administration' captures modern political action, its emphasis upon the social knowledge and the management capacities of enterprises and organisations, its eschewal of command and control policymaking and policy implementation, and its response to real social problems and to bottlenecks within the political system and its administrative machinery. This is the desired outcome but it is also the problem, the point at which 'is' and 'ought' part company and the search for a sustaining governance *legitimation* is revealed as a simple chimera. In the final analysis, governance is a tool of political science and not of (constitutional) law; its value within the material context of political science is precisely that it enables a necessary distinction between the efficiency of governance and its legitimacy. The European legal aspiration to marry governance to a programme of democratic legitimation could not but fail. The Commission and its advisors underestimated the weight of the underlying legal-normative question. They responded to the legitimacy question with the metaphor of 'good governance' and developed principles of openness, participation, accountability, effectiveness and coherence,[44] which, while individually worthwhile, merely reproduced the individual mechanics of administrative legitimacy, paying no corresponding attention to an overarching and coherent theory of constitutional legitimacy.[45]

Mainstream European legal thought remained trapped within the functionalist outlook, even returning to a traditional community method of centralised control as the failure to translate European governing praxis into a language of legitimacy found its counterpart in the return of the final version of the White Paper to the language of inherited legal categories. 'Strengthening the Community method!' – this was the *legal* leitmotiv of the White Paper as adopted in July 2001.[46] A simple legislative procedure, whereby Parliament and Council act as the legislature, was to be aspired to, and duly found its place within the Lisbon Treaty. The Commission is entrusted with 'implementing Community law' and is supported in this task by 'executive' agencies,[47] which by now number more than 40 and are active in fields ranging from the oversight of insurance to the defence of European borders,[48] forming the core of a burgeoning technocratic European administration, coordinated and overseen by the European Commission.

---

[44] Commission of the EC 2001, 10 f.
[45] Harlow 2002; Everson 2002.
[46] Commission of the EC 2001, 8.
[47] Commission of the EC 2001, 24 ff, 40.
[48] Vos 2018.

3.2 The Open Method of Coordination

With hindsight, the greatest paradox left to European legal posterity by the White Paper is the fact that its return to empty legal formulations only undermines the analytical bases for renewed normative legitimacy that the governance method might have provided. The Commission represented the 'administration' of the internal market, as if its sole purpose was to implement the will of a European sovereign through the mobilisation of expert support. The issues to which this 'administration' must respond are often politically sensitive and significant in economic terms, and also give rise to moral and ethical concerns. Seen in this light, the disconnect between the technical legal strictures of administrative law as they apply, in all their vagueness, to the dominant notion of good governance, and the demand for genuine constitutive legitimation only adds insult to injury: an incomplete innovation of false promise is a sticking plaster on the functionalist wound of technocratic administrative growth.

The European Commission was never insensitive to the disconnect between functionalist efficiency and constitutionalised (democratic) legitimation, similarly making reference to a notion of 'civil society' within its White Paper as some form of bridge between Europeans and their administration.[49] Nevertheless, even where European 'civil society' has itself become a useful hook upon which to hang contemporary legitimation theories of 'deliberative democracy',[50] or of 'democratic experimentalism',[51] too many questions remain unanswered: what gives those actors and expert communities 'included' within European governance a political mandate? How do they represent affected interests?

The pressing nature of such questions only grows when we make brief return to the vexed question of the Union's incomplete competence with regard to the policies of social distribution and to the relative failure of yet another mechanism of governance innovation, the Open Method of Coordination, established by the Treaty of Amsterdam in its new Title (VIII) on employment, with specific application to the national and Community coordination of employment strategies (Art. 125). Since the European Council in Lisbon in 2000 also recommended this method for social policy, the OMC has become the object of intensive discussion. Political scientists have had high hopes for it on both sides of the Atlantic,[52] and the OMC did appear to envisage a mode of governance which would avoid the institutional bottlenecks in European lawmaking and administration, simultaneously opening up new perspectives for legitimising the Union, especially by means of direct inclusion of the parties of civil society. However, the impacts of the OMC have been difficult to identify in all of the fields in which it has been deployed, and this is particularly true in the field of employment policy. It is difficult to find reliable information on the mechanisms that define it: is the autonomy that nation states enjoy in their search for means to achieve agreed upon targets really being used innovatively? Have criteria been discovered and defined which enable a 'benchmarking' which competitors will find convincing? Do political and societal

---

[49] Commission of the EC 2001, 14 f.
[50] Zeitlin & Trubek 2003.
[51] Sabel & Zeitlin 2003.
[52] Eberlein & Kerwer 2002, with many references.

actors really expose themselves to learning processes? Or does the OMC only erode core principles of constitutionalism, such as the regulative idea that governance should adhere to legal principles and the rule of law?

4. EUROPEAN LAW IN CRISIS: A CHRONICLE FORETOLD

Where the first decade of the new millennium was a period of promise for European law, incomplete innovations and promises, especially in the vexed realm of redistributive politics, and financial and sovereign debt crises only further exposed the continuing failure to bridge the gap between facts and norms, or the inability of European law to adapt itself to a moving target of political facts and real world happenings in a constitutively coherent manner. The effects are deeply troubling. We begin with a brief return to the Maastricht EMU construction, then comment on the current state of European studies, and conclude with a critique of the legalisation of European crisis politics by the CJEU, or, as we explained earlier, the death of law in facticity.

4.1 A Failing Constitutionalisation

Treaty amendments are the outcome of political bargaining processes. Unsurprisingly, they tend to be incoherent, even contradictory, and to leave thorny issues to the future. EMU, however, is a particularly troublesome example which has overburdened Europe's political equilibrium and its law.

(In)famously, the Maastricht Treaty only conferred monetary policy upon the Union. It is easy to understand why economic and fiscal competences were not transferred. Not a single Member State indicated an inclination to give up the 'power of the purse'. However, monetary policy and fiscal policy are interdependent, and in 1992 it was very clear that national socioeconomic constellations and political preferences differed considerably. The expectation that national economies and practices would converge due to the pressures of a common currency was unrealistic. This determined that a uniform European monetary policy would be required to confront differing fiscal and economic policies. The resulting conflicts were not of the vertical type for which the supremacy doctrine could be invoked, since the powers required to resolve such problems continued to be attributed to two distinct levels of governance. The form of conflict management foreseen in Article 119 TFEU is 'the adoption of an economic policy which is based on the close coordination of Member States' economic policies', as substantiated in Article 121 TFEU. As is plainly clear within the legal texts, this instrument was a *lex imperfecta.*

The formal provisions of the TFEU created a 'diagonal' conflict between the European and the national levels. This was not readily apparent. Tensions remained latent up until 2007 by virtue of political bargaining and sheer good economic luck. The true form of constitutional compromise was a praxis of muddling. Yet, at the same time, the common currency inevitably and inexorably intensified socioeconomic diversity within the eurozone, creating an explosive constellation. Europe experienced differential growth and inflation rates, as well as cyclical divergence with disastrous consequences; yet EMU foreclosed informed response to such clear problems. The fundamental design flaw and constitutional deficit within this regime was and continues to be the absence of a political infrastructure and institutional framework within which democratic political contestation might occur in order to legitimate the 'completion' of the imperfect regime established. The sad yet undeniable conclusion must be that the Maastricht arrangement was an ill-defined political compromise and not a sustainable achievement worthy of constitutional validity. Even more worrying: as the EMU provides no guidance, European crisis politics has been forced to operate *extra legem*. The first person to become aware of this dilemma was the former constitutional judge Ernst-Wolfgang Böckenförde.[53] The treatment of law, Böckenförde explained, was 'outrageous' (*abenteuerlich*). We leave exact details aside here,[54] and focus on what has happened to law and its operation. This has been articulated with notable clarity by Fritz W. Scharpf in a comment on the excessive imbalance procedure as adopted in the Six-Pack and Two-Pack regulations.[55] It is the very logic of this procedure, he submits, which

> dictates that it must operate without any pre-defined rule and that the Commission's *ad hoc* decisions must apply to individual Member States in unique circumstances rather than to EMU states in general. Regardless of the comparative quality of its economic expertise, the Commission lacks legitimate authority to impose highly intrusive policy choices on Member States.[56]

Are we really witnessing the 'ordoliberalisation of Europe', as so many observers believe?[57] Disregard of the rule of law and managerialism within the practice of crisis politics militate strongly against such assessments. What has to be conceded, however, is that the austerity politics which these politics impose on the south of the Eurozone echo the protestant reading of the ordoliberal tradition.[58]

4.2 Disintegration of European Studies

Scharpf is by background a lawyer, receiving a German *Habilitation* in the discipline which he has put behind him. It is all the more noteworthy that his diagnosis does not worry the mainstream of European legal studies. Quite to the contrary: 'After over half a decade of legal measures and prolific commentary on those measures, it is helpful to stand back and take stock. We will consider whether euro-crisis law … has by now mainly become simply the macro-economic law of the EU.'[59] Such complacency is not restricted to lawyers, however: many political scientists remain equally unconcerned, rediscovering conventional integration theories and focusing mainly on explaining the

---

[53] Böckenförde 2010.
[54] But see for an exemplary discussion Everson & Joerges 2017.
[55] See for a lucid summary of the pertinent documents by the Commission: http://ec.europa.eu/economy_finance/economic_governance/sgp/index_en.htm.
[56] Scharpf 2013, 139.
[57] See Biebricher & Vogelmann 2017, 9 ff and the many references in Hien & Joerges 2018.
[58] See Hien & Joerges 2018.
[59] Beukers, Kilpatrick & De Witte 2017, chapter 1.

aggregate institutional design outcomes,[60] avoiding normative evaluation of real world (crisis) politics.[61]

In a similar vein, scholars working at the intersection of law and political science have started to explore the extra-legality of Europe's 'crisis law' as a transnational form of exceptionalism that resembles, but in important ways also deviates from, the authoritarian kind of rule that Carl Schmitt advocated for the state of emergency.[62] Jonathan White has provided a particularly instructive diagnosis of current emergency politics, characterising it as

> a distinctive mode in which actions contravening established procedures and norms are defended – often exclusively – as a response to exceptional circumstances that pose some form of existential threat ... A sense of urgency pervades emergency politics, and is commonly used to excuse the pre-empting of debate and patient efforts to build public support. Necessity rather than consent is the organising principle.[63]

In contrast to the mainstream accounts, contributions in this critical camp share the view that the management of the euro crisis represents a deviation from, not a continuation of, European 'legal normalcy', since 'unconventional' measures of monetary policy (such as the ECB's bond-buying programmes and bailouts) and intrusive controls (such as *Troika* conditionalities) were adopted with reference to emergency conditions that are incompatible with the constitutional order of the EU.

4.3 Legalizing the Undecidable

The constitutionalisation saga began with the foundational jurisprudence of the ECJ in the 1960s. In our account, this saga is an unfinished story with no happy end in sight. This does not mean, however, that the Luxembourg Court has lost its prestige. To the contrary: following the very many political failures, as well as the failure of academic lawyers and political scientists to establish the validity of their arguments and the normative complacency of economics, the Court has been required to step up once again to fill the gap within legitimate authority in two judgments: first *Pringle*,[64] then *Gauweiler*.[65] Each judgment met with nearly unanimous approval. *Pringle* was praised, as Paul Craig put it, as a fine synthesis of 'conjunction of text, purpose, and teleology that informs legal reasoning'.[66] *Gauweiler* was celebrated as a thoughtful and nonpolemical examination of an arguably somewhat aggressive reference from the German Constitutional Court.[67] We remain unconvinced.

---

[60] Kreuder-Sonnen 2016.
[61] Joerges & Kreuder-Sonnen 2017.
[62] See Hufeld 2011; Dyson 2013; Kuo 2014, 2019.
[63] White 2015, 302–3.
[64] Case 370/12, *Pringle v. Ireland*, Judgment (Grand Chamber) of 27 November 2012, EU:C:2012:756.
[65] Case C-62/14, *Peter Gauweiler and others v. Deutscher Bundestag*, Judgment of 16 June 2015 (Grand Chamber).
[66] Craig 2013, 11.
[67] See Fabbrini 2016.

In its *Gauweiler* judgment the CJEU responded to a question submitted by the German Constitutional Court, this Court's 'first ever reference', as every commentator adds. The German reference, however, was less a question and more an insinuation that the ECB's explicit approval of the financial assistance programmes of the EFSF and the European Stability Mechanism had overstepped its monetary policy competence and interfered with the economic policy competences of the Member States. The German Court suggested similarly that the Outright Monetary Transactions programme (the OMT) had contravened the Treaty commitment to price stability (Article 123 TFEU) and infringed the budgetary autonomy of the Member States, which the German Court held to be 'constituent for the design of the monetary union' as evidenced by Article 125 TFEU.[68]

The ECB is a non-majoritarian institution, which enjoys unprecedented autonomy. Does autonomy imply unlimited discretionary freedom? Is there an external check upon the exercise of this discretion, or are such controls superfluous in the light of an inbuilt discipline of expertise? 'Monetary policy', so the Advocate General of the ECJ explained in his *Gauweiler* Opinion, is 'a highly technical terrain in which it is necessary to have an expertise and experience which, according to the Treaties, devolves solely upon the ECB'.[69] Two interrelated points are made here: on the one hand, monetary policy is suggested to be a technical operation justifying the notion of discretion and demanding judicial self-limitation; on the other, this expertise is declared to be uncontroversial or sacrosanct. It must not be contested or exposed to scrutiny by other bodies because the Treaty has assigned it to the ECB. Both points are as bold as they are unconvincing. Monetary policy is a very complex matter, but by no means a merely technical one, and certainly not uncontroversial.

The whole construction is such that the conferral of *de facto* unlimited discretionary powers upon the ECB and the necessarily 'epistemic' character of its discretionary decisionmaking powers attains the status of a command of the EMU design structure. That reasoning, so much the Court concedes, is incomplete in one respect. Economic and fiscal policy is still reserved to the Member States. There must therefore be some limit to ECB powers one is tempted to assume. But this would also require definition of the limits of monetary policy, which the Treaty fails to do. What is nevertheless clear under Articles 127(1) TFEU and 282(2) TFEU is the objective of monetary policy, namely the defence of price stability, and hence the mandate of the ECB to pursue that objective with the help of the instruments described in Chapter IV of the Protocol on the ESCB and the ECB.[70] In its reference, the German Court cited the passage of the *Pringle* judgment in which the Court of Justice had qualified the financial aid under the ESM Treaty as a matter of economic policy.[71] Once again the CJEU invokes the primacy of monetary policy objectives:

---

[68] BVerfG, 2 BvR 2728/13 vom 14.1.2014, §§1–105, www.bverfg.de/entscheidungen/rs20140114_2bvr272813en.html.
[69] Opinion of Advocate General Cruz Villalón in Case C-62/14 *Gauweiler*, para. 111.
[70] *Gauweiler* judgment, paras 42–5.
[71] Para. 64.

When the ESM buys up bonds on secondary markets, it is 'economic policy'. When the ECB does the same, and makes these purchases conditional on compliance with the ESM's 'macroeconomic adjustment' demands, it is 'monetary policy' ... it is the difference between the objectives of the respective operations, which is decisive.[72]

In plain English: the ESCB/ECB are entitled to define objectives and to determine means in full autonomy. This cannot be otherwise once it has been held that the conduct of monetary policy 'requires an expertise and experience which, according to the Treaties, devolves solely upon the ECB'.[73] Governance of the eurozone, we are told, is a technocratic exercise. By definition, this praxis can never be subject to democratic legitimacy requirements or the constraints of the rule of law.

What does this mean? Let us return to the 1905 dictum of Justice Holmes in the *Lochner* case:

> This case is decided upon an economic theory which a large part of the country does not entertain. If it were a question whether I agreed with that theory, I should desire to study it further and long before making up my mind. But I do not conceive that to be my duty, because I strongly believe that my agreement or disagreement has nothing to do with the right of a majority to embody their opinions in law.[74]

Europe's dilemma is that no such majority has ever been put in place; there is no alternative to technocratic rule.

5. EPILOGUE

If legal critique is argued to encompass bodies of thought that challenge legal orthodoxies or fictions, the study of European law is full of critical legal thinkers. Above all, the legal fiction of national sovereignty, or the constitutional concretisation of the sanitising myths of brute history, has repeatedly found its nemesis in the support of European legal scholars for the spontaneous constitutionalism of the European Court of Justice. European law is revolutionary in character. Yet, where the evolutionary river of European law has now emptied out into a functionalist sea devoid of normative character, the claim to 'critique' rings hollow as the giants of European legal scholarship rush to approbation of the empty reasoning of the *Pringle* and *Gauweiler* Court.

However, in the constructive critical perspective, the fault is not wholly one of European legal scholarship. Certainly, the dominance of the 'integration through law' movement has blinkered the sight of many a theoretically refined legal scholar, substituting the normative good of 'more Europe' for the quest for legitimated law. Nevertheless, as the failed struggle to respond to the legitimation deficit left by integration processes demonstrates, especially as regards the tantalisingly chimeric notion of 'governance', the search for validity is full of pitfalls.

---

[72] Schepel 2017, 96.
[73] Opinion AG Gruz Villalón, para. 111.
[74] *Lochner v. People of State of New York*, U.S. Supreme Court, 198 U.S. 45 (1905).

What then are the lessons of European law for the critical legal movement? At one level, the message is surely a simple one: critique has a value all of its own – would *Gauweiler* stand so immutably within the European canon as an adjudicative good were a strong critical movement at hand to unveil the shortcomings of law's reliance upon economic theory? At another level, however, a further lesson left to us by the *Gauweiler* saga stands as a challenge to the foundations of legal critique itself: almost uniquely, the German Constitutional Court judgment had its own dissenters, Justices Gerhardt and Lübbe-Wolff. The reasons given by Judge Lübbe-Wolff for her dissension are particularly instructive, where she urged that the German Court should not judge at all upon the provisions of the OMT because:[75]

> [To do so would be to go] beyond the limits of judicial competence under the principles of democracy and separation of powers (paragraph 3) … The more far-reaching, the more weighty, the more irreversible – legally and factually – the possible consequences of a judicial decision, the more judicial restraint is appropriate (paragraph 7) … Where for reasons of law the judges' courage must dwindle when it comes to the substance, they ought not to go into the substance at all (paragraph 27) … The democratic legitimacy which the decision of a national court may draw from the relevant standards of national law (if any) will not, or not without substantial detriment, extend beyond the national area. (paragraph 28)

Lübbe-Wolff's formulations are unashamedly formalistic in nature, founded in the limits to the competences of the law in general and the constitutional jurisdiction in particular; yet, in all their formalism, they both deliver one of the most stinging critiques of facticity *as* validity within national and supranational thinking and point the way forward to a refounding of European law.

Her final point is perhaps most telling: her critique in this instance is of the German Constitutional Court, and its determination to defend the budgetary competence of the German Bundestag while, by the same token, not caring at all for the rights of the Greek Parliament.[76] This is not an argument about proportionality and the limitation of discretionary decisionmaking. It concerns instead the jurisdictional mandate of constitutional courts. No national court is allowed to decide for the whole of the EU. Her preceding arguments are similarly weighty: no court is entitled to decide upon the survival of the common currency. The CJEU fails wholly to take note of this admonition, laying down instead a particular economic constitution for the eurozone. Governance of the eurozone, so the Court held, is a technocratic exercise, or a praxis which escapes the quest for democratic legitimacy and the constraint of the rule of law. The American law and political science scholar Alec Stone Sweet has characterised the foundational jurisprudence of the ECJ as a 'juridical coup d'état … a fundamental transformation in the normative foundations of a legal system through the constitutional lawmaking of a court'.[77] *Pringle* and *Gauweiler* continue this trend.

It is conceivable that the present transformation of the European polity deserves to be qualified as a constitutional moment. By the same token, however, we may be

---

[75] The following numbers go to the paragraphs of her dissent in BVerfG, 2 BvR 2728/13 vom 14.1.2014, §§1–105, www.bverfg.de/entscheidungen/rs20140114_2bvr272813en.html.
[76] See Everson 2015, 497.
[77] Stone Sweet 2007, 924 ff, italics omitted.

witnessing an unconstitutional amendment of the European legal order. These may be speculative deliberations, but the theoretical poverty of this revolutionary jurisprudence is nevertheless plain. One core assumption on which it builds is plainly wrong. Technical expertise cannot be neatly separated from, or insulated against, normative assessments and policy choices. A second weakness may not be so plainly visible. We have established in the eurozone a governance regime which does not content itself with the adjustment of interest rates and the use of other conventional monetary policy instruments. An irresistible logic is at work here. The ECB cannot restrain itself to a focus on price stability and leave financial stability operations to national governments. The Bank's concerns for financial stability are unlimited in their scope. They reach into the whole range of economic and social policies with requests for structural reforms and adjustments.[78] This not a correction of political processes – it amounts to their replacement. Would the course of events have been changed had the judiciary refused to legalise the new modes of European economic governance? It would have impressed neither the ECB nor the governments. However, it would have protected the integrity of the law, and, who knows, perhaps incentivised democratic political processes to finally refound the European legal order.

BIBLIOGRAPHY

Abelshauser, Werner (2016), 'Deutsche Wirtschaftspolitik zwischen europäischer Integration und Weltmarktorientierung', in: id. (ed), *Das Bundeswirtschaftsministerium in der Ära der Sozialen Marktwirtschaft. Der deutsche Weg der Wirtschaftspolitik* (Walter de Gruyter, 2016), 482–581.

Bellow, Gary (1977) 'Turning Solutions into Problems: The Legal Aid Experience', *NLADA Briefcase* 34: 106–22.

Beukers, Thomas, Kilpatrick, Clare & de Witte, Bruno (2017) 'Constitutional Change through Euro-Crisis Law: Taking Stock, New Perspectives and Looking Ahead', in id. (eds), *Constitutional Change through Euro-Crisis Law*, Cambridge: Cambridge University Press.

Biebricher, Thomas & Vogelmann, Frieder (eds) (2017) *The Birth of Austerity: German Ordoliberalism and Contemporary Neoliberalism*, London and New York: Rowman and Littlefield.

Blyth, Mark, (2013) *Austerity: The History of a Dangerous Idea*, Oxford: Oxford University Press, 2013

Böckenförde, Ernst Wolfgang (2010) 'Kennt die europäische Not kein Gebot? Die Webfehler der EU und die Notwendigkeit einer neuen politischen Entscheidung' (Does necessity not know rules? Design flaws of the EU and the necessity of a new political decision), *Neue Züricher Zeitung*, 21 June 2010.

Borger, Anne & Rasmussen, Morton (2014) 'Transforming European Law: The Establishment of the Constitutional Discourse from 1950 to 1993', *European Constitutional Law Review* 10, 119–225.

Commission of the EC (1985) 'Commission White Paper to the European Council on Completion of the Internal Market', COM(85) 310 final of 14 June 1985.

Commission of the EC (2001) 'European Governance – A White Paper', COM(2001) 428 final of 25.7.2001.

Craig, Paul (2013) 'Pringle: Legal Reasoning, Text, Purpose and Teleology', *Maastricht Journal of European and Comparative Law* 10, 2–11.

Dehousse, Renaud & Weiler Joseph, H.H. (1990) 'The Legal Dimension', in Wallace, William (ed.), *The Dynamics of European Integration*, London: Pinter, 242–60.

Dukes, Ruth (2014) *The Labour Constitution: The Enduring Idea of Labour Law*, Oxford: Oxford University Press.

Dyson, Kenneth (2013) 'Sworn to Grim Necessity? Imperfections of European Economic Governance, Normative Political Theory, and Supreme Emergency' (2013) *Journal of European Integration* 35, 207–22.

---

[78] See Feichtner 2016, 895.

Eberlein, Burkhard & Kerwer, Dieter (2002) 'Theorising the New Modes of EU Governance', *European Integration Online Papers* 6:5, http://eiop.or.at/eiop/texte/2002-005a.htm
European Council (2001) Presidency Conclusions, Counciöl Meeting at Laeken, 14 and 15 December 2001SN 300/1/01 REV 1.
Everson, Michelle (1995) 'Independent Agencies: Hierarchy Beaters', *European Law Journal* 1, 180–204.
Everson, Michelle (2002) 'Adjudicating the Market', *European Law Journal* 8, 152–71.
Everson, Michelle (2015) 'An Exercise in Legal Honesty: Rewriting the Court of Justice and the *Bundesverfassungsgericht*', *European Law Journal* 21, 474–99.
Everson, Michelle & Joerges, Christian (2004) 'Law, Economics and Politics in the Constitutionalization of Europe', in Eriksen, Erik O., Fossum, Johan E. and Menéndez, Agustín J. (eds), *Developing a Constitution for Europe*, London and New York: Routledge, 162–79.
Everson, Michelle & Joerges, Christian (2014) 'Who Is the Guardian for Constitutionalism in Europe after the Financial Crisis?', in Kröger, Sandra (ed.), *Political Representation in the European Union: Still Democratic in Times of Crisis?*, London: Routledge, 400–28.
Everson, Michelle & Joerges, Christian (2017) 'Between Constitutional Command and Technocratic Rule: Post Crisis Governance and the Treaty on Stability, Coordination and Governance ("The Fiscal Compact")', in Harlow, Carol et al (eds), *Research Handbook on EU Administrative Law*, Cheltenham: Edward Elgar, 161–87.
Fabbrini, Fabrizio (ed.) (2016) *The European Court of Justice, the European Central Bank and the Supremacy of EU Law. Maastricht Journal of European & Comparative Law* 23 (Special Issue).
Feichtner, Isabel (2016) 'Public Law's Rationalization of the Legal Architecture of Money: What Might Legal Analysis of Money Become?' *German Law Journal* 17, 875–906.
Giubboni, Stefano (2006) *Social Rights and Market Freedoms in the European Constitution: A Labour Law Perspective*, Cambridge: Cambridge University Press.
Habermas, Jürgen (2012) 'Afterword' in 'What Germany Thinks about Europe' (edited by Ulrike Guérot and Jacqueline Hénard), online publication of the ECFR, available at www.ecfr.eu/publications/summary/what_does_germany_think_about_europe.
Habermas, Jürgen (2015) *The Lure of Technocracy*, Cambridge: Polity Press.
Harlow, Carol (2002) 'Public Law and Popular Justice', *Modern Law Review* 65, 1–18.
Hien, Josef & Joerges, Christian (2018) 'Dead Man Walking? Current European Interest in the Ordoliberal Tradition', *European Law Journal* 24, 142–162.
Hufeld, Ulrich (2011) 'Zwischen Notrettung und Rütlischwur: der Umbau der Wirtschafts- und Währungsunion in der Krise', *Integration* 34, 117–32.
Ipsen, Hans Peter (1972) *Europäisches Gemeinschaftsrecht*. Tübingen: Mohr/Siebeck.
Isiksel, Turkuler (2016), *Europe's Functional Constitution. A Theory of Constitutionalism beyond the State*, Oxford: Oxford University Press.
Jachtenfuchs, Markus (2002) 'The Governance Approach to European Integration', *Journal of Common Market Studies* 39, 245–64.
Joerges, Christian (1994) 'Economic Law, the Nation-State and the Maastricht Treaty', in Dehousse, Renaud (ed.) *Europe after Maastricht: An Ever Closer Union?*, Munich: C.H. Beck, 29–62.
Joerges, Christian (1996) 'The Market without a State? States without Markets? Two Essays on the Law of the European Economy', EUI Working Paper Law 1/96, San Domenico di Fiesole, http://eiop.or.at/eiop/texte/1997-019-020.htm.
Joerges, Christian (1999) '*Der Philosoph als wahrer Rechtslehrer*. Review Essay on Giandomenico Majone, Regulating Europe (1996)', *European Law Journal* 5, 147–53.
Joerges, Christian (2008) 'Integration through De-Legalisation?', *European Law Review* 33, 289–312.
Joerges, Christian (2019) 'Sociological Shortcomings and Normative Deficits of Regulatory Competition', in Francesco Costamagna (ed.), *Regulatory Competition in the EU, European Papers* 4, No. 1 (forthcoming).
Joerges, Christian & Kreuder-Sonnen, Christian (2017) 'European Studies and the European Crisis: Legal and Political Science between Critique and Complacency', *European Law Journal* 23, 118–39.
Kreuder-Sonnen, Christian (2016) 'Beyond Integration Theory: The (Anti-)Constitutional Dimension of European Crisis Governance', *Journal of Common Market Studies* 54, 1350–66.
Kuo, Ming-Sung (2014) 'The Moment of Schmittian Truth: Conceiving of the State of Exception in the Wake of the Financial Crisis', in Joerges, Christian & Glinski, Carolai (eds), *The European Crisis and the Transformation of Transnational Governance: Authoritarian Managerialism versus Democratic Governance*, Oxford: Hart Publishing, 83–97.

Kuo, Ming-Sung (2019) 'Control by Aggregation? Critical Reflections on Global Constitutionalism in the Shadow of Looming Transnational Emergency Powers', forthcoming in *Constellations* 26. Available at https://ssrn.com/abstract=3340260.
Majone, Giandomenico (1989) 'Regulating Europe: Problems and Prospects', *Jahrbuch zur Staats- und Verwaltungswissenschaft* 3, 159–77.
Majone, Giandomenico (1994) 'The European Community: "An Independent Fourth Branch of Government"', in Brüggemeier, Gert, *Verfassungen für ein ziviles Europa*, Baden-Baden: Nomos, 23–44.
Majone, Giandomenico (2014) *Rethinking the Union of Europe Post-Crisis. Has Integration Gone Too Far?*, Cambridge: Cambridge University Press.
Mestmäcker, Ernst-Joachim (2007) *A Legal Theory without Law: Posner v. Hayek on Economic Analysis of Law*, Tübingen: Mohr/Siebeck.
Milward, Alan (2000) *The European Rescue of the Welfare State* (2nd ed), London and New York: Routledge.
Mussler, Werner (1998) *Die Wirtschaftsverfassung der Europäischen Gemeinschaft im Wandel: von Rom nach Maastricht*, Baden-Baden: Nomos.
Ruggie, John G. (1982) 'International Regimes, Transactions and Change: Embedded Liberalism in the Postwar Economic Order', *International Organization* 36, 375–415.
Sabel, Charles F. & Zeitlin, Jonathan (2003) 'Active Welfare, Experimental Governance, Pragmatic Constitutionalism', New York-Madison/WI, available at http://eucenter.wisc.edu/Calendar/Spring03/harvardomc.htm.
Scharpf, Fritz W. (2002) 'The European Social Model: Coping with the Challenges of Diversity', *Journal of Common Market Studies* 40, 645–70.
Scharpf, Fritz W. (2013) 'Monetary Union, Fiscal Crisis and the Disabling of Democratic Accountability', in Streeck, Wolfgang & Schäfer, Armin (eds), *Politics in the Age of Austerity*, Cambridge, UK: Polity, 108–42.
Schepel, Harm (2017) 'The Bank, the Bond, and the Bail-Out: On the Legal Construction of Market Discipline in the Eurozone', *Journal of Law & Society* 44, 79–98.
Schepel, Harm & Wesseling, Rein (1997) 'The Legal Community: Judges, Lawyers, Officials and Clerks in the Writing of Europe', *European Law Journal* 3, 105–30.
Schmitter, Philippe (2001) 'What Is There to Legitimize in the European Union … and How Might This Be Accomplished?' in Joerges, Christian, Mény, Yves & Weiler, Joseph H.H. (eds) *Symposium: Mountain or Molehill? A Critical Appraisal of the Commission White Paper on Governance,* Jean Monnet Working Paper No 6/01, 79 ff., 83 ff., available at www.iue.it/RSC/Governance/.
Stein, Erik (1981) 'Lawyers, Judges, and the Making of a Transnational Constitution', *American Journal of International Law* 75, 1–27.
Stone Sweet, Alec (2007) 'The Juridical Coup d'État and the Problem of Authority', *German Law Journal* 8, 915–28.
Tuori, Kaarlo & Tuori, Klaus (2014) *The Eurozone Crisis: A Constitutional Analysis*, Cambridge: Cambridge University Press.
Vauchez, Antoine (2013) 'Brokering Europe Euro-Lawyers and the Making of a Transnational Polity', *LSE Law, Society and Economy Working Papers* 19/2013.
Vos, Ellen (2018) 'EU Agencies on the Move: Challenges Ahead', SIEPS Working Paper 2018:1, available at www.sieps.se.
Weiler, Joseph H.H. (1981) 'The Community System: The Dual Character of Supranationalism', *Yearbook of European Law* 1, 267–306.
Weiler, Joseph H.H. (1991) 'The Transformation of Europe', *Yale Law Journal* 100, 2403–83.
Weiler, Joseph H.H. (1995) 'The State "über alles". Demos, Telos and the German Maastricht Decision', *European Law Journal* 1, 219–58.
Weiler, Joseph H.H. (2012, December) 'On "Political Messianism", "Legitimacy" and the "Rule of Law"', *Singapore Journal of Legal Studies*, 248–68.
White, Jonathan (2015) 'Authority after Emergency Rule', *The Modern Law Review* 78, 585–610.
Wissenschaftlicher Beirat beim Bundesministerium für Wirtschaft (1986) *Stellungnahme zum Weißbuch der EG-Kommission über den Binnenmarkt* (Schriften-Reihe 51), Bonn.
Zeitlin, Jonathan and Trubek, David M. (2003) *Governing Work and Welfare in a New Economy: European and American Experiments*, Oxford: Oxford University Press.

23. Critical law and development
Fiona Macmillan

> The idea of development stands like a ruin in the intellectual landscape. Delusion and disappointment, failures and crime have been the steady companions of development and they tell a common story: it did not work.[1]

1. INTRODUCTION: THE 'DEVELOPMENT CRISIS'

It is not uncommon to hear the international development project being referred to in terms of crisis. Strangely, however, the use of the word crisis in this context often seems to be somewhat non-urgent. After all, if the development project really is in crisis then it is a crisis that has been in course since at least the end of the Second World War. A very good case could even be made for the proposition that this crisis significantly predates the post-war decolonization process and, in fact, dates back to the colonial period. In 1922 Lord Lugard, a prominent colonial administrator, articulated the so-called dual mandate, according to which colonialism was justified as part of the universal historical mission of the imperial powers, which were under two moral duties:[2] 'to bring the blessings of Western civilisation to the inhabitants of the tropics and to activate neglected resources in "backward" countries for the benefit of the world economy'.[3] As this chapter will argue, these two principles continue, with some modifications, to be central to the development project, which has not only failed to address its own crisis but has also failed abysmally to address the crisis faced by a significant portion of the inhabitants of the planet.

Failing to understand the urgency of the development crisis somehow reflects the failure of the whole project. As if it does not matter that millions of people have been deprived of their social, cultural, political, economic and legal autonomy, not to mention the most basic of life's necessities; that after the succession of endless ideas, emerging from some strange coalition of theory and institutional politics, about what development might mean, or should be, we seem to have made no appreciable gains in achieving it in practice or even being quite sure what it is; that since the Washington Consensus, even that most arbitrary and unsatisfactory mode of measuring so-called development – by economic growth – has shown that the gap between developed and developing economies has on average grown for the first time since the end of the

---

[1] Wolfgang Sachs, 'Introduction' in Wolfgang Sachs (ed.), *The Development Dictionary: A Guide to Knowledge as Power* (Zed Books 2009).

[2] Lord Frederick J.D. Lugard, *The Dual Mandate in British Tropical Africa* (Frank Cass & Co, 1922).

[3] Jürgen Osterhammel, 'Colonialist Ideology' in *Colonialism: A Theoretical Overview* (trans. Shelley L Frisch) (Markus Winer 1997), 109–10.

Second World War.[4] Despite the plethora of international, intergovernmental and governmental bodies specifically dedicated to the development project, despite the focused attention to the question from nearly every other international and intergovernmental institution, despite an industry of nongovernmental organizations and civil society organizations working tirelessly, despite the combined efforts of the world's social, political, legal and economic elite gathered together annually at Davos under the auspices of the World Economic Forum[5] – in other words, despite the endless resources of all types poured into the development project – achieving, or imposing, development has proved remarkably elusive. Consequently, millions of people continue to live in material conditions that are unacceptable by any standard of decency.

On the other hand, as crises go this has been a rather successful one for the West.[6] The failure of the development process has allowed the Western world to maintain most of its historic geopolitical and material advantages, while at the same time leveraging the consequent weakness of the so-called developing world in order to find new ways of extracting resources and capital on advantageous terms. Understood this way, one might argue that the real crisis is that the enormous apparatus of the international development project is the very reason that a significant part of the planet continues to live in unacceptable material conditions. The role of law in this apparatus, both as a means of exporting Western norms and as a means of extracting resources on advantageous terms, is central. The pivotal issue here turns on the process by which the globalization of Western law, in the form of international law, has mediated the connection between colonialism and capitalism in the post-Second World War period.

2. INTERNATIONAL LAW AND THE POSTCOLONIAL CAPITALIST SYSTEM

2.1 Division between the Political and the Economic

The current international legal order, which emerged after the Second World War, embraces a kind of schism between international economic law and public international

---

[4] Julio Faundez, 'International Economic Law and Development: Before and After Neo-liberalism" in Julio Faundez and Celine Tan (eds), *International Economic Law, Globalization and Developing Countries* (Edward Elgar 2010), 25. On the inevitability of this, see Giovanni Arrighi, Beverley J. Silver and Benjamin D. Brewer, 'Industrial Convergence, Globalization and the Persistence of the North–South Divide' (2003) 38 *Studies in Comparative Economic Development* 3.

[5] See www.weforum.org/, accessed 27 December 2017.

[6] While accepting that broad descriptions such as 'the West' and 'the Global North/South' are unable to capture the complexity of global geopolitics, this chapter uses the expression 'the West' to describe that group of states currently regarded as being developed. There is an approximate identity between the group in question and the 35 states comprising the membership of the Organization for Economic Coordination and Development (OECD), see www.oecd.org/g20/g20-members.htm, accessed 27 December 2017.

law.[7] The United Nations organizations, which form the framework for what is referred to here as public international law, arose from the Dumbarton Oaks negotiations. The institutions of international economic law emerged from the Bretton Woods negotiations, which drew up the charters of the International Monetary Fund (IMF), the International Fund for Reconstruction and Development (which became the World Bank) and the International Trade Organization. From the beginning, the mandates of these two systems of international law were distinct. The Dumbarton Oaks institutions were to manage the international political order while the Bretton Woods institutions were to manage international economic relations. Thus, the Dumbarton Oaks institutions have taken charge of what have been described as 'state-making and war-making' functions.[8] In addition to this, the system of public international law that has been built up around the Dumbarton Oaks institutions has purported to establish international standards in areas such as the protection of human rights and of the environment.

This bifurcation of international law along the lines of the putative division between the political and the economic appears to be rooted in the origins of the Westphalia system. The principle that quarrels between sovereigns did not implicate non-combatant civilians was built into the Peace of Westphalia of 1648.[9] As a consequence, the treaties that built upon the Settlement of Westphalia abolished trade barriers and sought to protect private enterprises' rights to trade across state borders, even during times of war or other political turmoil. Arrighi remarks that '[t]his reorganization of political space in the interest of capital accumulation marks the birth not just of the modern inter-state system, but also of capitalism as world system'.[10]

Arrighi is far from being the only prominent commentator to have noticed that this division between the political and the economic is critical to the modern system of global capitalism.[11] This observation is fundamental to Hirschman's argument that among eighteenth century European political philosophers – making particular reference to Montesquieu and Sir James Steuart – the division between the political and the economic was regarded as being essential to controlling the power of despotic rulers in the pre-democratic period. The central point here is that, at least in the pre-democratic period, this division was a political question in the sense that the power of the economic system was regarded as a constraint on the operation of the political system.

---

[7] Sundhya Pahuja, 'Trading Spaces: Locating Sites for Challenge within International Trade Law' (2000) 14 *Australian Feminist Law Journal* 38; Fiona Macmillan, 'International Economic Law and Public International Law: Strangers in the Night' (2004) 6 *International Trade Law and Regulation* 115.

[8] Giovanni Arrighi, *The Long Twentieth Century: Money, Power and the Origins of Our Times* (Verso 2002), 275.

[9] Ibid, 43.

[10] Ibid, 44.

[11] See also, e.g., Karl Polanyi, *The Great Transformation: The Political and Economic Origins of Our Time* (first published 1944, Beacon Press, 2000); Albert O. Hirschman, *The Passions and the Interests: Political Arguments for Capitalism before Its Triumph* (Princeton University Press, 1977, reprinted 1997); Samir Amin, *Capitalism in the Age of Globalization* (Zed Books, 1998); John Gray, *False Dawn: The Delusions of Global Capitalism* (New Press, 1998); Ellen Meiksens Wood, *Empire of Capital* (Verso 2003).

In the nineteenth century, however, when Western politics had developed its own forms of democratic restraint, the economic system was liberated from its role in politics. But instead of democratic politics taking up the role of constraining the power of the economic system, under the influence of the neoclassical economists and the political economists that founded the Austrian School, the global capitalist system was liberated from much in the way of political restraint and so effectively depoliticized.[12] Bearing in mind that the system of international law that was remade at the end of the Second World War reflects the systemic division between the political and the economic, the depoliticization of the idea of the economic is crucial to understanding both the role of international economic law in relation to global capitalism and the place of the development project within the global capitalist system. With this point in mind, this chapter now turns to a closer engagement with the system of international economic law inaugurated at Bretton Woods.

2.2 The Bretton Woods System

The surviving Bretton Woods institutions are the IMF and the World Bank. Despite being the progeny of Franklin D. Roosevelt's 'one-worldism', the International Trade Organization never came into existence. Its death knell was the intense opposition that it engendered in the United States,[13] although the political and business interests ranged against it were not confined to those emanating from the US.[14] However, it metamorphosed into the 1947 version of the General Agreement on Trade and Tariffs (GATT) and was, accordingly, a precursor to the World Trade Organization (WTO). Together the IMF, the World Bank and the World Trade Organization make up what has been described as the 'unholy trinity'[15] of international economic law institutions. Each of these institutions has had, explicitly or implicitly, a significant role in the development project. This is perhaps most obvious in the role of the World Bank, which has a specific mandate with respect to development. Since the collapse of the fixed exchange rate system and the loss of its central function, the IMF has increasingly turned its attention to the question of development. Nowadays many of the explicit development strategies and policies are jointly operated by the IMF and the World Bank, and it can be no surprise that many of the most famous development disasters can claim a similar heritage.[16]

---

[12] Dimitris Milonakis and Ben Fine, *From Political Economy to Economics: Method, the Social and the Historical in the Evolution of Economic Theory* (Routledge 2009); Fiona Macmillan, 'The World Trade Organization and the Turbulent Legacy of International Economic Law-Making in the Long Twentieth Century' in Faundez and Tan (eds), n 4 above; Benjamin Selwyn, *The Global Development Crisis* (Polity 2014), ch. 5.
[13] See Arrighi, n 8 above, 276–7; Graham Dunkley, *The Free Trade Adventure: The WTO, the Uruguay Round & Globalism – A Critique* (Zed Books 2001), 26–8.
[14] See Dunkley, n 13 above, 26–8.
[15] Richard Peet, *Unholy Trinity: The IMF, World Bank and the WTO* (Zed Books 2003).
[16] See, e.g., B. Rajagopal, *International Law from Below: Development, Social Movements, and Third World Resistance* (Cambridge University Press 2003), ch. 5; Celine Tan (2008) 'Mandating Rights and Limiting Mission Creep: Holding the World Bank and the International

The role of the WTO is somewhat different as it has no specific mandate in relation to development, apart from a rather vague reference in the preamble to its constitutional agreement that refers to its role in the promotion of 'sustainable development', which presumably grounds the provisions in the WTO covered agreements on 'special and differential treatment' (SDT) for developing countries.[17] However, its role in the development debacle is more extensive than its constituent documents might lead one to believe. To understand this it is useful to make a brief reference to its antecedents, the failed International Trade Organization and the General Agreement on Trade and Tariffs (GATT). Both the rejection of the International Trade Organization in the post-war period and the subsequent arrival of the WTO 50 years later are part of a continuous process driven by the needs of capital accumulation. After the Second World War the introduction of a system of multilateral free trade was postponed in favour of the GATT's framework for the negotiation, on either a multilateral or bilateral basis, of the reduction of restrictions on international trade in goods. This is entirely consistent with the fact that the US embrace of free trade has always been largely rhetorical. Using the GATT, the US government was able to control the process of trade liberalization in ways that benefited US interests by internalizing international trade within the vertically integrated structures of multinational corporations. In this way, post-war international markets were reconstructed through the engine of foreign direct investment (FDI) rather than through 'free trade'. This is the beginning of the process which, as Arrighi notes, means that by the 1970s transnational corporations 'had developed into a world-scale system of production, exchange and accumulation, which was subject to no state authority and had the power to subject to its own "laws" each and every member of the inter-state system'.[18] So transnational capital neither needed nor wanted 'free trade' in the post-war period. The need for a selective free trade regime comes later in the US period of dominance and, as argued below, is directly connected to the process of capital accumulation and the generation of interstate competition for mobile capital.

2.3 Fragmentation and Depoliticization

In the present context there are two important consequences of the split between the political and the economic in the international law system. One of these, the depoliticization of international economic law, has already been mentioned but is worth some further attention. This is particularly so since the other important – if somewhat obvious – consequence, fragmentation of regulation, operates in tandem with depoliticization. The two are mutually supportive. The international law principles governing human rights, labour rights and development are, along with the protection of the

---

Monetary Fund Accountable for Human Rights Violations' (2008) 2 *Human Rights and International Legal Discourse* 79.

[17] See Donatella Alessandrini, *Developing Countries and the Multilateral Trade Regime: The Failure and Promise of the WTO's Development Mission* (Hart 2010).

[18] Arrighi, n 8 above, 74.

environment, particularly affected by the fragmentation of regulation. Arguably different concepts of human rights, for example, operate in the two parts of the system.[19] Maybe even worse, labour rights seem to have completely disappeared from the international economic law system. And specifically in relation to development, the dedicated instrumentalities are all part of the United Nations system, but the real action (or damage) is taking place in the international economic law system.

This fragmentation and depoliticization has enabled the imposition of conditions attached to lending by the World Bank and the IMF (the Bretton Woods institutions) in their role as lenders (often of last resort) to states. Structural adjustment using loan conditionality is one of the famous ways in which these institutions put pressure on developing countries (and other countries in need of emergency finance) to change their laws and institutions.[20] Distressing cases of the damage caused by this type of loan conditionality abound.[21] Conditionality has also crept into the aid agenda, where it has been used in relation to debt relief initiatives.[22] The conditional lending practices of the Bretton Woods institutions have changed their form over time, but the substance remains largely the same. Not only do these forms of conditionality require the Westernization of the law and institutions of the recipient states, they also reflect the tenets of the Washington Consensus and so are driven by ideas such as reduction of the public sector, low taxation, privatization of public services, limitation – or even elimination – of labour standards, liberalization of inward FDI and austerity. However, even within this straitjacket there is considerable room for variation and manoeuvre with respect to the type of conditionality imposed. Interesting work has been done on so-called rule of law conditionality which shows that the idea of 'the rule of law' in Bretton Woods rule of law conditionality, while being resolutely Western, differs substantially between instrumental (as suggested, for example, by Weber and Hayek) and intrinsic (for example, Dicey and Sen), and between institutional (for example, Weber and Dicey) and substantive (for example, Hayek and Sen).[23] It does not seem unreasonable to suggest that a particular form of rule of law conditionality exists not because we in the West have a political view that some versions of rule of law are better than others, but rather because some types of rule of law conditionality in certain circumstances fit better with the needs of global capital than others.

The use of the concept of the rule of law as a means to facilitate capital accumulation and drive interstate competition for mobile capital has also been achieved through WTO obligations, which require national laws to be brought into conformity with WTO rules. Here we can see the mutually supportive relationship between homogenization of

---

[19] Pahuja, n 7 above.
[20] See, e.g., Faundez, n 4 above; Peet, n 15 above, ch. 4; Celine Tan, *Governance through Development: Poverty Reduction Strategies, International Law and the Disciplining of Third World States* (Routledge 2011).
[21] See, e.g., Michel Chossudovsky, 'India under IMF Rule' (1993) 28 *Economic and Political Weekly* 385; Rajagopal, n 16 above.
[22] Celine Tan, 'Reframing the Debate: The Debt Relief Initiative and New Normative Values in the Governance of Third World Debt' (2014) 10 *International Journal of Law in Context* 249.
[23] Alvaro Santos, 'The World Bank Uses of the "Rule of Law" Promise in Economic Development' in David M. Trubek and Alvaro Santos (eds), *The New Law and Economic Development: A Critical Appraisal* (Cambridge University Press 2006).

markets through 'free trade' and homogenization of law. The effects of the fragmented system of international law and the depoliticization of international economic law are also fundamental in relation to the WTO. While the Bretton Woods institutions have, for example, developed their own concepts of human rights in order to discipline states to which they have given financial accommodation, the World Trade Organization appears to embrace the position that things like human rights and labour standards are simply outside its sphere of operation. Perhaps the honesty is refreshing, but the failure to acknowledge its role in the perpetuation of human misery as a result of downward pressure on labour standards, which are seen as constituting non-tariff barriers to trade, is not appealing.

2.4 Decolonization

A critically important process that informs the birth of the international economic law system, and especially its entanglement with development, is the process of decolonization, which begins after the Second World War and the remaking of the international law system. Thus, the first and most obvious point to make about this process is that the former colonies, which today have a substantial degree of identity with those states usually described as 'developing' or 'least developed',[24] had no role in the diplomatic conferences at Dumbarton Oaks and Bretton Woods and so no role in the remaking of the system into which they were born as new states. The remaking of the system was, of course, led by the US, which had emerged as the leading global power after the Second World War, displacing Great Britain, the leading imperial power of the nineteenth century.

The terms of the new relationship between the states comprising the great metropolitan powers, their satellites and the rest of the 'developing' world were set by the leader of the greatest power, President Harry S. Truman, when he famously gave voice to the concept of 'underdevelopment'. In a speech of 20 January 1949, he said:

> We must embark on a bold new programme for making the benefits of our scientific advances and industrial progress available for the improvement and growth of underdeveloped areas. The old imperialism – exploitation for foreign profit – has no place in our plans. What we envisage is a program of development based on the concept of democratic fair dealing.[25]

Of course, all this could only happen if the decolonizing and newly emerging states were woven into the fabric of the newly remade international law system.

The chronological coincidence of the invention of the concept of development, with its consequent drive to enmesh newly decolonizing states in the remade system of

---

[24] Or one might use the expression 'third world', as Chimni suggests, in a spirit of resistance: B.S. Chimni, 'Third World Approaches to International Law: A Manifesto' in Antony Anghie, B.S. Chimni, Karin Mickelson and Obiora Okafor (eds), *The Third World and International Order: Law, Politics and Globalization* (Martinus Nijhoff 2003).

[25] Harry S. Truman, Inaugural Address, 20 January 1949 in *Documents on American Foreign Relations* (Princeton University Press, 1967), quoted in Gustavo Esteva, 'Development' in Wolfgang Sachs (ed.), *The Development Dictionary: A Guide to Knowledge as Power* (Zed Books 2009), 7.

international law, and the process of decolonization are not accidental.[26] In particular, the loss of the colonies presented the former imperial powers and the new hegemon, the US, with the problem of how to continue to extract resources on favourable terms.[27] This question of extraction of resources is a critical theme in international economic law in a number of ways. First, the principle of most favoured nation (MFN) treatment in WTO law operates to protect extraction of primary resources by countries lacking them on favourable terms. Second, the doctrine of comparative advantage upon which the idea of free international trade is based (and more on this shortly) has forced many resource rich countries, mostly from the global south, into the position of suppliers of primary resources without having the opportunity to develop manufacturing capacity. This has undoubtedly meant that such states have been unable to extract some of the economic benefits that might have flowed from participation in the capitalist system.[28] Third, extraction of biological and knowledge-based resources seems to be one of the primary drivers behind the international patent system, which was reinforced with the conclusion of the WTO and its Agreement on Trade-Related Aspects of Intellectual Property (the TRIPS Agreement). If we accept the very plausible proposition that the WTO exists partly because of the two new major trade agreements that were created within its structure, the TRIPS Agreement and the General Agreement on Trade in Services (GATS)[29] (and more on this shortly as well), we might reasonably hypothesize that extraction of resources is one of the underlying concerns of the WTO system. Fourth, the system overall operates to extract capital from the global south. From the beginning of the period of decolonization it was necessary to enmesh the newly created states within both the international law system and, concomitantly, the capitalist system, by making them somehow dependent on these systems and the powerful states within them. Not only would this ensure that these states would provide markets for Western manufactured products and thus extract capital from them, but it would also operate to control and discipline them. The internalization of trade within the domains of multinational corporations which forms part of the post-Second World War global economic landscape has also operated to extract capital and other resources. This is because the direct relationship between multinational corporations and states of the global south has mostly taken place through a process of FDI, often on extremely disadvantageous terms.[30] The net result is that more capital and other resources go out than go in.

2.5 Development as Neocolonialism

Hopefully, at this point, more or less half way through the chapter, the case for development as neocolonialism is beginning to emerge. In the dual mandate of Lord

---

[26] Esteva, n 25 above.
[27] Cf B. Porter, *British Imperial: What the Empire Wasn't* (IB Tauris 2016).
[28] Dunkley, n 13 above.
[29] Fiona Macmillan, 'Looking Back to Look Forward: Is there a Future for Human Rights in the WTO?' [2005] *International Trade Law and Regulation* 163; Macmillan, n 12 above.
[30] E.g. (directly from the belly of the beast) WTO Working Group on the Relationship between Trade & Investment (2002) *Communication from China, Cuba, India, Kenya, Pakistan and Zimbabwe: Investors' and Home Governments' Obligations*, WT/WGTI/W/152, 19/11/2002.

Lugard 'justifying'[31] colonial rule we can see the two threads that not only create continuity between colonialism and the concept of development, but also hold together the story of international economic law. Colonialism was the export of Western concepts of the rule of law *par excellence*.[32] The extraordinary spread of the common law system in the Commonwealth countries, formerly colonies of Great Britain, is a tribute to the success of this project. In this way, in accordance with the first part of the Lugardian mandate, the 'blessings of civilization' were dispersed through the Empire. The postcolonial period has witnessed a comparable process through two central devices of international economic law. One of these is loan conditionality,[33] and the other is the requirement for states to bring their law into compliance with WTO standards. So far as the second part of the colonial dual mandate is concerned, the extraction of resources is a key factor in driving both the colonial enterprise and the development enterprise. The change in the political status of the former colonies after decolonization meant, however, that the task of extraction could no longer be achieved by simple plunder; rather, for this purpose, recourse has been made to international economic law.

While there is much debate about its desirability and morality, there seems to be very little about the fact of the relationship between the development project, including that part of it concerned with access to resources, and capitalist expansion. There is, on the other hand, a considerable amount of dispute and historical revision over the question of the extent to which the colonial project was driven by capitalist expansion. In a rather obvious sense, however, the argument that development is neocolonialism depends on establishing this link between the colonial and postcolonial periods. The argument, at least recently, that the significance of the capitalist impulse in the colonial period has been exaggerated tends to depend upon the claim that imperialism was a state, rather than an entrepreneurial capitalist, project.[34] However, this position critically underestimates the extent to which capital accumulation and state power were, and continue to be, linked. This is so even if the nature of the relationship between states and multinational enterprises has altered radically during the US period of dominance. In the colonial period this relationship was expressed through the joint stock corporations, which were state backed trading enterprises, the role of which was to advance both empire and capitalist expansion. These corporations were features of the international trade landscape at least from the establishment of the English East India Company in 1600 and its Dutch counterpart, the *Vereenigde Oost-Indische Compagnie* (VOC), in 1602.[35]

---

[31] See text accompanying n 2 above.
[32] Ugo Mattei and Laura Nader, *Plunder: When the Rule of Law is Illegal* (Blackwell 2008), 19.
[33] Sundhya Pahuja, 'Technologies of Empire: IMF Conditionality and the Reinscription of the North/South Divide' (2000) 13 *Leiden Journal of International Law* 749.
[34] See, e.g., Andro Linklater, *Owning the Earth: The Transforming History of Land Ownership* (Bloomsbury 2013); Porter, n 27 above.
[35] Arrighi, n 8 above; Fiona Macmillan, 'The Emergence of the World Trade Organization: Another Triumph of Corporate Capitalism?' in Richard Joyce and Sundhya Pahuja (eds), *Events: The Force of International Law* (Routledge 2010).

Arrighi in particular recognizes the role of these corporations in his argument that capitalism is a history of cycles of capitalist accumulation (meaning success in attracting mobile capital) dominated by a leading agency of capital accumulation in the form of a state.[36] The current dominant agency of capital accumulation is, of course, the US, which is the fourth of the cycles identified by Arrighi, and was preceded by the Genoese, Dutch and British dominated cycles. Arrighi links these cycles to the continual expansion of international trade and its domination by the leading state agency of capital accumulation. Thus, the trade ascendancy of the VOC in the seventeenth century was, like the power of the Dutch Empire, on the wane by the middle of the eighteenth century.[37] At this time, as the British Empire superseded the Dutch, the English joint stock companies began their domination of international trade.

In Arrighi's theory each of these cycles of state led capital accumulation follows the same trajectory. That is, when capital can longer be profitably employed by use in the development of new markets that expand the productive capacity of the existing markets, then a switch occurs and excess profits are ploughed into the trade in money. That is, a switch is made from trade to finance:

> The switch is the expression of a 'crisis' in the sense that it marks a 'turning point', a 'crucial time of decision', when the leading agency of systemic processes of capital accumulation reveals, through the switch, a negative judgment on the possibility of continuing to profit from the reinvestment of surplus capital in the material expansion of the world economy, as well as a positive judgment on the possibility of prolonging in time and space its leadership/dominance through a greater specialization in high finance.[38]

Arrighi argues that interstate competition for mobile capital has been essential to the material expansion of the capitalist world economy. However, Arrighi's gloss to this proposition is that capitalist power has intensified during each period of capitalist accumulation.[39] So, returning to the relationship between colonialism and capitalism, it is arguable that what happens in the colonial period is that, due to this intensification, international capitalism becomes part of the engine of state power in a way that was not previously seen.

2.6 The New International Economic Order and 'Neoliberalism'

This seems like a good moment to move onto a consideration of the current US-dominated cycle of capitalist accumulation. The key historical moments of this cycle are, first, the end of the Cold War and the *Pax Americana* or Washington Consensus, and second, the Uruguay Round of trade negotiations leading to the creation of the WTO in 1994. But the most important phenomenon of the entire American period is the modern multinational corporate enterprise, which is very much a creature of the constant intensification of capitalist power identified by Arrighi. The

---

[36] Arrighi, n 8 above.
[37] Arrighi, n 8 above, 139ff.
[38] Arrighi, n 8 above, 215.
[39] Arrighi, n 8 above, 12ff.

precondition of the ascendancy of the multinational enterprise was the twentieth century processes of vertical integration and internalization of international trade within those enterprises. And the dominance of multinational enterprises is crucially linked to interstate competition for investment and its adverse effects on countries of the global south, because it is this that puts pressure on the 'weakest' states to make their legal regimes 'welcoming' to the interests of capital.[40]

The so-called developing world did start to reorganize and fight back, agitating for changes in the world system to equal the unequal economic playing field, under the banner of a call for the famous, but never appearing, New International Economic Order (NIEO). This campaign was well placed to take advantage of the interruption to the process of corporate-led globalization as a result of the so-called exogenous shocks of the 1970s and 1980s, including the collapse of the fixed exchange rate system established under the auspices of the IMF and the OPEC crisis. As a result of these shocks, many states introduced non-tariff barriers to protect domestic production, which included such issues as labour rights, environmental protection, limits on the entry of foreign capital and differential taxation systems for foreign multinational corporations. The NIEO, however, never appeared, for the very simple reason that a political decision was taken to create the conditions for the re-intensification of corporate-led globalization and expansion of the capitalist system. This is a decision that we commonly call the Washington Consensus, which imposed on states fiscal discipline, tax reform, interest rate liberalization, trade liberalization, liberalization of inward FDI, reduction and redirection of public expenditure, deregulation, privatization and an almost religious zeal for the security of property rights. In the end, the only new international economic order to emerge was what is now referred to as neoliberalism.

2.7 The Uruguay Round, the WTO and Comparative Advantage

The Washington Consensus coincides historically with the beginning of the Uruguay Round of trade negotiations, which was primarily concerned with three things: first, removal of the nontariff barriers, which had been inhibiting the growth of international trade; second, putting in place a global intellectual property regime; and third, liberalizing trade in services, including financial services. These negotiations culminated in the birth of the WTO, which claims to promote free international trade based on the concept of comparative advantage, a doctrine of classical economics into which the neoliberal spirit has breathed new life. Derived from the ideas of Adam Smith and David Ricardo,[41] the modern version of the doctrine postulates that that optimal allocation of international resources will be achieved if each country uses its comparative advantage to produce only the commodities that it can most efficiently produce and trades those commodities with other countries in order to obtain the commodities that it does not produce.[42] Essentially, therefore, the argument is one about optimal allocation

---

[40] See n 30 above.
[41] See further Dunkley, n 13 above; Donatella Alessandrini, 'WTO and the Current Trade Debate: An Enquiry into the Intellectual Origins of Free Trade Thought' [2005] *International Trade Law and Regulation* 53; Macmillan, n 12 above.
[42] Dunkley, n 13 above, ch. 6.

of resources as a consequence of the operation of an unfettered market mechanism. Ultimately, it is argued, where there is optimal allocation of resources then economic welfare will be maximized. It is also frequently argued that economic growth will be stimulated and everyone will be better off in economic terms. However, even some prominent free trade advocates are doubtful about this proposition.[43] Non-economic benefits in the form of greater international cooperation and harmony are also postulated by adherents of the doctrine of comparative advantage and its concomitant of international trade free from government interference.[44] These non-economic benefits would, it is argued, flow from the fact of economic interdependence.

Leaving aside the deleterious social and welfare consequences of this doctrine, beautifully critiqued by Keynes and further addressed below,[45] a serious problem about its current applicability relates to its assumption that capital, along with skilled labour, is largely immobile.[46] The efficiency and welfare advantages predicted by the doctrine are based upon the movement of traded commodities, in the form of raw materials and manufactured goods, across borders. The twentieth century, however, marked an increase (that has continued unabated into the twenty-first century) in the movement of the means of production across borders. This generally occurs by means of FDI by multinational enterprises, which establish subsidiary undertakings in another country for this purpose.

In order to make some sense of these developments in systemic terms, it is useful to revisit one of Arrighi's insights, which is that every cycle of capitalist accumulation has a so-called signal point when the profits derived from trade become so poor that money switches from trade to investment capital. For the British dominated cycle the signal point came as the result of the intensification of competition from Germany and the US consequent upon the Depression of 1873 to 1896. For the Americans, in the 1970s and 1980s, the signal point was the economic challenge from Japan. These signal points and their accompanying switches are autumnal and generally inaugurate a period of economic turbulence. They do not, however, spell the immediate end of the dominant regime of capital accumulation.[47] In both cycles, the response of the dominant agency of capital accumulation to these signal points led to the establishment of international 'free' trade agreements and international agreements on the protection of intellectual property.[48]

In the current turbulent stage Arrighi argues that a combination of structural changes in the form of 'the withering away of the modern system of territorial states as the primary locus of world power', 'the internalisation of world-scale processes of production and exchange within the organizational domains of transnational corporations' and 'the resurgence of suprastatal world financial markets' has created a pressure to relocate state authority and counter systemic chaos through a process of

---

[43] See, e.g., Jagdish Bhagwati, *Free Trade Today* (Princeton University Press 2002), 41–3.
[44] Alessandrini, n 41 above; Dunkley, n 13 above, 110.
[45] John Maynard Keynes, 'Pros and Cons of Tariffs', *The Listener*, 30 November 1932, reprinted in Donald Moggridge (ed.) (1982), *The Collective Writings of John Maynard Keynes* (Macmillan 1982), Vol 21, 204–10.
[46] Gray, n 11 above, 82.
[47] Arrighi, n 8 above.
[48] Macmillan, n 12 above.

world government formation.[49] Going further and reflecting on the nature and ideology of the WTO, do these represent an attempt on the part of the US, in its death throes as the dominant agency of capitalist accumulation, to control interstate competition for mobile capital? Certainly, the chronological coincidence between Arrighi's post-switch phase in the US cycle of capital accumulation and the Uruguay Round negotiations is striking, as is the fact that the two new Uruguay Round agreements, the TRIPS Agreement and the GATS, are quite conceivably conceptualized as being essentially concerned with investment.[50]

2.8 Developing Countries in the Global Capitalist System

For developing countries, loan conditionality and structural adjustment requirements imposed by the Bretton Woods institutions, and also by the WTO as a condition of entry into the WTO system, are generally connected to gearing up for comparative advantage. This is notwithstanding the cogent criticisms that have been made about the ability of the doctrine of comparative advantage to deal with the obvious global disadvantage of developing countries.[51] The concern here, as Dunkley notes, is that 'in a world of uneven development free trade, or even trade *per se*, may be inherently unequalising'.[52] There is a range of economic arguments that explain why the doctrine of comparative advantage may be unable to deliver its promised welfare benefits to developing countries.

One of the important general arguments in this context is that comparative advantage is created and cumulative, rather than natural.[53] If this is so, then the cumulative comparative advantage of developed countries will ensure either that inequalities always remain or that they take an unacceptably long time to disappear. Another important school of economic thought postulates perpetual inequalities as a consequence of free trade. According to this argument, where there is low elasticity in demand for the exports of a country but high elasticity in domestic demand for imports, then export prices relative to import prices will result in a continuous trade deficit.[54] As this tends to describe the terms upon which at least some developing countries export their primary products and import manufactured products, this means that under free trade conditions these developing countries will remain trapped in a trade deficit, preventing them from realizing the welfare gains promised by free trade doctrine.[55]

It is, accordingly, the theory of comparative advantage and its concomitant doctrine of free trade that keep developing countries in the same economic position they have always been in: suppliers of primary products or suppliers of manufactured products made on the back of often appalling labour, environmental and human rights conditions. Domestic regulation to improve standards in these areas is not only directly

---

[49] Arrighi, n 8 above, 331.
[50] Macmillan, n 29 above, 178–80.
[51] See further Dunkley, n 13 above; Macmillan, n 12 above.
[52] Dunkley, n 13 above, 119.
[53] Dunkley, n 13 above, 122.
[54] John Stuart Mill, *Essays on Some Unsettled Questions of Political Economy* (Parker 1844), 21.
[55] Dunkley, n 13 above, 118 and 145ff.

constrained by the legal obligations placed on states through the international economic law system, but also by the need to survive in the international capitalist system by competing for mobile capital through FDI. The dominant state agencies, using the system of international economic law, have rigged the rules to give themselves a vast competitive advantage in the attraction of interstate mobile capital.[56] This rigging of the rules is quite consistent with the fact that the WTO is not really a free trade organization in any case. The GATT, for example, does not eliminate tariffs, but rather limits them subject to an exhortation to member states to reduce them over time. The latitude that this provides has been used by powerful states to keep up protectionist barriers with respect to both primary and manufactured products in order to protect domestic markets from competition from products imported from states, usually from the global south, with relevant comparative advantage. An outrageous example is the US refusal to drop its tariffs on cotton products. These tariffs protect the US cotton industry from exports from Benin, Burkina Faso, Chad and Mali, which have comparative advantage in the growing of cotton.[57]

The grotesque hypocrisy of the WTO – and of the powerful states that are responsible for the legal architecture of its agreements – aside, there is no compelling argument that things would be better for so-called developing countries in a true free trade regime. Apart from the economic arguments to this effect, some of which have already been canvassed, a free trade regime raises serious ethical concerns, especially in a vastly unequal world. A particular issue here is the exploitation of labour, whether by multinational corporate interests or by domestically based interests. The general issue, however, is the way in which free trade doctrine regards wealth maximization as the ultimate measure of human happiness and attainment.

The critique of free trade based upon the rejection of wealth maximization draws stark attention to the difficulty in attempting to divide the political and the economic. The decision to embrace a free trade regime is not, and can never be, a purely economic one. Rather, it is a political choice involving, among other things, economic considerations. In their failure to understand this point, as in so much else, modern free trade theorists appear to be embracing a type of intellectual foreclosure that dates back to the work of Adam Smith. Smith postulated non-economic effects of free trade, both positive and negative. On the positive side, both he and Ricardo cited cosmopolitanism and international harmony as a noneconomic benefit of free trade. Smith also saw that the pursuit of material wealth had less desirable effects.[58] He was, however, unable to resolve the conflict between this concern and his commitment to the expansion of wealth, cosmopolitanism and international harmony through international trade. He consequently appears to conclude that the primary motivation of humankind is to better its material condition. This conclusion set the parameters to the post-Smithian debate about international trade, which has been conducted around the question of whether

---

[56] See also Amin, n 11 above, 97.

[57] WTO, *Poverty Reduction: Sectoral Initiative in Favour of Cotton – Joint Proposal by Benin, Burkina Faso, Chad & Mali*, WT/MIN(03)/W/2, 15/8/2003; WTO, *Poverty Reduction: Sectoral Initiative in Favour of Cotton – Joint Proposal by Benin, Burkina Faso, Chad & Mali – Addendum*, WT/MIN(03)/W/2/Add.1, 3/9/2003.

[58] Hirschman, n 11 above, 106–7.

and to what extent international trade is capable of improving material wellbeing.[59] Somewhere along the way, the insidious idea that the maximization of material wealth is the ultimate human attainment seems to have become a foundational principle in this debate.[60]

3. IS THERE A WAY FORWARD?

As with free trade, so too with development: the idea of maximization of economic benefit as the holy grail has had a long history in development thinking. The early decades of international development policy were dominated by the idea that development meant an increase in gross national product.[61] A cynic might suggest that either or both the impossibility or the undesirability of achieving economic parity for that part of the world said to be lacking development has meant that the predominance of economic development thinking has gradually given way to other discourses variously labelled as human development, popular development, reflexive development, alternative development and so on.[62] Important contributions in understanding what a development process that is not dominated by economic objectives might look like have been made by commentators such as Amartya Sen and Martha Nussbaum.[63] Their 'human capabilities' approach has been influential in the creation of the United Nations Development Programme Human Development Index.[64] But none of this, desirable or not,[65] can gain much traction in the divided system of international law. As this chapter has sought to argue, whatever might be happening in the United Nations instrumentalities, the real theatre of development is international economic law. And there 'the idea that there are alternative development paths, and that therefore different pasts underlie different presents and may lead to different futures'[66] has gained no traction, except in the sense that the future for the so-called developing world looks much bleaker than that of the future of the so-called developed world.

In the context of this debacle, strands of critical theory grouped under the rubric of post-development have (in the same sentence)[67] been praised for their 'acute intuitions' and criticized for 'being directionless in the end, as a consequence of the refusal to, or

---

[59] Hirschman, n 11 above, 112.
[60] Alessandrini, n 41 above, 60.
[61] Esteva, n 25 above; Alessandrini, n 17 above, 41–55.
[62] Esteva, n 25 above; Pieterse, n 1 above.
[63] See especially Amartya Sen, *Development as Freedom* (Oxford University Press 1999) and, e.g., Martha Nussbaum, 'Capabilities and Human Rights' (1997) 66 *Fordham Law Review* 273.
[64] http://hdr.undp.org/en/content/human-development-index-hdi, accessed 27 December 2017.
[65] For an insightful critique of Sen, see Selwyn, n 12 above, ch 7.
[66] Boaventura de Sousa Santos, 'Beyond Neoliberal Governance: The World Social Forum as Subaltern Cosmopolitan Politics and Legality' in Boaventura de Sousa Santos and César A. Rodriguez-Garavito (eds), *Law and Globalization from Below: Towards a Cosmopolitan Legality* (Cambridge University Press 2005), 31.
[67] Those strands represented by the work of Gustavo Esteva, Arturo Escobar and their followers.

lack of interest in translating critique into construction'.[68] This verdict views calls for 'the expansion and *articulation* of anti-imperialist, anti-capitalist, anti-productivist, anti-market struggles'[69] as too aspirational and perhaps somehow lacking substance.[70] But practice must be informed by theory, and construction by critique. The particular contribution of critical legal theory, as this chapter has sought to demonstrate, has been to understand how the history and architecture of the international law system has dictated the real terms of the development project. It is clear, however, that we urgently need a theoretical framework that can open up a path ahead. Hopefully, it goes without saying that a just path ahead requires the abandonment of the current divided system of international law and the decoupling of international law and global capitalism. At this point, given the size and complexity of the task, it is easy to sympathize with theorists who have found themselves in difficulty in coming up with a constructive basis for advancing the battle. Nevertheless, in a spirit of grounded optimism (after so much pessimism), this chapter concludes by advancing two critical approaches, not necessarily completely mutually exclusive, that may indicate a way forward for critical legal theory in the development context. One of them focuses on a recast and reinvigorated role for the state and the other looks at ways of harnessing the power of global labour in order to create a more just global order.

New developmentalism, which places the state at its strategic centre, is essentially neo-Keynesian.[71] This means that new developmental theorists do not reject the idea of the market nor its role in capitalist growth. The particular target of new developmentalism is the Washington Consensus and the neoliberal policies introduced in its wake. It has a primary concern with the question of how best to regulate the market 'in order to achieve virtuous cycles of capitalist growth … devoid of the labour repression, climate change, gender inequality and state bureaucratisation characteristic of the first developmentalism'.[72] The central tenets of new developmentalism, the state and the capitalist market, make it an easy target of critique. So far as its adoption of a virtuous capitalist market is concerned, the line of attack is fairly obvious and centres on (important) things like the role of capitalist markets in systematically oppressing workers and denying their rights,[73] and the neo-imperialist nature of capitalism which means that it is inherently productive of uneven and combined development.[74] This is married to a characterization of the state as being an inherently repressive apparatus resting on unacceptable 'historical social relations of class, gender and race'.[75] Marxist

---

[68] Pieterse, n 1 above, 361.
[69] Arturo Escobar, 'Reflections on "Development": Grass Roots Approaches and Alternative Politics in the Third World' [1992] *Futures* 411, 431.
[70] Pieterse, n 1 above, 362.
[71] See S.R. Kahn and J Christiansen (eds), *Towards New Developmentalism: Market as Means Rather Than Master* (Abingdon and New York: Routledge, 2011).
[72] Thomas Marois and Lucia Pradella, 'Polarising Development – Introducing Alternatives to Neoliberalism and the Crisis' in Lucia Pradella and Thomas Marois (eds), *Polarising Development: Alternatives to Neoliberalism and the Crisis* (Pluto 2015), 8.
[73] See, e.g., Benjamin Selwyn, 'The Political Economy of Development: Statism or Marxism?' in Pradella and Marois, ibid.
[74] See, e.g., Alfredo Saad Filho, 'The "Rise of the South"' in Pradella and Marois, ibid.
[75] Pradella and Marois, n 72 above, 8.

critique is rightly sceptical of the idealistic view of the state as the moderator, in the name of some concept of the overall good, of capitalist development based on national comparative advantage.[76] Nevertheless, for a critical legal theorist considering the possibility of an institutional model upon which to remake the international system, perhaps the jettisoning of the concept of the state is a step in the wrong direction.

Marxist theories of labour-led development offer it as both a form of resistance to the current form of capital-centred development and a new theoretical framework for alternative development.[77] It is evident, however, that despite their rejection of the capitalist state, this theoretical position does not jettison the concept of the state. Instead this vision is represented by 'the capturing, holding and transformation of state power'.[78] Selwyn, following Marx, speaks of 'the reabsorption of the state by society'[79] but this does not mean the abolition of the state. Rather what is envisaged is, to paraphrase Marx, a political form of labour's social emancipation. This is a concept of the state that is, therefore, liberated from the burden of its repressive history. Working within this concept, Selwyn offers a plan for labour-led democratic development as follows:[80] banking, money and economic democracy; the introduction of a universal basic income; ecologically sustainable industrial policy; agrarian reform in order to ensure de-commodified food security; the protection of Indigenous Peoples and their knowledge; a nonaggressive foreign policy, which has both 'political' aims (to establish links with other social movements and support equivalent transformations globally) and 'economic' aims (to combat environmental destruction, control foreign trade and investment and use collective capacities at the international level with respect to trade and investment rules and environmental and labour standards);[81] reduction and equalization work; the elimination of gender inequality, nationalism and racism; and de-commodified cultural production as a form of personal and collective development.

Certainly, the concept of the state embedded in this vision shares no ground with the neoliberal idea of the state as one member of a constellation of actors, including private sector actors. Here the state reassumes importance as the central actor and carrier of a just and democratic vision. As should be obvious, however, this eminently desirable vision cloaks an enormous project for critical legal theory. Not only does it present a particular challenge to constitutional theorists, but in the context of the current chapter it can only be realized by the demolition (progressive or otherwise) of the post-Second World War divided system of international law. (If Arrighi is right and we are now in the terminal stage of the US led cycle of capitalist accumulation, perhaps we are already on the right track here.) A critical legal theory programme for international

---

[76] Pradella and Marois, n 72 above, 8.
[77] See, e.g., Benjamin Selwyn, *The Struggle for Development* (Polity 2017), especially chs 5 and 6.
[78] Selwyn, n 77 above, 126.
[79] Selwyn, n 77 above, 130. Cf Karl Marx, *The Civil War in France* (first published 1871, Peking Foreign Languages Press 1966): 'the reabsorption of the state power by society as its own living forces instead of as forces controlling and subduing it, by the popular masses themselves, forming their own force instead of the organised force of their suppression – the political form of their social emancipation'.
[80] Selwyn, n 77 above, 137–51.
[81] I, of course, would have described all of this as political.

development must, in any case, aim to decouple development both from the postcolonial constraints of the international law system and from its entanglement with the process of capital accumulation. A good first step would be the recognition that every initiative of the United Nations system is doomed to failure as a result of the systemic preeminence of international economic law. A second one might be, as the theorists of labour-led development suggest, the recognition that the current system has left us all 'underdeveloped'.

SELECTED REFERENCES

Alessandrini, Donatella, *Developing Countries and the Multilateral Trade Regime: The Failure and Promise of the WTO's Development Mission* (Hart 2010)

Anghie, Antony, B.S. Chimni, Karin Mickelson and Obiora Okafor (eds), *The Third World and International Order: Law, Politics and Globalization* (Martinus Nijhoff 2003)

Arrighi, Giovanni, *The Long Twentieth Century: Money, Power & the Origins of Our Times* (Verso 2002), 275

Arrighi, Giovanni, Beverley J. Silver and Benjamin D. Brewer, 'Industrial Convergence, Globalization and the Persistence of the North-South Divide' (2003) 38 *Studies in Comparative Economic Development* 3

Dunkley, Graham, *The Free Trade Adventure: The WTO, the Uruguay Round & Globalism – A Critique* (Zed Books 2001)

Esteva, Gustavo, 'Development' in Wolfgang Sachs (ed.), *The Development Dictionary: A Guide to Knowledge as Power* (Zed Books 2009)

Faundez, Julio and Celine Tan (eds), *International Economic Law, Globalization and Developing Countries* (Edward Elgar 2010)

Linarelli, John, Margot Salomon and Muthucumaraswamy Sornarajah, *The Misery of International Law: Confrontations with Injustice in the Global Economy* (Oxford University Press 2018)

Pahuja, Sundhya, 'Technologies of Empire: IMF Conditionality and the Reinscription of the North/South Divide' (2000) 13 *Leiden Journal of International Law* 749

Peet, Richard, *Unholy Trinity: The IMF, World Bank and the WTO* (Zed Books 2003)

Pradella, Lucia and Thomas Marois (eds), *Polarising Development: Alternatives to Neoliberalism and the Crisis* (Pluto 2015)

Rajagopal, B., *International Law From Below: Development, Social Movements, and Third World Resistance* (Cambridge University Press 2003)

Selwyn, Benjamin, *The Global Development Crisis* (Polity 2014)

Selwyn, Benjamin, *The Struggle for Development* (Polity 2017)

Tan, Celine, *Governance through Development: Poverty Reduction Strategies, International Law and the Disciplining of Third World States* (Routledge 2011)

24. International economic law's wreckage: depoliticization, inequality, precarity
Nicolás M. Perrone and David Schneiderman

1. INTRODUCTION

International economic law (IEL) gives expression to the ruling ideas of our time.[1] International trade and investment law, which we assimilate under the label of IEL, promotes the movement of goods, services and capital across borders with few qualifications. Though given expression in differing legal orders, each with its own set of complex legal rules and mechanisms of enforcement, they are cognate systems of law having more than coincidental points of resemblance. They constitute part of what can be called the legal culture of capitalism,[2] having as one of its objects the depoliticization of markets, rendering inequality within and between states and regions more difficult to address.

As with other law, trade and investment rules – together with the personnel who interpret them – express preferences about how social life should be organized. While different interests struggle over the negotiation and interpretation of these rules, only some are invited to the table to participate. Most others are subject to those rules.[3] Moreover, only certain rules from certain locales are candidates for adoption in the global arena, typically those associated with property and contract articulated in the Global North. In the case of international trade and investment rules, these preferences determine where raw materials will be produced, where goods will be manufactured and how foreign investors will be treated abroad. In other words, these rules determine who will benefit, who will lose and, perhaps more importantly, who will adapt to whom so as to render the policy goals of trade and investment rules most efficacious. The result is a world of winners and losers.

We aim to scrutinize these novel systems of global legal order through the lens of critical international political economy. This is a mode of analysis that interrogates relations between dominant and subordinate forces in international spheres. These relations are also referred to, variously, as those between the centre and periphery or

---

[1] KARL MARX, THE GERMAN IDEOLOGY 64 (edited by C.J. Arthur) (1989) and Walter Benjamin, 'Thesis IV' in MICHAEL LÖWY, FIRE ALARM: READING WALTER BENJAMIN'S 'ON THE CONCEPT OF HISTORY' 37 (translated by Chris Turner) (2016).

[2] David Singh Grewal, *Book Review: The Laws of Capitalism*, 128 HARV. L. REV. 626 (2014).

[3] DAVID KENNEDY, A WORLD OF STRUGGLE: HOW POWER, LAW, AND EXPERTISE SHAPE GLOBAL POLITICAL ECONOMY (2016).

between the Global North and Global South. We use these pairings interchangeably, though these territorial binaries are breaking down as the economically privileged in the periphery move closer to the centre and as labour forces in the centre look more like those in the periphery.

What is emphasized is the contingent nature of global legal orders, questioning, thereby, their 'aura of naturalness and necessity'.[4] While there has been much talk of the irreversibility of the rules and institutions of global economic integration, recent developments in the UK and US suggest that they remain contested and vulnerable to changes of direction. The critical mode of political economy allows us to probe these global legal orders, then, not as 'divinely ordained' nor as the outcome of fortuitous 'blind chance', but as the product of distributive and normative choices made by those granted privileged access to determining their content.[5] 'Structures are not "givens"', advises Cox, but are 'made by collective human action and transformable by collective human action'.[6] No grand theoretical project is pursued; instead, the aim is to reveal the specificity of power, rendering its mechanisms more vulnerable to resistance and rollback.[7] If the pessimist appreciates that there are constraints on future action, the 'pessimist as critic', Cox observes, seeks out 'contradictions in the status quo that might become triggers of change'.[8]

The frame we adopt enables us to better comprehend the impact of IEL regimes upon the precarious – those not granted any solicitude by its edicts. Precarity is the legally induced condition in which certain populations suffer more than others from failing legal networks of support, thereby being differentially exposed to economic impacts.[9] We speak of the poor – the 'part of those who have no part', in Rancière's evocative terms.[10] Precariousness, Butler adds, 'implies living socially' but in a disadvantaged state due to 'the fact that one's life is always in some sense in the hands of the other'.[11]

---

[4] ROBERTO MANGABEIRA UNGER, FALSE NECESSITY – AN ANTI-NECESSITARIAN SOCIAL THEORY IN THE SERVICE OF RADICAL DEMOCRACY: POLITICS, A WORK IN CONSTRUCTIVE SOCIAL THEORY, PART I 58 (1987).

[5] SUSAN STRANGE, STATES AND MARKETS, 2ND ED. 18 (1994). Joost Pauwelyn makes a similar argument, that investment law is a 'spontaneous order emerging from decentralized interactions' in Joost Pauwelyn, *At the Edge of Chaos? Foreign Investment Law as a Complex Adaptive System, How it Emerged and How it Can Be Reformed* 29 ICSID REV 372, 375–6 (2014).

[6] ROBERT W. COX, PRODUCTION, POWER, AND WORLD ORDER: SOCIAL FORCES IN THE MAKING OF HISTORY 395 (1987).

[7] Michel Foucault, *Powers and Strategies* in MICHEL FOUCAULT, POWER/KNOWLEDGE: SELECTED INTERVIEWS AND OTHER WRITINGS, 1972–1977 134–45, 145 (Colin Gordon, ed., 1980).

[8] Robert W. Cox, *Reflections and Transitions* in ROBERT W. COX WITH MICHAEL G. SCHECHTER, THE POLITICAL ECONOMY OF A PLURAL WORLD: CRITICAL REFLECTIONS ON POWER, MORALS AND CIVILIZATION 26–43, 37 (2002).

[9] JUDITH BUTLER, NOTES TOWARD A PERFORMATIVE THEORY OF ASSEMBLY 33 (2015).

[10] JACQUES RANCIÈRE, DISAGREEMENT: POLITICS AND PHILOSOPHY 11 (Julie Rose, trans. 1999).

[11] JUDITH BUTLER, FRAMES OF WAR: WHEN IS LIFE GRIEVABLE? 14 (2010).

With the ascendance of the neoliberal era, states are expected to be immunized from an 'overload' of fiscal demands placed upon them by citizens and interest groups.[12] States are persuaded, instead, to open up markets, privatize public services and give up on redistributing wealth.[13] The orders of IEL have emerged as constituent elements in this endeavour, promoting the spread of private economic power while turning a blind eye to its harsh outcomes – what we label its 'wreckage'.[14] The plan of action, in short, has been to disarm states and to weaponize IEL.

Key to the success of its programme is a rationale that renders this form of voluntary subordination tolerable.[15] The project is aided by invoking a legal rationale particular to the logic of the legal culture of capitalism. It is the distinction between law and politics. Weber famously distinguished between formally rational law, which enabled markets to spread in the occident, and law that was tainted by substantive values, such as socialism or utilitarianism.[16] It is the emphasis that Weber placed on depoliticized law that provides important discursive support for promoting the regimes of IEL.

Our argument is that depoliticization makes it more difficult to ameliorate the conditions giving rise to precarity. While the orthodoxy in policy circles is that economic globalization generates a 'rising tide' that lifts all boats, what has transpired is both persistent inequality in national income between regions and a discernible increase of inequality within states.[17] In section 2 we address depoliticization claims: that states no longer have a legitimate role in managing trade and capital movements and that disagreement over their distributive and normative consequences is to be emptied of politics. The end game is to naturalize and thereby internalize the depoliticization narrative. In section 3, we turn to a discussion of inequality by focusing upon disparities of wealth and influence between and within states. Our aim in these two parts is to elucidate linkages between depoliticization and the maintenance and reproduction of precarity. In section 4, we take up some basic elements of the hyperspecialized regimes of trade and investment law. In the course of describing their main features, we trace a trajectory common to each: global legal orders exhibiting a structural tilt that favours mobile economic wealth, precipitating legitimacy crises and kindred responses that aim to manage the fallout. Attempts at recalibrating trade and investment rules, however, have not managed so well at minimizing their deleterious

---

[12] MICHEL J. CROZIER, SAMUEL P. HUNTINGTON & JOJI WATANUKI, THE CRISIS OF DEMOCRACY: REPORT ON THE GOVERNABILITY OF DEMOCRACIES TO THE TRILATERAL COMMISSION (1975).

[13] 'To get a grip on the problems of poverty, one should also forget the idea of overcoming inequality by distribution', wrote an advisor to President Reagan. See GEORGE GILDER, WEALTH AND POVERTY 67 (1981).

[14] 'Where a chain of events appear before us, he [the angel of history] sees one single catastrophe, which keeps piling wreckage upon wreckage and hurls it at its feet': in Walter Benjamin, 'Thesis IX' in LÖWY, supra note 1 at 62.

[15] MICHEL FOUCAULT, THE POLITICS OF TRUTH 47 (Lysa Hochroth & Catherine Porter, trans. 2007).

[16] MAX WEBER, ECONOMY AND SOCIETY: AN OUTLINE OF INTERPRETIVE SOCIOLOGY 657 (Gunther Roth & Claus Wittich eds, 2 volumes, 1978).

[17] FACUNDO ALVEREDO ET AL, WORLD INEQUALITY REPORT 2018 65 (2017), http://wir2018.wid.world/files/download/wir2018-full-report-english.pdf.

effects. We conclude that, so long as schemes like IEL do not take inequality seriously, trade and investment rules will remain vulnerable to political blowback.

2. DEPOLITICIZATION

Each of the regimes of trade and investment law commits states to behave in accordance with particular norms, anything beyond which is unacceptable and results in the imposition of penalties. These regimes produce not soft law but hard law, interpreted and applied by international institutions, with variable enforcement mechanisms, rendering these regimes a formidable limit on state capacity. These legal regimes serve to separate politics from markets, having the effect of removing a variety of options from domestic policy tables which we associate with the movement towards 'depoliticization'. By depoliticization, we refer to processes 'that remove or displace the potential for choice, collective agency, and deliberation around a particular political issue'.[18] Such laws preempt state action. Tactics of depoliticization distinguish between the promotion of rules that render markets calculable, predictable and certain (rational law) and those which are labelled arbitrary, namely, those which result in new or 'abnormal' policy orientations (irrational law). Measures to promote social justice cannot, under this scheme, but be characterized as irrational and arbitrary.[19]

Policing the separation between law and politics was not always the main priority of IEL. There were periods, particularly in the postwar era, when developed and developing states had more room to manoeuvre. They were permitted to take measures that economically powerful states themselves had adopted in the course of their own development. This is what Amsden labels the first American empire, when states experimented with policies such as import substitution directed at developing nascent industry.[20] In this era, nonreciprocal rules of trade and investment eschewed conventional assumptions about equal opportunities for growth in favour of a view of the global state system as economically unequal.[21] These rules were not only more flexible; the available flexibility also resulted in more just distributions. This is the period Ruggie refers to as the era of the 'embedded liberalism compromise', where 'multilateralism would be predicated upon domestic interventionism'.[22]

By the time of the second American empire, associated with the ascendance of privatization and deregulation promoted by international financial institutions such as

---

[18] Paul Fawcett, Matthew Flinders, Colin Hay & Matthew Wood, *Anti-Politics, Depoliticization, and Governance* in ANTI-POLITICS, DEPOLITICIZATION, AND GOVERNANCE 3, 5 (Paul Fawcett, Matthew Flinders, Colin Hay & Matthew Wood, eds 2017).

[19] WOLFGANG STREECK, BUYING TIME: THE DELAYED CRISIS OF DEMOCRATIC CAPITALISM 59 (2014).

[20] ALICE H. AMSDEN, ESCAPE FROM EMPIRE: THE DEVELOPING WORLD'S JOURNEY THROUGH HEAVEN AND HELL (2007).

[21] See United Nations Conference on Trade and Development [UNCTAD], Report of the Secretary General [Raúl Prebisch], *Toward a New Trade Policy for Development* in PROCEEDINGS OF UNCTAD (II) 1964 E/CONF.46/141, 18–19.

[22] John Gerald Ruggie, *International Regimes, Transactions, and Change: Embedded Liberalism in the Postwar Economic Order*, 36 INT'L ORG. 379, 393 (1982).

the IMF and World Bank, the developmental state was looked upon with disdain.[23] Because of the insatiable demands being made upon social welfare states, on which they were incapable of delivering, there emerged a crisis of 'ungovernability'.[24] The only proper response was to disable states from having the capacity of responding other than through market mechanisms. States were expected to open up domestic markets to overseas goods, services and capital. Nothing less would be tolerated. After the fall of the Soviet Union and the end of the Cold War, this pressure only intensified. The resolution of distributional conflicts, insofar as they touched upon trade and investment, was removed to 'organizational settings' hard to reconcile with democratic theory.[25] Instead, national democratic politics would turn their attention to other salient noneconomic issues.[26]

The resulting governing paradigm, where all that is tolerable is markets freed from the requirement to respond to the demands of local citizenry, emerged as hegemonic. Political contestation would be displaced by outcomes the market would have produced, facilitating the depoliticization of distributive effects. To this end, at the macropolitical level, World Bank General Counsel Ibrahim Shihata declared that the Bank would assist states in developing their own laws so 'long as it is based on considerations of economy and efficiency'.[27] World Bank experts insisted upon legal frameworks that promoted market fundamentals. Other countervailing considerations would be off domestic policy agendas.

Each of the legal frameworks of trade and investment exemplify this hegemonic discourse. The Uruguay Round of the General Agreements on Trade and Tariffs (GATT), resulting in the establishment of the World Trade Organization (WTO), released states from the need to rely upon 'power-oriented' approaches, instead favouring 'rule-oriented' ones.[28] Jackson described this as a move away from the 'state of nature' to one of 'civilization' – a return to civilized justice, one could say.[29] For Jackson, what was neutralized was the power of hegemonic states relying upon coercive military might. Likewise, Shihata famously proclaimed that, with the establishment of the International Convention on the Settlement of Investment Disputes (the

---

[23] AMSDEN, supra note 20.

[24] CROZIER, HUNTINGTON, WATANUKI, supra note 12 and Clause Offe, *Ungovernability* in FRAGILE STABILITÄT – STABILE FRAGILITÄT 77–87 (Stephan A. Jansen, Eckhard Schröter, and Nico Stehr, eds 2013).

[25] Claus Offe, *The Separation of Form and Content in Liberal Democracy* in CLAUS OFFE, CONTRADICTIONS OF THE WELFARE STATE 162, 167 (John Keane ed., 1984).

[26] Timothy Hellwig, *Globalization, Policy Constraints, and Vote Choice*, 70 THE JOURNAL OF POLITICS 1128 (2008).

[27] Ibrahim Shihata, *The World Bank and 'Governance' Issues in Its Borrowing Members* in IBRAHIM SHIHATA, THE WORLD BANK IN A CHANGING WORLD: SELECTED ESSAYS, VOL. 1 53–96, 86 (1991).

[28] JOHN H. JACKSON, THE WORLD TRADING SYSTEM: LAW AND POLICY OF INTERNATIONAL AND ECONOMIC RELATIONS 110–11 (2nd ed. 1997).

[29] See David Schneiderman, *The Global Regime of Investor Rights: A Return to the Standards of Civilized Justice?*, 5 TRANSNAT'L LEGAL THEORY 60 (2014) and BENJAMIN ALLEN COATES, LEGALIST EMPIRE: INTERNATIONAL LAW AND AMERICAN FOREIGN RELATIONS IN THE EARLY TWENTIETH CENTURY (2016).

ICSID Convention), the result would be the depoliticization of investment disputes.[30] General Counsel to the International Bank for Reconstruction and Development, Aaron Broches, similarly declared that ICSID would 'insulate [investment] disputes from the realm of politics and diplomacy'.[31] The ICSID approach to investment disputes consists in granting foreign investors the right to sue host states for damages before international arbitration tribunals. Such legal innovation remains at the core of what is known today as investor-state dispute settlement (ISDS).

It is unfortunate that international lawyers would have recourse to the artifice of depoliticization when it was far from the reality on the ground. What the WTO's and ICSID's founders meant to say is that the traditional means for resolving disputes in international law, namely via interstate diplomacy, would be abandoned in favour of new institutional intermediaries enforcing rules intended to neutralize disagreement over market fundamentals. Disputes would no longer be subject to the political bargaining of locally elected officials responding to the inputs of their enfranchised citizenry. There was also a semblance of irreversibility in this transfer of power from below to above. Rather than being responsive to the demands of local populaces, enforcement mechanisms would bind citizens to rules of global good governance, those worthy of the appellation 'universal'.

The aim was to naturalize depoliticization and its distributive outcomes in much the same way as has Ricardo's hypothesis of comparative advantage.[32] According to Ricardo's simple formulation, states, like labouring individuals, should be expected to specialize in what they do best, such as textile production in England and wine production in Portugal.[33] Ricardo's argument was that specialization works to the comparative advantage of each nation – to 'capitalists' and to 'consumers', which 'diffuses to the general benefit'.[34] It turns out that gains from trade do not 'diffuse' to everyone but benefit certain privileged interests.[35] Nor does the theory match up well with successful paths to economic development. The evidence suggests that countries with a capacity to diversify are more likely to succeed economically rather than immediately specializing in industries in which there is some perceived advantage. It is only when countries are more highly developed that the advantages of specialization accrue to states and citizens.[36]

---

[30] Ibrahim Shihata, *Toward Greater Depoliticization of Investment Disputes: The Roles of ICSID and MIGA*1 ICSID REV 1, 4 (1986).

[31] ICSID, CONVENTION ON THE SETTLEMENT OF INVESTMENT DISPUTES BETWEEN STATES AND NATIONALS OF OTHER STATES, DOCUMENTS CONCERNING THE ORIGIN AND FORMULATION OF THE CONVENTION, VOL. II, PART I 242 (1968) (per Broches, December 16, 1963).

[32] Mill described Ricardo's 'doctrine [as] now universally received by political economists' in JOHN STUART MILL, PRINCIPLES OF POLITICAL ECONOMY WITH SOME OF THEIR APPLICATIONS TO SOCIAL PHILOSOPHY 348, fn. (1911 [1848]).

[33] DAVID RICARDO, ON THE PRINCIPLES OF POLITICAL ECONOMY AND TAXATION 135 (Piero Saffra ed. 1951 [1817]).

[34] Id. at 136.

[35] Dani Rodrik, *The Great Globalisation Lie* PROSPECT MAGAZINE (January 2018), www.prospectmagazine.co.uk/magazine/the-great-globalisation-lie-economics-finance-trump-brexit.

[36] DANI RODRIK, ONE ECONOMICS, MANY RECIPES: GLOBALIZATION, INSTITUTIONS, AND ECONOMIC GROWTH 103 (2007).

Ricardo overlooked important factors too – for instance, that comparative advantage requires that each country accept the production methods and labour standards of the other even if in violation of social norms in the importing country.[37] He was also misled about capital mobility. He described the insecurity of capital ('fancied or real'), together with a 'natural disinclination to quit the country of his birth and connexions, and intrust himself with all his habits fixed, to a strange government and new laws', as having the effect of 'check[ing] the emigration of capital'.[38] Yet English capital was, at the time, seeking new markets for its increased output,[39] including controlling the production and trading of Portuguese wine.[40] Comparative advantage, nonetheless, is the central peg around which modern trade orthodoxy hangs.

Depoliticized law results in the naturalization of these and other policy choices, unleashing the political power of multinational firms. Economic power thereby translates into political power. The challenge for critical scholars of law is to identify how these choices are made and then normalized. International trade and investment lawyers prefer that we overlook this partiality, in favour of rules having abstract and universal forms. They appeal, for instance, to the seemingly unobjectionable principle of national treatment or nondiscrimination in the GATT. This means that every member of the WTO has the same abstract right to export and to import goods. The principle is one of formal equality and overlooks what states can export or import, or whether they can export or import anything at all. While the principles of nondiscrimination and gains from trade appear universally appealing, they cannot have universal effects on the ground.[41]

There are, admittedly, special rules in some areas for countries in the Global South (called 'special and differential treatment'). For the most part, however, the abstract principle of nondiscrimination disregards the legacy of past imposed or unfair choices. In practice, countries in the Global North focus on high-skilled activities while Global South countries dedicate themselves to low-skilled labour. The GATT members' tariff commitments also favour the production of raw materials in the Global South and manufacturing of those resources in the Global North. These outcomes are encouraged by tariffs that increase to the extent that value is added to imported products (known as tariff escalation). It is in the interests of more economically powerful states that the average Organization for Economic Cooperation and Development (OECD) country tariff on imports from developing countries is four times higher than that on imports

---

[37] DANI RODRIK, HAS GLOBALIZATION GONE TOO FAR? 34 (1997).
[38] RICARDO, supra note 33, at 136.
[39] SVEN BECKERT, EMPIRE OF COTTON: A GLOBAL HISTORY 47–51, 76 (Vintage 2015).
[40] L.M.E. SHAW, THE ANGLO-PORTUGUESE ALLIANCE AND THE ENGLISH MERCHANTS IN PORTUGAL 1654–1810 141–57 (2017).
[41] Particularly in light of the legacies of colonialism. According to Peer Vries, 'what occurred in the nineteenth century with Western industrialization and imperialism was *not* simply a changing of the guard. What emerged was a gap between rich and poor nations, powerful and powerless nations, that was *unprecedented* in world history' (emphasis in the original). PEER VRIES, ESCAPING POVERTY: THE ORIGINS OF MODERN ECONOMIC GROWTH 46 (2013).

from other OECD countries.[42] These tariffs operate as inducements for producing cocoa and coffee beans in the Global South and manufacturing chocolate and coffee in the Global North.[43]

Such inducements are given even clearer expression in international investment law. The field is premised on the idea that foreign investment is good for development and that mitigation of political risk is required to lure investors. Foreign investors therefore require special protections, such as national treatment, because, after mixing (in Lockean fashion)[44] their ownership advantages with local resources, they are at the mercy of host state political forces (the so-called obsolescing bargain).[45] Foreign capital turns out not to be so vulnerable, according to empirical analyses. Relying upon World Bank data that draws on the experience of companies operating in 80 countries during the period 1999–2000, Aisbett finds that foreign firms are 'no more or less influential' than domestic firms and that 'both foreign and domestic multinationals are significantly more influential' than other firms.[46] This is not to say that states do not behave badly, only that large data sets do not support the obsolescing hypothesis. Nor do signing treaties often result in development outcomes favourable to host states. In a 2014 survey of 301 senior executives in companies with more than US$1 billion in annual revenue, respondents indicated that the existence of BITs was of far less importance in making investment decisions than the character of host state laws.[47] A meta-analysis of the existing empirical evidence exploring the correlation between signing BITs and attracting foreign direction investment (FDI) indicates that their effects appear to be 'economically negligible'.[48]

We maintain that the rules and institutions of IEL are intended to discourage, if not outlaw, policy options lying outside the range of what is considered 'normal'. The object, 'first and foremost', writes Lang, is to discredit 'the idea that economic governance ought to involve the mobilization and pursuit of collective goals and

---

[42] JOSEPH E. STIGLITZ & ANDREW CHARLTON, FAIR TRADE FOR ALL: HOW TRADE CAN PROMOTE DEVELOPMENT 47 (2005).

[43] See Nasredin Elamin & Hansdeep Khaira, *Tariff Escalation in Agricultural Commodity Markets* FAO COMMODITY MARKET REVIEW 101 (2003–4).

[44] For a critical discussion of the influence of Lockean theories of property in foreign investor rights, see Nicolás M. Perrone, *The Emerging Global Right to Investment: Understanding the Reasoning behind Foreign Investor Rights* 8 JOURNAL OF INTERNATIONAL DISPUTE SETTLEMENT 673 (2017).

[45] RAYMOND VERNON, SOVEREIGNTY AT BAY: THE MULTINATIONAL SPREAD OF U.S. ENTERPRISES 47 (1971).

[46] Emma Aisbett, *Powerful Multinational or Persecuted Foreigners: 'Foreignness' and Influence over Government*, Australian National University (Centre for Economic Policy Research Discussion Paper No 638 19, April 2010).

[47] Hogan Lovells et al, *Risk and Return: Foreign Direct Investment and the Rule of Law* (2015) 41, http://f.datasrvr.com/fr1/415/10099/10071_D4_FDI_Main_Report_V4.pdf. The survey results also indicated that the existence of a BIT affected investment decisions, which is hard to square with the fact that 'answers to other questions showed that they had indeed made investment in ... regions ... [where] no BITs were present' (id at 47).

[48] Christian Bellak, *Economic Impact of Investment Agreements*, Department of Economics, Vienna University of Economics and Business (Working Paper No 200, 19, 2015), https://epub.wu.ac.at/4625/1/wp200.pdf.

values'. The rise of imperial bureaucracies gives way to control by 'formal-technical governance, working through general legal principles, interpreted and applied in concert with technical knowledge', he writes.[49] All of this is aimed at dampening social and political imaginaries. The object is to internalize depoliticization. Politics is to be conducted not on the premise that 'here the people rule' but instead on the premise that 'we are open for business'. It signals not just governance without the people, but government without politics.[50]

It might be assumed that the object of IEL regimes is to constrain policy options to only those that metropolitan economic actors will tolerate. This suggests that not all programmes for egalitarian redistribution will be ruled out of order,[51] but rather only those that are deemed unacceptable to actors operating at the centre of the world trading and investment system. Something more, however, is expected from states in the periphery. They are not permitted to initiate policies that these states used 'to get where they are now'.[52] It becomes a matter, as Chang puts it, of 'kicking away the ladder' that home state governments climbed in order to secure their own economic success.[53] Even then, mostly similar policy initiatives will be more closely scrutinized if issued from states in the periphery rather than those in the core. Financial markets, for instance, are more sensitive and respond to a wider range of indicators in developing countries than is the case with developed countries. This disparity of treatment grants the latter states 'wider latitude to pursue a variety of policy objectives'.[54] The trick is to have the institutions of IEL apply rules in ways that do not precipitate a backlash within the powerful states that define the content of those rules.

Yet there remains an instability generated by the law's distributive functions, even within the 'civilized' states of the OECD. Legal strategies, it turns out, are not so successful in separating legitimate from illegitimate policy options. Of necessity, room for discretion must be built into these instruments that allows for the determination of what is in the common good. In most developed states property, for instance, is heavily regulated even though property rights might be entrenched constitutionally.[55] For this reason, exercises of policy discretion will remain deeply contested. Political disagreement will inevitably arise as these conflicts are played out on the transnational stage. Labelling the rules and processes of IEL 'depoliticized' misses this point entirely.

---

[49] ANDREW LANG, WORLD TRADE LAW AFTER NEOLIBERALISM: RE-IMAGINING THE GLOBAL ECONOMIC ORDER 7 (2011).

[50] JACQUES RANCIÈRE, HATRED OF DEMOCRACY 80 (Steve Corcoran, trans. 2006).

[51] E.g. Samuel Bowles, *Egalitarian Redistribution in Globally Integrated Economies* in GLOBALIZATION AND EGALITARIAN REDISTRIBUTION 120–47 (Pranab Bardhan, Samuel Bowles & Michael Wallerstein, eds 2006).

[52] HA-JOON CHANG, KICKING AWAY THE LADDER: DEVELOPMENT STRATEGY IN HISTORICAL PERSPECTIVE 127 (2002).

[53] Id.

[54] Layna Mosley, *Constraints, Opportunities, and Information: Financial Market-Government Relations around the World* in GLOBALIZATION AND EGALITARIAN REDISTRIBUTION, supra note 51, at 87, 96–7.

[55] LAURA UNDERKUFFLER, THE IDEA OF PROPERTY: ITS MEANING AND POWER (2003).

3. INEQUALITY

The economic and legal terrain has changed since Ricardo's time. Yet the gains from trade and investment, even when premised upon the equality of states, continue to cause social suffering. According to Pascal Lamy, former Director General of the WTO, trade 'works because it is painful ... [b]ut the pain is more poignant for the weak'. 'Appropriate policies', he acknowledges, 'are thus needed for social justice'.[56] The mechanics of free trade and investment provide cheaper and better products but only after allocating pain in notably unequal amounts. The preferences we formalize in trade and investment treaties generate precarity and contribute to inequality of wealth by creating 'losers' who are expected to catch up, often on their own, with global economic patterns.[57] The North American Free Trade Agreement (NAFTA), for instance, was a choice in favour of shifting manufacturing from the United States and Canada to Mexico. As Baldwin explains, this choice brought about a nearly unbeatable combination of US technology and cheap Mexican labour. The notable losers were the labour forces of the United States and Canada. These workers required either retraining, where available, or relying upon subsistence benefits at poverty levels.[58] What occurred can be described as the 'peripheralization of the labour force' at the core of the global economy.[59]

Similar outcomes can be seen in other places with comprehensive free trade agreements (FTAs) that include investment chapters. These agreements promote the offshoring of production to locales where labour is cheaper. Many proponents purport to take a global view and describe the loss of jobs as a tradeoff for more jobs and better salaries in the Global South.[60] But the evidence to date is not as convincing as proponents might think. It is true that overall inequality between states has declined, principally because of economic growth in China and, to a lesser extent, in India.[61] Nevertheless, inequality within most states, even within developed ones, has increased dramatically and shows no signs of easing off.[62] For many populations suffering as a consequence of these processes, the problem appears to be that the pain inflicted by these new circumstances appears to have no end in sight.

---

[56] Pascal Lamy, *Looking Ahead: The New World of Trade – Jan Tumlir Lecture* (ECIPE, Brussels, 9 March 2015) 2, https://pascallamyeu.files.wordpress.com/2017/03/2015-03-09-ecipe-brussels-speech-pascal-lamy-final.pdf.

[57] MICHAEL J. TREBILCOCK, DEALING WITH LOSERS: THE POLITICAL ECONOMY OF POLICY TRANSITIONS (2014).

[58] RICHARD BALDWIN, THE GREAT CONVERGENCE: INFORMATION TECHNOLOGY AND THE NEW GLOBALIZATION 237, 227 (2016). See also IMF, FISCAL MONITOR: TACKLING INEQUALITY (2017), www.imf.org/en/Publications/FM/Issues/2017/10/05/fiscal-monitor-october-2017

[59] Cox, supra note 6, at 324.

[60] BALDWIN, supra note 58, at 105–8. In 2000, Krugman made a similar argument in Paul Krugman, RECKONINGS; ONCE AND AGAIN, NEW YORK TIMES (January 2, 2000).

[61] BRANKO MILANOVIC, GLOBAL INEQUALITY: A NEW APPROACH FOR THE AGE OF GLOBALIZATION 122 (2016).

[62] THOMAS PIKETTY, CAPITAL IN THE TWENTY-FIRST CENTURY (2014); WORLD BANK GROUP, POVERTY AND SHARED PROSPERITY 2016: TAKING ON INEQUALITY (2016) and ALVEREDO ET AL, supra note 17, at 44.

The premise that states and peoples need to continuously adjust to global markets makes sense to most economists, who focus on economic growth and tradeoffs.[63] They purport to do value free empirical work with little or no appreciation of social costs, however. The problem, Rodrik observes, 'is that mainstream economics shades too easily into ideology, constraining the choices that we appear to have and providing cookie-cutter solutions'.[64] It is imperative, therefore, that legal scholars remain attentive to the role of law and the legal profession in contributing to the spreading tentacles of inequality. If the economics profession appears less concerned with the distributive consequences of legal rules, the same should not be said of lawyers, who like to speak in the language of 'fairness' and 'justice'.

Yet it seems as if lawyers are shying away from the debate on inequality. This is not good news for the precarious. Those economists who take inequality seriously conclude that politics, law and institutions are determinative in either exacerbating or easing inequality. Piketty notes that '[w]henever one speaks about the distribution of wealth, politics is never very far behind'.[65] Similarly, Milanovic reminds us that '[m]ost political battles are fought over the distribution of income'.[66] Rather than removing distributive questions from law and politics, they remain perpetually at the heart of contemporary social struggles. These struggles take place in the context of an economic and technological environment that has dramatically changed in the past few decades. This does not alter the political nature of distributional struggles, however. New technologies create economic gains and actors struggle to exclude others from these gains.

The social and political preferences that shape global distribution are the consequence of these battles. So as to rearrange these preferences, it is important to reconsider our approach to IEL. For one thing, this requires understanding each rule and its interpretation as a move in a broader terrain where different actors struggle for economic gain and control over the content of rules that govern their distribution. For another, the struggle is dynamic: each battle occurs in the shadow of previous victories and defeats. 'Over time', writes Kennedy, 'victories and defeats on the terrain of law add up, reproducing patterns of empowerment and disempowerment'.[67] These previous outcomes are distributive in material and in political terms. The final prizes are not merely economic gains but possibilities for politics.

As for the content of these depoliticized rules, as we suggest above, their substance is largely determined by those having the power and prestige to be invited to the table to participate in defining the rules of the game. This is a much smaller club than is usually acknowledged and contributes to an inequality of influence. It is 'global' only to the extent that the strategic sites for global calculation are mostly accessible to privileged actors within regions and states of the Global North. It is the law of those

---

[63] Milton Friedman, *Value Judgments in Economics* HUMAN VALUES AND ECONOMIC POLICY 85, 86 (Sidney Hook, ed. 1967).
[64] Dani Rodrik, *Rescuing Economics from Neoliberalism* BOSTON REVIEW (2017), http://bostonreview.net/class-inequality/dani-rodrik-rescuing-economics-neoliberalism.
[65] PIKETTY, supra note 62, at 10.
[66] MILANOVIC, supra note 61, at 86.
[67] KENNEDY, supra note 3, at 61.

states that gets taken up and represented as 'universal' standards that make up international law. These actors present their positions in the form of expert knowledge, namely, abstract, universal and depoliticized knowledge. This manoeuvre reflects an inequality in power/knowledge – an inequality in producing the regimes of truth that are considered reliable and trustworthy.[68] For this reason, states and their representatives are not disinterested in the outcome of the competition over who gets to name the content of the universal.[69] They have an interest in labelling the law of their rival competitors as 'local', giving expression only to parochial preferences, in contrast to those values labelled universal and representing global rules for good governance.[70] The local and the partial are relegated to 'social forms of non-existence', observes Santos, 'because the realities to which they give shape are present only as obstacles vis-à-vis the realities deemed relevant'.[71] By parading legal particulars as universal standards, international economic regimes not only serve particular local interests, but also perpetuate the inequality accorded to those denied the ability to make a contribution.

States are thereby restructured. If, as Polanyi explains, states are fundamental to the success of markets,[72] then the realignment of states generated by neoliberal legality produces a more narrowly cast agenda that can create conflict between international commitments and domestic political ones.[73] Gradually, however, the realignment of states serves precisely to control this conflict and occlude alternative choices. As Sassen explains, the increasing relevance of trade and investment disciplines has changed the organization of authority within states. It is not that states are not sovereign anymore but that this sovereignty is now organized differently.[74] 'Global capital has made claims on national states', she writes, 'which have responded through the production of new forms of legality'.[75] As competition for trade and capital grows, states 'shed some powers, but take [] on others'.[76] Trade ministries now rule the roost as they surveil other ministries, ensuring they do not act in violation of international

---

[68] Michel Foucault, TWO LECTURES in *Two Lectures* in FOUCAULT, POWER KNOWLEDGE, supra note 7, at 72, 93; Michel Foucault, ENTRETIEN AVEC MICHEL FOUCAULT in *Entretien avec Michel Foucault* in MICHEL FOUCAULT, DITS ET ÉCRITS II, 1976–1988 140, 158 (2001) and PAUL VEYNE, FOUCAULT: HIS THOUGHT, HIS CHARACTER 32 (Janet Lloyd, trans. 2010).

[69] TIM BÜTHE AND WALTER MATTLI, THE NEW GLOBAL RULERS: THE PRIVATIZATION OF REGULATION IN THE WORLD ECONOMY 12 (2011) and PIERRE BOURDIEU, PASCALIAN MEDITATIONS 65 (Richard Nice, trans. 2000).

[70] Boaventura de Sousa Santos, *Globalizations*, 23 THEORY, CULTURE & SOCIETY 393, 396 (2006).

[71] BOAVENTURA DE SOUSA SANTOS, THE RISE OF THE GLOBAL LEFT: THE WORLD SOCIAL FORM AND BEYOND 18 (2006).

[72] KARL POLANYI, THE GREAT TRANSFORMATION: THE POLITICAL AND ECONOMIC ORIGINS OF OUR TIME (Beacon Press 2001 [1957]).

[73] Cox, supra note 6, 221.

[74] Saskia Sassen, *The State and the Global Economy*, 6 THE JOURNAL OF THE INTERNATIONAL INSTITUTE 1 (1999).

[75] SASKIA SASSEN, LOSING CONTROL? SOVEREIGNTY IN AN AGE OF GLOBALIZATION 25 (1996).

[76] JOHN M. STOPFORD & SUSAN STRANGE WITH JOHN S. HENLEY, RIVAL STATES, RIVAL FIRMS: COMPETITION FOR WORLD MARKET SHARES 56 (1991).

trade and investment commitments. These changes reciprocally influence both internal and external relations. Trade and investment facilitation initiatives are a good example of this. The rules on facilitation aim to improve business climate and facilitate trade. Designated state agencies consequently bend over backwards to attract new economic activity by adopting what are considered best practices.[77] The rest of the population is expected to fend for itself as it faces similar, if not higher, barriers to accessing benefits, medical treatment or pensions. Though premised on the idea of level playing fields, the terrain of economic globalization is tilted, privileging those who already have an advantage.

This can be observed in the fields of trade and investment, which prompt a process of export and FDI-led restructuring of states. When it is determined that each country should focus on those goods and services that it produces efficiently, exporters gain a vital advantage over other domestic actors, contributing to inequality within states. Once a country signs a trade agreement, exporters have an incentive to invest and hire labour. Exporting sectors grow beyond the needs of the domestic market in their desire to supply global markets. This creates an inherent tension. As countries become more dependent on their exporting sectors, these sectors increasingly operate according to international determinants of prices and incentives. For the losers, the opposite is the case: they lose political influence. On occasion, the cost is higher than the closure of local businesses. In the case of food, cheap imports come at the cost of not only jobs but also food security.

As a result of admitting rice and corn imports under the WTO's Agreement on Agriculture, not only did rice production in the Philippines substantially decline, but corn production was 'wiped out'.[78] The dairy and edible oil sectors in India have been destroyed and replaced by a flood of cheap imports and substitutes.[79] High commodity prices result in a shift towards largescale export-oriented agriculture and ensuing domestic food shortages. The Agreement on Agriculture, after all, was structured by Northern states and works mostly to privilege Northern interests.[80] After unregulated trade triggered a food crisis in 2008, states began to rethink priorities, choosing food security and local production over access to global markets. This has led to a renewed focus on the agricultural trade agenda and the ability to raise limits on stockpiled food for security purposes as an aspect of special and differential treatment. An interim agreement was reached in 2013, permitting stockpiled increases above previously

---

[77] United Nations Conference on Trade and Development, *National Trade Facilitation Committees: Beyond Compliance with the WTO Trade Facilitation Agreement?* (2017), http://unctad.org/en/PublicationsLibrary/dtltlb2017d3_en.pdf.

[78] WALDEN BELLO, THE FOOD WARS 61 (2009).

[79] VANDANA SHIVA, YOKED TO DEATH: GLOBALISATION AND CORPORATE CONTROL OF AGRICULTURE 39 (2001).

[80] MATTHEW EAGLETON-PIERCE, SYMBOLIC POWER IN THE WORLD TRADE ORGANIZATION 130 (2013).

allotted amounts.[81] Because of its 'trade distorting' effects, however, these measures have not been made permanent due to US opposition.[82]

Large foreign investors enjoy similar advantages on this uneven playing field. States are expected to rely upon foreign investment in order to exploit natural resources and generate jobs. The rules that favour foreign over domestic investment, given expression in bilateral investment treaties, contribute to the creation of an overreliance on foreign investment. Discussing the importance of global value chains (GVCs) to improving development outcomes, the United Nations Conference on Trade and Development (UNCTAD) insists that many states 'may not have a choice'[83] other than to make efforts to join these GVCs and climb the value ladder. Attracting foreign investment and increasing exports, UNCTAD maintains, are both important to achieving macroeconomic stability and internal peace. But these objectives can come at the cost of land grabbing, overexploitation of natural resources ('neoextractivism') and precarious work. These policies may appear to be voluntarily embraced by states, but are in fact only 'choices' made under the constraints imposed by prior victories and defeats on the trade and investment terrain.[84]

The interplay between inequality and depoliticization is both material and epistemological. The result is predictability and flexibility for some and precarity for others. Actors struggle over the gains of trade and investment in ways that reinforce the narrative of depoliticization. As we discuss below, taking measures that speak in overtly political terms increases the odds of losing trade and investment disputes. Social and political preferences have more chances when they are planned, described and implemented in a seemingly depoliticized, expert manner that mimics the behaviour of private economic actors. We have also argued that previous victories and defeats constitute a terrain that occludes other social and political imaginaries. Certain arguments, certain ways of thinking, are forbidden. For the precarious, the regimes of IEL place them firmly at the margins.

4. RULES

The rules and institutions of IEL are productive in a number of different ways. First, they govern the world of legal possibilities – they aim to narrow the spectrum of policy

---

[81] World Trade Organization, *Public Stockholding for Food Security Purposes* (Ministerial Decision of 7 December 2013), www.wto.org/english/thewto_e/minist_e/mc9_e/desci38_e.htm.

[82] Indian Express, WHAT IS THE FOOD STOCKPILING ISSUE AT THE WTO? (December 13, 2017), http://indianexpress.com/article/what-is/what-is-the-food-stockpiling-issue-at-the-wto-4980749/. Also Michael Fakhri, *A History of Food Security and Agriculture In International Trade Law, 1945–2015* in INTERNATIONAL ECONOMIC LAW: NEW VOICES, NEW PERSPECTIVES (Akbar Rasulov & John Haskell eds 2019).

[83] UNITED NATIONS CONFERENCE ON TRADE AND DEVELOPMENT, WORLD INVESTMENT REPORT 2013: GLOBAL VALUE CHAINS: INVESTMENT AND TRADE FOR DEVELOPMENT xi, xxiv (2013).

[84] Some of these constraints and their implications are discussed in more detail in Nicolás M. Perrone, *UNCTAD's World Investment Reports 1991–2015: 25 Years of Narratives Justifying and Balancing Foreign Investor Rights,* 19 JOURNAL OF WORLD INVESTMENT & TRADE 1 (2018).

options to those deemed to fall within the range of the normal and acceptable. Second, they have distributive consequences that favour some interests over others. If we understand legal regimes of IEL as exhibiting a 'strategic selectivity',[85] they enhance the conditions of those privileged by its distributive tilt while rendering precarious those outside the ambit of its concern. In Butler's account, they 'maximize precariousness for some and minimize precariousness for others'.[86] Following from this last feature, the legal regimes of IEL produce the conditions giving rise to the regime's own legitimacy problems, even crises. In this section, we trace the outlines of two cognate regimes of IEL in order to disclose their structural tilt, the ensuing legitimacy crises and the responses of legal agents seeking to manage the fallout. In the course of doing so, we hope to show how policy choices are significantly constrained in order to favour mobile economic wealth. In Bentham's apt phrasing, there are state policy options that remain on the agenda while others are nonagenda items – these are options that continue to be treated as beyond the pale.[87]

A critical international political economy approach suggests that the constraints produced by these two regimes are not strictly technical, nor unavoidable. Rather, they are contingent and perpetually political. Their objectives are enhanced by allied governance institutions and dispute settlement bodies. They include global governance institutions dedicated to producing qualitative and quantitative indicators that contribute to state compliance with the rules of IEL.[88] Among them, the WTO regularly reviews the trade policies of its member states through its Trade Policy Review Mechanism. The OECD and UNCTAD assess the investment policies of selected countries. The World Bank has popularized the use of quantitative indicators via its Investing across Borders and Doing Business initiatives. Not only international organizations but also private institutions generate vital data about state behaviour. Credit rating agencies, for instance, ascertain sovereign credit risk and the likelihood that states will default on their debt. These agencies are also more interested in scrutinizing the behaviour of developing states than developed ones.[89] Overall, these public and private institutions set the table for the regimes of IEL. Few states can be indifferent to the information they produce as that data purports to shape trade and investment flows.

Despite increasing interest in indicators and governance, most scholarship has focused on the rules and institutions of IEL, undertaking detailed examination of the decisions of trade and investment dispute panels. These are worthwhile endeavours, as these details do matter. While we discuss selected cases below, we are not preoccupied with parsing their finer points. As Koskenniemi reminds us, the problem is not with the

---

[85] Bob Jessop's term in BOB JESSOP, STATE THEORY: PUTTING CAPITALIST STATES IN THEIR PLACE 260 (1990).

[86] BUTLER, FRAMES OF WAR supra note 11, at 2–3. Also Isabell Lorey, STATE OF INSECURITY: GOVERNMENT OF THE PRECARIOUS 20–1 (Aileen Derieg, trans. 2015).

[87] JEREMY BENTHAM, WORKS, Vol. III 41–2 (John Bowring ed. 1843).

[88] See, for instance, Kerry Rittich, *Governing by Measuring: The Millennium Development Goals in Global Governance* in SELECT PROCEEDINGS OF THE ESIL, Vol. 2, 463 (2008) and KEVIN DAVIS, ANGELINA FISHER, BENEDICT KINGSBURY & SALLY ENGLE MERRY (EDS), GOVERNANCE BY INDICATORS: GLOBAL POWER THROUGH CLASSIFICATION AND RANKINGS (2012).

[89] Mosley, supra 54 at 96–7.

cases but with the system.[90] For this reason, we undertake this analysis not for the purpose of bringing legitimacy to the regimes of IEL but in order to situate them in the larger project of repoliticizing IEL, thereby rendering its distributive consequences more vulnerable to contestation.

In undertaking these detailed analyses of the jurisprudence, mainstream scholars typically focus on IEL interactions with other systems, typically having to do with the environment, health or human rights (the so-called linkages debate). The research question often asked is whether regulatory chill or policy shifts result from either cognizance of the rules or from pending or resolved disputes. While we discuss the problem of the 'right to regulate' below, we are of the view that a focus on linkages misses the point. Framing the current debate in IEL through a sovereign right to regulate elides the fundamental question of what sort of regulatory imagination remains possible under regimes fashioned by a dominant political frame that aspires to unfettered economic freedom.

In contrast to rules intended to facilitate equality and social justice – those that better attend to the needs of the precarious – the rules and institutions of IEL are designed to remove barriers to international trade and investment flows. These forms of legality turn out not to give rise to many concerns on the part of most IEL scholars. Such legal innovations are rarely characterized as amounting to regulatory interventions in markets, despite the fact that they constitute regulatory givings (in contrast to regulatory takings) that facilitate business activities.[91] Most trade and investment literature worries instead about states' ability to curb negative externalities, address market failures and defend normative preferences embedded in local standards. The degree to which these run up against the systemic logic of IEL is the main preoccupation of scholars and dispute settlement bodies.

On the other hand, the terms of this debate have remained quite irresponsive to the demand for measures to protect the precarious – those harmed by global economic expansion, western imperialism or colonialism.[92] Such measures might be aimed at protecting indigenous lands or campesino property rights, or redistributing wealth to those who are disadvantaged by the regime's binding strictures. Similarly, the linkages and right to regulate debates have overlooked the possibility of opening up the policy toolkit of less wealthy states to catch up with the richer nations, to restore the ladder of development, so to speak. The discussion of WTO flexibility to promote new (or old) development policies is relegated to a marginal place in most trade law textbooks, which only briefly discuss measures that allow for special and differential treatment.[93] The general contours of the right to regulate, which overlook these other regulatory possibilities, are symptomatic of the significant role that IEL plays in normalizing rules that favour historic winners over historic losers, both between and within states. In

---

[90] Martti Koskenniemi, *It's Not the Cases, It's the System* 18 JOURNAL OF WORLD INVESTMENT & TRADE 343 (2017).

[91] See Abraham Bell & Gideon Parchomovsky, *Givings*, 111 YALE L.J. 547 (2001).

[92] Anghie has noted that international law has remained irresponsive to demands to compensate the injustices committed during formal colonial rule. See ANTHONY ANGHIE, IMPERIALISM, SOVEREIGNTY AND THE MAKING OF INTERNATIONAL LAW 2, 313 (2007).

[93] E.g. the popular text PETER VAN DEN BOSSCHE & WERNER ZDOUC, THE LAW AND POLICY OF THE WORLD TRADE ORGANIZATION (4th ed. 2017).

order to fill out the contours of IEL regimes, we turn next to a discussion of the content of two of its principal legal orders, those of trade and investment. Given the breadth of the subjects that could be covered, the discussion is meant only to be illustrative.

4.1 World Trade Law

Prior to the establishment of the WTO, trading rules under the GATT were enforced through interstate diplomacy. With the finalization of the Uruguay Round GATT in 1995, a new dispute settlement mechanism was initiated based on the 'rule of law' and lawyers. It consists of an initial panel to investigate and report on disputes and an Appellate Body to hear appeals against panel reports. Crucially, under the rule of negative consensus, WTO members must accept these decisions unless there is a consensus against.

At the height of the 'roaring nineties', outcomes in trade disputes were unabashedly about the primacy of markets over politics. The first dispute panel and Appellate Body reports emphasized the priority of eliminating market distortions, relying on the marketplace as the benchmark to decide vital legal questions. This is best illustrated by turning to interpretations of national treatment (the principle of nondiscrimination) and, in particular, the interpretation of 'likeness'.[94] Trading rules are organized around the idea of nondiscrimination and the prohibition of protectionism. Disputes resolved during the 1980s and 1990s, however, shifted the emphasis from curbing protectionism to upholding the requisite 'predictability needed to plan future trade'[95] and protecting the 'expectations of competitive opportunities'.[96] No matter the meritorious purposes motivating any given policy, if it resulted in discriminatory effects, it would run afoul of GATT Article I and III. What was of interest to dispute settlement bodies was whether a measure impeded competition from 'like' products – a determination that was to be made with reference almost exclusively to market factors. Another, more deferential line of authority associated with 'aims and effects' briefly made an appearance in this period. This mode of inquiry evaluates the measure in light of the policy's aims and effects. These decisions looked to the public purpose sought to be achieved as a crucial factor in assessing the measure's discriminatory effects.[97]

The dominant mode of interpretation, which favoured the rights of traders over other public policy rationales, precipitated a backlash in the late 1990s and early 2000s, exemplified by street protests at the 1999 WTO ministerial meetings in Seattle. By way

---

[94] E.g. GATT Article III, paragraphs 2 and 4, where the comparison is to 'like domestic products'.

[95] Panel Report, *United States – Taxes on Petroleum and Certain Imported Substances*, BISD 34S/136, adopted on 17 June 1987, para. 5.2.2.

[96] Panel Report, *Korea – Taxes on Alcoholic Beverages*, WT/DS75/R and WT/DS84/R, adopted 17 February 1999, para. 10.92.

[97] This second approach was accepted in two disputes against the United States, and in favour of this country, but was rejected by the WTO in Appellate Body Report, *Japan – Taxes on Alcoholic Beverages*, WT/DS8/AB/R, WT/DS10/AB/R, WT/DS11/AB/R, adopted 1 November 1996. See Panel Report, *United States – Taxes on Automobiles*, DS31/R, 11, unadopted, 11 October 1994; Panel Report, *United States – Measures Affecting Alcoholic and Malt Beverages*, DS23/R, adopted 19 June 1999.

of response, the WTO Appellate Body in 2001 suggested, in passing, that nonmarket factors could be significant in determining issues of 'likeness'.[98] This was developed in subsequent reports, where both Panels and the Appellate Body focused on whether the effects of a measure were the result of legitimate policy goals or, instead, were disguised restrictions on trade based on a product's foreign origins.[99] Mere market distortion was now insufficient to engage WTO rules on national treatment. What was now required was a determination that there was discrimination based on product origins. If, by so doing, the WTO Appellate Body appeared to be relaxing scrutiny of restrictions on trade, it did little to disturb the logic of the system of global trading rules. States were expected to open their borders to traders. Some policy aims would be tolerated – many would not. All would be subject to the oversight of trade lawyers.

A second response prompted by the legitimacy crisis that accompanied the rise of the WTO focused on the general exceptions clause in Article XX. This clause allows WTO members to discriminate against like products, enabling the breach of GATT Articles I and III if 'necessary' to achieve a closed list of nontrade goals, such as the protection of public morals or the protection of human, animal or plant life or health. Not included among general exceptions are those measures that might be characterized as advancing social justice – measures, for example, that are designed to enhance local employment opportunities or further the goal of economic redistribution. If the general exceptions clause was meant to tilt the inquiry in favour of public interest measures that deviate from trade strictures, the necessity test gave rise to the strictest of scrutiny. WTO institutions interpreted the clause as requiring that states adopt the least trade restrictive alternative. After all, as we have learned from similar inquiries undertaken by apex courts, it is quite easy for judges to imagine less restrictive alternatives. This precipitated all sorts of second guessing, even rejecting the advice of the World Health Organization on best practices to reduce cigarette smoking.[100]

Recognizing that strict scrutiny would not relieve the WTO of lingering legitimacy concerns, more recent Appellate Body reports have relaxed the requirement of necessity. In *Korea – Beef*, the Appellate Body crafted a balancing test similar to a three step proportionality inquiry.[101] In later cases, the Appellate Body even abandoned the last, overall balancing step of proportionality. In *EC – Asbestos*, the Appellate Body

---

[98] Appellate Body Report, *European Communities – Measures Affecting Asbestos and Asbestos-Containing Products*, WT/DS135/AB/R, adopted 5 April 2001, para. 100 [hereinafter Appellate Body Report, *European Communities – Asbestos*].

[99] Appellate Body Report, *Dominican Republic – Measures Affecting the Importation and Internal Sale of Cigarettes*, WT/DS302/AB/R, adopted 19 May 2005, para. 96; Panel report, *European Communities—Measures Affecting the Approval and Marketing of Biotech Products*, WT/DS291-3/R, para. 7.2499-&.2517. This was an interpretation of the GATT functionally equivalent to the aims and effects test, observes LANG, supra note 48, at 318.

[100] Panel Report, *Thailand – Restrictions on Importation of and Internal Taxes on Cigarettes, BISD 37S/200,* adopted on 7 November 1990, para. 75. Also Panel Report, *European Communities – Measures Affecting Asbestos and Asbestos-Containing Products*, WT/DS135/R, adopted 5 April 2001, para. 8.209.

[101] Namely, (i) suitability, (ii) less restrictive means, and (iii) weighing benefits against deleterious effects (proportionality *strictu sensu*). See Appellate Body Report, *Korea – Measures Affecting Imports of Fresh, Chilled and Frozen Beef* , WT/DS161/9/AB/R, WT/DS169/9/AB/R, adopted on 10 January 2001, para. 164.

noted that WTO members have the freedom to decide the level of protection they want concerning public morals, life or health.[102] Even as dispute bodies vacillated between strict and loose interpretations of general exceptions, the Appellate Body also has shown an interest, as indicated in its 1998 *US – Shrimp* decision,[103] in ensuring that due process has been accorded to foreigners. This turn to process, as in the turn to proportionality, is intended to underscore that dispute settlement review under the WTO is neutral, impartial and focused on the means rather than on the substantive ends which states choose to pursue. Yet, an emphasis on process disguises the values that are at stake. While the WTO appears not to want to impose its own preferences when weighing those values, it necessarily takes sides. As Lang observes, even if preoccupied with process, 'there is no conceivable way that WTO review can be neutral as to the substance of domestic regulation in anything but a trivial sense'.[104] This is underscored by the emphasis accorded to Article XX's chapeau, which directs dispute settlement bodies to remain attentive to 'arbitrary or unjustifiable discrimination' and to 'disguised restrictions on international trade'. Given the few instances in which Article XX has been successfully invoked, the balance remains firmly in favour of traders' rights.[105]

For developing countries, in addition, any flexibility in the GATT or other WTO agreements is weakened by the expectation that they adopt the standards of the developed world. As trade disciplines move from tariff to nontariff barriers, there is increasing awareness that access to developed country markets requires compliance with environmental, health and technical standards set out in the latter jurisdictions.[106] Litigation over sanitary and phytosanitary measures in the WTO suggests that only rich countries, such as the United States and the EU, can afford to have different standards. Most Global South countries will lack the resources to produce scientific evidence to either protect their standards or challenge those of other members. Global South countries, in this regard, can only aspire to receive technical advice to adapt to the standards of the Global North. In the meantime, local producers on the ground increasingly struggle to comply with private standards defined by global value chains or large multinational corporations.[107]

Despite these problems, a triumphalist narrative has taken hold in trade law circles in recent years. Whatever legitimacy crisis imperilled the trading regime had been vanquished by reason of the successful judicialization of trade disputes. The Appellate

---

[102] Appellate Body Report, *European Communities – Asbestos*, para. 168.

[103] Appellate Body Report, *United States – Import Prohibition of Certain Shrimp and Shrimp Products*, WT/DS58/AB/R, adopted 6 November 1998, para. 181. Also Appellate Body Report, *Brazil – Measures Affecting Imports of Retreaded Tyres*, WT/DS332/AB/R, adopted 17 December 2007.

[104] LANG, supra note 49 at 246.

[105] Appellate Body Report, *European Communities – Asbestos*. See Public Citizen, *Only One of 44 Attempts to Use the GATT Article XX/GATS Article XIV 'General Exception' Has Ever Succeeded: Replicating the WTO Exception Construct Will Not Provide for an Effective TPP General Exception* (August 2015), www.citizen.org/sites/default/files/general-exception.pdf.

[106] Lamy, supra 56, at 4–5.

[107] Id at 5.

Body had become the 'jewel in the crown' of the WTO.[108] As has often been the case in the WTO's short life, this state of affairs would not remain static. Trade insiders are, at present, worried about paralysis in WTO negotiations and attacks by the US upon the Appellate Body. As to the former, the WTO has made very little progress in furthering the multilateral trade agenda because of a 'too politicized' process and an overly complex agenda.[109] In respect of the latter, the Trump administration has blocked the appointment of new members, putting at risk the functioning of the WTO's judicial functions. At this pace, there is a likelihood that the Appellate Body will not have enough members to function properly or at all. Though the situation is turning critical, these problems predate President Trump's election. In 2016, the Obama administration expressed concerns with the Appellate Body's tendency to 'make law', accusing its members of using appeals 'as an occasion to write a treatise on a WTO agreement'.[110]

This complaint about 'making law' is a mantra familiar to conservative legal discourse in the US. Critical legal theorists, however, long have emphasized that the distinction between interpreting and making law is unstable and that 'judicial activism' is a character trait of common law judging.[111] It is unsurprising to learn that investment tribunals tasked with evaluating investor claims against host states similarly seized the opportunity to exercise typical judicial functions by filling in the content of laconic treaty text. In the course of so doing, tribunals have developed a body of law that is expansive in its reach, precipitating numerous legitimacy problems. We turn next to a discussion of these latitudinarian tendencies and consequent developments.

4.2 World Investment Law

This companion global legal order largely is the product of thousands of bilateral investment treaties signed in the two decades after the fall of the Berlin Wall. More than 3,000 are currently in force, having as their object the protection of foreign investors and their investments. While there is some variation amongst them, treaties commit states to: nondiscrimination (national treatment and most favoured nation), not impeding the transfer of funds, not imposing performance requirements (prohibiting preferences for local labour or services), not taking measures amounting to direct or indirect expropriation (not without full and immediately realizable compensation) and commitments to provide treatment in accordance with the minimum standard available under international law together with fair and equitable treatment (FET). The standards

---

[108] *The Separation of Powers in the WTO: How to Avoid Judicial Activism*, 53 INT'L & COMP. L.Q. 861, 861 (2004). We note the colonial connotations, which raise interesting questions not pursued here.

[109] International Centre for Trade and Sustainable Development & World Economic Forum, *The Functioning of the WTO: Options for Reform and Enhanced Performance. Synthesis of the Policy Options* (E15 Initiative, 2016), at 2, http://e15initiative.org/wp-content/uploads/2015/09/E15_no9_WTO_final_REV_x1.pdf.

[110] Statement by the United States at the Meeting of the WTO Dispute Settlement Body Geneva, 23 May 2016, www.wto.org/english/news_e/news16_e/ us_statment_dsbmay16_e.pdf.

[111] DUNCAN KENNEDY, A CRITIQUE OF ADJUDICATION [FIN DE SIÈCLE] 177 (1998) and ROBERTO MANGABEIRA UNGER, THE CRITICAL LEGAL STUDIES MOVEMENT: ANOTHER TIME, A GREATER TASK 16 (2015).

of expropriation and FET, which we discuss below, have emerged as core disciplines in international investment law. Most investment tribunals are responding to claims that either or both of these standards have been violated by host states.

As in the case of the Uruguay Round of the GATT, most standards of protection have been authored by powerful capital exporting states, oftentimes drawing upon their own legal standards of protection. As the United States Trade Representative put it, the US has not lost an investment dispute because its protections mirror those rights protected under its Bill of Rights.[112] This is what the US Congress ordered the executive branch to provide once Congress realized, in 2002, that the standards of protection in the event of an expropriation clearly exceeded standards provided in the US constitution.[113] The President was directed to negotiate new treaties incorporating the multifactor analysis identified by the US Supreme Court in *Penn Central* that helps determine when a regulation rises to a compensable taking.[114] Many other national states, and even regional political units such as the EU, have followed suit, seemingly unaware that they are promoting US constitutional law as global law.[115] It has been the case, then, that states in the Global South mostly have been rule takers rather than rule makers. According to Poulsen, many countries signed agreements seemingly unaware of their effects on regulatory space,[116] a puzzling fact given the long history of resistance to the content of international law promoted by countries of the North Atlantic.

In the late 1990s and early 2000s, when investors succeeded in their claims before investment tribunals, arbitrators seemed focused upon investor impacts, above all else. This was exemplified by a mode of analysis, developed in adjudicating expropriation claims, labelled as 'sole effects' doctrine.[117] In these cases, arbitrators were preoccupied with the effects of a measure upon an investment rather than upon any public policy rationales that were offered in support. The 'government's intention is less important than the effects of the measure' on the investor, the tribunal wrote in *Tecmed*.[118] The investment tribunal in *Santa Elena v. Costa Rica*, for instance, decided that the measure at issue, which aimed at preserving the rainforest environment, constituted an expropriation as it 'deprived the owner of his rights or has made those rights practically useless'. Even where measures are 'beneficial to society as a whole –

---

[112] United States Trade Representative, *The Facts on Investor-State Dispute Settlement*, TRADEWINDS: The Official Blog of the United States Trade Representative (March 2014), https://ustr.gov/about-us/policy-offices/press-office/blog/2014/March/Facts-Investor-State%20 Dispute-Settlement-Safeguarding-Public-Interest-Protecting-Investors.

[113] See DAVID SCHNEIDERMAN, RESISTING ECONOMIC GLOBALIZATION: CRITICAL THEORY AND INTERNATIONAL INVESTMENT LAW 80–3 (2013).

[114] See *Penn Central Transportation Co. v. New York City*, 438 US 104, 124 (1977). Those factors include the character of the measure, its duration, its economic impact and the extent to which it upsets investor expectations.

[115] Annex 8-A in CETA.

[116] This story is told in LAUGE SKOVGAARD POULSEN, BOUNDED RATIONALITY AND ECONOMIC DIPLOMACY: THE POLITICS OF INVESTMENT TREATIES IN DEVELOPING COUNTRIES (2015).

[117] Rudolf Dolzer, *Indirect Expropriations: New Developments?*, 11 NEW YORK UNIVERSITY ENVIRONMENTAL LAW JOURNAL 64 (2002).

[118] *Técnicas Medioambientales Tecmed SA v. Mexico* (ICSID ARB(AF)/00/2) Award, 29 May 2003, para. 116.

such as environmental protection', the tribunal concluded, the obligation to pay compensation remains.[119] It is not that arbitrators simply could ignore policy rationales. Rather, those rationales would be subsumed under investor effects or simply be dismissed as being driven by 'politics'. States were not permitted to behave politically but instead were expected to behave, and rewarded if they so behaved, in ways expected of rational economic actors.[120] Excising politics from state calculations enabled the regime's defenders to cast investment law as a legitimate constraint upon state action.

Given the impossibility of achieving such a state of antipolitics, some of these awards raised alarm bells for those country negotiators who had failed to appreciate the regime's muscularity. Nor, on the other hand, could states lose too often. Such an outcome would almost immediately heighten legitimacy concerns and deepen suspicion about the regime's structural tilt. There is some disagreement over the data but, according to UNCTAD, states prevail in 37 per cent of the cases while foreign investors win in only 28 per cent (in the so-called merits phase of an arbitration).[121] It is harder to account for settlements that, according to UNCTAD, occur in approximately 23 per cent of the disputes. We surmise, as do others, that a significant number of these settlements likely benefit investors.[122] In sum, it can be said that states and investors win in roughly equal amounts. This helps render the regime more palatable.

An emphasis on the economic effects of a measure alleged to be equivalent to expropriation, as opposed to an inquiry focused upon the aims or intentions of government, was quickly perceived by many actors as a threat to the right to regulate. Investment tribunals responded in two different ways. First, they purported to balance the effects of a regulation on investors against the importance of the public measure. In *LG&E v. Argentina*, for instance, the arbitrators admitted that 'there must be a balance in the analysis both of the causes and the effects of a measure in order that one may qualify a measure as being of an expropriatory nature'.[123] Alternatively, tribunals noted that regulations rarely had an effect equivalent to expropriation, reducing the frequency of regulatory expropriation to a few marginal cases. The *SD Myers v. Canada* tribunal, for instance, emphasized that '[e]xpropriations tend to involve the deprivation of ownership rights; regulations a lesser interference'.[124] By reducing the ambit for regulatory expropriations, investment lawyers turned to FET as a means of filling in the void. If the factors deemed determinative in characterizing an expropriation included,

---

[119] *Compañía del Desarrollo de Santa Elena v. Costa Rica* (ICSID Case No ARB/96/1) Award, 17 February 2000, paras 72, 76, 78.

[120] E.g. *Biwater Gauff (Tanzania) Ltd. v. United Republic of Tanzania* (ICSID Case No ARB/05/22) Award, 18 July 2008.

[121] 'UNCTAD, 'Investor–State Dispute Settlement: Review of developments in 2017,' *IIA Issues Note*, Issue 2 (6 June 2018), https://unctad.org/en/PublicationsLibrary/diaepcbinf2018d2_en.pdf.

[122] Thomas Waelde and George Ndi, *Stabilizing International Investment Commitments: International Law Versus Contract Interpretation* 31 TEX. INT'L L.J. 215, 260 (1996).

[123] *LG&E v. Argentina* (ICSID Case No ARB/02/1) Decision on Liability, 3 October 2006, 194.

[124] *SD Myers v. Canada* (NAFTA – UNCITRAL) Partial Award, 13 November 2000, para. 282.

among other things, investor expectations, the focus could now be directed exclusively upon the single factor of legitimate expectations. Arbitrators dutifully followed suit.

In awards such as *Occidental v. Ecuador I*, arbitrators interpreted FET as requiring that states offer stable and predictable business environments.[125] This, in practice, generated the equivalent of what is known in the law of state contracts as a 'stabilization' clause, rendering legal regimes irreversible without grandfathering affected investors or paying them compensation. With a focus on stability and predictability, arbitrators could rely upon what they characterized as the 'universal' doctrine of legitimate expectations.[126] Foreign investors are to be compensated when regulatory changes frustrate representations made by the host state – representations made by whatever means, including contract, licence, legislation or regulation – and relied upon by the foreign investor at the moment the investment is established.

While there have been attempts at narrowing the doctrine of legitimate expectations in subsequent awards, it continues to serve the interests of foreign investors who seek to challenge changes to existing regulatory frameworks. The doctrine of legitimate expectations, for instance, was crucial to investor success in a series of disputes against Argentina precipitated by its 2001 economic crisis. Having taken measures to lessen the effects of the economic and social crisis, no investment tribunal found Argentina liable for indirect expropriation. Most tribunals, instead, concluded that Argentina was liable for breaching FET by upsetting investors' legitimate expectations. These awards bring to the surface the distributive implications of this legal order. Investment law favoured foreign investors over not only domestic investors but also the rest of the Argentine population that could not claim to have an expectation to their jobs or salaries.[127] Ironically, these were the same Argentines who were pressured to open their economy, privatize public enterprises and sign bilateral investment treaties a decade earlier.

As in the case of the WTO, these awards were criticized for second guessing the substantive aims of state policy. An emphasis on process provided a way of eliding these critiques. Investment tribunals, not surprisingly, began to show an interest in procedural questions as a means of dampening critique. Arbitrators interpreted the procedural dimension of FET as requiring states to operate in a nondiscriminatory, transparent and nonarbitrary manner while penalizing states that did not provide to foreign investors the ability to participate in administrative processes that affected their interests. This focus on procedure has become useful as investment tribunals increasingly address disputes concerning the application and issuance of licences to exploit natural resources.

The case of *Clayton v. Canada* is emblematic of this turn towards process. It also underscores how intimately connected is process to substance. Canada was ordered to

---

[125] *Occidental v. Ecuador I* (LCIA Case No UN3467), Award, 1 July 2004, para. 183.

[126] As explained in the lengthy dissent of Thomas Wälde in *International Thunderbird Gaming Corporation v. Mexico* (Ad hoc – UNCITRAL Arbitration Rules) Separate opinion, 1 December 2005, paras 21–30. For a critical discussion of foreign investor legitimate expectations, see Nicolás M. Perrone, *The Emerging Global Right to Investment: Understanding the Reasoning behind Foreign Investor Rights*, 8 JOURNAL OF INTERNATIONAL DISPUTE SETTLEMENT 673 (2017).

[127] Nicolás M. Perrone, *The International Investment Regime after the Global Crisis of Neoliberalism: Rupture or Continuity?* 23 IND. J. GLOBAL LEGAL STUD. 603, 616–9 (2016).

pay compensation for violation of the North American Free Trade Agreement (NAFTA), having acted arbitrarily in refusing to permit the construction of a rock quarry and ferry terminal on sensitive shoreline in the province of Nova Scotia. While the US investor was encouraged to proceed with the investment, it was understood that the investment would have to go through environmental screening as required by local law. An independent review panel undertook this assessment, convening 13 days of hearings, and recommended the application be denied as the investment would cause harm to the marine, natural and human environments. The investment tribunal treated the review panel decision as procedurally flawed because it emphasized something the panel called 'community core values'. This was a focus denied to the panel by reason of its statutory authority, the tribunal concluded. This was by no means an obvious conclusion. It was, instead, a contentious interpretation of the panel's enacting authority. As dissenting arbitrator McRae pointed out, community core values described a set of statutorily mandated considerations. The majority of the tribunal, nevertheless, accepted the investor's claim that its discussion of community core values was an 'essential basis of the Panel's decision' and that the panel therefore acted in an arbitrary fashion.[128] This produced, according to the dissenting arbitrator, a 'disturbing result' leading to a 'remarkable step backwards in environmental protection'.

As in the case of WTO law and with the encouragement of scholars, some investment tribunals have turned to proportionality review as a means of securing legitimacy.[129] Neglecting this popular mode of inquiry, it is said, risks jeopardizing the future of investment arbitration.[130] Despite this urging to embrace proportionality, few tribunals have been receptive; nor, when they have been, have they performed this function very well. Instead, they have exhibited confusion by, for instance, assimilating proportionality into a determination of whether a treaty breach has occurred rather in relying upon it in the context of determining whether a deprivation of rights can be justified. Tribunals also have collapsed the requisite steps associated with the inquiry (suitability, necessity and proportionate effect).[131] In sum, proportionality as a response to legitimacy concerns has not worked out as hoped.

---

[128] *Clayton v. Canada* (Permanent Court of Arbitration (PCA) Case No 2009-04) Award on Jurisdiction and Liability, 17 March 2015, para. 548.

[129] Discussed in more detail in David Schneiderman, *Global Constitutionalism and its Legitimacy Problems: Human Rights, Proportionality, and International Investment Law*, JOURNAL OF LAW & ETHICS OF HUMAN RIGHTS (2018).

[130] Benedict Kingsbury & Stephan Schill, *Investor-State Arbitration as Governance: Fair and Equitable Treatment, Proportionality and the Emerging Global Administrative Law* in EL NUEVO DERECHO ADMINISTRATIVO GLOBAL EN AMÉRICA LATINA: DESAFÍOS PARA LAS INVERSIONES EXTRANJERAS, LA REGULACIÓN NACIONAL Y EL FINANCIAMIENTO PARA EL DESARROLLO 276 (Benedict Kingsbury et al eds, 2009), www.iilj.org/GAL/documents/GALBAbook.pdf.

[131] Erlend M. Leonhardsen, *Looking for Legitimacy: Exploring Proportionality Analysis in Investment Treaty Arbitration*, 3 JOURNAL OF INTERNATIONAL DISPUTE SETTLEMENT 124 (2012). See, e.g., *Técnicas Medioambientales Tecmed SA v. Mexico* (ICSID ARB(AF)/00/2) Award, 29 May 2003.

Yet another strategy for responding to nagging legitimacy concerns is the proposal for an investment court.[132] This is a project advanced by the European Commission in response to worries about arming US investors with the ability to launch disputes under the now stalled US–European trade and investment agreement (TTIP). After halting negotiations with the US and undertaking a European-wide consultation, the Commission returned with a proposal for an investment court having a tribunal of first instance together with an appellate body. Rather than exhibiting the features of a court, with security of tenure and independence, the European proposal appears to mimic, in its outlines, the dispute settlement bodies in the WTO. This is a strategy that appropriates the features of what is perceived to be a successful global legal order, having overcome some of its own legitimacy concerns. This could lend legitimacy to an allied regime that has yet to generate the same confidence. While only a couple of states, such as Canada and Vietnam, have shown a willingness to join in this project, we expect the EU will have some success in conscripting partners, given its economic influence, as it seeks to secure new trade and investment agreements and promotes the initiative in multilateral fora.[133]

Rather than relying on reforms having to do with process, some states have sought to refine treaty obligations by expressly incorporating a 'right to regulate'.[134] Such clauses have been proliferating in newly minted investment treaties with the hope, again, of imitating the experience under GATT Article XX. While such textual signals might make a difference to some investment arbitration outcomes, they are as likely not to make much difference. This is because investment tribunals have a lot of interpretive scope and can choose to do with such clauses what they will. In any event, each of the standards of protection in investment law purport to incorporate exceptions, such as a public interest justification under national treatment or a police powers exception under expropriation and nationalization. Standards already are interpreted so as to incorporate consideration of what might be called a right to regulate, and yet legitimacy concerns persist.

There is also little reason to be confident that an express adoption of a right to regulate will make much of a difference given another feature of investment arbitration. The regime is structured in such a way that arbitrators have an incentive both to accept jurisdiction (tribunals have this exclusive competence) and to interpret standards of protection widely. If we treat arbitrators as rational economic actors – they assume, after all, that everyone else is motivated by economic self-interest – we can assume that they would want to encourage new claimants to come forward. As the system is triggered only at the behest of investors, there is impetus for arbitrators to issue reasons that facilitates future arbitration business. As we have mentioned, this cannot mean that investors will win all of the time. Rather, arbitrators will endeavour to strike a balance between investors and states that will not drive either party away. Yet the system does not appear to serve even investors very well. There are persistent complaints that it is

---

[132] Discussed in more detail in David Schneiderman, *International Investment Law's Unending Legitimation Project*, 49 LOYOLA UNIVERSITY CHICAGO LAW JOURNAL 229.

[133] At present, European states are promoting a multilateral investment court at UNCITRAL Working Group III. See http://www.uncitral.org/uncitral/en/commission/working_groups/3 Investor_State.html'.

[134] See discussion in Schneiderman, supra note 129.

costly and slow and not easily available to small and medium sized enterprises. It turns out that investment dispute settlement best serves the interests of arbitrators, lawyers and some large multinational corporations.[135]

To conclude, IEL shows a growing convergence towards a single imaginary of the right to regulate. Even then, general, nondiscriminatory, reasonable measures to curb negative externalities and market failures are not so easily defended at the WTO or before investment tribunals. Whatever successes states and citizens can secure before these dispute resolution bodies are not sufficient to rebalance the costs and benefits of the global economy. IEL contributes to dampening the role of states and the potential for democracies to come to the defence of their populations. The people are, accordingly, limited in their ability to respond to the social costs of markets. The right to regulate grants states only a modest role. Interference with trade or investment transactions is discouraged, if not forbidden. Legal problems begin with any attempt either to reduce pain and precarity or to change the rules that unevenly distribute that pain and precarity.

5. CONCLUSION

We have argued that states are expected to behave in ways that do not encumber trade and investment flows. Should they do so, they will run afoul of global legal rules. Existing distributions of wealth thereby remain secure while the insecurities experienced by many remain unaddressed. The precarious condition of populations in both the developed and developing world is more difficult to address or is worsened. Yet states remain the most salient political actors in the world today and it is to them that the most vulnerable will look for protection.

By emphasizing the distributional effects of IEL, we hope to challenge both the triumphalist tone of the trade lawyers and the tepid response of investment lawyers to these challenges. According to Piketty, inherited wealth is coming to predominate over earned income in the twenty-first century, just as it did in the Belle Époque period. As this is a problem that traditionally is addressed by national taxation measures,[136] Piketty proposes a global wealth tax to supplement local income taxation. 'A progressive levy on individual wealth', he writes, 'would reassert control over capitalism in the name of the general interest'.[137]

Piketty does not seek out a remedy by addressing the governing legal rules of trade and investment. He does acknowledge, however, that a rise in foreign investment does not enhance equality but is instead likely to hinder it.[138] It is no coincidence, in our

---

[135] See Cecilia Olivet & Pia Eberhardt, *Profiting from Injustice: How Law Firms, Arbitrators and Financiers are Fuelling an Investment Arbitration Boom*, TRANSNATIONAL INSTITUTE (2012); Gus Van Harten & Pavel Malysheuski, *Who Has Benefited Financially from Investment Treaty Arbitration? An Evaluation of the Size and Wealth of Claimants* (Osgoode Legal Studies Research Paper No 14/2016).
[136] Piketty supra note 62, at 44.
[137] Piketty id at 532.
[138] Piketty id at 68, 70 (speaking of Africa).

view, that the period identified by Piketty as that in which wage inequality really takes off – the 1980s – is the very same period in which neoliberal values took hold in international financial institutions and those of IEL.

As states remove trade barriers and reregulate so as to smooth capital flows, they contribute to deepening inequality within their own countries. Indisputably, new technologies and increasing integration provide a different terrain for the global struggle over who wins and who loses. But this terrain is neither static nor preordained. For the critical lawyer, piercing the veil of the complex and expert discussions within IEL is not enough. It is also necessary to both consider recovering old and developing new legal imaginaries. In this regard, placing inequality at the centre of IEL is, for us, just the first step.

25. Can transnational law be critical? Reflections on a contested idea, field and method

Peer Zumbansen

[T]here is now emerging a modern international law that is in many respects a reflection of contemporary social, economic, scientific, and technological needs. There has been a movement away from unmitigated state sovereignty, war and neutrality, and the old-world diplomacy of the League Covenant, toward equality, universality, fundamental human rights, and the promotion of social welfare, economic progress, and interdependence, which has been impelled by modern communications, transport, science, and technology and of which the guiding light is increasing emphasis on the interests of the community of nations as a whole.[1]

If the dominant cultural paradigm of the early post-Cold War period was the end of history as a triumphant liberal internationalism flattened global geopolitical space, Trump's victory represents the end of this interregnum: a rearticulation of the primacy of the nation-state, a fracture in the postwar liberal internationalist consensus and a hardening of geopolitical revisionism.[2]

If you want to make God laugh, tell him your plans.[3]

1. LEGAL CONCEPTUAL ARCHITECTURES UNDER REVIEW

This chapter's title hints at the subject's potential for self-destruction and is serious about that. There is little reason to believe, at least at first and second glance, in transnational law's inherently critical stance. In fact, if anything, transnational law ('TL') is usually not taken as the label for a progressive, critically minded legal theory or legal concept; rather, the opposite appears to be the case. As TL is most commonly seen in close relation to the demographics and institutional formations of globalized business interests,[4] its reimagination as a 'critlaw' project is anything but intuitive. The

---

[1] T. Olawele Elias, *Modern Sources of International Law*, in: TRANSNATIONAL LAW IN A CHANGING SOCIETY. ESSAYS IN HONOR OF PHILIP C. JESSUP (Wolfgang Friedmann, Louis Henkin & Oliver Lissitzyn eds, Columbia University Press 1972), 34–69, at 67.

[2] Doug Stokes, *Trump, American Hegemony and the Future of the Liberal International Order*, 94:1 INTERNATIONAL AFFAIRS 133–50 (2018), 133.

[3] ABRAHAM VERGHESE, CUTTING FOR STONE (Verso 2009), 31.

[4] Arturo Ortiz Wadgymar, *Neoliberal Capitalism in the New World Economy*, 8 INT'L J. POL., CULT. & SOC'Y 295–312 (1994), 306: 'Globalization is the game of free play for powerful transnational interests, associated with one another or linked to second-class partners among local bourgeoisies, operating without regulation from national governments, and seeking to take control of international markets.'

evidence of the 'actors, norms and processes'[5] that are usually associated with TL surely points in that direction. Among the largescale shifts to private governance regimes, both as a domestic manifestation of post-Western welfare state transformation,[6] on the one hand, and the fast expanding realm of transnational private regulatory governance,[7] on the other, we are confronted with a continuously changing landscape of newly emerging power brokers; private norm makers; hybrid, public–private expert committees; standardization bodies; consultancies; and think tanks, all of which are deeply invested in new and extremely fragmented games of norm making and the creation of powerful regulatory regimes outside of the traditional frameworks of state-based governmental political administration.[8] This forms one part of the background to a present-day engagement with TL. The other facet of TL's complex discursive environment concerns, for short, theory. Theory,[9] we might say, plays a crucial role in the engagement with transnational law, especially as its status as *law* – a set of binding rules, created by a legitimate authority[10] – continues to be its Achilles'

---

[5] For an elaboration of the A-N-P triad as a central pillar of a transnational legal method, see Peer Zumbansen, *Defining the Space of Transnational Law: Legal Theory, Global Governance & Legal Pluralism*, 21:1 TRANSNATIONAL LAW & CONTEMPORARY PROBLEMS 305–35 (2012). For a recent application of this concept, see for example Kinnari Bhatt, *New 'Legal' Actors, Norms and Processes, Formal and Informal Indigenous Land Rights Norms in the Oyu Tolgoi Project, Mongolia*, TLI *Think!* Paper 63/2017, available at: https://ssrn.com/abstract=2995505.

[6] With regard to the US, see, for example, Mimi Abramovitz, *The Privatization of the Welfare State: A Review*, 31 SOC. WORK 257–64 (1986), and Jody Freeman, *The Contracting State*, 28 FLA. ST. U. L. REV. 155 (2001). Focusing on Germany and the UK, see Lutz Leisering, *Pension Privatization in a Welfare State Environment: Socializing Private Pensions in Germany and the United Kingdom*, 28 J. COMP. SOC. WELFARE 139–51 (2012).

[7] Benjamin Cashore, *Legitimacy and the Privatization of Environmental Governance: How Non-State Market-Driven (NSMD) Governance Systems Gain Rule-Making Authority*, 15 GOVERNANCE 503–29 (2002), and Philipp Pattberg, *The Forest Stewardship Council: Risk and Potential of Private Forest Governance*, 14 J. ENV. & DEV. 356–74 (2005).

[8] Critical insights in this regard have been provided by scholars in the field of international relations and (global) political economy: see, for example, the contributions to PRIVATE AUTHORITY AND INTERNATIONAL AFFAIRS (A. Claire Cutler, Virginia Haufler & Tony Porter eds, SUNY Press 1999), and TIM BÜTHE & WALTER MATTLI, THE NEW GLOBAL RULERS: THE PRIVATIZATION OF REGULATION IN THE WORLD (Princeton University Press 2011).

[9] See, for example, the intriguing survey by Fleur Johns, *International Legal Theory: Snapshots from a Decade of International Legal Life*, 10 MELBOURNE JOURNAL OF INTERNATIONAL LAW 1–10 (2009), and James T. Gathii, *TWAIL: A Brief History of Its Origins, Its Decentralized Network, and a Tentative Bibliography*, 3:1 TRADE, LAW AND DEVELOPMENT 26–64 (2011). See also the study by THOMAS SKOUTERIS, THE NOTION OF PROGRESS IN INTERNATIONAL LAW DISCOURSE (Springer, 2009), and the contributions to the OXFORD HANDBOOK OF INTERNATIONAL LEGAL THEORY (Anne Orford & Florian Hoffmann eds, Oxford University Press 2016).

[10] Tom Farer, *Toward an Effective International Legal Order: From Co-Existence to Concert?*, 3:5 SUR. INTERNATIONAL JOURNAL ON HUMAN RIGHTS 150–71 (2006), 152–3: 'An authoritative legal system certainly is more than an archipelago of functional regimes. However effectively a blend of rules and principles, sometimes embedded in formal bureaucratic institutions, may as an observable matter stabilise behaviour and expectations concerning a wide array of subject areas as diverse as the uses of the seas and the protection of the chicken-breasted

heel. While TL is associated with continuing forms of state transformation – which tend, as was just mentioned, to be depicted through ideas around globalization, deregulation, privatization and eroding state sovereignty[11] – there is an even larger set of suspicions surrounding the notion of a 'transnational *law*'. Such suspicions feed on the everyday experience of state transformation but have their origin in something deeper still. It is here that TL is being scrutinized, more than anything, as a challenge to a more generally accepted, if not altogether universalized, understanding of law as such. The stuff of such anxieties is that of 'new', supposedly 'nonstate' actors that not only have become involved in legal norm creation but have in fact become authors of legal norms themselves. Another cause for concern is the apparent expansion and proliferation of norms which, while they might not be 'law' proper, appear to be treated and functioning as such nevertheless.[12] The contention that legal pluralism – that is, the coexistence of different legal orders – must be present at the outset of an adequate understanding of law is central here.[13] And while legal pluralism and all the jurisprudential headaches it seems to generate are often not even addressed as such, its underlying assertions of normative plurality and conflict are close to the surface. The most productive approaches to a discussion of TL's relationship to normative pluralism, then, seem to come from within the sociolegal triangle of legal sociology, legal anthropology and 'law in context'. And it is against this background that TL as a jurisprudential challenge can begin to appear in a new light. With a view to what would be a legal philosophical engagement with transnational law, Roger Cotterrell very astutely formulated this point thus:

---

sloth, they will not constitute a legal order unless they are seen as instances of a general system of authority that applies reasonably effectively to all states and addresses the existential concerns of human communities which include but is not limited to the question of who may use force under what circumstances.'

[11] Martin Loughlin, *The Erosion of Sovereignty*, 45:2 NETHERLANDS JOURNAL OF LEGAL PHILOSOPHY 57–81 (2016), 57: 'Many of the assumptions underpinning the modern system of nation-states are now being placed in question. Increased global flows of capital, intensified networks of social interaction, and the emergence of transnational regulatory regimes on a significant scale are affecting the ability of national governments to regulate their economic conditions and improve their citizens' well-being.'

[12] See also Steven Wheatley, *A Democratic Rule of International Law*, 22:2 EUROPEAN JOURNAL OF INTERNATIONAL LAW 525–48 (2011), 546: 'The idea of a conflict of laws might, then, be reformulated in terms of an evaluation of the democratic legitimacy claims of conflicting assertions of authority. There is no reason to conclude that an autonomous legal order would regard another legal order as being inherently superior; if that were the case it would presumably amend its legal order better to reflect the version of political justice manifested in the other legal system. Whether a legal system will defer to another cannot be determined in abstraction; it must be undertaken on a case-by-case basis. A legal order might recognize the assertion of authority by another as falling more clearly within the other's domain. Alternatively, a legal order might be persuaded by the authority of the conflicting norm, i.e., that it represents a better approximation of a political truth. In other words, the legal system might be open to the possibility that it has erred in the adoption of the regulation.'

[13] Boaventura de Sousa Santos, *Law: A Map of Misreading. Toward a Postmodern Conception of Law*, 14:3 JOURNAL OF LAW AND SOCIETY 279–302 (1987). And see the intriguing paper written from the perspective of international relations theory by Geoffrey Swenson: *Legal Pluralism in Theory and Practice*, 20 INTERNATIONAL STUDIES REVIEW 438–62 (2018).

Since conceptual study of law has been so central to legal philosophy (insofar as it has aimed to develop philosophical theories of the nature of law), the issue is whether legal philosophy's explanations of law can cope with the new (or newly prominent) phenomena of transnational law, or whether its ignoring of these phenomena ... undermines the whole legal theoretical house of cards that the philosophers have built.[14]

Of course, the depiction of jurisprudential architectures as so ephemeral as to be comparable to a house of cards risks missing at least some of what is 'the point' in analytical jurisprudence. A crude confrontation of theories of law that are interested in the nature, the concept and the system of law with an ethnography of law's functions, implementations and failures will end up being more polemical than helpful in re/opening channels of communication. It might then be helpful to consider how much is gained by maintaining such differently oriented endeavours in play – not for the purpose of seeing one emerge as victorious and the other vilified, but instead to continue to appreciate the different aspects of law which become visible through the work in each of these undertakings.

The crux is that for both approaches – roughly speaking, analytical jurisprudence and socio-legal studies – the endgame of the transnationalization of regulatory arrangements, that what will be the ultimate result of an increased interpenetration of state-based and nonstate orders as well as of the continuing proliferation of competing epistemologies of knowledge, especially from a post-colonial perspective, is not even remotely predictable. While the globalization of human and institutional, material and immaterial affairs is widely accepted to have prompted, inter alia, significant challenges for inherited conceptual frameworks of societal ordering, the contours of what will replace them remain nebulous at best. Globalization has shaken the edifices – however real or 'merely' symbolic they themselves may be[15] – of a political order which is based on an understanding of a relationship of interdependence between 'state' and 'society'.[16] Meanwhile, the prescriptive dimension of "TL" as a label for these newly

---

[14] Roger Cotterrell, *What Is Transnational Law?*, 37 LAW & SOCIAL INQUIRY 500–24 (2012), 504.

[15] Michel-Rolph Trouillot, *The Anthropology of the State in the Age of Globalization*, 42:1 CURRENT ANTHROPOLOGY 125–38 (2001), 126: 'Is the state a "concrete-concrete," something "out there?" Or is it a concept necessary to understand something out there? Or, again, is it an ideology that helps to mask something else out there, a symbolic shield for power, as it were?'

[16] See the first chapter in JÜRGEN HABERMAS, THE POST-NATIONAL CONSTELLATION (MIT Press 2001). See also Timothy Mitchell, *The Limits of the State: Beyond Statist Approaches and Their Critics*, 85:1 AMERICAN POLITICAL SCIENCE REVIEW 77–96 (1991), 78: 'Rather than searching for a definition that will fix the boundary, we need to examine the detailed political processes through which the uncertain yet powerful distinction between state and society is produced. The distinction must be taken not as the boundary between two discrete entities, but as a line drawn internally within the network of institutional mechanisms through which a social and political order is maintained. The ability to have an internal distinction appear as though it were the external boundary between separate objects is the distinctive technique of the modern political order. The technique must be examined from a historical perspective (something prevailing approaches fail to do), as the consequence of certain novel practices of the modern age. This approach can account for the salience of the state phenomenon, but avoids attributing to it the coherence, unity, and absolute autonomy that result from existing theoretical approaches.'

emerging regulatory formations is inseparable from a critical project of calling into question the conceptions of political, legal and economic order which had their origin in the postrevolutionary, Westphalian age of sovereignty of the eighteenth century and as they unfolded through the course of the 'long nineteenth' and the divisive twentieth centuries. Regardless of whether we draw on optimistic or critical accounts of social theory's dealings with globalization,[17] we are struck by the prominence and presence of conceptual building blocks that owe their historical and symbolic capital to a long tradition of 'state theory', 'modernization' and 'development'.[18] Among those, the inherited concepts of the state and its relation to 'the market' and to 'society', or of 'the public' and 'the private',[19] constitute crucial sites of conflict and contestation in the present struggle over the fate of democratic sovereignty and public regulatory competences.[20] So, while we are drawn to observe that '[t]he state-centrism and the nation state/inter-state framework that informs much theorization and analysis of world politics, political economy, and class structure is ever more incongruent with twenty-first century world developments',[21] this is not yet saying much about what might take its place. Under the tip of a formula such as 'the state in an age of globalization'[22] lies a vast iceberg of interdisciplinary work which continues to unfold and which seeks to map and engage the complex correlation and interdependence of global marketization and 'state transformation'.[23] This analysis *of* and critical engagement *with* the prospects and limits of transnational governance regimes, in other words, is the background and context to the research which has been unfolding in legal scholarship and elsewhere in response to the 'globalization challenge'.[24]

---

[17] Compare MARTIN WOLF, WHY GLOBALIZATION WORKS (Yale University Press, 2nd ed., 2005), with QUINN SLOBODIAN, THE GLOBALISTS (Harvard University Press 2018).

[18] For a discussion of these dimensions, see Amanda Perry-Kessaris, *Prepare Your Indicators: Economics Imperialism at the Shores of Law and Development*, 7:4 INTERNATIONAL JOURNAL OF LAW IN CONTEXT 401–21 (2011).

[19] WOLFGANG FRIEDMANN, THE CHANGING STRUCTURE OF INTERNATIONAL LAW (Columbia University Press 1964), 190: 'The neat distinction of the categories of public and private law has long ceased to be expressive of the realities of contemporary municipal, as well as international, law, even though the distinction still dominates the teaching curricula of law schools.'

[20] See the introduction in: Walter Mattli & Ngaire Woods, *In Whose Benefit? Explaining Regulatory Change in Global Politics*, in: id (eds), *The Politics of Regulation* (Princeton University Press 2009), 1–43.

[21] William I. Robinson, *Debate on the New Global Capitalism: Transnational Capitalist Class, Transnational State Apparatuses, and Global Crisis*, 7:2 INTERNATIONAL CRITICAL THOUGHT 171–89 (2017), 171–2.

[22] Trouillot, above note 15.

[23] See the contributions to Aradhana Sharma & Akhil Gupta (eds), THE ANTHROPOLOGY OF THE STATE: A READER (Blackwell 2006). See also Martin Shaw, *The State of Globalization: Towards a Theory of State Transformation*, 4:3 REVIEW OF INTERNATIONAL POLITICAL ECONOMY 497–513 (1997), 498: 'just as states have not always been nation-states, so their transformations in recent times have produced state forms which go far beyond the nation-state as classically understood.'

[24] See Harry W. Arthurs, *Law and Learning in an Era of Globalization*, 10 GERMAN LAW JOURNAL 629–39 (2009) [Special Issue on 'Transnationalizing Legal Education']. See also Morag Goodwin, *Embracing the Challenge: Legal Scholarship in a Global Era*, 4 TRANSNATIONAL LEGAL THEORY 686–99 (2013), 689: 'First, our starting point must be an

2. THE CONTESTED 'WHAT' AND 'WHERE' OF TRANSNATIONAL LAW – STILL?

In that regard, we are at a point in time where the jury is still out with regard to its verdict on whether transnational law should be considered a field, a concept or an (likely promarket, neoliberal) ideology. Casting doubt on TL in terms of being either a neatly demarcated and regularly adjudicated field of doctrinal law or a conceptual elaboration which we would locate somewhere between private and public international law in the way outlined by Philip Jessup in the 1950s,[25] it is crucial to take seriously the lingering and persistent claims which situate TL in the greater transformation of state-based, political governance of economic affairs and the continuing trend towards privatization and corporate ownership of formerly public regulatory prerogatives. Seen as part of a wholescale shift to private governance, forum shopping and the curtailing of state "intervention", TL is today often squarely associated with an intensifying constellation of globalized markets in which the authority of regulatory agency – at least from the early 1980s until very recently – seemed to widely shift to private actors.[26] Acknowledging the weight of such assumptions, we need to not only reconsider law's and legal theory's receptivity to normative critique but also trace more carefully the lines of these longstanding concerns about TL.

It comes as no surprise that the growth and expansion of private regulatory governance in institutional and spatial dimensions continues to be the subject of extensive critical analysis.[27] What is noteworthy, however, is the changing scope of such critique, as it unfolds in response to an increasingly complex and multilayered

---

acknowledgement of the magnitude of the challenge and recognition that we lack adequate responses to the need for a new, global legal perspective. We are at the beginning of our explorations and there can be no quick solutions, no simple fixes to the question of what the impact on our understanding of law is or will be, or, moreover, how we should respond as lawyers. Secondly, relatedly, we cannot therefore simply cling to the old assumptions or attempt to transpose them to the global or transnational realm. Instead, we need to recognise that the challenges to our understanding of what law is and how it functions are profound. This requires us to eschew grandiose responses or claims to have uncovered an over-arching theory of global law. Rather, an open starting position means accepting the possibility that we will fail to find shared understandings that are true in all places and at all times upon which law can rest.'

[25] For an attempt to critically revisit and interrogate Jessup, see the contributions to Peer Zumbansen (ed.), THE MANY LIVES OF TRANSNATIONAL LAW: CRITICAL ENGAGEMENTS WITH JESSUP'S BOLD PROPOSAL (Cambridge University Press 2020).

[26] For an optimistic endorsement, see Jan Dalhuisen, *Legal Orders and Their Manifestation: The Operation of the International Commercial and Financial Legal Order and Its Lex Mercatoria*, 24 BERKELEY JOURNAL OF INTERNATIONAL LAW 129–91 (2006). More sceptically: Daniela Caruso, *Private Law and State-Making in the Age of Globalization*, 39 NYU JOURNAL OF INTERNATIONAL LAW AND POLITICS 1–72 (2006).

[27] See, for example, the important and groundbreaking work by Saskia Sassen, including TERRITORY, AUTHORITY, RIGHTS: FROM MEDIEVAL ORDERS TO GLOBAL ASSEMBLAGES (Princeton University Press, 2005), and A. CLAIRE CUTLER, PRIVATE POWER AND GLOBAL AUTHORITY: TRANSNATIONAL MERCHANT LAW IN THE GLOBAL ECONOMY (Cambridge University Press 2003).

regulatory 'assemblage'[28] which is prompting the creation of an altogether new or fundamentally revamped analytical vocabulary and conceptual toolkit to capture its object of analysis. But, while the proliferation of these new *actors* and their increasingly diversified and deepened involvement in regulatory activity, innovation and intervention is the stuff of sociological study,[29] it is the consideration of the newly emerging materialities of regulatory *norms*, and the wide-eyed acknowledgement of the varied types of *processes* through which such norms come into existence and are disseminated, enforced and contested, which prompts the development of interdisciplinary conceptual frameworks in order to more adequately grasp the advanced degree of complexity in the forms of social organization surfacing here.[30] The breathtaking speed and scope of functional and geographical differentiation of legal-regulatory regimes is a hallmark of law in a complex global context. The legal anthropologist Mark Goodale depicted this reality with regard to the post-Second World War aspirations for a worldwide effective human rights system in the following manner:

> Eleanor Roosevelt, the chair of the inaugural United Nations Commission on Human Rights, had hoped that a 'curious grapevine' would eventually carry the idea of human rights into every corner of the world, so that the dizzying – and regressive – diversity of rule-systems would be replaced by the exalted normative framework expressed through the 1948 Universal Declaration of Human Rights. In fact, the curious grapevine of non-state and transnational actors did emerge in the way Roosevelt anticipated, but the resulting networks have been conduits for normativities in addition to human rights. Ideas, institutional practices, and

---

[28] Gilles Deleuze, in an interview in 1980, reframed his idea of 'assemblage' thus: 'In assemblages you find states of things, bodies, various combinations of bodies, hodgepodges; but you also find utterances, modes of expression, and whole regimes of signs.' Gilles Deleuze, *Eight Years Later: 1980 Interview*, in: TWO REGIMES OF MADNESS (MIT Press 2006), 176–7. Partly drawing on Deleuze's work on assemblage, sociologists, political theorists and lawyers have more recently been applying the concept to the multifarious and nonunified governance regimes in what systems theory scholars term functionally differentiated systems of specialization. See, for example, SASKIA SASSEN, TERRITORY, AUTHORITY, RIGHTS: FROM MEDIEVAL TO GLOBAL ASSEMBLAGES (Princeton University Press 2006), and Gavin Sullivan, *Transnational Legal Assemblages and Global Security Law: Topologies and Temporalities of the List*, 5 TRANSNATIONAL LEGAL THEORY 81–127 (2014), 82: 'The concept of assemblage has been rarely used in legal theory because its emphasis on materiality, distributed agency and heterogeneity challenges received notions of legal formalism and the way international norms are ordinarily thought to be constituted, transmitted and contained. Yet I suggest that it is precisely these qualities that provide the assemblage with analytical advantage in understanding how this listing regime functions in the transnational context.'

[29] Gráinne de Búrca, Robert O. Keohane & Charles Sabel, *Global Experimentalist Governance*, BRITISH JOURNAL OF POLITICAL SCIENCE 1–10 (2014).

[30] De Búrca, Keohane & Sabel, previous note, at 5: 'Institutional inertia and political deadlock, the rise of non-hierarchical organizations, and the proliferation of linkages between international organizations and civil society actors – all fomented by and contributing to greater uncertainty – have led to the emergence of a variety of higher-order governance arrangements, the most representative of which are regime complexes … Regime complexes, including different mixes of states, sub-state units, international organizations, civil society organizations and private actors, have in various issue areas replaced more tightly integrated international regimes … and have been identified in the areas of climate change, food security, refugee policy, energy, intellectual property and anti-corruption.'

policies justified through a range of distinct frameworks and assumptions – social justice, economic redistribution, human capabilities, citizen security, religious law, neo-laissez faire economics, and so on – come together at the same time within the transnational spaces through which the endemic social problems of our times are increasingly addressed.[31]

What this suggests is that even a legal field – human rights – whose appeal is so fundamentally based on its principled, nonpartisan, generalized normativity 'lives' in fact in the tiniest detail of locally and substantively diverse and destabilizing struggles for voice, recognition, and identity.[32] And it is here that TL reveals its deep roots in an anthropological – however problematic, contested and charged[33] – engagement with the living material of social processes, institutional developments and human interaction.[34] It is through the invocation of something like 'transnational law'[35] that one can point to the transformation of law's architectures through an increasing interpenetration of local, national and international, formal and informal, state and nonstate-based norm making processes. Transnational law's doctrinal grounding follows from the functional area in which a legal conflict arises and is shaped through the increasingly precarious and volatile competition and power struggle between different actors over regulatory and interpretive authority. It is in that sense that one may speak, for example, of 'transnational' labour law, when referring to the border crossing processes of hard and

---

[31] Mark Goodale, *Locating Rights, Envisioning Law Between the Global and the Local*, in: THE PRACTICE OF HUMAN RIGHTS: TRACKING LAW BETWEEN THE GLOBAL AND THE LOCAL (Mark Goodale & Sally Merry eds, Cambridge University Press 2007), 3.

[32] See, for example, Helen Quane, *Legal Pluralism and International Human Rights Law: Inherently Incompatible, Mutually Reinforcing or Something in Between?*, 33:4 OXFORD JOURNAL OF LEGAL STUDIES 675–702 (2013), highlighting the tensions between international human rights law and legal pluralism. Ibid, at 677. This is further illustrated by the analysis respectively provided by Marc Galanter, *Justice in Many Rooms: Courts, Private Ordering, and Indigenous Law*, 19 JOURNAL OF LEGAL PLURALISM 1–47 (1981), and Rosemary Nagy, *Transitional Justice as Global Project: Critical Reflections*, in: LAW IN TRANSITION: HUMAN RIGHTS, DEVELOPMENT AND TRANSITIONAL JUSTICE (Ruth Buchanan & Peer Zumbansen eds, Hart Publishing 2014).

[33] Akhil Gupta & James Ferguson, *Discipline and Practice: "The Field" as Site, Method, and Location in Anthropology*, in: Akhil Gupta & James Ferguson (eds), ANTHROPOLOGICAL LOCATIONS: BOUNDARIES AND GROUNDS OF A FIELD SCIENCE (University of California Press 1997), 1–46, at 8: 'Anthropology, more than perhaps any other discipline, is a body of knowledge constructed on regional specialization, and it is within regionally circumscribed epistemic communities that many of the discipline's key concepts and debates have been developed ... More than comparativists in other fields – political science, sociology, literature, history, law, religion, and business – anthropologists combine language learning and regional scholarship with long-term residence in "the field."'

[34] Sally Merry, *Anthropology, Law, and Transnational Processes*, 21 ANNUAL REVIEW OF ANTHROPOLOGY 357–79 (1992). See also, for example, the programme of studies in 'Transnational Processes' at the University of Chicago: https://sociology.uchicago.edu/content/transnational-processes.

[35] This section draws in small parts on Peer Zumbansen, *Transnational Law, With and Beyond Jessup*, in: Peer Zumbansen (ed.), THE MANY LIVES OF TRANSNATIONAL LAW: CRITICAL ENGAGEMENTS WITH JESSUP'S BOLD PROPOSAL (Cambridge University Press 2020).

soft law norm production, the emergence of norm-creating and norm-resisting coalitions of workers, employers and their multifarious cascades of multinationals and supply chains, governments, unions, NGOs and diverse activists. Unmoored, as it were, from a constitutionally embedded framework of labour and employment law, of industrial relations and from the recognition that labour conflicts are essential test cases for a national political economy, transnational labour law today unfolds in an extremely contested and fragmented sphere of declining and increasingly deferential state regulation, on the one hand, and the de-legalization, privatization and precarization of work and employment relationships, on the other.

Similarly, it seems adequate to refer to 'transnational climate law' in an effort to depict the complex and constantly evolving architecture of public and private regulatory innovation that ranges from forms of state regulation of tax incentives or emission standards to a wide diversity of civil society and market-based initiatives to mitigate climate change.[36] As in the case of transnational labour law, a label such as transnational climate law can hardly over up the fantastic levels of demagogy and horse-trading that occur under its auspices. Finally, whatever we – and, here, bear in mind that our current students include those who were born after 9/11 – have come to associate today with 'transnational anti-terrorism law', remains a highly diversified, seemingly intractable and overwhelmingly intransparent set of transnational regulatory regime complexes that – based on the crudely simplifying policy choice 'between security and freedom' – have forever transformed national and global political economies.

Transnational law, in other words, offers a valuable perspective on the differentiation of lawmaking processes across a wide range of core legal-regulatory areas, while at the same time prompting us to look more closely at the constituting dynamics out of which rules and standards arise.

But, in light of the just mentioned three areas of TL – labour, the environment, terrorism – it also becomes clearer how TL should not be seen as a self-standing edifice of legal rules, somewhere 'out there' in global space. TL offers a sobering perspective on the ongoing transformation of law and of its normative and institutional foundations. TL strikes us as inherently precarious and as a work in progress, but it should really remind us of how law is always already unstable and vulnerable. Transnational law, thus, emphasizes the need to critically challenge the idea that a particular legal field not only displays but, arguably, represents and guarantees theoretical and doctrinal coherence. Transnational law challenges the possibility of such coherence by scrutinizing the dynamics at the heart of a legal field. The law with which we engage in this space of self-critique is never complete or 'finished'. Rather, as legal 'field', it is an unstable ground on which competing claims are negotiated with regard to values, societal expectations, doctrinal coherence and 'system' as well as the field's openness to future challenges. Seen that way, a legal field prompts an inquiry also into the process through which we reengage with what law is, should be, can be. The space, then, in which this self-critique – and new forms of careful, open-minded and mutually respectful

---

[36] Stephen Minas, *Climate Change Governance, International Relations and Politics: A Transnational Law Perspective*, in: Peer Zumbansen (ed.), *Oxford Handbook of Transnational Law* (Oxford University Press 2020, *forthcoming*).

interaction among lawyers from different backgrounds, along with critical theorists, anthropologists, sociologists, geographers and literature theorists[37] – can occur, becomes the foundation of the engagement with the new form and practice of law which we here call 'transnational'.

This process is already underway, across the connection of legal subfields among themselves and with other disciplines, through the critical elaboration of problem-based and problem-driven 'new' legal areas, through legal practice in unchartered territories, through the fusing of different legal strategies of litigation, advocacy and reform and through a recognition of the importance of access to facts. Transnational law, then – as a methodology of law in (global) context – unfolds across an ongoing engagement with manifestations of transnational regulatory normativity,[38] legal pluralism (in its domestic, transnational and global iterations)[39] and nonstate and 'unofficial' law,[40] with intricate ethnographies of local ordering,[41] the 'spatialization' of human and institutional activities and law's varied associated adaptive processes,[42] and 'recursivity' as the intricate, interloping processes of up- and downloading of norms between local, national and international regulatory levels – with its challenging consequences for the shape and driving dynamics of the emerging transnational architecture of politics and

---

[37] EDWARD SAID, ORIENTALISM (Vintage 1978); Amanda Ruth Waugh Lagji, *Transnational Law and Literatures: A Postcolonial Perspective*, in: Peer Zumbansen (ed.), OXFORD HANDBOOK OF TRANSNATIONAL LAW (Oxford University Press 2019, *forthcoming*).

[38] Here, the demarcation lines between what is referred to as 'global' and 'transnational law' are oftentimes blurry. See, for a good discussion, Eric C. Ip, *Globalization and the Future of Law of the Sovereign State*, 8:3 INTERNATIONAL JOURNAL OF CONSTITUTIONAL LAW 636–55 (2010), 643 ff.

[39] See, for example, John Griffiths, *What Is Legal Pluralism?*, 24 JOURNAL OF LEGAL PLURALISM AND UNOFFICIAL LAW 1–55 (1986); Sally Engle Merry, *Legal Pluralism*, 22:5 LAW & SOCIETY REVIEW 869–96 (1988); Paul Schiff Berman, *Global Legal Pluralism*, 80 SOUTHERN CALIFORNIA LAW REVIEW 1155–1237 (2007); Ralf Michaels, *Global Legal Pluralism*, 5 ANNUAL REVIEW OF LAW AND SOCIAL SCIENCE 243–62 (2009); Peer Zumbansen, *Transnational Legal Pluralism* 1:2 TRANSNATIONAL LEGAL THEORY 141–89 (2010).

[40] Boaventura de Sousa Santos, *A Map of Misreading: Toward a Postmodern Conception of Law*, 14:3 JOURNAL OF LAW AND SOCIETY 279–302 (1987); Ralf Michaels, *The Re-State-ment of Non-State Law: The State, Choice of Law, and the Challenge of Global Legal Pluralism*, 51 WAYNE STATE LAW REVIEW 1209–59 (2005).

[41] Prabha Kotiswaran, *Sword or Shield? The Role of the Law in the Indian Sex Workers' Movement*, 15:4 INTERVENTIONS: INTERNATIONAL JOURNAL OF POSTCOLONIAL STUDIES 530–45 (2013).

[42] PHILIP G. CERNY, THE CHANGING ARCHITECTURE OF POLITICS: STRUCTURE, AGENCY, AND THE FUTURE OF THE STATE (SAGE 1990); MICHAEL LIKOSKY (ED.), TRANSNATIONAL LEGAL PROCESSES: GLOBALISATION AND POWER DISPARITIES (Butterworths 2002); Saskia Sassen, *The Embeddedness of Electronic Markets: The Case of Global Capital Markets*, in: Karin Knorr-Cetina & Alex Preda (eds), THE SOCIOLOGY OF FINANCIAL MARKETS (Oxford University Press 2005), 17–37.

the 'formal properties of global law'[43] – as well as in the fast evolving architectures of 'transnational legal orders'.[44]

It should have become clear that close scrutiny of the instability of evolving 'transnational' regulatory arrangements reveals the relations between these arrangements and the law, which are otherwise taken for granted or, at least, taken as comparably more stable, 'historically grown' and grounded in the domestic context. Such a perception is based in part on the misconception of law as a principled edifice which, in its doctrinal, normative and philosophical dimensions, stands distinctly. While a sociologist like Niklas Luhmann would agree with the relative autonomy of law 'as a system', even ascribing to it a fairly high degree of idiosyncrasy,[45] this is not the kind of autonomy that analytical as well as mainstream jurisprudence has in mind. By contrast, for systems theory sociology, it was always clear and, indeed, crucial for the appreciation of law's nature and function that law's operational closure – the self-referential systematic processing of specific distinctions – co-exists with law's cognitive openness – meaning the never-ending challenge of and, even, assault on relied-upon legal meanings and truths by competing knowledge systems.

The mainstream account of law's nature remains quite distinct from both a systems theory and transnational law one. While for the former law is forever part of and caught in a conflict of different rationalities in the wider context of a functionally differentiated (world) society, TL is here understood as a methodological laboratory in which to scrutinize law's alleged distinctiveness from and superiority over other systems of social ordering. Both then take issue with the mainstream's regularly unquestioned association of law with the nation state, from which follows a host of additional, consequential assumptions. When it comes to law's fate in an era of 'globalization', the stubbornness with which the law-state nexus is defended comes at a price. Not only becomes law tied to the state in its now overdrawn symbolic dimension as gate keeper and guardian of purportedly (democratically) legitimate politics, but law itself becomes somehow reified as a body of norms, principles and institutions, which need to be protected from the corroding forces of globalization's acidic, decomposing effect. The 'state', too, becomes caught up in the reification. By ascribing to the jurisdictional, in the end wholly constructed, boundary between 'the domestic' and 'the international' (let alone, 'the global') the qualities and characteristics of a real border, the actual nature of this boundary becomes wholly elusive. Ironically, perhaps, such border drawing repeats the moves that have gone into erecting the ideological boundaries

---

[43] Terence C. Halliday, *Recursivity of Global Lawmaking: A Sociolegal Agenda*, 5 ANNUAL REVIEW OF LAW AND SOCIAL SCIENCE 263–89 (2009), 265.

[44] Gregory Shaffer, *Transnational Legal Ordering and State Change*, in: ibid (ed.), TRANSNATIONAL LEGAL ORDERING AND STATE CHANGE 1–22 (Cambridge University Press 2013); TERENCE C. HALLIDAY & GREGORY SHAFFER (EDS), TRANSNATIONAL LEGAL ORDERS (Cambridge University Press 2015).

[45] Niklas Luhmann, *Law as a Social System*, 83 NORTHWESTERN UNIVERSITY LAW REVIEW 136–50 (1989), 140: 'In a way that no other system does, the law processes normative expectations that are capable of maintaining themselves in situations of conflict. The law cannot guarantee, of course, that these expectations will not be disappointed. But it can guarantee that they can be maintained, as expectations, even in case of disappointment, and that one can know this and communicate it in advance.'

between 'state' and 'society'.[46] One of the most problematic results of such a literal understanding of the idea of border and boundary is that the very choice by which domestic law has been situated, effectively, as existing 'apart' and in a state of solid and reliable beauty has itself become invisible. Both 'the state' and its role as host to 'the law' have become self-evident, unquestionable truths.

Against such crude line-drawing between what law allegedly is, has been and should be, 'here' in 'the nation state' on the one hand, and in the face of the horrors of what law cannot and should not be, 'out there' in the vacuous wilderness of the global space on the other, we want to argue for a different conception of law. In effect, we want to argue that the instability which is ascribed to the chaos of 'law and globalization' – aka TL – is not inherent to this particular concept or 'field' but, rather, that this kind of institutional and normative instability is an inherent and unavoidably characteristic part of law's evolution in the context of a changing society. While TL prompts us to investigate the particular manifestations of its natural instability with a greater emphasis on the spatialization of human and institutional interactions,[47] and on the 'places' in which political (and, along with it, legal) agency is being claimed and fought over[48] – as we, in Mark Goodale's and Sally Merry's words, 'track it between the Global and the Local'[49] – we can look at the longstanding body of work by legal sociologists and critical legal scholars to appreciate the very 'local' roots of this instability that plagues law's institutional and normative framework. It is important, then, to resist the idea that TL serves as a stand-in for the conceptual turmoil and doctrinal riddles that 'law and globalization' has been bringing about. TL, understood in that vein, is then not a result *of* or an answer *to* the problem of law's globalization. Instead, TL should be recognized as a methodological framework that engages with law's ever changing social – as well as political, cultural and geographic – conditions.

TL – to the degree that it encompasses the actors, norms and processes implicated in the generation, dissemination, implementation and contestation of legal norms – has its roots in the realm of political economy and the myriad local, 'national' and spatial battlegrounds where political agency is invoked, imposed and resisted and rights are claimed, denied, struggled for. TL, so understood, bears considerable elective affinities with critical legal scholarship as it unfolded in the US throughout the 1970s, against the background of the more recent revival of the legal realists' critique of legal formalism in a climate of dramatic societal conflict over racial and gender equality and political as well as social and economic rights, but also bears affinities with the German late nineteenth century strands of interest jurisprudence and the post-Second World War sociological jurisprudence as it unfolded at law schools in Frankfurt and Bremen.[50] It is

---

[46] Mitchell, *Limits of the State*, above note 16.

[47] EVE DARIAN-SMITH, LAWS AND SOCIETIES IN GLOBAL CONTEXTS (Cambridge University Press 2013).

[48] CHANTAL MOUFFE, AGONISTICS: THINKING THE WORLD POLITICALLY (Verso 2013). See also Brendan Hogan, *Agency, Political Economy, and the Transnational Democratic Ideal*, 3:1 ETHICS & GLOBAL POLITICS 37–45 (2010).

[49] Goodale & Merry, above note 11.

[50] Christian Joerges, David Trubek & Peer Zumbansen, *Critical Legal Thought: An American-German Debate: An Introduction at the Occasion of Its Republication in the German Law Journal 25 Years Later*, 12:1 GERMAN LAW JOURNAL 1–33 (2011).

against that background that TL emerges as part of a tradition of *political* legal theory in the aftermath of various strands of legal realism, critical legal studies, feminist legal studies and critical race theory, as well as, more recently, Third World approaches to international law (TWAIL) and science, technology and society (STS) approaches. TL's European roots can be found, for example, in the elaboration of a critical concept of 'economic law' that was undertaken in Germany between the 1960s and 1980s,[51] seeking to overcome the conservative line-drawing between an interventionist (as well as, eventually, redistributive) state and an apolitical market.[52] Meanwhile, transnational law lives across geographical spaces and jurisdictional boundaries, drawing together social practices of norm creation and norm contestation, 'state making', renewal, reform and revolution.

With the benefit of legal–anthropological and legal–sociological insights, the question regarding the type and orientation of a legal theory that can capture this assemblage of actors, norms and processes across the time and space of a globally connected yet deeply divided world poses itself in a new light. At once, such a legal theory would have to be able to both make sense of the *spatial* dimensions of specialized regulatory regimes and be sensitive and receptive to their local and never fixed idiosyncrasies. It would appear, then, that a suitably globally minded and locally grounded legal theory would have to serve a number of functions. For one, it would have to be an ordering framework through which the different building blocks that form part of border crossing yet locally idiosyncratic and diverse regulatory regimes can be accounted for and be made amenable for conceptual as well as practical use. In other words, such a legal theory would have to provide a platform on which to deliberate the conceptual coherence of the theory's scope and normative orientation. This sounds more obscure than it has to, as we already have a number of comparable examples at our disposition: think of, for example, commercial law and property law, or of administrative and constitutional law. While the former two are within the core of what is generally considered 'private law', the latter are said to belong squarely to the realm of 'public law'. Each of these fields exists, in highly varied forms, both 'globally' and locally. It is the genius, one might say, of commercial law to provide an effective and comprehensive regulatory apparatus which spans both domestic and transnational dealings through an elaborate institutional and normative framework.[53] And it is the

---

[51] See Rudolf Wiethölter, *Social Science Models in Economic Law*, in: Gunther Teubner (ed.), CONTRACT AND ORGANISATION: LEGAL ANALYSIS IN THE LIGHT OF ECONOMIC AND SOCIAL THEORY (Walter de Gruyter 1986), 52–67; ibid, *Artikel Wirtschaftsrecht*, in: Axel Görlitz (ed.), HANDBUCH ZUR RECHTSWISSENSCHAFT (Darmstadt 1972); Christian Joerges, *Vorüberlegungen zu einer Theorie des Internationalen Wirtschaftsrechts*, 43 RABELS ZEITSCHRIFT FÜR AUSLÄNDISCHES UND INTERNATIONALES PRIVATRECHT 6–79 (1979); ibid, *Europe's Economic Constitution and the Emergence of a New Constitutional Constellation*, ZenTra Working Paper in Transnational Studies 06/2012, available at http://ssrn.com/abstract=2179595.

[52] See JOERGES, TRUBEK & ZUMBANSEN, CRITICAL LEGAL THOUGHT, above note 50.

[53] See, for example, Clive M. Schmitthoff, *International Business Law: A New Law Merchant*, 2 CURRENT LAW AND SOCIAL PROBLEMS 127–53 (1961); Graf-Peter Calliess, Hermann Hoffmann & Jens Mertens, *The Transnationalisation of Commercial Law*, in: STATE TRANSFORMATION IN OECD COUNTRIES (Heinz Rothgang & Steffen Schneider eds, Palgrave Macmillan 2015), 127–42.

486 Research handbook on critical legal theory

intricacy of a field such as property law that allows it to be at once a core doctrinal dimension of private law, a central category in economic theory, an ideological token in development policy and a contested concept in political theory.[54] Whereas private law has always been seen as a more suitable candidate for its border crossing expansion and migration, we have witnessed a significant degree of spatialization in public law areas such as administrative and constitutional law as well.[55] Placing such legal fields 'in global context' should not be understood as a manual of how to *move* a certain toolkit from one physical space into another. Instead, what is required is a problematization of law's understanding of 'the global'. How does law, in other words, construct and operationalize the difference between what is taken – uncritically, automatically, most often – as its habitat and what is considered to lie outside of it?

3. TRANSNATIONAL LAW'S PLACE IN POSTCOLONIAL LEGAL THEORY

And it is at that moment that we can sense the growing suspicion that an amalgam such as TL ('transnational' and 'law') must be *connected to* and become *part of* this congregation of disciplines, investigative strategies and heterogeneous research frameworks with which we are grappling in light of a host of phenomena that are not only extremely wide-ranging and diverse,[56] but also contested with regard to their underlying epistemologies and inherent ideologies. The larger universe of critical theory, post-colonial studies and post-colonial legal theory is a crucial reference point in this regard. How does TL fit into this mix? If postcolonial theory has 'taught' us anything, we must acknowledge that a depiction of a 'problem', a 'crisis' and a particular 'affectedness' always occurs from a certain standpoint and perspective. What from a Western perspective might constitute 'pressing' challenges in the shape of 'disembedded' markets, the globalization of financial capitalism and the seemingly unstoppable erosion of social safeguards might be depicted very differently and with contrasting

---

[54] Priya S. Gupta, *Transnational Property Law*, in: OXFORD HANDBOOK OF TRANSNATIONAL LAW (Peer Zumbansen ed., Oxford University Press forthcoming 2020); Priya S. Gupta, *Globalizing Property Law*, UNIVERSITY OF PENNSYLVANIA JOURNAL OF INTERNATIONAL LAW (forthcoming 2019).

[55] Benedict Kingsbury, Nico Krisch & Richard B. Stewart, *The Emergence of Global Administrative Law*, 68 LAW & CONTEMPORARY PROBLEMS 15–61 (2005). See the critical discussion of the 'GAL' project by Susan Marks, *Naming Global Administrative Law*, 37 NYU JOURNAL OF INTERNATIONAL LAW AND POLITICS 995–1001 (2006), Bhupander S. Chimni, *Co-Option and Resistance: Two Faces of Global Administrative Law*, 37 NYU JOURNAL OF GLOBAL ADMINISTRATIVE LAW 799–827 (2006).

[56] Garrett W. Brown & Ronald Labonté, *Globalization and Its Methodological Discontents: Contextualizing Globalization through the Study of HIV/AIDS*, 7 GLOBALIZATION & HEALTH 1–12 (2011), 1–2: 'traditional approaches to the study of globalization often fail to capture many facets involved within its multifarious and complex processes: that whatever globalization is, it is not something that is easily definable or reasonably encapsulated by a single trend (or bundle of trends) associated with global interconnection. It is more appropriate to think of globalization as a pluralistic phenomenon with indeterminate idiosyncrasies and anomalistic permutations' (references omitted).

accentuations, explanations and allocations of (political, historical) agency from within alternative, 'subaltern' framings.[57] When we start challenging, relativizing and decentring the usual state/law-nexus against which so many of the dominant depictions of a 'crisis of law in an age of globalization' are rendered,[58] a very different universe of reference points begins to emerge. Instead of confirming the prevailing viewpoint from which law is challenged through waves of internationalization with regard to inter- and intragovernmental collaboration,[59] as well as through border crossing subject areas,[60] on the one hand, and through the proliferation of private, 'nonstate' actors in the context of norm creation, on the other, we are confronted with deep-reaching challenges to the dominant characterizations of 'the normal' and 'the exception'. While some of these challenges manifest themselves under the umbrella of a postcolonial critique of (Western) law[61] – take the example of public international law, which has been exposed to an important critique of its colonial and imperialist legacies, for

---

[57] The critique of a market having become disembedded from society goes back, of course, to KARL POLANYI, THE GREAT TRANSFORMATION (Beacon Books, 1946). For a present-time engagement, see the contributions to Christian Joerges & Josef Falke (eds.), KARL POLANYI, GLOBALISATION AND THE POTENTIAL OF LAW IN TRANSNATIONAL MARKETS (Hart Publishing, 2011) On financial capitalism, see, e.g., the astute observations by Eric Helleiner, *Explaining the Globalization of Financial Markets: Bringing States Back In*, 2 REVIEW OF INTERNATIONAL POLITICAL ECONOMY 315–41 (1995), and now the brilliant book by MARIANA MAZZACUTO, THE VALUE OF EVERYTHING: MAKING AND TAKING IN THE GLOBAL ECONOMY (Allen Lane, 2018), esp. chpts 4 et seq. On the 'social question' in a transnational context, see, e.g., Gary Spolander et al, *The Implications of Neoliberalism for Social Work: Reflections from a Six-Country International Research Collaboration*, 57 INTERNATIONAL SOCIAL WORK 301–12 (2014).

[58] See, for example, Eric C. Ip, *Globalization and the Future of the Law of the Sovereign State*, 8 INTERNATIONAL JOURNAL OF CONSTITUTIONAL LAW 636–55 (2010), 637: 'Two major developments highlight the international legal system's partial withdrawal from its established state-centric orientation and its embrace of globally relevant concerns: the proliferation of specialized regimes of international law, which extend into major domestic policy areas, and the rising prominence of transnational regulatory regimes enacted by nonstate actors. The rise of nonstate regulation of issues previously monopolized by state legal control raises important questions about the future of state law.'

[59] Jonathan I. Charney, *Universal International Law*, 87 AM. J. INT'L L. 529–51 (1993), 529: 'In this shrinking world, states are increasingly interdependent and interconnected, a development that has affected international law.' ANNE-MARIE SLAUGHTER, A NEW WORLD ORDER (Princeton University Press, 2004).

[60] Frank Biermann, Philipp Pattberg & Harro van Asselt, *The Fragmentation of Global Governance Architectures: A Framework for Analysis*, 9:4 GLOBAL ENVIRONMENTAL POLITICS 14–40 (2009), 16: 'the notion of global governance architecture in particular for this reason: because it allows for the analysis of (the many) policy domains in international relations that are not regulated, and often not even dominated, by a single international regime in the traditional understanding. Many policy domains are instead marked by a patchwork of international institutions that are different in their character (organizations, regimes, and implicit norms), their constituencies (public and private), their spatial scope (from bilateral to global), and their subject matter (from special policy fields to universal concerns).'

[61] Alpana Roy, *Postcolonial Theory and Law: A Critical Introduction*, 29 ADELAIDE LAW REVIEW 315 (2008); Eve Darian-Smith, *Postcolonial Theories and Law*, in: LAW AND SOCIAL THEORY (Hart Publishing, 2nd ed., 2013) (Reza Banakar & Max Travers eds), 247–64.

example under the auspices of TWAIL[62] – their critical and transformative significance is far greater. It is as much political as it is epistemological.[63] While the former results in radically 'complicating' the place that law, its doctrines, its concepts – as well as the legal profession itself – is occupying in the world,[64] the latter has been pointing to the potential of calling into question and destabilizing the entirety of the Western liberal legal paradigm in its intertwinement with a long and bloody trajectory of imperialist

---

[62] Obiora Chinedu Okafor, *Critical Third World Approaches to International Law (TWAIL): Theory, Methodology, or Both?*, 10 INTERNATIONAL COMMUNITY LAW REVIEW 371–8 (2008), 373: 'Regarding its predictive-ness, much TWAIL scholarship tends to offer windows into international law's tomorrow. Drawing from the empirical history of international law's engagement with third world peoples, such scholarship tends to imagine and predict the ways in which international law will behave toward the "third world" (or some part thereof) in the near and long term'; James T. Gathii, *TWAIL: A Brief History of Its Origins, Its Decentralized Network, and a Tentative Bibliography*, 3 TRADE, LAW & DEVELOPMENT 26–64 (2011), 30: 'TWAIL scholarship, more than any other scholarly approach to international law, has brought the colonial encounter between Europeans and non-Europeans to the center of this historical re-examination of international law. 14: In doing so, 'TWAIL scholarship has not only rethought international law's relationship to the colonial encounter, but has also challenged the complacency in international law to treat the colonial legacy as dead letter, overcome by the process of decolonization.'

[63] For a political critique, see James Thuo Gathii, *Neoliberalism, Colonialism and International Governance: Decentering the International Law of Governmental Legitimacy*, 98 MICHIGAN LAW REVIEW 1996–2055 (2000), 1997: 'This third world approach thus not only disrupts the hegemonic approaches to the study of international law, but also partly embodies the political goals of the third world, as I see them. It is thus as legal as it is political.' Eve Darian-Smith, *Postcolonialism: A Brief Introduction*, 5:3 SOCIAL & LEGAL STUDIES 291–9 (1996), 292: '(…) postcolonialism operates as a chronological marker and method of periodization. It optimistically suggests the transcendence of nineteenth-century imperialism, and a greater balancing of respective political and economic power between the West and developing countries. This temporal approach to postcolonialism is explicitly political since it involves contested interpretations of what it does and does not represent.' See, for an engagement with the epistemological dimensions of colonization and de- as well as post-colonization, Boaventura de Sousa Santos, *Beyond Abyssal Thinking: From Global Lines to Ecologies of Knowledges*, EUROZINE 1–41 (2007), 4/33: 'the colonial zone is, par excellence, the realm of incomprehensible beliefs and behaviours which in no way can be considered knowledge, whether true or false. The other side of the line harbours only incomprehensible magical or idolatrous practices. The utter strangeness of such practices led to denying the very human nature of the agents of such practices. On the basis of their refined conceptions of humanity and human dignity, the humanists reached the conclusion that the savages were sub-human.'

[64] MARTIN LOUGHLIN, SWORD AND SCALES: AN EXAMINATION OF THE RELATIONSHIP BETWEEN LAW AND POLITICS (Hart Publishing 2000), 50–1: 'The logic of legal discourse yields a particular interpretation of events, but that interpretation is invariably susceptible to challenge from what may be called a political perspective. […] Between the naïve belief that political events can be understood entirely in terms of legal discourse and the blind conviction that the normative world of law can be dismissed as empty rhetoric, there remains a multiplicity of perspectives which might be advanced.' See also PHILIP ALLOTT, EUNOMIA: NEW ORDER FOR A NEW WORLD (Oxford University Press, 1990), 8.16 (p.128): 'Time and space are thus a consequence of the human being's ability to conceive the world in consciousness and to conceive of it as a world of possible willing and acting.'

and, eventually, neoliberal expansion.[65] This critique goes to the core of the matter, as it not only aims to uncover the victims, the bloodshed and the collateral damage of liberal law's travels into farflung corners of the world, but also targets colonialist and exclusionary legal effects within domestic, local legal cultures and instruments.[66] It does so through scrutiny, engagement, often also refutation of inherited, canonical views of how 'the law' has evolved as part of the 'progress' of human society – with alternating and intersecting associations of 'civilization', 'modernization' or, simply, 'development'.[67] Susan Buck-Morss, in an important article, asked:

> why is it of more than arcane interest to retrieve from oblivion this fragment of history, the truth of which has managed to slip away from us? There are many possible answers, but one is surely the potential for rescuing the idea of universal human history from the uses to which white domination has put it. If the historical facts about freedom can be ripped out of the narratives told by the victors and salvaged for our own time, then the project of universal freedom does not need to be discarded but, rather, redeemed and reconstituted on a different basis.[68]

An important tenet of the colonial critique is to identify and expose the black holes within and the gaps between these different narratives – both within the explicitly outward-oriented, expansionist and interventionist colonializing context and within core liberal doctrines in the here and now of Western law. An important aspect of such a

---

[65] Robert J.C. Young, *What Is the Postcolonial?*, 40:1 ARIEL: A REVIEW OF INTERNATIONAL ENGLISH LITERATURE 13–25 (2009), 14: 'Postcolonialism's concerns are centred on geographic zones of intensity that have remained largely invisible, but which prompt or involve questions of history, ethnicity, complex cultural identities and questions of representation, of refugees, emigration and immigration, of poverty and wealth – but also, importantly, the energy, vibrancy and creative cultural dynamics that emerge in very positive ways from such demanding circumstances. Postcolonialism offers a language of and for those who have no place, who seem not to belong, of those whose knowledges and histories are not allowed to count. It is above all this preoccupation with the oppressed, with the subaltern classes, with minorities in any society, with the concerns of those who live or come from elsewhere, that constitutes the basis of postcolonial politics and remains the core that generates its continuing power.'

[66] See, for example, John Borrows, *With or Without You: First Nations Law (in Canada)*, 41 MCGILL L.J. 629 (1996), and Monique Mann & Angela Daly, *(Big) Data and the North-in-South: Australia's Informational Imperialism and Digital Colonialism*, TELEVISION & NEW MEDIA 1–17 (2018), 2: 'Despite Australia's geographical position within the Asia-Pacific, and the enduring presence and richness of Aboriginal and Torres Strait Islander cultures, Australia's social and political backdrop neglects these in favor of Northern/Western influences, thereby perpetuating the marginalization of Indigenous peoples.'

[67] Susan Buck-Morss, *Hegel and Haiti*, 26:4 CRITICAL INQUIRY 821–65 (2000), 851–2: 'It has long been recognized that Hegel's understanding of politics was modern, based on an interpretation of the events of the French Revolution as a decisive break from the past and that he is referring to the French Revolution in The Phenomenology of Mind, even when he does not mention it by name. Why should Hegel have been a modernist in two senses only: adopting Adam Smith's theory of the economy and adopting the French Revolution as the model for politics. And, yet, when it came to slavery, the most burning issue of his time, with slave rebellions throughout the colonies and a successful slave revolution in the wealthiest of them – why should – how *could* Hegel have stayed somehow mired in Aristotle?'

[68] Buck-Morss, *Hegel and Haiti*, previous note, 864–5.

critique is that it is grounded in the present-day political economies of postcrisis, neoausterity and nondying neoliberal arrangements.[69] By directing critical attention to ideas such as contract, consent and autonomy, and to the way they play out in the context of legal and judicial interpretation and reaffirmation, it becomes possible to identify the structural violence of such universalizing concepts vis-à-vis the vulnerability of marginalized groups.[70] The creation of identities, of a 'we' as opposed to 'others', and the resistance against such creation, is crucial here. As Alpana Roy put it:

> postcolonial theory challenges the view of Otherness proffered by Western culture, and focuses on identities which have been constructed independently from the dominant narrative. Indeed, this issue of identity is fundamental, as the historically marginalised insist upon the recognition of their own construction in this postcolonial world. While postcolonial theory is critical of the colonial and imperial projects, and the continuing hegemonic position of Western economies and cultures, it actively engages in the formation of positive new political identities.[71]

---

[69] See the astute analysis by Gurminder Bhambra & John Holmwood, *Colonialism, Postcolonialism and the Liberal Welfare State*, 23:5 NEW POLITICAL ECONOMY 574–87 (2018), 575: 'the liberal welfare state exemplifies a general tendency in understandings of the welfare state to separate the "economic" from the "social" and the "political" and to assign to the former an impersonal logic of the market. The "social" is then understood as the locus of "identities", which are mobilized through the "political" process to intervene in the "economy" to moderate its outcomes. Most approaches, then, represent commodification and its correlative categories of economy, market and class to operate in a way that looks forward either to the erosion of discrimination (standard liberal accounts) or to a universalism beyond "race" contained in class-based opposition to the commodity form (for example, as in Marxist-oriented accounts). We seek to show that "commodification" is racialised in itself and not simply by the operation of external "social" modifications that may contingently prove stronger than any tendency to resolve them. In this way, we argue that markets are racialised as a consequence of the commodity form, rather than despite it.'

[70] Anne O'Connell, *My Entire Life Is Online: Informed Consent, Big Data, and Decolonial Knowledge*, 5:1 INTERSECTIONALITIES: A GLOBAL JOURNAL OF SOCIAL WORK ANALYSIS, RESEARCH, POLITY, AND PRACTICE 68–93 (2016), 70: 'Many of our institutional and government responses to ethical concerns are instrumental approaches for the "how to" of consent, autonomy, and privacy. While online and digital research protocols are being introduced in relation to these issues, the foundational questions about the communities we want to live in persist … What kind of ethics are we moving toward when our face-to-face encounters are computer mediated, while the body itself is increasingly compartmentalized, exteriorized, and commodified through a tissue economy that includes biobanks … transplant tourism … the human genome project, and reproductive technologies … ? In an age of increased abstractions, how do categories of race and racisms appear less visible or hyper-visible, with little interrogation into the concrete ways they are formed and used to organize knowledge production and ways of ruling?" See also ibid, *Building their Readiness for Economic 'Freedom': The New Poor Law and Emancipation*, 36:2 JOURNAL OF SOCIOLOGY AND SOCIAL WELFARE 85–103 (2009).

[71] See Alpana Roy, *Postcolonial Theory and Law: A Critical Introduction*, 29 ADELAIDE LAW REVIEW 315–57 (2008), 320.

It is here that the postcolonial historical assessment of the 'where' and the 'who dunnit?' becomes key.[72] But, importantly, it no longer remains confined to the countries to which we attribute the label 'decolonized'.[73] Legal history becomes an important battlefield on which competing and opposing narratives get tested against the background of their incorporated assumptions regarding progress but also 'centre' and 'periphery'.[74] Colonial critique unfolds in a repeated calling into question of generally accepted ascriptions of historical reason and meaning. In that regard, Walter Mignolo has astutely observed: 'That "civilization" is somewhat related to "globalization" and "modern/colonial world system" is obvious. How it is related is not obvious. I submit that the colonial difference is one of the missing links between civilization, modernization, and modern/colonial world system.'[75]

Whether, to highlight just two areas of considerable contention, it is the idea of human rights being 'universal' in contrast to pluralist, subaltern human rights conceptions,[76] or whether it concerns the contention that it is the central role of 'the state' not

---

[72] See, for example, Makau wa Mutua, *Conflicting Conceptions of Human Rights: Rethinking the Post-Colonial State*, Proceedings of the Annual Meeting, 89 ASIL, 'Structures of the World Order', 487–90 (1995), 487: 'It is becoming increasingly apparent that sovereignty and statehood are concepts that may have trapped Africa in a detrimental time capsule; they now seem to be straightjackets with time bombs ready to explode. The imposition of the nation-state through colonization balkanized Africa into ahistorical units and forcibly yanked it into the Age of Europe, permanently disfiguring it. Unlike their European counterparts, African states and borders are distinctly artificial and are not the visible expression of historical struggles by local peoples to achieve political adjustment and balance. Colonization interrupted this historical and evolutionary process.'

[73] For a riveting analysis of the gap between the 'legal' and the 'political'/'economic' decolonization on the part of formerly colonized states after the Second World War, see SUNDHYA PAHUJA, DECOLONIZING INTERNATIONAL LAW (Cambridge University Press 2011).

[74] See the account by Renato Ortiz, *Notas sobre la problemática de la globalisacíon de las sociedades*, 41 DIÁLOGOS DE COMUNICACÍON (1995), ms p. 1: 'Es el caso cuando hablamos de relaciones internacionales. Esta noción presupone la existencia de naciones autónomas interactuando entre sí. La dinámica global derivaría de movimiento de las partes. Cada una de ellas, en su integridad actuaría en el contexto mundial. Las mismas premisas subyacer a los conceptos de colonialismo y de imperialismo. En cada uno de ellos destacamos un centro (el imperio o la nación industrializada) como elemento propulsor de movimiento de expansión. El mundo sería así el cruzamiento de las diversas intenciones, transimperiales o transnacionales que, de forma diferenciada incidirían en las colonias o en los países periféricos. Una aplicación común de este tipo de raciocinio es la comparación entre el momento actual y algunos periodos de la historia pasada. Por ejemplo, la analogía de la ascención y la caída de un país, como los Estados Unidos, a la del Imperio Romano. En los dos casos tenemos la expansión de una civilización, norteamericana o romana, de una lengua, el inglés o el latin, hacia un conjunto de territorios apartados de su núcleo irradiador. Las relaciones de contacto entre esta «periferia» y el «centro» se harían por tanto de acuerdo con normas de dominación elaboradas por los países o por los imperios colonizadores.' (Available at: https://www.infoamerica.org/documentos_pdf/ortiz02.pdf)

[75] WALTER MIGNOLO, LOCAL HISTORIES/GLOBAL DESIGNS: COLONIALITY, SUBALTERN KNOWLEDGES, AND BORDER THINKING (Princeton University Press 2000), 278.

[76] See, for example, the seminal text by C.L.R. JAMES, THE BLACK JACOBINS: TOUSSAINT L'OUVERTURE AND THE SAN DOMINGO REVOLUTION (Random House, 1963; 2nd revised ed., Vintage Books, 1989), and, more recently, one of the foundational works in the TWAIL movement: ANTONY ANGHIE, IMPERIALISM, SOVEREIGNTY AND THE MAKING OF INTERNATIONAL

only to contain and administer the legal order but also to be the 'reservoir' of the people and of a democratic populace,[77] the colonialist critique goes to the roots of the dominant historical narratives and the central tenets of Western law. What we might learn in this regard from the intriguing coexistence of human rights disillusionment and steadfast revival is the importance of continuing 'close encounters' between competing and too often insulated theoretical approaches, on the one hand, and down to earth, locally sensitive ethnographies of how, where and why human rights work or fail. As Ben Golder observed:

> When operating in this mode, much critical theorising about human rights actually ends up attempting to reimagine (and in doing so, reinforce) the human rights project itself. After having exposed its false claims to universality, its investment in and reproduction of a narrow liberal ontology, its propensity to circumscribe the field and possibility of politics, its inability to break with global capitalist ordering, its indebtedness to and repetition of colonial history, and a host of other related criticisms (in short: the critique of human rights as a particular form of Western political liberalism that gets exported globally with great violence), critical commentators on human rights nevertheless make a curious return to human rights. In this post-critical redemptive guise, human rights emerge in spite of their evident historical and political limitations as the site of reinvestment, reimagining and of futural possibilities.[78]

A central focus of critique in this regard is the perpetuated distinction between a 'European' law, existing in a timeless and immaterial, abstract space of universal validity, and the various localities of 'non-European' peoples in which underdeveloped, nonenlightened custom and tradition prevailed:[79]

LAW (Cambridge University Press 2005), and Rebecca Adami, *On Subalternity and Representation: Female and Postcolonial Subjects Claiming Universal Human Rights in 1948*, 6 JOURNAL OF RESEARCH ON WOMEN AND GENDER 56–66 (2015), 58: 'United Nations delegates from non-Western and Western societies met on an international arena and agreed to disagree on the values that underscore the moral justification of the universality of human rights. Human rights were referred to as practical principles, compatible with divergent cultural value systems. What was under critical consideration in the United Nations by the delegates in 1948 was the disrespect of human rights in national legislation around the world, in Western as well as non-Western countries.'

[77] See, for a critique, Makau wa Mutua, *Politics and Human Rights: An Essential Symbiosis*, in: THE ROLE OF LAW IN INTERNATIONAL POLITICS (Michael Byers ed., Oxford University Press 2000), 149–75, at 166–7: 'There are fundamental defects in presenting the state as the reservoir of cultural heritage. Many states have been alien to their populations and it is questionable whether they represent those populations or whether they are little more than internationally recognized cartels for the sake of maintaining power and access to resources.'

[78] Ben Golder, *Beyond Redemption? Problematising the Critique of Human Rights in Contemporary International Legal Thought*, 2 LONDON REVIEW OF INTERNATIONAL LAW 77–114 (2014), 79.

[79] ANGHIE, IMPERIALISM, above note 76, at 5: 'European states were sovereign and equal. The colonial confrontation, however, particularly since the nineteenth century when colonialism reached its apogee, was not a confrontation between two sovereign states, but rather between a sovereign European state and a non-European society that was deemed by jurists to be lacking in sovereignty – or lese, at best only partially sovereign.'

Part of the problem has been the production of a binary between the enlightened space of 'abstract universal law' and the specifically located site of ('non-Western') culture and tradition. International law has in this way been both claimed to reflect the embodiment of 'Western' Enlightenment principles and simultaneously abstracted to assert a universal applicability.[80]

Furthermore, then, a central test ground of postcolonial critique is its ability to expose continuities and recurrences of colonialist categories in the present-day exclusionary politics in the context of migration governance,[81] racialized policing,[82] and the 'war on terror' without confining its investigation to historically colonized states. As before in the cases of 'law and development',[83] critical comparative law,[84] and certain strands of legal pluralism,[85] it is through postcolonial legal theory's inward turn that it becomes

---

[80] Kiran Grewal, *Can the Subaltern Speak Within International Law? Women's Rights Activism, International Legal Institutions and the Power of 'Strategic Misunderstanding'*, in: NEGOTIATING NORMATIVITY (N. Dhawan et al, eds, Springer 2016), 27–44, at 28.

[81] See Ratna Kapur, *The Citizen and the Migrant: Postcolonial Anxieties, Law, and the Politics of Exclusion/Inclusion*, 8:2 THEORETICAL INQUIRES IN LAW 537–69 (2007), 539: 'The subaltern is not merely a marginalized subject or a minority member, as understood within the terms of classical liberal thinking. The subaltern emerges from the specific ways in which the liberal project and imperialism operated during the colonial encounter, exposing the "dark side" of the liberal project and its exclusionary potential. The insights provided by the colonial past enable us to understand the operation of power through knowledge and how it sets the terms of inclusion and exclusion in the postcolonial present, though this understanding is not confined to postcolonial states.'

[82] ANDREW GUTHRIE FERGUSON, THE RISE OF BIG DATA POLICING: SURVEILLANCE, RACE AND THE FUTURE OF LAW ENFORCEMENT (New York University Press 2017). See also, for a slightly less pessimistic view, Sarah Brayne, *Big Data Surveillance: The Case of Policing*, 82:5 AMERICAN SOCIOLOGICAL REVIEW 977–1008 (2017), 982: 'Data-driven policing is being offered as a partial antidote to racially discriminatory practices in police departments across the country … However, although part of the appeal of big data lies in its promise of less discretionary and more objective decision-making … new analytic platforms and techniques are deployed in preexisting organizational contexts … and embody the purposes of their creators … Therefore, it remains an open empirical question to what extent the adoption of advanced analytics will reduce organizational inefficiencies and inequalities, or serve to entrench power dynamics within organizations.'

[83] David M. Trubek & Marc Galanter, *Scholars in Self-Estrangement: Some Reflections on the Crisis in Law and Development Studies in the United States* (1974) WISCONSIN LAW REVIEW 1062–1102; ibid, *Law and Development: Forty Years after 'Scholars in Self-Estrangement'*, 66 UNIVERSITY OF TORONTO LAW JOURNAL 301–29 (2016); Chantal Thomas, *Critical Race Theory and Postcolonial Development Theory: Observations on Methodology*, 45 VILLANOVA LAW REVIEW 1195–1220 (2000).

[84] Günter Frankenberg, *Critical Comparisons: Re-Thinking Comparative Law*, 26 HARV. INT'L L. J. 411–55 (1985); Peer Zumbansen, *Comparative Law's Coming of Age? Twenty Years after 'Critical Comparisons'*, 6 GER. L. J. 1073–84 (2005).

[85] Sally Merry, *Legal Pluralism*, 22 LAW & SOCIETY REVIEW 869–96 (1988), 869: 'The intellectual odyssey of the concept of legal pluralism moves from the discovery of indigenous forms of law among remote African villagers and New Guinea tribesmen to debates concerning the pluralistic qualities of law under advanced capitalism.' Geoffrey Swenson, *Legal Pluralism in Theory and Practice*, 20 INTERNATIONAL STUDIES REVIEW 438–62 (2018), 445: 'Complementary Legal Pluralism does not disappear in a state with a high-capacity, effective legal system, but it

possible not only to see 'the South in the North'[86] but to thereby also gain a more adequate grasp of, and a platform on which to resist,[87] the neocolonial regulatory dynamics unfolding in 'settler colonial' states.[88]

The proliferation of postcolonial legal theory – despite its lingering at the outer periphery of mainstream legal thought (and pedagogy)[89] – has the potential of fundamentally challenging the universalist and abstract assumptions of law in both theoretical and, indeed, highly practical terms.[90] Both in a wide range of specialized legal subfields and in the increasingly unruly realm of 'legal theory' we can witness a breathtaking intensification of law's engagement with and, subsequently, its transformation *through* interdisciplinarity, politics, history and social theory.[91] Transnational law, love or hate the term, might work as a convening framework to engage with law in this difficult context.

---

is complementary. In other words, nonstate is subordinated and structured by the state because the state enjoys both the legitimacy to have its rule accepted and the capacity to actually enforce its mandates.'

[86] Amar Bhatia, *The South of the North: Building on Critical Approaches to International Law with Lessons from the Fourth World*, 14 OREGON REV. INT'L L. 131 (2012).

[87] GLEN SEAN COULTHARD, RED SKIN WHITE MASKS: REJECTING THE COLONIAL POLITICS OF RECOGNITION (Minnesota University Press 2014), 3: 'I argue that instead of ushering in an era of peaceful coexistence grounded on the ideal of *reciprocity* or *mutual recognition*, the politics of recognition in its contemporary form promises to reproduce the very configurations of colonialist, racist, patriarchal state power that Indigenous peoples' demands for recognition have historically sought to transcend.'

[88] See, in that regard, Noura Erakat, JUSTICE FOR SOME. LAW AND THE QUESTION OF PALESTINE (Stanford University Press 2019), and Alexandre Kedar, Ahmad Amara & Oren Yiftachel, EMPTIED LANDS. A LEGAL GEOGRAPHY OF BEDOUIN RIGHTS IN THE NEGEV (Stanford University Press 2018). See also Adrian A. Smith, *Temporary Labour Migration and the 'Ceremony of Innocence' of Postwar Labour Law: Confronting 'the South of the North'*, 33:2 CANADIAN JOURNAL OF LAW AND SOCIETY 261–77 (2018), 274: 'Just as Canada's migration approach functions in ways consistent with colonialism, it too performs the work of settler colonial hyper-exploitation, displacement and dispossession. The production of migrant labour occurs as a basis for preserving if not deepening the colonial settlement project in Canada.'

[89] For a promising counterpoint: Paul Jonathan Saguil, *Ethical Lawyering across Canada's Legal Traditions*, 9:1 INDIGENOUS LAW JOURNAL 167–87 (2010). But, see John Strawson, *Orientalism and Legal Education in the Middle East: Reading Frederic Goadby's 'Introduction to the Study of Law'*, 21:4 LEGAL STUDIES 663–78 (2001).

[90] See, for example, the contributions in Mark Goodale & Sally Merry eds, THE PRACTICE OF HUMAN RIGHTS: TRACKING LAW BETWEEN THE GLOBAL AND THE LOCAL (Cambridge University Press 2007).

[91] An impressive display of such a comprehensive approach can be found in Boaventura de Sousa Santos ed., *Another Knowledge Is Possible: Beyond Northern Epistemologies* (Verso 2005), and more recently in: LAW AND SOCIETY IN LATIN AMERICA: A NEW MAP (César Rodríguez-Garavito ed., Routledge 2015).

26. Critical legal theory and international law
Bill Bowring

Critical legal theory has generated a vast and diverse English-language scholarly literature, in part because of its unusual eclecticism and heterogeneity, and in consequence it is, as we shall see, very hard to pin down. So this short entry does not propose a complete and detailed overview or anything like it.[1] Familiar landmarks will make their appearance, hopefully with new perspectives, and in context. But the aspect which interests this writer in particular is the apparent disjuncture between two worlds: that of heterodox legal scholarship, and that of radical international lawyering.

1. CRITICAL THEORY AND PRACTICE IN THE US

Critical legal studies had emerged in the United States in the late 1970s, and was put firmly on the map by Roberto Unger with his 1983 article 'The Critical Legal Studies Movement', published in the *Harvard Law Review*.[2] The following year Duncan Kennedy and Karl Klare published their 'Bibliography of Critical Legal Studies'[3] and Mark Tushnet his 'Critical Legal Studies: A Political History', both in the *Yale Law Journal*. With reference to international law in particular, in 1999 Martti Koskenniemi referred to the prizewinning 1991 essay by Nigel Purvis, 'Critical Legal Studies in Public International Law',[4] as an authoritative overview of the field.[5]

In the United States, for a decade, 'critical legal studies' took the form – or, as Koskenniemi put it, 'was more commonly classed under the label'[6] – of the New Stream, or New Approaches to International Law (NAIL). David Kennedy (its founder) proclaimed NAIL 'done' in 1998. Ntina Tsouvala remarked,[7] in her 2016 review of an

---

[1] With kind permission of the editors, this chapter utilises materials taken from Bowring, Bill (2011) 'What is Radical in "Radical International Law"?' in 'Debate: What is Critical Legal Practice?' v.22, *Finnish Yearbook of International Law* (Hart Publishing, 2013) 3–29.

[2] Unger, Roberto Mangabeira (1983) 'The Critical Legal Studies Movement' v.96, n.3 *Harvard Law Review* 561–675.

[3] Kennedy, Duncan and Karl E. Klare (1984) 'A Bibliography of Critical Legal Studies' v.94, n.2 *Yale Law Journal* 461–90.

[4] Purvis, Nigel (1991) 'Critical Legal Studies in Public International Law' v.32 *Harvard International Law Journal* 81.

[5] Koskenniemi, Martti (1999) 'Letter to the Editors of the Symposium' v.93 n.2 *American Journal of International Law* 351–61.

[6] Ibid, at 352.

[7] Tzouvala, Ntina (2016) 'New Approaches to International Law: The History of a Project' v.27 n.1 *European Journal of International Law* 215–32 – review of Beneytto, Jose Maria and

'obituary' of NAIL edited by Kennedy and others,[8] that NAIL had 'material bases'.[9] In other words, it was to be found in a few exclusive locations on the planet: these included Harvard University, home of David Kennedy, and its *Law Review*, initially with the European Law Research Centre, followed by the Institute for Global Law and Policy. Other bases for NAIL included Brown; the London School of Economics and the School of Oriental and African Studies (SOAS) – the 'London corridor'; Cornell, Bogota, Melbourne, Sydney, Toronto; the American University in Cairo; and the Erik Castren Institute in Helsinki, the home of Martti Koskenniemi. But it was very much a Harvard enterprise.

In 1999 the editors of a symposium on 'method in international law', to be published in the *American Journal of International Law*, invited Koskenniemi to participate with a contribution on 'critical legal studies'. Instead of a contribution, he sent a Letter to the Editors,[10] declaring that

> it was impossible for me to think about my – or indeed anybody's – method in the way suggested by the symposium format … you may, of course, have asked me to write about 'CLS' in international law irrespectively of whether I was a true representative of its method (whatever that method might be).[11]

Critical legal studies was, he added, more commonly classed under the label 'new approaches to international law', or NAIL. Indeed, for Koskenniemi, new writing in the field was 'so heterogenous, self-reflective and sometimes outright ironic that the conventions of academic analysis about "method" would inevitable fail to articulate its reality'.[12]

It is no surprise, then, that in the reissue of *From Apology to Utopia*, published in 2006 with a new epilogue,[13] Koskenniemi explicitly distanced himself from 'critical legal studies' and from NAIL. According to Nigel Purvis, NAIL's 'critical analysis of international law has demonstrated the incoherence of the liberal ethical basis of

---

David Kennedy (eds) (2012) *New Approaches to International Law: The European and American Experiences* (TMC Asser-Springer).

[8] Beneytto, Jose Maria and David Kennedy (eds) *New Approaches to International Law: The European and American Experiences* (TMC Asser-Springer, 2012).

[9] See Rasulov, Akbar, 'New Approaches to International Law: Images of a Genealogy?' in Beneytto, Jose Maria and David Kennedy (eds) *New Approaches to International Law: The European and American Experiences* (TMC Asser-Springer, 2012) 151–91.

[10] Koskenniemi (1999).

[11] Ibid, 351.

[12] This started with the seminal 1988 text by David Kennedy, initiating NAIL: Kennedy, David (1988) 'A New Stream of International Law Scholarship' v.7 n.1 *Wisconsin International Law Journal* 1–49. For an overview of NAIL, he suggested a number of texts, including his own. See also Purvis, Nigel (1991) 'Critical Legal Studies in Public International Law' v.32 *Harvard International Law Journal* 81; Korhonen, Otti (1996) 'International Law: Silence, Defence or Deliverance?' v.7 *European Journal of International Law* 1; and the essays in 'Special Issue: New Approaches to International Law' (1996) 65 *Nordic Journal of International Law* (Martti Koskenniemi ed.); and Kennedy, David and Chris Tennant (1994) 'New Approaches to International Law – A Bibliography' v.35 *Harvard International Law Journal* 417.

[13] Koskenniemi, Martti, *From Apology to Utopia: The Structure of International Legal Argument* (with a new epilogue, Cambridge University Press, 2006).

international law, international law's constricting intellectual structure, the indeterminacy of international legal argument, and the self-validating nature of international law's authority'.[14] In his 1999 Letter to the Editors, Koskenniemi explained that when he wrote *From Apology to Utopia*, he wanted to describe the following key property of international legal language – its simultaneously strict formalism and substantive indeterminacy – in terms of a general theory, drawing on (classical) French structuralism.[15] Koskenniemi was writing from the position of working as a practitioner of international law at a very high level.

Peter Goodrich once commented acerbically, if a little unfairly: 'The American law professor is too well paid to be politically committed, too status conscious to be intellectually engaged, and too insular – too bound to the parochial and monolingual culture of the law review – to be scholarly.'[16] If, for Goodrich, the American academy had remained aloof from the engagement that might or perhaps should have informed *critical* legal work, the same cannot be said of its activist lawyers.[17] American activist practitioners have for many years organised effectively in the National Lawyers Guild,[18] founded on 20 February 1937 as an association of progressive lawyers and jurists who believed that they had a major role to play in the reconstruction of legal values to emphasize human rights over property rights.[19] In 2017 it celebrated '80 Years of Law for the People'.[20] As a result of its work in the USA and internationally, it became a focus of attention for the American secret services. In 1989 the Guild won a case against the FBI for illegal political surveillance of legal activist organizations, including the Guild. The case, which was filed in 1977, revealed the extent to which the government had been spying on the NLG. Since 1941, the FBI had used more than 1,000 informants to report on NLG activities and disrupt Guild meetings and conferences. FBI agents broke into the National Office and into private law offices of key NLG members. The bureau released derogatory and misleading information about the Guild to judges, the press and the public. As part of the 1989 settlement, the FBI turned over copies of roughly 400,000 pages of its files on the Guild, which are now available at the Tamiment Library at New York University.

The NLG is closely connected with the Center for Constitutional Rights.[21] The CCR litigates in the US courts, and its victories have established major legal precedents,

---

[14] Purvis (1991) 127.
[15] Koskenniemi Letter (1999) 355.
[16] Goodrich, Peter (1993) 'Sleeping with the Enemy: An Essay on the Politics of Critical Legal Studies in America' v.68 n.2 *New York University Law Review* 389–425, at 399.
[17] Antony Carty was an exception, during the 1980s. See Carty, Anthony, *The Decay of International Law: A Reappraisal of the Limits of Legal Imagination in International Affairs* (Manchester University Press, 1986).
[18] www.nlg.org/.
[19] www.nlg.org/about/history/.
[20] www.nlg.org/nlg80/.
[21] http://ccrjustice.org/. 'The Center for Constitutional Rights is dedicated to advancing and protecting the rights guaranteed by the United States Constitution and the Universal Declaration of Human Rights. Founded in 1966 by attorneys who represented civil rights movements in the South, CCR is a non-profit legal and educational organization committed to the creative use of law as a positive force for social change.'

from *Filártiga v. Peña-Irala*,[22] which opened US courts to victims of serious human rights violations from anywhere in the world, to *NOW v. Terry*,[23] which established a buffer zone around abortion clinics. In a recent example, on 5 April 2018 a settlement was reached in *Hassan v. City of New York*. A group of Muslim-owned businesses, mosques, individuals and student groups finalized a settlement agreement with the New York Police Department in this federal lawsuit challenging the suspicionless, discriminatory surveillance of American Muslims in New Jersey.[24]

As far as this author is aware, there is little to no evidence of engagement in the US, in the field of international law, between critical legal scholars and the kind of activist legal work I have just described.

2. THE BRITISH CRITICAL LEGAL STUDIES MOVEMENT AND ITS CRITICS

The history of the CLS movement in Britain has been documented in a number of notable papers by Peter Goodrich (1999),[25] Tim Murphy (1999)[26] and Costas Douzinas (also in this volume),[27] the latter having moved intellectually from study of the French deconstructionist Jacques Derrida in 1991,[28] to the ethics of alterity of Emmanuel Levinas in 1996,[29] to the Marxist utopianism of Ernst Bloch in 2000,[30] to the Slovenian Lacanian Slavoj Žižek, to Jacques Lacan and psychoanalysis, and most recently to the controversial conservative Catholic theorist and erstwhile Nazi Carl Schmitt, and his successor Giorgio Agamben, in 2007.[31]

It is hard to escape the conclusion that CLS in England has been devoted more to eclecticism and the encouragement of approaches such as law and literature than to any radical or overt political critique. In 1999 Peter Goodrich, one of the movement's founders, published an acerbic critique captured in this summary:

---

[22] 630 F.2d 876 (2d Cir. 1980).
[23] 159 F.3d 86 (2d Cir. 1998).
[24] https://ccrjustice.org/home/what-we-do/our-cases/hassan-v-city-new-york.
[25] Goodrich, Peter (1999) 'The Critic's Love of The Law: Intimate Observations on an Insular Jurisdiction' 10(3) *Law and Critique* 343–60.
[26] Murphy, W.T. (1999) 'Britcrits: Subversion and Submission, Past, Present and Future' v.10 *Law and Critique* 237–78, and https://slideheaven.com/britcrits-subversion-and-submission-past-present-and-future.html.
[27] Douzinas, Costas and Adam Gearey, *Critical Jurisprudence: The Political Philosophy of Justice* (Hart Publishing, 2005).
[28] Douzinas, Costas, *Postmodern Jurisprudence: The Law of the Text in the Texts of the Law* (Routledge, 1991).
[29] Douzinas, Costas, *Justice Miscarried: Ethics, Aesthetics and the Law* (Edinburgh University Press, 1996).
[30] Douzinas, Costas, *The End of Human Rights* (Hart Publishing, 2000).
[31] Douzinas, Costas, *Human Rights and Empire: The Political Philosophy of Cosmopolitanism* (Routledge Cavendish, 2007). For a critique of Douzinas' more recent work see chapter 8, '"Postmodern" Reconstructions of Human Rights' in my *The Degradation of the International Legal Order? The Rehabilitation of Law and the Possibility of Politics* (Routledge Cavendish, 2008).

Lacking academic identity, political purpose and ethical conviction, critical legal scholarship in England has been too insecure in its institutional place and too unconscious of its individual and collective desires to resist absorption into the institution. Critical legal studies – as distinct from feminist legal studies, gay and lesbian studies or critical race theory – has tended to teach and so reproduce the core curriculum in a passive and negative mode. Resistant, ostensibly for historical and political reasons, to self-criticism and indeed to self-reflection upon their institutional practices, critical scholars have ended up repeating the law that they came to critique and overcome.[32]

Akbar Rasulov has made a similar point regarding the influence of poststructuralism in international law.[33] He concludes as follows:

What is going to be the effect of the poststructuralist intervention in international law? Will it be to encourage international lawyers – by reminding them that now, as ever before, everything in the international arena is only a transient product of a contingent combination of traces and hegemonic self-exertions – to experience their everyday work as an ongoing exercise of power? Or will it be to discourage all but the most dedicated of them, with its confusing vocabulary and uncritical interdisciplinarism, from performing any other kind of intellectual operations than a linear explication of the established dogma? Or will it, perhaps, simply tire them with its dogged insistence that the existing tradition is too outdated and a new method has to be created?[34]

Despite misgivings of this kind, which are anything but rare, and despite the fact that CLS effectively died in the US several years ago, it is still alive – indeed, in rude health – in Britain. The journal *Law and Critique* continues to publish a wide range of critically inclined theoretical scholarship. The annual Critical Legal Conference, the first of which took place at the University of Kent in 1986,[35] has long outlasted its US counterpart;[36] it takes place at a different campus each year, with recent conferences held in South Africa, India, Finland and Sweden.

Theoretically, both the journal and the conference are highly eclectic. Marxist or Marxian scholarship is a continuing but relatively very small component, with many more scholars motivated by postmodernism in various forms. The London-based website Critical Legal Thinking, Law & the Political,[37] established in 2009, is also a showcase for the flourishing of many schools of thought, with 6,384 subscribers at the time of writing. It describes its purpose thus:

This is our time, the time of protest, of change, the welcoming of the event. Critical (legal) theory must be re-linked with emancipatory and radical politics. We need to imagine or dream a law or society in which people are no longer despised or degraded, oppressed or

---

[32] Goodrich (1999).
[33] Rasulov, Akbar (2006) 'International Law and the Poststructuralist Challenge' v.19 *Leiden Journal of International Law* 799–827 – this is a review essay on Fitzpatrick, Peter and Patricia Tuitt (eds), *Critical Beings: Law, Nation and the Global Subject* (Ashgate, 2004); Cheng, Sinkwan (ed.), *Law, Justice, and Power: Between Reason and Will* (Stanford University Press, 2004).
[34] Rasulov (2006) 826–7.
[35] See www.jstor.org/stable/1410297 for the paper given by Nikolas Rose at that conference.
[36] Goodrich (1993) 389.
[37] http://criticallegalthinking.com/.

dominated and from that impossible but necessary standpoint to judge the here and now. (Legal) critique is the companion and guide of radical change.[38]

Is it in fact the case that there is such a 'companionship' between legal theoretical critique and 'radical change'? In the context of the CLC we encounter again a notable disjuncture between theory and practice, between heterodox legal scholarship and radical – or socialist – 'lawyering'. Take the following revealing example from the 'call of papers' of the 2012 Critical Legal Conference that invited critical scholars to explore:[39]

> a plurality of justice gardens that function together or that are at times at odds with each other. There are for instance well ordered French gardens, with meticulously trimmed plants and straight angles, but that also plays tricks on your perception. There are English gardens that simultaneously look natural – un-written – and well kept, inviting you to take a slow stroll or perhaps sit down and read a book. There are closed gardens, surrounded by fences, and with limited access for ordinary people. There are gardens organized around ruins, let's call them Roman gardens, where you can get a sense of the historical past, but without feeling threatened by its strangeness. There are Japanese stone gardens made for meditation rather than movement. There are zoological gardens, where you can study all those animal species that do not have a proper sense of justice, no social contracts, no inequality and social injustice, and no legal systems. There is, indeed, the Jungle, a real or imaginary place outside the Gardens of Law.[40]

In an article placed on the Critical Legal Thinking site, Paul O'Connell offered the following indictment of the critical legal 'project' thus envisaged:

> At a time at which global and national elites are engaged in an unprecedented assault on the living conditions and rights of working people, when democracy, even in its 'low intensity' form, is in retreat, the leading lights in critical legal inquiry are retreating into the gardens of their own imagination, and abandoning the less pristine, less genteel footpaths and public squares of politics.[41]

3. RADICAL LAWYERING IN BRITAIN

O'Connell's indictment resonates with my sense of the failure of the critical legal 'project' on this side of the Atlantic to engage with the strong tradition of left political lawyering in England. I have addressed above the similar disjuncture in the United States. In the English context I have in mind both political lawyers engaging in radical

---

[38] The website is regularly updated with fascinating material, primarily by young scholars, and a significant number of reports from activists. It has established a publishing house, CounterPress, and its Twitter feed has nearly 3,500 followers. However, only a small minority of the articles posted on it tackle international law.
[39] The 2012 CLC took place in Stockholm under the unifying theme 'Gardens of Justice'.
[40] www.csc.kth.se/clc2012/.
[41] Paul O'Connell, 30 April 2012, 'Trouble in the Garden: Critical Legal Studies & the Crisis' at http://criticallegalthinking.com/2012/04/30/trouble-in-the-garden-critical-legal-studies-crisis/.

legal practice, and a long tradition of lawyers who played vitally important roles in other capacities.

The Haldane Society of Socialist Lawyers was founded in 1930,[42] as an organisation of lawyers active in the Communist Party and the left wing of the Labour Party. It has been 'a legal thorn in the side of every government, lobbying for law reforms, civil liberties and access to justice for all; supporting national liberation movements against colonialism and campaigning against racism and all forms of discrimination'.[43] It has always worked closely with the National Council for Civil Liberties (founded in 1936, now named Liberty) and with the trade union movement. The Society never saw itself as an independent political force, nor did it conceive of law as inherently revolutionary or as capable of being moulded into revolutionary theory; rather, it saw the role of politically active lawyers as serving the interests of the working class and the oppressed. In all of this it is very close to the National Lawyers Guild in the US. Haldane lawyers were particularly active in support for the miners in their strike of 1984–5, and proudly provided services to the National Union of Mineworkers. They consistently campaigned for human rights in Northern Ireland and against internment without trial. They challenged the miscarriages of justice experienced by the Guildford Four, the Birmingham Six, Judith Ward and others. They were also instrumental in calling for a public inquiry into the Bloody Sunday massacre, and represented the families and survivors at the inquiry.

Internationally, members of Haldane provided free legal assistance to the African National Congress (ANC) and South West Africa People's Organization (SWAPO) members throughout the long years of the struggle against apartheid, and regularly picketed South Africa House.

The Haldane Society has succeeded in attracting new generations of campaigning lawyers, and young Haldane lawyers represent defendants accused of public order offences and provide monitors for antifascist and antiracist demonstrations. It publishes its journal *Socialist Lawyer* several times a year.

Both the National Lawyers Guild and the Haldane Society of Socialist Lawyers are member organisations of the International Association of Democratic Lawyers. Awareness of the existence of the IADL and of the tradition of active political engagement of legal practitioners and scholars (more the former than the latter) is almost entirely lacking in the many works of critical scholars. Indeed, to my knowledge, no NAIL or CLS scholars have participated in international campaigning, or attempted to contribute their insights to political legal practice.

A few words on the IADL. It was founded on 24 October 1946 in Paris by lawyers from 24 countries. It remains active, despite the loss since 1991 of the substantial subsidy it received from the USSR and from, for example, the Algerian FLN – which paid for a headquarters building in Brussels, and (minimal) staff. In the past 20 years, congresses have taken place in Cape Town, Havana, Paris, Hanoi and Brussels. It has played an important role in promoting the right of peoples to self-determination – that 'revolutionary kernel of international law' that enshrines in international law the principles formulated by Marx and Engels in the second half of the nineteenth century

---

[42] See www.haldane.org; it was named after the first Labour Party Lord Chancellor.
[43] www.haldane.org/our-history.

and developed by Lenin in the period immediately before the First World War.[44] Through the bloody struggles for decolonisation which followed the Second World War and came to a peak in the 1960s, these principles became a legal right as common article 1 to the two International Covenants on human rights of 1966.

Mainstream Western scholars' hostility towards the IADL was exemplified in an outspoken article published in 1960 by Professor Elliot Goodman of Brown University, author of *The Soviet Design for a World State*,[45] in which, having ignored the contributions of Marx, Engels and Lenin, Goodman declared: 'The idea of national self-determination, fathered by political theorists like Mazzini and Wilson, is, of course, Western in origin. But in an age of nation-building in the Afro-Asian world, skilful Soviet use of this concept presents Western diplomacy with a formidable and continuing challenge in the East.'[46]

He continued:

> As a result of Soviet initiative, the issue of self-determination for non-self-governing peoples became enmeshed in the numerous deliberations on human rights. Basic to the enjoyment of any human rights, the Soviet delegates insisted, is the right of national self-determination, which must be realized in the colonial and non-self-governing territories of the West.

By 1952, said Goodman, 'it was abundantly clear that the venerable complex of ideas associated with national self-determination had been fashioned into a blunt political weapon by a Soviet-Afro-Asian entente'.[47]

Why is it that these political struggles – encompassing the planet as a whole – which have profoundly changed the content of public international law have remained beyond the horizon of so many scholars of international law, including its CLS exponents?

4. AN ATTEMPT TO LINK THEORY AND PRACTICE

One important attempt to link theory and practice was the 1992 publication of the *Critical Lawyers Handbook*,[48] edited by Ian Grigg-Spall and Paddy Ireland.[49] A special

---

[44] See chapter 1, 'Self-Determination – The Revolutionary Kernel of International Law' in Bill Bowring, *The Degradation of the International Legal Order? The Rehabilitation of Law and the Possibility of Politics* (Routledge Cavendish, 2008); and Bowring, Bill (2011) 'Marx, Lenin and Pashukanis on Self-Determination: Response to Robert Knox' v.19, n.2 *Historical Materialism* 113–27.

[45] Goodman, Elliot (1960) 'The Cry of National Liberation: Recent Soviet Attitudes Toward National Self-Determination' v.14, n.1 *International Organization* 92–106.

[46] ibid, 92.

[47] ibid, 92; but see my 'The Soviets and the Right to Self-Determination of the Colonized: Contradictions of Soviet Diplomacy and Foreign Policy in the Era of Decolonization' in Dann, Philipp and Jochen von Bernstorff, *Battle on International Law – International Law in the Decolonization Period* (Oxford University Press forthcoming).

[48] Grigg-Spall, Ian and Paddy Ireland (eds) *The Critical Lawyers Handbook* (Pluto Press, 1992).

[49] My own first short essay, 'Socialism, Liberation Struggles and the Law', was published in the Handbook. The themes of my essay were concretised and extended in Bowring, Bill, *The*

feature of the Handbook was its three part structure, comprising Critical Theory, Critical Legal Education and Critical Legal Practice. Alan Thomson provided a foreword, 'Critical Approaches to Law: Who Needs Legal Theory?',[50] introducing the eclecticism which was already characteristic of British CLS. Robert Fine and Sol Picciotto's chapter was entitled 'On Marxist Critiques of Law' and featured an account of Yevgeniy Pashukanis,[51] and Costas Douzinas and the late Ronnie Warrington contributed, in ironic postmodern mode, 'The (Im)possible Pedagogical Politics of (the Law of) Postmodernism'. The section also contained Anne Bottomley on feminism, Sammy Adelman and Ken Foster's 'Critical Legal Theory: The Power of Law' and Peter Fitzpatrick's 'Law as Resistance'.

The second section, on Critical Legal Education, started with a senior representative of US critical legal studies, Duncan Kennedy, writing on 'Legal Education as Training for Hierarchy';[52] it continued with Alan Hunt's 'Critique and Law: Legal Education and Practice', Alan Thomson on contract law, Alan Norrie on criminal law, Joanne Conaghan and Wade Mansell on tort law, and chapters on property law, company law, labour law, constitutional law and European law. A thorough antidote was provided to the usual black letter textbooks.

My own essay was in the third section, on Critical Legal Practice. The outstanding human rights lawyer Michael Mansfield QC, now President of the Haldane Society, contributed 'Critical Legal Practice and the Bar';[53] Kate Markus, then at the highly political Brent Law Centre (later a barrister at Doughty Street Chambers) and Chair of Haldane, wrote on 'The Politics of Legal Aid';[54] David Watkinson, now retired from Doughty Street Chambers, provided the chapter 'Radical Chambers, Wellington Street: A Personal View';[55] and John Fitzpatrick wrote two chapters, 'Legal Practice and Socialist Practice'[56] and 'Collective Working at Law Centres'.[57]

I have no doubt that the publication of the *Handbook* was the high point of critical legal scholarship in Britain. It was followed by an attempt at a joint conference of the CLC and the Haldane Society in the 1990s at Kent University, which was memorable for a sharp clash between John Fitzpatrick, then a member of the Revolutionary Communist Party, and Stephen Sedley QC, then still a member of the Communist Party, before his appointment to the High Court Bench.[58] But the critical scholars and

---

Degradation of the International Legal Order? The Rehabilitation of Law and the Possibility of Politics (Routledge Cavendish, 2008).

[50] *Handbook* ibid pp. 2–10.
[51] *Handbook* ibid pp. 16–21.
[52] *Handbook* ibid pp. 51–61.
[53] *Handbook* ibid pp. 157–61.
[54] *Handbook* ibid pp. 184–90.
[55] *Handbook* ibid pp. 167–72.
[56] *Handbook* ibid pp. 149–56.
[57] *Handbook* ibid pp. 173–8.
[58] John Fitzpatrick founded and leads the successful Legal Clinic at Kent University, and has been awarded an OBE; Stephen Sedley recently retired as a judge of the Court of Appeal.

the radical lawyers were oil and water, or chalk and cheese: no crossfertilisation was achieved on that occasion or those that followed.[59]

A single exception to the disjuncture as far as critical international law is concerned was the presence of B.S. Chimni at the 2008 CLC conference that took place at Glasgow University. Chimni, well known as the author of the splendid *International Law and World Order*,[60] delivered a provocative keynote speech entitled 'Prolegomena to a Class Approach to International Law'.[61] It was an opportunity for him to elaborate the idea that 'Marxism still constitutes the most beneficial vehicle for the humanistic grounding of a new jurisprudence', an argument that had been advanced in the 2007 paper 'The Past, Present and Future of International Law: A Critical Third World Approach',[62] where he argued that 'a third world approach to international law, or TWAIL as it has come to be known, represents in general an attempt to understand the history, structure and process of international law from the perspective of third world states'. His ambitious project was 'that the discipline of international law be transfigured. International lawyers must, going beyond human rights law, consistently engage with the existential world of the global poor and oppressed. Ordinary life must become the focus of the entire discipline of international law.' The 2008 keynote speech, published in 2010 by the *European Journal of International Law*, proposed a 'class approach to international law', to get away from the state-centred mainstream and to focus 'besides states on social groups and classes which are shaping and have historically shaped international law'. This would enable 'international lawyers to practise the discipline of international law as if people mattered'.[63]

An extended version of Akbar Rasulov's response to this was published in the same year in the *Finnish Yearbook of International Law*.[64] Rasulov neatly summed up his perspective as follows:

> Done correctly, a class-analytic re-theorization of international law can supply the international law CLS community not just with a new brilliant theoretical apparatus, but with an apparatus that could give us both a highly effective instrumentarium for debunking any number of rightwing ideological mystifications and a highly reliable analytical platform for constructing practically implementable counter-hegemonic strategies.[65]

---

[59] I helped to organise Critical Legal Conferences at the University of East London in 1995 and again at the University of North London in 2001, both with Marxist streams and a few practitioner activists; but the predominant tone was eclecticism.

[60] Chimni, B.S., *International Law and World Order: A Critique of Contemporary Approaches* (Sage, 1993). A long-awaited second edition will soon appear.

[61] Chimni, B.S. (2010) 'Prolegomena to a Class Approach to International Law' v.21, n.1 *European Journal of International Law* 57–82.

[62] Chimni, B.S. (2007) 'The Past, Present and Future of International Law: A Critical Third World Approach' 8(2) *Melbourne Journal of International Law* 499–515.

[63] Chimni (2010) 58.

[64] Rasulov, Akbar (2008) 'Bringing Class Back into International Law – A Response to Professor Chimni', available at SSRN: http://ssrn.com/abstract=1675447, later published as '"The Nameless Rapture of the Struggle": Towards a Marxist Class-Theoretic Approach to International Law' v.19 *Finnish Yearbook of International Law* (2008) 243–94.

[65] ibid, 3.

He continued:

> Where a generation and a half ago, most of the practical momentum in the international law leftwing projects came in the fields of international diplomacy and political activism, a vast majority of all leftwing efforts in international law today are limited to the field of academia ... We have lost every connection our predecessors' predecessors had with the world of activist politics and practical diplomacy.[66]

And as for the academy: 'The global class structure has long immunized itself against any destabilizing action that could come from the esoteric writings of a marginalized group of Western academics, especially as disorganized as the international law CLS people are.'

5. FINAL REFLECTIONS

In this chapter I have explored the evident disjuncture, or disconnect, between academic writing and legal practice in radical or progressive approaches to international law. I conclude with some final comments on that broken relationship, with an emphasis on what two theorists have said about the practitioners.

David Kennedy leads the Institute for Global Law and Policy at Harvard Law School,[67] and organises its regular Workshops. He writes on its website: 'Since we began in 2010, more than 331 young scholars representing 83 countries and more than 100 universities have participated in The Workshop. It has been an amazing experience.'[68] Among those who have been profoundly influenced by Kennedy's style and approach are many of the younger generation of the UK's critical international law scholars. They have benefited from Harvard's wealth to participate in the Workshop, in many cases several times.[69]

It is from David Kennedy's allusion to the enigmatic figure of the 'practitioner-being' that we take our lead. S/he appears in the context of the way in which most scholarly work in the international law field presents itself. Kennedy explains:

> The key here is that there is another group of people, called 'practitioners', for whom scholars are doing this work and who will judge its persuasiveness and ultimate value. However argumentative and critical this work may be, it will ultimately be judged not by other scholars on the basis of its arguments, but by practitioners on the basis of its usefulness. When scholars do judge this sort of work, they do so by reference to the often imaginary eye of the practitioner.[70]

---

[66] ibid, 6.
[67] http://iglp.law.harvard.edu/.
[68] http://iglp.law.harvard.edu/iglp-the-workshop/.
[69] One such is Akbar Rasulov. He refers approvingly to a seminal text of David Kennedy's from 2000: 'When Renewal Repeats: Thinking against the Box' v.32 (1999–2000) *New York University Journal of Law and Politics* 335–499.
[70] Kennedy (2000) 399.

Kennedy continues in ironical vein:

> Nevertheless, when practitioner-beings assess things, they do so with their eyes wide open, unaffected by the fashions and egos that can befuddle scholars. Their focus is relentlessly on the real world where the rubber meets the road, and it is their judgment, or predictions about their judgment, that guarantees the pragmatism and political neutrality of the field's development.[71]

Section IV of this article is headed 'Critical Performativity: New Approaches to International Law', while the final part of the article is entitled 'The Project: Making New Thinking and Making It Known'. What is this 'new thinking'? After a lengthy autobiography (including details of how he achieved tenure at Harvard), Kennedy describes how in establishing NAIL he wanted to differentiate the new group from 'critical legal studies', which seemed to his students 'at once passé, dangerous, too politicised, too much associated with a "line" of some sort'.[72] He closed down the NAIL project quite deliberately in 1998. What, writing in 2000, did he have to offer for the future? In his view, a project like NAIL must have 'a shared sense that description matters, that things are terribly misrepresented, and that correcting, changing and influencing what is understood, what is seen, what can be asked, can be a matter of passion and politics'.[73] This is a different world to that of radical practitioners.

As noted above, Koskenniemi, more than most international legal scholars, has combined theory and practice. His view of the practitioner contrasts sharply with Kennedy's when he suggests that international lawyers would be better advised to search for 'more concrete forms of political commitment' which might 'engage them in actual struggles, both as observers and participants, while also taking the participants' self-understanding seriously'.[74] In his 2011 *Politics of International Law*,[75] having discussed the roles of the international *judge* and the government legal *adviser*, Koskenniemi turned to the *activist*. 'The activist participates in international law in order to further the political objectives that underlie his or her activism. The principal commitment of the serious activist is not to international law but to those objectives.'[76] In Koskenniemi's view, the lawyer activist who fails to 'think like a lawyer' and to 'internalise the law's argumentative structures' will inevitably be marginalised.[77] For Koskenniemi, the academic finds herself in a 'position ... much less stable than that of the activist or the adviser'.[78]

Moreover, legal indeterminacy may occasion doubt about the academic pursuit altogether: is not law precisely about the daily practice of political/government

---

[71] Kennedy (2000) 399.
[72] Kennedy (2000) 489.
[73] Kennedy (2000) 498–9.
[74] Koskenniemi, Martti (1996) '"Intolerant Democracies": A Reaction' v.37 *Harvard International Law Journal* 234–5; Marks, Susan, *The Riddle of All Constitutions* (Oxford University Press, 2000) 141.
[75] Koskenniemi, Martti, *The Politics of International Law* (Hart Publishing, 2011).
[76] Koskenniemi (2011) 289.
[77] Koskenniemi (2011) 290–1.
[78] Koskenniemi (2011) 291.

decisionmaking, weighing pros and cons in a world of limited time and resources, and not about the academic's abstract norms?[79]

Koskenniemi does not go as far as to ascribe any transformative role to the critical legal theory of international law. But he also, famously, declares his faith in international law, in the final chapter of the book, under the title 'The Fate of Public International Law: Between Technique and Politics':

> I often think of international law as a kind of secular faith. When powerful states engage in imperial wars, globalisation dislocates communities or transnational companies wreak havoc on the environment, and where national governments show themselves corrupt or ineffective, one often hears an appeal to international law. International law appears here less as this rule or that institution than as a place-holder for the vocabularies of justice and goodness, solidarity, responsibility and – faith.[80]

In this position, Koskenniemi appears remarkably close to David Kennedy, whom he also cited with approval. For the most part, the bloody military reprisals of the colonial powers and the contradictory and fraught effort on the part of the USSR to give content to the anticolonial struggle are missing from his text. But the text contains one passage on self-determination, buried away in a rather abstract discussion of instrumentalism and formalism, which to some extent resonates with my own position – even if Koskenniemi, like so many of his peers, entirely left out the political content, including Lenin's contribution to the theory and practice of the 'right of nations to self-determination':

> 'self-determination', typically, may be constructed analytically to mean anything one wants it to mean, and many studies have invoked its extreme flexibility. Examined in the light of history, however, it has given form and strength to claims for national liberation and self-rule from the French Revolution to decolonisation in the 1960s, the fall of the Berlin Wall, and the political transitions that have passed from Latin America through Eastern Europe and South Africa.[81]

This is very close to my own position.

BIBLIOGRAPHY

Beneytto, Jose Maria, and David Kennedy (eds) (2012) *New Approaches to International Law: The European and American Experiences* (TMC Asser-Springer)
Carty, Anthony (1986) *The Decay of International Law: A Reappraisal of the Limits of Legal Imagination in International Affairs* (Manchester University Press)
Goodrich, Peter (1993) 'Sleeping with the Enemy: An Essay on the Politics of Critical Legal Studies in America' v.68 n.2 *New York University Law Review* pp. 389–425
Kennedy, David (1980) 'Theses about International Law Discourse' 23 *German Year Book of International Law* pp. 353–91
Kennedy, David (1987) *International Legal Structures* (Nomos Verlagsgesellschaft)

---

[79] Koskenniemi (2011) 292.
[80] Koskenniemi (2011) 361.
[81] Koskenniemi (2011) 261.

Kennedy, David (1988) 'A New Stream of International Law Scholarship' v.7 n.1 *Wisconsin International Law Journal* pp. 1–49

Kennedy, Duncan and Karl E. Klare (1984) 'A Bibliography of Critical Legal Studies' v.94 n.2 *Yale Law Journal* pp. 461–90

Koskenniemi, Martti (1999) 'Letter to the Editors of the Symposium' [Symposium on Method] v.93 n.2 *American Journal of International Law* pp. 351–61

Koskenniemi, Martti (2011) *The Politics of International Law* (Hart Publishing)

Purvis, Nigel (1991) 'Critical Legal Studies in Public International Law' v.32 n.1 *Harvard International Law Journal* pp. 81–127

27. Nihilists, pragmatists and peasants: a dispatch on contradiction in international human rights law
Margot E. Salomon

This chapter engages theory to help human rights advocates see what they may not have seen before. It focuses on the new UN Declaration on the Rights of Peasants, drawing on insights offered by one critical legal theory in particular – the commodity form theory developed by the Soviet jurist Evgeny Pashukanis. It is through this lens that an analysis of the contradiction inherent in what is at times a radical normative project in developing international human rights law is presented. Here, critical legal theory helps reveal the paradoxes that have ostensible human rights successes perpetuate the suffering they seek to confront. The concluding section offers what appears to be the only solution to the conundrum that shows our most important human rights gains also to be our losses.

1. INTERNATIONAL LAW AND ITS CONNECTION TO CAPITAL

There is a fundamental tension at the heart of modern international law; it questions the foundational limits of international law as an enfranchising venture and, as such, the costs that come from deploying it. The tension can be expressed through a debate between nihilists who reject international law for its capitalist, structural bias and pragmatists who are nonetheless willing to utilize it for its gains to the disenfranchised, pyrrhic as they may be. The core of the nihilists' thesis, as this paper calls it, was set out a century ago by the radical Soviet jurist Evgeny Pashukanis and recently adopted most notably by the international law and relations scholar China Miéville. A number of international legal scholars take inspiration from its central claim as to the 'commodity form theory' of international law, including both nihilists and pragmatists. This is where our dilemma begins.

The thrust of the dilemma comes from the premise that there exists a structural connection between capitalism and law, including international law. As Pashukanis frames it, '[m]odern international law is the legal form of the struggle of the capitalist states among themselves for domination over the rest of the world'.[1] Here the key insight is that the logic that guides modern interstate relations is the same logic that regulates individuals in capitalism, because 'since its birth, and in the underlying

---

[1] Evgeny B. Pashukanis, 'International Law' in P. Beirne and R. Sharlet (eds) *Pashukanis: Selected Writings on Marxism and Law* (PB Maggs tr, Academic Press 1980) 168, 169.

precepts of international law, states, like individuals, interact as property owners'.[2] The imperial economic power and expansion of European states in the seventeenth century saw the formation of international law tethered to the spread of capitalism.[3] The principles of international law today presuppose the legal concepts of private property and the arrangements necessary to protect and profit from them[4] – the formal equality of states that cloaks their substantive and material inequality,[5] sovereignty and territory in international law as functionally analogous to property ownership,[6] and the tenets of private property and thus contract that underpin the rules of international economic law and global finance.[7] Commodification is woven into the form and fabric of international law, with its constant need for new methods of private appropriation and geographic and material opportunities for capital investment.[8] The logic of capital as it

---

[2] China Miéville, *Between Equal Rights: A Marxist Theory of International Law* (Brill 2005) 54.

[3] See Pashukanis, 'International Law', *supra* note 1, 171–2: 'The spread and development of international law occurred on the basis of the spread and development of the capitalist mode of production.' See further James Anaya, *Indigenous Peoples in International Law* (Oxford University Press 2000); Antony Anghie, *Imperialism, Sovereignty and the Making of International Law* (Cambridge University Press 2004); Michael Fakhri, *Sugar and the Making of International Law* (Cambridge University Press 2014); John Linarelli, Margot E. Salomon and Muthucumaraswamy Sornarajah, *The Misery of International Law: Confrontations with Injustice in the Global Economy* (Oxford University Press 2018).

[4] International law, like liberal law more generally, presupposes the legal concepts of private property and thus contract. See Duncan Kennedy, 'The Role of Law in Economic Thought: Essays on the Fetishism of Commodities' 34 *American University Law Review* (1984–5) 939, 978.

[5] Pashukanis captures the point: 'Bourgeois private law assumes that subjects are formally equal yet simultaneously permits real inequality in property, while bourgeois international law in principle recognizes that states have equal rights but in reality they are unequal in their significance and power … These dubious benefits of formal equality are not enjoyed at all by those nations which have not developed capitalist civilization and which engage in international intercourse not as subjects, but as objects of imperialist state's colonial policy.' Pashukanis, 'International Law', *supra* note 1, 178.

[6] 'Sovereign states co-exist and are counterposed to one another in exactly the same way as are individual property owners with equal rights. Each state may "freely" dispose of its own property, but it can gain access to another state's property only by means of a contract on the basis of compensation: do ut des.' Pashukanis, 'International Law', *supra* note 1, 176. The rules addressing the prohibition on the use of force in international law are likewise rooted in the protection of property framed as territory.

[7] See Linarelli et al, *The Misery of International Law*, *supra* note 3.

[8] See A. Claire Cutler, 'New Constitutionalism and the Commodity Form of Global Capitalism' in Stephen Gill and A. Claire Cutler (eds) *New Constitutionalism and World Order* (Cambridge University Press 2014) 45, 49. In his writing Miéville argues further that claims, disputation and contestation are a necessary element where the commodity form exists, since private ownership implies the exclusion of others and thus coercion ('violence') is required to enforce what is mine and not yours. Defence of what is mine is essential lest there be nothing to stop it becoming yours. Coercion is implicit. China Miéville, 'The Commodity-Form Theory of International Law' in S. Marks (ed.) *International Law on the Left: Re-Examining Marxist Legacies* (Cambridge University Press 2008) 92, 112–13 and ff 115.

plays out in the *structure* of international law exposes as facetious the conventional presumption that international law is ahistorical, apolitical and neutral.

The material *content* of international law reflects social relations founded on commodity exchange,[9] and commodity exchange under capitalism is based on – just as it reproduces – exploitative class relations of production.[10] A contemporary take would add also the role of capitalism in sustaining the 'overlapping subjugations' of gender, race and nationality, including through the exploitation of low pay or no pay labour, that grease the wheels of global capitalism.[11] This is not to say that economic interests are all that matter in international legal relations or that the *content* of international law cannot reflect public interests, or that the judicial interpretation of rules cannot favour the disenfranchised. But it does highlight how 'international law's constituent forms are constituent forms of global capitalism',[12] and as such international law's presuppositions give legal expression to the rapacious, endlessly expansive and exploitative features that make up capitalism. Grasping the nihilist mantle, Miéville takes the position that no 'systematic progressive political project or emancipatory dynamic' can be expected from international law.[13]

While the nihilist doesn't necessarily deny that international law can be put to reformist use, it can only ever be of limited emancipatory value; given its legal form, it can only ever 'tinker' at the surface level of institutions.[14] The pragmatist, alive to the commodity form of international law and its hazards, finds value in that 'tinkering' – tinkering that prevents war, makes people less hungry, recognizes local culture. But the cost of this engagement is to legitimate and help sustain the international legal system that undergirds such exploitation and alienation in the first place.[15]

If law is part of the problem, pragmatists offer up solutions that would have the conscience of international law – international human rights law – pursued not because

---

[9] Miéville citing Chris Arthur, *Between Equal Rights*, *supra* note 2, 119.

[10] Ibid, 92.

[11] On feminist materialism in international law see the incisive essays by Miriam Bak McKenna, 'Blood, Breastmilk, and Dirt: Silvia Federici and Feminist Materialism in International Law (Parts One and Two)' *Legal Form* blog (2018). in the reference above McKenna draws on Chandra Talpade Mohanty, *Feminism Without Borders: Decolonizing Theory, Practicing Solidarity* (Duke University Press 2003) 28.

[12] China Miéville, 'The Commodity-Form Theory of International Law: An Introduction' 17 *Leiden Journal of International Law* (2004) 271.

[13] Miéville, 'The Commodity-Form Theory of International Law', *supra* note 8, 130.

[14] Ibid, 130–1.

[15] Recognition as to danger of 'valorizing the currency' of international law through its deployment is not new and need not draw exclusively on its ties to capitalism (although even if not explicit, capitalism is often just below the surface of critique): 'Why were we encouraging faith in international law as an agent of justice and peace when we know that it helps to legitimate oppression and justify violence, and we devote a considerable portion of our energies to showing how? One response to this might be that there is surely not a coherent, unified currency here. International law also has the potential to help those trying to resist oppression and curb violence. In other words, it works in more than one dimension, and so therefore must we. Or is this just rationalization?' Matthew Craven, Susan Marks, Gerry Simpson and Ralph Wilde, 'We Are Teachers of International Law' 17 *Leiden Journal of International Law* (2004) 363.

it is 'law' per se, but to advance the aims of progressive constituencies – here, as Robert Knox would have it, international human rights law is a tool of 'principled opportunism', nothing more.[16] In his own efforts to reconcile legal activism with the limits of law, Bill Bowring concludes that lawyers should 'employ legal competence and skills modestly in the service of collective resistance and struggle'.[17] This is to use law not because it is law, but in spite of law.[18] While nihilists and pragmatists agree on capitalism's deep inscription upon international law, they disagree on whether or not to reject it as a result. The tension between nihilist and pragmatist lawyers is ultimately intractable.

The commodity form theory that Pashukanis presents posits private law as the 'fundamental, primary level of law'[19] and applies it to international law. Insofar as international legal theorizing in this area remains a work in progress and the complexities of international law might expose its limits,[20] the commodity form theory of international law functions as a potent heuristic device. For current purposes, it helps us to appreciate how international law, viewed as the clashes and claims of states defending 'private' interests, underpins efforts to elaborate a progressive normative content of international human rights law in the cutting edge domain of the rights of peasants and indigenous peoples, and how access to and control over productive resources are both central to the negotiations between states and between states and local communities.

International law is a product of the market just as the invisible hand of the market is made possible by the visible hand of law,[21] shaping and cohering capitalism in ways that other social institutions could not.[22] To an international lawyer, this foregrounds the role of international law in instantiating the relationship between law and money; it invites us to consider how contemporary international law produces and hardens the terms under which the global economy operates – a global economy marked by great poverty, inequality, environmental devastation and violence. A central function of international law is to secure transnational access to profit and to control

---

[16] Robert Knox, 'Marxism, International Law, and Political Strategy' 22 *Leiden Journal of International Law* (2009) 413, 433.

[17] Bill Bowring, 'What is Radical in "Radical International Law"' 22 *Finnish Yearbook of International Law* (2011) 3, 29.

[18] Grietje Baars, '#LesbiansAreHot: On Oil, Imperialism, and What It Means to Queer International Law' 7 *Feminists@law* (2017). http://journals.kent.ac.uk/index.php/feministsatlaw/article/view/398/990.

[19] Miéville, 'The Commodity-Form Theory of International Law: An Introduction', *supra* note 12, 283; Evgeny B. Pashukanis, *Law and Marxism: A General Theory* (1929 Ink Links tr 1978).

[20] Just as Pashukanis' legal nihilism – attacking law and the rule of law and advocating for the replacement of the bourgeois state with administrative regulation – paved the way for Stalin's repression.

[21] On the latter point, see Quinn Slobodian, 'Ordoglobalism: The Invention of International Economic Law', Scales of Economy Conference, University of Sydney (2016). www.academia.edu/28283843/Ordoglobalism_The_Invention_of_International_Economic_Law.

[22] Honor Brabazon, 'Introduction: Understanding Neoliberal Legality' in H. Brabazon (ed.) *Neoliberal Legality: Understanding the Role of Law in the Neoliberal Project* (Routledge 2017) 1, 2.

over resources, including land. It works through a system of expanding commodification globally and into new areas of activity. Competition, comparative advantage and the international division of labour, and deep economic integration are among its techniques; exploitation, alienation and dispossession are among its costs. Accumulation aimed at higher rates of profit and control over raw materials seeks to expand overseas markets for one's own products, and, for those with the necessary military clout, to deploy it towards a host of aggressively self-interested ambitions. In short, the commodity form of international law and the corresponding world that international law has helped to construct expose the constraints against which international human rights lawmaking – and, more specifically for current purposes, peasant and indigenous rights lawmaking – operate.

The concern highlighted by nihilists and pragmatists serves as an illuminating heuristic device in the study of the rights of peasants and indigenous peoples, the focus of this chapter. Rejecting human rights for coconspiring with capitalism's voracious and expansive tendencies would be an elitist project that removes a potentially valuable tool from the toolbox of the oppressed. But insofar as its deployment deepens the hold of capitalism, curtailing the emancipatory potential of human rights law and driving away real alternatives that go beyond contemporary capitalism, using it has a substantial cost.

2. THE COMMODITY FORM THROUGH THREE APPROACHES TO THE PEASANTS' DECLARATION

The theory that the form of international law presupposes predatory capitalism suggests that the structural features connecting capitalism to international law delimit the options available for juridical reinvention by its victims. Although Pashukanis himself (and the nihilist thesis) opposed the 'pseudo-radicalism' that claimed 'bourgeois law' could be replaced by 'proletarian law',[23] being alerted to the embeddedness of capitalism in the international legal project facilitates an appraisal of the content of bottom up efforts at progressive international human rights law and how far it departs from the features of the legal form to become something significantly and lastingly different. A review of the draft UN Declaration on the Rights of Peasants is insightful in this regard.

In 2012 the UN Human Rights Council (HRC) established an intergovernmental Working Group to negotiate a Declaration on the Rights of Peasants and other People Working in Rural Areas. On 26 September 2018, at its 39th session, the HRC adopted the Declaration and sent it on to the UN General Assembly, recommending its parent organ do likewise.[24] Civil society, including the representatives of peasant communities

---

[23] Chris Arthur, 'Editor's Introduction' in Pashukanis, *Law and Marxism*, supra note 19, 9, 18.

[24] UN Doc. A/HRC/39/L.16, 26 Sept 2018. For the purposes of the Declaration, 'a peasant is any person who engages or who seeks to engage alone, or in association with others or as a community, in small-scale agricultural production for subsistence and/or for the market, and who relies significantly, though not necessarily exclusively, on family or household labour and other non-monetized ways of organizing labour, and who has a special dependency on and attachment

– among them the Via Campesina peasant consortium comprising 167 organizations and 200,000 individual members – has contributed forcefully to the Declaration and will seek to defend the instrument during the final negotiations in the General Assembly. The Declaration emerged in response to the impact of globalization on peasants and other people working in rural areas as an attempt to salvage their relationships to the land, water and nature to which they are attached and on which they depend for their livelihood and their way of life. As with indigenous peoples, this Declaration is to offer a normative articulation of the claims of peasants given their traditional role in conservation and improving biodiversity – including with regard to food production – to their overrepresentation among the poor.

The debates during the sessions of the Working Group display many of the usual cleavages, as well as the entrenched and familiar positions of various states on particular issues. These include concern over the language of 'free, prior and informed consent' (Russian Federation), given the fear of devolving real influence or even a veto to communities; the rejection of collective rights in international human rights law (United Kingdom[25]); and the defence of the right to development by a mix of countries from the Global South (e.g. Pakistan, China, South Africa). Invariably the content and specifics of the Declaration will reflect compromise given the respective interests of states and between states and the fervent views of civil society. That much is predictable. But one might also anticipate that the Declaration will make some notable normative contribution expounding the rights of peasants.

A review of the advanced draft Declaration exposes at least three approaches to confronting the plight of peasants that are in tension with each other. These tensions offer paradigmatic insights of the legal form at work in a progressive legal project. The first approach – and a revolutionary one – might be framed as the rise of rights against global capitalism. Here we see included in the right to an adequate standard of living 'facilitated access to the means of production', as well as 'a right to engage freely … in traditional ways of farming, fishing, livestock rearing and forestry and to develop community-based commercialization systems'.[26] There are rights of peasants to land, including 'the right to have access to, sustainably use and manage land and the water bodies, coastal seas, fisheries, pastures and forests therein, to achieve an adequate standard of living, to have a place to live in security, peace and dignity and to develop their cultures'.[27] State action is required 'to provide legal recognition for land tenure rights, including customary land tenure rights not currently protected by law' and 'to recognize and protect the natural commons and their related systems of collective use and management'.[28] There is a 'right to seeds', which includes '[t]he right [of peasants]

---

to the lands'. United Nations draft Declaration on the Rights of Peasants and Other People Working in Rural Areas. Ibid, Art. 1(1).

[25] The UK voted against the Declaration in the HRC as a result. See the UK's explanation of the vote, UN Media 28 Sept 2018. On the UK's position generally see Chair-Rapporteur Report of the open-ended intergovernmental working group on a draft United Nations declaration on the rights of peasants and other people working in rural areas, A/HRC/35/59 (3rd session, 20 July 2016) para 74.

[26] UN Doc A/HRC/39/L.16, 26 Sept 2018, Art. 16(1).
[27] Ibid, Art. 17(1).
[28] Ibid, Art. 17(3).

to save, use, exchange and sell their farm-saved seed or propagating material'.[29] Although the 'right to biodiversity' found in the February 2018 version of the draft Declaration, which stated that peasants 'have *the right* to maintain their traditional agrarian, pastoral and agroecological systems upon which their subsistence and the renewal of biodiversity depend, and the right to the conservation of the ecosystems in which those processes take place',[30] did not survive, a stated requirement to 'take appropriate measures to protect and promote' those and other systems 'relevant to the conservation and sustainable use of biological diversity' was retained.[31] These and related articulations are not without their state detractors, of course. Argentina, Colombia and the EU fought (not entirely successfully) to have references to the right to food sovereignty replaced by the term 'food security', which lacks the elements of local control and decommodification,[32] and the stronger participation standard of 'free, prior and informed consent' found in the Declaration on the Rights of Indigenous Peoples and widely supported by judicial and quasi-judicial human rights bodies had already been contested and dropped from the draft Declaration well before it reached the HRC. Japan proposed the weaker language of 'access' to seeds over 'right' to seeds in order to avoid any interpretation that would undermine international agreements on intellectual property.[33]

These rights as advanced by peasants are not casual linguistic preferences; they reflect articulations that contest the logic of (transnational) capitalism – of private property, contract, accumulation and the exploitation of people and natural resources. They express alternatives to the standard technique of forced displacements, largescale land and water grabs and speculative land investments, and impacts that include climate disruptions and environmental devastation, rapid urbanization, the obliteration of culture and the creation of food insecurity in rural communities as well as widespread hunger, with women its greatest victims globally.[34] The recent history of peasants in India and their struggle over seeds provides a telling example of the lived experience that underpins the rise of rights against global capitalism captured in this approach to the Declaration. In 1998 the World Bank Structural Adjustment Programme had India

---

[29] Ibid, Art. 19(1) and 19(1)(d).
[30] UN Doc. A/HRC/WG.15/5/2, 18 Feb 2018, Art. 20(1).
[31] UN Doc. A/HRC/39/L.16, 26 Sept 2018, Art. (20)(2): 'States shall take appropriate measures to promote and protect the traditional knowledge, innovation and practices of peasants and other people working in rural areas, including traditional agrarian, pastoral, forestry, fisheries, livestock and agroecological systems relevant to the conservation and sustainable use of biological diversity.'
[32] For the international food sovereignty movement's six defining principles of food sovereignty: www.globaljustice.org.uk/six-pillars-food-sovereignty.
[33] Report of the open-ended intergovernmental working group on a United Nations declaration on the rights of peasants and other people working in rural areas UN Doc. A/HRC/39/67 13 July 2018, 44 and 76.
[34] Women play a crucial role in the food security of households, producing between 60 and 80 per cent of food crops in developing countries and cultivating more than 50 per cent of food grown globally. While the great majority of women work in agriculture, as much as 70 per cent of the world's hungry are women. Moreover, they rarely receive any recognition for their work. Indeed, many are not even paid. Human Rights Council Advisory Committee, UN Doc. A/HRC/19/75, 24 Feb 2012, para 22.

open up its seed sector to multinational corporations. Farm saved seeds were replaced by seeds from Monsanto and other multinational corporations, including genetically modified organisms, which need fertilizers and pesticides and cannot be saved.[35] Corporations prevent seed savings through patents and by engineering seeds with nonrenewable traits that cause them to die. As a result, poor peasants have had to buy new seeds for every planting season, driving up their costs. What was traditionally a free resource available by putting aside a small portion of the crop, allowing also for biodiversity as opposed to monoculture, became a commodity. There are a host of other problems, including poor yields; a shift from indigenous varieties, for example of cotton, that are rain fed and pest resistant to corporate crops that require irrigation and pesticides; and a dramatic fall in agricultural prices due to international trade 'dumping'. Poverty and sheer desperation led to a spate of suicides: this is Vandana Shiva's 'suicide economy'.[36] It is against multiple registers of capitalist dispossession – material and spiritual, as well as the dispossession of hope – that we can locate the rise of rights against global capitalism in the draft Peasants' Declaration. These rights against global capitalism reflect an effort to challenge the forced shift from nonmarket to global market economies and values. The dominant understanding of 'development' and 'progress' is still coterminous with the idea of industrialized, Western and modern development. Its contribution is to see the dismantling of nonmarket access to food and self-sustenance and the universal establishment of transnational market-based economies.[37] This first approach of the draft Peasants' Declaration offers normative claims against those dominant values, values that reflect the structural connection between international law and commodification.

The second approach taken in the draft Peasants' Declaration, in contrast to the first, is one that can be said to legitimate and sustain the terms of globalization against which the peasants strive. The General Obligations of States require that they 'elaborate, interpret and apply international agreements and standards, including in the areas of trade, investment, finance, taxation, environmental protection, development cooperation and security, in a manner consistent with their human rights obligations'.[38] A paradox presents itself: legal regimes that constitute and sustain global capitalism are retained, indeed, reinforced in the draft Declaration. International law that has served peasants so poorly is taken as a given and validated. Here, the Peasants' Declaration anchors its demands to the continued existence of the regimes against which they struggle.

---

[35] Monsanto alone controls 90 per cent of the global market in genetically modified seeds. Ibid, para. 36.
[36] Vandana Shiva, 'From Seeds of Suicide to Seeds of Hope: Why Are Indian Farmers Committing Suicide and How Can We Stop This Tragedy?' *Huffpost Blog*, 25 May 2011. www.huffingtonpost.com/vandana-shiva/from-seeds-of-suicide-to_b_192419.html.
[37] See Farshad Araghi and Marina Karides, 'Land Dispossession and Global Crisis: Introduction to the Special Section on Land Rights in the World-System' 18 *Journal of World-Systems Research* (2012) 1; Rob Nixon, *Slow Violence and the Environmentalism of the Poor* (Harvard University Press 2011).
[38] UN Doc. A/HRC/WG.15/4/2, 6 March 2017, Art. 2(4). Subsequent versions of the draft Declaration reflect some amendments but do not alter the central idea. See UN Doc. A/HRC/39/L.16, 26 Sept 2018, Art. 2(4).

This technique of seeking normative assurances that human rights will be brought to bear on other areas of international law that have a direct and often egregious impact on the exercise of rights is commonplace among (academic) activists and UN human rights bodies, and is an approach that is not limited to the outcomes of intergovernmental negotiations. The celebrated Maastricht Principles on the Extraterritorial Obligations of States in the Area of Economic, Social and Cultural Rights, adopted by 40 human rights legal experts in 2011,[39] reflect the same approach, one that validates international economic law and other agreements in the first instance – agreements against which human rights compliance must be sought.[40] Even in the most progressive area of the Principles, the obligations of international cooperation to fulfil socio-economic rights globally, compliance with the obligation to create an internationally enabling environment is to be achieved through 'the elaboration, interpretation, application and regular review of multilateral and bilateral agreements as well as international standards'.[41] That the endorsers of the Maastricht Principles were circumscribed in the nature and extent of their pronouncements by having agreed to reflect the state of the juridical art, rather than go beyond it with proposals to restructure radically the global economy, highlights another layer in the paradox at the centre of this chapter. Not only do the Maastricht Principles at times unwittingly accept the economic status quo and the inevitability of economic globalization, but if the Maastricht endorsers were ever going to offer a progressive account of extraterritorial obligations that is *consistent* with the current state of international human rights law, they could do nothing else. The problem identified here is, quite simply, that if one is to rely on the law *as it is*, then one is bound by its terms. As such, the best one can do is to seek to soften its hazardous features and, as the pragmatists know all too well, the cost is one of legitimating the system that one seeks radically to change.[42] In light of the pragmatist's dilemma, James Harrison can be seen to have presented a profound proposal when he suggested, in his consideration of the fragmentation problem, replacing the 'coherence mindset' for one of 'investigative legal pluralism'.[43] He advises that before any attempt at reconciliation is even proffered, the place to begin (including among judicial bodies) is with an honest exploration of frictions between the

---

[39] Disclosure: The author was a member of the Maastricht Principles' Drafting Committee.

[40] Maastricht Principles, Art. 17. 'States must elaborate, interpret and apply relevant international agreements and standards in a manner consistent with their human rights obligations. Such obligations include those pertaining to international trade, investment, finance, taxation, environmental protection, development cooperation, and security.'

[41] Ibid, Art. 29.

[42] While drawing on substantive dimensions of the Maastricht Principles (and not at all times entirely convincing examples), Ralph Wilde draws interesting conclusions, highlighting comparable concerns to those above. He warns, moreover, that the 'modest nature' of the legal claims in the Maastricht Principles (which graft discrete areas of liability onto the existing structures of global economic relations) not only functions to bolster the status quo but 'can now be further legitimated by states through claims to being "human rights compliant"'. Ralph Wilde, 'Socioeconomic Rights, Extraterritorially' in E. Benvenisti and G. Nolte (eds) *Community Interests across International Law* (Oxford University Press 2018) 381, 394.

[43] James Harrison, 'The Case for Investigative Legal Pluralism in the International Economic Law Linkages Debate: A Strategy for Enhancing International Legal Discourse' 2 *London Review of International Law* (2014) 115.

values and priorities of the different regimes. Only then should any further legal inquiry proceed to the second stage regarding whether the diverse analytical lenses allow for an accommodation of normative visions and practices. This, Harrison indicates, is both to open up the possibility of real reconciliation and to avoid an artificial attempt at coherence where reconciliation is impossible.[44] From this vantage point comes the possibility of moving beyond alleged fixes to globalization towards offering up entirely alternative imaginaries. To sum up so far: the first approach identified in the Peasants' Declaration embraces new imaginaries; the second makes them impossible.

The third approach, like the second, demonstrates through the terms of 'benefit sharing' how the draft Declaration suffers from capitalism's rootedness in international law. In realizing the rights of peasants to the natural resources present in their communities, the Declaration provides '[m]odalities for the fair and equitable sharing of the benefits of such exploitation that have been established on mutually agreed terms between those exploiting the natural resources and the peasants and other people working in rural areas'.[45] But, contrary to the first approach that seeks to define rights against the logic of global capitalism, here 'benefit sharing' requires a continuation of, rather than a break with, the logic of commodification underpinned by exclusive property rights.[46] Further, challenges to the status quo are permanently deferred through the granting of economic concessions: this is hegemony through the consent of the governed.[47] It is not for outsiders to stand in judgement as to what concessions are necessary or preferred, and indigenous peoples have elsewhere made the case that engagement allows for 'demonstrating how to do this right', or how indigenous people can 'pave a middle way for developing resources responsibly'.[48] Yet through the technique of 'benefit sharing' the alienations and antagonisms produced by capital accumulation can merely be managed, and the 'solution' invariably becomes an indispensable aspect of sustaining the processes of capitalist exploitation and accumulation. The turn to benefit sharing in this way represents an instantiation of Gramsci's passive revolution – socialization and cooperation by the ruling class in the sphere of production that nonetheless does not touch upon their appropriation of profit, nor their control over the 'decisive nucleus of economic activity', thereby ensuring that the elite interests prevail.[49]

---

[44] Ibid.

[45] UN Doc. A/HRC/39/L.16, 26 Sept 2018, Art. 5(2)(c).

[46] See generally Georges Abi-Saab, 'Permanent Sovereignty over Natural Resources' in M. Bedjaoui (ed) *International Law: Achievements and Prospects* (UNESCO/Martinus Nijhoff 1991) 600, 601; Sundhya Pahuja, *Decolonising International Law: Development, Economic Growth and the Politics of Universality* (Cambridge University Press 2011) 125.

[47] See Joe Wills, *Contesting World Order: Socioeconomic Rights and Global Justice Movements* (Cambridge University Press 2017) 11, for a valuable exploration that brings 'neo-Gramscian' insights to bear on socioeconomic rights.

[48] Ashifa Kassam, 'First Nations Group Proposes Oil Pipeline that Protects Indigenous Rights' *The Guardian* (18 Sept 2018). www.theguardian.com/world/2018/sep/08/canada-oil-pipeline-first-nations-proposal-indigenous-rights.

[49] Antonio Gramsci, *Selections from the Prison Notebooks* (ed. and trans. Q. Hoare and G. Nowell Smith) (Lawrence & Wishart 1971) 119–20, 161.

This embrace of benefit sharing found in the Peasants' Declaration is not unusual. Reading the 2007 UN Declaration on the Rights of Indigenous Peoples into the African Charter on Human and Peoples' Rights, in what is widely considered a landmark case, the African Court on Human and Peoples' Rights found a violation by Kenya of the right of the indigenous Ogiek community to 'occupy, use, and enjoy their ancestral lands' under Article 14 of the African Charter on the right to property (the creative interpretation of the right to property to protect collective rights of indigenous peoples having been spearheaded by the Inter-American Court of Human Rights).[50] The African Court also found a violation of the right of indigenous peoples 'to freely dispose of their wealth and resources' given that the community was deprived by the state, through the pursuit of economic exploitation and displacement, of the right to enjoy and dispose of the 'abundance of food produced on their ancestral lands'. This was the first time that the African Court found a violation of the right of peoples to natural resources. This first indigenous rights case before the African Court reflects a number of novel elements, perhaps most notably an interpretation that the right of indigenous peoples to natural resources includes the right to their traditional food sources. Yet alongside its innovative normative dimensions sits the compensation request by the Ogiek applicants for royalties from existing economic activities in the Mau Forest, where they have lived since time immemorial, and the request to ensure 'that the Ogiek benefit from any employment opportunities within the Mau Forest'.[51]

Benefit sharing is developed in other international instruments, and in the case of the Convention on Biological Diversity and its Nagoya Protocol on Access to Genetic Resources and the Fair and Equitable Sharing of Benefits Arising from their Utilization,[52] many indigenous communities and organizations have expressed commitment to the project despite its alien, Western legal rationale, assumptions and concepts.[53] Notwithstanding arrangements less disturbing of indigenous and local communities' land, way of life and traditional knowledge, and promises of conservation, sustainability and poverty reduction, the Nagoya Protocol is in many ways a status quo masterwork: 'fair and equitable sharing of benefits' is premised on the 'economic value of the ecosystem and biodiversity'[54] and based on a relationship between 'providers' (indigenous peoples and local communities) and 'users' (unnamed entities providing the R&D)[55] to whom the indigenous peoples and local communities cede traditional knowledge, innovations and practices that are associated with genetic resources in order

---

[50] *African Commission on Human and Peoples' Rights v Kenya*, Appl No 006/2012, judgment of 26 May 2017.

[51] The Court's ruling on reparations is awaited.

[52] Convention on Biological Diversity (1992) entered into force 1993, 196 states parties at September 2018; Nagoya Protocol (2011) entered into force 2014, 111 states parties at September 2018.

[53] 'Our ceremonies, offerings, prayers, chants, reciprocal support, and tears helped us, the Indigenous women from Latin America and the Caribbean, to continue calmly in these tiring, technical, and difficult dialogues under an umbrella of Western paradigms' (F. López, personal communication to Terán, 12 April 2010). Maria Yolanda Terán, 'The Nagoya Protocol and Indigenous Peoples' 7 *The International Indigenous Policy Journal* (2016) 1, 12.

[54] Nagoya Protocol, Preamble.

[55] Ibid.

to receive returns, either monetary (for example, upfront payments, royalties) or non-monetary (for example, a 'contribution to the local economy'), derived from their 'utilization', that is, their financial exploitation.[56] The hard won indigenous rights standard of 'free, prior and informed consent' in decisions that affect them and their lands and territories is thinned out in the Protocol, rendered subject to 'domestic law', with the state required merely 'to take measures, as appropriate, with the aim of ensuring that the prior informed consent or approval is obtained for access to genetic resources where [indigenous peoples and local communities] have the established rights to grant such resources'.[57] In this treaty, the doctrine of prior, informed consent in an uncompromising version becomes applicable to states 'in the exercise of sovereign rights over natural resources'.[58] The ability of indigenous peoples and local communities to rely on their customary use and exchange of genetic resources and associated traditional knowledge within and among their communities is exercisable only 'in so far as possible'.[59]

In its best light, the indigenous standard of participation gives disenfranchised local communities greater say in decisions that affect their rights and their way of life, at times to the point of veto.[60] But the important Gramscian insight is that the political rights to effective participation in decision making for the sharing of benefits are consistent with international human rights law while opening up the distinct possibility of coopting the rightholders. There is a real risk that arrangements to come from participation in the design of a benefit sharing scheme require acceptance of the capitalist logic of natural resource exploitation (in contradiction to indigenous and local culture and way of life).[61] As such, it is through the very exercise of those rights that

---

[56] Ibid, Art. 2(c): '"Utilization of genetic resources" means to conduct research and development on the genetic and/or biochemical composition of genetic resources.'

[57] Ibid, Art. 6(2). See similarly Art. 7 with regard to access to traditional knowledge associated with genetic resources.

[58] Ibid, Art. 6(1): 'In the exercise of sovereign rights over natural resources ... access to genetic resources for their utilization shall be subject to the prior informed consent of the Party providing such resources that is the country of origin of such resources or a Party that has acquired the genetic resources in accordance with the Convention.'

[59] Ibid, Art. 12(4).

[60] See the UN Declaration on the Rights of Indigenous Peoples (UNDRIP) (2007) Arts 10 and 29(2) and *Poma Poma v Peru,* Comm 1457/2006, UN Doc CCPR/C/95/D/1457/2006 (HRC 2009) para. 7.6: 'The Committee considers that participation in the decision-making process must be effective, which requires not mere consultation but the free, prior and informed consent of the members of the community.' But cf Arts 19 and 32(2) of UNDRIP, the latter providing merely: 'States shall consult and cooperate in good faith with indigenous peoples ... in order to obtain their free and informed consent prior to approval of any project affecting their lands or territories and other resources.'

[61] Of course, this is not unique to indigenous rights and peasants' rights. The right of peoples to the exploitation of their natural resources – understood initially as a right of states – can be found in the 1950s norm of permanent sovereignty over natural resources and in common article 1 of the two human rights covenants.

indigenous peoples and local communities serve to validate and entrench the rationalities and mechanics of global capitalism while deferring wholesale challenges to them.[62] The Nagoya Protocol sees traditional knowledge commodified and intellectual property rights granted to indigenous peoples and local communities, drawing them into the global market with rights to profit financially from their culture; contrary to the philosophy that defines their communal way of life, it encourages the use of those newfound rights in their own self-interest and to the exclusion of others.[63] As one indigenous participant in the Nagoya negotiations put it:

> In our vision the plants, animals, rivers, everything is related and interconnected. We believe that the resources from Mother Earth are for the well-being of humanity. Consequently, it was very painful for us to understand these initial discussions on the commercialization of our resources and to put a price on genetic resources and traditional knowledge.[64]

Rights against global capitalism may yet emerge from standards on biological diversity and benefit sharing but it is an uphill battle to have intellectual property reimagined internationally.[65] Under the terms of the Convention and Protocol there is scope for sui generis protections distinct from dominant intellectual property systems (for example, patents) that are responsive to the needs and worldviews of indigenous and local communities and protect local communities against misappropriation by third parties while making the knowledge available for wider benefit.[66] And indigenous and local communities are providing clear guidelines on the content of a suitable sui generis

---

[62] Comparable scenarios play out in other areas. The controversial response of the World Bank to concerns over the impact of (foreign) land acquisition on local populations, smallscale farmers and fisher people is largely how to manage it: to facilitate the consultation of those affected, avoid increasing their vulnerability, and share the value of responsible agroinvestment.

[63] See Ciupa, in this case referring to UNDRIP: Kristin Ciupa, 'The Promise of Rights: International Indigenous Rights in the Neoliberal Era' in H. Brabazon (ed.) *Neoliberal Legality*, *supra* note 22, 140, 157; Tobias Stoll, 'Article 31: Intellectual Property and Technology' in M. Weller and J. Holman (eds), *The UN Declaration on the Rights of Indigenous Peoples: A Commentary* (Oxford University Press 2018), 299, 314–15: 'Indigenous peoples might consider to seek intellectual property protection for their traditional knowledge themselves' (precisely the concern implied in Ciupa). Yet 'a rule might emerge … that third parties are barred from applying for, obtaining, and exercising intellectual property rights which are based on traditional knowledge or traditional cultural expressions of Indigenous Peoples and obtained or used without their prior and informed consent'. Ibid, 327.

[64] Naniki Reyes as cited in Terán, 'The Nagoya Protocol and Indigenous Peoples', *supra* note 53, 9.

[65] Notably, the WIPO Intergovernmental Committee on Intellectual Property and Genetic Resources, Traditional Knowledge and Folklore has been discussing the possibility of a sui generis system internationally to protect traditional knowledge since 2001.

[66] Convention on Biological Diversity, Art. 8(j): 'Subject to its national legislation, respect, preserve and maintain knowledge, innovations and practices of indigenous and local communities embodying traditional lifestyles relevant for the conservation and sustainable use of biological diversity and promote their wider application with the approval and involvement of the holders of such knowledge, innovations and practices and encourage the equitable sharing of the benefits arising from the utilization of such knowledge, innovations and practices.' The preamble to the Nagoya Protocol recalls the relevance of Art. 8(j) of the Convention on Biological Diversity.

system, including by safeguarding the free exchange of resources, recognizing collective custodianship, ensuring systems that primarily seek to address the subsistence and cultural needs of communities rather than commercial objectives, and respecting customary laws for benefit sharing that emphasize equity, fairness, helping those in need and conservation values.[67]

The Secretariat of the Convention on Biological Diversity and the Nagoya Protocol explains that the treaties were aimed at regulating internationally bioprospecting activities undertaken for commercial and noncommercial purposes, as well as the privatization and marketization of new medicines that are based on discoveries from natural products and traditional knowledge. Herbal products, for example, are a multitrillion dollar industry; the commercialization of local plants and knowledge generates enormous profits for transnational drug companies, with no returns to locals. Lack of implementation of the Nagoya Protocol is a live concern; on the account described, implementation is another.

What the indigenous examples above demonstrate, as for the Peasants' Declaration, is that benefit sharing on dominant terms comes at a cost: it masks the structural subordination at the heart of contemporary capitalism just as it contributes to its continuation. It draws into global capitalism its most passionate opponents and those with the greatest experience to spearhead alternatives. With this third dimension of the draft Peasants' Declaration one can see how the Declaration sustains the very terms against which it also militates, throwing into doubt whether it amounts to a meaningful departure from global capitalism and the deeper problems engendered nationally and internationally.

The second approach taken in the Peasants' Declaration demonstrates how the commodity form of international economic law is brought to bear on international human rights law. This third approach taken in the Peasants' Declaration exposes a number of fault lines through which twenty-first century capitalism is taken as a permanent, unspoken feature of international human rights law. These two approaches beg the question as to whether the status of the disenfranchised is merely and always an object of the 'completed transaction' that is capitalist globalization – a central claim of nihilists.[68] If the first approach taken in the Peasants' Declaration reflects a protest against global capitalism, the second and third inadvertently reflect an affirmation of it.

---

[67] *Sui Generis Systems for the Protection of Traditional Knowledge*, Information for the Secretariat of the Convention on Biological Diversity Submitted by: IIED, Kechua-Aymara Association for Nature and Sustainable Development (ANDES, Peru), Fundacion Dobbo Yala (Panama), University of Panama, Ecoserve (India), Centre for Indigenous Farming Systems (India), Herbal and Folklore Research Centre (India), Centre for Chinese Agricultural Policy (CCAP, China), Southern Environmental and Agricultural Policy Research Institute (ICIPE, Kenya), Kenya Forestry Research Institute (31 October 2005). http://pubs.iied.org/pdfs/G02378.pdf.

[68] See Pashukanis, 'International Law' *supra* note 1, 172.

3. EYES WIDE OPEN

Advances that tame the injurious tendencies of capitalist globalization also normalize the status quo. This takes place through the legitimating function of international human rights law in the area of indigenous and peasants' rights, including through the pacification of protest that accompanies concessions. As we have seen, the approaches that seek to bring human rights to bear on globalization's juridico-institutions of trade and investment and the increasingly popular model of benefit sharing, any shallow ameliorative functions notwithstanding, reflect the strategic logic of the capitalist, imperial state – imperial in its defence of the interests of transnational capital, to the ultimate disadvantage of the states and peoples of the Global South.[69] But the greatest loss reflected in the latter two approaches of the Peasants' Declaration is how they might serve the ancillary function of narrowing the possibility even to imagine alternative forms of social organization and alternative arrangements to global capitalism. Where the rise of rights against global capitalism – the first approach in the Peasants' Declaration – reflects the antideterministic reach of the content of human rights law and its normative openness,[70] against the juridical backdrop of global capitalism, the second and third approaches make the existence of that backdrop essential to their claims.

The dilemma faced by international human rights lawyers in search of a transformed world cannot be resolved. To engage with international (human rights) law is to engage with international (human rights) law, capitalist warts and all. Not to engage with international law – as per the nihilist position – is of course tacitly to engage with international law by leaving it as is, absent oppositional, revolutionary voices. As the strategic proposals advanced by pragmatists effectively demonstrate, there is no real pragmatic compromise to be had at all; one is either in or out, and to do nothing is also to take a position. This has prompted insightful if not openended soul searching as to the role of the critical legal enterprise, suggesting its value must lie in alerting people of good heart as to what is at stake.[71] I alluded to this need for attentiveness when writing in an earlier work about the paradox that comes from having the protection of socioeconomic rights and social protection floors rely on capitalist growth, with all its attendant harms – as it does without exception. I suggested that to begin the process of overcoming that paradox, it needs to be consistently exposed. Thus, along with its mandate to protect the most vulnerable, the UN Committee on Economic, Social and Cultural Rights could endorse social protection floors, but it should also state that in

---

[69] For apposite reflections on what is meant by 'imperial', see B.S. Chimni, 'International Institutions Today: An Imperial Global State in the Making' 15 *European Journal of International Law* (2004) 1, 1–2.

[70] See generally Emilios Christodoulidis herein on law and 'the leverage that critique is afforded under the conditions of normative closure and legal self-reference'. Emilios Christodoulidis, 'Critical Theory and the Law: Reflections on Origins, Trajectories and Conjunctures' in E. Christodoulidis, R. Dukes and M. Goldoni (eds) *Research Handbook on Critical Legal Theory* (Edward Elgar 2019).

[71] Craven et al, 'We Are Teachers of International Law', *supra* note 15, 374, asking but not answering: 'does the distinctiveness of the critical enterprise lie in the fact that it raises these issues, it prompts these anxieties, but precisely does not resolve them?'

doing so it does not necessarily endorse the means by which the needed redistribution is made possible. The 'predistributive' requirements would then be the subject of a separate and related inquiry into compliance with the Covenant.[72] In his introductory chapter to this edited volume speaking to what critical legal theory can do, Emilios Christodoulidis draws the same conclusion, and the only one to adopt in confronting – not the dilemma between nihilists and pragmatists, since, as this chapter has shown, no material impasse between them actually exists – but the dilemma of international human rights law that the tension between nihilists and pragmatists has exposed. What critical legal theory can do is bring the human rights lawyer to her rendezvous with international human rights law with eyes wide open.

---

[72] Margot E. Salomon, 'Sustaining Neoliberal Capital through Socio-Economic Rights' *Critical Legal Thinking* (Oct 2017). http://criticallegalthinking.com/2017/10/18/sustaining-neoliberal-capital-socio-economic-rights/; Linarelli et al, *The Misery of International Law, supra* note 3, chapter 7.

Index

actor-network theory 243, 247, 252–3
Adorno, Theodor 4, 5, 9, 11–12
  Metacritique 15
  Negative Dialectics 185
aesthesis 207–208
  decolonial aestheSis 210
  renewed focus on the particular 212
aesthetic turn 5, 201–3, 229
  law as image conscious 210
  as legitimation 202
  political and ontological consequences 202, 214
  as return to the origins of aesthetics 208
  shift from aesthetics to aestheses 207–8, 211–12
    as grounding 213
aesthetics 229–30
  aesthetic economics 213–14
  affect
    as aesthesic 220
    as emotion 220
    as goal-oriented 220
    as symbolic 220
  affective turn 210
  Aristotelian 208
  choice as not choice 219–20
  decolonial 210
  English 211
  feminist 209
  Kantian 208–9
  legal *see* legal aesthetics
  minoritarian 209–10
  as shifting 201
  sources of 210–11
  subverting norm of 211
  of withdrawal 218–19
affect
  collective 215
  diverging 215
Althusser, Louis 13, 96
  as anti-Hegelian structuralist 109
  capitalist/ideological state repression differentiation 109
  on commodity fetishism 109
  contesting bourgeois democracy 109
  definition of ideology 226

  structuralism 6–7
'anti necessitarian' thinking 13
Arendt, Hannah
  freedom 181
  On Revolution 21
  on public sphere 146
atmosphere 214–17, 215
  affective excess 221–2
  attracting while excluding 220
  of contractual freedom 215–16
  definition 215
  distinction of 220
  engineered 217
    maintaining predetermined positions 220
  fragility of 211
  freezing effect of 218
  generating cycle of addiction 216
  legal 215
  of legitimacy 215
  naturalised 217–18
  relying on circumvention of rationality 217
  self-maintaining 221
atmospherics
  atmospheric engineering 215, 216–17, 221
  atmospheric partitioning 216
  and move to aesthesis 217
  power of 221
  preserving the status quo 217
  self-dissimulation 217–19
  and synaesthesic disorientation 217
Austin, John 266, 278
Autonomia movement 4

Badiou, Alain 4, 6, 237
Balkin, Jack 153, 303, 304
Barthes, Roland 152, 155, 396, 398
Beard, Charles on economic origins of American constitution 99–100
Bell, Derrick A Jr, 67–8
Benjamin, Jessica
  Beyond Doer and Done To 398
  inherent tension between self-assertion and recognition 404
  juridical law/lawfulness distinction 398
  moral third 398–9
    embodied 399

failed/dead 399–400
hollow 400
public 399, 400
rhythmic 399
Benjamin, Walter 5, 190, 195, 231
  mythical/divine violence distinction 193, 202
Blackstone, Sir William 163, 260, 261, 263, 266, 268, 270–71
  Commentaries on the Laws of England 262
  exclusivity axiom 261, 266
  ten-to-one ratio 193
Bloch, Ernst 231, 235, 498
Böhme, Gernot 210–11, 213–14
Bottici, Chiara 152, 161–2
Bottomley, Anne 46–7, 48
Bourdieu, Pierre
  on linguistic interactions 86–7
  magic of performative speech 86
Boyle, James 276, 314
Bretton Woods
  conditional lending practices of 433
  International Monetary Fund 431
  World Bank 431
  see also development
Brown, Wendy 364–6
  human rights scepticism 365–6
Burke, Edmund 201, 206, 211
Butler, Judith
  distinguishing rules from norms 83
  rejecting Bourdieu's study of linguistic interactions 86

Camus, Albert 183–4, 190
capital accumulation 437
  cycles of
    Dutch-dominated 437
    English-dominated 437
    signal point 439
    trajectory 437
    US-dominated 437–438, 439–40
citizenship 375
  development of 375
  as egalitarian idea and agent 378
  principle of equality 375–6
  /private property tension 376–7
    social rights as solution to 377
  retrospective self-understanding 375–6
  see also civil rights; social rights
civil rights 367–8, 368–9, 370–71
  equal freedom 375–6
  as negative rights 371
  and social rights *see* social rights

understanding of taxes 372
Cohen, Felix 31, 309
  'transcendental nonsense' 305
Cohen, Morris 35, 38, 140
colonialism
  decolonisation 434–5
  dual mandate 428, 436
  joint stock corporations 436–7
  see also development
commodity form theory 509, 512, 513
  and draft Declaration on the Rights of Peasants *see* draft Declaration
  as heuristic device 512
  private law as primary level of law 512
communicative turn 5
contract
  doctrines 39
  enforcement 39
  freedom of 34–5, 36, 38
  law *see* contract law
contract law 283–4
  bargain theory
  consideration
    bargained-for 284–5
    benefit/detriment test 285
    first restatement 285–6
    past 286
  equitable estoppel 286
  form/substance link 288
  promissory estoppel *see* promissory estoppel
contradiction 21
Convention on Biological Diversity 519
  aims 522
  and intellectual property 521–2
  Nagoya Protocol 519
    commodifying traditional knowledge 521
Convention on the Settlement of Investment Disputes *see* ICSID
Cooper, Davinia 90–91
co-originality 5
Copyleft 307
copyright
  Baker v Selden 312
  binaries of 315
  choreographic 317
  critical legal history 310
  critical perspectives 320
  Deeks v Wells 312
  Donaldson v Beckett (1774) 264
  escalating significance of 318
  exclusivity 310

and aesthetics 317–18
  creating and maintaining inequalities 318
  feminist perspectives 321
  gendered protection of 312, 317
  Hinton v Donaldson (1773) 264
  indeterminacy of 314
  merger doctrine 312
  Millar v Taylor (1769) 263
  Nichols case 312
  originality threshold as gatekeeping fiction 310
  postcolonial perspectives 321
  problematisation of collective/collaborative products 317
  public domain as essential to 310
  public/private domains 311–12, 314
  shifting the benefits of 319
  Statute of Anne (1709) 262–3
  Tonson v Collins (1761) 263
  user rights as restraint on 319
  where not granted 310–11
corporate governance 343–4
  antagonism 325, 325–6, 328
  Cadbury Committee Code (1992) 325
  code revisions 335
  codetermination 330
  Companies Act 2006 (UK), sec (172) 335, 336
  corporate culture
  Corporate Governance Code (UK) 325
    amendments 336
  corporate social responsibility 330–31, 336
  critical company law/governance opposition 339
  directors' duties 336, 337–8
  early history 324–5
  end of history thesis 333–4, 335, 337
    pressures on 334
  entity theory 330
  external auditors
  external pressures 337
  G20/OECD Principles for Corporate Governance 325
  Greenbury Report (1995) 325, 326
  Hampel Report (1998) 324
  implications of social/institutional accounts of the company 331
  indicative events 328–9
  juridical features of the company 329
    carrying controversial forces 329–30
  new governance 337
  nonexecutive directors 325, 335

  NYSE Corporate Governance Standards 325
  pay and social reporting
  promoting success of company 331
  R (People & Planet) v HM Treasury 338
  recent history 325–6
  shareholder-orientated model 334–5, 340
  as site of antagonism 325–6, 327
  social and environmental reporting 336
  stakeholder
    engagement 336
    theory 330
  Walker Report 325
Cossman, Brenda 48–9, 53
countervailing values 34–5
Crenshaw, Kimberlé W. 47, 73
criminal justice 379, 405–6
  contradictory poles of 402
  criminal responsibility 401
  and emancipatory promise 380
    emancipation 380
  freedom as limited and problematic 381
  and liberal law 402–3
  the moral third 398–9, 405
    broken 399, 400, 403–4
    relationality invoked by 402
    see also Benjamin, Jessica
  persecutory nature of 402
  and psychoanalytic shadow 402–3
  punishment 401
  reconciliatory/persecutory balancing 396–8
  retributive 390–91, 404
  and social shadow 403
  and structural violence 401–2, 404
criminal justice theory 380–81
  critical 381
  liberal 381–2
  moral psychology *see* moral psychology
criminal law 379
  formal morality of 394
  hermeneutics of suspicion 379
  as limiting and embodying authoritarianism 401–2
critical company law 344
  alienation 342
  alternative corporate forms 333
  capitalist development 340–41
  challenge facing critical 330
  challenging notion of companies as shareholder property 332
  commoning the company 332, 333, 343
  commons theory of the company 330

company as social actor/-economic
    institution 330
concentrations of voting power 329
corporate governance *see* corporate
    governance
critique of intended but unrealised effects
    341–2
critiques of capitalism 341
doux commerce
    expectations 342–3
financialisation 335
history of expectations 341
Karl Marx on exchange economy 328
rise of marketisation 340
self-regulating markets 339
shareholders
    enforced modesty 331
    no longer risk bearers 332
    not owners of company 331–2, 333
    say-on-pay 335
    schizophrenic dimension 332
    shareholder primacy 332–3, 334, 335,
        337
    shareholder-led governance 334, 335
social character of production 330, 331
stakeholders' overlapping property rights
    333
writing company purposes into law 332
critical engagement 17
critical international political economy 446–7,
    471–2
    contingent nature of global legal orders 447
    depoliticisation 448, 449
        defining 449
        first American empire 449
        internalising 454
        results of 452
        second American empire 449–50
        tactics of 449
    dominant/subordinate relations 447
    free trade agreements 455
    IEL rules 460–62
        contingent/political constraints 460
        creating precariousness 460
        dampening role of states 471
        dispute resolution 462–3
        legitimacy crisis 460
        objectives 461
        and quantitative indicators 460–61
        right to regulate 461, 462
    inequality 455–9
        /depoliticisation interplay 459
        destruction of production 458–9

    favouring of foreign investment 459
    increasing 455–6
    neoextractivism 459
    peripheralization of the labour force 455
    in power/knowledge 457
    realignment of states 457–458
    relegating national law to social forms of
        non-existence 457
    within states 458
law/politics distinction 448
    policing 449
linkages debate missing the point 461
policy discretion 454–5
precarity 447, 456
    linkages debate irresponsive to 461
special and differential treatment 452–3
tariffs 452
    tariff escalation 452–3
trade and investment facilitation 458
world investment law *see* international
    investment law
world trade law 462–5
    access to markets dependent on
        compliance 464–5
    dispute settlement 462–3
    dominant mode of interpretation 463
    early enforcement 462
    likeness 462, 463
    nondiscrimination 462
    prohibition of protectionism 462
    triumphalist narrative 465
    WTO *see* WTO
wreckage 448
see also GATT; international economic law;
    WTO
critical labour law 345–7
    collective bargaining 347, 348, 349–50
        Germany 349–50
        as measure of democracy 348
        as regulatory process 348, 349
        UK 350
    current 354
    defining 346
    elements of 345–6
    emergence 347
    essentials of working relations 352
    individual employment relation 347
        essentially contractual 349
        imbalance of power in 348
    legal pluralism 347, 349–50
        nature of 350
    legal scepticism 347, 350–51
        crisis in labour law 351

as mainstream 345, 346, 359
   see also labour law
Marxist influence on 345
Oxford School 352
rejection of public/private divide 347–9
  interpretation of labour law 349
  labour codes 348
  labour law as corrective to private law 348
  necessary autonomy of labour law 351
  precondition of emergence of labour law 347
sociolegal approach 347, 352–3
  law in context 353
  law/social reality distinction 352
critical legal feminism 304, 312
  call for shift in analytical frameworks 47
  commitment to antiessentialism 46, 48
  diversity of 61
  engagement in normative projects 56–7
  engagements with law 51
    critical discourse analysis 55
    critique of discursive power of law 54–6
    critique of exclusion 52–4
    deconstruction 55
    immanent critique 51–2
  fem-crits 46, 47
  /feminist critical project in law distinction 45–6, 48
  and identity politics 47
  imperative to move beyond critique 56
  need for 45
  origins 46–47
  postmodern turn 54
  problematizing law reform efforts 48, 49–50
  reconstruction 57
    judgment projects 59–61
    provocation defence 57–8
    sex workers 58–9
  scope of 45
  utopian projects 56
  value of legal reform 57–60
  see also feminism
critical legal studies 63, 288–9, 293–4, 304
  American
    Center for Constitutional Rights 497–8
    National Lawyers Guild 497
    New Approaches to International Law 495–7, 506
    New Stream 495
    origins 495
  British 498–500

    BritCrits 232
    Critical Legal Conference 228, 499, 500
    Critical Legal Thinking, Law & the Political 499–500
    critique of 498–9, 500
    eclectic nature of 499
    failure of critical legal project 500–501
    Haldane Society of Socialist Lawyers 501
  Critical Lawyers Handbook 502–3
  David Kennedy *see* Kennedy
  European
    aesthetics 228, 229–30
    development 228–9
    ethics 228, 230–32
  first wave 232, 239
  form and substance 291–2
  form/substance link in rhetorical conventions 288
  fundamental contradiction of self and other 245
  ideological dimension of legal analysis 287
  individualism/altruism conflict 287–8
  legal indeterminacy 506–7
  legal realism *see* legal realism
  linguistic turn 153
  Martti Koskenniemi *see* Koskenniemi
  movement 27
  new scholarsip 27
  patterned conflict 288–9
  political nature of legal categories 305
  politics and resistance 228, 232–5
  post- *see* postcritical legal studies
  practitioners 505–6
  race theory *see* critical race theory
  radical lawyering 500–502, 506
    see also radical lawering
  revolutionary impulse 199
  second wave 240–41
  theory/practice disjuncture 500, 504, 505
  truth impulse 199
  see also legal critique; postcritique
critical legal theory
  aim of 225
  characteristics 303–4
    expanded rhetoric 151–2
    indeterminacy 292–3
    political 303
    producing perjorative conception of law 304
    reification 303
  creativity of affect and expression 151
  exit from law 151

ignoring rhetoric and semiotics 154–5
Kantian 224
Marxian 224–5
melancholegalism 151
object of 225
post-Marxian 225
recognition of limits of critique 151
type and orientation of legal theory 485–6
see also legal critique; postcritique
critical race theory 63, 304, 312
   analysis of policing and racial profiling 77
   analysis of postracialism 76–7
   Black/White binary 74
   case law
      Adarand Constructors, Inc. v Peña 68
      Brown v Board of Education 67
      City of Richmond v J.A. Croson Co. 68
      Civil Rights Act 69
      Fisher v University of Texas (Fisher I) 69
      Fisher v University of Texas (Fisher II) 69
      Gratz v Bollinger 68
      Grutter v Bollinger 68
      Parents Involved in Community Schools v Seattle School District No. 1 68
      Regents of the University of California v Bakke 68
      Ricci v DeStefano 68–9
      Shelby County v Holder 69
   challenging mainstream beliefs 66
   conceptual toolkit 66
   critique of civil rights/antidiscrimination law 67–70
      adoption of perpetrator's perspective 68
      colorblindness 68–9
      confirmation of validity 68–9
      as convergence of White & Black interests 67–8
      discriminatory intent 68
      hate speech 70
   critique of critical legal studies 70–72
      failure to address role of racism as hegemony 71–2
      intellectual and racially determined divide 72
      introducing reconstructive minority perspective 72
      rights-critical approach 70–71
   expansion
      of analyzed groups 74
      geographical analyses 74–5
      inherent risks 76
      material scope 75–6
   grounded in praxis 66
   interest convergence
   intersectionality 73
   LatCrit 65, 74, 76
   main aim 65
   methodology 66
   origins 63–5
      in radical feminism 64
      in USA 63–4
   postmodernity of 63–4
   skepticism regarding dominant claims 65
   tenets 65–7
      challenging ahistoricism 65
      challenging presumptive legitimacy of social institutions 65
      critical race feminism 72–3
      eclecticism 66
      racism as endemic rather than deviation 65
      recognizing experiential knowledge & critical consciousness of people of colour 65
      rejection of essentialism 72
      Whiteness studies 73–4
   Washington v Davis 68
critical reflexivity 13, 18
critical state theory 114–15, 131–2
   capital accumulation 131
   Continental European tradition 114–15
   definition of the state 115
   economy/politics separation 131
   Foucaultian *see* Foucault
   Gramscian *see* Gramsci
   key issues 114
   legal aspects to the state 131
   market/state separation 131
   Marxian *see* Marxian critical state theory
   Marxism-Leninism dominant tradition 114
   Pashukanis on *see* Pashukanis
   Poulantzas on *see* Poulantzas
   reproduction of bourgeois society 131
critical theory
   embracing dialogue 30
   feminist *see* critical legal feminism
   history 1–5
   immanent critique *see* immanent critique
   irreducible contradictions 22
   and law 22–6
      gaps conflicts and ambiguity 31
      role in legal thought 24
      thematising law 22
      see also critical legal theory
   modern 5

necessity in 18–19
   promise of recuperation 20–21
   renegotiating contingency/necessity boundary 6
   social production and reproduction in 22
   of the state *see* critical state theory
   /traditional theory comparison 16
   universal concepts in 18
critique 246
   endurance of 244
   immanent *see* immanent critique
   internally fractured logic of 245
   as juridical technique 255
   legal *see* legal critique
   limits of 245
   path of 255
   as political mode of thought
   post- *see* postcritical legal studies; postcritique
   pragmatic sociology of 247
   self-reflexive drive 244–5
   tools of 246

Davies, Margaret 56, 58
   Law Unlimited 251–2
Deakin, Simon 332–3
Debord, Guy 160–61
deconstruction 166
   and Critical Legal Studies movement 168
   Derridean *see* Derridean deconstruction
   focusing on textuality of texts 166
   meaning
      interrogating selection of process 166
      reactivating potentiality of 166–7
      texts deactivating potentiality of 166
   politics of 167–8
   sole concern 167
   usefulness for legal theory 168
Deleuze, Gilles 202, 210
   pure semiotics 163
Derrida, Jacques
   influence of Heidegger on 170
   Spectres de Marx 176, 177
   undecidability 194–5
Derridean deconstruction 167, 168, 169
   conception of justice 178
   concern with *différance* 177–8
   concern with the event 177–8
   disruptiveness of the event 177, 178
   ethics of 173
   impossibility of the possible 171
   of Kantean *summum bonum* 170–71
   and legal theory 178–9
   of logocentrism 195
   of metaphysics of presence 170
   non-traversable divide with law 168
   nothing outside the text 173, 177
      as double-edged 175–6
      phenomenology 174–5
      structural linguistics 175
      world of meaning 174
      writing as origin of meaning 173–4
   possibility of the impossible 171–3
      categorical divide in 172–3
      impossibility of justice 172
      impossible gift 172
      interpreting concept 171–2
      spectral concepts 173
   quasi-names 176–7
   textuality 176–7
      confronting limits of 176
   thinking of the outside 175
development 428
   /colonialism continuity 436
      decolonisation 434–5
      resource extraction 435, 436
   comparative advantage 440, 451–2
      cumulative 440
      /free trade as concomitant of 440
   conditionality 450
      aid 433
      loan 433, 436, 440
      rule of law 433–4, 436
   crisis 428–429
      failure to understand urgency of 428
   doctrine of comparative advantage 435
   failure of process 429
   foreign direct investment 432, 435, 441
   and free trade
   and global capitalism 440–42
   human capabilities approach 442
   labour-led 444–5
   and maximisation of economic benefit 442
   most favourved nation principle 435
   as neocolonialism 435–7
   new developmentalism 443–4
      central tenets 443
   New International Economic Order (NIEO) 438
   perpetual inequalities as result of free trade 440
   political/economic separation 429–31
      consequences of 432–4
      critical to global capitalism 430
      depoliticisation of international economic law 431, 432

enabling imposition of lending conditions 433
fragmentation of regulation 432–3
origins 430
post- 442–3
role of unholy trinity 431
special and differential treatment 432
structural adjustment 433, 440
UN Development Programme Human Development Index 442
underdevelopment 434
Uruguay Round 438
Washington Consensus 428, 438
World Bank mandate 431
WTO role 432
dialectic 10–11
central to critical theory 10
role of negation 10, 14
system or method 10
dialectical imagination 23
dialectical method 3
Douzinas, Costas 154, 186, 189, 212, 498, 503
draft Declaration on the Rights of Peasants and Other People Working in Rural Areas 513–514
benefit sharing approach 518–22
deferring challenges to status quo 518
hegemony through consent 518
indigenous rights 519–20
risks of 520–21, 522
loss reflected in 523
rise of rights against global capitalism approach 514–16, 522
articulations contesting logic of capitalism 515
food sovereignty 515
land tenure 514
right to adequate standard of living 514
right to biodiversity 515
right to follow traditional ways 514
right to seeds 514–15
seed saving 515–16
as sustaining terms against which it militates 522
validation of globalisation approach 516–18, 522
seeking assurances on human rights 517
see also human rights
Dumbarton Oaks institutions 430

École Normale Supérieure Paris 4, 109
emancipation 380–81

enclosures 269, 273
land grabs 276
privatisation of public land 276
second movement 276–7
still occurring 276
Engels, Frederick 9, 96, 501, 502
estoppel
equitable 300
promissory see promissory estoppel
ethical turn 181, 184–5, 193, 195–6, 199–200
Achilles' heel of 198
ambiguities of 196
as consequence of inability to let go of faith in reason 198–9
as consequence of loss of faith in reason 198
as irreversible 231
knowledge as contingent social act in 195
post- 185–6
pre- 185
preresponsibility 186–7
consequence of 187
self-conscious 186
as turn away from structuralism 185
ethics 230–32
Categorical Imperative 183
of compassion 181, 184
ethical I 192, 193
ethical Other 191, 194
ethical respect 188
ethical responsibility 184, 191
preresponsibility 187, 194
role of 183
third person in 191
concept of the third person 191
as contested 181
and critical legal scholarship see ethical turn
disruptive potential of senseless kindness 186
as elaborate subterfuge 187
ethical turn see ethical turn
exposing meaning 195
as first philosophy 186
Golden Rule 183
and justice 191–2
Colloredo twins case 192–3
legal guilt 193
moral guilt 193
political/legal incompatibility 190–91
problem of the passage 192
ten-to-one ratio 193
as uneasy relationship 198

Levinasian *see* Levinas
moral responsibility 188
neglecting compassion 183
neo-Platonic interpretation 183
   criticism of 183–4
philosophical/meta- 189
   definition 183
   formal structure of 184
and poststructuralist scepticism 188
proper subject matter for 188
rational 181, 183, 187
   subversion of 187–8
threat to weaponise 197
unbounded compassion as origin and ultimate justification 187
ethnomethodology 250
EU
   Commission 413
      task of 417
      Working Programme 417
   Communities as purposive associations for functional integration 411
   competence, incomplete 418
   constitutionalisation 421
   crisis politics 420
   and distributive politics 411
   European Central Bank 422
      reach 425
   European Financial Stability Facility 422
   European Stability Mechanism 422
   ever closer union 412–13
   extra-legal developments 416
   functionalist efficiency/constitutionalised legitimation disconnect 418
   governance
      technocratic administration 417, 418, 424
   internal market policy 412
   law *see* EU law
   Lisbon Treaty 417
   Maastricht Treaty (1992) 412–13
      broadening community competences 413
      as ill-defined political compromise 420
      only conferring monetary policy 419
   as market without state 410
   monetary policy 422
      European Monetary Union 415, 422
      objectives 422–3
   more Europe/more market tension 411, 412
   no alternative to technocratic rule 423
   ordoliberalisation of Europe 410
   Outright Monetary Transactions programme 422
   regulatory intervention 413, 414
   as regulatory state 411
   Single European Act 413
   social Europe 412–13
   strengthening of social regulation 413
   as supranational legal community 409
   TFEU 413, 419, 422
   Treaty of Amsterdam 418
   as union of stability 413–15
EU law 407–8, 423–5
   and assignment of competences 414–15
   Brunner v European Union Treaty 414
   Cassis de Dijon case 412, 413
   constitutionalisation 412
   in crisis 407, 412, 419
      crisis law 407, 420–21
      failing constitutionalism 419–20
   dominant orthodoxy of 409
   ECJ 412, 413
   as ECJ invention 409
   gap within legitimate authority 421
   integration through law orthodoxy 408–9, 411
      challenge to 414
      dominance of 423
      flaws in 409
      hidden agenda 409–10
      as success story 409
   jurisdictional mandate of constitutional courts 424
   and legal critique 423–5
   legitimation deficit 423
   mutual recognition doctrine 412, 413
   Open Method of Coordination 418–19
   Peter Gauweiler and others v Deutscher Bundestag 421, 422
   Pringle v Ireland 421
   reform 415–16
      governance 146–7
   as revolutionary 408, 423
   trapped within functionalist outlook 417
exchange value, dominance 145

Felski, Rita 89, 90, 91
feminism
   antipornography campaign 55
   carceral 50
   complex equality 53–4
   critical legal *see* critical legal feminism
   critical race 48
      role in critique of legal exclusion 52–3
   as force rather than identity 48
   governance 50
   implications of deconstruction for 56

and law reform 49–50
    danger of cooption of concerns 50
    legal, discursive effects of 48–9
    lesbian 48
    moving theory to the intersection 53
    postcolonial 53
    poststructural 48
    Western, fetishization of Third World women 48–9
feminist legal theory 63
fetish phenomenon 13
forum shopping 145
Foucault, Michel
    articulation of the economic and political 130–31
    advocacy of bottom-up approach to social power 128
    Collège de France lectures 129
    criticism of state theory 128
    disciplinarity 129
    disciplinary normalization 130
    Discipline and Punish 130
    governmentality 129
    History of Sexuality 130
    hostility to orthodox Marxism 128
    power mechanisms
        consolidation/institutionalisation of 130
        dispersion of 130
        strategic codification 130
    problematic of government 128
    rise of governmental state 129–30
    Security, Territory, Population 128
    Society Must Be Defended 128, 130
    sovereignty 129
    The Birth of Biopolitics 128
    thinking of the outside 174
France, malaise des banlieues 19–20
Frankfurt Institute for Social Research *see* Frankfurt School
Frankfurt School 3, 7, 9, 146, 225
    negative dialectic 109
    turn to/from Marxism 4
free trade doctrine
    non-economic effects of 441
    wealth maximisation
        critique of 441
Freedom, Arendtian definition 181
Freud, Sigmund
    Civilization and Its Discontents 386
Frug, Mary Joe 39, 54, 55

GATT 431
    Art I 462
    Art III 462
    Art XX
        flexibility, weakening of 464
        general exceptions 463 464
        tariff commitments 452–3
    Uruguay Round 450
        protection standards 466
Gay Liberation Front Manifesto 85
genealogy 15–16
    archaeological method 16
    associated with 'subjugated knowledges' 15
    Foucaultian definition 15
    and law's powers of 'homology' 23–4
    possibility in 15–16
    urgency in 15
General Agreement on Trade and Tariffs *see* GATT
Gilson, Ronald 324–5, 327, 328, 342
global financial crisis 334
Goodrich, Peter 229, 254, 304, 497, 499
Gramsci, Antonio 4
    class domination
        force 121
        hegemony 121, 122–3
        intermediate forms 121
    influence of 121–2
    notion of the integral state 122
    respecification of approach 122–3
        metagovernance 122
        politicisation 122–3
        state power 122
Gray, Kevin 268, 272, 276, 277, 278
Grey, Thomas 260, 268, 280, 281

Habermas, Jürgen 5
    critical public sphere 146
    mode of formation of public sphere 146–7
    objective illusions 139
Hale, Robert 140, 141, 272
Hegel, Georg 3, 98, 103, 116, 183
    dialectic method as prone to mystification 104
    Hegelian Marxism 2, 4, 108–9
    history as a 'slaughter bench' 400
    Karl Marx's critique of *see* Marxist legal theory
    Philosophy of Right 104, 223
    state as an achieved synthesis of ethics 104
    systematic philosophy 10
    transcendental moment 18
    understanding/reason distinction 3
hegemony 121–3
    as class domination 121–2

creation and reproduction of active consent
    of dominated groups 121
  crystallisation and mediation of 121
  forms of 121
Heidegger, Martin
  Being and Time 196
  Geworfenheit thesis 182
  metaphor of the turn 196–7
  metaphysics of presence 169–70
  question of Being 196, 197
Hirschman, Albert 327, 340–42, 430
Hobbes, Thomas 13–14, 149, 223, 270
Horkheimer, Max 2, 3, 16, 109
  The Eclipse of Reason 11
human rights 224–5, 479–80, 509
  African Charter on Human and Peoples'
    Rights 519
  benefit sharing 519–20, 523
    African Commission on Human and
      Peoples' Rights v Kenya 519
    commodifying traditional knowledge
      521
  Filártiga v Peña-Irala 498
  Hassan v City of New York 498
  as integral part of power relations 234
  law
    dilemma within 523
    as tool of 'principled opportunism' 512
  as neoliberal phenomenon 366
  as offering global minimalist utopia 366
  right to an adequate standard of living 514
  right/access to seed in India 515–16
  rise of rights against global capitalism 523
Hume, David 136, 137, 271
Husserl, Edmund 174–5, 176, 188
hyperconnected markets 338

ICSID 450–51
  investor-state dispute settlement 451
  transfer of power 451
ideology 12–13
  definition 226
  /function relation 12
image
  as affect 163
  cinematic
    expansion allowed by 164
    as movement-image 163
    postauditorium 164
  as independent medium of transmission
    163
  as intermediary 163
  as memory 165

movement-
  desire 164–5
  effects 163–5
  fragmentation 163–4
  mobility 164
new media undoing juridical tradition 163
as threat 165
imaginal law 160–63
  as affective 162–3
  change in medium signalling change in
    order 160
  change in theatre signifying change in
    theory 161, 162–3
  as democratising 161
  as disruptive power 161
  at heart of legal policy 162
  as interventionist 162
  as positive 162
  semiosis of 163
  visual and virtual jurisprudence 160
  see also image; rhetoric; semiotics
immanence 5, 19, 232
  of knowledge 191
immanent critique 3, 5–6, 16, 21, 238
  contradictions 24
    between categories of rights 25
    constituent/constituted power 24–5
    criminal procedure 25–6
  critical legal feminist 51–2
    contributions to debate 51
    juxtaposing law and women's lives 51
    understanding of masculine power of law
      52
  embeddedness in experience 19
  features of 26
implicit submission 144
indeterminacy thesis 29–30
Institute for Social Research (Frankfurt) 5
intellectual property 276, 305–6, 319–20
  conceptual task of 301
  copyright *see* copyright
  corporate 276
  critical legal history 301–2, 304, 312–13
  critical resistance 320–22
  deconstruction of 306–10
  exclusive rights 309, 315
    precluding enjoyment of equal access
      315
  fair use, gendered/racialised protection 312
  law 318–19
  legal fictions in 301
  as legitimising label 309–10

legitimizing function of legal rhetoric in 307
manufacturing artificial scarcity 309
as metaphorical construct 306, 307–8
  result of rejecting 309
as performing political functions 307
pervading questions 305–6
politics of 310, 320
  misappropriation of traditional knowledge/cultural resources 315–16
  public debate around 302, 309
  public domain 309, 310, 319
    see also public domain
  public/private divide 311, 315–20
  racialisation of cultural production 316–17
  redirecting discourse 319
  reinforcing exploitative power structures 318
  reproducing gender bias 315, 317
  as second enclosure movement 276–7
  user rights 319
protection of
  increasing 307, 308, 312
  limits of 313
real property analogy 310
scholarship 321–2
theoretical perspectives 322
International Bank for Reconstruction and Development 451
international economic law 446–9
  bilateral investment treaties 459
  and comparative advantage 451–2
  depoliticisation 448–9, 457
    internalising 454
  and global distribution 456
  global value chains 459
  governing paradigm 450
  as hegemonic 450–51
  instability generated by law's distributive functions 454
  international trade and investment rules 446
    recalibrating 448
  investment law 446
    national treatment 453
  as legal culture of capitalism 446
  legal regimes
    legitmacy problems 460
    and precariousness 460
  nontariff barriers 464
  obsolescing hypothesis 453
  right to regulate 461, 462, 471
  suicide economy 516
  systemic logic of 461
  tariffs
    move away from 464
  trade law 446
    weaponising 448
  see also critical international political economy; international investment law
international investment law 465–71
  bilateral investment treaties 465–6
  Clayton v Canada 469
  dispute resolution
    arbitration tribunals 470–71
    emphasis on process dampening critique 468–9
    multifactor analysis in 466
    proportionality review 469–70
    settlements 467
    'sole effects' doctrine 466–7
  distributive implications 468
  expropriation 466, 467
    LG&E v Argentina 467
    SD Myers v Canada 467–8
  fair and equitable treatment 466
    Occidental v Ecuador I 468
    as legitimate constraint on state action 467
    legitimate expectations 468
    minimum standards 466
  nondiscrimination 465
  performance requirements 466
  promoting US constitutional law as global law 466
  proposed investment court 470
  right to regulate 470
  Santa Elena v Costa Rica 467
  subsuming policy rationales 467
  transfer of funds 466
  see also GATT; international trade law; WTO
international law
  central function 512–13
  commodity form see commodity form theory
  constituent forms as forms of global capitalism 511
  embeddedness of capitalism in 513
  fundamental tension in 509
  material content 511
  nihilist thesis 509–11
  pragmatic theory 511
    offering solutions to law as problem 511–12
    as product of the market 512

techniques of 513
irrationalities of class society 7–8
Italian Marxism
  Autonomia
    project of destruction 110
    resistance to hegemonic representational orders of capitalism 110
    working class self-valorisation 110
  operaismo movement 110
  revolutionary syndicalism 109

jurisprudence 226–7
  business of 227
  as combination of descriptive and prescriptive 227
  general 227
  liberal 231
  restricted/ontological 227
justice
  miscarriage of 226

Kafka, Franz 223, 232, 246, 247–8
Kahn-Freund, Otto 346, 348, 350–52
Kant, Immanuel 2
  Critique of Practical Reason 224
  hermeneutic deficit 2–3
  summum bonum 170
  transcendental idealism 244
Kelsen, Hans
  critisism of Marxist theory of law
    as constradictory 100–101
    as unsustainable 101
  ideology as false representation 101
  methodological disagreement with Marx 101
  pure theory of law 101, 168, 227
Kennedy, David 505–6, 507
Kennedy, Duncan 36, 153, 162, 287, 288, 292, 456
Klare, Karl 135, 349, 354–5, 357
Klein, Melanie
  on guilt 386
    depressive/reconciliatory 292, 293, 294
    persecutory 392–3, 394
  moral psychology 385, 386–9
    depressive position 387–8
    neither reductive nor moralising 389
    originary psychic situation 386–7
    retributive blaming 390
    unconscious phantasy structures of experience 388–9
  see also moral psychology

Koskenniemi, Martti 461, 495, 496, 497, 506–7

labour law 359
  collective agreements 356
  critical *see* critical labour law
  current 354
  dominant discourse 354
  gig economy 356
  and human rights 357
  influences on 354
  legal pluralism 356
  legal scepticism 357
  maximising flexibility 356
  methodological innovation
    economic sociology 359
    political economy approaches 358–9
  reassertion of public/private divide 354–6
    deregulation 355
    globalisation narrative 355
    liberalisation 355
    new economic orthodoxy 354
    privatisation 354
  recolonisation of the public by the private 355, 358
  resurgence of the contract 356
  shortcoming of scholarship 359
  spider's web of transnational standards regulation 356
  zero hours contracts 356
Lacey, Nicola 55, 56, 141–2, 394
Lassalle, Ferdinand 98–9
Latour, Bruno 92, 242
law
  as affect 201–2
  allocation of speakability 88
  anthropology of 253
  biopolitical 233
  cannot be understood in isolation 54
  as commodity value 203
  as complex of pathways 252
  conferring official visibility 88
  construction of by lawyers and judges 31–2
  creating atmosphere of contractual freedom 215
  criminal *see* criminal law
  critical exit from 151
  as critical mode of attachment 238
  /critique relationship 223–4
  as disciplinary influence 83
  discursive power 54, 55
    feminist challenges 54–6
  dissimulation as nonlaw 218–19

dissipation of text of 152
dividing lawful from unlawful 223
and economics 63
effective 84
/emancipation relationship 379–80
as endogenous to human behavior 36
formalism of, confronting 236
of gesture 158
as having no morality 226
and humanities 232
as ideological practice 226
imaginal *see* imaginal law
as important component in new materialist thinking 251
as institutional affect 214–15
instrumental view 239–40
international *see* international law
invocation of as something already known 241
-life 233–4
and literature movement 63, 227
matching expectation of consumerist society 216
materiology 253
as mode of social control 379
and new media 151–2
pedagogy of 156
as pivoting on notion of performativity 252
positive 223, 226
relative autonomy 319
remediation of 165
rhetoric being 152
  see also rhetoric
rules of *see* rules of law
scriptural, imaginal ruptures with 163–4
socially constitutive power of 36–7
/society relationship as indeterminate 35, 36
sociology of action 253
as source of contestation/subversion 83
staging 212–14
  itself as contractual 213
  media of 214
  value 203, 214
  see also aesthetics; aesthetic turn
  value 203, 214
and structural violence
as subject formation device 83
and systems theory sociology 483
theatre of 158
  see also theatrocracy
as tool 248
validity of 234

as visual phenomenon 159
lawscape 218, 221
legal aesthetics 204–7
  as affective 201–2, 207
  and art 206–7
  atmospherics 214–17
    engineering atmosphere of legitimacy 215
    see also atmospherics
  and critical legal theory 205–6
  as definitional 210
  distinction in 219–20
  phenomenological visual/legal connection 212
  plethora of literature on 204–5
  prime movement of 218
  staging law 212–14
  see also aesthetics
legal consciousness 28
legal constraint 30
legal constructs, reification of 305
legal critique 238
  denunciation of law 241–2
  first wave CLS 239
  form-of-law construct in 239–40, 241
    as suspect device 240
  as having run out of steam 242
  immanent critique *see* immanent critique
  object of 239
  postcritical 241–2
    see also postcritique
  second wave CLS 240–41
  supposed death of 238–9
  as tied to dominant conception of law 241
  weaknesses of 241
  see also critical legal studies; critical legal theory
legal culture 28–9
  accepted interpretive maxims 32–4
    precedent 32
    stare decisis 32–3
  mechanical rule application in 30
  settled understandings in 30
legal decision making
  abuse of deduction 32
  and bend points 31–2
legal morality 397
legal necessity 30
legal norms, not determined by social/political set-up 35–6
legal philosophy 226
legal realism 27–8
  critical 27–8, 29–30

core claim 29
  formalist error in 28
  preoccupation with legal arguments 28
  promoting modernist and postmodernist social and cultural theory 27
  recovering and extending techniques of legal criticism 27
 critique of propertisation 305
legal reasoning 28, 29
legal responsibility 397
legal rules *see* rules of law
legal theoretical deconstruction 179
Levinas Emmanuel 196
 affective dimension of existentially concrete 186–7
 close identification of ethics with compassion 189
 concept of the third person 191
 criticism of 189–90
 ethics/justice distinction 194
 Heidegger's influence on 196
 incompatibility between political and legal justice 191
 infinite ethical responsibility 187
  consequences of 189
 philosopher of compassion 186
 prerespensibility 187, 194
 on subjectivity 189
 see also ethical turn; ethics
liminal 6
liminality 6
linguistic immediacy 182
 irreducable 182–3
Llewellyn, Karl 32, 34, 83
Local 1330 v U.S. Steel 294–6
 early symptom of neoliberal/neoformalist turn 295
 judicial reasoning 269
  inapplicability to the facts at hand 300
  profitability as condition precedent (district court) 295
  profitability as promise (Supreme Court) 298–9
  reasonable expectability test in 296–7
  reliance 297–8
Luhmann, Niklas 23, 223, 483
Lukács, Georg 4, 9, 10, 109

Marcuse, Herbert 3–4, 7, 11
 One-Dimensional Man 13
marriage
 as political weapon 88
 same sex *see* same sex marriage debate

Marshall, Thurgood 69, 368–9, 372, 375–6, 377
Marx, Karl
 analysis of 1871 Paris Commune 116
 Critique of Hegel's Philosophy of Law 116
 18th Brumaire 10, 110
 Capital 97–8, 102, 105, 116–117
 critical state theory *see* Marxian critical state theory
 Critique of Political Economy 97
 Draft Plan for a Work on the Modern State 117
 form analytical approach 116–18
 Introduction to the Critique of Hegel's Philosophy of Right 116
 legal theory *see* Marxist legal theory
 on material/phenomenal relation 98
 methodology 100
 Paris Manuscripts 4
 rejection of theoretical work as means of social change 9
 state as alienated form of political organization 116
 The Class Struggles in France 1848–1850 117
 The Critique of Hegel's Doctrine of the State 103
 The German Ideology 95, 97
 Theses on Feuerbach 3
  4th thesis 21
  11th thesis 3, 8, 14, 199
Marxian critical state theory
 analyses of the repeal of the Corn Laws 18
 analysis of introduction of factory legislation 118
 capital logic school 118
 critique of Hegel 116
  duality of constitutional state 117
  exploitation of class conflicts 116
  form analysis approach 116, 117
  fragmented 115
  moral/social critique of use of legal power 115–16
  separation of rulers and ruled 116–17
 form analysis approach 116–18
  duality 117
  economic class struggles 118
  form problematising function 117–18
  influence of 118
  not merely formal 117
  political class struggles 118

social relations of production shaping
social relations of domination and
servitude 117
fundamental contradiction in democratic
constitution 117
Marxian legal theory 100
Marxism 95
accumulation as outcome of capitalist mode
of production 102
anti-Hegelian 109
capacity for agency of labour 104, 105
commodity fetishism 108
economy as base of every society 95–6
fetishisation of labour 106–7
Hegelian 2, 4, 108–9
subject as agent of emancipation 109
see also Hegels
history made by and through class struggle
103–4
Italian *see* Italian Marxism
legal fetishism 108
Marxist-Leninist treatment of the state 114
structuralist 109
Western 6
Marxist legal theory
bourgeois law 106–7
capital logic school 118
constituent power 108–11
constitutional and labour law 110
juridical reductions of 111
promise of 110–11
question of subjectivity in 108
constitutive role of property as legal
relation 103
core of capitalist developments 104–5
criticism of
Carl Schmitt 101
Hans Kelsen 100–101
see also Kelsen; Schmitt
critique of Hegel's dialectic 104
idealised concept of the state 104
mystification 104
dialectic materialism 111
dismissing will-based conception of law 97
essence /appearance distinction in 101
intertwining of modes of appropriation &
production 103
law not necessarily rational 104
the legal illusion 97
legislation/class struggle connection 105
marginal impact of 100
materialist understanding of the social order
111–12

consequence of solidity/contingency of
legal order 112
political economy 112
relation between the legal order and
society 112
negation 103–4
as constitutive act for the formation of
subjectivity 103
not systematic 101
Pashukanis' contribution to 106
see also Pashukanis
proletarian law 105–8
as reductionist 95, 97
criticism of 95–6
qualifying 96
sidelining of 111
mediation 11–12, 14
as abstraction 14
of legal meaning 23
melancholegalism 151
melancholia of the lawyer 223
metaphysics of presence 169, 170
moral hermeneutics 231
moral politics 230
moral psychology 381, 382–3
blaming practices 384
the moral third 385
persecutory anxiety 390, 391
retributive blame 384, 390–91
coming of age 383
Freudian guilt 385–386
guilt 384, 389, 397
healthy/unhealthy distinction 393–4
narcissistic 392
persecutory 392–3
reconciliatory 392, 393, 394, 395
Melanie Klein 385, 386–9
see also Klein
moral retributivism 392
reductive traps 383
reparation 384, 389
of responsibility 395
responsibility practices
holding responsible 384, 395, 396
taking responsibility 384–5, 389, 396
morality of law 230
Moyn Samuel 366, 367
mutual understanding 3

NAFTA 455, 469
National Labor Relations Act (USA) 299
negation 22
function of 19

Negri, Antonio 109–10
  on constituent power 110–11
  Il potere costituente 110
  on revolutionary subject 109
neoliberalism
  Anglo-Saxon 410
  German 410
  v democracy 378
new constitutionalism 275, 279
Nietzsche, Friedrich 183, 187, 223, 383, 390, 392
  On the Genealogy of Morality 386
No Feedback 219
norms 83–4
  background 37
  gender as 84
  as generalizations 83
  providing grid of intelligibility 83–4
North American Free Trade Agreement *see* NAFTA

Operaismo movement 4
Oppen, George 181–2
ordoliberalism 410
Organization for Economic Cooperation and Development 453

Pashukanis, Evgeny
  bourgeois law
    as constitutive 107
    withering away under socialism 107–8
  capitalist law and the state 118–20
    bourgeois law 119
    bourgeois state 119
    modern tax state 119–20
  criminal & public law as derivative extensions of private law 107
  criticism of 120
  disappearance by Stalinist regime 108
  on fetishisation of labour 106
  on repression 120
  on subject of rights 107
  The General Theory of Law and Marxism 106
Peace of WEstphalia (1648) 430
Piketty, Thomas 274, 277, 334, 456, 471–2
Plato 170, 173, 183, 189, 226
political rights
  expanding freedom 376
political turn 223, 228, 232–5
  after collapse of new world order 232
  biopolitical law 233
  and justice 224
  law and resistance 235–7
  politics of resistance 235
  revolution as normative principle 237
positivism 227, 230–31
postcolonial legal theory 486–94
  central test ground 493–4
  challenges 486–8
  core of the matter 489
  core tenet of 489
  creation of identities 490
  critique grounded in current political economy 490
  focus of 492–3
  human rights 491–2
  inward turn 493
  legal history as battlefield 491
  proliferation of 494
  reference points 487
postcritical legal studies 247–8
  actor-network theory in 252–3
  critical postcritical thought 254
  and ethnomethodology 250–51
  juridification of mechanism 249
  materiological/materialist distinction 252–3
  mechanisation of law 248–9
  new materialist 251–2
  postcritical politics 255–6
    neoliberalism 256
  production of legal doctrine 248
  proper object of 254
  STS-based approaches 250, 251
postcritique 241–2
  as ante-critique 253–4, 256
  detachment 244–6
  lacking unity 243, 255
  lacking utility 243, 247
  logic of substitution in 245
  need for empiricism of attachments 246–7
  new materialist 251
    account of law 251–2
  not necessarily reconstruction-after-deconstruction 255
  weakening tools of critique 246
  wide-ranging 247
  see also critique; legal critique
postmodern legal movements 63
Poulantzas, Nicos 126–128
  authoritarian statism 125–6, 127–8
  combination of form analysis and class analysis 126–7
  constitutive absence of class from the bourgeois state 127

criticism of Marx 123
critique of 127
exceptional regime 124–5, 127
hegemony 124
influences 126–127
'isolation effect' 123
juripolitical ideology 124
law and the state 126
normal state 124, 127
power bloc 124, 125
private individuation and public unity 123–4
state as a social relation 123, 127
praxis 7–9, 23
/theory connection 8–9
/theory distinction 7
promissory estoppel
application of chosen rule in 296
/bargain theory tension 287–8
critical legal history 287–2
argument in 288–289
flipping 290
framing 290
nesting 289–90
paired arguments 289
central lesson 296
critique of 296–300
tension in 269
facts
application of particular 289–90
framing 290
flipping 290–91
Local 1330 case *see* Local 1330
mainstream 284–5
realist 285–7
first restatement 285–6
relegation of 291
reliance crucial to recovery 292
required elements 292
unbargained-for reliance 289
see also contract law
property 260–2
as bundle of rights 261, 266, 267, 274, 278
appealing to statists 279–80
effects of 268
exclusivity axiom 272
qualities of 267
in contemporary capitalism 281–2
contested nature of 261, 268, 281
detachment from tangible objects 267
financial 273–5
effects of 273–4
investor protection 275
social-relational dimensions 275
valuation 274–5
intangible 262, 263, 266
IP *see* intellectual property
undermining property/obligation boundaries 266–7
law 486
as legal construct 308
limits on 277
as originating in labour 273
physicalist conception of 260–61, 263, 264
as problematic 261, 262, 266
as power 272–5, 280, 281
delegated private government 272
publicly constituted and enforced 272
private 34, 269, 270
as basis for self-governance 279
as central to civil society 279
conversion of productive resources into 276
as expression of personality 279
extensions of 277
as prerequisite for operation of free market 279
rise of 271
problem defining 266
public law character of 272
rights *see* property rights
as social relation 261–2, 267, 269, 280–82
as storytelling 309
Sunday Times/Forbes 'rich lists' 260, 274
thingification of 305
as thing-ownership 269–70
belief in special nature of property 278
ideological attraction of 277–80
revival of 278, 279–80, 281
property rights
(less than) absolute property in land 262, 269
choses in action 264–5, 273–4
change in nature of 265
nonassignability 264
as personal rights against specific persons 264
transferability 265
common land 268
contested nature of 261, 268–71
corporeal/incorporeal distinction 263
emergence and extension of 269–70
and enclosures 269, 273
see also enclosures
as exclusive rights 271, 272
intellectual 276–7

copyright 262–264
  see also copyright
corporate 276
extension of as second enclosure
    movement 276–7
in means of production 272–3
personal possessions/productive resources
    distinction 272
private 261, 278
  as special 278, 279
and privatisation 270–71
reification of 265
as rights against persons 267
rights to receive revenues 264, 273
*Securities and Exchange Commission v W.J.
    Howey Co.* 272
as social relation 268–9
specific use rights 262
psychoanalytic shadow 402–3
public domain 310
  as a socio-legal construct 314
  as an environment 314
  as legal divide 310
  legal history 313–14
  as metaphorical construct 313–15
  politics of 310–13
    cultural product flow 315
    gender bias 315
    misappropriation of traditional
        knowledge/cultural resources 315–16
    plasticity of 316
    redirecting IP discourse 319
  as positive entity 313
  romance of 314–15
  see also copyright; intellectual property
public sphere
  capacity of law 143–4
  changes in content 145
  changes in form 145
  contemporary 146
  distinctive quality of 147–8
  dual orientation 147
  epiphenomenal character of 136
  formation of 'opinion' in 137
  juridical security 149
  legitimatory terms 143
  omnipresence of state in 137
  potentialities 149
    challenging reducibility of public sphere
        148
    dependency 146, 147
    invoking possibilities of unconstituted
        public 149

latency 146–7
mode of actualisation 146, 147
protection of personality dignity and reason
    143
quality of law 135–6, 137
roots 146
sacred element to 143
vulnerability of 148, 149
  to capture by private interests 149
  to direct attack 148
  to the role of law in contemporary
      thinking 148–9
public/private distinction
  as a form of political rhetoric 135
  accountability in 145
  as analytical tool 135
  challenging 136
    how the 'public' comes about 136–7
  and law see public/private distinction and
      law
  private sphere
    individualized private existence 144
    as outside turned inside 144
  as qualitative distinction 142
  refeudalisation 144–5
  Roman influence on 142–3
public/private distinction and law 135
  coercive distinction 140
  coercive role of law of property 140
  feminist critique 141–2
  Justinian 142
  mutuality of public and private 142–3
    maintaining 143–4
  private interests depending on public
      institutions for juridical form 143
  private sphere 144
    Arendtian understanding 146
    contemporary 146
    and critical legal theory 146
    publicspiritedness 146
    roots 146
    subordination of to public sphere 143
  public sphere
    capacity of law 143–4
    quality of law 135–6, 137
    see also public sphere
  state as public actor 137–8
    distribution of coercion from public to
        private actors 140–41
    freedom by detour 139
    immunity 138
    monopoly on legitmate use of force 140
    sovereign power 141–2

state as transcendent mediator 139
theological dimension 138–9
universal equality 139–40
symbolic distinction 139–40

queer theory 79
antisocial theories 82, 85
debunking the normal 88–9
Freudo-Marxism 81, 85, 91
/radical constructivism differences 82
law of no avail to queer people 83
minority practices 91
postcritical 89–92
demanding methodological change in law 92
looking at the particular 91–2
paranoia/suspicion criticism 89–90
reparative readings 90–91
post-Foucauldian 82
queer as a displacement 79–80
queer as critical proximity 90, 91
queer as potential 90–91
queer/law relation 83–4
radical constructivism 81–2
political potential 82
resignification 91
same sex marriage debate *see* same sex marriage debate
see also sexuality

radical lawyering 500–502
Haldane Society of Socialist Lawyers 501
International Association of Democratic Lawyers 501–2
mainstream hostility towards 502
National Lawyers Guild 501
see also critical legal studies
Rancière, Jacques 5, 6, 7, 20, 161, 207, 215
recuperation of reason 17–18
reduction-achievement 23
regulation and normalisation as ubiquitous 233
revolutionary agency 6
marxisant expression 6
as struggle for recognition 6
rhetoric
allure of 155
constraint of 156
rhetorical delivery 155–6
ancient 152

contraction into academic pedagogy 152–3
critical 158
failure of 154–5
revival of forgotten 152, 155
rhetorical delivery
form/substance link 288
politics of legal performance 157–8
roots of 156–7
theatricality 157, 158
as semiosis 154
visual 165
see also image; imaginal law; legal semiotics; theatrocracy
Ricardo, David 438, 451–2
right(s)
formal 235
to insubordination 235–6
legal 235, 236
enforcing individual will 236
political 235
sources of 235, 236
rights
civil *see* civil rights
human *see* human rights
political *see* political rights
social *see* social rights
Riles, Annelise 248–50, 251
rule of law 143–4, 226, 240
reduction of 233
rule sets 35–6
rules of law
affecting distributive outcomes 37–9
background, transformative potential 40–41
cultural and psychological impact 39–40
private 38
privileging employers 38–9

same sex marriage debate 79, 84–9
deconstructing privilege attached to marriage 88
defects in recognition
domesticating effect 87–8
either/or positions 88
heteronormativity 86
homonormativity 86
igniting broader official/unofficial law interaction 88
problematizing nature of social change through law 86
reasserting conventional relationships 85
as turning point in queer community 84–5
Schmitt, Carl 169

criticism of Marxist legal theory 101–2
    as excessively reductive 102
    Nomos of the Earth 102
    Political Theology 102
    sequence of creation/development of legal orders 102
science, technology and society *see* STS
Scoular, Jane 50, 54, 58, 59
Sedgwick, Eve Kosofsky 80, 89, 90
self-regulating markets 339
semiotics
    of contemporary law 165
    legal 153–4
        demise of 154
        as exercise in mapping linguistic presuppositions of legal theory 153
        restriction to linguistic model 153, 154
sexuality
    gender identity dysphoria 84
    and legal recognition 79
    queer theory *see* queer theory
    regulation of gender 83
    same sex marriage debate *see* same sex marriage debate
    struggle for sexual equality 84
    transexuality 81
Sinzheimer, Hugo 346, 348, 350–51, 352
Smart, Carol 50, 51–2, 54
    Feminism and the Power of Law 49
Smith, Adam 270, 340, 438
social rights
    as 20th century concept 369
    as actionable rights 373
    aim of 377
    as challenge 367–9, 372, 377
        to inequality 377
        to neoliberalism 377
    civil rights
        asymmetry between 370–71
        and citizenship 368–9
        /political rights continuity 367–8, 375–6
        see also civil rights; citizenship
    conservative critique 371
    creating decommodified spheres 377
    as decommodifying some human needs 369
    defining feature of 371
    depoliticising conditions giving rise to 365
    dominatory power of 365
    early/human rights distinction 366
    emancipatory potential of 365, 367, 371
    human rights *see* human rights
    judicialisation 373–4
        countering 373–4
    juridifying language of social rights 374
    neutralising rights 373
    not bringing social transformation 373
    South Africa v. Grootboom 374
    weak/dialogical form 373–4
    leftist critique 364–6
        emancipatory value 364
        Karl Marx 364
        Samuel Moyne 366
        Wendy Brown 364–6
    as minimums 369–70, 374
    in neoliberal age 363
    neoliberalism v democracy 378
    neutralisation 370–71, 374
    as part of legal architecture of inequality 369–70
    as positive rights 371
    as problematic 364
    progressivism 370, 371–2
    as safety net 369
    as solution to citizenship/private property tension 377
    theory of constitutional rights 374
    understanding of taxes 372
    as utopian 374–5
    whether emancipatory 367
Spinoza, Baruch 183, 210, 211, 221
Stalin, Joseph
    defeat of Left Opposition 108
    New Economic Programme 108
    socialist legality 106
structural violence
    of universalising concepts 490, 492
STS 249–50, 485
    ethnomethodology in 250
Supiot, Alain 142–3
    refeudalization 144–5
syndicalism
    Italian 109

theatrocracy 158
    and contemporary transmission of law 158
    expanding 160
    imaginal law *see* imaginal law
    law as visual phenomenon 159
    place of the camera in 158–9
    videosphere 160–61, 162
        symbolic economy of 161
theory
    emancipatory element of 5
    /practice distinction 7–9
Third World Approaches to International Law *see* TWAIL

traditional theory 16–17
  /critical theory comparison 16
  necessity in 18
  object not affected by theory that describes it 18
  perceived facts in 17
  pervading fragmentation 17
  separation of questions of fact from questions of value 16
  universal concepts in 18
transmission of theory 19
transnational law
  analytical jurisprudence 476
  anthropological engagement 480
  anti-terrorism law 481
  anxieties over 475
  border and boundary in 483–4
  changing scope of critique 478–9
  climate law 481
  commercial law in 485
  contested nature of 478
  curtailing state power
  discursive environment 474–5
    changing legal landscape 474
    legal pluralism 475
    suspicions of concept 475
    theory 474–5
  doctrinal grounding 480
  engagement with transnational regulatory normativity 482–3
  globalisation challenge 476–7, 478
  interdisciplinary conceptual frameworks 479–80
  as jurisprudential challenge 475–6
  labour law 480–81
  as legal field 481–2
  as methodological framework 483, 484
  as part of tradition of political legal theory 485
  and postcolonial legal theory *see* postcolonial legal theory
  precarity of 481, 483
    not inherent 484
    potential for self-destruction 473
    roots 484
  prescriptive dimension 476–7
  private law in 485, 486
  property law in 486
  public law in 485, 486
  roots of 484–5
  shift to private regulatory governance 478
  socio-legal studies 476
  unpredictability of 476

TWAIL 485, 488, 504

United Nations 430
  Committee on Economic, Social and Cultural Rights 523–4
  Conference on Trade and Development 459
  Declaration on the Rights of Indigenous Peoples 515, 519
  Development Programme Human Development Index 442
  draft Declaration on the Rights of Peasants *see* draft Declaration on the rights of Peasants and Other People Working in Rural Areas
Universal Declaration of Human Rights (1948) 366
USA
  Black Lives Matter movement 77
  Equal Protection clause 68, 70
  freedom of speech 70
  selective embracing of free trade 432
  US–European trade and investment agreement 470
  Voting Rights Act 69
  see also critical race theory

van Marle, Karin 53–4, 56, 58
voluntary agreements, enforcing 35

Warrington, Ronnie 186, 189, 228, 229
Weber, Max 140, 183, 187, 198, 433, 448
Western legal tradition 225, 240, 519
will 236–237
World Bank
  Doing Business initiative 460
  Investing across Borders initiative 460
  Structural Adjustment Programme 515–16
World Economic Forum 429
WTO 431, 438, 450
  Agreement on Agriculture 458
  Agreement on Trade-Related Aspects of Intellectual Property (TRIPS) 435
  Appellate Body 463
    EC – Asbestos case 464
    as jewel in the crown 465
    Korea – Beef case 464
    and necessity rule 463–4
    tendency to make law 465
    US attacks on 465
    US – Shrimp case 464
  comparative advantage doctrine 438–9
  dispute resolution 463–4

Appellate Body *see* above
  not impartial 464
  Panel 463
flexibility 461–2
GATT *see* GATT
General Agreement on Trade in Services
  (GATS) 435

hypocrisy of 441
legitimacy crisis 463, 470
national treatment rules
paralysis in negotiations 465
Trade Policy Review Mechanism 460

Yates, Joseph 263–4